# Liberalism at Large

# Liberalism at Large

*The World according
to the Economist*

Alexander Zevin

London • New York

This paperback edition first published by Verso 2021
First published by Verso 2019
© Alexander Zevin 2019, 2021

1 3 5 7 9 10 8 6 4 2

**Verso**
UK: 6 Meard Street, London W1F 0EG
US: 20 Jay Street, Suite 1010, Brooklyn, NY 11201
versobooks.com

Verso is the imprint of New Left Books

ISBN-13: 978-1-78873-962-7
ISBN-13: 978-1-78168-626-3 (UK EBK)
ISBN-13: 978-1-78168-625-6 (US EBK)

**British Library Cataloguing in Publication Data**
A catalogue record for this book is available from the British Library

**Library of Congress Cataloging-in-Publication Data**
A catalog record for this book is available from the Library of Congress
Library of Congress Control Number: 2019946698

Typeset in Sabon by MJ & N Gavan, Truro, Cornwall
Printed and bound by CPI Group (UK) Ltd, Croydon CR0 4YY

# Contents

Introduction: The *Economist* and the Making of
  Modern Liberalism 1

## I  PAX BRITANNICA

1. Free Trade Empire: From Hawick to Calcutta 21

2. Walter Bagehot's Dashed Doubts 71

3. Edward Johnstone and the Aristocracy of Finance 115

4. Landslide Liberalism: Social Reform and War 138

5. Own Gold: Layton and the League 177

## II  TRANSLATIO IMPERII

6. Extreme Centre 225

## III PAX AMERICANA

7. Liberal Cold Warriors 277

8. Globalization and Its Contents 332

Conclusion: Liberalism's Progress 375

*Acknowledgments* 398
*Notes* 400
*Index* 531

# Introduction

## The *Economist* and the Making of Modern Liberalism

The *Economist* is not like other magazines; it does not even call itself one. No 'newspaper' – as it styles itself – has been anywhere near as successful in the internet age, nor able to defy digital gravity for so long. As print media shed audiences and advertisers, foreign bureaus and paid journalists, the *Economist* added them. How had 'a magazine with a sleep-inducing title' and 'sometimes esoteric content', asked National Public Radio in 2006, posted readership gains of 13 per cent the year before, comparable only to celebrity tabloids?[1] Four years on, circulation in North America topped 820,000, a tenfold increase since it began an additional printing there in 1981. The global total surged, nearing 1.5 million, or fifteen times the figure in 1970.[2] Editors and publishers at *Time, Atlantic, Newsweek, Businessweek* and *US News* all agreed on the need to emulate the *Economist*, while in Europe similar refrains echoed at *Der Spiegel, L'Express* and *Panorama*.[3] But what was the secret, and why try to steal it from a paper a century older than any of them, edited from London continuously since 1843?

For some, it was the clever covers, wry humour, strong editorial line. For the *New York Times*, the answer was simpler: slick marketing. Red-on-white banners tugged at the insecurities of striving readers, making the *Economist* a status symbol for the would-be well-heeled. Its ads said everything. '"I never read The Economist." Management Trainee. Aged 42,' ran one ad from 1988. Another quipped, 'It's lonely at the top; but at least there's something to read.'⁴ This view owed much to James Fallows, whose 1991 broadside in the *Washington Post* argued that the *Economist* peddled conventional wisdom to US professionals too besotted by its snooty British accent and 'Oxbridge-style swagger' to be able to tell. A few other journalists sounded sceptical notes over the next two decades, when the *Economist* seemed unstoppable. For Jon Meacham, ex-*Newsweek* editor, it failed 'even to attempt to do original reporting'. At the *New York Observer*, one reporter struggled just to open his copy, then quickly shut it – finding leaden editorials, airy adjectives in place of evidence, layouts so dense they recalled the telephone book – and wondered if others who swore to read it might be pretending.⁵

The *Economist* does not walk on water, and in 2014 paid sales dipped for the first time in at least fifteen years. But in response, the *Economist* did what few other magazines could: it raised subscription prices 20 per cent to $180 for the electronic edition alone, making it the most expensive weekly in the US, with operating profits to match. At £54 million in 2017, these were still 60 per cent higher than they had been a decade before, despite the general collapse of ad revenues in the intervening years.⁶ But even if *Economist* readers are richer and more status-driven than most, the draw of the paper is about more than symbolic prestige, as a glance at its Letters to the Editor section might suggest. Here articles are nitpicked by whatever corporate, academic or government authority they incensed the week before: a lesson in the law from Philip Morris; a territorial protest from the Azerbaijani Ambassador; a budget clarification from South Korea's Ministry of Finance; the case for a US weapons system from the ex-general in charge; a professor's pained explanation that Chinese is logographic, *not* ideographic. Too busy to write, Angela Merkel speaks to the editor when she is 'cross'.⁷ Before her, George H. W. Bush could be seen with a copy pressed to his chest, striding up the White House lawn.

Not all readers are this powerful, but many have plans to be. In Anthony Powell's novel *A Dance to the Music of Time,* Sunny Farebrother – stockbroker, entrepreneur, amateur geo-statesmen – serves to satirize the type, retiring from dinner at the manor house he is visiting to scan the *Economist*. He has so annoyed the other guests, expatiating on everything from how 'to handle the difficulties of French reoccupation of the Ruhr, especially in relation to the general question of the shortage of pig-iron on the world market' to 'professional boxing', his host tells him to shut up: 'Farebrother, you are talking through your hat.'[8] Buyers usually do more than walk around with their copies, in other words: whether he or she is the leader of the free world, a business magnate, college freshman or, apparently, Sarah Palin and Steve Bannon – they also read it.

Investigative journalism is not a strength of the paper. What readers expect from the *Economist* are sharp didactic summaries and surprising numbers, which it provides on a grand scale. In a single issue, one may flit past e-commerce in China, mortgage fallout in Las Vegas, peace negotiations in the Middle East, the search for life on Mars, a new art museum in Qatar, and an obituary for an obscure South African explorer eaten by a crocodile. The first paper ever to compile and publish wholesale prices, it still devotes its back pages to data sets that change like shifting prisms onto the world economy: greenhouse gas emissions, growth forecasts, global remittances, the cost of a Big Mac. Treatment of any single issue is limited, outside of special reports, and articles can descend into parody – 'as if the writer started out knowing that three steps must be taken immediately – then tried to think what those steps should be'.[9] Range is accompanied by relentlessness: sucked under the foaming waves, the unfortunate explorer was served up as a fine specimen of the entrepreneurial spirit.[10]

Yet this strong institutional character, which sees an act of creative destruction in death, is also what makes it unique, preserved as it is by an equally unusual ownership structure designed to 'let the editor run the paper as though it belonged to him'. In place since 1928, this structure gives the editor power over policy, salaries and employment; and puts between him or her and the board of directors four trustees, who sign off on share transfers and the appointment of chairmen and editors. In 2016, when Pearson sold its half of the Economist Group for £469 million to existing shareholders, this charter came into play, with voting rights capped at 20 per cent for the largest of them. Insulated from business pressure, editors have swelled the business. In 176 years, just seventeen have filled the position: all but one a man, and for the last hundred years almost exclusively graduates of Oxford and Cambridge. At least one staffer has called the striking lack of diversity in this 'common room' an asset, making it easier to maintain a stable, collective voice. The need for that will be obvious to any reader, as the most distinctive feature of the *Economist* by far is that articles in it are unsigned. With few exceptions, the hundred or so staff in London and abroad toil anonymously – common enough at nineteenth-century newspapers, but almost unheard of today. Individualism may be the editorial line, but as a result of this Victorian holdover, the editorial leaders are written in an unusually cooperative and collegial manner, as if guided by invisible hands.[11]

Anonymity was always designed to amplify the voice of the *Economist*. Today, so do the covers, with Photoshop acting as a slingshot for pop-cultural lèse-majesté: Kim Jong Il blasts into space as 'Rocket Man'; Angela Merkel appears as Kurtz, groaning in horror at Greeks in 'Acropolis Now'; Hu Jintao and Barack Obama are the cowboy lovers from *Brokeback Mountain*. The more hated the figure, the more lurid the caricature: Vladimir Putin has been a prohibition-era mobster with a gas pump for a gun, a chess piece, a spider, an ice cube, a shirtless tank driver. Faced with this sort of barrage, Silvio Berlusconi sued. Hero worship is less common, if not unknown. 'Freedom Fighter', above a halo of hair, was its memorial to a monochrome Margaret Thatcher.

Both covers and articles are belligerent but conversant with politicians and governments; whole countries are blamed or praised with breezy self-assurance. But this is not mere posturing. When a new leader appears on the global stage, especially one unknown to capital markets, or from a developing country that needs to tap them, he or she will make a pilgrimage to the offices of the *Economist*. Even Hugo Chávez paid homage in 2001, trying to 'chat up the receptionists, two young black women, as if they were Venezuelan voters'. Luiz Inácio da Silva got a warmer welcome in 2006 for his plans to promote market reforms in Brazil, as well as asides about his diet. Michelle Bachelet had her tête-à-tête in 2014 'over herb tea in the Moneda palace' in Santiago, assuring the *Economist* she would never put equality before growth.[12] Latin

American leftists are one thing. The paper is naturally still more solicited at home, where each year Britain's Chancellor of the Exchequer briefs it on the budget over lunch at Downing Street.[13] In the US, Barack Obama was the first president to write a signed editorial for it in 2016, before departing the White House.

'How do you write like the *Economist*?', a nervous new recruit, trying to compose his first leader for it, once asked. Simple, a senior editor replied. 'Pretend you are God.'[14]

## A Power unto the Powerful

This quality of omniscient narration was not dreamt up by sales managers, and even if they could account for the success of the paper in circulation terms, this would be a misleading measure of its importance. What truly sets the *Economist* apart is the way it has shaped the very world its readers inhabit, by virtue of three close relationships: to liberalism, to finance, and to state power. Launched at a watershed in the historical development of each, the *Economist* opened a new front in the mid-nineteenth century battle against the Corn Laws in Britain, aimed less at partisans of the free trade in grain than at those wariest of it, above them: 'the higher circles of the landed and monied interests', in particular the commercial and financial hub of the City of London.[15]

That perspective paid. The *Economist* not only made money – turning a regular profit after just two years – it also made a name for its founder, James Wilson, a Scottish hat manufacturer who used the paper to catapult himself into politics. Elected to parliament in 1847, Wilson became a powerful financial secretary to the Treasury, and the first 'Chancellor of the Indian Exchequer', tasked with putting the British Raj on a sound fiscal footing in 1859. As Wilson stepped onto the steamer that would take him to India, the Chartered Bank he had co-founded – in part from *Economist* profits – was opening branches in Calcutta, Bombay, Shanghai and Hong Kong, with an eye to the opium traffic into China; this would become today's Standard Chartered Bank, with over $660 billion of assets.[16] By that time his paper had become indispensable as a conduit between a nascent Liberal Party in

Whitehall and Westminster and the parts of the City of London most concerned with imperial and foreign affairs. This caught the attention of Karl Marx, who read the *Economist* not just for its indexes on global trade, but for its political worldview – the most striking depiction in Europe of the concerns of the 'aristocracy of finance', whose stake in 'public credit' required it to keep close track of 'state power'.[17]

Over time, the *Economist* became even more deeply embedded in these circuits of money, power and ideas: editors advised chancellors on the currency, devised ground rules for running central banks and responding to financial panics, scanned the horizon for threats to British rule and British capital everywhere from Ireland to Egypt and Argentina – offering up the sort of political advice that markets themselves might, if only they could speak. Up to 1943, the paper had 10,000 subscribers, no more. But, as one editor pointed out at the time, in the past decade these had included Franklin D. Roosevelt, Benito Mussolini, Manuel Azaña, Heinrich Brüning and Adolf Hitler's finance minister. Its centenary celebration in wartime London was stuffed to bursting with bankers, politicians, economists, diplomats and foreign dignitaries, eating smoked salmon, puffing cigars. 'Never has so much been read for so long by so few,' quipped another editor, riffing on Winston Churchill.[18]

In the second half of the twentieth century, the *Economist* reached across the Atlantic: the role it once played in the British Empire, it now undertook in the American. A literal bridge between them, star reporters now passed apprenticeships on Wall Street and in Washington, where they enjoyed special access from the start – collared by John F. Kennedy or Lyndon B. Johnson in the marble corridors of Congress, enjoying personal lines to Ronald Reagan's White House via George Shultz, Henry Kissinger and other pillars of the foreign-policy establishment. The intimacy of its advocacy of US hegemony, all the more powerful for coming from a global rather than merely national point of view within the US, is one reason why a new history of the *Economist* is needed, and American readers have cause to be interested in it. If much of what follows is a history of liberalism in a British sense and a British setting, this matters in the US too – as parallel and preamble to a doctrine that came to explicitly dominate the political landscape there after 1945. Many now lament that this post-war liberal order is under threat; but very rarely do they define liberalism, still less disambiguate it for Americans, who may take it to mean several different and contradictory things at once.

## What Is Liberalism? Barriers to a Better Definition

The *Economist* has long defined itself as a lodestar of liberalism. In the aftermath of Trump and Brexit in 2016, it took great pains to renew and recast that commitment in a series of online debates, podcasts, films and profiles of liberal philosophers, culminating in a bold manifesto for its 175th anniversary in September 2018. Made complacent by their very success in spreading 'freedom and prosperity', the paper declared, liberals had to rediscover their best traditions to 'rekindle the spirit of radicalism' these contained.[19] But what is liberalism? Who are liberals? If American readers are confused, they are not alone; so are scholars, who are partly responsible for the muddle.[20] Before proceeding, it makes sense to consider some of the shortcomings in studies of this difficult-to-define 'ism', not only to explain how a work on the *Economist* may help to avoid them, but also to set us on the path to a more accurate conception. The barriers are roughly three: anachronism, decontextualization, and lack of comparison.

   Political theorists usually treat liberalism as a boundless body of thought, loosely and adaptively adhering around a few abstract principles of freedom, to be found in this or that canonical text or great thinker. In one recent indicative survey, liberalism is said to begin with John Locke, who supplied its first capacious axiom: men are 'born in a state of perfect freedom, to order their actions and dispose of their possessions, and persons, as they see fit'. The writings of this seventeenth-century English philosopher, for whom liberalism as a developed doctrine was totally unknown, are then stretched into political formulae fit for today: 'committed to democracy tempered by the rule of law, a private-enterprise economy supervised and controlled by government, and equal opportunity so far as it can be maintained without too much interference with the liberty of employers, schools, and families.'[21] The dangers of this approach are clear, and do not arise through want of erudition.

Perhaps the best-known account of liberalism in this key, and for many an inspiration, is Isaiah Berlin's 1958 Oxford lecture, 'Two Concepts of Liberty'. There were two diverging branches of the political philosophy, argued Berlin: one based on negative and another on positive freedom. The first, greatly to be preferred, meant 'non-interference' – by individuals, a ruler, the state, a 'minimum area of personal freedom which must on no account be violated'. John Locke and John Stuart Mill, Benjamin Constant and Alexis de Tocqueville lit up this path. The second was darker, and held that men could be made free, in conformity with their 'true' or 'rational' selves, even if they do not desire it. This was the legacy of Plato, Auguste Comte, Jean-Jacques Rousseau, Hegel, Marx, and in certain moods even Immanuel Kant and Mill. Here, the issue of decontextualization – thinkers plucked from across time and space, to be arranged like flowers in a vase – met anachronism, as Berlin applied 'profoundly divergent and irreconcilable attitudes to the ends of life' to the two camps in the Cold War.[22] The procedure may have been useful for normative purposes, but as one of Berlin's students later acknowledged, it could not be justified on the basis of what liberals had actually thought.[23]

Rejecting in principle (if not always in practice) arbitrary bricolages of this kind, the so-called Cambridge School of historians has sought to re-contextualize political thinkers in their national, linguistic and temporal space, so that who counts as a liberal at any given moment will depend on the available concepts, arguments and terms.[24] This approach has produced remarkable histories of early modern republicanism, extending across epochs and frontiers, but has never been successfully applied to liberalism, of which its leading practitioners have markedly different, not to say incompatible, views. No comparative tracing of the transnational development of liberal ideas across borders has been offered by this tradition. Attempts to bridge this gap have come from other kinds of scholarship, but have been few and far between.[25] For our purposes, a brief retrospect of early uses of the word liberalism in nineteenth-century Europe can suffice to set the historical stage for the birth of the *Economist*.

## Liberalism's Origin Story: A Historical and Comparative View

The morphology of liberalism developed in three stages. 'Liberal', as adjective, has been current in English since the fourteenth century, though for most of that time it had little to do with politics. In common with *liber*, its Latin root, 'liberal' distinguished free men and their cultivated pursuits – 'liberal arts and sciences' – from the rough manual labour of the lower classes. A compliment, it was always positive in connotation: to be liberal was to be generous, munificent, tolerant, broad-minded, or freespirited. Politicization came much later, applied first to persons and ideas, only then to parties.[26] Finally, the adjective became a noun: liberal-*ism* as a doctrine or system. How and when did this last jump take place? The answer lies in the Napoleonic era and its aftershocks, rippling across Spain, France and England.

As Napoleon's armies overran the old regime in Spain, reforming and absolutist deputies clashed in the Cortes of Cádiz (1810–1812) over what kind of political order was required to expel them. The first faction, describing themselves as *liberales* and their opponents as *serviles*, called for a constitutional monarchy, press freedom, universal male suffrage, indirect elections, and the breakup of church lands. Spanish 'liberals' drew on the French constitutions of 1791 and 1795 for this programme, which survived the restoration of Absolutism in 1814 as an inspiration to critical spirits in Spain and elsewhere in Southern Europe.[27]

In France, Napoleon had seized power on the 18th Brumaire (9 November 1799) in the name of 'idées conservatrices, tutélaires, libérales'. But of this trio only the last term resonated: the Parisian press was writing of 'liberal ideas' as 'fashionable' within a month, and outside the capital such ideas, associated with his Consulate, took some root in French-ruled Germany and Italy. Under the Empire they migrated towards critics of the regime like Benjamin Constant and Madame De Staël. But it was not until the Bourbon Restoration that 'liberal' as a collective political term acquired

more general currency – at first to pillory those deemed insufficiently ultra in their royalism and clericalism (when liberal was
virtually equated with Jacobin), then adopted by more moderate conservatives as a positive mark of opposition to the reign of
Charles X. In the 1820s 'liberal*ism*' came to describe the outlook
of such figures, *doctrinaires* (as they were called) like François
Guizot and Pierre-Paul Royer-Collard, later pillars of the July
Monarchy, from whom Tocqueville inherited central ideas.[28]

French liberalism was thus different from the Spanish in two
respects. Firstly, it positioned itself self-consciously as a centrist
political viewpoint, the enemy of two extremes: both ultra-
royalism and Jacobinism, both the ancien régime up to 1789, and
the calamitous popular radicalization of the revolution against
it. Spain did not experience an upheaval on this scale, so liberals
there were somewhat less fearful of the masses, allowing for a
wider suffrage than the *doctrinaires* ever envisaged. Secondly, the
French version was much more sophisticated intellectually, producing major bodies of political theory.[29]

This French political thought had little or no connection with
the economic theory of the free market that generated doctrines
of laissez-faire. That slogan-concept was formulated under the
ancien régime by the Physiocrats, whose legacy passed to Jean-
Baptiste Say during the Napoleonic period, and then to Frédéric
Bastiat (one of Marx's bêtes noires) under the July monarchy, who
produced major bodies of work attacking state interference in
the economy and trumpeting the virtues of self-regulating market
exchange. But without a strong class of manufacturers in support
of it, French political economy remained a marginal force, its free
trade doctrines handicapped by the threat of industrial competition from a more advanced Britain, prior traditions of French
mercantilism personified by Louis XIV's minister Jean-Baptiste
Colbert, and a generally more positive view of the State on both
right and left.[30] Its one significant achievement, the Anglo-French
Treaty of 1860 lowering tariffs between France and Britain –
negotiated by Richard Cobden and Michel Chevalier, once a
disciple of Saint-Simon – would boomerang politically, as it came
to be identified as the inaugural act of the final phase of Napoleon
III's rule, self-proclaimed as the 'Liberal Empire', whose collapse

in the disgrace of the Franco-Prussian War ten years later covered the term with discredit. So no Liberal Party ever emerged in the Third Republic, unlike in Germany or Italy in the same period. 'Liberalism' acquired a toxic odour that, despite strenuous efforts by the deeply unpopular current ruler of the country, it has yet to overcome in France today.

In Britain, Adam Smith and David Hume were using 'liberal' in its pre-political sense in the late eighteenth century to describe their favoured free market system.[31] Politically, however, the word arrived late – carried back from the Peninsular Wars in Spain, and as a result viewed with suspicion in Tory Britain. Lord Castlereagh detested the Cádiz *liberales,* nominally English allies, considering them little better than Jacobins. This impression was only confirmed when Leigh Hunt and Lord Byron, notorious subversives, founded *The Liberal,* and championed Greek independence. For Robert Peel in 1820, 'liberal' was still 'an odious phrase', albeit an intelligible one. Three years later, the first English essay on 'liberal*ism*' was a virulent attack on it as a destructive, alien doctrine wreaking havoc on the continent. Gradually, though, the Whig writers of the *Edinburgh Review* domesticated the term to describe their standpoints.[32] But naturalization moved slowly for two reasons: first, the Whig-Tory dichotomy was deeply entrenched as the national political polarity; second, outside it, the term 'Radicals', referring loosely to the Benthamites, already occupied the space of innovation. It was not until the 1830s that John Stuart Mill wrote, privately, of the contrast between liberalism and conservatism, and not until the 1850s that 'Liberal' superseded 'Radical' as a political calling card in Britain.[33]

And yet when 'liberal*ism*' as such finally arrived in Britain, it was far stronger than anywhere else in Europe. For here alone there was a totalizing fusion of the political ideas of rule of law and civil liberties with the economic maxims of free trade and free markets, in theories of 'limited government'. The synthesis that was missed in France is captured in Mill, who authored the *Principles of Political Economy* (1848) as well as *On Liberty* (1859) and *On Representative Government* (1861). The leap from ideology to organization then took place with the demise of

Whiggery, and the birth in 1859 of the Liberal Party, to be led by the charismatic Gladstone.

What produced this exceptional ideological-organisational double development? On the one hand, the dynamism of British industry, generating a feistier manufacturing class than on the continent, well capable of pursuing its own economic agenda, as in the Anti-Corn Law League.[34] On the other, the absence of revolutionary plebeian traditions, with Chartist mobilizations quickly divided and deflated. British Liberalism remained poised between landowners and workers, as elsewhere, but with much less to fear from the latter. It could thus move more boldly to 'disembed the market' from society, in Karl Polanyi's sense, than its European opposites, and to supplant earlier strains of Ricardian socialism with a fully capitalist free trade fetishism in popular consciousness itself. Political economy became, as *Economist* editor Walter Bagehot enthusiastically put it, the 'common sense of the nation'.[35]

The singular consummation of liberalism in Britain is underscored by the fact that in Germany, Italy and France, the term remained so predominantly political that a separate coinage was typically used to indicate the economic creed central to British liberalism. In Germany, where the bourgeoisie of the *Vormärz* and 1848 were primarily bureaucratic and professional, not industrial, *Manchestertum* stood in for the cult of the free market. In Italy, Benedetto Croce coined *liberismo*, to distinguish it from *liberalismo*. In France, the conventional term was always *laissez-faire* – notably absent from Tocqueville, the country's best-known defender of political liberalism.

### Liberalism in America: A Detour

In America, on the other hand, no crystallization of liberalism as an explicit doctrine occurred, because many of its basic tenets were taken for granted from the start. As Louis Hartz and Eric Voegelin famously argued, the absence of either feudal and aristocratic barriers to capitalism above, or working class and socialist threats from below, obviated the need for systematic liberal theories or organizations in nineteenth-century America.[36] Liberalism was not entirely unknown – a group of Liberal Republicans split from the Republicans, albeit for just two years, in 1870 – but it was not until almost half a century later that it began to acquire political salience. The *New Republic,* looking for alternatives to the word 'progressive' after the defeat of its candidate, Theodore Roosevelt, in 1912, chose the term. Eager to court its influential editors, and to justify his entry into the First World War, Woodrow Wilson began to describe his foreign policy as 'liberal' in 1917.

This fairly light symbolic baggage made 'liberal' attractive in the 1930s, when Franklin Roosevelt hit on it as a tag for his New Deal policies, in part to distinguish them from the efforts of his Progressive predecessors to end the Great Depression. The alternatives were less appealing: social democratic, let alone socialist, was far too extreme, and anyway sounded foreign, while progressive was too redolent of Republicans and smacked of laissez-faire for most Democrats. Liberal, in contrast, had positive if vague associations with British 'New Liberals' such as Lloyd George, whom members of Roosevelt's Brain Trust saw as paving an economic middle way between unbridled capitalism and oppressive statism. This appropriation of the term provoked an immediate reaction from right-wing critics, however, who claimed – as purer adherents of free markets – to be the 'true' liberals.[37] Upset by collectivist departures from laissez-faire, but losing this battle to define liberalism in the 1930s, American conservatives eventually managed to invert the term, such that today 'liberal' often implies a leftist departure from American liberty, rather than its fulfilment.

### Classical Liberalism: Three Unanswered Questions

The core ideological complex of classical liberalism that emerged in Britain combined economic freedoms – the right to unconditional private property; low taxes; no internal tariffs; external free trade – with political freedoms: the rule of law; civil equality; freedom of the press and assembly; careers 'open to talent'; responsible government. While this was a coherent, integrated agenda, it left unresolved three large questions.

First, to whom was government to be responsible? Who should parliaments, essential to the new constitutional system, actually represent? The classical liberal response was a censitary suffrage: votes only for those with sufficient means and education to form an independent judgment of public affairs. But how should liberals react when those without them pressed for inclusion in the political process? Second, how far should the liberal order extend, not just to the lower classes within the constitutional state, but to territories beyond it? By the mid-nineteenth century, the modal type of liberal state was national. Could it also be imperial, with overseas possessions? If so, did liberal principles apply to them? Finally, what was the role to be accorded by liberal political economy to activities not regarded as productive of value – neither agriculture, nor industry, nor trade, but lending and borrowing, and speculation? Was money a commodity like any other, with banks no different from farms or factories? If business cycles were normal in a market economy, what of longer-lasting crises and depressions?

How, in other words, would liberals respond to the rise of democracy, the expansion of empire, and the ascendancy of finance, none of which figured in the core doctrine?

### The *Economist* as Touchstone

Other studies have examined a single point in this triad. Scholars have shown how methodically liberals opposed democracy, defending a limited suffrage on the basis of education, and turning to an emphasis on economic over political liberties as socialist ideas spread after 1848.[38] The concept of 'empire' has recently garnered more attention than in the past. Liberals are now acknowledged to have been deeply interested in the imperial project, even as debate rages over the nature of that interest, and whether it constituted a fundamental 'urge' or was liable to constant shifts and shadings.[39] Recent histories of finance capitalism have added to our knowledge of the City of London, though they remain rather hesitant to credit an ideological perspective to the varied actors operating within it.[40]

The *Economist*, however, unlike particular thinkers or themes, offers a continuous record of the confrontation between classical liberalism and the challenges of democracy, empire, and finance across the better part of two centuries – and can claim far greater intellectual success than any other expression of liberalism, with a world-wide reach today. Reading it is an antidote to the standard eclecticism of most accounts of liberal ideas, whose effect has been to *noyer le poisson*, as the French say, adducing everything and its opposite in a grab-bag going back at least to Smith, if not to Locke or earlier. From the time when the term first truly became part of political discourse, the paper has pressed imperturbably forward under the banner of liberalism – sometimes a little ahead of ideological shifts, at others a little behind them. What the history of the *Economist* reveals is the *dominant* stream of liberalism, which has had other tributaries, but none so central or so strong.

## On Method

Writing the intellectual history of a newspaper that covers the entire world and has come out on a weekly basis for the last 176 years has not been simple. Nor has it been a straightforward matter to choose how to organize and narrate that history, so that both general and specialist readers can hope to move through it with relative ease. What began as an article, turned into a dissertation and became a book has threatened at each stage to exceed the frame to which it was fitted – as in the famous Borges story, in which an obsessive group of cartographers draws a map of the world that expands until it is the same size as what it seeks to represent. Contrary to appearances, given the length of the present volume, principles of selection were applied to avoid that outcome.

Alternative paths could have been taken: that of a more or less traditional publishing history; or one that set the paper in a media studies frame, among the literary quarterlies, business journals and mass circulation dailies that have appeared and disappeared in London since the Victorian age. While I do discuss the location, production and distribution of the *Economist* – and the way other periodicals have competed with it for writers, readers and renown – my focus has been on ideas, and on connecting these to the broader material and ideological forces that have shaped 'actually existing liberalism' since 1843: radical demands for democracy, the ascent of finance in the global capitalist order, and imperial expansion, conflict, cooperation and continuing dominion. Three official books, and a few academic articles, have been written on other aspects of the *Economist*, or its attitude to one theme or another: railways, statistics, drugs, laissez-faire, America.[41] Now that every issue has been digitized and made available online, future works can explore other subjects, sketched too lightly – or left out – of the portrait I have drawn here. To name just two cases, much more could be said on the way its views have evolved on climate change, or on the project of European integration.

In writing the history of the *Economist* as a history of liberalism, I confronted challenges particular to my source material: not just continuously and collectively published, but almost all of it anonymously. I have worked to attribute some of its most significant articles, and to explain the editorial environment in which they were composed, through extensive research. That has meant sifting the letters, memoirs and other papers which editors left behind, at archives in London, Cambridge, Oxford, Stanford and elsewhere. Since most were prolific authors outside of the *Economist,* I have also made use of their books, articles and speeches, which range from treatises on the stock market and unemployment to politics, religion and even spy fiction, in my assessments of them and the paper. (Often these titles have helped to determine the authorship of articles – or to discern a disagreement – within the *Economist* itself.) From around the middle of the twentieth century, these sorts of sources could be supplemented with another: interviews. Between 2011 and 2018, I conducted over two dozen interviews with current and former *Economist* staffers. Robustly confident in their convictions, they were always generous and open, never troubling to inquire too deeply into the nature of my research, nor worry whether my findings might cast their work in a critical light. How could it? This book is richer for their insights: not just because of the colourful stories and character sketches they shared, but for their inside perspectives on the debates and turning points in the recent history of the *Economist,* from the Vietnam War to the drive for circulation in America, the decisions to endorse Thatcher and Reagan to the invasion of Iraq. The one cache of material I have been unable to access is the *Economist*'s own, which – largely destroyed in the Blitz, haphazardly stored since – is still being catalogued. As it is, a largish body of notes can be found at the back of this volume. This is where publishers insist on putting them, even if they contain – as they do here – not just sources, but vivid quotations, biographical asides, and historiographic discussions. My apologies for the inconvenience of their location to readers who take an interest in such things: *commerce oblige*, as today's wisdom has it.

This study follows the *Economist* through the sequence of its editors, whose tenures organize the narrative, tracing the tone and direction that each has given to the paper. Variation in the texture of the story is one consequence, reflecting contrasts between different incumbents and their eras – yielding, for example, here a finer-grained sense of British politics or newsroom disputes, there a broader brush on wars or economic conjunctures. I start with a detailed contextual account of the *political* origins of the *Economist* and its links to the organized campaign for free trade in mid-nineteenth-century Britain, and a consideration of the extraordinary figure of its founder, James Wilson – whose life and writings have been edulcorated in the few latter-day accounts we have of him. Then I pass to the paper's famous second editor, Walter Bagehot, whose output and reputation are in a class by themselves in the history of the *Economist*, overtopping it, so that here uniquely it becomes the story of effectively one person. This sets the stage for the paper's emergence as the voice of British finance capital at its global peak, punctuated by the exceptional tenure of Francis Hirst, who opposed Britain's entry into the First World War and was fired in 1916. Disputes between interwar editor Walter Layton and John Maynard Keynes over the gold standard and how to respond to the Depression presage Britain's global decline and the passing of the imperial sceptre to the United States. After the paper's turn to America during the Second World War came an all-out commitment to Washington as the

Cold War escalated, a fealty consummated in the eras of Ronald Reagan and George W. Bush. Moving into the present, the story ends with what is now – rightly or wrongly – widely perceived as the contemporary crisis of liberalism, and looks at the ways the *Economist* has contributed to and tried to surmount it. In doing so, it pulls back to survey the long history of liberalism according to the *Economist*, and lays out a counter-narrative to which its actual record points. No one book can have the last word on the *Economist*. But I hope enough is said in these pages to alter whatever may come after them.

# I

## PAX BRITANNICA

# 1

## Free Trade Empire

### *From Hawick to Calcutta*

The 1830s and 1840s were the most tumultuous decades in the history of modern Britain: during this period, a social order forged in the seventeenth century came closer to being overturned than at any subsequent point. Yet in the end it bequeathed that order, albeit in modified form, to the present. Pressures bubbled during the Napoleonic Wars, and nearly boiled over after 1815, as twenty years of rising prices gave way to sharp trade depressions, deflation and discontent, amidst the upheavals of the Industrial Revolution. From 1816 to 1819, protest spread in waves through northern manufacturing towns and rural parishes, with the smashing of power-looms and threshing machines, and bread riots involving laid-off operatives and farm labourers. The famous clash at St Peters Field on 16 August 1819 showed how quickly tensions in the country became political: reformers called a rally to demand parliamentary representation for the large towns and votes for working men, and more than 60,000 people packed into the centre of Manchester. Peterloo was the name given to the killings that followed, an ironic nod to the brave hussars who charged an unarmed crowd.

A decade later dissent once more assumed an organized form, this time briefly uniting the middle and working classes in urban political unions, just as agricultural workers were exploding into riot throughout the south of England. For the aristocracy that dominated the House of Commons, the three years from 1829 threatened an upheaval whose terrors it associated with the French Revolution. In 1832 a Reform Bill was passed whose purpose was to reconcile a rising middle class, 'the intelligent and independent portion of the community', with an oligarchic system and so divert it from any alliance with the masses below.[1] In this at least it succeeded. Radical MPs from the industrial towns trickled into the Commons, which continued to divide along the same Whig-Tory party lines.

But electoral concessions did not stop pressures for reform, even if those who were aggrieved now pursued their goals separately, and as often at odds with each other. Agitation revived at the onset of the economic crisis of 1837, with the almost simultaneous birth of Chartism and the Anti-Corn Law League. The Chartists focused popular anger into six demands, including universal male suffrage and the ballot; what Engels called the 'first proletarian party' mobilized new factory workers and once skilled craftsmen now threatened by penury behind it. But the strikes it bred were swiftly repressed, and its petitions fizzled out.[2] Based in the manufacturing middle-class, the Anti-Corn Law League was both more 'respectable' and far more effective. Avoiding any broader issues, what it demanded was the repeal of the laws that British landowners had imposed in 1815 to keep foreign competition in wheat out of the country, and domestic prices high. This aristocratic tariff squeezed the industrial cotton masters of Lancashire during a severe depression, and obstructed their pursuit of export markets. In the League they created a formidable machine to overturn agrarian protection and move Britain toward unilateral free trade. If its programme was much narrower than that of Chartism, its organizing capacity – drawing in not only manufacturers, merchants and middle-class professionals, but a good many workers too, attracted by its promise of cheaper bread – greatly outstripped it.

Between 1839 and 1843 the League petitioned parliament over 16,000 times, collecting nearly six million signatures. From a Manchester warehouse it shipped 9 million pamphlets, posters, newspapers, almanacs and every other kind of printed matter in 1843 alone. Lecturers fanned out to hundreds of local chapters across the country. There were banquets, balls, conventions, tea parties, bazaars – precursors to the great exhibitions, whose celebrations of technical progress drew hundreds of thousands of visitors. In 1845 Covent Garden was dressed up as a Gothic hall, with industrial displays, libraries, raffles, puppet shows, and stands selling Anti-Corn Law-themed crockery, tablecloths, thimbles, handkerchiefs, scarves, razors and stickers to seal letters at the post office: 'Free communication with all parts of the empire is good: free trade with all parts of the world will be still better.' The money involved was staggering: a budget of £25,000 in the first three years, £50,000 in 1842–1843, £100,000 in both 1844 and 1845, with a goal of £250,000 (or £29 million in today's money) for 1846.[3] By then a pressure group seeded in a single chamber of commerce, controlled by factory owners in search of lower labour costs at home and new markets abroad, had convinced much of the rest of the country that repeal was vitally in its interest too, as a master-key to general prosperity. It had also shown how far the issue of free trade could travel, and the passions it aroused. Consciously echoing earlier agitation against the slave trade, and its dissenting and evangelical overtones, the League built links abroad – including to American free-traders, who nonetheless remained a minority in the US well into the twentieth century.[4] In no other country would the forces that came together under the banner of the League prove so successful, or enduring, as in Britain.[5]

Credit for repeal of the Corn Laws, when it came in 1846, went to one League leader above all, Richard Cobden. A calico printer turned politician, Cobden had risen from a clerk in a City of London warehouse to the smoggy heights of Manchester's cottonopolis: in 1836, five years after moving from commission to factory production, his firm had £150,000 in turnover, with profits of £23,000, a hint of the sums to be made from textiles in flush times.[6] John Bright was the other outspoken leader of the League, born, unlike Cobden, to a prosperous family of Quaker cotton spinners in the town of Rochdale in Lancashire. Both were eloquent and tireless proponents of free trade, though in each case – untypically – their radicalism reached past the Corn Laws, to electoral and land reform, an end to primogeniture, and religious disestablishment. 'The colonies, army, navy and church are, with the Corn Laws, merely accessories to aristocratic government', wrote Cobden in

1836. 'John Bull has his work cut out for the next fifty years to
purge his house of those impurities!'[7] Long before victory over the
Corn Laws was in sight, however, Cobden and Bright met James
Wilson, a Scottish hat manufacturer and author, whose powerful
vision of a free trade world, first set out in 1839, gave their campaign its winning argument.

## James Wilson's Winning Argument

Wilson was born in Hawick, a busy town in the Scottish Borders,
whose River Teviot powered the textile mills that sprang up along
its banks in the 1700s. His father, William, a devout Quaker,
owned one of these establishments and secured from it a very
respectable livelihood. His mother, Elizabeth, died giving birth
for the fifteenth time in 1815, leaving five surviving daughters
and five sons, of whom James, born in 1805, was the fourth. His
education was brief. For four years he attended a school run by
the Society of Friends in Ackworth where, an aunt recalled, he
was 'exceedingly clever … but never excelled in play'. The austerity there agreed with him: at fifteen he wanted to become a
schoolmaster, though he soon thought better of it. After a year at
an Essex seminary he wrote home to his parents, 'I would rather
be the most menial servant in my father's mill than be a teacher.'
He and his older brother were apprenticed instead to a hatmaker,
a business their father eventually bought them.

It was during this period, from ages sixteen to nineteen, that
Wilson seems to have read most of the authors on whom he would
later draw as editor. Adam Smith, James Mill, Thomas Tooke,
David Ricardo and the Frenchman Jean-Baptiste Say supplied a
mix of moral philosophy and political economy.[8] The title he later
chose for his paper indicates how far these fields of inquiry over-
lapped. 'Economist' had yet to acquire its modern meaning; its
sense was 'the economizer', he who does not waste money and
manages resources efficiently. Wilson was a talented economizer.
Walter Bagehot described his approach to intellectual matters in a
memorial. 'For some years at least he was in the habit of reading
a good deal, very often till late at night. It was indeed then that

he acquired most of the knowledge of books he ever possessed. In later life he was much too busy to be a regular reader, and he never acquired the habit of catching easily the contents of books or even of articles in the interstices of other occupations. Whatever he did, he did thoroughly. He would not read even an article in a newspaper if he could well help doing so.'

These habits may seem strange in someone Bagehot also described as a 'great *belief producer*', but were in fact the precondition for his passionate faith. 'He was not an intolerant person but the qualities he tolerated least easily were flightiness and inconsistency of purpose. He had furnished his mind, so to say, with fixed principles, and he hated the notion of a mind which was unfurnished.'[9] Wilson was already a busy, practical man of affairs before his twentieth birthday, with all the theoretical knowledge about political economy he considered useful. In 1824 he and his brother left Hawick to set up Wilson, Erwin and Wilson in London, each with a further £2,000 of paternal capital in pocket. His father must have been extremely wealthy to give such generous gifts – the equivalent today of around £400,000 – to just two of his sons. In 1831 Wilson bought out his partners, renaming the hatter James Wilson & Co, and the following year Wilson married Elizabeth Preston and so into a line of Yorkshire gentry then living in Newcastle, members of the Church of England. His conversion to Anglicanism opened the way for his nuptials and a career in politics. Four years later Wilson and his new family moved from a house near the factory in Southwark to a mansion in Dulwich Place. By 1837 Wilson had amassed a fortune of £25,000. But, in a sign of the speculative financial turn his business interests were taking, that year he lost most of his wealth betting on the price of indigo, which fell when he had expected it to rise. The firm was on the line: in a global financial panic, with unlimited liability, he rushed to satisfy his creditors. This he managed to do, though the manner in which he mortgaged certain assets to raise capital raised awkward questions later on.[10]

Wilson refused to despair over this setback. Instead he began to investigate what he saw as their general cause, publishing his first pamphlet in 1839, *Influences of the Corn Laws as Affecting All Classes of the Community, and Particularly the Landed Interests.*

Cobden and Bright were impressed with this text, which also marked a turning point in the repeal debate, in arguing that free trade would usher in an organic harmony of all economic interests. The aim and effect of repeal was not to remove the advantages of the landed interests, as both those who were for and those who were against it had been saying since at least 1815. 'We cannot too much lament and deprecate the spirit of violence and exaggeration with which this subject has always been approached.' Rather it was protection – a flawed, unnatural system of government interference with commerce – that was the enemy, 'prejudicial to all classes of the community'.[11] It was not a matter for 'class enmity ... the interest of all classes was the same', and Wilson spoke privately, on this score, of 'the rubbish they have been talking at Manchester'.[12] It is unlikely Cobden and Bright were ever won over to this line of thinking, so different from their broadsides against the parasitism of rent-seeking aristocrats. Cobden even ventured a small criticism at the time. 'I think you have lost sight of one gain to the aristocratic land-lords ... the *political* power arising out of the present state of their tenantry – and political power in this country has been pecuniary gain.'[13]

Whatever its flaws, however, the pamphlet proved strategically invaluable. The League and the *Leeds Mercury* (a leading voice of provincial Whiggism) reprinted it. Cobden praised Wilson for 'labouring to prove to the Landlords that they may safely do justice to others without endangering their own interests.'[14] J. R. McCulloch, the chief disciple of David Ricardo, called it 'one of the best and most reasonable of the late tracts in favour of unconditional repeal'.[15] It was even quoted by certain Tories, then the party of protection, including the prime minister Sir Robert Peel. Such was its power to transform debate and attract formerly committed foes of free trade in the countryside that, for a time, even Cobden adopted its language. 'I am afraid, if we must confess the truth, that most of us entered upon this struggle with the belief that we had some distinct class interest in the question, and that we should carry it by a manifestation of our will', he told a Manchester crowd in 1843. 'If there is one thing which more than another has elevated and dignified and ennobled this agitation, it is, we have found, that every interest and every object which every part of the community can justly seek, harmonize perfectly with the views of the Anti-Corn Law League.'[16] In Wilson the League discovered that in pursuing its own class interests it was pursuing those of all classes.

Yet it is just as easy to see the appeal his early tracts against protection held out to enterprising landowners. In *Influences,* his clearest point was conveyed in statistical tables which claimed to show that production costs in England were competitive with Europe; given other variables, like soil conditions and cost of transport, foreign grain was unlikely to flood the home market.[17] Still more significant, however, were the theoretical foundations for this claim. In contrast to Ricardo and Thomas Malthus he did not see class conflict as an inherent fact of economic life: from the former he discarded or modified the theory of marginal rents and wages, and from the latter the pessimistic forecast that population always outpaces food supply. Ricardo suggested that landed capital gained at the expense of industrial capital, and Malthus that working-class wages tended towards the bare minimum necessary for survival. Wilson favoured a model of rapid growth, in which rent, profits and wages all rose in tandem – provided that a free trade system was in place, allowing Britain to exchange its finished goods for the raw materials of less advanced nations. The less advanced nations could then buy even more from Britain. Given such a system, Ricardo had written, 'it is difficult to say where the limit is at which you could cease to accumulate wealth and to derive profit from its exploit'.[18] If this blueprint for growth owed much to Ricardo, however, the universal identity of class interests it presaged belonged to Adam Smith.

Wilson posited a theory of price fluctuations to explain a status quo that only *appeared* to benefit agriculture at the expense of capital and labour. High grain prices ensured by protective tariffs encouraged farmers to over-cultivate during good times, only to see their surplus grain mouldering during subsequent crashes. Worse, falling prices meant a reverse cycle of abandoned fields and diminishing investment. As prices began to rise again the home grower had little to sell; foreign wheat was then called in and *it* reaped the profits. Landowners suffered nearly as much, faced with the unpalatable options of accepting steeply reduced rents, ruining their tenants without being able to find new ones, or taking over the fields themselves.[19] Manufacturing would also be served by reform, though not in the way many Leaguers assumed. Repeal was not going to lower the price of provisions or labour. Quite the contrary, since prices were bound to climb in step with the general prosperity attendant upon a more productive application of labour and capital and the rise in exports. What of the workers? Price swings were, finally, most regrettable for their effect on 'the moral and political condition of the labouring population of all kinds.' No one could forget the terror which swept the countryside during the last crisis: 'the awful and mysterious midnight fires ... anonymous letters; secret societies to fan and inflame the worst passions; highway robberies and personal attacks.' And all this carried out by the indigent peasants whose miseries 'were really much more apt to excite our pity than our blame'. Factory workers were even more cruelly used, lulled by 'the temporary possession of comforts and luxuries far beyond what their average condition will enable them to support'.[20]

### Backing the *Economist*: Wilson and the Whig Grandees

Armed with such arguments Wilson became a regular speaker at meetings of the League, where Archibald Prentice of the *Manchester Times* remembered him as 'relying more upon statistical figures than on figures of speech, and trusting more to facts and reasoning than to rhetorical flourishes.' Yet his audience 'had come to learn and not to be excited by flashes of oratory', listening with 'deep interest for three quarters of an hour'.[21] Wilson for his part preferred the pen to the podium, and continued publishing, with *Fluctuations of Currency, Commerce, and Manufactures: Referable to the Corn Laws* in 1840. The assemblies were noisy and drew too many 'Manchester School extremists'. After a meeting at the Drury Lane Theatre in London, in which Cobden, Bright and Daniel O'Connell took front stage, he confided to his family that this was 'not to his taste, and he would be sorry to see other political questions settled that way'.[22]

Wilson was aware that his voice carried farther than the theatre pits of the capital. His writings had caught the attention of a group of Whig politicians sympathetic to the goals of the League, if not to its noisy proceedings. In 1839, lordly letters began to stream into Dulwich Place. Charles Villiers, the radical MP for Wolverhampton, asked for help in drafting his annual motion for repeal in the House of Commons, a solitary ritual, usually voted down by a margin of several hundred. Would Wilson, he added, be kind enough to call on his brother George, fourth Earl of Clarendon, at the Athenaeum Club? William Pleydell-Bouverie, third Earl of Radnor, wrote from Longford Castle requesting anti-Corn Law arguments he could use against the surrounding squires in Wiltshire.[23] Radnor, who took an almost fatherly interest in Wilson – nominating him to the Reform Club in 1842, and helping him take his first steps into politics – prided himself on being the most radical of all grandees. At the age of ten a terrified witness of the French Revolution, Radnor later became convinced (after repairing to Edinburgh and Oxford and studies of Smith, Blackstone and Montesquieu) that progress was possible without reliving those scenes of democratic chaos: the cause of individual liberty was best served by laissez-faire economics coupled with the political rule of an enlightened aristocracy.[24] On a visit to Radnor's vast demesne near Salisbury, built up on investments in the Levant trade, the French statesman Alexis de Tocqueville observed that the Radnor family embodied the eminently commercial character of the English nobility.[25]

One drawing room after another, in town and country, opened its doors to Wilson, who passed through them to find the backers he would need to start the *Economist*. His message was that complete free trade would mean an end to the trade cycle itself, a thesis whose utopian flavour is evident in all his major works between 1839 and 1841 – from *Influences* and *Fluctuations* to *The Revenue; or What Should the Chancellor Do?*[26] The idea of starting a newspaper arose soon after the last of these pamphlets appeared, for it was clear that neither corn nor the League offered sufficient scope for Wilson to develop his unique vision. 'There never was a time when an *independent* organ was more required,'

Villiers insisted in the spring of 1843. Meeting at his club, Wilson
found him 'very fond of the thing, – but from what he said I fear
we shall have some difficulty with the League – it appears they are
extremely jealous of their importance and will want it a League
Paper, and as such I will have nothing to do with it.' Cobden was
meanwhile reporting to Bright that 'James Wilson has a plan for
starting a weekly Free Trader by himself and his friends'. The two
tried to persuade him to edit the *Anti-Bread Tax Circular* instead.
Newspapers, Cobden informed Wilson, were *'graves de fortunes*
in London ... have you made up your mind to a great and continuous pecuniary loss?' To Bright he wrote in slight bemusement,
'Wilson has a notion that a paper would do more good if it
were *not* the organ of the League but merely their independent
support.'[27] Still, he noted, Wilson was reluctant to act without
their approval.

Wilson desperately needed the League for its subscribers
and distribution networks and so tried to explain his reasoning
at a meeting with Bright and George Wilson, chairman of the
League, to which he also invited Radnor. To his Anti-Corn Law
colleagues he promised new and more influential converts than
could be reached by any journal bearing the direct imprint of the
League. His intended audience, he told Cobden in June, in what
was probably his most compelling pitch, was 'the higher circles of
the landed and monied interests'.[28] Wilson's other partners came
from just these social heights, and they wanted a moderate journal
free of the faintest traces of populism. From Radnor he obtained
£500, while the League, with the aim of winning both the City of
London and the countryside, agreed to order 20,000 copies.[29] For
Cobden the journal would be another means of putting pressure
on opinion within parliament – and of altering its composition,
since a crucial by-election pitting a free-trader against a protectionist was coming up in the City.[30]

To ensure the success of his venture Wilson imposed some
drastic personal economies. He rented out one of his homes, and
ordered a halt to pineapples in the hothouses. By shipping his wife
and six daughters to Boulogne to take the waters and dismissing
all servants – save nurse, maid, housekeeper and errand boy – he
raised a further £800. In a letter to his wife in France, Wilson

confided another reason for his drive for independence: 'no question will ever arise as to the property, or to whom the benefit of the paper will belong after it shall have risen to a good circulation which I hope it may do in time.' From the start the *Economist* was a business and had to make money.[31]

Yet its founding was also a milestone in political and economic thought, a bugle blast of the first age of global capitalism. Wilson and his newspaper became more than mouthpieces for the Manchester school: they developed and disseminated the doctrine it embodied – laissez-faire liberalism – in its clearest and most consistent form. It was with this aim in mind that Wilson refused to work for the League. 'My paper would not do for that purpose … mine must be perfectly philosophical, steady and moderate; nothing but pure *principles*.'[32] Thus a footnote in the history of the Anti-Corn Law movement quickly eclipsed it: of the millions who now read the *Economist* how many have heard of the forces that made it possible, or the principles by which it found distinction?

## The Original Cast of the *Economist*

The economic historian Scott Gordon thought he saw the force of an idea, steady if not moderate, in a portrait of Wilson painted a year before his death:

> He sits stolidly in his chair, his hands folded in finality. His round face is benevolent, but there is the unmistakable mark of doctrine in the eyes, close set and steady, and there is that thin, firm mouth. 'There is no nonsense about me,' they say. 'I know what is right, I work hard, and I do my duty.' 'What is this man's passion?' one wonders, for surely he has one: good portraits do not lie about that. Is it Temperance? Abolition of slavery? Prevention of cruelty to animals? Education? It is all of these things and many more, for it is the one thing, the one principle, which will make the whole world a harmonious and beneficent order. It is laissez-faire.[33]

Wilson controlled the *Economist* and wrote much of its content. 'He worked on it indefatigably,' remembered Herbert Spencer,

sub-editor from 1848 to 1853, 'and, being a man of good business judgment, sufficient literary faculty, and extensive knowledge
of commercial and financial matters, soon made it an organ of
the mercantile world, and, in course of a relatively short time,
a valuable property.'[34] His collaborators were perhaps the only
men whose doctrinal commitments exceeded his own. Thomas
Hodgskin was the most influential editor between 1844 and 1857,
followed by Spencer and William Rathbone Greg, a leader-writer
starting in 1847. Several other distinguished individuals made
occasional contributions, including Charles Villiers's brother-in-
law Sir George Cornewall Lewis, Poor Law Commissioner and
later Chancellor of the Exchequer in Palmerston's first government, for whom Wilson worked as financial secretary. Lewis was
also a classicist, linguist, philologist and political theorist, whose
key public service had been to extend the English Poor Law of
1834 to Ireland – condemning claimants of state assistance to
workhouses, to be made as unpleasant as possible to teach their
inmates self-reliance. Nassau Senior, the main author of the
Poor Law and one of the most eminent economists of his day,
was another contributor; for Wilson he seems to have written on
foreign affairs.[35] Together they extended laissez-faire in every conceivable direction, embellishing and amending it in the process.
These were the original voices hidden behind the anonymous,
imperious judgments for which the *Economist* would become
famous.

Hodgskin may seem oddly out of place among them, given
his reputation as a Ricardian socialist and radical anarchist,
whose texts from the 1820s so inspired Marx. When Wilson
met Hodgskin, however, he was no longer arguing that capital
and labour were locked in a battle to the death, or explaining
that the labour theory of value showed how the former shamelessly cheated the latter of its moral right to the whole of what it
produced.[36] By 1843 Hodgskin had retreated from such attacks
on capital, and the Ricardian reading of class conflict that fired
them. What remained was an anarchic individualism: a profound
distrust of all government and legislation, no matter how enlightened, and a deistic faith in natural law. That year he published a
free trade tract praising the League in terms that would have made

sense to Wilson; repeal of the Corn Laws, it argued, was merely a first step in beating back the Leviathan of the state, 'a huge system of injustice, all of which must be removed'.[37] Even as a young man Hodgskin had distinguished himself from other socialists in seeing the free market, not mutual aid, as the only way for workers to secure the full fruits of their labours. In the 1830s he no longer imagined that this would come about as a result of victory over the middle classes, but by workers being absorbed into its ranks.

> Now we find, in consequence of the respect for the natural rights of property, that a large middle class, completely emancipated from the bondage of destitution which the law ... sought to perpetuate, has grown up in every part of Europe, uniting in their own persons the character both of labourers and capitalists. They are fast increasing in numbers; and we may hope, as the beautiful inventions of art gradually supersede unskilled labour, that they, reducing the whole society to equal and free men, will gradually extinguish all that yet remains of slavery and oppression.[38]

'All these changes have been effected in spite of the law,' he added, driving home his point that the middle class, if left alone, could achieve what no earthly government could. Hodgskin wrote book reviews as well as leaders, rebutting social reformers on everything from the Poor Law and Factory Acts to health and sanitation committees, and questions of crime and penal law.[39]

Herbert Spencer was twenty-eight in 1848. He had yet to formulate his famous theories of social evolution but was groping towards them, and Wilson was favourably impressed by his first efforts, a series of letters to the *Nonconformist* published as the pamphlet *The Proper Sphere of Government* in 1843. In it Spencer argued that the state was originally designed to do almost nothing, except 'defend the natural rights of man – to protect person and property'. Its proper sphere was definitely 'not to regulate commerce; not to educate the people; not to teach religion; not to administer charity; not to make roads and railways'.[40] He put the *Economist* together each week, working and sleeping at the Strand offices, where he sometimes dined with Hodgskin.[41] He contributed little of his own writing. But he did soak up the atmosphere, even if he preferred going to the Royal Italian Opera, or crossing the street to see *Westminster Review* editor John Chapman. Through Chapman he met the leading radical thinkers of the day, and a publisher for his first book in 1850.

*Social Statics* owed more to his *Economist* colleagues than his new friends, however. Both in its hostility to Utilitarian concepts of law and morality and style, direct and flippant, Spencer's book was exactly like an *Economist* leader. The visible hand of the state was slippery: what began with 'tax paid teachers' was bound to end in doctors and scientists, 'government funerals', and things so absurd only the French could have dreamt of them, 'public ball rooms, gratis concerts, cheap theatres, with state-paid actors, musicians, masters of ceremonies'. Meddling with the market-place was far from a laughing matter, however. It had truly dire consequences, upsetting a natural process of adaptation on which all material progress depended: 'principles that show themselves alike in the self-adjustment of planetary perturbations and in the healing of a scratched finger – in the balance of social systems and the increased hearing in a blind man's ear – in the adaptation of prices to produce and the acclimatization of a plant.'[42] A strong utopian element was evident. Spencer maintained that out of these harsh and slightly mysterious mechanisms of adjustment would emerge a perfect society of sexual equality, intellectual cultivation, and an end to private ownership of land.

This last point went too far for Hodgskin, who noted, in an otherwise glowing review in the *Economist*, 'the right of each individual is not to use the land ... but each to use his own fac-ulties'.[43] Laissez-faire nevertheless received an important new justification in Spencer, who, as one historian has argued, wished to show that 'the individualistic competitive society of Victorian England had been ordained by nature and was the sole guarantor of progress'.[44] If some elements of his positivist social philosophy postdate his time at the *Economist* – for example, his juxtaposi-tion of Lamarckian evolution and Darwinian natural selection after 1859, when he coined 'survival of the fittest' – these would be taken up with growing frequency in its pages.

One conduit for social evolutionary theories in the *Economist* was William Rathbone Greg, who came up with his own applications of them. In fact, Greg had met Darwin before Spencer, when, as classmates at the University of Edinburgh, both Darwin and Greg joined the freethinking Plinian Society. Where Spencer stressed the internal, class dynamics of Social Darwinism – the struggle for survival in nature applied to economic competition between individuals in the nation – Greg pushed it in other directions: to the competition between races and nations and even sexes. It was this version, very often opposed to that of Spencer, which had a major impact on the next editor, Walter Bagehot.

Greg authored some of the paper's most ardent laissez-faire positions, applied indiscriminately to the Irish, the Gospels, the working class and women. Like Wilson he was the son of a mill-owner turned publicist for the League, winning its praise for his 1842 essay *Agriculture and the Corn Laws*. He was even more socially conservative, while indulging in more Victorian symptoms and mystic fads than Wilson would have thought decent. A mesmerist, he also claimed to be able to magnetize livestock, and experienced melancholia, dyspepsia, neuralgia and vapours. He claimed to abhor fornication, especially in women. Under similar psychological pressures his wife and brother went mad.[45] Greg soldiered on, consoled that these and other traits could be discerned from inspection of the human skull – something he was glad to do at parties as a practising phrenologist. He also found time to write books and articles for the *Economist*, the *North British Review*, *Westminster Review* and *Edinburgh Review*.

Greg seems to have fallen out with most of the women he met in these liberal circles – a fact linked not only to his hobbies but his influence on the paper. One reason may have been an 1862 article entitled 'Why Are Women Redundant?', which argued that unmarried British women – all 1.5 million – should be asked to emigrate. 'He is very pleasing,' wrote his *Westminster Review* editor George Eliot, 'but somehow he frightens me dreadfully'. She praised his temperament and brain. 'But when you see him across a room, you are unpleasantly impressed, and can't believe he wrote his own books.'[46] The popular political economist and writer Harriet Martineau was more forthright. Greg was insolent, his mind unbalanced. She condemned his view of blacks as inherently inferior, and suspected him of writing *Economist* pieces

with 'mistakes of the grossest kind on the American constitution
... always on the slaveholding side'. Despite all contrary evidence,
she added later, 'he will go on supposing the Negro to be always
sucking cane sugar in the sun ... one might easily show him and
Carlyle negroes considerably less "savage" than themselves.'
At least Thomas Carlyle was a 'gentleman' where women were
concerned. Greg 'philanders vulgarly & on the other hand uncon-
sciously regards them insultingly'.[47]

After Wilson, Hodgskin and Greg, one of the most important
early contributors to the *Economist* was a foreigner who never
actually worked there – Frédéric Bastiat, the leading advocate
of free trade in France. Bastiat was a French complement to
Wilson, whom he met alongside other leaders of the Anti-Corn
Law League on his trips to England in the 1840s. The *Economist*
reported on his *Association pour la Liberté des Echanges* (modelled on the League), quoted from its journal, *Le Libre-Echange*,
reviewed his books – *Harmonies Economiques* was a special
favourite. Dubbed 'the Cobden of France', Bastiat's ability to distil
laissez-faire principles into epigrams surpassed that of anyone in
England. 'The state', he wrote in a style that captivated Wilson, 'is
the great fiction by which everybody tries to live at the expense
of everybody else'.[48] Bastiat considered the *Economist* a model.
'There never was a periodical in which all the questions of political economy were treated with so much depth and impartiality. It
is a precious collection of facts, doctrine and experience mutually
support each other in its columns: its diffusion on the continent
would have excellent effects.'[49] On his death the paper returned
the compliment, devoting an entire leader to 'the most consistent
and sturdiest opponent of Government action who has appeared
in our time, or, perhaps, has ever appeared in the world'.[50]

### The Belief Producer: 'Free trade principles most rigidly applied'

Such was the intellectual universe of some of the main characters: what did their efforts look like in the *Economist*, which
first appeared as a prospectus and preliminary number in August
1843? In it, Wilson promised 'original leading articles in which

free-trade principles will be most rigidly applied to all the important questions of the day'. His language conjures up images of
a crusade more readily than a business journal. Abroad he saw
'within the range of our commercial intercourse whole continents and islands, on which the light of civilization has scarce yet
dawned'; at home, 'ignorance, depravity, immorality and irreli-
gion, abounding to an extent disgraceful to a civilized country'.
In both cases the civilizing medium was free trade, which 'we seriously believe will do more than any other visible agent to extend
civilization and morality – yes, to extinguish slavery itself'. 'We
have no party or class interests or motives', he continued, in the
spirit of his pamphlets, 'we are of no class, or rather of every class:
we are of the landowning class: we are of the commercial class
interested in our colonies, foreign trade, and manufactures'. One
day, finally, it would be as difficult to understand the case for protection 'as it is now to conceive how the mild, inoffensive spirit
of Christianity could ever have been converted into the plea of
persecution and martyrdom, or how poor old wrinkled women,
with a little eccentricity, were burned by our forefathers for witch-
craft.' This was free trade as a mission, a worldview, which the
Economist promised to serve and spread.[51]

In its first two years the fledgling paper was true to its word,
examining the deleterious effects of tariffs on the supply, quality
and cost of sugar, wool, wheat, wine, iron, corn, cochineal, silk,
fish, lace, coal, coffee, wages, currency, tailors, slaves and French
linen. Information was conveyed in two densely packed columns,
beneath the ornate Gothic letterhead, The Economist: or the
Political, Commercial, Agricultural, and Free Trade Journal. The
paper gradually put on weight: sixteen pages the first year, twenty-
four the next, and twenty-eight for two decades afterwards. These
contained new sections, responding to reader requests and business
trends: banking and railway reports, a monthly trade supplement,
followed eventually by the first wholesale price index, statistical data on the terms of foreign trade, industrial profits, shipping
rates, insurance shares, capital issues, and anything else that could
be measured. Wilson altered the subtitle after less than two years
to the Weekly Commercial Times, Bankers' Gazette and Railway
Monitor, a Political, Literary, and General Newspaper – a signal

of his constant search for wider horizons, outside and beyond the League. Around that time a small notice began to appear, making the same point. 'The *Economist* from its extensive and increasing circulation among Members of Parliament, Bankers, Merchants, Capitalists, and the Trading Community, is well adapted as the medium for advertisements intended to meet the attention of those numerous and respectable classes.' Civil servants and professionals could have been added to the list. By the 1850s circulation was around 3,000 – small, even by contemporary standards, but held in the most powerful hands in the country and already sent to capitals in Europe and North and South America.[52]

The *Economist* addressed itself to the same social transformations that had given rise to Chartism – 'this great national leprosy … want and pauperism and hunger'. Yet in contrast to these other agitations it declared itself above class. It alone could speak disinterestedly, and it implored readers – the very ones with the power to do so – not to interfere with a divine order: 'personal experience has shown us in the manufacturing districts the people want no acts of parliament to coerce education or induce moral improvement … we look far beyond the power of acts … and the efforts of the philanthropist or charitable.'[53] From its point of view the danger was never just the protectionists in parliament but the quorum there of gentle souls totally ignorant of the laws of political economy.

The *Economist* considered it a duty to instruct the latter, starting with the abolitionists, 'that *body of truly great philanthropists*', of the unintended consequences of their campaign to end slavery. The boycott they proposed of all goods made using slave labour would hurt British consumers and punish slaves. It would decimate foreign trade: half was in textiles, most spun from slave cotton, and must logically extend to gold, silver and copper imports from Brazil; rice, indigo, cochineal and tobacco from the US, Mexico and Guatemala; and sugar and coffee from Cuba. To really help slaves, and encourage masters to offer them wages, the answer was free trade, which would demonstrate to slave owners that free labour was in fact cheaper than the bonded kind. Britain could do its part by ending special treatment for its own West Indian colonies, which practically forced others to use slaves as a way to stay competitive. 'That is a very doubtful humanity', it concluded, which 'seeks to inflict *certain* punishment upon poorer neighbours ... for some *speculative* advantage on the slaves of Brazil'.[54]

Almost all the social reform movements of the Victorian era, intent on actively improving the lot of the lower classes at home, received this sober going-over from the *Economist*. The editorial reaction to the railway and factory legislation is indicative, though by no means exhaustive. In obliging companies to provide once a day a third tier of service for working-class passengers, who had formerly to travel in exposed freight cars, the 1844 Railway Act meddled in a problem best left to market competition. 'Where the most profit is made, the public is best served ... limit the profit, and you limit the exertion of ingenuity in a thousand ways.'[55] That same year a Factory Bill limiting the workday for women to twelve hours, the same amount as for teenagers, was denounced as confused, illogical, harmful; proof that 'no consistent medium between *perfect freedom* of capital and labour, and that princi-ple which would regulate wages, profits, and the whole relations of life by acts of legislation – between perfect independent self-reliance and regulated socialism – between Adam Smith and Robert Owen', was possible. As if that were not emphatic enough the next week it declared, 'the more it is investigated, the more we are compelled to acknowledge that in any interference with industry and capital, the law is powerful only for evil, but utterly powerless for good.'[56]

The movement for a ten-hour day for adult males was there-fore little less than criminally insane, abetted by demagogues, and sentimental old Tories like Lord Ashley, who in fact favoured a more modest measure aimed only at women and children. This caveat made no difference. The result would be to reduce the supply of labour, raise wages, increase the cost of manufactures, undercut British goods in foreign markets, and ultimately destroy all employment and industry. As Lord Ashley's Ten-Hours Bill was taken up in 1846 the *Economist* reminded workers their interests were identical with those of their employers, and asked them to refrain from sniping about greed, for it 'must be remembered that the capitalists of England are exposed to a keen competition, not

only among themselves, from which no individual can escape –
and that capitalist is sure to go to the wall who is less sharp and
exacting than his fellows – but also to a similar competition with
the capitalists of other countries.'[57] The *Economist* attacked the
bill long after it had passed into law: for the factory inspectorate it
created – 'busybodies' who treated businessmen like 'thieves and
vagabonds' – and for infringing on the rights of women and children to spend as many hours as they wanted working, in whatever
way, be it at night or in relays.[58] The paper's influential tirades
helped opponents in parliament water down this and similar
measures.

Marx, a dedicated reader of the *Economist,* mocked its editor
mercilessly for his apocalyptic predictions about the effects of
these industrial regulations. In *Capital,* 'James Wilson, an economic mandarin of high standing', had simply rehashed the old
shibboleths of Nassau Senior in 1836, among them the notion that
'if children under 18 years of age, instead of being kept the full 12
hours in the warm and pure moral atmosphere of the factory, are
turned out an hour sooner into the heartless and frivolous outer
world, they will be deprived, owing to idleness and vice, of all
hope of salvation for their souls.'[59] A reduction in the working day
for children under nine had not, Marx added, forced cotton mills
to run at a loss. If Wilson and his writers applied the same kind
of logic to every legislative demand, even to those from which its
readers stood to benefit – the *Economist* was against patent law,
copyright protection or funding for scientific research, and for a
time against what is now considered basic company and banking
law[60] – it was measures to alleviate the lot of the worst off that
attracted its most ferocious objections.

In 1847 the newspaper opposed the creation of a board of health.
'We quite agree as to the evils', went a leader, listing common
urban plights such as narrow lanes, fetid pools of waste, and dingy
and badly ventilated housing, 'but the principle of *laissez-faire*
compels us to disagree with those who promote Lord Morpeth's
Board of Health Bill as the remedy'.[61] As the regulatory zeal of
the Board intensified, so did the hostility of the *Economist,* which
accused it of 'lapsing into protection' when it sought to merge the

water companies of London or require new sewer systems in large towns. 'Water is as much food as bread, and if the government must control the supply of the one, why not the other?' Recent cholera epidemics were but 'momentary terrors', and should not be allowed to 'suppress all the moral convictions which have been tangibly the experience of ages'.[62] A book review criticized 'the sanitary movement' for its 'shallow philosophy', bound to aggravate the two main causes of disease. If the first was poverty (for which the remedy was free trade),

> the second is that the people have never been allowed to take care of themselves. They have always been treated as serfs and children, and they have to a great extent become with respect to those objects government has undertaken to perform for them, imbecile ... Besides, it makes them demand things from government – such as regulation for labour, for rates and wages – which no government can possibly accomplish. There is a worse evil than typhus or cholera or impure water, and that is mental imbecility.[63]

Some wondered if there was a role for central or local authorities to play in the disposal of 'town guano'. 'Certainly not. We are now agreed that it should not feed the people: why should it clear away their dirt? Every man is bound to remove his own refuse.'[64] Attacks against public health officials and doctors grew violent and no one aroused such ire as the commissioner of the Board of Health, Edwin Chadwick, 'a man of sincere benevolence', but with 'one mental peculiarity that utterly disqualifies him for the executive services of his country ... he is essentially a despot and a bureaucrat'. The *Economist* rejoiced when he was forced to resign in 1854, but felt 'free-born Britons' were unsafe from his 'frightful pertinacity' so long as he remained in the country. The solution was to send him to Russia, as a gift, 'to preside over and reform her corrupt but far stretching bureaucracy'.[65]

The *Economist* was not only opposed to public education of any kind. It even objected to charity schools which, by providing for children, removed all restraint on the appetites of their parents, who begat more of them. In London alone, 80,000 clogged the streets. 'The houseless, deserted children have benevolence to

thank for tempting their parents from the path of duty', the paper
opined. Alms and the state were poor substitutes for nature and
reason; the truly compassionate were advised to let the struggle
for survival run its course.

> The whole history of the poor – weekly doles of loaves and soup;
> labour rate acts; the whole vast scheme of protecting their indus-
> try; charitable education, as well as alms-giving in the streets;
> factory acts; visiting the poor in their abodes; plans of emigration,
> and plans of penal reformation, have all in time been intended to
> promote the wellbeing of the poor, and have all ended in produc-
> ing the population, which, according to Lord Ashley's description,
> is about the most degraded in Europe.[66]

The *Economist* reiterated this position, even as pressure mounted
in parliament for some form of national education bill in 1850
and 1851. 'To be successful education must be sought from self-
interest, and obtained by self-exertion.' Common people should be
'left to provide education as they provide food for themselves'.[67]

Editorials often went beyond denouncing particular laws as
misguided: they also laid out grand theoretical statements, as in
a series of articles asking, 'Who is to Blame for the Condition of
Society?' After weighing in turn the role of the lower classes, the
capitalists, the landowners and the state, the *Economist* found
that the first and last shared responsibility – but unevenly. For in
a world in which 'each man is responsible to nature for his own
actions', and for learning from them, the poor were fully culpable for their misery, wasting wages and free time on sex, drink
and gambling instead of practising thrift and self-improvement.
'Looking to their habits, to their ignorance, to their deference to
false friends, to their unshaken confidence in a long succession of
charlatan leaders, we cannot exonerate them. Nature makes them
responsible for their conduct – why should not we? We find them
suffering, and we pronounce them at fault.' The capitalists and
landlords, taken together, were selfish, but so much the better, 'for
the larger their income, the greater is the quantity of net produce
provided for the food of the community, and the greater is the

quantity of employment and the amount of wages for the labouring classes.' As for the state, it was simply unable to comprehend this complex social organism, and by attempting to enact laws whose effects no one could predict in advance, undertook a task 'rather fit for God than man'. The reality was that 'the desire for happiness, or what is called self-interest is universal. It is not confined to man – it pervades the whole animal kingdom. It is the law of nature, and if the pursuit of self-interest, left equally free for all, does not lead to the general welfare, no system of government can accomplish it.' A more total and radical justification of individual responsibility in a market society is hard to imagine.

That all of these prescriptions could seem unfeeling the *Economist* was aware. But that they were anything other than absolutely true and ultimately humane was out of the question. Political economy was a science and so certain was the newspaper that its laws had been discovered, and by whom, that it argued repeatedly for changing its very name.

> The application of the adjective *political* to the science of 'The Wealth of Nations' is of French origin; and never was an epithet more misapplied; for the distinguishing feature of Smith's science is the proof it continually supplies that all policy – unless *laissez-faire*, or standing idle and religiously refraining from interfering, can be called a policy – is erroneous, injurious to the production of wealth, and repudiated by the science.

Political economy was a contradiction in terms because economics was the absence of political interference as such. 'All matters connected with politics being but tradition, guess-work, assumption, fancy, usurpation, or expediency, there is no other science in politics but political economy.' A review, penned by Hodgskin, of Cornewall Lewis's *Treatise on the Methods of Reasoning and Observation in Politics,* criticized Lewis for accepting the very term, for 'the principles of the science of the production of wealth may altogether be contrary, as we know they are in many cases, to the practices of political society, and, far from being subservient to it, may be destined to subvert it.'[68]

## Free Trade's Triumph, Ireland's Tragedy

Despite holding to this essential antagonism between politics and economics, and the primacy of the second over the first, Wilson followed leaders of the League into parliament. Stockport, just outside Manchester, returned Cobden to the House in 1841, the year Sir Robert Peel formed a Tory government after a decade of Whig rule under Lords Melbourne and Grey. Bright joined from Durham, farther north, in 1843. Together they made the lower chamber echo with free trade motions, though both were surprised by the speed of their triumph, as well as its instrument. Peel split the cabinet and shocked and angered his own party with a bill to phase out the Corn Laws in 1846. What had caused this volte-face? In his last speech as prime minister, Peel gave the credit to Cobden, 'the name which ought to be, and which will be associated with the success of these measures'. Cobden was more modest, reckoning that 'despite all the expenditure on public instruction, the League would not have carried the repeal of the Corn Laws when they did, if it had not been for the Irish famine'.[69] For Peel, the immediate impetus was indeed Ireland, England's oldest and longest-suffering colony. Here the appearance of an unknown, virulent fungus, which quickly turned healthy potatoes into black decaying mush, was set to expose the failings of English rule – imposed over three centuries of conquest and colonization, to the benefit of a ruthless Protestant elite. By November 1845 it was clear that at least half the crop of potatoes in Ireland was infected, 'either destroyed or unfit for the food of man', that the same would hold next year, and that this spelled doom for Irish peasants, who unlike the English or Scottish relied almost entirely on potatoes for food. On the brink of a major crisis and with all the accumulated arguments in its favour, the pressure to allow the free entry of grain into Ireland had been enormous.

To pass his repeal of the Corn Laws, Peel had relied on support from the Whigs, almost as angry with him for stealing their signature issue as the Tories were for his somersault on it. Both parties conspired to topple him the next year. The Whigs won the election that followed, and Wilson was among the new arrivals: sent from Westbury in Wiltshire, a constituency Radnor had found him, in which he beat the West Indian planter Matthew Higgins by 21 votes. Months later Wilson was appointed to the India Board. The *Economist* was now edited from the heart of government, just as the new Whig regime faced full-scale famine in Ireland. What role did the *Economist* play in the official response to it? In accordance with the laissez-faire outlook of the ministers in charge of the emergency, cheap provisions were expected to flow from the act of repeal straight into Ireland.[70] Would these suffice? Late in November 1847 the *Economist* grew alarmed at rumours that a grant of £3 million was about to be made to Ireland to allow it to buy food, urging its countrymen to reflect that this would increase the price of grain, not the supply, causing hardship in England to alleviate it in Ireland. 'Charity was a natural English error.' But it could be corrected. The only ways to mitigate scarcity were '*to procure more food or eat less*'. Or to at last throw open the ports, in which case, 'any supply that America could afford would then be brought hither by the regular course of trade, and employment – not eleemosynary aid – would enable people to purchase it.'[71] The result of following the *Economist*'s prescriptions was a utopian social experiment on par with the better-known holocausts of the twentieth century.[72] During the worst of the famine years of 1845–1849, one and a half million people died out of a population of 8 million, and another million fled.

The British government showed its commitment to the invisible hand of the market throughout, with the *Economist* critical of even the smallest departure from its rigours. In 1845–1846 Peel had shown insufficient firmness. He had ordered small batches of Indian corn to be bought discreetly by Baring Brothers in North America, as a reserve to keep prices in check; but the severity of the famine forced him to release small dribbles at select government depots. In 1846–47 the Russell administration, in which Wilson served, announced that it would buy no more foreign grain: Charles Wood, Chancellor of the Exchequer, and Charles Trevelyan, Assistant Secretary, blamed Peel's purchases the year before for paralysing trade by deterring dealers and merchants from importing adequate supplies on their own.[73] No forgiveness was to be shown to small tenants unable to pay rent, or who faced starvation if they did. Under no circumstances were exports to be restricted, as some in Ireland were demanding. True, even as people scrounged for nettles, thousands of tons of wheat, oats, cattle, pigs, eggs and butter were sailing out of the country. Yet this was all for the best. For in a free trade world the high prices these articles obtained abroad would allow merchants to buy and import cheap food to make up the lost potatoes.[74] In practice what private enterprise there was in Ireland never imported enough, or at prices most could afford.

The correspondence between high officials was laden with nostrums lifted from the *Economist,* as the paper itself acknowledged when reviewing a parliamentary selection of them in 1847. But this only spurred it to attack compromises made on humanitarian grounds, in full knowledge of the errors committed. 'We totally deny that what is wrong in *principle can* be right in practice. If a principle be true there can be no exception to its application, and least of all can it be abandoned or neglected in an *extreme* case.'[75] The paper was aware that Adam Smith had sanctioned public works in like situations. But it doubted if he would still approve, and defended him from a hostile pamphlet, *The True Cure for Ireland,* which called it 'perfect folly to be dancing a Will-o'-the-wisp dance, after the abstract principles of political economy, as laid down by Adam Smith, for it ought to be remembered he wrote for a country advanced in social position and high civilization.' On the contrary, retorted the *Economist,* 'Smith wrote for all time, and of all time'.[76]

Wilson not only ensured that his paper constantly firmed up civil servants and politicians over Ireland: he soon enlisted them to craft the *Economist* itself. George Villiers, the fourth Earl of Clarendon, and one of his original backers, was appointed Lord Lieutenant of Ireland in the spring of 1847. He was in constant touch with Wilson, feeding him data on the famine – from potato yields to confidential reports on Irish Poor Law returns intended for cabinet eyes only. On taking up his post in relatively optimistic mood, Clarendon asked for *Economist* articles on landlord-tenant relations. Did Wilson have 'any hints' on the ideal form of lease? A few months later he asked him to 'prepare the public mind' for his plans to effect large scale emigration out of Ireland. As one ostensibly liberal policy after another failed to do any good, however, both began to despair of the whole race. A crackdown was needed.[77]

When a number of landlords were assassinated in the winter of 1847, Clarendon became convinced an armed insurrection was brewing and threatened to resign unless he was given extraordinary powers to protect life and property. The *Economist* supported him: the 'special duty' of government in such a country was not to tamper with the labour or money markets but to counter the turbulence that 'had driven away capital'; 'the more dangerous the state of society becomes the more necessary it is that order and security should be enforced.'[78] A Coercion Bill received the royal assent in December, and as Engels observed, 'the Lord Lieutenant was not slow in taking advantage of the despotic powers with which this new law invests him.'[79] In the summer of 1848, Clarendon wrote to Wilson that the bill was a 'complete success', thanking him for articles 'exhibiting your accurate knowledge of Ireland and friendly feeling towards myself'. As for the country he was ruling, he felt 'like the governor of an ill-guarded jail … they have been made a nation of political gossips instead of agricultural labourers, and as they sow idleness so they reap misery'.[80]

When an uprising did occur that summer it was not the work of the starving masses, as officials had feared, but of a small band of intellectuals in Tipperary calling themselves Young Ireland, easily subdued by local constables. They were 'the laughing stock of the world', jeered the *Economist*. Still, the precautions taken by government – suspending habeas corpus, dispatching an extra 15,000 troops and ordering the fleet to patrol the coast – were sensible.[81] The *Economist* urged their extension for twelve months and that martial law be declared. Trials by jury should be cancelled: military tribunals alone could be relied on to punish rebels. 'It is liberty, not despotism, which acts as an irritant to the Irish constitution. It simply, as doctors say, *does not agree with it*. The oriental element – mental prostration before power – is paramount.' 'Powerful, resolute, but just repression' would render the Irishman 'not only submissive, but content'. It continued:

These suggestions will sound strange in English and in liberal ears. But it is time the truth should be spoken boldly out that

the ideal of equal laws for England and Ireland is a delusion,
a mockery and a mischief ... not till Ireland has been trained
and inured to respect and obey the law by years of rigid and
severe enforcement, will she have learnt those lessons of justice,
honesty, truth, and subordination, which can alone entitle her,
by sharing English virtues, to share English liberties and English
institutions.[82]

This was enough to make even Clarendon hesitate: 'I would like
to hear how your articles have been received by the middle classes
in England, and whether they are prepared to go your lengths.
Pray let me know this as it may to a certain extent guide my proceedings.' Clarendon had earlier voiced doubts about the lengths
to which Wilson was taking laissez-faire in Ireland, feeling that
repression must be coupled with relief, and by 1849 he implored
Russell not to leave the Irish, in Trevelyan's phrase, to 'the operation of natural causes'.[83]

Revolutionary disturbances were not confined to Ireland in 1848,
as upheavals swept across Europe, threatening not just continental
monarchies but alarming even the crown-in-parliament in Britain,
where Chartism saw a brief, unnerving revival. The *Economist*
could find no words harsh enough to describe 'a movement around
which are aggregated all the turbulence, all the rapscallionism, all
the demagogic ambition of the nation'. Its demands would hand
power to the 'one class exclusively, the most open to corruption
and deception ... partial, unfair, fatal, despotic'. Editorials argued
that electoral reform would only infantilize the lower orders yet
further: 'it unteaches the people the great lesson of self-dependence;
it encourages them to look to government rather than themselves,
both for the causes and the remedies of their sufferings'. Political
leadership belonged to the middle classes. They paid the most tax
and practised the virtues, 'frugality, industry and forethought', on
which the prosperity of all other classes depended.[84]

The appalling tumult in European capitals, on the other hand,
put these domestic troubles in perspective. If there was some hope
in Germany, since the revolution there was 'led by the nobles, and
consecrated by the priests', France was lost: it had too many state

employees, no respect for property (or credit: deposits had been frozen), and was obsessed by the wrong kind of freedom, 'equality ... without the slightest care for personal liberty ... the right of unfettered action and speech'. Compared to the Irish or the French, the English were relatively safe: 'order is beloved; property is sacred; we respect the rights of others.' In private Wilson was even more scathing about the French, 'a weak, puerile and despicable race ... the only thing that will do them any good is the iron grasp of a sturdy but wise despot'.[85]

## City, State, Empire: Joining the Gentlemanly Capitalists

The *Economist*'s influence grew in lockstep with that of its editor. Wilson sat on the parliamentary committees – Commercial Distress, Banking, Currency, Life Insurance – crafting the policies on which his paper pronounced each week. His aristocratic colleagues, a little unsure about the rudiments of political economy, leant on him. The ageing Duke of Wellington, victor of Waterloo and a monument to Tory reaction, required a private tutorial before agreeing to let repeal of the Navigation Laws pass through the upper chamber. The Whig imperialist Lord Palmerston took his lessons on early morning strolls back from Whitehall; his amusing banter more than making up for his 'belligerent propensities'.[86] Lord Grey, grudging sponsor of electoral reform in 1832, passed colonial news – Guiana, the Cape, a lecture by Lord Elgin on the progress of Upper Canada – to the paper. The diplomat Lord Howden paid a visit before setting sail for Argentina and Brazil to negotiate lower sugar duties, promising news of his progress.[87] Wilson carried these intimacies into the countryside, first in Wiltshire, then in Somerset, with hunting, ponies for the girls, gentlemanly pursuits – judging sheep contests – rounding out the days.

This change in status was accompanied by a shift in interest from industry, where his father had given him his start, to finance – destined in the framework of the British Empire to benefit from free trade to a greater extent than any other branch of commerce. In 1852, during a brief interlude of Tory rule under

Lord Derby, Wilson went to work on a new venture, which he
must have partially funded from *Economist* profits: the following year the Banker's Gazette section of the paper announced
the founding of a Chartered Bank of India, Australia and China,
initial capital £1 million, prospects 'unrivalled', success 'beyond
doubt'.[88] Wilson's pieces for the *Economist* on the 1847 financial crisis – published as *Capital, Currency and Banking* the same
year – pointed out, in the wake of so many bank failures, a field
for profitable investment in the Far East, and lessons on avoiding a similar fate there. For the official historian of Standard and
Chartered Bank, this explains a charter initially restricting its
exchange activities. Wilson showed 'grave caution', and emphasized that the note issue would be covered by 'public securities
and bullion on the same principle as was observed by the Bank
of England'.[89] Wilson insisted the bank be pan-Asian and include
India, a case he made directly to Gladstone in a letter lobbying for
a royal charter over the objections of the East India Company and
the Board of Control.[90] In the next few years the Chartered Bank
expanded rapidly, driven by the growth of trade within Asia, most
importantly in Indian opium, for the sake of which Britain would
fight a second war with China.

At almost the same moment, Wilson was promoted to high
government office in the Peelite-Whig coalition headed by Lord
Aberdeen. As Financial Secretary to the Treasury until 1857, he
assisted Gladstone in drafting his first budgets. To these landmarks in fiscal minimalism he contributed consolidation of
customs duties, reducing or ending levies on soap, tea and apples,
and cutting and simplifying all other import rules, a long-standing
demand of City merchants whose realization Wilson viewed as
a capstone of the free trade movement in England.[91] In 1855
Cornewall Lewis succeeded Gladstone as Chancellor, making the
Treasury an *Economist* stronghold. An academician whose deliv-
ery was described by a contemporary as 'enough to dishearten
any political assembly ... nearly inaudible, monotonous, halting',
which yet 'covered very powerful resources of argument, humour
and illustration',[92] he once told his friend: 'You see, Wilson, you
are an animal, I am only a vegetable.'[93] The self-deprecation was

not to be taken seriously: Wilson held him in high regard, and with Lewis's help was about to stamp his ideas on the map of the world.

Now ensconced at the pinnacle of the state, Wilson was in a position to survey the empire it had acquired, and was continuing to expand. A series of wars to defend and augment its borders, secure bases, trading rights and routes, and check the progress of rivals, coincided with his new vantage point. British imperial power started to become central to the liberal worldview of the *Economist* in ways it had not been before. In the 1840s the paper had viewed even white settler colonies like Canada either as burdens that cost more to defend than they were worth, or as simple outlets for trade and investment, over which it was unnecessary to exert direct control. (In this spirit, it once wanted to dismiss the entire diplomatic corps and replace it with merchants, who 'may feel petty slights in intercourse with foreigners' but never got so worked up as to risk their lives, while 'inflated representatives excite strife and bloodshed on account of dignity'.)[94] This was a position that could draw on Adam Smith and the Physiocrats, for whom colonies were among the most misguided and pernicious forms of protection. To their anti-mercantilist agenda, the *Economist* of these years added its theory of natural harmony, according to which free trade meant peace and goodwill not just at home between classes, but among the nations of the world as well.

Once Wilson was in government, however, the *Economist* revised this earlier vision of laissez-faire. Where imperial interests were at stake, war could become an absolute necessity, to be embraced. This conversion split the free traders of the 1840s, escalating into an epic confrontation with the most profound consequences for the *Economist* and the liberalism it embodied, which played out over a run of interconnected imperial conflicts from 1853 to 1860. Wars against Russia and China, and conflicts in India, rocked British liberalism at home and recast it abroad. Since then, the *Economist* has rarely wavered from the view that laissez-faire may best be furthered through the barrel of a gun.

## Crimean Turning Point: Liberals Fall Out

Though little remembered today, the Crimean War was by far the largest armed conflict in the century between 1815 and 1914, involving pitched battles between the major powers in Russia and the Balkans, and naval clashes from the Black Sea to the Baltic and the Arctic to the Pacific. The war was ostensibly triggered by religious quarrels in Ottoman-controlled Palestine, and at stake was the fate of the Ottoman Empire itself – a large part of which still stood in south-eastern Europe – and which of the rival predators would dominate or dismember it: Russia in the East, or Britain and France in the West. War fever took hold of the British press late in 1853, when news reached London of the destruction of the Ottoman fleet at Sinope on the Black Sea, after a surprise naval bombardment by Russia. The *Economist,* however, had been clamouring for an armed solution to the 'Eastern Question' – i.e. war with Russia – a year prior to the 'disgraceful and melancholy butchery' at Sinope: before, that is, much of the press – from the *Westminster Review* and the *Spectator* to the *Times* – took up the same cry.

Its editorialists dismissed the religious dimension of the question: disputes between the Russian Orthodox, French Catholic and Protestant Churches over control of holy places in Jerusalem and Bethlehem were an excuse for their respective nations 'to peck at the unfortunate carcass of the Porte'. The issue lay elsewhere. If Britain failed to intervene to prop up the Ottomans against the Russians, its own empire in the Near East was in danger:

> Russia will have command of Constantinople and the Dardanelles ... she will be closer to the Levant than ourselves ... her command over the Ottoman Court might at any time induce it to close off the Isthmus of Suez to us, or oblige us to engage in war to prevent such a catastrophe. It is perfectly obvious that our interest imperatively require either that Egypt shall be in our own hands, or in those of a naturally friendly and really independent power.[95]

In building its case for war the *Economist* blazoned its break with those who held that free trade automatically meant peace, or counselled the 'hideous and shallow doctrine' of non-interference in foreign affairs, even in the face of 'barbarous sovereigns oppressing their subjects, or powerful states bullying and partitioning their weaker neighbours'. Ethical and commercial justifications for war with Russia were one. 'Turkish independence', 'territorial integrity', 'justice, honour and national existence' appeared side by side with warnings to British businessmen of the consequences of letting Tsar Nicolas take Constantinople.

> That anyone who values India and is prepared to maintain and defend it, who regards England as a great empire and not as a little workshop, and who knows how much even of our safety depends upon our naval and especially our Mediterranean supremacy, should profess willingness to permit Russia to plant herself on the Bosporus and the Aegean, and regard it as a matter of indifference whether the key of our Eastern communication be held by a harmless friend or by a formidable rival – this, we confess, passes our powers of comprehension.[96]

The sooner war broke out the better, for a 'precarious and ill-conceived peace is almost as fatal and discouraging to commerce as actual hostilities'.[97]

By the turn of 1854 Palmerston and his war party in parliament and the press had pushed a cautious cabinet headed by Aberdeen into striking an ambitious blow against Russia, with a scheme to shore up British interests in the Near East by offering swathes of the Baltic to Prussia, of the Balkans to Austria, and of the Caucasus to Turkey. Britain and France fought as allies, each loath to see the other benefit by the outcome, Britain eyeing with particular suspicion France's competing claims in the Levant. The elderly British commander, Lord Raglan, who had lost his right arm at Waterloo, sometimes confused the French and Russians.[98] From beginning to end the joint expedition was a disaster. French and British soldiers arrived in the pestilential Danube Delta in summer, and were sent on to the Crimea without maps, proper kit, food or medicine; they froze at the onset of winter. The battles of the Alma and Balaclava were beset by tactical errors; the siege of Sebastopol became the longest at that time in recorded history.

The same papers that had bellowed for war now sent back, for the first time, horrifying images and stories from the front line.

The *Economist*, however, was not among them. 'Our Gallant Army in the Crimea' depicted a dying Maréchal Saint-Arnaud, deeply stirred by the behaviour of his British opposite number at the Alma. 'The bravery of Lord Raglan', he said, before breathing his last, 'rivals that of antiquity. The rest of this item was a dispatch from ... Lord Raglan.'[99] As expectations of a quick victory dissolved, its coverage attempted to rally public opinion behind a Homeric struggle which 'may task all our endurance ... the commencement of that great conflict between liberty and despotism which Canning and Napoleon alike predicted as inevitable'. It reminded readers of the nature of the enemy, 'whom we know to be the resolute, instinctive, conscientious foe of all that we hold dearest and most sacred – of human rights, civil liberty, enlightened progress'. Worse still, 'freedom of trade, freedom of movement, freedom of thought, freedom of worship – all are proscribed as deadly sins in the Decalogue of Muscovy'. Giving thanks to the country's ally, it explained: 'France and England alone venture to make head against the terrible Colossus', which, but for their courage, 'would reign over Europe from the Ural Mountains to the Alps and Apennines, if not to the Pyrenees, without a rival and without check'.[100]

Diplomatic efforts for a negotiated peace were shot down from the beginning. The *Economist* sided with Palmerston, now prime minister, who wished to keep France in the war at all costs – with 310,000 men-in-arms compared to 98,000 for Britain, France's will to fight started to flag earlier – and to expand operations, fielding an army to attack Russia through the Baltic. 'Peace at any price or war at any cost?' This was the wrong way of looking at the problem. 'The correct mode is to inquire whether the objects we aim at be just? If they be, they must be fought for to the last drop of our blood and the last sovereign in our coffers.'[101] Around this time the *Economist* finally acknowledged that cholera and typhus were killing more soldiers than the Russians. Yet the paper found Britain, at least, 'was never served by abler or more zealous or more honest men', and with the benefit of hindsight was even able to pull some lessons from the wreckage.[102] Thanks to 'the unimpaired resources of empire', it declared in February 1856, shortly before the Peace of Paris was signed with its grudging assent, 'never was there a year of greater or more uniform prosperity'.[103] In the end, 21,000 British soldiers died, 16,000 from disease, exposure or starvation, along with 100,000 Frenchmen, 120,000 Turks and 450,000 Russians.[104]

Some of the *Economist*'s bellicosity can be explained by the fact that Wilson and Greg were government agents, making the paper a scrapbook of their wartime service. Setting aside previous scruples, Wilson defended Cornewall Lewis even when the latter caused an outcry among free traders for raising duties on sugar, spirits, coffee and tea in 1855.[105] A £5 million loan to Turkey was needed, which Wilson helped to negotiate. He sprinkled lead articles with details of his meetings in Paris with Lord Cowley, ambassador to France, and Achille Fould, French finance minister. He secured the post of Commissioner of the Customs for Greg – also in Paris, transcribing his chats with the former premier François Guizot. Wartime London was a similar whirlwind of Allied loans and socializing, with Wilson near the centre: balls in honour of Louis-Napoleon, medal ceremonies for crippled heroes, and dinner parties; at one Ferdinand de Lesseps pitched his plans for the Suez Canal to Wilson over pudding as the poet Matthew Arnold, another guest, looked over the proposal.[106]

Neither Wilson's editorial interventions nor his social life passed unnoticed in the wider liberal world, with which he had sometimes disagreed on foreign policy as early as 1850.[107] Cobden and Bright furiously opposed the Crimean War, and had savage things to say about former brothers-in-arms who lent it support. Wilson was in a class apart, however; his betrayal was both personal, in light of the help they had given him to found the *Economist*, and political. All three had once shared a view of empire as a feudal residue. In Cobden's early pamphlets free trade was perhaps less pronounced a theme even than the evils of foreign wars. *England, Ireland and America*, written in 1835 when he was thirty-one, summed up his position, which did not change. Trade was 'the grand panacea', the only thing, in stark contrast to misguided meddling abroad, likely to spread liberal institutions: 'not a bale

of merchandise leaves our shores, but it bears the seeds of intelligence ... to the members of some less enlightened community; not
a merchant visits our manufacturing industry, but he returns to his
own country the missionary of freedom, peace and good government'.[108] In the *Economist*'s early years Wilson devoted countless
leaders to demonstrating how this process worked in practice. In
the House of Commons, Cobden aimed to cut defence budgets;
outside, he became an active member of the Peace Society. Free
trade, peace and goodwill was his motto – the first naturally fostering the second, and vice versa. The idea that one country might
force another to trade freely, let alone be free, never appealed to
Cobden. Calling on the Royal Navy to pry open foreign markets
or protect trade routes and lines of communication struck him as
outrageous and hypocritical; now, though, the very liberals with
whom he had fought against the Corn Laws were taking up this
call. That Wilson was among them, formerly the most rigid expos-
itor of laissez-faire principles imaginable, was a shock.

For Cobden the language used by the *Economist* and the rest
of the hawkish press – 'integrity of the Turkish Empire, balance
of power' – were 'words without meaning, mere echoes of the
past, suited for the mouths of senile Whiggery'.[109] Wilson was a
'Whig valet', his defection symptomatic of a general desertion of
wealthy Leaguers.[110] Asked if he had read the latest *Economist*,
which had backed a belligerent ultimatum to Russia, in December
1855, Cobden replied, 'I never see the *Economist* though I have it
on my conscience that I was mainly concerned in starting it. It was
always a dull stupid paper even when it was honest. But to read
sophistical arguments in no better style than Wilson's is a task I
would not condemn a dog to.'[111] Writing to Bright, he asked: 'Have
you heard Greg has got a commissionership of the Customs, given
him by Wilson, worth I suppose £1,200 a yr., & nothing to interfere with his literary pursuits? The state into which our press has
fallen is scandalous, dangerous to all sound public opinion, & it
ought to be ripped up with the tomahawk of exposure.'[112]

For its part the *Economist* battered Cobden and Bright week
after week. When Cobden published a letter in the *Leeds Mercury*
maintaining that the war was as unpopular as it was badly run, the
paper commented, 'Few idols have ever so grieved or disappointed

their worshippers as the member for West Riding ... Cobden is becoming disingenuous ... an ordinary demagogue.'[113] In 1853 it had welcomed his pamphlet criticizing Britain's annexation of Burma, 'How Wars are Got Up in India'. Now, in 1856, much the same stance applied to Crimea in 'What Next – and Next?' was 'irrational, feeble, and flagitious'.[114] As for Bright and his 'immoral moralizing', it was in danger of running out of epithets – he was 'the tool and sycophant of the Great Disturber of the peace', the 'intrepid advocate and reckless ally of the Czar' and 'worth a dozen regiments'.[115] When a lead article in the paper fulminated against his and Cobden's acts of deceit against the nation in arms – the article was entitled 'The Enemies of Free Institutions' – Bright directly addressed the *Economist* in the House of Commons, in a speech attacking the Turkish loan that Gladstone and Wilson had arranged behind the backs of parliament. 'It is understood by the occupants of the Treasury bench, that when the country is at war the House of Commons is to be a shadow.' Mocking the editorial anonymity behind which Wilson hid, he remarked:

If you want to know the opinions of Gentlemen upon the Treasury bench on this subject, I will give it you from a journal of great influence, which is supposed to be under the control of an hon. and very able Gentleman who sits upon that bench. Here is a paragraph which appeared in a leading article of that paper upon the 30th of December, 1854, and, of course, things are worse now – 'It is difficult to say whether the leaders of the Radicals or the leaders of the Tories – whether Lord Derby, Mr. Bright, or Mr. Disraeli – have done most to awaken us to a perception how mischievous, at critical conjunctures, free legislative assemblies may become. The plain truth is, that Parliamentary government is, in time of war, an embarrassment, a danger, and an anomaly, and we have to thank the advocates of an extended suffrage and the supporters of rotten boroughs for making it so plain. Legislative bodies are needed for legislation and control. They are not needed, and they are not fitted for executive action, especially in moments of peril and difficulty. The seldomer Parliament meets, and the shorter time it sits during actual hostilities, the better for the country which it represents, and the better for its own dignity and influence.' Now, that is a paragraph from the *Economist* newspaper.[116]

Bright had little doubt where the loan to fund an unjust war would end up. The money raised would not be given to the Turks directly, he noted, but to a French and English commission:

> If we could by possibility, with the knowledge which we possess of the history of the past, conceive ourselves in the Ottoman Empire and subject to its rule, with two of the Powers of the West coming and, under the pretence of defending us from an enemy, taking first the revenues of Egypt, then that of Syria, then that of Smyrna, the inlet and outlet of their commerce, and then appointing a commission to sit in our capital city to expend the money necessary to defray the expenses of our army, should we not say, the glory of the nation had departed, and with it the last shadow of our independence? Should we not say, that the nations pretending to assist us were but treacherous friends … ? [117]

Bright felt sure that behind the rhetoric of friendship lurked the desire for profit and territory, and he predicted that it would not be long before Britain and France made expansionist moves in the Near East. There he was wrong. The two allies in the Crimea turned their gaze instead to the Far East, where another backward and despotic empire was in need of liberal lessons in free trade.

## The Second Opium War

The signal for the Second Opium War was given in October 1856, when Chinese police arrested the Chinese crew of the *Arrow*, a *lorcha* (a type of junk) in Canton accused of piracy. The British consul claimed, falsely, that the vessel was flying the Union Jack, that it was registered in Hong Kong, and so based on a treaty signed in 1843 (in the wake of the First Opium War) the Chinese had no right to detain anyone on board. Sir John Bowring, the plenipotentiary, chief superintendent of trade, governor, commander-in-chief and vice-admiral of Hong Kong, then

sent a fleet to bomb Canton into submission – despite the fact
that its governor had already released the captives and agreed
to his terms, refusing only to apologize, since, as Governor Yeh
stated, the *Arrow* was Chinese. For this, three weeks of fire rained
down on Canton, followed by a four-year invasion ending in the
sacking of Beijing. Thus was China opened to Western trade and
culture.[118] France, Russia and the US joined in the attack, but
Britain and its special interest in one commodity gave the war its
name. British revenue from opium was so vast at the time that it
not only kept afloat the state machine in India, where most of the
opium was grown, but turned a trade deficit with Asia in silk, tea
and ceramics into an overall surplus.[119] Chinese opium addicts
were in demand, their supply limited by the ban the Qing dynasty
had imposed on this powerful narcotic.

The pretext for invasion, and a widespread suspicion that the
drug trade stood to benefit, sparked an uproar when news of
the 'Arrow' incident' reached London in 1857. The Conservative
opposition leader Lord Derby brought forward a motion on 24
February condemning British behaviour as 'the arrogant demands
of overweening, self-styled civilization', which was narrowly
rejected in the upper house.[120] Richard Bethell, Attorney General,
privately advised ministers, 'a very serious case against us on the
points of international law could be, and probably would be,
made in the Commons'.[121] Cobden stepped in with a censure
motion days later; carried by sixteen votes in a marathon debate,
it toppled Lord Palmerston's government, and an election was
called.

Behind the scenes Cobden exhorted his press contacts to expose
not only the illegality of British actions but also the free trade
arguments with which some justified them. 'There is no great
empire where our trade is a quarter as free', Cobden wrote, comparing the low duties charged in China favourably with Europe,
and rounding on those close to Wilson, from Clarendon to Porter.
Cobden denounced all groups backing war, from 'Manchester
fire-eaters' and 'the Liverpool China Association' to the intrigues
of Paris, London and Washington and the missionaries in league
with them. 'God help the Christians who think of making their
religion acceptable in the rear of an opium war', he wrote, 'for

surely nothing but an interruption of the laws of human nature by especial divine interposition could ever have that result!'[122]

This time the liberal backlash against any criticism of Britain's action abroad was still more venomous than over Crimea. Bowring, the official at the centre of events, was a liberal intellectual of high standing, onetime editor of the *Westminster Review*, disciple and literary executor of Bentham, a member of the League and the Peace Society, a non-conformist, ex-radical MP, who once exclaimed to a crowd in Bolton, 'Jesus Christ is Free Trade, and Free Trade is Jesus Christ.' He had also been a close friend of Cobden and Bright.[123] The *Economist* defended Bowring.[124] He had acted a little 'precipitously', but it would only sow mischief to reprimand or recall him: besides, even if he had been in error, and his actions were technically illegal, and even if, 'as regards that illicit trade our hands are not clean' – an allusion to opium – 'all declare that satisfactory, safe, and dignified intercourse with those arrogant and cruel people is impossible till they have met with severe chastisement'. The paper did not fear for Europeans resident in China, 'for the same mail that carries out this news will carry out such reinforcements as will put opposition and danger at defiance'.[125] In retrospect, there was a thread that ran between the wars in Crimea and Canton. 'Trade is as much a necessity of society as air or food or clothing or heat.' Interventions were therefore akin to humanitarian operations.

> We may regret war ... but we cannot deny that great advantages have followed in its wake. As the improvement both of Turkey and Russia will be consequent on the war now happily at an end; so any war with China that results in bringing her people more completely into trade communication with all other nations ... relieving them from the temptation to put infants to death, to allow the aged to die for want of food, and to exterminate great numbers from their standing in each other's way.[126]

The *Economist* and its allies prevailed, so far as public opinion was concerned, despite Cobden's victory over Palmerston in the House. In the ensuing election, Palmerston took his campaign to the country, with an endlessly reprinted manifesto that ran, 'An insolent barbarian wielding authority in Canton has violated the British flag.' Virtually the entire 'peace party' was swept from office – Cobden, Bright and Thomas Milner Gibson among them.[127] The *Economist* was exultant. Here was proof of who really represented the middle classes; not Manchester relics 'extinguished' by their pacifism, but the new Liberal Party. Bright ought to reflect on the 'unrepented sin' of his 'disregard of all patriotic feeling and decorum', rather than blaming electors who were just as interested in Peace, Retrenchment and Reform as ever, but stood firm for the flag. Ten years on from the repeal of the Corn Laws it was not they, but Bright who had changed. He did not understand the real men of Manchester, and the *Economist* endeavoured to educate him.

As a body wealth is not their *sole* pursuit, they are patriots as well as manufacturers. They think that there are higher objects both for men and citizens to strive for than mere material well-being. They did not grudge their hundred or thousand pounds subscription to the League for the defeat of Protection, and they were not likely to grudge their hundred or thousand pounds to the National Treasury for repelling Russian aggression. They did not like to be held up to the scorn and odium of the world as men who had no idea and no aim beyond their ledgers – as the incarnation of cold, hard, and narrow selfishness.[128]

Cobden drew more radical lessons from his defeat than Bright, and he advised the latter to take a break from politics and abandon his seat in Manchester. 'The great capitalist class formed an excellent basis for the Anti-Corn-Law movement, for they had inexhaustible purses, which they opened freely in a contest where not only their pecuniary interests but their pride as "an order" was at stake', Cobden reflected. 'But I very much doubt whether such a state of society is favourable to a democratic political movement.'[129] In another letter he complained bitterly of what the *Economist* had become, and of its role in pushing the government line on the war.

Jemmy Wilson wrote dull pamphlets and made duller speeches, but still he showed some Scotch pertinacity in keeping alive the agitation in the metropolis. When we dissolved our organization, a lithographed circular was sent to all its subscribers recommending them to support the *Economist*. This was the foundation of Wilson's fortune, which was in a sickly state previously ... [it] became the stepping stone to Office ... What so natural as that the paper should be the obsequious servant of the government, or the *Economist*'s pages should be employed in assailing the two men who laid the foundation of all this success, if they happen no longer to be in favour with the dispensers of patronage?[130]

Bright ignored the *Economist,* and only partly listened to Cobden, agreeing a few months later to stand for a vacant seat in Birmingham – as news reached Britain in 1857 of a bloody uprising in India.[131]

## India and the Indian Mutiny

In the climate of fear and vengeance that reports of the Indian Mutiny produced, criticisms of empire risked becoming still more unpopular, jeopardizing Bright's chances of re-election, and Cobden urged him to moderate his tone, at least in public. In private, both condemned 'the depraved, unhappy state of opinion', Cobden wondering what point there was in taking to the stump: 'I consider that we as a nation are little better than brigands, murderers, and poisoners in our dealings at this moment with half the population of the globe.'[132] Once back in parliament, however, Bright grew bolder, informing his Birmingham constituents that the Empire 'is a positive loss to the people' and 'neither more nor less than a gigantic system of outdoor relief for the aristocracy of Great Britain'. The rationale for fighting Russia and China, 'introducing cotton cloth with cannon balls', were 'vain, foolish and wretched excuses for war'. India, moreover, was a 'country we do not know how to govern', and Indians were justified in rebelling against British rule in the subcontinent, where the conquest of Oudh, 'with which our Government had but recently entered into a solemn treaty' was 'a great immorality and a great crime, and we have reaped an almost instantaneous retribution in the most gigantic and sanguinary revolt which probably any nation ever made against its conquerors'.[133]

Wilson found this last strophe on India so alarming that when he saw Bright in the Commons a few months later he obtained assurances from him that he had been 'carried away much further than he intended'. Wilson relayed these assurances to Cornewall Lewis, who wanted to know if Bright would cooperate on electoral reform should the Tories be turned out and a new Liberal ministry formed – inevitably including Palmerston or Russell, the very men Bright was castigating for criminal misconduct in imperial and foreign affairs.[134]

From 1857 the *Economist* was as fixated as the rest of the press on the horror stories pouring out of British India – where a mutiny of Indian soldiers, or sepoys, against their European officers in Meerut rapidly grew into a full-fledged rebellion against the British East India Company. By this time the quasi-private company, founded under Elizabeth I, ruled about two-thirds of the Indian subcontinent, in exchange for a £630,000 annuity to London on the revenue the land under its control generated. Three separate armies marched under its banners, one for each of the presidencies into which India was subdivided: Bengal, Bombay and Madras, totalling 232,000 Indians and 45,000 Europeans. The first of these was the largest and most homogeneous, recruited since the mid-seventeenth century from Hindu peasants in Bengal, Oudh, Bihar and Benares. These men mutinied in far greater numbers than anywhere else; a fact contemporaries attributed to an unwitting religious insult, infantry in Meerut – it was said – refusing to bite cartridges greased with cow and pig fat, offensive to Muslims and Hindus alike. In reality, their grievances were structural: both in the army – low pay, poor living conditions, an inability to rise through the ranks, in which the most senior Indian officer was obliged to obey the most junior European – and in the surrounding society, whose once formidable textile economy had collapsed under the onslaught of British manufactured cloth, while being subjected to an East India Company business model based on the predatory chase after new revenues and territories.[135]

The *Economist* was just as ruthless with Indians as with the Irish or Chinese. As Elgin ordered troops en route to China to double back to Calcutta, the paper looked forward to swift justice being meted out to the mutineers for their treachery in 'undiscriminating destruction of hospitals and barracks, of helpless women and children', which it contemptuously attributed to the 'native character ... half child, half savage, actuated by sudden and unreasoning impulses' more than to any coherent motivation or design.[136] It thought the worst was probably over by mid-July when the fall of Delhi to the rebels failed to ignite a general uprising. 'Three-fourths of the Bengal army – the whole of the Madras and Bombay – and the entire non-military population from Cape Comorin to the Himalayas, have stayed aloof ... could there be stronger evidence that, in spite of numerous errors, British rule is regarded by the natives of India as a blessing rather than a curse?'[137]

Even the 'barbarous and treacherous massacre of the garrison at Cawnpore', which, unlike the *Times* it declined to describe in detail, scarcely troubled its confidence in the future of empire.[138] In fact, the mutiny was soon viewed as little less than a blessing in disguise. A month later, it offered 'The Bright Side of the Picture' in a tone of elated Benthamite optimism. The English character perhaps required such a shock to 'startle and energize us' – 'a Crimean winter to convince us of the defects in our military administration, and a universal mutiny to open our eyes in India'. The sheer scale of the disaster gave British statesmen that rare thing, '*carte blanche* – an unencumbered field ... we are free to act as on the first day of our Imperial existence'.[139] This notion became the refrain of the *Economist.* 'No event less horrible could have strengthened our hands so powerfully.' If the sepoys had only committed garden-variety cruelties, 'the Government would have been assailed at once by a strong party likening the revolt to that of the American colonies, and recommending the nation not to resist a patriotic movement ... Eloquent voices would have been raised as Mr Bright's was formerly, to warn the nation that a due retribution had come upon them for a selfish feeling of grasping ambition.'

Yet now all these doubts and fears are absolutely stilled ... Every Englishman knows that to abandon India, would be to commit a far worse sin against the millions of Hindoos than against our own nation ... to the horrors of a military anarchy compared with which the reign of terror in the French revolution was a model of justice and mercy ... In Europe too they see how helpless are the Indian races to restrain their own superstitions and their own passions – that no reverence for law, and civil order, and social obligations, adequate for the rudest form of self-government is yet written on their minds ... Commerce with India would be at an end were English power withdrawn.[140]

British forces regained the initiative at the turn of 1858, with the active help or acquiescence of princely states in upper and central India, and the diversion of regiments from Crimea, Persia and China. Imperial troops, reconquering or relieving besieged cities – in Delhi, Cawnpore, Lucknow and elsewhere – exacted terrible revenge on whole populations deemed guilty of aiding rebels. The *Economist* noted with approval 'the stern vigour afforded by daily executions of mutineers of every rank' – some were shot from the mouths of cannons – but wondered whether journalists and officers calling for the head of every sepoy in a mutinous regiment, even those who had committed no violence, had thought through the domestic reaction that might ensue: 'it is at least worthy of consideration', it submitted, 'whether the deliberate execution of 35,000 men or more is a measure which the people and Government of England are prepared for'.[141] When the East India Company itself failed to survive the uprising, London henceforward assuming direct control of the new British Raj, the *Economist* gave the change a warm welcome.

## Noblesse Oblige: Wilson in India

One reason why the *Economist* embraced the new model of government for India became clear a month after a state of peace was declared. 'James Wilson', the *Times* announced on 5 August 1859, had consented to become 'Chancellor of the Indian Exchequer', tasked with mopping up the cost of the mutiny. As in Crimea this had exceeded *Economist* estimates, with the death toll from

the disproportionate British retaliation against Indian troops
and civilians in the hundreds of thousands.[142] The new appoin-
tee, the *Times* opined, 'will carry with him habits of business and
financial ability hitherto but too rarely exhibited on the banks of
the Hooghly, and if he succeeds in making India solvent, and in
proving that she can pay her own way, he will have rendered a
public service which cannot be too highly appreciated.'[143] Wilson
went on a farewell tour. He appeared with Bowring at a banquet
given by the mayor of Liverpool. The Cotton Supply Association
met with him in Manchester. Bradford's Chamber of Commerce
asked him to induce the Indians to clip their sheep only once
in nine months for finer fabrics. And after thirty-five years he
returned to Hawick. Around '70 Scotch gentlemen' were there
to toast him, and amidst their cheers he summed up his work
since leaving home. 'We have at last solved that great problem in
politics – that the real interests of society, well understood, were
common to all alike.' In India – whose interests were also 'to an
extent, identical' with those of Britain – he promised to raise revenues and cut the cost of the army, which had more than doubled
from £11,000,000 in 1855. 'I say if you cannot govern the country
and keep the internal peace for less than £21,000,000 you must
abandon it altogether.'[144]

During his valedictions Wilson gave effusive thanks to
Palmerston, who had interceded on his behalf many times since
1848. Confessing that he had initially declined the offer of a position as secretary at the Board of Control, a parliamentary body
that supervised the East India Company, he reported that 'the
noble Lord begged that I reconsider' telling him that 'a man who
enters public life must not confine himself to those few questions
of which he considers himself master'. In 1856, Queen Victoria
had blocked Wilson from a governorship in Australia, considering
it bad form for a commoner to run a place bearing her name. But
in 1859 Palmerston, now prime minister, made him vice-president
of the Board of Trade, before offering him such an exalted post
in India – sweetened with promises of a title and cabinet place
within five years.[145] Yet it was his time on the India Board, Wilson
reflected, without which 'I could not have assumed the duty which
has now devolved upon me'.

In that earlier stint in the Commons Wilson had indeed pushed for the kind of economic development the East India Company had been slow or unwilling to pursue. Railway construction was his main concern, sharing the view of Bright and other Manchester men that this would open the vast interior to British industrial goods and ease extraction of raw materials like flax, wool, indigo, sugar and above all cotton, where Britain was too reliant on the American South. His daughter Emilie remembered her father 'planning these Indian lines of railway on the dining-room table – lines over which eleven years later he himself was destined to travel'.[146] He pressed administrators to open the port of Karachi, hoping to tempt 'native dealers from Kabul', and personally carried wool and cotton samples to factories in Leeds. But to these goals Wilson added another, a direct extension of his concerns as editor and proprietor of the *Economist*, and now Chancellor of India: security of investment.[147]

'Wilson believed that he originally suggested', Bagehot – his successor at the *Economist* – would record, 'the peculiar form of state guarantee upon the faith of which so many millions of English capital have been sent to develop the industry of India.'[148] Peculiar because, as Wilson realized even before his arrival there, and with no less an authority than Mill to back him up, for liberal outcomes a compromise with liberal principles might be needed – at least when it came to what were commonly considered backward races.[149] Bagehot, who was even more alive to this problem, praised Wilson for his pragmatism: 'the necessity on the one hand, in an Asiatic country where the state is the sole motive power, of the Government's doing something – and the danger on the other of interfering with private enterprise, by its doing, or attempting to do, too much'.[150] Wilson took leave of Britain telling his audiences, 'I am one of those who believe that what is right in one part of the world cannot be wrong in another', for 'human nature is human nature the world over'.[151] In practice, however, he behaved as though India required very different measures to springboard capitalist development.

Wilson arrived in Calcutta in November 1859 with his wife and three eldest daughters, before setting out to meet the new viceroy of India, Lord Canning, on a tour of the Upper Provinces. He soon got to work, seeking to apply in under one year policies that had taken decades to enact in England. His first budget – with its dual task of raising revenue and keeping order – included policies Wilson had once opposed. He proposed a paper currency, for example, modelled on Peel's Act of 1844. Income tax would also be assessed, starting at 200 rupees, even as millions of pounds in spending were slashed. 'I am putting the screw on very strongly', he admitted.[152] He sought to do so with tact. Recycling his strategy from *Influences of the Corn Laws*, he tried to show Hindus that being taxed was as one with their own ancient laws, codified in the *Manu-Samhita*.[153] In the army he aimed to reduce the ratio of native Indians by shifting some to 'a great police system of semi-military organization', which, he claimed, would be 'cheaper by half a million', and safer for Europeans.[154] Finally, he set up an English system of public accounts, with estimates, annual budgets, and a national audit.

It is no coincidence that these moves all tended to increase the confidence of overseas investors. Wilson was such an investor, and that was his intention. As if to underscore the byways between empire and finance, Wilson arrived in India even as his Chartered Bank was opening branches in Calcutta, Bombay, Shanghai and Hong Kong, buoyed by the opium pouring into China, as well as those more benign-sounding commodities, which in contrast it actually named in its prospectus, circulating between China, Java, Ceylon, India, Manila, Australia and the rest of the region.[155]

His reforms did more than incorporate India into the formal structure of empire: they made it into that structure's financial cornerstone. Without the Indian Army, and the Indian revenues that paid for it, Britain could not have projected its power in Africa and the Middle East, let alone Central, South and East Asia. Nor could the international system of multilateral settlements and payments that emerged after 1858 have looked nearly as favourable to the City.[156] A stabilized British Raj pulled in capital from London: £286 million, or 18 per cent of the total invested in the empire from 1865 to 1914. The presence of so much foreign capital, in turn, made it crucial to maintain stability, and therewith investor confidence. India was expected above all to 'keep faith' with its creditors. Between 1858 and 1898 remittances averaged nearly half of exports, with 20 per cent alone going to debt service and Home Charges, an ingenious system by which Britain debited India for the cost of exploiting it. Meanwhile, the trade surplus India ran with much of the rest of the world allowed it to settle its trade deficit with Britain; and for Britain, in turn, to settle around two-fifths of its own trade deficit, mainly with Europe and North America.[157]

If his special mission concerned finance, Wilson was far from indifferent to the trappings of empire this brought with it. He was excited by the challenge of India, and his own power to act there, in contrast to London. He described the 'increased capacity of the mind when removed to a new scene of action ... I cannot tell you with what ease one determines the largest and gravest question here compared with in England', exulting that 'the Indian Exchequer is a huge machine. The English Treasury is nothing to it for complexity, diversity and remoteness of the points of action.'[158] Taking to his new imperial role with gusto, he relished the subtleties of frontier diplomacy as much as he enjoyed the dusty chaos of the financial files before him:

It is a most unwieldy Empire to be governed on the principle of forcing civilisation at every point of it. One day it is the frontier of Scinde and a quarrel with our native chiefs which our Resident must check: another, it is an intrigue between Heraut and Cabul, with a report of Russian forces in the background: the next, there is a raid upon our Punjab frontiers to be chastised: then come some accounts of coolness, or misunderstanding, or unreasonable demands from our ally in Nepaul: then follow some inroads from the savage tribes which inhabit the mountains to the rear of Assam and up the Burrampootra: then we have reported brawls in Burmah and Pegu, and disputes among the hill tribes whose relations to the British and the Burmah Governments are ill defined: then we have Central India, with our loyal chiefs Cindiah and Holkar, independent princes with most turbulent populations, which could not be kept in order a day without the presence of British troops and of the Governor-General's Agent.[159]

On his departure for India, Wilson relinquished nominal control
of the *Economist* first to Greg, and then to Bagehot's best friend,
Graham Hutton, who stayed on as editor during his absence in
Calcutta. In reality, the paper served the ambitions of its founder
and owner till the end. When controversy arose over his first
budget, Hutton and Bagehot leapt to defend it, attacking Charles
Trevelyan, now Governor of Madras, who publicly objected to
its steep spending cuts, tax rises and large procurements for the
army.[160] Wilson was outraged at this attempt to undermine his
authority, but he scolded his surrogates, accusing them in one of
his last letters of hurting his chances by going overboard in the
dispute.

Trevelyan was recalled for insubordination, yet the budget was
swept further into the political storm. In London, Bright and Sir
Charles Wood, secretary of state for India, backed the recalled
governor. All three put some blame for the mutiny on an overly
centralized bureaucracy and in Wilson's budget they saw those
tendencies exacerbated. Trevelyan had been the official most in
charge of 'relief efforts' during the Irish famine, and later Wilson's
colleague at the Treasury, where both had preached the purest
laissez-faire. Yet personally they did not get along. To Trevelyan,
Wilson was an unscrupulous climber whose sole aim in India was
to become Chancellor of the Exchequer back in Britain. 'Ordering
a salute and giving him a sort of public reception would be funny',
he wrote to Wood, anticipating Wilson's arrival in Madras. Wilson
saw Trevelyan as impulsive and vain, 'thinking himself able equally
to command a squadron, lead an army, or regenerate the civil government of a country'.[161] Obituaries for Wilson strongly implied
that this last administrative quarrel, and the advent of the rainy
season, caused a fever-gripped Wilson, murmuring to Canning
about 'his income tax' and in early August arranging his will, to
go to 'bed never to rise from it again'.[162]

# 2

## Walter Bagehot's Dashed Doubts

Founder, owner, editor, political high-flyer – no other leader of the *Economist* wore as many hats as James Wilson. But the name most associated with the paper he started is not his, which faded after his death in India in 1860. Lasting fame instead awaited his son-in-law and successor, Walter Bagehot, who remains not only the best-known editor of the *Economist,* but a totemic figure in and beyond its pages. Drawn as much to religion, literature, art, history and political gossip as the effect of tariffs on the price of salt, Bagehot forms a vivid contrast to Wilson, with far broader interests. In addition to money market summaries, Bagehot wrote two and often three or four leading articles a week on current events for sixteen years; in 1861 he wrote at least thirty-one just on the American Civil War. From these anonymous articles, as well as signed essays in the *National Review, Fortnightly Review* and other journals, Bagehot spun three major works between 1865 and 1873: *The English Constitution* and *Physics and Politics,* describing the subtle and secret evolution of government in England, and the world; and *Lombard Street,* on the causes and management of financial crises. *Economic Studies*, a guide to political economy and the lives of its most famous theorists, was unfinished at his death in 1877.

This prospectus has landed Bagehot on the reading lists of the Anglo-American ruling class since the late Victorian period. The jurist James Bryce called Bagehot 'one of the greatest minds of his generation' and ranked his constitutional insights above those of Tocqueville and on a level with Montesquieu.[1] 'The greatest

Victorian' pronounced the historian G. M. Young, after scanning a list that included Eliot, Tennyson, Arnold, Darwin and Ruskin.[2] While John Maynard Keynes had some doubts about his art criticism, he warmly recommended Bagehot's behavioural studies of the middle-class men who flourished in nineteenth-century Britain. 'Bagehot', Keynes noted in 1915, 'was a psychological analyser, not of the great or of genius, but of those of a middle position, and primarily of business men, financiers, and politicians.'[3] More fulsome praise came from across the Atlantic, where Woodrow Wilson was a devoted reader. In 1895 and again in 1898 the future president enthused about Bagehot in the *Atlantic* as a sheer pleasure to read: witty, prophetic, and the basis for his own analysis of the flawed American Constitution. Wilson kept a portrait of Bagehot on his study wall at Princeton, deriving from it 'much inspiration'.[4]

As the twentieth century progressed, so did Bagehot's reputation. In 1967, Labour prime minister Harold Wilson fondly recalled his student days at Oxford, preparing for a prize essay, reading *Economist* articles on state regulation of the railways by Bagehot – 'the most acute observer of the political and economic society in which he lived'.[5] In 1978, Harold Macmillan addressed the staff of the *Economist* on the subject of Bagehot. The former Tory prime minister, now eighty-four, mulled over Bagehot's virtues: 'gifted amateur', 'solid, sensible, perfectly straightforward' – 'because if you want to become the editor of a newspaper what can you do better than marry the daughter of the proprietor' – who didn't go in for 'theories and dreams' or 'extraordinary doctrines'. After losing the thread in a long complaint against the BBC, which had falsely reported Macmillan's death the summer before, prompting a daydream about withdrawing his money from Coutts and disappearing to 'a nice little estaminet' in the south of France to play boules, Macmillan concluded: Bagehot was 'the kind of man we'd awfully like to have known'.[6]

Today the picture is much as the elderly Macmillan left it. In 1992, the writer Ferdinand Mount still found Bagehot 'full of manly common sense' on the English Constitution; 'often witty, very often charming, he is never silly'.[7] A fictional memoir arrived in 2013 that was so true to life, the reviewers had trouble discerning its real author: historian Frank Prochaska, who presented Bagehot as 'the Victorian with whom you'd most like to have dinner'.[8] Bagehot's biographers have seen him in the same candlelit glow, with one searing exception, and have generally had a personal or professional interest in doing so, usually connected to the *Economist*.[9] That is hardly surprising. The *Economist* cannot be understood without Bagehot; neither can he, without it. Fifteen volumes of *Collected Works* make attributing authorship easier than for any other editor, and reveal three broad ways in which he changed the *Economist*, and through it, liberalism. The first was a sharper focus on the changing facets of finance; second, a comparative approach to political systems and institutions, with the explicit aim of discovering the ones best adapted to sustaining the phenomenal growth of finance – both at home, where the defeat or neutralization of the democratic demands of the working class was his top priority; and, finally, abroad, where he assessed the costs and benefits of empire.

## Walter Bagehot: Born Banker

Bagehot was born into a prosperous, well-connected provincial banking family in 1826. Vincent Stuckey, his maternal uncle, ran the bank, and Thomas Bagehot, his father, was a partner whose marriage to the widow Edith Stuckey had merged the leading shipping, mercantile and financial families of Langport in Somerset. Banking formed a backdrop to their lives, but for their son and 'greatest treasure' the Bagehots hoped for even wider vistas. His father, a plainspoken Unitarian, assigned history and philosophy in English and French. When Walter turned five, a governess introduced novels and Latin. His Anglican mother took up his moral education, bringing him to church on Sunday afternoons, though she inadvertently taught him about 'darker realities' too, during 'attacks of delirium'.[10] Little Walter was unruly, rode a pony named Medora, and climbed trees and would not come down.

His formal schooling built upon this liberal home life. In 1839 he left Langport Grammar School for Bristol College, where he studied classics, math, German and Hebrew. Three years later, at

sixteen, he enrolled at University College, London, where noncon-
formists sent their sons (unlike Oxford or Cambridge it had no
doctrinal test). He chased down still more subjects: after history,
poetry and math, he took a first in classics, followed by political
economy, metaphysics and, two years later, a gold medal in philosophy. He and his friends started a debating society, wrote each other
sonnets, and went to meetings of the Anti-Corn Law League.[11] At
one gathering the biggest stars of the movement spoke. Bagehot
was stunned by their oratorical skill. 'I do not know whether you
are much of a free-trader or not', he told a friend. 'I am enthusiastic about, am a *worshiper* of, Richard Cobden.'[12]

After graduating with his master's in 1848, he studied law, and
was called to the bar in 1852. In between he began to write articles on political economy for the *Prospective Review*. One of his
most audacious assessed the brand-new treatise by John Stuart
Mill, *The Principles of Political Economy*. 'I am in much trouble
about John Mill, who is very tough, and rather dreary', he told
his best friend, Richard Hutton. 'I am trying to discuss his views
about the labouring classes.'[13] Bagehot's own opinion of them was
not high. He wrote to his mother of his duties as a volunteer con-
stable in London, where a Chartist revolt was expected on 10
April 1848. Though unexcited at 'muddling about Lincoln's Inn
field with an oak staff', and by the Chartists, whose 'very violent
language is delivered to the world gratis by men in dirty shirts',
he found the government's precautions prudent: 'with the mass
of wretchedness in London, the slightest spark is dangerous and
must not be neglected.'[14]

It was a chance encounter in Paris, however, that led him to
turn his back on the law, while also reinforcing his distrust of
the popular political movements that flowered between 1848 and
1851, when artisans, workers and peasants supplied the thrust
for the liberal revolutions that briefly shook the autocratic capitals of Europe.[15] Bored in London, Bagehot left for the French
capital in the fall of 1851, witnessing a last-ditch effort to defend
the republican regime installed three years earlier. What Bagehot
saw – uneducated workers building barricades to defend the
Second Republic against Louis-Napoléon's coup d'état, before they
were crushed by the army – affected him deeply. He took notes,

and seven 'letters' from Paris appeared in the *Inquirer*, a Unitarian journal. Their provocative intent was to justify the coup to liberal opinion in England, as a way to restore confidence among shop-keepers, tradesmen, housewives, 'stupid people who mind their business, and have a business to mind', acutely worried that 'their common comforts were in considerable danger'. 'Parliament, liberty, leading articles, essays, eloquence' – he went down the list of liberal virtues – 'all are good', but in such a climate, 'they are secondary' for 'the first duty of government is to ensure security of that industry which is the condition of social life'.[16]

Bagehot's letters 'were light and airy, and even flippant on a very grave subject', Hutton recalled, and 'took impertinent liberties with all the dearest prepossessions of the readers of the *Inquirer*'.[17] In private, Bagehot was even glibber. 'I was here during the only day of hard fighting', he informed one correspondent, 'and shall be able to give lectures on the construction of a barricade if that noble branch of Political Economy ever became a source of income in England.'[18] 'M. Buonaparte is entitled to great praise', he told another. 'He has very good heels to his boots, and the French just want treading down, and nothing else – calm, cruel, business-like oppression to take the dogmatic conceit out of their heads.'[19]

The stir caused by the letters kindled his ambition, but with no clear path into politics Bagehot heeded his father's urgings and returned to Langport to work at the family bank in 1852. Luckily, the man who ran it, his uncle Vincent Stuckey, was no ordinary banker: a political career at the Treasury; friendships with two prime ministers, Pitt and Peel; three times mayor of Langport; and as a bonus, a taste for epigrams. 'Bankers are mortal, but banks should never die.' Stuckey had converted the bank into one of the first joint-stock operations and made it into a regional force. By 1909, when merged with Parr's Bank of Lancashire, it had £7 million in deposits, and a note circulation second only to the Bank of England.[20] Heartened by the precedent, Bagehot slogged on for seven years in a variety of jobs, including as manager of the Bristol branch.

After years cultivating his mind in London, however, Bagehot found bookkeeping a chore. He complained to a school friend of 'being rowed ninety-nine times a day for some horrid sin against the conventions of mercantile existence'. 'My family perhaps you know are merchants, ship-owners, and bankers, etc., etc.', he continued. How much better if they 'would admit that sums are a matter of opinion'.[21] Among number crunchers, he was a poet. When confronted by intellectuals, however, he played the practical, no-nonsense philistine. On a business trip he was invited to a dinner party, where an aged scholar declared his intention to get at 'the kernel of all the machinery by which we were governed'. Bagehot piped up after a pause, 'My impression is that the kernel is *the consolidated* fund, *and I* should like to get at *that*!' If someone was taking too long constructing an elegant phrase, he would interrupt them, asking, 'How much?'[22]

Bagehot's articles from these years were mainly portraits of English writers: Cowper, Coleridge, Shakespeare, Macaulay, Shelley, Scott, Dickens, Milton and others. Aside from Bagehot's interpretation of business success as a criterion of literary merit, what is striking is the relation of all these lives to his own. As an historian Scott was preferable to Macaulay, because the former gave the Cavalier his due: 'a thrill of delight; exaltation in a daily event; zest in the "regular thing".' Shakespeare, meanwhile, was made to share in his view of common folk. It was fun to mix with the lowly, 'the stupid players and the stupid door keepers'. But at the end of the day 'it was enough if every man hitched well into his own place in life', as in *Much Ado About Nothing*. For, 'if every one were logical and literary, how could there be scavengers, or watchmen or caulkers, or coopers?'[23]

Essay-writing in his spare hours from the bank was not enough. It was as a banker, though, and not an intimate of artists, that Bagehot freed himself from the daily chores of the counting house. Richard Hutton, now co-editor of the *National Review,* wrote from London in 1856 to say he had received a tentative offer from William Rathbone Greg to edit the *Economist*. Hutton was unsure, and thought of visiting the tomb of his wife in the West Indies before deciding: what did Bagehot think? 'Offers of this kind are not to be picked up in the street every day', Bagehot replied. 'You have an opportunity of fixing yourself in a post, likely to be useful and permanent, and give you a fulcrum and position in the world which is what you have always wanted and is quite necessary to comfort in England. I do not think you ought to risk it for the sake of a *holiday*.'[24]

Hutton set out for Barbados. Bagehot, however, wrote to their mutual friend James Martineau, who secured him an introduction to Greg, who in turn obtained an invitation to Claverton Manor, James Wilson's pile in the country. After a visit in January 1857, Bagehot was asked to write a series of letters on banking. He also caught the eyes of the six girls in the house, for making fun of their German governess, 'an egg', and for his appearance: black wavy hair, long bushy beard, tall, thin, 'very fine skin, very white', a 'high, hectic colour concentrated on the cheek bones ... he would pace a room when talking and throw his head back as some animals do when sniffing air.'[25] A year later he was engaged to the eldest daughter, Eliza.

Hutton got to work as editor after his return, but it was Bagehot who quickly imposed himself as the heir apparent. Wilson liked Bagehot, and was so thrilled with an essay of his in the *National Review* in 1859 – warning of the dangers of any but the most limited extension of the franchise to the top layers of the working class – he threw him a dinner party in April, inviting Lord Grey, Lord Granville, Sir Richard Bethell, Sir George Cornewall Lewis, Edward Cardwell, Thackeray and Gladstone – 'a very fine collection of political animals', Bagehot observed contentedly.[26] And it was to Bagehot that Wilson turned in 1859 'to interpret his great work in India to the public in England through the pages of the *Economist*' – even as Hutton remained nominal editor for two more years.[27] When Wilson died, Bagehot was offered his job in India. He declined, looking forward to greener and more pleasant political pastures at home. Though he resigned as bank manager, he stayed on as a director, and now oversaw all of Stuckey's business in London.

Bagehot took after Wilson in another respect, with the clear intention to use the *Economist* as a springboard into politics. He stood for parliament four times as a Liberal: in Manchester in 1865, Bridgwater in 1866, and twice at London University, his alma mater, in 1860 and 1867. All were unsuccessful, but on his third try he came within a hair's breadth – just seven votes behind his Tory opponent. Bagehot did not lose the Bridgwater by-election, however, as fable has it, 'because he refused to bribe the electorate'. An 1869 investigative commission declared him 'privy and assenting to some of the corrupt practices extensively prevailing'. Nor did he accept this censure with good grace. He blamed the voters, these rustics, and did a droll impersonation of them for the commissioners: 'I won't vote for gentlefolks unless they do something for I. Gentlefolks do not come to I unless they want something of I, and I won't do nothing for gentlefolks, unless they do something for me.'[28] After admitting he had paid out £1,533 10s. 2d. via his solicitor to cover 'retrospective' campaign expenses, he wrote to Hutton in triumph, with news that his reputation had been 'much raised' by his examination. 'They say, "Ah! Mr. Bagehot was too many for them. They broke Westropp but they could not break him." They regard it as a kind of skill independent of fact or truth. "You win if you are clever, and lose if you are stupid," is their idea at bottom.' It was an idea Bagehot seemed to share.[29]

While a seat in the Commons eluded him, Bagehot received ample confirmation of his standing outside it – elected to Wyndhams and Brooks's, the Metaphysical Society, Political Economy Club and finally in 1875 the Athenaeum. As editor he was a trusted advisor to two Chancellors of the Exchequer. These varied and prominent roles in Victorian political, economic and cultural life came to an abrupt close in the spring of 1877. Bagehot, then fifty-one, came down with a cold. It was the last in a chain of respiratory ailments – caught, some believed, in the draughty drawing room at 8 Queens Gate Place in London, awaiting drapes custom-designed by William Morris. Bagehot returned to his family home at Herds Hill, where he died on 23 March, and was buried in the family vault beside his mother at All Saints Church.

## Liberal Lines: Bagehot Steers the *Economist*

Bagehot became director of the *Economist* the year the Liberal Party emerged from its chrysalis among the Whigs in 1859. He was editor at the zenith of Victorian liberalism, with Liberals in power for thirteen out of seventeen years. At the Treasury, William Gladstone drafted one masterpiece of budgetary discipline after another – winning high praise from Bagehot for his 'flowing eloquence and lofty heroism', 'acute intellect and endless knowledge'.[30] In the country at large, trade and employment picked up briskly after the downturn of 1848, while the threat of revolution receded along with it. Liberal rule seemed the benign backdrop to this era, to such an extent that Bagehot was stunned when Conservatives interrupted it in 1874.[31] This context helps to explain a marked shift in tone and outlook at the *Economist*. Bagehot displayed the knowing nonchalance of a young banker, without the solemnity veering into bombast that had characterized Wilson or William Rathbone Greg. As editor, he brought his literary and professional tastes and interests to bear on the look and feel of the *Economist,* with tangible results.

In 1861 Bagehot added a Banking Supplement and in 1863 a Budget Supplement. A year later he hired William Newmarch to compile an Annual Commercial History and Wholesale Price Index; and in 1868 he brought Robert Giffen on board to assist him in expanding coverage of the money market, including an *Investors Manual,* which cost an extra sixpence a month. By 1873, with the *Economist* itself at eightpence and circulation at 3,600, Bagehot could boast that the previous year 'was the most profitable in the history of the paper'. He made the link between its financial health and that of the markets in a confidential memorandum to the Wilson family, who held the paper and other assets in trust. It was both a business plan and manifesto.

Since 1859 net income had increased from just under £2,000 to £2,765, with Bagehot's salary at £400 plus half of all profits over £2,000 – giving him, on average, £780 since 1862. Yet trustees should never mistake this 'delicate' source of income for 'funded property or land', Bagehot warned, pointing to the 1866 financial crisis, after which profits declined.[32] At first he had feared that competition from other business papers, nearly non-existent in 1843, was to blame. But he had changed his mind. 'I believe it to have been owing to the dull state of the money market which was so motionless for nearly four years that there was nothing to tell the public about it.' When trading volumes picked up again the *Economist* 'recovered its position', while the 'other papers made nothing of their chance at all'. This he attributed to the fact that, as a member of Stuckey's, 'which always has large sums in London, I have better means of knowing than a mere writer what is happening and what is likely to happen.'[33] Insider knowledge and a reputation for honesty ('a reason why its management must never be left to a salaried Editor', who might be bought off) set the *Economist* apart in the now crowded field of business journalism.

As for coverage, political analyses of the sort businessmen 'would care to read' were 'a material support to the paper and strengthen its circulation'. 'Indeed if politics were abandoned there wd. be a universal impression that the paper had changed its character and was going down.' So far as profits were concerned, however, all subjects must be viewed in relation to changes in the money market, 'because they affect all men of business, and all are anxious to see what will be their course'. What free trade and commercial legislation had been under Wilson, the money market would be for the era and editors that followed Bagehot.

The most remarkable change was not so much the sharper focus on finance, however, as the way this transformed the laissez-faire worldview of the *Economist*. Bagehot disliked the doctrinaire fanaticism he had found in the *Economist* in his youth, and as its editor showed a readiness to bend when it came to the basic principles of political economy. In 1871 he took stock of scientific developments since his youth – remembering Nassau Senior, and the school of political economy he represented, in a review of his journals. 'I was myself examined by him years ago, at the time of the strict school, at the London University', he wrote. 'If it could have been revealed to him that persons of authority would dare to teach that profit had no tendency to become equal in different trades, – that the Ricardo theory of rent was a blunder and a misconception, – that it was unnecessary for bankers to keep a stock of gold or silver to meet their liabilities, but that they should buy gold in the market when they wanted it, I think Mr. Senior would have been aghast. Yet such is the present state of the science, and naturally the rise of the heresiarchs has diminished the dignity of the orthodox heads.'[34]

Up to a point, innovation was welcome. As an undergraduate Bagehot had registered his own doubts about the strict school, which included Wilson. Laissez-faire was 'useful and healthy when confined to its legitimate function – watching the government does not assume to know what will bring a trader in money better than he knows it himself,' he argued in 'The Currency Monopoly' in the *Prospective Review* in 1848. He continued:

> but it is a sentiment very susceptible of hurtful exaggeration: in the minds of many at this day it stands opposed to the enforcement of moral law throughout the *whole* sphere of human acts: to the legislative promotion of those industrial habits which conduce to the attainment of national morality or national happiness at a sacrifice of national wealth: to efforts at a national education, or a compulsory sanitary reform: to all national aid from England towards the starving peasantry of Ireland: to every measure for improving the condition of that peasantry which would not be the spontaneous choice of the profit-hunting capitalist. Whoever speaks against these extreme opinions is sure to be sneered at as a 'benevolent sentimentalist': and economists are perpetually assuming that the notion of government interference is agreeable only to those whose hearts are more developed than their brains: who are too fond of poetic dreams to endure the stern realities of science.[35]

Wilson's *Economist* was not only guilty of overstating the free trade case, it crudely caricatured any who asked 'if there be no exception to it within the limits of political economy itself'. At twenty-two Bagehot thought he had uncovered such a case: government, not private entities, should enjoy a monopoly on coining precious metals and printing paper money – absent which, financial crises like the one just past in 1847 would be more frequent and severe.[36] 'It is a duty of a wise state to secure the mass of the nation against evils produced by the selfishness of individuals so far as it is possible: to bring within government control even the most limited causes of commercial convulsion.'[37]

Once editor, he nudged the *Economist* in the same direction. In 1861 the paper came out in favour of a permanent, graduated income tax, on the grounds that in its form at the time the tax failed to distinguish between different kinds of wealth: a barrister who earned £1000 annually was not as well off as a landowner or fund holder who earned that amount. 'People with secure incomes are richer than people with only precarious ones.' Fairness was an issue: 'People think that the more rich should be taxed more than the less rich.'[38] In 1864 the *Economist* reversed its earlier insistence under Wilson that all factory legislation, even to protect children from overwork or injury, amounted to an assault on free trade.[39] The next year it endorsed state ownership of railways, comparing the plan to the penny-post reform, which ensured a cheap, efficient, national parcel network.[40] Trade unions *did* restrain trade, but they were 'real forces of the industrial world which the law did not make, and which it cannot unmake'; better to recognize them, with special laws to punish intimidation and sabotage by their members.[41] Even women, after hesitations and qualifications, got some sort of break – though Bagehot's admirers are stretching the truth when they call him an advocate of female suffrage. Votes for women on any wide basis was an absurdity that only John Stuart Mill took seriously, he wrote in 1865. Five years later, Bagehot was ready to concede only 'a certain legal plausibility in the claim' that unmarried female property owners might obtain the vote on the same grounds as men – even if he thought very little of the 'political intelligence' of the 'spinsters', 'widows' and other 'lonely women' that would exercise it.[42]

For all this Bagehot did not count himself among the 'heresiarchs': by showing greater flexibility he hoped to update laissez-faire at the *Economist*, not overturn it. In the part of *Economic Studies* he had completed by 1876, he celebrated the 'wonderful effect' of 'English political economy' since the publication of Adam Smith's *Wealth of Nations* a hundred years before. 'The life of almost everyone in England – perhaps of everyone – is different and better in consequence of it. The whole commercial policy of the country is not so much founded on it as instinct with it.' Indeed, 'no other form of political philosophy has ever had one thousandth part the influence on us,' he went on, 'its teachings have settled down into the common sense of the nation, and have become irreversible'.[43] Bagehot criticized newer rivals to this 'English-school' of political economy: on the one hand, the 'enu-merative' or 'all case method' of the German Historical School; on the other, the neo-classical or marginal revolution that was just starting to take off. 'Mr Jevons of Manchester, and M. Walras of Lausanne, without communication, and almost simultaneously, have worked out a "mathematical" theory of political economy', Bagehot wrote of the latter school; 'and anyone who thinks what is ordinarily taught in England objectionable, because it is too little concrete in its method, and looks too unlike life and busi-ness, had better try the new doctrine, which he will find to be much worse on these points than the old.'[44]

Bagehot's mission as *Economist* editor was to teach a common sense science of political economy, 'the science of business', whose chief merit was its ability to adapt to changing circumstances – in his era, the increasing weight of global finance in Victorian capi-talism. Export of capital on a large scale was a new phenomenon in Britain, coinciding with Bagehot's career: from low levels of 1 to 1.5 per cent of gross national product in the forty years prior to 1850, average net foreign investment leapt to 2.1 per cent in the 1850s and to 2.8 per cent in the 1860s; and as Bagehot foresaw, it kept rising, averaging 4.3 per cent between 1870 and 1913, at which point net overseas assets accounted for 32 per cent of national wealth – a larger share than for any country before or since. If the surpluses for this boom arose in part from Britain's early industrial monopoly, it soon developed dynamics of its own.[45] 'Banking in England goes on growing, multiplying, and changing, as the English people itself goes on growing, multiply-ing, and changing. The facts of it are one thing today and another tomorrow.'[46] 'England has become the settling place of interna-tional bargains much more than it was before', he observed. 'But whose mind could divine the effect of such a change as this, except it had a professed science to help it?' A new wave of investment in 'half-finished' and 'half-civilised communities' flowed abroad. 'Who can tell without instruction what is likely to be the effect of the new loans of England to foreign nations?' Such easy access to credit, and on a global scale, was unprecedented in human history. It fell to Bagehot's *Economist* to map this new world, tracing the

theoretical insights of political economy to the people and places
men of business were sending their money.[47]

## Central Banking Rules

It was in the halfway-house between theory and practice that
Bagehot made his contributions to financial history, where the
legacy of his editorship was the construction of a role and set of
rules for central banking in the age of global capital. On these
matters, his opinion carried great weight. Gladstone dubbed him
a 'supplementary Chancellor of the Exchequer' and consulted
him on policies such as the Bank Notes Issue Bill, with Bagehot
promising 'the entire assent and substantial support of the issuing
bankers'.[48] Contemporaries credited him with inventing the
Treasury Bill in 1877, when he advised Gladstone's successor as
Chancellor, Sir Stafford Northcote, to replace 'Exchequer Bills'
with a modern, easily traded instrument, to 'resemble as near as
possible a Bill of Exchange'. 'The Treasury has the finest security
in the world, but has not known how to use it', Bagehot explained
privately. 'Such a Bill would rank before a Bill of Barings.'[49]

The *Economist* was the source of this authority as well as
the most important outlet for his views on bringing stability
to the financial system – which by all accounts needed more of
it: crises were frequent, either beginning in the City of London
or passing through it infinitely magnified, as the spoke around
which international finance now turned. At home, the panic of
1866 was among the most spectacular, dominating *Economist*
coverage of the money market long afterwards. In that year one
of the City's great wholesale banking houses, Overend, Gurney
& Co., failed soon after it had raised large sums by incorporating as a company with limited liability. After the stock market
crashed, a bank run ensued. For Bagehot, the episode demonstrated beyond a doubt that the Bank of England, which at first
refused to intervene, was unlike all other banks and discount
houses, and Bagehot told Gladstone as much during the crisis,
over breakfast on 31 May.[50]

Bagehot also developed this argument in countless *Economist* leaders, distilled into a standalone book in 1873, *Lombard Street*. Since it was backed by government and held the nation's reserves, the Bank of England had an important duty. When credit dried up during a crisis like the one that felled Overend, Gurney & Co., it must act as lender of last resort, until confidence returned, using two guiding rules: advances must be at a 'very high rate of interest' and made on 'all good banking securities', thereby limiting the bailout pool to 'solvent' but 'illiquid' banks, and encouraging rapid repayment.[51] The Bank of England's directors were 'trustees of the public', whose actions had a major effect in and beyond Britain. 'A large deposit of foreign money in London is now necessary for the business of the world.' Yet this also meant that a rush to withdraw by foreign individuals, businesses or states could determine 'whether *England shall be solvent or insolvent*'.[52] The Bank of England would require larger reserves in the light of the vast new scale of British financial commitments and could no longer be governed by an elderly bench of part-timers, drawn from a class of reputable but amateur City merchants.[53]

The French answer was nationalization. That, obviously, would not pass muster with the English. Such a move also had the demerit of exposing government to criticism in a crisis, or subjecting policy to political pressure, 'as chance majorities and the strength of parties decide'.[54] In an ideal world, he conceded in *Lombard Street* – with a nervous glance over his shoulder at Wilson – the Bank of England would not even exist. Like any other trade, state meddling harmed the banking business. 'The best thing undeniably that a Government can do with the Money Market is to let it take care of itself.' Since it did exist, though, better not to upset markets by any too-radical change. 'You might as well, or better, try to alter the English monarchy and substitute a republic', he added archly. Yet the analogy between the function of credit and that of a constitutional monarch was deliberate – and revealing. Bankers had faith in the Bank of England as implicitly as 'Queen Victoria was obeyed by millions of human beings'.[55] There was no good reason to accept either, in other words.

But since people did believe, and their belief was essential to the smooth running of the banking and political systems, Bagehot looked to the monarch as a model. The appointment of a permanent deputy director to the Bank with the requisite experience, sitting under a rotating, ceremonial governor, would ensure consistency and independence enough to instil confidence in the nation's credit. But where to find the deputy? The custom by which bankers were excluded from the Bank's governing body dated from an era in which all banks, including the Bank of England, were in competition. 'This is a relic of old times.'[56] Now bankers could work together, and as the principal depositors, with an interest in a large reserve to safeguard their assets, they were ideal candidates.[57] The point was to remove the old commercial oligarchs from the board of the central bank as well as any threat of parliamentary interference. Major powers – to set interest rates, determine and maintain adequate reserves, and to bail one another out in a pinch – would fall to the bankers themselves.

For Bagehot, banking was the mirror image of politics. Both depended, in the final instance, on a powerful illusion from which everyone benefited – even if only a discerning few were able to chuckle about it. In his lifetime better known as a banker (*Lombard Street* took just three years to reach a sixth edition), Bagehot is more widely read today for what he had to say about the other side of this looking-glass. His writings on the English Constitution represent just a small sample of his political output, however. The *Economist* took him further afield, towards two political systems that contrasted with Britain: Louis-Napoléon's imperial dictatorship in France, and the partisan democracy in America. By the 1870s both France and the US were just beginning to challenge the monopoly Britain had enjoyed over industrial production for the world market, while entirely new nation-states appeared alongside them, in Germany and Italy, whose leaders sought to unleash the productive forces latent in their own societies. The *Economist* cheered these developments, which would require ample investment capital to be realized. But it also identified a new problem, thanks to Bagehot, on which its comparative political judgments of them hinged. In an age where new and older nation-states were attempting to play catch-up to Britain, in part with British capital, the role of political institutions in fostering this growth – or hindering it – became pivotal; and for *Economist*

readers, a way of evaluating the potential return on their investment, and its security. Historians have noted how this wave of
capital transformed the world economy – pushing frontiers of
food cultivation in North America and Eastern Europe, cotton
production in India, mineral extraction in Australia, ranching in
Argentina, and railways nearly everywhere, cheapening the transport cost of all these goods.[58] Fewer have remarked on the form
of liberal politics that was its corollary, and which had no clearer
tribune than Bagehot's *Economist*.

## Confidence Tricks: The English Constitution and the Dangers of Democracy

On its own the *English Constitution*, first released as a book in
1867, ensures that Bagehot is required reading for any soul bold
enough to inquire into the arrangements by which Britain persists
in being governed. In it, he presents an alternative view of the
parliamentary system, in which it is divided into two parts, as
opposed to three, and the traditional theory of checks and balances between them is discarded. There are the dignified parts,
'which excite and preserve the reverence of the population', and
the efficient, 'by which it in fact works and rules'.[59] The Queen
and House of Lords belong to the former category, with the crown
placed at the head of a 'parade' or 'theatrical show' meant to distract and gratify 'the mob' below. This 'disguise' allows the 'real
rulers' – not the House of Commons but the Cabinet, a 'committee of the legislature' chosen by it – to conduct the business of the
nation in relative peace and quiet.

Business is the operative term. Bagehot repeatedly emphasized
how much this committee resembled a 'board of directors' – its
greatest virtue, in his eyes – with the royal family there to smooth
out its one comparative shortcoming: the fact that cabinet
members could be removed suddenly based on shifts in public
opinion. Since most people, he said, *'really believe that the Queen
governs'*, the real rulers came and went 'without heedless people
knowing it', avoiding the unrest or uncertainty such reshuffles
might otherwise provoke. The upshot was as cynical as it sounds.

A vindication of the 'plutocratic' upper and lower houses and a strong executive shrouded in secrecy were the wonders of political science in England.[60]

Yet Bagehot's classic work – revered by jurist Albert Dicey as the first to explain 'in accordance with actual fact the true nature of the Cabinet and its real relation to the Crown and Parliament' – must be considered in the context of the *Economist*.[61] For over five years before the serialization of the *English Constitution*, Bagehot had been writing on politics, evaluating constitutional structures in terms of their tendency to help or hinder different states on their paths of capitalist development. Wilson had first encouraged Bagehot to take on this role, expanding his original banking brief at the *Economist*, based on his 1859 *National Review* essay entitled 'Parliamentary Reform', which showed how far they agreed on the need to limit democracy. In it, Bagehot had argued that any extension of the franchise be limited to a top layer of rate-paying artisans in the largest towns – with artisans in smaller towns, farm workers and all unskilled labourers shut out, so as not 'to deteriorate the general character of the legislature'. This was fair, he insisted, in his recalibration of natural law, for '*every person has a right to so much power as he can exercise without impeding any other person who would more fitly exercise such power.*'[62]

From that point on, Bagehot used the *Economist* itself to denounce the democratic tendencies of reform plans put forward by both Tories and Liberals, which, he said, risked turning a sensitive deliberative body into 'class-government', 'a mere reflex of the popular cry'. 'True Liberalism' was at odds with 'the extreme left of the Liberal party', he wrote in the spring of 1860, with its 'superstitious reverence for the equality of all Englishmen as electors' based on a 'glaringly false assertion', that 'the talents and attainments of the lowest peasant and mechanic are the measure of the electoral capacity of the most educated man in the land'.[63]

In a review of Mill's *Considerations on Representative Government*, he hailed the first section, which he called 'an exceedingly able protest, by the only living thinker of much authority among English Liberals, against that helpless and reluctant drifting of the Liberal party into pure democracy which is so melancholy a sign of their political imbecility.'[64] This rhetoric forced the *Economist* to defend itself against charges of being 'impractical, doctrinaire, theoretic' and of promoting 'Tory views' – a reminder that it was uncommon for Liberals to be quite so openly anti-democratic.[65] In 1860 Bagehot had even sent a signed letter to the editor, wishing to express himself categorically on the proper attitude of Liberals towards any further reform. 'The question now is, what securities against democracy we *can* create; none are easy; none are perfect; which is the least defective and the least difficult to attain?'[66]

Bagehot tinkered with his answer to this question in the *Economist* before folding the results into the *English Constitution*. Early on, he was prepared to accept a slightly wider suffrage, provided there was also 'a double test of numbers and property, giving every householder a vote, but taking property as the index of social station, and giving higher classes, therefore, a number of votes.'[67] He soon had second thoughts about this, however. In a leader from 1864 he suggested a net transfer of members from 'stagnant' boroughs to industrial towns, which alone would enjoy a greater degree of popular participation.[68] 'A Simple Plan of Reform' then became the appendix to the 1867 edition of the *English Constitution*.[69]

Here Bagehot gave a detailed rationale for the schemes he had posited in the *Economist*.[70] For the efficient secret of the constitution to be kept, two things were required: the lower classes must not know it, and the upper classes must fully understand it, not falling for pious 'paper descriptions' of their government as one of perfectly calibrated checks and balances. So Bagehot made clear just how wide the chasm was between rulers and ruled. With the exception of an educated and propertied elite amounting to no more than ten thousand men, most were 'no more civilized than the majority of two thousand years ago, narrow-minded, unintelligent, incurious' and 'unable to comprehend the idea of a constitution'. Giving them votes would spell disaster, for that would mean 'the rich and the wise are not to have, by explicit law, more votes than the poor and stupid' – or, in big towns, the workers, whom he dubbed 'the members for the public houses' (i.e. pubs).

It is useless to pile up abstract words. Those who doubt should go into their kitchens. Let an accomplished man try what seems to him most obvious, most certain, most palpable in intellectual matters, upon the housemaid and the footman, and he will find that what he says seems unintelligible – that his audience think him mad and wild when he is speaking what is in his own sphere of thought the dullest platitude of cautious soberness. Great communities are like great mountains – they have in them the primary, secondary, and tertiary strata of human progress; the characteristics of the lower regions resemble the life of old times rather than the present life of the higher regions.[71]

Bagehot's defeat in his third attempt to be elected a Liberal MP in 1866, just as he was finishing up the *English Constitution,* gave to it this very bitter edge, with masters advised to 'go into their kitchens' to confirm the witlessness of their servants. Passage of the Second Reform Act the next year – by the Tories, no less – surprised him and deepened his gloom. A change in tone is clear from the 1872 edition of the *English Constitution.* 'What I fear is that both our political parties will bid for the support of the working-man.' There was no worse misfortune 'for a set of poor ignorant people than that two combinations of well-taught and rich men should constantly offer to defer to their decision'. Or, rather, there was one: the poor and ignorant conferring among themselves. 'In all cases it must be remembered that a political combination of the lower classes, as such and for their own objects, is an evil of the first magnitude.'[72]

Yet once again it was in the *Economist* that Bagehot first registered his shock and disgust at the bill that Benjamin Disraeli, the Conservative leader in the Commons, crafted and pushed through both Houses in 1867. The Second Reform Act increased the number of working-class male voters in the towns and cities by extending the vote to occupiers (renters) paying at least £10 a year – in a move that altered neither the basis of the franchise in property, nor the balance of class forces in parliament. 'We shall not be supposed to like a Reform of the present pattern. We have opposed it for years', ran an *Economist* leader, comparing the debate over reform to a botched shareholders' meeting.[73]

Bagehot's constitutional theory was on the line, just a year after it was published. 'We are not so great a political people as we thought,' he wrote, 'or we could not on a sudden change our deepest thoughts upon the most familiar and important of political questions.'[74] 'Why has the "Settlement" of 1832 So Easily Melted Away?' contained a mixture of bitterness, and swipes at the British elite for misunderstanding the constitution, despite his attempts to enlighten it:

> The English people have been told by the received authorities on their Constitution, that it contains, apart from the House of Commons, and in a position to resist that House, great conservative forces on which they might rely. Most people believe that no great change could be effected in a democratic direction, because of these old powers. 'The Queen would not *let* it,' is believed by many more than a London politician fancies, and 'Thank God we have a House of Lords' has passed into a cry. But now when it comes to business, these book checks are of no use.[75]

Bagehot cited the recently published correspondence between William IV and Lord Grey at the time of the 1832 Reform Bill, and commended the latter: here was a minister 'able to manage his sovereign without a trace of artifice, and without impairing his peculiar patrician austerity'. But this only revealed how much had changed. 'We talk of Mr. Disraeli's wonderful manipulation both in the Cabinet and the House of Commons. But the very name of Victoria is not mentioned, though in 1832 William was prominent and constant in everyone's mouth. The check of royalty upon democratic change has turned out to be a fancy.'

Yet this was exactly what Bagehot had been saying it was all along. In the *English Constitution* he had urged the Queen to remain 'hidden like a mystery', a relic, 'not to be brought too closely to real measurement'. Now in the *Economist* even he lamented her powerlessness. 'Who cares about managing the Queen? She goes away to Scotland, and the world hardly knows where she is.'[76] His objection to the 'paper description' of the constitution was that it took the idea of checks and balances at face value. His theory, however cheeky, was not so different: checks and balances were illusions, of course, but given the mental haze of the housemaids and footmen of England, he had counted on them being effective blocks on democratic change.[77]

## The French Constitution

The trade-offs between democracy and socioeconomic stability were even more glaring in France, where the Second Empire exercised a lifelong fascination for Bagehot. Indeed, no one in history has made the case for Louis-Napoléon – the portly, preening nephew of the first Emperor, whose rule over France ended in a catastrophic defeat to Prussia in 1870 – quite like him. Bagehot never shared the view of much of the press: that 'Plonplon', Louis-Napoléon's nickname, was an adventurer and a slightly ridiculous facsimile of his famous uncle. The *Economist*, on the contrary, treated him as a genius, who understood the French better than an elected assembly ever could.

Bagehot began his complex love affair with Louis-Napoléon in 1851, excusing his coup d'état as the surest way to restore 'confidence' and 'security of industry' to France, in the *Inquirer*. At this time, Bagehot based his support for a regime in Paris that he would never have tolerated in London on the concept of 'national character'. Frenchmen were too 'excitable, volatile, superficial, over-logical, uncompromising' to enjoy the same freedoms as the English.[78] What the aftermath of the 1848 revolutions in Europe had 'taught men' was just the opposite: 'that no absurdity is so great as to imagine the same species of institutions suitable or possible for Scotchmen and Sicilians, for Germans and Frenchmen, for the English and the Neapolitans.'[79]

As editor of the *Economist,* Bagehot was somewhat more sober in his praise of Louis-Napoléon, but consistently backed his regime in France – a restless, revolutionary nation, in need of a firm hand to force down the bitter medicine of political economy.[80] What nuance did enter the picture during the 1860s had more to do with the intellectual situation in England. Here disciples of the positivist French philosopher Auguste Comte were winning converts, Bagehot worried, with arguments that rapid material progress backed by a strong central state in France held lessons for overly individualistic, market-oriented England. In 1867 Bagehot attacked these thinkers, whose support for the Second Reform Bill was bad enough. They also believed, he said, 'Parliamentary government is complex, dilatory, and inefficient. An efficient absolutism chosen by the people, and congenial to the people, is far better than this dull talking.'[81] In *Physics and Politics,* he named 'the secular Comtists, Mr. Harrison and Mr. Beesly, who want to "Frenchify English institutions" – to introduce here an imitation of the Napoleonic system, a dictatorship founded on the proletariat.'[82] The *Economist* aimed at a similar audience of Francophiles, but tried to teach them different lessons: the point was to admire the view across the English Channel, not to import what they saw there.

Bonapartism, or Caesarism, as Bagehot often called it, ensured stability now, but in the long run no one could predict what would happen after Louis-Napoléon – now Napoleon III – died; and it was too democratic, cutting out the urban educated middle class, in favour of direct appeals to the 'dumb majority', the 'populace, the peasantry and the army'.[83] The ultimate sign of its shaky foundations? A few times a year the *Economist* was confiscated in Paris. 'At one time any article with "French despotism" in it was seized, no matter what followed, and though it were laudatory', Bagehot complained of censors too dim to tell a friendly editor from a subversive. 'If the *Economist* would make a revolution, what would not make a revolution?'[84] The English system was better, then, provided the people living under it were English. Any country would be wise to adopt the '*true* British constitution', he said – that is, the secret one – but few could.

Yet despite his attempts to warn 'young Englishmen' off Bonapartism, its appeal in England had a lot to do with the *Economist,* where each week Bagehot reported the progress of France under Napoleon III in vivid detail. In 1863 'The Emperor of the French' informed English Liberals of the popularity of this 'Crowned Democrat of Europe'.[85] In 1865 it hailed him as a progressive, vastly superior not just to the ancient 'democratic despot' Julius Caesar but the old monarchs of Europe as well. 'Louis Napoleon is a Benthamite despot. He is for the "greatest happiness of the

greatest number."' His regime was renowned for 'orderly dex-
terity', his 'bureaucracy is not only endurable but pleasant.' And
whereas the English intellect was freer than the French, and better
able to 'beat the ideas of the few into the minds of the many',
it 'has rarely been so unfinished, so *ragged*'. In Parisian society
'higher kinds of thought are better discussed than in London, and
better argued in the *Revue des deux Mondes* than in any English
periodical.'

Above all Napoleon III had kindled an economic miracle to
'amaze Europe and France itself'. 'No government has striven to
promote railways, and roads, and industry, like this government.
France is much changed in twelve years.'[86] The usual objection
to despotism was that it made property insecure. But the modern
model erected in France had nothing to do with this 'coarse
Asiatic despotism'. The Emperor handled property rights with
'ostentatious care', being 'too wise to kill the bird which lays the
golden egg', and 'is as good a free trader as there is in France'. As
for a 'common English notion that such freedom stimulates the
demand for political freedom', Bagehot wrote, with a wink, he 'is
aware that very often it does nothing of the kind'.[87]

Readers could be forgiven for wondering what if anything
was wrong with 'Caesareanism as It Now Exists', the title of
one *Economist* leader. To Bagehot there was a major flaw, which
he identified in 1865. '*Credit* in France, to an Englishman's eye,
has almost to be created.'[88] In the summer of 1867 the French
and Austro-Hungarian emperors seemed to be plotting a war
against Prussia. 'Every bourse in Europe is trembling', he wrote
in 'The Mercantile Evils of Imperialism', for their intentions were
'incalculable'. Parliaments had their uses, after all: furnishing businessmen with '*data* to spell the future'. The *Economist* brimmed
with illustrations of what this stunted financial development
meant for France. 'An English traveller sees nothing incalculably
inferior to England. Means of communication, trade, agriculture,
are all excellent.' Only, 'the French banking system is childish.'
Napoleon III had merely postponed the day of political reckoning
that retarded the growth of financial capitalism. 'A French banker,
in answer to all comments upon his timidity, has a single reply:
he says, "It is all very well for you to talk in England; but *we* in

Paris, have revolutions; you were not here in 1848, *I* was."' Paris 'is a great place of pleasure, – she is an inferior place of lending business.'[89]

## Nations, Nationalism and the Franco-Prussian War

If Bagehot was clear in his political prescriptions for France, his predictions went hopelessly astray. His evaluation of the emperor suggested a war was impossible between France and Prussia. 'A singular mixture of tenacity and hesitation, of daring and timidity', Napoleon III was, the *Economist* assured readers, the last statesman liable to do something rash. 'We may feel very confident that he will never face Europe, or run any risk of acting in such a fashion as to combine all Europe against him.'[90] In 1867 it counted on his 'sagacity and self-interest' to hold back the warlike masses. While the Italian liberal nationalists Mazzini and Garibaldi crafted 'mischievous projects' in Italy, the wise rulers of France and Prussia beamed at one another from across the Rhine.[91] Just months before Napoleon III was duped into a war in which he allowed his army to be trapped and himself taken prisoner, Bagehot wrote that the future would judge him the greater of the two Napoleons. The career of his uncle was 'more sudden and brilliant and meteoric' but though 'an exciting story' it did 'not to our minds furnish one half so singular and unexampled in history as that of the present Emperor's plodding, painstaking, uphill, intellectual efforts to gauge and adapt himself to both the superficial tastes and permanent demands of the French people.'[92]

Bagehot was momentarily chastened at the outbreak of hostilities. Maybe those who had called Plonplon 'a gambler and a desperado' had been right after all.[93] Just a month later, however, he noted that what had failed in France was not 'personal government' – since Prussia was ruled by a military autocracy at the pleasure of a king. It was Caesarism: a plebiscitary despotism that had cut out the middle classes, courting 'the favour of the ignorant peasantry'.[94] Bagehot remembered Napoleon III fondly at his death in exile three years later. His defeat at Sedan was excused, attributed to a painful bladder stone that had impaired his usual 'clearness of insight'. The muse of history blessed the fallen hero. 'To declare him a great man may be impossible in the face of his failures, but to declare him a small one is ridiculous. Small men dying in exile do not leave wide gaps in the European political horizon.'[95]

What of those gaps? Just before the collapse of the Second Empire, Bagehot had advised Liberals to refrain from trying to topple it, to 'defer all ideas of a republic'.[96] Rather, 'thinking Liberals' should 'engraft upon it rational and liberal principles' because the republic they wanted – sober, 'with no nonsense in it' – was impossible in France. Under pressure from workers it would turn red, demanding 'equal division of property'.[97] After the fall of the Empire, socialists took power in Paris in 1871, declaring a revolutionary republic and vowing to fight on against the Prussian invaders in defiance of their own government, which had surrendered. The *Economist*, predictably enough, recoiled in horror. The Paris Commune was a gang of 'artisans and working men', 'desperate poor', 'mad with rage and envy'. It only prayed they could be stopped before their 'settled design to destroy the Tuileries, the Louvre, the Palais Royal' was realized.[98]

The *Economist* was thus grateful to Adolphe Thiers, provisional president of the French national government, for marching 60,000 loyal troops on Paris, aided by the Prussian chancellor Otto von Bismarck, who released them for this task at Thiers's urgent plea. In the ensuing bloodbath, around 20,000 civilians were killed – many shot without trial, to be burnt or dumped in open graves, as the opening act of the French Third Republic. The fact that Thiers, a self-avowed republican, had given orders to massacre so many fellow citizens was encouraging. France owed 5 million francs in reparations to a newly united Germany and needed to show markets, where it would have to raise much of the cash, who was in control.[99] Above all, the defeat of the Commune 'effectively severed the *name* of the Republic from the creed of the delirious Republicans. It left it perfectly open to M. Thiers to identify the idea of the Republic with the soberest possible conceptions.'[100]

Till the end Bagehot never thought a republic could succeed, however, and welcomed signs of a return to enlightened dictatorship. 'Why an English Liberal May Look without Disapproval on the Progress of Imperialism in France', a leader from 1874, argued that while a parliament was just right for England – where a new ministry 'does not change consols an eighth', and a monarch sits 'behind the ministry, to preserve at least an appearance of stability' – this would never do for the French.[101] In a friendly mood, he nevertheless offered to advise the National Assembly meeting at Versailles. He printed his own constitutional template in the *Economist*, 'drawn up by one who has great experience in such matters'.[102] In it, Bagehot urged the French delegates to vest power in a strongman, elected by an assembly, but who could in turn dissolve it – reminding readers that this was the secret 'mainspring' of the English Constitution. The document the Assembly actually adopted in 1875 earned his admiration on this basis. The 'Conservative Republic' looked forward – incorrectly, as the history of the Third Republic would show – to an executive more powerful than the US president and British prime minister combined. 'Indeed, it is not very easy to conceive, outside Russia, a position of more influence and grandeur', he wrote, thinking the model of the Czar to be an appropriate outer limit for a leader whose aim was to liberalize France.[103]

National character may have been a key category in comparative explorations of political order for Bagehot. But to nationalism as a leading force of the period he was relatively blind. A necessary precondition for a great nation was, of course, he granted, 'accordance in sentiment, language and manners' – but he was unwilling to endorse the existence of pure nationalities, or place them above these looser categories of national belonging. The term was unscientific, 'a vague sort of faith to vast multitudes – a vague sort of implement to some plotters'. Yet it was also useful, so long as it was helping to build modern states – as in Germany and Italy. As a rallying cry for 'alien fragments of old races', however, nationalism was pernicious. 'To set up the Basque nationality, or the Breton, or the Welsh, would be injurious to the Basque, the Bretons, and Welsh, even more than to Spain, France and England.'[104] Its point was to release talented

men cooped up in the administration of tiny nations ('small politics debase the mind just as large politics improve it'), into larger
ones, somehow leading to smaller, efficient government – and
peace, with big countries less tempted to go to war to snap up
weaker neighbours.[105]

What interest Bagehot's *Economist* did take in nationalism
was usually focused on its leading proponents. In Mazzini, the
founder of Young Italy and champion of Italian unification, it
saw a 'true zealot', more in love with himself than Italy, obsessed
with the name of a republic, and too stubborn to accept its
reality under the guise of a constitutional monarch. The brilliant military commander Garibaldi was a dimwit, who fought
'with windmills instead of giants'. In both cases Bagehot refused
to recognize the popular forces backing Mazzini and Garibaldi
up and down the Italian peninsula.[106] The *Economist* registered
patriotic fervour in France and Prussia, meanwhile, but thought
statesmen there would act to restrain lowborn passions at the last
moment; in reality, Bismarck manipulated them – while Louis-
Napoléon tried and failed to do the same, at home and as far afield
as Mexico.[107]

Nowhere was the misreading of nationalism more pronounced,
however, than in America, and the form this drive took in
Lincolnism. And here the stakes were highest: of the 800 million
pounds of cotton British mills consumed each year, 77 per cent
came from the slave plantations of the American South, in which
one-tenth of British capital was sunk. The outbreak of the Civil
War in April 1861 cut off these supplies, endangering the most
important industry in Britain, which added up to near half of
exports. Anxious industrialists, merchants and investors turned
to the *Economist* not just for analysis of the American situation,
but for reports on markets as far afield as Egypt and India, where
capital raced to open up new sources of cotton cultivation, leading
to a cycle of boom and bust that transformed peasant agriculture
and merchant trading networks around the world.[108] For Bagehot
the conflict also prompted a third constitutional investigation,
setting the efficient secret of the English system against the grim
realities of the American.

## The American Constitution and the Civil War

Of all the politicians whose portraits Bagehot painted, his estimate of the US president, Abraham Lincoln, was at first lowest.
'The President is unequal to the situation in which he is placed',
judged the *Economist* flatly at the end of 1861. 'He has received
the training of a rural attorney, and a fortuitous concurrence of
electioneering elements have placed him at the head of a nation.'[109]
The federal government had 'fallen into the hands of the smallest,
weakest and meanest set of men who ever presided over the policy
of a great nation at the critical epoch of its affairs.' Their collective wisdom was a 'concatenation of paltry arts which their own
word "dodge" and no other will describe'.[110] By the time of his
re-election in 1864 Bagehot considered Lincoln the best candidate
but made it clear this was not saying much. 'It is not even contended that Mr. Lincoln is a man of eminent ability. It is only said
that he is a man of common honesty, and it seems, this is so rare a
virtue at Washington that at their utmost need no other man can
be picked out to possess it and true ability also.'[111] Bagehot did
not even value his literary style, the ultimate insult, comparing
'the dignified and able State Papers of Jefferson Davis to the feeble
and ungrammatical prolixity of Abraham Lincoln'.[112]

Bagehot looked down his nose at Lincoln, but it was the
American Constitution he blamed for putting him in charge,
and for the seeming inability of the more prosperous and pop-
ulous North to suppress a rebellion of eight million backward
Southerners.[113] The contrast with the efficient political reflexes of
the English system was constant in his leaders for the *Economist,*
and formed a considered corpus of work beyond it. 'The American
Constitution has puzzled most persons in this country since the
remarkable course of recent events has attracted a real attention to
American affairs.'[114] Bagehot would explain its mysteries. Indeed,
his disclosure of the efficient secret of English parliamentarianism
depended on a prior act of exposure in America, where the Civil
War revealed the horrific administrative, military, and financial
consequences of wrong constitutional theories.

The US founding fathers had built upon an interpretation of the
English Constitution that Bagehot would attack as false – with the

perverse result that, here, checks and balances were *real*, limiting efficient government without restricting the suffrage. Americans had trusted to 'paper checks and constitutional devices' to 'resist the force of democracy' but 'either could not or did not take the one effectual means of so doing; they did not place the substantial power in the hands of men of education and of property'.[115] Congress, meanwhile, lacked the dynamic powers that might have made it an effective check either on the people or the president. With respect to the latter, it had an 'extreme remedy' only, 'the power of refusing supplies'. The Founders had misunderstood their model. For 'the framers of this clause in the American Constitution copied it from the traditional theory of the English Constitution.' They had not understood that though it was 'a deadly sleeping weapon', in practice 'a lesser instrument had been annexed to it, and was always used instead of it – that of choosing the executive'.[116] Their mistaken reading meant the president had a '*lease for years*' and stayed for all four no matter how 'unfit, incompetent, and ignorant'.[117]

Congress, with a power almost 'too terrible to use', put America at a disadvantage in the new age of global capitalism. 'The use of it stops the whole machinery of government, and the mere fear of its use annihilates public credit. Since the creation of large national debts, which did not exist in the times when the English House of Commons acquired its power, it is questionable whether a successful use of the power of withholding supplies could be effectually made with safety to the state.'[118] The evils were legion: presidential impunity, the poor quality and limited 'educating capacity' of Congress, and apathy even among those supposed to be leading citizens.[119] To Englishmen this was the most astonishing facet of the Northern character. 'They bear defeat in their armies, fraud in their contractors, incompetence in their generals and statesmen, with a stoicism which would be admirable if it rested on philosophy or reason, if it were anything but ignorant patience.'[120]

Given this barrage of bad press, readers must have been stunned to open the *Economist* at the end of April in 1865 and find an encomium to Lincoln, after he was shot by an assassin during a performance in Washington, D.C. 'We do not know in history such an example of the growth of a ruler in wisdom as was exhibited by Mr. Lincoln. Power and responsibility visibly widened his mind and elevated his character.' In taking a second look at the dead president Bagehot found his hidden greatness to have been his ability to make the constitution work – a document even more wretched than he had imagined at the outset of the Civil War.

'The difficulty of creating a strong government in America', able 'to do great acts very quickly, is almost insuperable.' The national character was dead set against both efficiency and dignity. 'The people in the first place dislike government, not this or that administration, but government in the abstract, to such a degree that they have invented a quasi philosophical theory, proving that government, like war or harlotry, is a "necessary evil."' States impeded any central initiative. 'To make this weakness permanent they have deprived even *themselves* of absolute power, have first forbidden themselves to change the Constitution, except under circumstances which never occur, and have then, through the machinery of the common schools, given to that Constitution the moral weight of a religious document.' Lincoln seemed the one man, 'by infinitesimal chance', capable of managing this infernal machine. 'The President had, in fact, attained to the very position – the dictatorship – to use a bad description, required by revolutionary times.'[121]

The *Economist* made a post-mortem exception for Lincoln, but it entertained few doubts about the low character of his compatriots and hoped that one outcome of the Civil War would be to humble them. Above all it had called for a speedy end to the conflict, and resumption of cheap and unrestricted flows of raw cotton to the shuttered mills of Lancashire, cut off from their supplies by the blockade of Southern ports. While Bagehot stopped just short of calling for Britain's Royal Navy to reopen them, he had welcomed the dissolution of the Union in 1861 and looked forward to a future with two 'less aggressive, less insolent, and less irritable' trading partners.[122] In many ways a lucid critic of American politics, he was less perceptive about the impact of the ultimate victory of the North, in part because the *Economist* had a profound interest in the economic and imperial consequences of the outcome for Britain.

Bagehot had personally sympathized with the Confederacy and maintained it could not be defeated, scoffing at the idea that '5 or 6 millions of resolute and virulent Anglo-Saxons *can* be forcibly retained as citizens'.[123] He urged Russian or French or English mediation, for 'there is not the slightest prospect of their forcible subjugation'. The brilliant victories of the South had earned it 'the right to be admitted into the society of the world as a substantive and sovereign State. Certainly, neither Belgium, nor Greece, nor the Spanish colonies of the New World, manifested in anything like the same degree the qualities and resources which enable nations to maintain freedom and command respect.'[124] With the Confederate capital of Richmond in flames, he saluted its 'vanquished gallantry which appeals to the good side of human nature'.[125]

Southern courage contrasted with Northern cowardice. 'They are a *wholly untried people,* they have never yet faced a really formidable foe.' In the war of American independence, it was true, they had shown 'pluck', but 'the indescribable imbecility of their enemies was yet more wonderful than their own vigour'. The only triumph since 1783 had been in the War of 1812, a short conflict in a minor theatre of Britain's war against Napoleonic France, when the future president Andrew Jackson 'defended a walled city against an inadequately-provided invading force lodged in an unhealthy swamp' outside New Orleans – not exactly bad odds. 'All their other contests have been against naked Indians and degenerate and undisciplined Mexicans: these were *raids* rather than wars.'[126] The *Economist* flew into a rage at US interference with British shipping, which was 'very like insanity' for Northern officials to condone.[127] When two Confederate diplomats aboard the *Trent* were taken prisoner en route to London in 1861, it demanded their release and an apology, 'or we have no alternative save war'. The incident was blamed on 'the voting, electioneering, spouting, rowdying public' in the North, which actually believed it could beat the South, 'lick Great Britain in the bargain', and add 'Canada to Texas'. 'The depth of their ignorance is unfathomable. The height of their frenzy is inconceivable.'[128]

The *Economist* repeatedly predicted the collapse of the Northern war effort at the turn of 1862 for lack of funds. 'With a revenue of twelve millions they are spending one hundred and twenty millions; indirect taxes bring in next to nothing; direct taxes are not even yet voted; the loans required are not taken up; and already they have resorted to the desperate, ruinous, and speedily exhausted contrivance of inconvertible paper money.' There was no need to intervene: 'mere want of funds must almost infallibly bring them to a stand in twelve months – probably in six.'[129]

Nor did Bagehot accept the casus belli of the Union, and he steadfastly denied the charge levelled against the *Economist* as a result – that it was condoning slavery. Lincoln had made it quite clear, he reminded readers, that the North was not fighting to extinguish this peculiar institution. If the choice were 'between the preservation of the Union and the perpetuation of slavery; if "Union" meant negro emancipation as surely as "secession" means negro servitude, – then, indeed, we should be called upon to take a very different view of the subject.'[130] He scoffed at the Emancipation Proclamation a year later, a strategic ploy to stir slave rebellions behind enemy lines and score humanitarian points abroad. 'Half-hearted and inconsistent', it would disgust public opinion in Europe. This 'shibboleth of Emancipation', which freed slaves in enemy but not loyal states, 'is so curiously infelicitous, so grotesquely illogical, so transparently *un*-anti-slavery, that we cannot conceive how it could have emanated from a shrewd man.' Lincoln had confirmed 'the servitude of those whom he *might* set free, and he decrees the freedom of those whom neither his decree nor his arm can reach!'

Britain and the *Economist* sincerely desired to see slavery abolished, without a thought as to the price of raw cotton, Bagehot insisted. Still, the paper made some surprising claims about what would tend to that end – perhaps reflecting the fact that, as one biographer puts it, its editor 'did not take a high principled abstract view on slavery'.[131] The surest route to abolition, argued the *Economist*, was the success of the South. 'It is in the independence of the South, and not in her defeat, that we can alone look with confidence for the early amelioration and the ultimate extinction of the slavery we abhor.'[132] The paper was no friend of 'the fanatics who hope to found a great empire on the basis of slavery', it clarified, for 'we do not believe that predial slavery

such as exists in the slave states is a possible basis for a good
and enduring commonwealth'. But it was unclear why, in that
case, Southern independence was desirable. 'We wish the area of
slavery should be so small that, by the sure operation of economical causes, and especially by the inevitable exhaustion of the soil
which it always produces, slavery should, within a reasonable
time, be gradually extinguished.'[133]

In the end slavery was a side note, however. Far more important
in the paper's warnings about a Northern victory was the inter-
twining logic of empire and economics. Two states were better
than one, and would balance the naturally grasping character
of each: 'reckless Southerners may talk of seizing on Mexico,
Nicaragua, and Cuba; unprincipled and inflated Northerners may
talk of seizing on Canada; but there will be some hope that we
may leave them to each other's mutual control, and smile at the
villainous cupidities of both.'[134] Harriet Beecher Stowe and her
abolitionist ilk were thus wrong to accuse London of rooting
for the South: 'The effectual discomfiture of either party would
answer our purpose equally well.'[135] If the *Economist* looked
slightly more favourably on the South, this was because it had
a right to leave the Union, was 'more decent and courteous' to
Britain, and because it desired 'to admit our goods at 10 per cent
duty, while their enemies imposed 40 per cent'.[136] Not just a geopolitical check, then, but freer trade would flow from the Southern
states' independence. In articles for the *New York Daily Tribune,*
Marx had mocked the *Economist* up to this point for rationalizing slavery; now he gave it an ironic salute, as 'honest enough to
confess at last that with it and its followers sympathy is a mere
question of tariff'.[137]

Bagehot continued to push British Liberals to acknowledge
that, despite their distaste for slavery, 'the experiment of one
nation for one continent has turned out on the whole far from
well.' America was an only child, with 'no correct measure of its
own strength', and having never played with others, 'indulges in
the infinite braggadocio which a public school soon rubs out of
a conceited boy'.[138] It was, in other words, a dangerous imperial
rival, a point nicely captured by his image of the English public
school, where playground bullying was preparatory to a career in

the Empire. By the turn of 1865 the victory of the North looked imminent, 'exciting the brains of Americans', based on a mania for 'empire and exclusive possession of a continent'. Bagehot was hostile to this outcome. The rest of the world, he wrote ruefully, 'could not look with much favour or anticipated comfort on the formation of a new power thus motivated and thus clenched – a power whose two fundamental rules of action and raisons d'être would be, to defy its neighbour, and to annex its neighbour's land.'[139]

## The British Empire

If Bagehot viewed America through the prism of the British Empire and its interests, what did he have to say about the latter? Bagehot's editorship was less rich in incident than Wilson's – sitting between bursts of warfare and annexation in the 1850s and 1880s–1890s – and Bagehot showed the same breezy, flexible confidence in imperial destiny as he did in English political economy. Whether in Canada, the Cape, New Zealand or Australia, he admitted that colonists could be difficult, demanding, costly, and confrontational with natives. But he opposed the idea of cutting them loose. 'We are pre-eminently a colonizing people. We are, beyond all comparison, the most enterprising, the most successful, and in most respects the best, colonists on the face of the earth.'[140] He countenanced force wherever that valiant spirit was obstructed by recalcitrant subjects, or non-Westerners, though in such cases he preferred it to be moderate, and directed from London.

Closest to home, he backed Gladstone's efforts to 'pacify Ireland' after 1868: disestablishing the Church of Ireland – Protestant, in a country four-fifths Catholic – and passing very limited tenure reform to give evicted farmers compensation for their improvements to the land. Any step outside the 1801 Act of Union, however, was anathema. The *Economist* attacked both the Fenian Brotherhood, made up of armed republicans in America and Ireland, as well as the Home Rule League, which sought greater autonomy through conventional parliamentary forms.

Gladstone was right to 'tread out the Fenian folly' following an uprising in 1867, which proved that the organization preferred sowing strife to practical politics. But since Home Rule was a 'gigantic and impossible constitutional revolution', it was hardly less of a folly. A parliament for Ireland would tear down the entire edifice of the British state, creating a federal instead of imperial parliament in London, unable to override the Irish one 'without provoking something like a rebellion on every separate occasion'. Home Rulers would 'be imprudent, but they would be far more logical, if they were to raise a cry at once for an independent Irish Republic'.[141] The one consolation for the defeat of the Liberals in 1874 that so shocked Bagehot was, 'at least it delivers us from the rule of the faction which is anti-English in essence, and which wishes to destroy the Empire'.[142] His idea for political reform in Ireland was to suppress the office of viceroy: concentrating the symbolic majesty of the British state in such a person lent credence to the claim of Irish nationalists to live in a subjugated colony – as if Dublin were no different than Delhi.[143]

Perhaps the most far-reaching colonial crisis during the period was not in Ireland, but in the West Indian colony of Jamaica. Here, in 1865, Governor Edward John Eyre responded to an uprising of former slaves in Morant Bay with brutal force, declaring martial law and deploying troops, who burned and looted over a thousand homes, and killed several hundred black Jamaicans, including a mixed-race member of the Jamaica Assembly. This looked like an organized lynching designed to shore up the power of white sugar planters, whose fortunes had declined since the advent of free labour, free trade and lower-cost sugar a generation earlier – and these events caused massive controversy when news of them reached Britain. Though Bagehot rebuked black rebels as 'negro Fenians', he was much more critical of Governor Eyre. For a time he made common cause with John Stuart Mill, who in 1866 set up the Jamaica Committee to press for Eyre to be put on trial; a host of liberals joined Mill, including John Bright, Charles Darwin, Herbert Spencer and many others. Opposite them stood Thomas Carlyle and the members of the Governor Eyre Defence and Aid Committee. Bagehot attacked Carlyle in the *Economist* for defending Eyre's 'carnival' of violence as 'the worship of brute force', and a threat to law, justice and liberty – not just in Jamaica, but in England. 'On Mr. Carlyle's principles of judging human actions, as exemplified in this Eyre case, Philip II and Alva have a right to the honour and thanks of posterity.'[144] But as might be expected, his objection was not primarily moral. Bagehot agreed that blacks were inferior to whites, and acknowledged the importance of maintaining order in the Empire. To assure this in keeping with the needs of capital, however, required some cooperation from subject peoples. The *Economist* pointed to the tantalizing investments to be made in China's railways, canals, tea planting, silk growing, and steam navigation, 'beyond any experience we have yet acquired', and similar opportunities in 'Japan, Indochina, Persia, Asiatic Turkey' and Africa, 'from Abyssinia to the Cape'. To unlock these treasures, one point had be kept in mind – 'that very large bodies of dark laborers will work willingly under a very few European supervisors'.[145]

As it turned out, gaining access to these markets involved more than investment prospectuses. It required armed compulsion, especially in East Asia. Bagehot saw British and French interventions in China to prop up the tottering Qing dynasty against Taiping rebels – a radical millenarian rebellion that spread from rural Guangxi to convulse the country, in part due to prior Western wars to force it open – as a regrettable necessity; but with Englishmen 'leading the fleets and armies, and administering the finances of the Celestial Empire', soon to be 'Governors and Viceroys over vast provinces', its violent repression had a silver lining. Farther east in Japan, trade – and the sort of extraterritorial legal treatment that British merchants should expect – was also at stake, in a nation that had shown still stronger distrust of Westerners than China. The *Economist* was unsure if the Royal Navy had legitimate grounds to bombard Kagoshima in 1863, to punish the 'Daimio Satsuma' for the death of a British merchant. But once begun, the paper pushed for widening the war. 'Possibly we may have to bombard the Spiritual Emperor as well as the Feudal Baron, if his palace lie within a mile or two of the shore. Anyhow we are in for it: we must now hold our ground and make good our position; and we must do this by force and at the cost of blood.'[146] As the smoke settled afterwards, it worried that in continuously shelling a town of 150,000 ('as large as Sheffield') for over forty-eight hours 'we do seem to have outstepped all the now recognized boundaries of civilized and credible warfare'. Satsuma's representatives later put the death toll at 1,500.[147]

Not all imperial undertakings were military during these years. Bagehot grumbled in 1875 when Disraeli, as prime minister, opted to buy 176,602 shares in the Suez Canal from the Khedive of Egypt, bringing the total Britain owned to just under half. As an investment yielding 5 per cent it was sound, and would allow the Khedive to 'reform his finances'. But Bagehot was unsure if it would solve the problem it was meant to address – making sure the passage to India stayed open, and in British hands. 'We do not know what will be the course of history or the necessities of future times.' 'If we are prepared to take hold of Egypt, will this share in the Suez Canal help us in so doing? Will it not be better to take the country when necessary, without making public beforehand our intention to do so?'[148] India itself was non-negotiable, whatever route was taken there, as Bagehot affirmed in 1863 at the death of Elgin – the man sent east to break Chinese resistance in the Second Opium War and open Japan, subsequently appointed viceroy of India. His successor, Sir John Lawrence, had the 'single quality' needed to 'keep a vast population which wants to recede, perpetually advancing'. What was that? 'Force'.[149]

Perhaps the most revealing example of the open-ended imperialism of the *Economist* under Bagehot was its enthusiasm for the least successful of all such ventures: the invasion of Mexico at the end of 1861 by France, with support from Spain and Britain. It applauded Napoleon III for rebuilding a failed state unable to pay its creditors in Europe, and for balancing the US, with its back turned fighting the Civil War. The installation of an Austrian archduke, Maximilian, on Mexico's throne three years later, was a particular stroke of brilliance – a better administrator than 'any obtainable half-caste or Indian president', whose rule would ensure the export of everything from silver to apples, and timely interest payments on Mexico's sovereign debt.[150] Three years later Maximilian was executed by firing squad in Querétaro, after French forces hastily withdrew.

In *Physics and Politics,* Bagehot explained his approach to empire in more theoretical terms, as a complement to these snapshots in the *Economist.* Applying his take on positivism and the natural sciences to human societies around the world, he divided them into three evolutionary epochs: a 'preliminary age', primitive, tribal and customary; a 'fighting age', in which some nations prevailed over others thanks to their martial qualities; and a third, progressive, industrial and peaceful 'age of discussion', where the 'higher gifts and graces have rapid progress'. This, of course, was Victorian Britain: the class rule of the ten thousand educated members of society that Bagehot had outlined in the *English Constitution* found an evolutionary basis in 'adaptation' and 'natural selection'. Bagehot added that some law of imitation must operate inside nations to account for their success in the world – a copying process, working its way from 'predominant manners' down and then inherited, in a Lamarckian sense. Bagehot was himself copying social evolutionists – not least Herbert Spencer and John Lubbock – by making such claims, and then extending them outwards. British wars were justified in China, for example, since its ancient civilization had been arrested at an earlier stage of development. There, to 'crack the cake of custom' might indeed require cannonballs.[151]

## Bagehot and the Faces of Liberalism

Bagehot endowed the *Economist* with his tone as well as his point of view. 'He is not only clever himself', wrote one biographer, but he 'gives a distinct impression that he is one of a band of like-minded conspirators, to which the reader is invited to attach himself.'[152] What was this band of conspirators, and where did Bagehot's editorial positions place the *Economist* on the spectrum of liberalism in the 1860s and '70s? Other liberals were far more open to democratization of the British political system, more critical of the Second Empire in France, less hostile to the American republic, and less complicit with imperialism. These stances reinforced each other, so that the radicals within the Liberal Party – the same men with whom Wilson had so spectacularly fallen out in the 1850s – continued to embody all that Bagehot and the *Economist* opposed.

Bagehot's views brought him into conflict with various shades of liberal thinkers, journalists and statesmen. Frederic Harrison, a barrister and one of the English Comtists whom Bagehot despised, was a radical who gave free courses to workers as well as refugees from the Paris Commune. In 1867 he used the *Fortnightly Review* to attack the *Economist* editor, that 'able constitutionalist' who 'in these pages could scarcely defend without a smile' the House of Lords, the bench of bishops and the throne, 'as the "theatric part" of the constitution'. But that, Harrison pointed out, was itself a mystification: 'a fiction which covers a fiction', for behind all 'parliamentary play' was 'the hard fact of an aristocratic regime'. Where was the 'efficient secret' Bagehot described? It had scarcely a single significant accomplishment since the repeal of the Corn Laws (and that had been 'forced on the House of Commons at the price of revolution', he noted): 'no national education, no efficient poor law, no reorganised army, no law reform, no contented Ireland'. Bagehot was unconscionably embellishing a moneyed, undemocratic status quo. 'If we are going to tear down shams, let us be consistent, and know where we are going.'[153]

Bagehot, for his part, evaluated other liberals – even allies – in terms of their proximity to radical elements of the Liberal Party. Gladstone, drafting his budget of 1860, was told that to become a great statesman he must learn 'not to object to war because it is war, or to expenditure because it is expenditure' – to reject, in other words, the liberalism of Cobden and Bright. 'It may be that the defence of England ... is one of our duties; if so, we must not sit down to count the cost.'[154] Bagehot may have praised Cobden as a 'sensitive agitator' at his death in 1865, but he still used the occasion to sharply rebuke the former leader of the Anti-Corn Law League: 'his mind was very peculiar and had sharp limits', in particular an 'insufficient regard for the solid heritage of transmitted knowledge' contained in the 'dignified' parts of the constitution.[155] Cobden had also been wrong to oppose the Crimean War. 'There are occasions when a war itself does its own work, and does it better than any pacification. The Crimean War was an instance of this', which, Bagehot argued, 'destroyed the prestige and the pernicious predominance of Russia. At the end of it, what were to be the conditions of peace were almost immaterial.'[156]

The richest, most revealing comparison between Bagehot and a compatriot thinker is with John Stuart Mill – who Bagehot read more carefully than any other, and whose liberalism troubled him greatly the more it diverged from his own. At twenty-two, the future *Economist* editor praised Mill's *Principles of Political Economy* as a thoroughly modern foundation for the dismal science, combining all that was logical about Ricardo with the worldliness of Smith. Bagehot was already puzzled, however, by Mill's plans to improve the labouring poor, which placed too much stress on their 'intellectual cultivation'. What workers needed was not so much education – especially in those 'depots of temptation', the great towns – than a 'restraining discipline over their passions and an effectual culture of their consciences'.[157] As 1848 rolled on, and revolutions swept the capitals of Europe, the gap between them widened. Mill was thrilled, seeing the uplift of workers and democratic reform in Britain as tied to the republican experiment in France.[158] Inspired by the Fourierist socialists, Mill quickly revised his *Principles* to emphasize support for workers' co-operatives, and hailed 'the capacity of exertion and self-denial in the masses of mankind' when 'appealed to in the name of some great idea'.[159] Writing from Paris in 1851, Bagehot saw these associations as bad jokes or worse – a polarization that only grew more marked two decades later during the worker-led Paris Commune, which Mill defended and the *Economist* denounced.[160]

If the paper endorsed Mill when he stood for parliament in 1865, it was because of the crucial ways in which their conceptions of liberalism did coincide: on empire. 'Differing as we do in the strongest manner from many of Mr Mill's political opinions' – including a franchise that would extend to the labouring classes almost half of national representation – 'we should vote for him in preference to any other candidate'. Why? In his address to the electors of Westminster, it saw an indictment of the 'official creed of the advanced Liberals', 'shattering into dust those Radical fallacies' of 'Mr. Bright and the Manchester School'. Mill promised to vote for defence outlays, and in contrast to the radicals – who argued that 'England must never interfere in foreign affairs' except

in 'her own national interest' – declared that 'interposition on the
side of liberty, to countervail interposition on the side of oppression, is a right and may become a duty.'[161] As the Governor Eyre
controversy gripped parliament, Bagehot took Mill's side against
Eyre. But this was not only because his rampage in Jamaica
undermined the rule of law: both Mill and Bagehot accepted that
white colonial administrators should continue to rule over black
Jamaicans, treating the episode as an isolated infraction. Shared
support for the imperial order as given went beyond one event or
policy. Bagehot's civilizational hierarchy in *Physics and Politics,*
in which Britain might force societies at arrested stages of development to advance, echoed Mill's voluminous writings on the
backwardness of Indians and Irish and the progressive purpose
behind London's unrepresentative rule over them.[162]

But even here, Bagehot found Mill too easily swept along
by revolutionary currents. In 1868, the latter responded to the
Irish nationalist upsurge of the year before with a proposal that
addressed what he considered the root grievances of the Fenians,
whom he wished to stamp out: creation of quasi-peasant proprietors, with fixity of tenure, via state guarantee or purchase – as
much out of moral obligation for past misrule by England
as to maintain that rule, through the imperial Act of Union.[163]
Scathing in his review of Mill's pamphlet, Bagehot pointed to
the contradictions that undermined the ultimate goal he shared
with it. Not only was possession of land in itself unlikely to cure
the misery of Irish peasants, given their ingrained habits of idleness, but it handed them a potent new weapon. 'Suppose that at
a moment of political excitement – at such a crisis, say, as this
of Fenianism – the whole Irish people do not pay their rent to
the English Government. What is to be done? You cannot serve
a writ of eviction upon a whole nation.' In Bagehot, the cause of
liberal imperialism had a harsher, but also a more consistent and
unfussed champion, who prided himself on this temperamental
contrast with the great philosophic radical. On Ireland, Mill had
shown himself to be 'easily excitable and susceptible; the evil that
is in his mind at the moment seems to him the greatest evil, – for
the time nearly the only evil – the evil which must be cured at all
hazards', wrote Bagehot.[164] 'Mr Mill is, of course', he could muse

in 1871, 'the standing instance of a philosopher spoilt by sending him into Parliament, and the world.'[165]

Perhaps the most revealing international comparative insight into the liberalism of the *Economist* under Bagehot comes from France – only fitting given the coverage devoted to it. 'The English thinker with whom Tocqueville can be most properly compared is Bagehot', wrote A. V. Dicey, and the two men are still often classed together on account of an allegedly shared distrust of democracy.[166] In fact, they had less in common on democracy than they did in according a central importance to empire in the competitive environment of mid-nineteenth century Europe. Indeed, it was in part his recognition that democratic change could not be halted – in contrast to Bagehot, who bitterly resisted it – that led Tocqueville to advocate the merciless conquest and colonization of Algeria, as a 'great task' capable of unifying France in a post-revolutionary and egalitarian age. Elected to the Chamber of Deputies in 1839, Tocqueville applied himself with singular energy to erecting a French empire in North Africa, and fulminated against just the sort of radical critics that Bagehot excoriated in the pages of the *Economist* – for John Bright, read Amédée Desjobert.[167] As foreign minister for the Second Republic, he showed no qualms about using force in Europe either, if the end of national prestige justified it – overseeing the dispatch of troops to revolutionary Rome in 1849 to topple a sister republic on behalf of Pope Pius IX, in violation of the French constitution; in the aftermath, he connived at the illegal prolongation of powers of Louis-Napoléon that ended in his overthrow of the republic in France itself.

In reacting to this coup d'état, however, Tocqueville and Bagehot did hint at ways in which their liberalism differed. In his *Recollections* Tocqueville offered a vivid account of the revolution of 1848 right up to the moment of the coup in December 1851. In contrast to Bagehot's sarcasm in the *Inquirer*, Tocqueville earnestly participated in the February uprising – upbraiding his fellow national guardsman, observing with approbation the handiwork of *barricadiers*, being lectured at by a working-class man outside the National Assembly (without, however, rendering his speech in cockney), and deploring the pious egotistical ravings of his sister-in-law, 'concerned only with the good God, her husband, her children and especially her health, with no interest left over for other people'.[168] Bagehot's ode to 'common comforts' and 'stupid lives' in a national emergency was, for Tocqueville, selfishness. Though he helped pave the way for the coup that displaced the moderate republic he claimed to defend, when it came he denounced Louis-Napoléon in a letter smuggled out of France. 'If the judgment of the people of England can approve these military saturnalia', wrote Tocqueville, addressing the same audience of middle-class liberals that Bagehot was also trying to reach, 'I shall mourn for you and for ourselves, and for the sacred cause of legal liberty throughout the world.'[169]

For Bagehot, crippling commercial uncertainty awaited societies unable to contain the democratic elements in their constitutions. Tocqueville, more concerned with moral and religious liberties and whether these could survive in democracies, was less intransigent. The spread of democracy to the 'Christian nations of our day' might be cause for anxiety, but for the author of *Democracy in America* it was also inevitable, an edict of providence that might even – provided it did not put equality above liberty, as he accused socialists in France of doing – be beneficent.[170] Bagehot read and admired Tocqueville, and met him at least once in 1857. Yet he could not help suspecting that a man who took such a dim view of 'money-making', even criticizing the individualism it bred as a threat to the preservation of liberty, 'might be thought to be the expression, if not of a disappointed man, then of a disappointed literary class'.[171] Where was liberalism headed? Tocqueville was an aristocrat with a manor in Normandy, Bagehot a banker, whose favourite pastime was riding to hounds. The coup d'état of 1851 obliged the former to retire from politics, and set the latter on his path to the *Economist*.

# 3

## Edward Johnstone and the Aristocracy of Finance

Karl Marx read the *Economist*, starting at least as early as the summer of 1850, when he acquired a pass to the reading room of the British Museum.[1] The revolutionary surge of two years earlier, the 'springtime of the peoples', had fizzled, and to the author of the *Communist Manifesto* the back issues of the fiercely free trade *Economist* suggested why: after two years in which poor harvests and high grain prices, a downturn in trade and a credit crisis had fuelled popular and middle-class discontent, the business climate began to improve in mid-1848, strengthening conservatism and dampening protests against it all over Europe. Yet Marx took more than raw economic data from the *Economist*. In it he identified a sector of liberal opinion with a distinct worldview and cosmopolitan wealth, so fearful of further popular upheaval that by 1851 it was ready to welcome an illiberal but orderly dictatorship in the revolutionary capital of the nineteenth century, France.

'The position of the aristocracy of finance is most strikingly depicted in a passage from its European organ, the London *Economist*', Marx wrote of events leading up to the coup d'état in the *Eighteenth Brumaire of Louis Bonaparte* in 1852. On 1 February 1851, the paper's Paris correspondent had noted 'the sensitiveness of the public funds at the least prospect of disturbance, and their firmness the instant the executive is victorious'. 'In its issue of 29 November', he continued, 'The *Economist* declares in its own name: "The President is the guardian of order, and is now recognized as such on every

Stock Exchange of Europe".'² If its perspective – that of 'the loan promoters and the speculators in public funds' and 'the whole of the banking business' – was far from new, the scale of the invested capital was: 'If in every epoch the stability of the state power signified Moses and the prophets to the entire money market, why not all the more so today, when every deluge threatens to sweep away the old states, and the old state debts with them?'³

Marx was, in short, in perfect agreement with Bagehot, the future editor then writing his letters from Paris, in claiming that market uncertainty was leading 'even the most ordinary liberalism' to be denounced as socialism by middle-class Frenchmen.⁴ In another sense, Marx was ahead of the curve, for it was not until Bagehot took the helm that the *Economist* truly articulated the political wisdom of the 'financial aristocracy' as such. The turbulent years that followed Bagehot's death in 1877 saw an amplification of the dynamic that Marx had registered. Indeed, the advice Bagehot left behind, scrupulously adhered to by trustees and editors alike, was to focus on the frothy money markets of the City of London – and what seemed their most important new lines: settling 'international bargains' and floating foreign loans, with Britain ('the country of banks') pressing the latter upon 'civilised' and 'half-finished' nations much like 'London money dealers' on 'students at Oxford and Cambridge'.⁵

The next two editors built on this blueprint. But their joint appointment, which was intended to re-create the twin talents of Bagehot, was troubled and brief. Daniel Conner Lathbury, graduate of Brasenose, Oxford, a trained barrister turned journalist, was tasked with writing political leaders. His liberalism pivoted on the politics of the Anglican High Church, however – and in contrast to Bagehot, who took an impish, intellectual interest in religious subjects, Lathbury was drawn deep into earnest debates on the Catholic revivalism of the Oxford movement.⁶ He was dismissed in 1881. Robert Harry Inglis Palgrave handled the money market and trade statistics, staying on two years after his ex-co-editor. Palgrave seemed exactly what Bagehot had in mind: his family were bankers from Great Yarmouth, who financed their four sons' forays into poetry, history, imperial diplomacy, economics, and politics.⁷ The only son to go into the family business instead of to university after Charterhouse, a minor public school, Palgrave even sounded like Bagehot – at least when contemplating 'the union of pecuniary sagacity and educated refinement' that fell to the country banker, whose work left him free to contemplate Elizabethan sonnets on 'the long winter evenings, the half hour in the shady garden in summer, the quiet times on the deck of the yacht', or on the way to the office.[8]

## The New Financial Press

Neither Lathbury nor Palgrave, alone or together, could achieve the lively synthesis of politics and finance the trustees wanted. There was a profit to be made reporting on the money market, and the paper was now attracting stiff competition. In 1859 a weekly *Money Market Review* began to appear; ten years on, in response to a rush of listings fuelled by the Companies Act, its owners started the daily *Financier,* and a monthly *Bondholders Register.* The rival *Bullionist* launched in 1866. The *Daily News* and the *Times* devoted increasing if not always disinterested space to the City of London.[9] But the fiercest challenger arose from within: Robert Giffen, Bagehot's assistant from 1868 to 1876, declined to succeed him, and instead founded the *Statist,* which fought the *Economist* for writers, advertisers, and statistical scoops until 1967.[10] One difference between the *Economist* and these newcomers is hinted at by its address for most of this period: not Fleet Street, the traditional home of London's newspapers, nor the bankers' Square Mile, but the Strand, sandwiched between a cigar importer and a wine merchant, near music halls and literary magazines, in the bustling heart of London.

It took six years for the *Economist* trustees to agree on a new model, during which time Wilson's brother George, sons-in-law Greg, Shipley and Barrington, and daughter Eliza played leading roles. At various points they consulted the economist Stanley Jevons, and contemplated offering the post to John Morley, then editor of the *Pall Mall Gazette.*[11] But in 1883 it was Edward Johnstone, veteran City hand for the *Scotsman,* and financial stringer for Bagehot, Palgrave, and Morley, who got the job – at first with the future Liberal prime minister Herbert Henry Asquith as his political editor – and held it, for a record twenty-four years.

Johnstone came to London in 1874. His university studies in Edinburgh had focused on political economy, and though he also qualified as an actuary, he seems not to have practised this trade.[12] At thirty, he was a 'comely, fresh-faced young Southern Scot', according to a *Times* editor who read his letter of introduction and sent him along to the manager of the *Economist*. There are few other remembrances. John St Loe Strachey – a cousin of the Bloosmbury biographer Lytton Strachey – described Johnstone as an editor 'who told you exactly what he wanted' and 'made it so very clear that one was expressing not one's own views, but the views of the *Economist*' and that 'whether they were in fact right or wrong they certainly deserved full consideration'. He remembered just one alteration Johnstone made to his writing in nine years: in a review of Bagehot's collected works, Strachey compared Bagehot's 'perfection of style' to Robert Louis Stevenson, 'who at the time was held to be our greatest master of words'; Johnstone removed the passage, not for going too far, but because 'he feared Mr Bagehot's family might think that the writer was not properly appreciative of Bagehot's work if he compared it to that of Stevenson!' Though a great journalist – Strachey reported with mild understatement – Johnstone was 'not a man who had paid any attention to literature'.[13]

Instead his focus was on the *Economist*, which also provides our main clues about Johnstone. Its obituary to him makes this seem almost intentional, noting his 'direct, forcible, and unassuming' prose and 'retiring disposition', roused by hatred of 'tautology', 'hyperbole', and those he suspected of 'writing for lineage'. His 'fidelity to the high traditions which he had received from Wilson and Bagehot' kept the *Economist* distinct in an era of intense competition – where 'there was a danger that the English press might become shallow and subservient', a 'mouthpiece of financiers and share-pushers, the enemy instead of the friend of the investing classes'.[14] Johnstone sought not to make 'readers fortunes', but to recall 'governing principles' and 'guide them clear of blunders'. As the *Financial News* and *Financial Times,* founded in 1884 and 1888 respectively, battled over which 'puffed' shares harder (both took their rough-and-tumble tactics from the Wall Street press), the *Economist* was coolly 'devoted to the higher interests of finance'.[15]

## The Foreign Investor's Friend

Johnstone became editor in the midst of the first Great Depression, a worldwide fall in prices and profits, which lasted roughly from 1873 to 1896. The deflationary trend puzzled contemporaries, in part because production, investment and trade continued to grow. Too much of the latter was, in fact, likely to have been responsible for the former, as foreign industrialists began to battle Britain for control of markets, advances in railroad and marine transport opened up farmlands in North America and Russia, lowering food prices, and the gold standard limited the money supply.[16] Alongside a class structure that favoured savers over consumers, this malaise may also have spurred further overseas investment – which rushed forward in spurts, towards higher rates of return. British assets abroad grew from £200 million in 1850 to £700 million in 1870, £2 billion in 1900, and £4 billion in 1913. Capital outflow averaged over 4 per cent of national income over this period, at its close generating about £200 million in interest, or 8 per cent of national income.[17] Bagehot had wondered how British loans and investments might affect 'half-finished' civilisations abroad. In the end, Britain was itself transformed. No other country has ever sent such a large portion of its wealth abroad, or received such a large share of it back.

The *Economist* had no doubt that it was profitable to invest overseas, and its weekly, monthly, and annual data sets have always been central references for economists and economic historians trying to determine the overall quantity and direction of capital flows to and from late nineteenth-century Britain – not to mention their possible causes and effects.[18] Yet few have paid attention to how the *Economist* itself interpreted the data – a significant oversight, given its instrumental role not just in purveying information, but in constructing knowledge about the world as an interlinked market, which it wished to expand in and beyond the formal empire. The paper circulated, after all, among the most powerful class of Victorian and Edwardian savers, the 'gentlemanly capitalists' clustered in south-east England, who made their livings in finance, banking, trade, and shipping, or as politicians, administrators, and landowners, and showed a marked preference for income derived from safe overseas assets like railway and government securities.[19] They turned to the *Economist* not for news in the narrow sense but for political analysis to help them evaluate the risks and rewards of placing capital abroad. What did they learn?

Revenues and yields were calculated annually, in part to defend 'liberal imperialism' against both its critics and those who wanted to pursue it for frivolous ends. Total colonial investments of £620 million yielded an average return of 5 per cent in 1883. Charts abounded, calculating total interest payments by region – Australasia, North America, India, Africa – and type: government loans, railways, provincial cities, harbours and gas, banking, mortgage, agency, and others. Colonial government loans brought in only slightly more than 4 per cent, excusable because low in risk; railway and municipal bonds and stocks were excellent at over 5 per cent; banks and mortgage companies were galloping away at over 6 per cent. 'Nearly one half of our subscriptions in 1883 were to colonial loans and to colonial enterprise', it reminded readers, 'and the growth is so certain to continue, that the whole question cannot be too carefully considered.'[20]

The lack of movement on the Stock Exchange over the same period gave rise to similar formulas. An encomium to speculative virtues praised the social utility of the risk-taker who 'will subscribe for new securities – such as the Indian gold mines and electricity companies already mentioned – which without him would certainly never have been subscribed at all'. In the midst of stagnating prices, one was obliged to wait until 'the savings of the investing classes increase'. A dazzling securitized vista would then open up: 'New Guinea and the Western Pacific may someday be pictured as teeming with wealth; South America, where we have already sunk over £150,000,000, will offer an indefinite field; so will all our colonies.'[21]

Weekly reports on the money market moved to the front page for

the fin de siècle. Subsequent sections tied political news to investment. The headlines from 13 January 1883 were typical: 'Suez
Canal Dues and Traffic', 'The Finances of Eastern Roumelia', 'The
Condition of the Peasantry of the Deccan', 'Roumanian Progress',
'Industrial Enterprise in Turkey'. Links were explicit. In the 1880s
the *Economist* regularly assessed the creditworthiness of Russia
and Italy, then embarking on major railway expansions. On
Europe's fringe, the instability of the Sublime Porte was a source
of acute anxiety, even after it emerged from default in 1881 under
the budgetary supervision of foreign bondholders. One appraisal
of the Imperial Ottoman Bank concluded that its holding of government securities – despite high annual dividends and a stake in
the profitable state tobacco monopoly – made it vulnerable in the
event of political turmoil. 'When the crash does come, it will be
best for those institutions standing most clear.'[22]

Still greater scrutiny was reserved for Central and South America,
where 20 per cent of British foreign investment was tied up by
the 1880s.[23] Brazilian and Uruguayan deficits it eyed warily on
behalf of European bondholders.[24] Past mistakes in Mexico were
forgiven; the growth in railway stock revived hopes that, 'with its
vast natural resources, it would speedily become an orderly State,
and therefore a State in which English capital might profitably be
invested.'[25] It anxiously watched Peru's borders lest supplies of
phosphorus-rich bat guano be disrupted.[26] In Argentina it fretted
not only over the government's ability to finance its external debt
– incurred largely through railway loans from England – but also
at the erosion of British exports faced with goods emanating from
France and Germany.[27]

News arrived regularly from Buenos Aires, as its share of
British overseas investment bounded ahead between 1880 – when
General Roca became president, pledged to 'order and progress' after his genocidal 'Conquest of the Desert' – and 1890,
to 40–50 per cent of the total.[28] Although the *Economist* hailed
Roca's administration, doubts grew under his successor, if not
soon enough about the famed British merchant bank floating his
loans.[29] Baring Brothers actually blandished a politician with a
free subscription to the *Economist*, and the governor of Buenos
Aires with a stallion, to win this business. The horse, ten years

older than advertised, and bandy-legged, turned out the wiser bet. The *Economist* rebuked the bank's partners when the collapse of the property boom in Argentina revealed the extent of the risks they had taken: the bank was highly leveraged, invested in unstable mortgage-backed bank bonds, and overexposed, with 75 per cent of its portfolio in the River Plate region. As the value of its assets sank, Barings secretly approached the Bank of England – which spearheaded a huge £17.1 million guarantee fund with the City's largest firms and joint-stock banks, to slowly liquidate Barings' liabilities.[30] Johnstone played a direct role in devising this plan, which avoided panicking money markets. 'So great was the public desire to become acquainted with its opinion of the event', recorded the *Bankers' Magazine,* that 'numerous reprints were required of the issue of the *Economist* following the announcement of the breakdown.'[31]

Nor was this the only display of its standing in the City. The Barings Crisis also signalled the end of a long investment boom in Australia, which for the next decade struggled to export enough to service its debt.[32] In 1898 an *Economist* report exposing gold mining companies in West Australia, one of the few bright spots in the economic picture, as a 'conspiracy to deceive investors' led to a libel case against it. Johnstone agreed to withdraw any aspersions on Scott Lings, a Manchester cotton promoter and chairman of Golden Link Mines, but maintained the report had 'been fully justified by events' since the much-touted 'main lode' had still not been struck. Both parties, strangely enough, confirmed the special status of the paper. A simple retraction would not do, explained Lings's lawyer, for 'the very fact that the *Economist* has never had a libel action brought against it, and that it is a highly respectable and responsible newspaper, made it imperative' that its statements 'should be withdrawn in the most public way possible'.[33]

The *Economist* may have been more prudent than the competition, but it was no less optimistic about the overall direction of investment. It could become downright sanguine, in fact, when the capital in question was in good hands – a tone set by Bagehot, for whom the emigration of young men 'with English capital' to 'manage English capital' was one of 'the great instruments of world-wide trade' and 'binding forces of the future'.[34]

South American investments had not only been profitable, but from this perspective, quite secure: it reminded readers that most of the 'railways, tramways, gas, mining, improvement' and other companies 'in which our money has been sunk *are purely English*, in so far as the directorates and shareholders are concerned'.[35]

These statements hinted not only at the scale of British holdings, if direct investments are added to the portfolio type, but at the potential threats to them from rival national capitals.[36] The problem was practical. Between 1878 and 1914, European territorial empires expanded massively, adding 8.6 million square miles throughout Asia, the Middle East and Africa. Germany, Italy, Japan, the US and even Belgium, as latecomers to the imperial stage, now joined older powers such as France and Russia to compete with Britain for land, resources and markets; the risks involved in the 'new imperialism' were manifestly higher. For Johnstone's *Economist*, analyzing investment prospects also meant deciding what limits, if any, to place on this growth; when and where inter-imperial conflict could make way for cooperation; and how newly subject peoples ought to be treated.

### A Liberal Scramble for Empire?

The imperial landscape was already shifting rapidly – and taking more newsprint to cover – in the years leading up to Johnstone's tenure. In 1877, Disraeli made Queen Victoria Empress of India, a move intended to rally India's princelings to the British Raj. The *Economist* did not see what difference it made to Indians what she was called – 'a great army and navy was behind the name, and that is enough for them' – but it did wonder at a Conservative prime minister tinkering with the 'magic' of the English Constitution.[37] The 'Eastern Question' re-emerged at the same time, as Russia launched a new war against the Ottomans that threatened to redraw the map of south-eastern Europe in its favour, and undermine British naval predominance in the Mediterranean. The *Economist* favoured intervention to avoid this outcome in 1878 – first welcoming a diplomatic convention to backstop Ottoman rule in Asia, then endorsing the Congress of Berlin, which divided up most of the

Balkans between the Europeans, and handed Cyprus to Britain.[38]
A new skirmish with Russia irrupted almost immediately, however,
when the Tsar sent his 'envoys' to Afghanistan. Britain promptly
invaded, with the paper calling for an 'irresistible demonstration
of our power' to depose 'Ameer Shere Ali' in Kabul and shore up
the north-western frontier with India in the Second Anglo-Afghan
War.[39] At the same time, Britain also pressed forward in Africa, brutally uprooting the Zulu nation in 1879, clearing a path for white
settlers hungry for its land and labourers. The Dutch-descended
Boers in the neighbouring Transvaal then rebelled against the prospect of being annexed too, temporarily checking British expansion
at Majuba in 1880 during the First Boer War.[40]

The *Economist* tried to take stock of the frenetic pace of imperial activity the year Johnstone took full control of the paper in
1883, sounding a more prudent note than before: London needed
room for manoeuvre in imperial affairs, but should carefully
weigh further territorial commitments. 'The air is thick with projects of annexation. In Africa, in Asia, and in Australasia, schemes
of conquest or of colonisation are being pressed forward.' Though
some chances could not be passed up – 'to such enterprises as the
opening up of the Congo we cannot, of course, be indifferent'
and there could be no red lines 'where we can say thus far and no
farther' – on the whole, 'consolidation and development rather
than fresh adventure' was the wisest course. It reminded readers
of the vast possessions already under British sway – an expanse
sixty-five times the size of the British Isles, twice the area of Europe,
with an estimated populace of 217,695,000. 'Our interests will be
better promoted by international agreements as to freedom of
trade, than to extend our dominion over new land.'[41] Let latecomers, 'under an emotion of tropical territory', fight for leftovers,
as Britain and the *Economist* focused on the invisible bonds of
capital being laid by the City of London. This was not because territory was unimportant to the paper, but because Britain already
had the best bits, 'holds all coaling stations on the two routes to
the far East' and the 'keys of the Mediterranean, of the Red Sea, of
the Persian Gulf, the Straits of Malacca, the Eastern Archipelago,
and rules in unquestioned and practically lonely sovereignty the
people of India'.[42]

If the paper favoured indirect forms of imperial control based on trade and investment, it recognized the necessity of the territorial strings often attached to them. After Egypt had followed Turkey into default in 1876, its main creditors, Britain and France, had imposed a 'Dual Control' over its budget.[43] This violation of Egypt's sovereignty stoked a nationalist movement, led by Colonel Arabi Pasha, which the creditor nations promptly resolved to crush. The *Economist* had pondered a joint expedition even before the deaths of fifty Europeans in Alexandria in June 1883, during riots that broke out when British and French warships appeared off the coast.[44] Now that law, order and European lives were at stake, action could not wait. Admiral Seymour's shelling of the city the next month was 'an act not of aggression, but of self-defence', while the 'burning and pillaging' it triggered among the Egyptians – 'pure vandalism', 'no strategic purpose' – showed that Arabi and his followers were 'not high-minded patriots' but 'military adventurers, capable of any excesses, and caring little what injury they inflict on their country'.[45]

The *Economist* considered the 'preservation of our right of way through the Suez Canal' a matter of life and death for Britain. But in making the case for a swift invasion of Egypt, it also insisted on unselfish motives: dutifully reporting on the risks of disorder to 'the City and businessmen', it dismissed these as a casus belli. Britain was acting on liberal principles. Egyptians had registered anger at their '"exploitation" by bondholders'. 'But bad as some of its features may have been', surely they 'would be glad to return to it' – given the 'paralysis of industry', 'growth of official corruption', 'revival of torture', 'diminishing security of life and property', and 'other Oriental abominations'.[46] Any new regime in Cairo would, meanwhile, be submitted to all the powers of Europe for 'sanction' – a point to which it returned even as it cheered the rout of Arabi by 31,000 Anglo-Indian troops in September.[47] Here tutelage proved unavoidable: 'we have tried to govern Egypt through its treasury, and the attempt has failed.'[48] So during the 'temporary occupation' that followed, the paper tinkered with different policies to make 'financial control' both inconspicuous and inescapable.[49]

In practice, the *Economist* rarely paused to draw a critical breath between colonial wars, even when these arose from the unintended consequences of a previous one. Invading Egypt further weakened the Khedival ruling structure, for example, opening the door to a rebellion in Egypt's own southern colony of Sudan. When the capital Khartoum fell to the jihadi forces of the Mahdi in 1885, the paper demanded vengeance – in uncharacteristically shrill tones – for a no less messianic figure, General Gordon, who had stayed in the city despite orders to evacuate: 'The Englishmen in the Soudan have shown the best qualities of the national character, and their achievements will always hold a conspicuous place in the annals of British heroism.'[50]

More typical of the *Economist*'s justification of British imperial greed was the case it made a few months later for the seizure of the rest of Burma not already coloured red, and the destruction of a monarchy and monkhood that had structured its society for over a millennium. King Thibaw could not be allowed to defy Westminster by pursuing independent policies, whether with France, Russia or China, on the north-eastern border of India, or in commercial matters – where a fine levied on the Bombay Burma Trading Co. amounted to a violation of free trade.[51] Lord Dufferin, viceroy of India, who had amassed an army to carry this last point home to Thibaw in October 1885, was 'a moderate man', who 'must be trusted'.[52] As in Egypt, 'opening up new outlets for trade' was unacceptable as an official motivation for conquest. What *was* at stake, however, was the sacred right of contract, and contrary to the harrumphs of radicals like John Bright, 'we are surely bound to guard against arbitrary and illegal spoliation of our subjects.'[53]

Getting the rationale for imperial expansion right was important for the *Economist*, since narrowly nationalistic, commercially self-interested arguments played into the hands of Britain's rivals – already liable to pursue empire for the wrong reasons, and with increasing assertiveness. Germany could be a productive partner on the world stage – as in 1884, when Bismarck worked to settle the status of the Congo and the Niger at the Berlin Conference.[54] But in 1888 the paper questioned if its leader 'directed or utilised the national desire for colonies with any wisdom', having selected neither places where surplus population could settle, 'nor ones which promise to greatly increase the volume of national trade'.[55] Russia was untrustworthy, madly expansionist, and backward.[56] France, with whom Russia allied in 1894, was tetchy and impulsive – a portrait that grew darker towards end of century, as Paris and London clashed repeatedly throughout Africa and Asia.

France's Tonkin Expedition of 1883 was a foolish land-grab, which was bound to ignite a war with China and damage trade, causing a rise in the price of tea 'felt in every English cottage' and an interruption to flows of Indian opium, product of 'a century of care and skill, akin to Lafitte among clarets, or Havannah cigars among tobaccos'.[57] In 1898 it asked if French behaviour in the Fashoda Crisis was 'worthy of a great nation' – for, besides 'annoying England', why would Major Marchand, 'with his 120 negroes from Timbuctoo', dare tangle with General Kitchener's mighty army over a 'swamp at the bottom of Ethiopia'?[58] Anglo-Egyptian forces had marked out this terrain in blood, tracking the Nile up to Omdurman – where they finally avenged Gordon by killing 11,000 dervishes, and exhuming and torching the remains of the Mahdi.[59] 'France has an enormous colonial empire', it granted after the crisis was defused, 'but she makes so little of it that it is a burden rather than a source of profits', since it was 'overrun by officials and soldiers, and hampered by unwise tariffs'.[60]

The *Economist* was ambivalent about American imperialism, which also reared its head in 1898 during the Spanish-American War. It advised Europe to let 'second-rate' Spain nurse its losses, and accept America's seizure of Cuba, Puerto Rico, the Philippines, not to speak of Hawaii, Guam and Wake Island; at least the US would promote economic development – or 'the interests of humanity and the higher civilisation' – in these places.[61] But the paper harboured few illusions about American exceptionalism, pointing to the wide gap between the country's constitution and its territorial ambitions, which made it ill-suited to be an empire. Under President McKinley the US was taking a 'momentous step' that was 'not in harmony with the spirit or letter of American institutions', in 'violating the inalienable right to liberty' of the native populations of the islands it had seized. More fundamentally, for the *Economist* the US was compromised by the character of its national political economy. For if it resembled 'the mother

country' in seeking a commercial empire (a need for new markets
was '*the* fundamental economic fact' in the US), its 'people have
never been guided by free trade principles'.[62]

This was a major shortcoming in what looked likely to be the
next inter-imperial feeding frenzy, over China, a 'dying nation'
after its drubbing by Japan in the Sino-Japanese War in 1895,
whose corpse the Western powers hungrily circled – including
America, its 'Open Door Policy' in East Asia mere window dress-
ing, in the *Economist*'s opinion.[63] The *Economist*'s response to
the 1899 Boxer Rebellion – an anti-Western uprising that swept
through north China, cresting in Beijing, where a rebel siege of
foreign legations lasted for months – was at once an admission
of Britain's overreach elsewhere, and an illustration of what
distinguished its Empire from the others. Boxers ought to be
'extinguished' for killing Western diplomats and missionaries, but
unlike in Africa, Europeans could cooperate in this stern duty. The
aim was to restore order with a multi-national armed response,
but to avoid partition: not just because the Chinese were clearly
better able to resist than, say, Egyptians, but because the ruling
Manchu dynasty was not to be jeopardised.[64] Foreign investment
in railways, mines, banks and the like required political stability, which outright control, in China, would undermine. If the
*Economist* deplored the treaty that ended the expedition, it was
not for exacting a huge indemnity from the 'bloodthirsty' Empress
Dowager, but because it did so in violation of liberal precepts, on
the back of higher customs duties. Afterwards, the paper deplored
the protectionist leanings of the French, German, Russian and
Italian businessmen who poured into China, and their cynical
reasoning that if the country were 'really and honestly thrown
open' – 'the Anglo-Saxon will beat us in the Chinese market as
he has in every other market in Asia'. In the end, it was a little
disappointed with this inter-imperial experiment, which 'future
historians will describe as without precedent ... the first time
since the Crusades the whole white world joined in an attempt to
punish an Asiatic power for a grave outrage'.[65]

In all these instances British imperialism was peerless, avoiding
the vainglorious preening of the French, the shifting *Weltpolitik*
of Germany, or the hypocrisies of America. What distinguished

it was liberalism, a talent for promoting trade, investment and 'higher civilization'. Yet as the scramble for territory reached fever pitch in the late nineteenth century, obscuring this civilizing commercial mission, criticism of imperialism was never to be found in the *Economist*. It could not be, since the reproduction of national as well as international wealth was inconceivable for the paper under Johnstone outside the imperial framework, and the invasions, pacifications, occupations and annexations necessary to construct, preserve and extend it. Whether imperialism was an 'urge' or a 'tension' internal to liberalism, or one twist in its 'convoluted trajectory', as several scholars would have it, what is abundantly clear is that in the second half of the nineteenth century it was central to the mainstream of liberalism – to which the *Economist* gave authoritative expression.[66] Empire structured the world economy and made it safe for capital, even outside the zones under its direct control. And though the *Economist* faced criticism from radical Liberals over the policies this governing reality led it to endorse, such voices only looked (even momentarily) strong enough to challenge its dominance after 1899, when the Second Boer War shook the British Empire.

As Beijing burned, Britain faced a war in South Africa entirely on its own, in what turned into its costliest military engagement since the time of Napoleon. Not only was its performance in the Second Boer War unsteady, so was its pretext for the war, which seemed to many critics at home and abroad like a plot to grab the gold and diamond mines of two small independent Boer republics, the Transvaal and Orange Free State.[67] The *Economist* had doubts about the official reason offered by its erstwhile contributor, High Commissioner Alfred Milner. At Bloemfontein in June 1899 it was Milner, not the Boer leaders, who refused compromise over the status of Britain's Uitlander expatriates in their territory, provoking the paper in a rare burst of candour to call the issue of their voting rights in the Transvaal a red herring, 'moneyed interests standing in ambush behind a political movement'. Cecil Rhodes, at once prime minister of the neighbouring British Cape Colony, director of the British South Africa Company, speculator in diamond and gold, and the architect of the botched Jameson Raid four years earlier, symbolized this 'unhappily close connection between politics and capitalist interests'.[68] Rhodes's enablers in London were nearly as bad, especially Colonial Secretary Joseph Chamberlain, whose brash style unsettled diplomacy and markets.[69] The annexation these men were pushing for was above all short-sighted. For surrounded by British colonies, inundated by British migrants bearing British capital, both Boer republics would be absorbed into a British-controlled Union of South Africa inside a generation.[70] 'Do not let an exaggerated Imperialism make us ridiculous before the world', the paper initially remonstrated. 'Our Empire was not built up that way.'[71]

But in a trice the Second Boer War proved no different from the other colonial conflicts – for the *Economist* abruptly changed tack when the Transvaal's president Kruger served an ultimatum to the British to halt their troop build-up in October 1899. No matter how just their cause, if the Boers 'once presume to attack a British colony', the country 'would be united in a war which would be literally waged *saigner à blanc*. There would be no compromise, as in 1881; the Boer State would be wiped out of existence by general consent.'[72] From 'stock-breeders of the lower type', such a 'horrible blunder' might have been expected: average Boers 'knew less than people like the Afghans'; but their leaders believed 'as Muslim fanatics believe', and were 'possessed with the idea that Englishmen want their mines – which, we may remark, Englishmen own already'. Boers may have thought like 'Orientals' but counted on being treated as white men, in a 'war with limited liability'. 'They know perfectly well that the English will neither execute them, nor take their farms, nor subject them to special taxation.'[73] When this proved untrue, and revelations about the use of concentration camps emerged, the *Economist* fell silent. Thereafter, criticism was confined to calls for more and better guns, more and swifter transport, and a larger, better-paid standing army.[74]

## Imperial Unity and Liberal Splits

Johnstone presided over a less predictable political scene than past editors, as the old quarrels over empire between the *Economist* and its onetime backers, Cobden and Bright, suddenly took hold of the entire Liberal Party; the succession of far-flung colonial wars, joined to the simmering of nationalism in Ireland, added up to a full-blown crisis. The paper remained militantly hostile to any hint of 'radical pacifism' and any Liberals who espoused such views in parliament. Sir Wilfrid Lawson, the temperance campaigning MP, and a 'small knot' of 'advanced Liberals' were inexcusable in their 'blind' and 'mischievous' opposition to Gladstone's seizure of Egypt in 1882–83.[75] Bright was dismissed for 'denouncing our interference' in Burma in 1885 since he was merely venting 'his favourite dogma on the essential criminality of war'.[76] John Morley, who had nearly become editor of the *Economist*, was admirably Cobdenite when it came to free trade, but took the likeness too far – asking 'foolish' and 'illogical' questions about British scorched earth tactics in the Sudan.[77]

Critiques of empire that hadn't had much impact in the past now seemed to be gaining ground in the Liberal Party and straining its unity. So much so that when Gladstone himself announced a belated conversion to Home Rule for Ireland in 1885, the party imploded – nearly one hundred of its MPs formed a breakaway Unionist faction. In this crisis, the *Economist* knew where it stood, and expressed itself without hesitation. Almost overnight Gladstone turned from a great Liberal hero into an ageing demagogue, dragging his party and country down a sinkhole. Liberals that stood with him over Home Rule had struck a 'fanatical alliance' with nationalist Irish Parnellite MPs, fomenting 'a war against all payment of rent in Ireland', the 'very foundations of contract', to 'hand that unhappy country over to the strife of rival factions, the bitter play of religious animosities, and the keener conflict of class hatreds'.[78] By 1893, the split between the Liberal Unionists and the Liberals was so severe that the *Economist* stopped calling for a reconciliation between them: Unionists needed to throw their full force behind the Conservatives to stop Gladstone's second Home Rule Bill – a 'step towards the disintegration' of the Empire, this time crushed only by the merciful intervention of the House of Lords.[79]

The early editors of the *Economist*, Wilson and Bagehot, had been pillars of the Liberal Party, both of them intimates of

Gladstone. Under Johnstone, the *Economist* now issued its liberalism from a distance, as the paper switched to support for the Conservatives, who soon absorbed the Liberal Unionists (the latter agreeing to drop the prefix 'Liberal' in 1890), and ruled Britain with brief interruptions for the next twenty years.

Disraeli stepped down in 1880 and was remembered with surprising fondness at his death a year later, given that the *Economist* had 'resisted half his proposals' – for he had a sharp mind, 'fought his way amidst great disadvantages to the top', and showed the country and the Liberals (with their 'tendency to forget the importance of force in human affairs') that 'a small nation which governs a great Empire must make sacrifices' and 'occasionally do high-handed things'.[80] Salisbury, the most powerful Conservative statesman of the last third of the nineteenth century, enjoyed even better press, at least by his third stint as prime minister, as the paper acquired a taste for this strangely 'sardonic man'. The marquis had stood up to Germany in South Africa, France in Egypt, and all of Europe over Crete; and he had held fast to his Liberal Unionist allies on Irish Home Rule, living down an earlier reputation for weakness – while resisting 'injudicious adventures'.[81] His nephew and protégé seemed at first a disappointing contrast. Arthur Balfour, who became prime minister in 1902, possessed his uncle's hauteur and 'scant respect for popular government', without his political instincts, or a grasp of economics.[82]

The Liberal politicians of the period faced much harsher criticism, in part because the *Economist* doubted their hold over the party – with the 1886 split having by no means settled imperial policy outside Ireland. The paper backed the Unionists-cum-Conservatives in 1886, 1892, 1895, and 1900. In the last, a 'khaki election' during the Second Boer War, it found the official Liberal opposition in a 'sad way' – 'incurably divided by personal dislike, with followers who upon the leading question of Imperialism really form two, if not three, parties'.[83] Henry Campbell-Bannerman, the leader of the Liberals, was 'obviously not the man to govern this particular situation'; his infamous 1901 speech, denouncing the farm burnings and concentration camp roundups inflicted on Boer civilians as 'methods of barbarism', made him a pariah at the *Economist*. It praised the Liberal Imperialists who defied his leadership to walk out of the House of Commons rather than support a radical motion condemning these camps. Their parliamentary leader, the erudite, horse-racing Lord Rosebery, was far superior – but, for reasons it could not fathom, refused to mount a serious challenge to Campbell-Bannerman for control of the party.[84]

Not until 1906 did the paper break with the Unionists and Conservatives – and then reluctantly, at the last minute, driven to it only when the leader of the former, Joseph Chamberlain, forced the latter, under Arthur Balfour, to adopt 'tariff reform' as the price of an electoral pact between them. This swerve away from free trade and towards protection turned out to be as suicidal in the ensuing general election as the *Economist* predicted. The remarkable fact, however, is that on the eve of the greatest electoral triumph for Liberalism, when it won 400 out of 670 Commons seats, the *Economist* failed to endorse it. Conservatives, under a Chamberlainite 'delusion' the Empire could be bound with reciprocal tariffs, were no longer trustworthy on free trade; sound on trade, Liberals seemed to lack the nerve to defend the Empire, most damningly in Ireland.[85] So far as the paper was concerned, the election of 1906 was a choice between the devil and the deep blue sea.

## Asquith, Ireland and the New Radicalism

One of the editors responsible for leading the *Economist* to this impasse had, paradoxically, just assumed high office in the new Liberal government. Herbert Henry Asquith, as Chancellor of the Exchequer and then as prime minister from 1908, would lead the party during the legislative battles that defined New Liberalism in power. Asquith had begun writing at least one leader a week for the *Economist* in 1880, as a young barrister in need of extra money. He got the job, which paid £150 a year, through Bagehot's old friend and co-editor, Richard Hutton, for whom Asquith also wrote at the *Spectator*. Before crossing the Strand to the *Economist* offices, Asquith would wax on classical themes – 'The Art of Tacitus', say, or 'The Age of Demosthenes' – as well as on contemporary topics like fair trade, land reform and Ireland.[86] At the *Economist* he set down his ideas on the future of liberalism, at this stage under the heading of 'New Radicalism', intended to head off the very schism that precipitated his own exit from both the *Spectator* and the *Economist* in 1885.

A Liberalism fit for the times would, Asquith argued, take on board some progressive social demands without endangering international free trade, while banishing any concerted opposition to interventions overseas, which was as unrealistic as it was unpopular. In the first place, the idea was to revise the strict laissez-faire injunction the *Economist* had laid down under Wilson: 'that the duty of the State begins and ends with protection of life and property and the enforcement of contracts'.[87] To Asquith, fresh from Balliol at Oxford, where the idealist philosopher T. H. Green was a tutor and the art critic John Ruskin had engaged students in social experiments like digging roads, this sounded out of date. That point was underscored at the time by Asquith's meetings with Herbert Spencer, once Wilson's assistant editor at the *Economist*. Spencer was still writing essays, Asquith recalled, 'with such titles as "The Coming Slavery" and "The Great Political Superstition," attacking, with all the fervour of an uncompromising Individualist, the Liberal party for having forsworn its faith in personal freedom'.[88]

In advanced industrial societies the state now had a positive responsibility, Asquith replied in his *Economist* pieces, 'to some undefined degree, for the distribution of comfort and social well-being'. Old radicals like Mill, Macaulay, Bright, Cobden and Wilson, were in a way responsible for this turnabout: after their victory in the 'crusade against the follies of paternal government' at mid-century, the ensuing 'generation of perfect industrial freedom' had stimulated new wants and new evils at the century's close. Free education, sanitation, well-mannered, apolitical trade unions – insofar as these were possible, it was by 'direct action of the State alone'.[89] This Asquithian prospectus included a wider franchise and some redistribution of seats from country to town. The 1884–85 Reform Bills were, after all, far from the populist earthquakes Bagehot had feared back in 1864: even after their passage, at least 4.5 million adult males could not vote, in what remained a franchise system tied to property, not universal rights. Democracy could act as a hedge against disorder, Asquith argued. But that was because he still understood democracy in such a limited sense: 'universal suffrage, which so fetters continental politicians, takes little hold on Englishmen.'[90]

New Radicalism was meant, on the other hand, to sever once and for all the connection between free trade and peace posited by the 'Manchester School of foreign policy'. Abolition of war was not on the cards; ensuring uninterrupted flows of capital, goods, and people within and among the empires actually required such 'shows of force'. Thankfully, 'younger Radicals are obviously indisposed to the idea of non-intervention' – having accurately taken the pulse of the 'new constituencies' created by the latest Reform Bills. Popular opinion not only grasped how important it was to secure the route to India: 'No anxiety is shown to reduce the numbers of the Army; strong measures, like the dispatch of a fleet to Smyrna, to secure the surrender of Thessaly to the Greeks, are not resisted; and in recent Egyptian difficulties the country has been, on the whole, in favour of high-handed action.'[91]

Ireland was the pivot on which both sides of this New Radical realignment – social reform at home, imperial unity abroad – hinged: it was thus significant for both the *Economist* and for liberalism that Asquith grew so exasperated with the place, backing a wave of repression that set the tone at the paper long after he departed. The Land League, which began to urge Irishmen on to economic disobedience in 1880, calling for rent strikes, boycotts and bank runs, was the object of his special hatred. To eradicate these 'terrorists' posing as 'public benefactors', responsible for all kinds of 'agrarian outrages', no measures were too harsh: indefinite suspension of habeas corpus and jury trials, curfews, round-the-clock police and army patrols, deportations, collective punishment. 'Nor do we feel much sympathy with the rather pedantic constitutionalism' of those Liberals who objected to the results: about six hundred Irishmen in jail without trial by 1882, including Charles Parnell, leader of the Irish Home Rulers in parliament.[92]

Asquith accepted that 'pacifying' Ireland depended on settling the land question by creating more 'peasant proprietors'. But he condemned plans to set up such a class without fully compensating present owners of the land as 'unblushing robbery' (whether Irish peasants had also been robbed in the past was a footnote).[93] Englishmen should be generous to the Irish, not on account of any historical wrong – there was none – but because the former might, in near future, 'have to choose between holding Ireland as they hold India, or letting her go altogether'. To nudge 'English democracy' away from this precipice, 'we wish the working classes to feel they have a just claim on Irish gratitude', which was 'the best attainable security that, if the time for making the choice should ever come, they will insist that three kingdoms shall not be reduced to two'.[94] In this vision, the newly enfranchised workers would become allies in the cause of imperial unity, and opponents of Irish Home Rule.

After Asquith, the language was less decorous, but its sense was similar.[95] From 1889 to 1898, John St Loe Strachey wrote the *Economist* leaders on this and other political subjects – as a staunch 'democratic imperialist', who quit the Liberal Party in 1886 in opposition to Home Rule, putting him 'in entire agreement' with Johnstone, even if the latter was somewhat 'less strongly Unionist'. To explain how he felt about the 'sacred character' of the Empire, and its 'incomparable service to humanity' for 'maintaining stable government' in India and Africa, Strachey recounted a stormy meeting with the unscrupulous mineral magnate and politician Cecil Rhodes at a Mayfair Hotel. Strachey told Rhodes off for having given £10,000 to Charles Parnell's Irish Nationalists, so that Rhodes could secure a charter for his South Africa Company in the House of Commons. 'I was an imperialist, I pointed out', whereas Rhodes had given 'money to the Irish enemies of Britain and the Empire, and that I could never forgive. "The Parnellites were engaged in a plot to ruin the British Empire. You knew it, and yet you helped them. You gave them the means to arm and fortify their conspirators and assassins."'[96] The *Economist,* in contrast, was *sincerely* imperialist.

Why Asquith broke with the *Economist* and the *Spectator* in 1885, a year before standing as a Liberal candidate for parliament, remains something of a puzzle, since his position on Ireland was all but indistinguishable from that of Strachey, who took over for him at both publications. It was Joseph Chamberlain, the Unionist leader, who showed the exemplary toughness that Asquith saw as the road to electoral success for Liberalism in the 1880s.[97] One historian suggests party discipline, which Asquith defended in the *Spectator*, dictated his actions.[98] If so, his work for the *Economist*, and his party's long exile from office after it, help explain why he was in no hurry to push Home Rule to the front bench in the election of 1906. By then the *Economist* had itself reached a dead end, at least in party-political terms, with protection at least as great a threat to its brand of liberalism as the dimming prospects for devolution in Ireland. When Johnstone suffered a stroke in 1907, the *Economist* trustees replaced him with a young editor they thought could redirect the paper towards the triumphant New Liberalism. But they chose just the sort of Liberal who had never followed Asquith in renouncing the 'Manchester School of foreign policy'. The question of empire was no 'exhausted volcano': seven years into the editorship of Francis Hirst, it would erupt with enough force to render the Liberal Party all but extinct.

# 4

## Landslide Liberalism

### *Social Reform and War*

Of the three general election landslides to have transfigured twentieth-century British politics, the one in 1906 remains in many ways the most remarkable. The Liberal Party had tasted office for just three of the last nineteen years, while the rivalry within it between Imperialists – grouped around the Liberal League – and radicals – in the Liberal Federation – made improving on that record seem just as remote. Liberal disarray over the Second Boer War was such that, six years earlier, it had failed to contest almost a quarter of seats.[1] Arthur Balfour, the Conservative prime minister, resigned in December 1905, hoping that strife would cripple his 'pro-Boer' opposite, Henry Campbell-Bannerman, leading Liberals to another electoral drubbing. Liberal Imperialists did try to displace Campbell-Bannerman, but failing in that promptly agreed to serve under him at the Foreign Office, the War Office, and the Treasury.[2] Infighting was kept at bay, even over Irish Home Rule, where Liberals had learned to be vague.

Conservatives were partly responsible for this surprising display of unity. Voters showed signs of fatigue with them, especially after a series of unpopular measures, from education and licensing acts that enraged religious dissenters, to the arrival of 50,000 Chinese labourers in South Africa in the aftermath of the Boer War – a government scheme to cheaply man mines there, which inflamed working class opinion.[3] It was the maverick politician Joseph Chamberlain, however, who gave the election shape and colour, turning it into a referendum on free trade. In his younger days a radical mayor of Birmingham, where he owned a screw factory, he later bolted from the Liberal Party over Ireland, and became a leading Liberal Unionist. By 1903, he put his Conservative allies on notice by resigning as colonial secretary to pitch his case for tariff reform directly to the British people – proposing import duties on food that gave preference to the colonies, with the aim of binding them more tightly to Britain, while shielding British industry from foreign rivals. Balfour resigned late in 1905 when it became clear that Chamberlain, who led the largest group of Unionist MPs, would withdraw his support unless the government went 'whole hog' for tariff reform.[4]

This was a Christmas gift to the Liberals, who rallied round the flag of free trade, associated with the heroic Anti-Corn Law struggles from which their party was forged. It was the Tories' turn to fall apart: nine Unionists defected, including Winston Churchill, and ninety-seven seats went uncontested. In an election pitting songs of 'Tariff Reform Means Work for All' against cries that what it really entailed was a 'dear loaf', the latter won out. Here it was Herbert Henry Asquith, widely seen as the best orator on behalf of free trade, who led the charge – entirely appropriate from the former political editor of the *Economist*. Conservatives lost over half their seats on a swing of 10.6 per cent. Liberals made gains almost everywhere – even in formerly hostile parts of Lancashire and London – adding 224 more seats since the khaki election of 1900. They now enjoyed an outright majority of 130, and with their Irish Nationalist and Labour allies, this rose to 356 – the widest margin since 1832.[5]

Yet the 1906 landslide had its origins in more than a negative defence of free trade. Liberals took active steps to win their historic victory, as evidenced by the widespread expectation that it was about to usher in a new era of social reform. Even as the franchise in Britain remained deeply undemocratic up to 1918 – with four and a half million lower class men unable to vote, 500,000 or so plural votes to property owners in the boroughs and counties, and women excluded – after 1885–86, about half the electorate was working-class.[6] By the turn of the century, the growing trade union movement was attempting to organize the working class as an independent political force – a development Liberals vigilantly watched and tried to head off. In 1903 the party signed a secret agreement with the Labour Representation Committee, freeing the latter to fight in 30–40 races unopposed in exchange for its campaign war chest and urban support. Labour expected reform as part of this bargain: two-thirds of Liberal candidates called for restoring legal immunity to trade unions (overturned in the 1901 Taff Vale case), creating old age pensions and more.[7] Internally, these welfare commitments bound the Imperialists and the radicals together, even if the former put the accent on 'efficiency' and breeding up a strong imperial race.[8] Chamberlain was also after working-class support, pressuring Liberals from the right. In addition to mitigating unemployment, he argued, tariffs would generate cash to spend on social programs – a problem Liberals would have to face *without* touching free trade.[9]

The efforts of a generation of Liberal intellectuals to address this issue – of whether (and if so, how) the state should take steps to raise moral and material living standards, leaving behind laissez-faire – is the final element in understanding 1906. Philosopher T. H. Green often gets credit for introducing Hegel and thus a version of continental idealism to Oxford in the 1880s – with the aim of breaking the individualist mould of liberalism, or at least reconciling it to an ethics of communal obligation and legitimate state action.[10] Scholars have, more recently, questioned if Germans are necessary to explain this drift in thought. New Liberals had plenty of native sources upon which to build their plans for reform: from Bentham, an interest in human happiness and in the state's legislative power to increase it; and from Mill, a notion of equality of sacrifice in taxation that lent itself to proportional and distributional schemes. Even Darwin and Spencer were sources, after whom New Liberals fashioned evolutionary models for societal – not just individual – development, believing this could be consciously directed towards cooperative ends.[11]

Contact with the labour movement played no part in the generation of these ideas. They arose in the cloistered setting of Oxford and aimed to pre-empt attacks on private property, viewed as an extension of human personality, not to abolish it. As a result, in 1906 Liberals claimed the most dynamic set of 'organic' intellectuals of any political grouping in Britain – students of Green,

Toynbee, Ruskin and others, prominent among them J. A. Hobson and L. T. Hobhouse, who had graduated to a national stage as journalists, academics, and politicians. Francis Hirst, the new editor of the *Economist,* was one of these. Though less known than Hobson and Hobhouse, two friends and colleagues, Hirst was integral to the makeup of New Liberalism, from the context that shaped it, to the tensions that beset it after 1906, to the disaster of war that broke it in 1914. At the *Economist,* Hirst plunged into the battles that defined Liberalism in office, as the crucial link to a City of London divided by all that was 'New' in it.

## Hirst and the Golden Days of Liberalism

The third of five children from a nonconformist family with a wool-stapling business in West Yorkshire, Hirst had a familiar profile. His divergence from the path of past editors, in the matter of education, became the rule for future editors: in 1892, after Clifton College, he was sent up to Oxford. A dissenting father and doctrinal tests had closed this route to Bagehot. Yet it was the great man himself whom Hirst otherwise resembled. As an undergraduate at Wadham he was as uninterested in captaining the boats as he was in the cricket eleven, Rugby fifteen or Association eleven. 'Not one of those distinctions pointed the way to leadership in Church or State.' The portraits in the hall of the Oxford Union, in contrast, showed the heights to which its officers could aspire. Hirst became president, enlivening debates that blended seriousness – 'that this House heartily welcomes Mr. Gladstone's intervention in the Armenian agitation' or 'the time has come for the substitution of arbitration for war' – with what passed for humour – 'that *ladies* should propose'.[12] Tall and broad, Hirst dressed well for literary society dinners, in a light-blue waistcoat with gilt buttons, and joined the Russell Club, known as a gathering spot for advanced Liberals.

The Union was his centre of gravity, serving up exalted references and role models. Gladstone, a 'majestic presence' with a 'deep and still musical voice', returned to cheers in 1892, with a beguiled Hirst on hand to observe that sixty-two years had elapsed since the 'Grand Old Man's' stint as president. Four years later, Hirst was puffing on cigars with Asquith, then Home Secretary, who had just led a debate on voluntary schools. Chamberlain, on a similar occasion, invited Hirst to lunch and a tour of his orchid houses. At 'Teddy' Hall he ran into Ramsay MacDonald, a 'handsome young fellow with curly black hair and bright black eyes', a 'wild man', who was priming 'dare-devil undergraduates with dangerous thoughts'.[13] By the time he left Oxford in 1896, Hirst had demonstrated a rare mix of intellectual qualities – earning a double first in classics, while excelling in the subtleties of 'abstract economics' under F. Y. Edgeworth.[14]

Hirst's classmates were just as central to his political development, and at this stage they held to a very traditional view of the liberal creed, proudly at odds with many in their cohort who wished to overhaul its philosophic and economic foundations. In 1897 Hirst, then a teacher 'bubbling over with zeal' at the London School of Economics, was the organizing force behind *Essays in Liberalism by Six Oxford Men* – a rallying cry for the Liberal Party to return to first principles after its latest electoral rout in 1895. 'Is it possible to revert at this hour to the simple doctrines which formed the strength of our first leaders? Most undoubtedly it is.' Hilaire Belloc wrote on the Liberal Party's free trade ideals, which must be pressed against both the 'economic absolutism of the landlord' entrenched in the House of Lords, as well as the socialists, who would 'dissolve thrift, and self-control, and the personal honour which keeps a contract sacred'.[15] J. A. Simon, J. S. Phillimore, J. L. Hammond and P. J. Macdonell laid down the line on labour, foreign policy, and education – while Hirst, in the longest, most polemical piece, dismissed as faddish all attempts to alter the core doctrine (whether Social Democratic, Primrose League imperialist, or Social Evolutionist). Liberals, acting in the names of Bright, Cobden, Mill and Gladstone, were the only real reformers, with an outstanding record of fifty years of 'uninterrupted progress' since repeal of the Corn Laws.[16] Any intervening changes to liberalism had, notwithstanding appearances, left it unaltered: Factory Acts, Death Duties, the right of workers to combine in trade unions, free and compulsory education, even a graduated income tax – in each case, Liberals had justified state action only to 'prevent men, women, or children from suffering in their capacity of wealth producers'.[17]

Hirst conceived this early book as a provocation to new social varieties of liberalism, and tried to secure a preface from an 'eminent Liberal' to amplify it. While Morley and Asquith politely declined – the latter citing its 'declaration of war' on party members who had 'gravitated towards' collectivism – Gladstone agreed to bless the 'efforts on behalf of individual freedom and independence' of these six Oxford men.[18] *Essays in Liberalism* made an impact, even as it elicited mainly critical reactions from the Liberal press. If the *Speaker* found it 'refreshing', the *Daily News* and *Daily Chronicle* objected to its 'narrow' liberalism and caricature of socialism.[19] Sidney Ball, the least 'woolly' leftist at Oxford, according to Hirst, replied for the Fabians – arguing that socialism was the realization of liberal individualism, not its antithesis, under new economic conditions, and for the many, not just the few.[20] *Essays in Liberalism* put Hirst and his friends at the centre of debates in the party and press over New Liberalism, with a clear position on just how little it ought to depart from the old.

Morley was delighted with the book, which bore a dedication to him, and in 1898 asked Hirst to assist him in his latest literary endeavour – a biography of the recently departed Gladstone. The sifting of thousands of old letters served as an unlikely turning point for Hirst: not just 'the best time he ever had' with the living 'embodiment of philosophic Liberalism', but an eye-opening experience, because it took place amidst the Second Boer War. Hirst fervently opposed this conflict – as much on Cobdenite grounds of peace and economy as in a Gladstonian defence of small nationalities – at meetings for the League of Liberals Against Aggression and Militarism, and in the *Speaker,* which he and J. L. Hammond took over in 1899.[21] Hirst changed in important ways a result of his anti-war activities. As the Imperialists in the Liberal Party lined up behind government diplomacy in South Africa, with Lord Rosebery leading Haldane, Grey and Asquith to endorse annexation of the Boer Republics, the collectivists Hirst had derided two years earlier in *Essays in Liberalism* became his political allies and friends.

## Pro-Boer Liberalism

Hirst now asked Leonard Hobhouse, with whom he had felt 'rather far apart in politics' at Oxford, to extend his *Manchester Guardian* work for the *Speaker,* remarking that he 'thinks very differently now of Cobden and Bright'. H. W. Massingham, a harsh critic of *Essays in Liberalism,* became a friend, as a lead writer for the *Daily News* (and later at the *Nation,* which Hirst helped to set up with money from the Quaker sweets manufacturers the Rowntrees).[22] In the League, Hirst came to share platforms as well as columns with the political economist J. A. Hobson; and this widened his political orbit beyond Morley – whose 'sore throat' during the war frustrated his followers – to include a 'rather daring' Lloyd George, and the unexpectedly inspiring 'pro-Boer' Campbell-Bannerman.[23]

The war not only brought young Cobdenites and collectivists closer together in a battle to control the party: it forced them to explain what had caused it. That urgency was palpable in *Liberalism and Empire* (1900), where the internationally-minded Oxford classicist Gilbert Murray joined Hirst and Hammond in condemning military aggression as a betrayal of the liberal tradition in foreign affairs. Hirst's contribution, 'Financial Imperialism', owed much to Hobson, whose *War in South Africa* appeared earlier that year, as well as to the satirical broadsides of Belloc and G. K. Chesterton.[24] Attacks on the Transvaal and Orange Free State were only the latest 'unjust and uncalled for wars' Britain had fought, stirred by the basest instincts of 'adventure, conquest, mastery, and race-pride' and 'strangely wedded with speculative finance'.[25] The scramble to partition Africa in the decades leading up to the Second Boer War had no other basis, Hirst argued, and was especially misguided on commercial grounds. British trade with foreign nations was worth three times as much as the Empire. 'Trade follows the flag', he wrote, mocking a standard imperialist trope, 'over jungles, swamps, deserts' and even 'flies after it in the face of facts, arguments and arithmetic'.[26]

Hirst conceded that a small group of capitalists did stand to gain from such policies: arms-makers, spoiled sons (of free-trading fathers) who had become 'sleeping partners in limited companies and supporters of Mr Chamberlain', and 'international financiers'.[27] They had the political clout, moreover, to see their interests enacted. The most pernicious specimen of this group was Cecil Rhodes, who had parlayed a few diamond mines in Kimberley into the mighty De Beers monopoly, buying up not only the press and political machinery of the Cape Colony – but also of Britain, where bribes had secured him a royal charter, a seat on the Privy Council, honours from Oxford, and apparent immunity for his crimes, including the 1895 Jameson Raid, a botched first attempt to force Britain to annex the Transvaal. This time, Rhodes and his largest investors had set the whole Empire in motion in order to snatch the Transvaal's mines, and bring in the men to work them. 'Democratic as it may appear on paper', wrote Hirst, in a distorted echo of Bagehot, 'the British Constitution is very little better than a pretence. It is only a mask over the face of plutocracy'.[28]

Hobson may have developed the more sophisticated critique of finance capital, and the unequal distribution of wealth feeding it, as the 'taproot' of imperialism. But Hirst gave this theory his own accent, and imparted it to the *Economist*.[29] In his essay from *Liberalism and Empire*, imperialism emerged as the single greatest danger to Liberalism, both old and new. The need to pay off huge debts after the war would, he predicted, serve as an excuse for the Conservatives to scrap free trade, raising tariffs and other taxes, at the same time as ever-higher spending on the navy and army took precedence over productive investments in education and health. 'Radical change' was now the only alternative to this scenario: writers should share in the ownership, and control the policy, of their papers; election expenses and salaries must be paid; and a graduated income tax was no longer just about fairness, but 'self-defence', reducing the political reach of wealth along with its concentration. The Second Boer War fuelled Hirst's attack on imperialism in and outside the party, marking his conversion to an advanced brand of New Liberalism.[30]

Four years after the end of the Boer war, the Liberals took power in a landslide, with Hirst among its most effective propagandists. In the interim, he wrote for the *Speaker*, the *Nation*, the *Manchester Guardian*, and as City editor for the short-lived

Liberal daily, *The Tribune*. He also penned lively books updating the Cobdenite trinity of peace, retrenchment and reform for a new era in *Free Trade and Other Fundamental Doctrines of the Manchester School* in 1902, *Local Government in England* (co-authored) in 1903, *Adam Smith* in 1904, *Monopolies, Trusts, and Kartels* in 1905. *Arbiter in Council*, written in 1906, was a Socratic dialogue on war from biblical times to the present. It made the case for international arbitration, and raised his profile with yet another strata of liberals: the legal scholar F. W. Maitland, the world's richest man Andrew Carnegie and his Endowment for International Peace, and Sir Robert Reid, future Lord Chancellor, with whom Hirst worked on proposals to revise maritime law (for the free passage of merchant ships in wartime) at the second Hague Conference in 1907.[31] Amidst all this he married Helena Cobden, Richard's great-niece, in 1903 – and travelled widely. In Italy, he befriended Luigi Einaudi, the economist, journalist and future president, whom he would recruit to the *Economist*; in Austria, Josef Redlich, the law professor, Liberal politician and finance minister, who also became a correspondent for it; and eventually eminent Americans, including Herbert Hoover, with whom Hirst struck up a lifelong friendship.[32] Hirst stepped still closer to the centre of this liberal universe when Sir Robert Giffen, a fellow member of the Political Economy Club, advised Eliza Bagehot to make him the next editor of the *Economist* in 1907.[33]

Hirst was one of the most prolific authors ever to become editor, and the most ideologically driven since the first. In contrast to James Wilson, however, that laser focus included a commitment to peace, not just prosperity, with Hirst as adamant about the former as the latter. Hirst has been misjudged on both counts. Characterization of him as having 'automatically associated finance with speculation, gambling, luxury, and corruption', and as a pacifist far outside the Liberal mainstream make it hard to explain how he was hired at all, since blanket hostility to finance or force would have ruled him out at the *Economist*.[34] In reality, even Hirst's fiercest attacks on 'the gold-reefed City' were aimed less at the stock market than at its 'rigging' by the likes of Rhodes, who 'duped honest investors' and used the state to bail himself out. Nor was his antipathy to the Liberal Imperialists based simply on their readiness to intervene abroad: Palmerston and Gladstone had both seen that morality might demand action on behalf of oppressed minorities, in Greece or Armenia; neither, however, would have condoned 'for one moment a war with two free Republics'. Hirst and his friends, 'blind neither to the glories nor yet the responsibilities of the British Empire', found the 'teachings of modern imperialism' to be 'inconsistent with the greatness and safety of the Empire'. The Empire was a *liberal* achievement, which imperialist schemes for territorial expansion or tariffs actively threatened.[35]

## A Campaigning *Economist*: Between Cabinet and City

Hirst brought immediate change to the *Economist* when he took the chair Johnstone had vacated. Gruff consistency gave way to playful sparring, as Hirst added flair to the principal leaders: a stanza of Milton to introduce a budget, Bentham to explain social reform, Mill political economy, or Burke for foreign policy. Headlines often ran as rhetorical questions, as in a debating club – in 1908, 'What Causes a Revival of Trade?', or 'What is Waste?' The focus shifted from the money market to politics, with the latter set in a wider frame. 'The Significance of Karl Marx' was condescending, but curious – only dismissing the man and his ideas after explaining that his proletarian heirs in Germany, France, and England had sensibly replaced revolutionary social-ism with evolutionary … liberalism.[36]

Hirst enlarged the staff, recruiting the sort of young people he liked from Oxford and Cambridge, many of whom stayed on for decades: Walter Layton in 1908 and his brother Gilbert in 1911, for statistical expertise; Leonard Reid, as a leader writer, in 1912; for briefer spells, Dudley Ward, C. K. Hobson and Richard Lambert.[37] In 1913, Mary Agnes Hamilton, the first female editor, was a striking choice: a classicist, translator and novel-ist, she was also a suffragette, who days before the outbreak of the First World War defected to Labour, later representing it as an MP for Blackburn. Her description of Hirst says much about what it was like to work at his *Economist*, where doctrine and debate somehow coexisted. His 'heroic pertinacity', she observed, was the 'power of seeing what he wishes to see' – noting how his view of women as 'in essence irrational' was unaffected by her, or his sisters, who held university posts. 'Anyone who has any truck with Socialism must be intellectually flabby', he remarked to Hammond; 'it was like him not to notice the imputation also covered me.' When, arguing with Hirst, she suggested 'it could be useful to define what one meant by a principle, his reply was "Free Trade is a principle" – more need not be said'.[38] 'A true fanatic', wrote another intellectual opponent, albeit with affection.[39]

As dramatic as the rejuvenated staff and style was the sudden shift in editorial line. Hirst did more than shepherd the *Economist* back into the Liberal fold after two decades; he turned it into one of the party's most vocal backers, especially in the City of London. This, combined with his own Cobdenite linking of peace and free trade, overturned its line on imperialism. Plans to build more Dreadnoughts, praised as instruments of peace up to 1906, were henceforth decried as wasteful and dangerous; Germanophobia as well as Francophilia – the paper showing signs of both during the Boer War and the Moroccan Crisis in 1905 – were anathema; and it now looked forward, at some unspecified date, to Home Rule for Ireland.[40] These changes in position ramified throughout the paper. Reducing armaments was not just a question of foreign policy. For Hirst, it was *the* crucial step to achieving social reform while maintaining 'liberal finance' at home, with more direct but still low levels of taxation.

After 1906, the *Economist* cheered progress on the social and economic fronts, paying close attention to the fiscal policies outlined in each budget. Liberal achievements piled up after year one: 'they have re-established the sinking fund', 'nearly put an end to borrowing for works', 'removed the coal duty, lowered the tea duty' and 'reduced the income-tax on earnings by 25 per cent'. Hirst gave much of the credit to Campbell-Bannerman who, along with a 'genial and imperturbable temper', possessed 'an insight into human nature, a sympathy with the anxieties and aspirations of the common people, a good humoured indifference to the opinion of smart society'.[41] The paper hailed Asquith for introducing old-age pensions for the poor in 1908, even as he lowered the sugar duty and reduced the debt – and went on to attack 'Lord Northcliffe and his army of journalists' for their sudden concern with thrift, in reality sour grapes over Asquith's triumphant example of 'free trade finance'.[42]

Nor did the *Economist* stop at these early efforts, which struck many party radicals as modest. If Asquith glided into Downing Street almost automatically when Campbell-Bannerman died in 1908, radicals nonetheless believed they had gotten their choice for Treasury.[43] Lloyd George's 'People's Budget' of 1909–10 was 'bold', 'ambitious' and 'equitable' – offsetting spending with indirect taxes on luxuries like motor cars, tobacco and liquor, and direct ones on income, estates and land.[44] With health insurance, introduced in 1911, Lloyd George had not only 'captured the imagination of the man in the street', but asked him to do his part. Equality of sacrifice was also a feature in Churchill's unemployment insurance, guaranteeing that 'millions of the working classes to whom a few weeks sickness or unemployment now mean poverty and distress, will be able to meet such time with comparative fearlessness.'[45]

Hirst always stressed the fiscal chastity of these social schemes – audacious as well as economical – in ways that point to the unique role the *Economist* now played in selling New Liberalism to the City.[46] Budgets were the paper's main focus, reflecting the intense polarization these engendered. By 1910, the overwhelmingly Conservative House of Lords – having gutted Liberal education, plural voting, land and licensing bills – rejected outright its latest, People's Budget, as little better than socialism and plunder. In the ensuing constitutional crisis – which subsided only after two general elections, and a threat to flood the Lords with Liberal peers – the party and paper found new purpose. But the latter walked a tight rope: railing against a 'hereditary oligarchy of sumptuous and leisured men' in the upper chamber, it also tried to win over the gentlemanly capitalists who made up its traditional readership.[47]

The *Economist* worked to assuage, cajole, even threaten holdouts in the City, hoping in this way to win it back to Liberalism, or at least free trade – even as hostility grew inside the Square Mile to the entire agenda of the Liberal Party. A Budget Protest

League formed, drawing up a petition that attacked the use of the sinking fund for social insurance, and the new spate of taxes which threatened 'the safety of capital' – signed by thirty-six bankers and presented by Lord Rothschild in parliament.[48] *Bankers' Magazine,* already fuming at the unabated fall in the price of consols (the main reserve security for the financial system) gave space to an anxious former *Economist* editor Inglis Palgrave, who warned that excessive taxation could send Britain down the same slope of decline as eighteenth-century Holland.[49]

'The bankers and brokers and shippers, merchants and financiers of the City need ever and anon to be reminded', replied the present editor, 'that although the increasing burden of direct taxes upon their incomes is naturally exasperating, it is infinitely preferable to indirect taxes upon their trade and commerce which will take away their business, hand it to foreign centres, and inevitably destroy the supremacy of London.'[50] Each fiscal innovation elicited a reassurance that social reform was very far from socialism, indeed as English as warm beer and cricket:

> It may be wrong to tax very rich men at a higher rate than men with only moderate incomes, but it is not Socialism. It may be wrong to relieve landlords of income-tax, but it is not Socialism. It may be wrong to tax wind-falls, but it is not Socialism. It may be wrong to tax the still rather than the teapot, but the crime is not Socialism. If this Budget were Socialism, the public may be sure that it would have been welcomed by the *Morning Post* and torn to pieces by the *Economist.*[51]

Hirst was not alone in advocating reform in the face of protests from within the City. In fact, the *Economist*'s most successful offshoot and competitor, the *Statist,* also carried the Liberal torch; behind the scenes, its editor, George Paish, became a close advisor to Lloyd George in dealing with the City from 1909 to 1914, and often worked with Hirst.[52] The latter arguably had a higher profile – leading the City's Free Trade Committee, drawing into it eminent bankers such as Lord Avebury, Sir Felix Schuster and Frederick Huth Jackson, even contemplating their idea that he contest a City seat in one of the two general elections of 1910.[53]

While Hirst declined to run on this occasion, his *Economist* broadcast the official Liberal line in and outside the City up to 1914, with only two significant divergences along the way: suffrage and military spending. Whereas the bulk of the Cabinet did its best to evade the suffragettes, whose spectacular demonstrations aimed to puncture this studied indifference, Hirst railed against the idea that women had a right to vote. Members of the Women's Social and Political Union, or WSPU, were 'educated' and 'refined', he observed in horror: 'what is it that allows or compels them to lay aside these qualities' and turn into 'the shrieking, struggling, fighting viragoes of the Ladies' Gallery and Albert Hall?'[54] Only lower-class men surrendered to passion, he concluded, whereas even well-born females had no 'safeguard against' their impulses, displaying an incapacity for political reason. Around the time he began to compare suffragettes to Russian and Turkish marauders – pillaging 'solemn vows, ties of love and affection, honour, romance' – his wife, Helena, took up with the WSPU. Not long after admitting to several American dinner guests 'that she should prefer to avoid burning the house of an anti-suffragette friend, but would do so if necessary', she was arrested for throwing stones at a minister's window. The story landed in the press, a row ensued, and she left home.[55] In the end, it was Hirst with the passionate feelings that plunged his personal life into crisis: he implored his friend John Simon, the Attorney General, to convince Helena to come back. Earlier, he had shocked J. A. Hobson by arguing that both men should resign from a committee of the New Reform Club if it supported the 'revolutionary', 'unconstitutional', 'Anti-Liberal' cause of 'women suffrage'.[56]

If on the issue of suffrage Hirst was far behind his radical friends, on the military budget he was ahead, criticizing Liberals relentlessly for their failure to reverse spending. In 1907, he privately wrote to the prime minister: in his new capacity as editor of the *Economist*, which 'compels me to watch trade and finance very closely' – Hirst was compelled to urge Campbell-Bannerman to back 'Lord Willy' (Harcourt) in Cabinet, and 'make it the policy of the Government to return to the pre-war level … cutting four millions at least off army and navy this year'.[57] Behind the scenes, he tried to light a fire under Asquith, who sought in turn to calm

Hirst by sketching his fiscal plans from 1906 to 1909.[58] Even as the *Economist* used Liberal budgets to pitch free trade finance to the City, so it criticized party leaders for 'procrastination in bringing about a return to peace establishments'.[59] For Hirst, it was Campbell-Bannerman's death in 1908 that altered the balance of forces in Cabinet, weakening resistance to the naval panic that crashed over it the next year. Hirst furiously denounced calls for four, let alone eight, new Dreadnoughts, the number exhorted by Balfour, the Sea Lords and 'Big Navy' Liberals. He mocked the fantasy of an imminent German invasion by which the *Daily Mail, The Times,* and even the *Clarion* and *Daily News,* sought to justify them.[60] And he recalled 'two or three facts' to those in the City, including the Rothschilds, 'who seem almost as much frightened as *The Standard,* which talks of a hundred million loan' and '82 millions' for the navy. The spectre of the Boer War loomed, as he and Massingham at the *Nation* descried the influence of the international armament firms in this latest panic.[61]

Hirst was no mere commentator. As editor he fought pitched battles on behalf of his allies in the Cabinet, who then included Lloyd George, Churchill and Morley. In 1912, Morley leaked Hirst an account of his rows with the Liberal Imperialists – Haldane, Grey, and the 'defunct economists' McKenna and Asquith. 'You might like to know for your own information how opinion is divided at the moment', relayed Hirst to the head of the Liberal Federation, Sir John Brunner, asking him to send a 'firm letter' to Asquith that if he endorsed the latest ship-building program, 'you would feel conscientiously bound to summon a meeting of the Federation in the hope of bringing Liberal opinion to bear upon this fatal and provocative policy'.[62] Such internal pressure stood a chance, he believed, for outside the Cabinet, 'old fashioned Liberals and modern radicals' outnumbered Imperialists.[63] His activities continued right up to the war, not only at the Federation, through which he tried to organize the backbench opposition, but also chambers of commerce, reform clubs, ad hoc committees. He at least managed to extend the anti-armaments drive far beyond the pages of the *Economist* – obtaining funds to send one of its journalists, Dudley Ward, to Berlin in 1911 to 'act as press-correspondent' for all the Liberal dailies 'with the object of promoting friendly relations between Germany and England'.[64]

And yet despite these efforts, the relationship between Liberalism as a force for social reform and imperialism had turned out to be just the opposite of what he had envisioned in 1907. Lloyd George and Churchill finally won the backing needed in Cabinet to press forward with health and unemployment insurance, land, death and super taxes, not by halting the naval race with Germany, but joining with the Imperialists on its escalation.[65] After the People's Budget, neither they nor the naval budget ever looked back.

## Empire of Finance or Financial Imperialism?

As a result of the escalation of the arms race, the *Economist* was obliged to fight two imperialisms at once – contending that both endangered, instead of strengthened, the Empire. On the one hand, the Chamberlain-Milner-Rhodes variety would lead to wars on the scale of the Boer conflict, not to speak of protection; on the other, Liberal Imperialists, though free traders, seemed ready to commit Britain to France and Russia in a still more foolhardy confrontation with Germany. Grey's secretive diplomacy as foreign minister caused anxiety on this score. So did his public acts – adding to the Anglo-French Entente of 1904 an agreement with Russia in 1907 fixing up their spheres of influence in Persia and Tibet.

To counter the first threat, of imperial preference – a campaign that Chamberlain had begun in the downturn of 1903, and his sons Austin and Neville carried on – the *Economist* insisted that free trade had become so fundamental to the imperial order that the two could not be safely disentangled. To abandon 'our policy of the open door' and 'knowledge that wherever British sovereignty is exercised foreign commerce can come and go freely on equal terms' would invite 'envy, hatred, and malice', the 'hostility of the world'.[66] What mattered most were the *invisible* ties binding the colonies and dominions to England. Above and beyond culture, sentiment and security – if Canada and Australia were 'left to themselves, how long would the one hold her own against the United States, the other against Japan?'– there was

*capital.* The question of how freely to invest it abroad now set
the *Economist* on a collision course with tariff reformers inside
the City – not just over the effect of capital exports on Britain's
growing trade imbalance, or the price of consols, but over its
power in the broadest sense.[67]

The opening salvo in this conflict was Lloyd George's People's
Budget, which elicited hand-wringing over the 'safety of capital'
from bankers like Lord Rothschild and other members of the
Budget Protest League. The notion that 'socialistic finance' was
'driving' capital abroad furnished another rationale for tariffs,
originating in the City but with a potent appeal extending up to
the industrial North. Instead of allowing the unrestricted outflow
of British savings, which funded – critics argued – the industrial
and imperial expansion of rival powers, tariffs and capital controls could direct those savings to the home market, which was
starved for investment and in need of modernization. The proof?
German, American and even Japanese firms were now outcompet-
ing their British counterparts on everything from pottery to steel,
iron to chemicals.[68]

Here the *Economist* played its best card on behalf of a liberal
empire – for no better authority on the ebb and flow of capital
within it existed. Asquith might respond to financiers complaining
of Liberal mismanagement by pointing out that consols had fallen
even further under the Unionists, or to his own strides in cutting
the national debt. But the *Economist* had been eyeing overseas
investment since before Lloyd George was born, putting even
a relatively 'flat' period for foreign issues since the early 1890s
into perspective.[69] In it, readers found a careful breakdown of
the interest on foreign and colonial government securities, as
well as company dividends, income disclosed by bankers, coupon
dealers, persons, firms, public companies and railways. Close tabs
were kept on the top customers for debt, which, with the notable
exception of the United States, were formal or informal colonies:
India, South Africa, Australasia, Canada, and Argentina.[70]

'Surely we can look composedly upon the exports of British
capital as the surplus profits of an enormously wealthy country,
whose trade spreads all over the world', argued the *Economist* on
Smithian lines, putting the total at over £3 billion in 1909. 'There

is no fear of our home industries being starved. Capital is cheaper here and credit more abundant than in any other country.'[71] Unionist politicians, journalists and bankers attempting to smear the budget argued the opposite, using the *Economist*'s own figures to show that London sent abroad over eight times what it raised for domestic purposes. 'They omit to explain that most sections of British industry are never publicly financed, but draw on private men', syndicates, insurers and provincial banks, the paper retorted.[72] It feigned surprise to hear Lord Revelstoke, head of Barings, bewail the 'exodus' of British capital on account of 'wicked' Lloyd George, 'to quarters where it is more warmly welcomed'. 'We fancy that the largest foreign loan in London since this Government came into office was issued by Baring Bros' to Russia – where high risk and high returns, not security, had attracted it. It was poor countries that borrowed in London, and this was a boon for Britain, Hirst argued in step with Paish at the *Statist,* and with Hobson: pushing back distant frontiers would yield a new bounty of cheap food to workers (a rise in prices since the mid-1890s had hurt their buying power), raw materials to industry, and a steady demand for British exports.[73]

Whatever stigma Hirst had ascribed to finance at the turn of the century had vanished by 1909, with the City emerging as a bastion of free trade dynamism and British 'soft' power – uniting the Empire and the world through investment and trade rather than brute force. The reissue of Bagehot's *Lombard Street* in 1910 was a moment to savour the City's global reach, and celebrate the great banker and editor who had anticipated its turn to foreign flotation and investment. The Boer War may have been a setback, swallowing £160 million, or two years of British savings, but

> Wall Street's boastful anticipations that it would succeed London as the centre of the financial world were humbled to the dust by the crisis of 1907, when all the banks of the United States suspended payments. Never was the City of London's hegemony more plainly demonstrated. The Bank of England's rate controlled the world. London attracted gold from every part of the compass and doled it out to New York and Chicago as a good doctor distributes drugs to suffering patients.[74]

In the *Stock Exchange,* an investment guide from 1911, Hirst beamed with pride at 'the banking and financial centre of the world', where 'our merchants and shippers seek profit in every corner of the globe; our investors large and small have interests in every continent, and the London Stock Exchange List is itself a sort of key to the distribution of trade and capital'.[75] While he might be accused of a bias in favour of small investors, he added, 'I would beg to assure the reader that he and I have no better friends than the numberless bankers, brokers, dealers and promoters of new undertakings who practice callings so useful and so indispensable with the highest sense of honour'. The need to educate the public about this 'vast and delicate' system revolving around the City, he explained by way of an epigram from Burke: 'great empires and little minds go ill together'.[76]

### Misreading the Tea Leaves: Liberal Imperialists and the Run-Up to War

Taking on the Liberal Imperialists was always the more delicate task. Hirst found it hard to gain the true measure of his foes inside the party – in part because allies such as Morley turned out to be weak, or in the case of Churchill, Harcourt or Lloyd George, hardened imperialists themselves; in part because he and other radicals overestimated their own strength based on the outcome of key Cabinet debates, so that a curious optimism muted their alarm at the galloping naval budgets up to 1914.[77] Campbell-Bannerman's grant of self-government to the defeated Boers in 1906 showed 'splendid courage' and 'magnanimity', paving the way for the Union of South Africa in 1910. This was a 'happy outcome' – even if the state that resulted deprived black South Africans of all civil rights – because it rebuked Grey, Haldane, Asquith and other Liberal supporters of the Boer War and the policy of 'unconditional surrender' they had thought necessary to win it.[78] India was another example of the liberal empire at work – at least once Hirst's mentor John Morley was appointed Secretary of State for the subcontinent at the end of 1905. The *Economist* heartily approved his actions there, which combined severe repression of anti-British rioting in Bengal and the Punjab in 1907, with limited political concessions. The Morley-Minto reforms added a token layer of elite native representation in India in 1909: from zero to one on executive councils of the viceroy and governors, with separate appointed and elected spots for Hindus and Muslims on the legislative councils.[79] The aim of these reforms was not to prepare the way for Indian self-government under the British flag – as in South Africa – but to make such demands redundant. For Hirst, they proved that liberalism could triumph over jingoism while still pursuing vital imperial work.[80] The Raj was just as central to the economic side of this vision, and Hirst used it to poke holes in the case for imperial preference.[81] Revealingly, on the issue of India, this defence of Morley put the *Economist* on the same side as Grey. For the foreign minister, that had been the point: Morley's 'unimpeachable' record of hostility to 'the Jingo' as the 'devil incarnate', wrote Grey, shielded the government from 'sentimental' Liberal critics of imperialism and the repression of Indian nationalism.[82]

To radicals, even the Agadir Crisis in 1911 could be made to look like a victory, once the dust had settled on this major diplomatic spat. When France landed troops in Morocco en route to Fez, nominally to restore order in violation of prior treaty obligations, the other European powers descended: Spain occupied Larache, and Germany dispatched a cruiser to the port of Agadir. Britain sent a battleship, not only to track this German boat, the *Panther*, but to stiffen the will of the French: even Cabinet radicals worried that the latter might, without consulting them, make damaging concessions to the Kaiser in the form of a naval base on the Mediterranean.[83] At the height of the crisis on 21 July, Lloyd George delivered a hawkish, pro-French speech to a City crowd, which Hirst tried to minimize as 'a few words taken out of context'. The Chancellor had concluded his remark that Britain had the greatest financial stake in the prosperity of other countries, and thus in peace, with a warning that followed from this premise: 'It is essential in the highest interest not merely of this country but of the world, that Britain should at all hazards maintain her place and her prestige among the great powers.' To be treated 'as if she were of no account in the Cabinet of Nations', continued Lloyd George, in a threat aimed at Germany lest it steamroll France and ignore British interests – 'peace at that price would be a humiliation intolerable for a great country like ours to endure.'[84]

In private, Hirst was shaken. Even as he assured readers that such a 'notorious pacifist' as Lloyd George had never intended war, Hirst built a sweeping case against what he had said in the *Economist*. Britain had less to fear from German imperialism than French. It occupied no moral high ground, having failed 'to resist or protest against the buccaneering expedition of the French to Fez', and had no casus belli, 'unless, indeed, this nation is to tie itself to the apron-strings of France, with whom our jingoes were not very long ago anxious to go to war over a miserable swamp in Fashoda'. Moreover, £54,864,811 of trade with Germany would cease in a dispute over Morocco, which took in £1,404,741, 'less than half our exports to Java'. If a general war ensued, it would blanket the North Sea and Baltic shipping lanes, destroy eastern ports, shutter factories, double debt, and treble taxation. Liberty, humanity, justice, the mitigation of suffering, fostering civilization – all these might justify a call to arms; a 'sordid squabble, a scramble for concessions and commercial monopolies' on behalf of France did not.[85]

The *Economist* saw another way out of the bitter rivalry between France and Germany, which linked its attack on the two imperialisms, protectionist and free trade. Given the financial panic that gripped Berlin that summer, attributed to French bank withdrawals – a stock market crash, bank runs, a drain of gold abroad – all but forcing the Kaiser to back down in North Africa,[86] it was a remarkable suggestion: categorically rejecting the idea that Paris was intentionally turning a 'financial screw' on its German neighbour, the paper argued for *more* French capital to cross the Rhine.[87] Throw open the Paris Bourse to German industrial listings, spinning ties of mutual interest not unlike those the City wove with the British Empire.[88] As tensions over Agadir eased – France ceding patches of West Africa for effective control in Morocco – Hirst was emboldened, sensing radicals had drawn a line in the sand. Grey, whose approval of secret military talks with France surfaced soon after, agreed under intense pressure in

Cabinet to suspend them, and to make no formal commitments to Paris or St Petersburg in the event of a war on the continent.[89]

By the summer of 1914, the great danger to the liberal imperial order seemed to come from Ireland, where Hirst thought the radicals and Imperialists agreed. If so, neither produced a Home Rule Bill before 1910, when Liberals lost their majority and came to rely on the Irish Nationalists to form a government.[90] The *Economist* now gave more space to the issue, seeing only a small minority of Ulster Protestants, or Orangemen, barring the route. In its view, the Anglo-Irish landed class was no longer a factor; many had turned into Home Rulers, along with 'heroes of our imperialist press' like Cecil Rhodes, as a scheme to buy land holdings, and enfranchise Irish peasants, took effect.[91] The reality was far more contentious than the *Economist* made it seem.[92] Home Rule's passage through the Commons in 1914 set the stage for civil war – with a mutiny of officers at Curragh, fomented by generals in London, point blank refusing to enforce the bill. The words of the Conservative opposition leader Andrew Bonar Law, who warned Liberals of forces 'stronger than parliamentary majorities', echoed in the Tory press: loyalist volunteers must arm without delay to defend the Empire. Days before the outbreak of the First World War in Europe, the *Economist* was transfixed by 'men with machine guns' marching through Dublin and Belfast.[93]

## Great War, Great Illusions

Archduke Franz Ferdinand, heir to the Austro-Hungarian throne, was assassinated along with his wife Sophie on a visit to Sarajevo on 28 June 1914. Nearly a month later, Austria issued an ultimatum to neighbouring Serbia, accusing it of sponsoring the nationalists who carried out the killings. Focused on Ireland, like most of the press and political elite in Britain, the *Economist* was slow to catch up with this new chapter of the Eastern crisis. Mary Agnes Hamilton recalled the atmosphere:

There was an argument in the *Economist* office about the subject of the leader for the last week in July. The staff – at that time,

Leonard Reid, Gilbert Layton, A.W. Wright and myself – thought
it must be about Ireland, where armed rebellion seemed to be preparing and there had just been an affray in which the King's Own
Scottish Borderers were involved. F.W.H. insisted that it must be
about the expiry of the Austrian ultimatum to Serbia – which we
had forgotten. Even he, however, was calmly planning a summer
holiday which was to take him to visit the battlefields of Europe.
He was going to Waterloo, Sedan, and so on. I can see him, now,
in the brown linen suit which a very hot day and the imminent
prospect of departure made suitable.[94]

On 1 August, the day Germany declared war on Russia, the
*Economist* went to press predicting a short war in the Balkans,
and found nothing outrageous in Austria's readiness to fight given
the gravity of the attack that had taken place in its wayward
province of Bosnia-Herzegovina. Would Britain have reacted any
differently to an Afghan plot to raise a rebellion in Northwest
India? If the Prince and Princess of Wales had been slain, instead
of the Archduke and his wife, 'the cry for vengeance would have
been raised'.[95]

Yet the *Economist*'s tone was calm, arguing in the same vein
as the bestselling author and peace campaigner Norman Angell,
that global economic integration had gone so far as to make
war suicidal for all involved. Hirst did cancel his vacation, on
which he was due to stop at Lucerne for a special meeting of the
Carnegie Endowment for Peace, having just produced an inquiry
for it into the Balkan Wars of 1912–13.[96] His fear that Britain
might be dragged into the latest one, however, let alone a wider
conflagration, was much less acute than it had been three years
earlier during the Agadir Crisis. Warmongering by the *Times* and
*Daily Mail* was typical, but as 'utterly opposed to the interests of
the business community' as 'the instincts of the working classes'.
Churchill's 'sensational orders to the fleet to stand fast' on 26 July
were deplorable, but showy and absurd, 'as if whatever happened,
any British Government was entitled to plunge this nation into the
horrors of war, in a quarrel which is no more of our making and
no more our concern than would be a quarrel between Argentina
and Brazil or between China and Japan'.[97] Hirst concluded, based

in part on information passed to him from the Cabinet, that British neutrality was assured.

Britain entered the war three days later on 4 August 1914, ostensibly over Germany's violation of Belgian neutrality en route to Paris – in reality over pledges to the latter, with Grey threatening to resign and bring down the government if these were not honoured.[98] Hirst heard the news with John Burns, the only workingman in the Cabinet, who had resigned two days before, anticipating its decision for war. Both men burst into tears.[99] Morley quit a day later, along with junior minister Charles Trevelyan, earning them emotional praise from Hirst.[100] These defections were a far cry, however, from the eleven (out of nineteen) members another ally, Harcourt, had counted a week earlier, a 'Peace Party which if necessary shall break up the Cabinet in the interest of our abstention'.[101] To underscore the collapse of any such opposition, John Simon, Attorney General (and Hirst's former marriage counsellor), tearfully withdrew his resignation less than twenty-four hours after submitting it, while Harcourt, the Peace Party's supposed leader, had none to retract: he took the plunge just behind Grey and Asquith, drafting plans the next day to seize German East Africa and South-West Africa, Togoland, the Cameroons, New Guinea, Nauru and Samoa.[102]

Bitterness and anger are etched in every line Hirst wrote for the *Economist* from this moment until his firing two years later. 'Since last week millions of men have been drawn from the factory to slay one another by order of the warlords of Europe. It is perhaps the greatest tragedy of human history.' The *Economist* had implored its own government to lead the way in halting the arms race. 'It is now too late. The explosion has come. Look where you may you can see no ray of comfort. Death, anguish, starvation, and despair are written over Western Europe. It is the triumph of diplomacy over common sense, of force over reason, of brutality over humanity.' By 8 August, Hirst accepted that war could not be avoided, and urged those who had tried to prevent it to 'keep our tempers' in the name of a 'common patriotism'. Emphasizing thrift – deer parks into vegetable gardens, luxury taxes, competitive war contracts – he also nodded at Belgium: the defence of small nationalities was a 'consolation' to those looking for an honourable basis for the war. But he never endorsed this as an explanation of its cause, which was rather 'the deliberate policy of Ministers, undertaken from a sense of obligation to France', nor that it was worth the loss of British life and treasure.[103]

Until then a loyal propagandist for the Liberal Party, Hirst and the *Economist* now diverged sharply from it. The effective suspension of the Bank Act, the printing of small paper bills by the Treasury to shore up circulation, the closure of the Stock Exchange, a moratorium on repayment of bills of exchange and other contracts, direct subventions to banks unable to make or receive payments on far-flung and frozen balance sheets during the global panic of July-August – decisive measures that earned wild plaudits for Lloyd George in much of the City – simply confirmed the *Economist*'s dire predictions about the effects of a major war on the delicate architecture of world finance, and above all Britain's hegemony over it.[104] For the next two years the paper attacked one betrayal of liberalism after another, with the financial bailout of 1914 as original sin: martial law, censorship, tariffs, taxes, conscription, compulsion – all followed, like so many nails in the coffin.[105]

Not only did the *Economist* criticize these domestic policies, it encouraged peace overtures from the moment French and British forces had halted the German advance towards Paris. On the last day of the Battle of the Marne, it urged the Allies to throw out the treaty they had signed, which enjoined each to 'fight to the finish'. Negotiate separately, avoid preconditions: casualties were just too high, at 40,000 a day, to go on for a single year. Germans possessed 'physical bravery and daemonical courage', while fraternization between troops in facing trenches 'bring home to the imagination the cruel absurdities of war, and suggest to some a hope that from the soldiers in the field there might come a protest against the indefinite prolongation of its horrors'.[106]

Dissent reached a fever pitch with the fall of the Liberal government and the rise of a coalition in 1915 – which Hirst greeted with sardonic approval, as the latest treachery from Asquith. Desperate to remain prime minister, Asquith had agreed to share power with the Conservatives, so as to avoid tough questions about his responsibility for munitions shortages and the disastrous expedition to the Dardanelles that May.[107] 'I am not sorry to see the organised hypocrisy of Liberal Imperialism based upon the unholy alliance of Jingoism and Socialism falling to pieces', Hirst told C. P. Scott, owner of the Liberal *Manchester Guardian,* heaping scorn on the 'foul Lord Northcliffe pogrom of people with German names' and the imperialists of all parties, 'with their idiotic resolution of destroying the German nation'.[108] Mounting calls for conscription had a simple goal: 'discipline and enslave the working class and keep down Ireland'.[109] By 1916, Hirst hoped that the Conservatives would take over the leadership: let them take the blame for breaking strikes, military blunders, and the brutal repression of the Easter Uprising in Ireland. If Lloyd George wanted to join the Conservatives in this work, still better: then his reputation would be tarnished, not that of Liberalism.[110] That proud tradition lay vanquished. 'Faith without deeds is vain', Hirst wrote in his last full *Economist* leader. 'But what of a political creed whose apostles work against it?'[111]

Hirst was not alone in advocating neutrality before war was declared, but his intransigence after it had started set the *Economist* apart. Even many of his oldest friends from Oxford or pro-Boer days rallied to a moral defence of little Belgium. Hobhouse, Hammond, Murray and Massingham all lined up against Prussian militarism, while by 1916 Scott's *Manchester Guardian* was backing Lloyd George to achieve victory 'in a nation marshalled and regimented for service'.[112] Hirst travelled a different path – urging neutrality to calm global financial markets and racing between Neutrality Committees in August, and thereafter the Union of Democratic Control. Alongside J. A. Hobson and other war critics, he published Bertrand Russell. The Cambridge philosopher and pacifist admired Hirst for his work at the Carnegie Endowment. Together the two men set out to secure a meeting with Woodrow Wilson – Russell calling on the American president to act as peacemaker to Europe in a letter to the *Economist* in December 1914 – while Hirst raised funds to defend Russell in his trials under the Military Services and Defence of the Realm Acts.[113] In the *Economist,* Hirst pushed back not just against the persecution of conscientious objectors like Russell, but also censorship, xenophobia, and the 'starvation blockade' of Germany.

This may not have impressed Lenin – who, reading the *Economist* in 1915, called it 'a journal that speaks for British millionaires' and 'stands for peace just because it is afraid of revolution' – but it earned Hirst powerful enemies.[114]

Chief among them was the *Times,* whose attacks on the *Economist* probably counted for most in Hirst's dismissal. The *Economist*'s line on conscription was one flash point, especially as it came into force in 1916. For the *Times* it was an obvious necessity, if only to end the chaotic practice of sending the best workmen to the front while leaving a mass of potential soldiers at home. 'This, we suppose, is what the *Economist* means when it professes to think that we shall win the war through "the admirable elasticity of a free community". The soul of Carthage was lulled by such specious phrases.'[115] But it was over 'financial patriotism' that the *Times* landed the hardest blows. A column, 'Through German Eyes', began appearing, which quoted German journalists quoting unreliable English ones. The *Cologne Gazette* took heart from an *Economist* leader arguing that Britain would be unable to recover lost markets after the war, and that an imperial customs union to balance Germany was off the table now that colonies were being forced to develop their own wartime industries.[116] In another, the *Lokalanzeiger* used 'the authoritative London financial journal' to show that the City favoured an early peace.[117]

This campaign quickly took its toll, and by the end of June, *The Times* broke a story it had helped to create. 'Questions are being asked in the City as to the prospects of a change in the editorial attitude of the *Economist* towards the war', it wrote on 28 June, announcing Hirst's imminent dismissal and replacement with Hartley Withers – from whom it expected a 'distinct lack of continuity in this respect'.[118] Hirst responded defiantly at first, citing the *Economist*'s 'circulation and letter bag' to show that its push for peace talks was 'rapidly gaining ground in business circles'.[119] Many letters did indeed arrive, though not necessarily from businessmen: Keynes, reacting to the *Times,* wrote, 'I for one have thought the leading articles in the *Economist* amongst the very best things that have been written about the progress of the War and the proper attitude of decent people towards it.'[120] But a week later on 8 July, Hirst was out. Given just half a column on page eleven to make closing remarks, he proudly accepted the accusation that he had imparted a 'distressingly pacifist' policy to the *Economist*. 'If I could believe that I had hastened its advent by one day', he wrote, referring to letters he had published in favour of peace negotiation, 'and saved the precious lives and limbs that are lost in 24 hours, I should feel myself to have won a prize worth all the titles that Emperors shower on their favourites or Ministers on their supporters.'[121] Unbowed, he immediately set up the journal *Common Sense* to keep up his campaign, with backing from the Liberals Hugh Bell, Percy Molteno and R. D. Holt: by 1917 the journal was a meeting spot for the 'Lansdowne set', which Hirst saw as the best chance to form a broad 'Peace Party' to displace the Lloyd George coalition that was committed to delivering a 'knockout' blow to Germany.[122]

At the *Economist,* it was not just Hirst's hostility to the war that had to be erased, but his financial pessimism – in a sense the more serious crime, with the trustees intensely nervous that this would destroy the paper's circulation in the City. 'You know how much we regret losing you', wrote the elderly Eliza Bagehot somewhat sheepishly. 'A newspaper is a curious property to be in', but 'the Economist is so + we have no choice but to submit to what the trustees arrange.'[123] For Hirst, finance and liberalism died a twin death in 1914 – a point captured by Walter Layton, then a young staff editor, recalling the mood at the *Economist* at the start of war that August:

> Turning up the file for 1871 to see what had happened in the Franco-Prussian war, I came across a dispatch sent from Paris by a correspondent who had lived through the siege. In the course of his letter he said that from beginning to end of the war no bank in Paris ever closed its doors. I took the article in some excitement to the editor and suggested that we should reprint this extract to help to restore confidence on the financial front. He brushed it aside with the remark that 'Grass will be growing in Lombard Street before the end of the year.' I sadly left the office and did not return until I was appointed editor three years after the war ended.[124]

### Hartley Withers and Financial Patriotism: Rebuilding City Bonds

'By 1916, Hirst had brought the proprietors of the *Economist* to the point of revolt', according to Mary Agnes Hamilton.[125] If so, their choice of Hartley Withers to replace him may have carried the fingerprints of two trustees in particular, Walter Wilson Greg and Eliza Bagehot. Withers's book *The Meaning of Money* had 'struck oil as a financial best seller' in 1909, inviting comparisons to Bagehot, so that Eliza had asked him to follow it by writing the introduction to a new edition of *Lombard Street* in 1910.[126] A seasoned financial journalist, Withers was an editor at the *Times* for five years, before stints at the *Morning Post,* the merchant bank Seligman Brothers, and as director of financial inquiries at the Treasury. Withers was also a patriot, according to his old paper: not only had he launched a National Committee for War Savings in 1916, as the author of 'an excellent little new book on "International Finance"', he 'also differs considerably from the rather gloomy forecasts with which the *Economist* has lately been identified'.[127]

If his expertise was somewhat narrower than that of Hirst, Withers shared important traits with him. Born to a Liverpool banker father in 1867, Withers attended Westminster and Christ Church, Oxford, before clerking for a stockbroker, and writing – mainly on finance – for outlets running from Liberal to Unionist, the *Westminster Gazette* and *Economist* to the *Pall Mall Gazette* and *Spectator*.[128] Like Hirst, he had criticized British imperialism in South Africa, opposing both Boer wars, and mocking their justification on the basis of equal rights for English outlanders.[129] In *Stocks and Shares* in 1910, he too dismissed fears of British industrial decline, and advised against the restriction of foreign investment, given the tangible benefits industry derived from it.[130] *Poverty and Waste*, published in April 1914, prefigured one line of editorial continuity between past and future editors – funding the war from taxation rather than borrowing, eliminating wasteful luxury, to ensure fairness and keep inflation low. Withers praised most tax and welfare programs undertaken by the New Liberal state after 1906, even as he wanted to limit their expansion much more than Labour, or the Fabian socialists Sidney and Beatrice

Webb.[131] Nor was he hostile in principle to 'peace and goodwill' among nations, albeit after the First World War had revealed just how damaging modern warfare could be to the global trade and financial settlement systems. In a break with the past, national governments no longer paid their debts to enemy subjects, making it imperative to avoid another conflict on this scale. [132]

Less partisan in tone, with an affable, aphoristic turn of mind, what most distinguished Withers were his views on war and finance. Hirst's *Economist* had mocked *Poverty and Waste*, finding the problem Withers addressed real enough – riotous living, the rich snapping up motorcars as the poor starved – but the remedy absurd: appealing to the better natures of the better-off to save and invest (so as to produce working-class necessities like houses or boots), without making any demands on them in the form of higher taxes, or curbing outlays on the army or navy.[133] Though Withers conceded the arms race in Europe was an 'appalling' and 'barbarous' waste, it was 'not self-indulgence, but a sacrifice cheerfully born' and 'a small affair' compared to the 'aggregate of our individual expenditure on extravagance and luxury'. Angell argued 'war does not and cannot pay'; but he had failed to prove, put in Withers, 'that it does not pay better to win than to be beaten'.[134] In 1915 *War and Lombard Street* was just as pragmatic, explaining how manfully the City had faced the crisis in the days leading up to war in August 1914 – this 'thunderbolt from a clear sky', whose successful earthing was 'the greatest evidence of London's strength as a financial centre that it could have desired or dreamt of'.[135]

Withers was a compelling choice for the *Economist* trustees, nervous that City readers might desert the paper after two years of relentless criticism and prophecies of doom. Withers's *International Finance,* which came out just before he took the post, was a prospectus of the paper as he would run it, extolling the heroism of the City at war, and offering an optimistic vision for it afterwards. In it he pointed out the inconsistency of the charges levelled against besieged bankers – both of having started the war through the aegis of secret diplomacy, and of plotting to end it early in a negotiated peace. His work as a journalist covering financers had shown him that 'the popular delusion that depicts them as hard, cruel, ruthless men, living on the blood and sweat of humanity' was 'about as absurd a hallucination as the stage Irishman'. Much of this was simply anti-Semitism, 'that miserable relic of medieval barbarism'. Not all charges against finance were baseless, of course: Britain's interventions in Egypt and South Africa had pecuniary motives. But in both cases bond-holders and speculators 'might have whistled for their money until the crack of doom if it had not been that their claims chimed in with Imperial policy'.[136] The political reach of finance was minus-cule where national honour was concerned; the half-empty Stock Exchange, restrictions on new listings, reduced broker fees, under-writing taken over by the central bank, all showed how much it had suffered from the present war.

The post-war City would emerge even stronger from this expe-rience, however, and in contrast to Hirst, Withers was prepared at this stage to see it bend somewhat on free trade. Greater concern would be needed on the part of underwriters to make *productive* loans, not loans for foreign nations to build battleships or cover deficits. 'England may find it necessary', he added, 'to consider the policy of restricting the export of British capital to countries with which there is no chance of her ever being at war, especially to her own Dominions overseas.' His assertion that finance was a 'mere piece of machinery which assists, quickens, and lives on produc-tion' even left open the possibility that speculation was something quite different from the system of credit that kept international trade turning over. What he did not doubt was that the City could defeat Germany and stave off the challenge of Wall Street. 'If the war teaches her to work hard and consume little, so that when peace comes she has a great volume of goods to export, there is no reason why [London] should not retain much if not all of its old prestige in the world.'[137] Doubts about the future of civilization, to say nothing of English bills of exchange, were banished.

On the second anniversary of the war, and his first full issue as editor, the *Economist* announced its conversion. 'And yet when all has been said that can be said concerning the awfulness of the calamity of this war', it declared on 5 August 1916, 'it would have been still worse for mankind if Germany's claim to dominate Europe had been accepted, and if her brutal attack on Belgium had called in vain for an avenger.' The blush of honour re-emerged. Allied exploits were praised – the 'magnificent resistance by our French Allies at Verdun'; 'glorious successes of the Russians'.[138] Hirst had depicted Germans as worthy adversaries, if unlikely to win a drawn-out conflict with Britain. 'No one needs to be told that if Germans beat us in the field or at sea, civilization is doomed', blared the paper under its new editor, for the Central Powers stood 'for ruthlessness and the rule of force, domination and destruction'.[139] It now rejected peace overtures outright, or parsed them for weakness: 'a mere stratagem designed to gain time, so that our enemies may improve their defences on the Western Front', a 'kite flown for the benefit of public opinion'.[140] It scorned Wilson's peace plan late in 1916 as a mask for American self-interest, spurred by fears of ethnic strife and unrestricted submarine attacks. Britain would formulate its own demands; in the meantime, a bloodletting might do it good.[141] 'Generations of prosperity had fattened us and weakened us' – leaving 'us' vulnerable to Prussian militarism as well as industrial competition. 'The war's experience is, or ought to be, training us into lean and lusty commercial athletes, ready to work as hard as anybody, and to put as much care and keenness into the task of restoring our trade position.'[142]

Withers's most important editorial move was not so much his backing of the war, however, as his flattering focus on the role the City could play in winning it. This required more panache than regurgitating old slogans from the summer of 1914. On the one hand, the paper had to dispel a perception that profiteering was taking place. On the other, it sought to show that finance was just as important an asset to national prospects as adequate munitions, gas masks, naval convoys or conscripts. Curtailing extravagance was paramount on both fronts. Women in minks were as morally distressing as men slurping oysters. One leader pointed to an infamous article in the *Herald*, 'How They Starve at the Ritz', to indicate how 'keenly organs of working-class opinion appreciate the manner in which the well-to-do classes are meeting the war needs by personal self-sacrifice'. Perceived lapses stirred up 'a very critical and dangerous spirit' among the poor, 'which is expressing itself in crude and inequitable proposals for taxing capital'. And yet the notion that capitalists were growing rich was a fallacy. 'The classes in receipt of rent and interest will receive a gross income which will be higher by the income payable to them on the various war loans', it granted, 'but, owing to a much higher level of taxation and the rise in prices, the net income of those who live on rent and interest will be considerably reduced.' Against these ravages, *rentiers* had no defence, and the paper rejected the idea of adding to their pain by increasing capital gains, even to raise revenue.[143] 'We shall have to find for our Allies and ourselves well over £2,000 millions in 1917.' Arthur Pigou, Alfred Marshall's successor at Cambridge, was on the right track, urging in his recent letters to the *Economist* 'a really vigorous use of the income tax ... and a much higher and wider taxation of luxuries of all kinds'.[144]

'The extent of its financial strength has, indeed, astonished', the *Economist* proudly observed of the City, all the while warning that its 'staying power' depended on battling inflation.[145] Average wage rates nearly doubled between 1914 and 1918 – outpaced only by the cost of living – with tight labour markets, rising rates of unionization, and unprecedented levels of spending.[146] Anticipating this trend, the paper advocated joint action on the part of the City and the Treasury to soak up wages before they were spent, preferably on war loans. 'We cannot more eloquently prove to our enemies our determination to maintain the cause of freedom and justice to a triumphant end than by rolling hundreds of millions into the coffers of the Treasury.' The *Economist* shamelessly hawked loans to finance the war as 'a rare and varied feast', while all were invited to become 'investors', including the humblest. Terms were attractive, with guaranteed 5 per cent interest on thirty-year loans in the form of bearer bonds or registered stock, which could be used to pay death duties, and were tax-exempt for residents abroad.[147] A speech from Chancellor Bonar Law explaining the reaction he expected from large investors to these offerings – as long as there was money, the war would not be hampered for lack of it, even if the government had to confiscate it – enchanted the *Economist*. 'The enthusiasm with which this frank threat of financial compulsion was received by the Guildhall audience was remarkable evidence of the readiness of the City to suffer all things for victory.'[148]

The same determination suffused its political outlook, liberal principles giving way for the next two years to a more pragmatic agenda: 'will it tend to increase the efficiency of the nation for achieving victory?' When Lloyd George stuck a knife into the hapless Asquith to form a new win-at-all costs coalition in December 1916, the *Economist* backed the energetic Welshman on these grounds.[149] By the time the Armistice and khaki election arrived in 1918, however, it had little good to say about Lloyd George or any other political combine: certainly not Labour, with its 'astonishing and perverted passion for nationalising things', nor the Conservatives angling to make wartime tariffs permanent, nor Lloyd George. The latter seemed ready to promise anything to anybody – protection to his coalition partners, a land 'fit for heroes' to soldiers and, 'going back on our pledged word', at Versailles he now demanded that Germany pay for the entire war. Along with Keynes, the *Economist* denounced peace terms negotiated in France as vindictive and self-defeating.[150] Such benevolence did not extend as far as Soviet Russia, excluded from the peace conference after the Bolsheviks bowed out of the Eastern Front in 1917. The *Economist* saw Russia's revolution mainly through the prism of debt. The October, if not February, upheavals so menaced the credit Britain had advanced its formerly tsarist ally – £571.6 million, over 30 per cent of the total post-war loan book – that it entertained all options for obtaining repayment, including a blockade and invasion to crush the new regime.[151]

The *Economist* now insisted on returning to free trade, as the basis of peace and prosperity prior to 1914, with tariffs and other measures of coercion justified only by the life-and-death struggle that had followed. It endorsed the Cunliffe Report without hesitation in 1918, including its call for a quick return to gold convertibility at the old par rate, state withdrawal from money and capital markets, and a run of budget surpluses to pay off debt.[152] Until 1921, the most striking political feature of the paper was its avoidance of politics – a remarkable feat, given the crisis in Ireland at the time, postmarked from that supposed pre-1914 golden age. After sweeping the Irish Parliamentary Party into oblivion for backing Britain in the war, Irish Republicans erupted against British rule in 1919, sparking a bloody guerrilla war that raged until independence in 1921.[153] That September, Withers slipped away, taking up a lucrative position at the *Saturday Morning Post*. A year later, the Conservatives ejected Lloyd George – marking the end not only of his premiership, but that of any other Liberal: on its own, the party has never again captured power in Britain.

### The Strange Death of Liberalism?

Liberalism went from a landslide victory in 1906 to eclipse by 1922, a rise and fall historians have struggled to explain. Though it had been common to ascribe its 'strange death' to ideological exhaustion, as it faced the discomfiting twentieth-century developments of trade unionism, women's rights, and a spirited nationalism in Ireland, the pendulum has since swung in the other direction.[154] Not only were its formidable intellectual resources put to bold use advancing social reform; its subsequent collapse had little to do with any failings therein.[155] On this view, the fall of the last Liberal government, set in motion by its own leaders in 1916, was contingent. It arose from a clash of personalities, not policies. The wish to 'get rid' of Lord Kitchener at the War Office, and the unbridled ambitions of Lloyd George, split the party and drove it into permanent electoral exile.[156] In this telling, of course, the First World War is itself purely contingent – a bolt from the blue, crashing down on Britain and the unsuspecting Liberals who happened to be ruling it. If Hirst gave voice to a major current of the Liberal Party that achieved office in 1906, his sacking by the *Economist* in 1916 implies a more complicated, structural picture of the conflicts and culpabilities that led to its demise. The issue of war was an integral element in the struggle to direct and define New Liberalism up to 1914 – with empire, finance, and democracy the key terms in that debate.

Hirst and his allies certainly overestimated their strength, perhaps in part because of their control of levers of opinion, from the Liberal Federation to the press. But while radicals may have set the pace at home, from the outset New Liberalism was in quite different hands abroad. Here Liberal Imperialists strove for 'continuity' with the Conservatives, who had concluded by the turn of the century that with the rise of competing imperial powers in Europe – above all Germany; but Russia in Asia too – it was no longer possible to preserve the British Raj worldwide without allies.[157] In office, the Liberals maintained the formal alliance with Japan; acting in secrecy, they extended the kind of agreement reached with France to Russia in 1907 – drawing Britain relentlessly thereafter into an unspoken Triple Entente, arrayed against the Central Powers of Germany and Austro-Hungary, even as Grey constantly denied it, insisting Britain had its 'hands free'. Each time Hirst thought that radical Liberals had checkmated the Imperialists – from Campbell-Bannerman's apparent defeat of their plot to remove him in 1905 onwards – the latter recoiled like a spring, only to jump forward with greater force.[158]

Though British diplomacy masked its determination to defend the Empire against what it took to be the gathering challenge of Germany, it is difficult to maintain that radicals were simply bamboozled in 1914 – as their failure to oppose Britain's plunge into the carnage to any effect suggests. Outside the Cabinet, pious invocations of Gladstone had the desired effect, with many of Hirst's allies rallying behind Belgium after Grey invoked the Grand Old Man to argue Britain had a moral duty to defend it. Leonard Hobhouse came to see the war in this light, trying to explain his shift from pro-Boer to anti-Hun by 1914 to his sister Emily: 'Nearly all those who sympathised with the Boers as a small nation struggling for freedom now sympathise with the Belgians struggling for freedom'.[159] Inside the Cabinet, Belgium had no part in the decision for war, taken two days before its invasion, though as a pretext its merits were seen. 'Simplifies matters', Asquith wrote. For Lloyd George, his mistress reported, it was 'to be cynical, a heaven-sent excuse'.[160] Gladstone's shade had a different lesson for ministers: frugality. Churchill played a hand that had won him many a trick when he passed Lloyd George a note on 2 August: 'The naval war will be cheap – not more than £25 million a year.'[161] Intervention would be good value for money, with a quick campaign on the high seas.

Hirst was unmoved either by the appeal to morality in international affairs, or the enticement that war could be had on the cheap. Yet his basic assumption about liberalism – that it entailed a free trade empire, kept that way on the one hand by finance capital, and on the other by a powerful navy– had none of the inherently pacific force he attributed to it. Japan, as Hirst was aware, had been tapping the London money markets to finance a war with Russia in the Far East, where its stunning victories on land and sea raised its credit high enough by 1905 to carve out an empire in Asia.[162] Tokyo borrowed £84 million between 1897 and 1913, becoming the City's single best customer in the years up to the First World War.[163] Lloyd George was very explicit about the connection between foreign investments of this sort and Britain's status as a great power. His Mansion House speech of 1911 might have served as a warning to Hirst that free trade finance could just as easily justify war as create 'hostages for peace'.[164] Norman Angell's optimistic theory of capital export, which Hirst and Paish (and Hobson) also avowed, was no more persuasive before than after August 1914, when events seemed to correspond to the inverted analysis of 'monopoly capital' that Lenin posited. The self-satisfied assumptions of a liberal empire – set against a deplorably aggressive imperialism – also propelled Britain toward a confrontation with Germany, in other words, even if Hirst, Paish and Hobson had the personal rectitude to oppose entry into a war against it.[165]

Given the absolute priority of capital export to the Liberal vision of free trade and empire, it is surprising to see how seriously contemporary scholars take the 'falling out' between the party and the City over taxes, old-age pensions and so forth.[166] Many bankers, traders, merchants and others no doubt abandoned Liberalism, judging by voting patterns in the City, and on logical if rather short-sighted grounds. Between even mild increases in their tax bill, and tariffs – which might also mitigate risk on their sizable imperial investments – they opted for protection and Tories.[167] Liberals, however, were not so flighty. While a quick glance at the *Economist* shows obvious tensions between it and sections of the financial community over the People's Budget, a closer look reveals a more striking fact: the pleading tone, the passion to keep the City of London the beating heart of global financial and commercial exchange. A propensity to compare bankers to penguins, or fume at individual actors like Lord Rothschild, ought not be confused with opposition to the City as such. Nor should it obscure the central place of finance in the fiscal-political constitution of New Liberalism, as Lloyd George demonstrated very clearly in the summer of 1914. At that moment, he carried out an unprecedented rescue of the City, in what one commentator has called 'the most severe systemic crisis London has ever experienced – even more so than 1866 or 2007-8'. In a month, the Bank of England doled out £133 million, or 5 per cent of GDP, to banks and discount houses, taking a third of the entire discount market off their books.[168]

What of the 'democratic promise' of the party during these years, which has also been positively reappraised since Dangerfield gave his biting assessment of it: stalling on voting rights for women and working men, and opportunistic neglect of Home Rule for Ireland? Here, thanks to analyses of the Liberal budgets, and the changes in taxation they ushered in from 1905 to 1914, a clearer picture emerges of its claims to represent fairness and progress. Neither, as it happened, was incompatible with unequal burdens of taxation. Workers in 1914 continued to pay a larger portion of their income in indirect taxes than almost anyone else, and if the People's Budget introduced old-age pensions, it also taxed workers' 'luxuries' such as spirits and tobacco, while three-quarters of new unemployment and health insurance was funded out of wages. The greatest beneficiaries of New Liberal finance were neither the poor, nor the very rich – who, above £10,000, did see taxes on unearned incomes rise – but the middle classes, most of whom paid less in 1914 than in 1905, 'when the income tax, as yet undifferentiated, had stood at 1s. in the £'.[169] It is odd to treat social reform and the differentiation and graduation of taxes as watershed moments for Liberalism, but not the wartime interventions that also took place under it, dwarfing these earlier forays. Liberals, whose last peacetime budget of £207 million was considered a fiscal revolution, spent over half that bailing out the banks, before sending a quarter-million men to their deaths in the First World War, to the tune of £9.5 billion.[170]

A look at its relationship to empire, finance, and democracy gives a different picture of the rise and fall of liberalism. What is perhaps most striking about that story is its aftermath: survival of the central tenets of liberalism, and their re-emergence after the war as virtually hegemonic. Rarely in history has the political power associated with a current of thought given way without its intellectual legitimacy faltering too. 'By the autumn of 1916, economic liberalism was played out', asserted the historian A. J. P. Taylor. 'The only logical alternatives were to abandon liberalism or abandon the war.'[171] The *Economist* is a testament to just how fleeting this judgment was. Not only did the paper successfully insist on liberal economic policies being maintained so far as possible during the war, and then re-imposed after the Armistice, but in the almost hundred years since, its circulation and influence have flourished as never before.

# 5

## Own Gold

### *Layton and the League*

Walter Layton quit the *Economist* in August 1914, after the editor Francis Hirst refused to use it to harness the City of London to the war: 'Grass will be growing in Lombard Street before the end of the year' was Hirst's view. Late in 1921, Layton returned to the *Economist*, but in a world littered with signs that Hirst had been right – that four and half years of total war had dealt a serious blow to the liberalism the *Economist* embodied, starting with the international free trade order over which Britain presided as top imperial nation.

From Flanders to the Dardanelles, the map of Europe was stained with blood. Approximately 750,000 British soldiers had died, along with 250,000 from across the colonies and dominions. The Empire was bigger than ever, with Britain acquiring vast territories from the defeated Germans and Ottomans, stretching in an 'irregular semi-circle' from South West Africa to the Middle East and on to the Pacific.[1] But now a wave of anti-colonial nationalism had spread just as far, sapping the legitimacy of imperial rule and raising the cost of its enforcement. In 1919, *Wafd*-led demonstrators, frustrated at being locked out of peace negotiations in Paris, took to the streets in Egypt. In India, a British general ordered troops to fire into an unarmed crowd at Amritsar – mowing down at least 500, inflaming Indian nationalists, and giving Afghan king Amanullah a pretext to invade from the north.[2] Arabs and Jews alike rioted in newly-mandated Palestine. By 1920, open revolts had erupted in Mesopotamia, Persia, and Ireland – where thousands of ex-servicemen, in paramilitary outfits like the Black and Tans and the Auxiliaries, sowed terror in attempts to flush out republican rebels from Balbriggan to Cork.[3] Lloyd George's coalition finally dissolved in 1922 as the Conservatives and Dominion leaders refused to follow him into another imperial fracas – this time with Kemalist nationalists in Turkey surging towards the Allied-occupied Straits.

Even more alarming than colonial insurgency for the prospects of liberal civilization as understood in London was the apparent crumbling of its economic basis. Free trade was under attack both abroad and at home, where tariffs to safeguard so-called strategic industries, from wireless valves to chemicals, succeeded those on wartime luxuries like clocks and motorcars. Cheap government, meanwhile, lay buried under £7.5 billion of debt: at 40 per cent of GDP, state expenditure had risen thirteen-fold in four years, with loans paying for two-thirds of it.[4] The fact that Britain had borrowed so heavily, not just on its own account but also for allies, carried profound implications. By 1918, it owed $1.3 billion to the US, heretofore recipient of the largest share of its capital, reflecting a liquidation of stockpiled assets there that undermined, in turn, the London-managed gold standard. Convertibility of the pound sterling into gold was *the* symbol of sound money and security in global exchange: but with convertibility suspended at the war's outset, in March 1919 the pound was freed to float against the American dollar, and fell – a sign of the dwindling confidence Britain's currency now inspired relative to the greenback.[5]

If these interlocking pieces of pre-war political economy could not be put back together again, it stood to reason that neither could world trade, which up to 1914 had relied on the City of London to underwrite, finance, ship, and intervene to keep it running. Britain was no less dependent on that trade; by the time Layton became editor of the *Economist* in August 1921 a heady restocking boom had fizzled, and unemployment was at an unprecedented 17 per cent, rising to twice that in the old staple industries of coal, iron and steel, shipbuilding and textiles.[6] The concentration of misery in export trades was all the more troubling, as these had been under pressure since the 1870s, when German and US manufacturers, under cover of rising tariffs, began to erode their share of world markets. What war had now greatly weakened was Britain's ability to cover, as before, the resulting trade deficits with invisible income piped through the City.[7]

Not only did the liberal order face threats of a kind almost unimaginable to previous editors of the *Economist,* but these converged on its home ground: the world of commerce and finance, its institutions, markets and men. And yet, as surprising as it may seem, this liberalism pivoting on the City emerged more ideologically determined after the war – energized by men like Layton – *because* and not in spite of their experience of it. The *Economist* reflected this confidence, embedded in the broader perspective of those who read and wrote it, that to each of the challenges the Great War had thrown up – and to three in particular: preserving peace, reviving global trade, and handling demands for democratic self-determination – liberalism offered not just the best but indeed the only credible solutions.

## Liberalism's 'Strange' Rebirth

To the first and most pressing question – how to prevent anything like the First World War from happening again – the official response of the period took shape during the fighting itself, and was the brainchild of a scion of Britain's leading imperial statesman of the previous generation, Salisbury himself. On coming to power in 1916, Lloyd George ramped up the war effort. Joining the coalition government, Lord Robert Cecil, Salisbury's third son, a Conservative free-trader, became Minister for the blockade of Germany – designed to starve it into submission, should it not succumb to the Entente armies' 'knock-out blow' promised by Lloyd George. Cecil proposed that a League of Nations be created once victory was achieved. By 1918 the Cabinet had come round to the idea, after Woodrow Wilson was persuaded of it – the inter-Allied committees coordinating everything from shipping to finance henceforward serving, for their staffs, as models of the global governance the League could bring.[8] Cecil, responsible for the death of some 400,000 German civilians who succumbed to starvation or disease during the blockade, would in due course be given the Nobel Peace Prize for his contribution to birthing the League.

For Cecil, the League would act as the linchpin of a *Pax Anglo-Americana* after the war. Wilson made this British vision his own. 'Liberalism is the only thing that can save civilization from chaos', intoned the US president, scholar of Gladstone and Bagehot, en route to the peace treaty talks on the outskirts of Paris: 'it must be more liberal than ever before, it must even be radical', to counter the 'poison' of Bolshevism that the Russian Revolution of 1917 had released.[9] Once at Versailles, ignoring his own advisors, Wilson fell in with the South African premier Jan Smuts, architect of apartheid, who posited the British Empire as a model and partner for the League, with mandates 'nursing' peoples 'either incapable of or untrained in the power of self-government' to inoculate them against 'that despair of the State which is the motive power behind Russian Bolshevism'.[10] The League may have missed its original vocation when the US Senate rejected the Versailles treaty. But by 1922 Britain had itself restored a measure of order to its empire, in the process adopting recipes Smuts had recommended: combining grants of formal independence to Egypt and Iraq with treaties locking down Britain's military, economic or political interests in them; homeopathic reforms to stabilize control of India; greater say for the white Dominions, Ireland now included; airplanes replacing gunboats in the liberal repertoire of technological domination on the cheap.[11]

Back in the centre of the Empire, meanwhile, cheapness in the form of budgetary discipline was itself a weapon of choice for social domination, in the face of popular pressures. If war had weakened the international standing of the City, this was by no means the case at home, where its prestige – refurbished by the legend of 'financial heroism' to which the *Economist* under Hartley Withers had contributed – stood perhaps higher than at any point since the defeat of Napoleon. As in 1815, while the costs of war had left a trail of inflation and social unrest behind them, they also offered a means for bringing these to heel: austerity. That meant sharp deflation and a swift return to gold, comporting net transfers of wealth to well-off, mainly domestic holders of government debt.[12] The difference with the early nineteenth century lay in the character of the threat from below: a newly enfranchised and organized working class, on strike in record numbers, with Russian Bolsheviks rather than French Jacobins as inspiration or spectre abroad.[13] Politicians, civil servants, bankers and economists recast the gold standard in light of this unprecedented political predicament. Gold became 'knave proof' – acting, in a democratic age, as a 'constitutional barrier' that would submit the social spending of any future Labour government to its automatic rigours.[14]

In 1919, under Lloyd George's call to root out all public 'waste and extravagance', the turn to deflation began. After two years of swingeing cuts, the removal of import and exchange controls, and a rise in bank rate to 7 per cent, a £1690 million budget deficit was transformed into a £231 million surplus, given over to debt reduction.[15] Austerity did more than balance budgets; it put the financial and mercantile interests of the City in control of economic policy to an even greater extent than before, with the Bank retaking hold of short-term interest rates, while a Treasury veto over government spending was elevated for the first time into virtually a constitutional principle.[16] The order of economic priorities was set for the decade: even with unemployment at over 10 per cent, interest rates stayed up and almost 40 per cent of the budget serviced the debt. All talk of a capital levy on the recipients of the interest on that debt vanished.[17]

But if a liberal empire and a liberal economy emerged more or less intact from the war, the party that had launched the war did not. Irreparably divided by Lloyd George's war-time nuptials with the Conservatives, and the 'coupon' election he called after the Armistice, the Liberals were routed in the polls of 1924, winning a mere forty seats, and less than twenty more in the subsequent election of 1929. Labour had taken their place as the alternative to Conservative rule; the Liberals were henceforward a minor third party, of little consequence in the Commons. Paradoxically, however, the political eclipse of Liberalism masked its continuing intellectual grip on the minds of those who were its beneficiaries. This was less true of the Conservatives, whose new leader, Baldwin, jettisoned free trade for tactical reasons, than it was of Labour, whose ostensible commitment to socialism should have ruled out any straightforward acceptance of it, but whose leaders adopted its economic orthodoxy as a matter of faith: at the Treasury, Philip Snowden was unsurpassed in his zeal for budgetary rectitude. This consensus at the top reflected the peculiar emplacement of Labour as a party: not just closer than any counterpart in Europe to its bourgeois predecessor, but emergent as an electoral force under its tutelage, so that its relation to Liberalism, as one historian argues, 'was less one of hostility than of apostolic succession'.[18] Absent any real party-political alternative, Bagehot's 'common sense of the nation' would become its pathology, with crisis, breakdown and a 'doctor's mandate' in 1931.[19]

## Walter Layton and Interwar Liberalism

Far from limiting the reach of the *Economist*, the parliamentary weakness of the post-war Liberals actually helped to extend it: all three parties could call on the new editor, whose applied knowledge of statistics was legendary and useful to any of them. Walter Layton's cursus began when he was just nineteen at University College, London, where he gathered data on working-class wages for the Board of Trade. His obvious ability led to similar work at Trinity College, Cambridge, where he studied with the legendary neoclassical political economist Alfred Marshall and sat the new Economics Tripos in 1906. Trinity was a leap, for unlike past editors of nonconformist stock, Layton's parents were professional musicians. A Congregationalist choirboy from Chelsea who sang at Gladstone's funeral, Layton won prizes and played the organ to pay for school fees. At university, he dipped a careful toe in the currents that were carrying his friends away, visiting the local Fabian socialists while protesting his 'fidelity to sound economic truth', or attending 'highbrow' *conversazioni* with Apostles such as Bertrand Russell, Lytton Strachey and John Maynard Keynes, even as he found their moral, aesthetic and carnal interests 'not really my cup of tea'. Layton lost his part in a production of *Faust* to poet Rupert Brooke because he was studying railway wages for the Board of Trade.[20] (A pattern that continued after university, when Lady Violet Bonham Carter, observing him sipping lemonade at parties, dubbed him 'the handsomest little grey mind in Europe'.) Layton found his level instead among New Liberals in discussion groups run by the political scientist Lowes Dickinson and Alfred Marshall, where he met Hirst, who asked Layton for a piece on the Liberals' 1907 Licensing Bill for the *Economist*. A year later, Layton was assistant editor, just as he and Keynes began to lecture for Part II of the Tripos under Marshall's successor in the chair of political economy, Arthur Pigou. In this dual role, Layton met his wife, Dorothy Osmaston, who was reading history and economics at Newnham College, and published his first and only purely scholarly work, *An Introduction to the Study of Prices,* in 1912.[21]

Both jobs came to an abrupt end in August 1914. As Layton strolled along Kings Parade, stunned by the declaration of war, he was nearly run down by a motorcycle combination with Keynes in the sidecar. 'They stopped to tell me that Maynard had been summoned for consultation by the Treasury ... my own call quickly followed.'[22] Seebohm Rowntree and William Beveridge, at the local government and Board of Trade respectively, put Layton's expertise in wage statistics to use in taking labour censuses. But it was at the Ministry of Munitions that he shone, rising to be right-hand man to Lloyd George, then Churchill – and emerging as one of a new breed of civil servant experts, along with Josiah Stamp, Arthur Salter, Jean Monnet, Eric Drummond and others, whose hopes for a post-war League of Nations were based on their experience in directing a supranational war effort.[23] On the Milner Mission to St Petersburg in February 1917, Layton found Russian supply statistics as threadbare as the Tsar's banquet at Tsarskoye Selo, observing an official stuff sweet meats down his pants a week before the revolution. Two months later, Layton made the rounds in Washington and New York with the Balfour Mission to plan arms production and bank credits with newly-at-war America. The *New Republic* compared him – a 'fine-faced, sensitive, quiet-voiced professor' – to the sort of men H. G. Wells 'used to delight in imagining', 'cool in a cosmic upheaval', 'organizing America for destruction as an engineer might deliberate lining a leaky tunnel with copper ... it was he and a few men like him who had made it feasible for amateur armies to loop round an empire a burning rain of steel'.[24]

'Profound Professor Layton', as Churchill called him, inspired confidence – not in voters, who failed to elect him three times as an MP, but in the politicians that they did elect.[25] In 1920, Lloyd George made Layton acting head of the Economic and Financial section of the League of Nations, and for thirteen years, Conservative, Labour and National governments alike sent him abroad to conferences in Europe – on German reparations and inter-Allied debt, currency stabilization and tariff unions; as financial assessor to the Simon Commission to India (1928); as Ramsay MacDonald's economic aide for talks with Roosevelt in Washington (1933).[26] By then, he was not only editor of the *Economist,* but also chairman of the *News Chronicle,* the largest Liberal daily newspaper in Britain, with a circulation near 1,400,000. His sway over liberal opinion was greater, in terms of reach, than that of anyone, including his friends Keynes and Hubert Henderson at the *Nation,* or Ernest Simon, director of the *New Statesman.*

Yet it was the *Economist,* with still just 5,000 subscribers, that gave Layton the greatest leverage, as both an outlet for and pressure point on policy elites and insiders, increasingly to be found not only in Whitehall or the City, but among those dependent in some way on what happened there: from the League secretariat in Geneva to the halls of power in Berlin, Rome or Vienna. It was his professor Alfred Marshall who saw the potential for the *Economist* to serve these men of affairs in a broad sense, prodding Layton early on to move it towards them. 'There is a growing interest among businessmen in the treatment of business questions from a point of view intermediate between that of the newspaper and the academic lecture-room', Marshall advised in 1910, 'and you might do good service to the *Economist* by writing on that intermediate line'. Bagehot, he added, had done both: 'and I am inclined – being a mere old fogey – to suggest as a motto, LIVE UP TO BAGEHOT'.[27]

Layton barely had a choice, returning to the magazine at the start of a decade 'packed with political issues'. He later claimed that in his first leader on the Washington Naval Conference in November 1921 'the tone of international politics was set for the seventeen years of my editorship'.[28] The *Economist* strongly supported the agreement to emerge from Washington, which discarded the old balance-of-power alliance with Japan for joint acceptance that the US would dominate the Pacific, but in an agreed ratio of capital ships between the three states: this was a concrete example of 'collective security', to be pursued henceforward through the League, and a brilliant American contrast to the 'elusive manoeuvring and ungenerous compromise' of the Europeans at Versailles.[29] Lloyd George's fall nine months later turned on the same issue: a looming 'military collision' between British and Turkish troops at Chanak was a direct result of the prime minister's 'immoral practice' of playing Greece as a 'pawn in the game of British foreign policy', outside the League or even the Entente.[30] Layton briefly broke with Lloyd George, his political mentor, shedding few tears for the passing of his coalition in the *Economist*. At least a Conservative government would 'restore consistency of outlook to national affairs', while hastening a realignment around the only genuine alternative to it – an alliance between the Liberals and Labour, centred on free trade, international 'reconciliation' through the League, and better industrial relations.[31]

### Finance and Hegemony: Restoring Confidence, Debating Keynes, 1921–31

In the event, Layton's *Economist* focused mainly on reviving international markets and stabilizing currencies on the basis of a return to free trade and gold, and of placing the City back in charge of both. If many historians now see the painful adjustments this imposed on Britain as sacrificing industry to cosmopolitan finance, the *Economist* reminds us that for their proponents at least, the sacrifices were to be borne as much by the City, in terms that denied the possibility of a split between it and the rest of the economy.[32] As Britain failed to regain its export footing in the 1920s, this orthodox view came under scrutiny, but, significantly, from one of its former adherents. It was Keynes who began to challenge his fellow Liberals at the *Economist* over positions they had shared prior to 1914, in a series of bruising debates about the very nature of economics, amidst a slump it seemed powerless to explain or to cure. If the obstacles Keynes faced from the reigning intellectual consensus are now well-known, the part the *Economist* played is much less so. Reconstructing the back-and-forth between them reveals two important points about the long road to the 'Keynesian revolution', and the mainstream liberal response to it. First, their debates turned to a greater extent than is realized on issues of finance and empire; second, both agreed on the need to revive the City for Britain to remain a Great Power, but differed over whether Keynes's novel proposals would hurt or help in that effort. Wary of anything that threatened 'sound finance', the *Economist* would emerge as a highly qualified convert to Keynesianism by the late 1930s, with a correspondingly limited vision of the supposed post-1945 consensus.[33]

Keynes and Layton drew their liberalism from the same deep reservoir of culture, ideas and social milieu, even as their personalities formed a nearly complete contrast. There was nothing grey about Keynes. A brilliant student from a prominent upper-middle class household in Cambridge – his father was a lecturer in moral sciences and university registrar, his mother a graduate of Newnham and the city's first female mayor – Keynes was just as curious about art as economics, and preferred to pass his private life in unconventional pursuit of the former as part of the Bloomsbury circle. Still, he and Layton shared a great deal: intellectually, not just their Cambridge apprenticeships under Marshall, but links stretching back almost as far to the *Economist*. Keynes was indeed a devoted, in a sense ideal, reader of the paper, and his famous description of the 'happy age' before 1914 is almost a parody of himself in the act of perusing it: this inhabitant of London, who, 'sipping his morning tea' in bed, could 'adventure his wealth in the natural resources and new enterprises of any quarter of the world'.[34] To retrace Keynes's dialogue with the *Economist* is to watch someone change their own mind – showing us both how much Keynes moved after 1914, and how much he had, and would go on having, in common with the *Economist*.

Keynes had been a presence at the paper since 1909 after his post at the India Office made him an authority on currency and investment questions for the subcontinent. A champion letter writer, he also dashed off periodic articles to his 'anonymous pulpit' – the guinea he earned from his first effort pleasing him enough to preen about in a letter to his friend, the Bloomsbury painter Duncan Grant.[35] Both Keynes and Layton recoiled from Hirst's line on the First World War. Layton walked out, objecting not just to Hirst's defeatism, but to 'his prognosis of its economic consequences'; three weeks later, Keynes wrote to his father, vexed that the *Economist* editor was such 'a violent pacifist, passionately incensed at our being in the war, and far more interested in these political questions than in finance' (though Keynes grew more sympathetic as the war dragged on).[36] In this sense, both had more in common with Hirst's replacement, Hartley Withers, concurring that the City could and should do all in its considerable power (except submit to a capital levy) to win the war. Keynes was indeed first to the mark here, accusing London's joint stock banks of failing in 'courage and public spiritedness' for hoarding gold and exacerbating the financial crisis in August 1914.[37] If war sent Hirst to the margins, where even his own past support for unemployment insurance began to look to him like socialism – by the end, welfare was that 'Beveridge Hoax' – it endowed Layton and Keynes, in contrast, with extraordinary new powers of economic planning. It confirmed their shared New Liberal outlook, which dissociated laissez-faire at home and free trade abroad, discounting the former in favour of the latter.[38]

Thus, the *Economist* walked arm-in-arm with Keynes into the era of post-war reconstruction. It gave ample coverage to his bestselling attack on the Treaty of Versailles, *The Economic Consequences of the Peace* in 1919. And though it criticized him for going overboard with personal attacks on the statesmen at Versailles, the *Economist*'s own view was not so different. Politicians, accountable to vengeful electorates, were probably not the best peacemakers: the 'alternative to dissolution and economic collapse in much of Europe' was for economic experts and central bankers to take the lead in negotiating debt forgiveness and a loan to revive trade and to stabilize currencies.[39] Under Layton, the paper praised Keynes's follow-up in 1922, *The Revision of the Treaty* – a reminder that for both, the problem with the Versailles Treaty was never just its harsh punishment of Germany, but that it left in place loans the Allies had made to one another. US pressure for full and prompt repayment from Britain and France, and of both to third countries to which they had lent, led to the unreasonably large reparations demands upon Berlin.[40] A solution to this three-cornered debt and reparations tangle was the first step to getting the British and world economies back on their feet.

Yet when Arthur Balfour, the stand-in foreign secretary, issued a note in August 1922 making this plain and insisting that Britain was ready to ask of its Allies and Germany only what it was obliged to pay to the US, the *Economist* attacked him. It was 'deplorable' to insist that 'Britain's debt policy was contingent upon that of America', and the transatlantic cables were already abuzz with the 'unfortunate effect upon American opinion such insistence was bound to produce'.[41] At the first Liberal Summer School put on by Layton and Ramsay Muir at Oxford, Keynes agreed Britain should demonstrate the leadership that creditor status gave it in Europe, forgiving its allies' debts regardless of what the US did.[42] Both praised the new Chancellor, Stanley Baldwin, another Conservative, who called for a 'discussion as businessmen' with the Americans, Keynes differing only when the repayment terms he obtained proved so miserly. Privately Keynes urged Prime Minister Bonar Law to hold out for better than 80 cents to the dollar. 'It is the debtor who has the last word in these cases.'[43] The *Economist*, in contrast, worried the settlement was *too* generous, almost a 'confession of weakness': 'an appreciable reduction in what the United States Government is entitled to ask us to pay', it 'should be accepted not only with good grace but with gratitude'. The City, it reported, greeted news that Cabinet had signed on to the deal not with 'gloomy forebodings of disaster' – as might have been expected of a plan that exacted over £32 million a year for sixty-four years while earning the Americans a handsome profit – 'but by marking up the prices of British Funds'.[44]

The severity of the settlement seems in fact to have been the chief argument in its favour: a dramatic, determined step to restore confidence in the nation's credit and currency. When Keynes published *A Tract on Monetary Reform* the same year, this was the sticking point. Although the *Economist* saw 'immense advantages' in his proposal for a flexible system of fixed exchange – linked to gold but based on a 'tabular standard' of key commodities – it also worried, 'if the great trading nations of the world did not follow our lead they would not be likely for a long time to recognise that the pound sterling was the most stable unit in the world, and, in the meantime, London would lose her financial pre-eminence.' Not only did gold compel nations to keep 'balances in London', it was safer than giving 'absolute discretion' to the Treasury and the Bank of England, as Keynes's plan entailed.[45] Whether the *Economist* really believed the gold standard ever operated independently of these institutions, the *idea* that it did mattered. Without this political cover, every decision to ease or restrict credit could be questioned by industrialists and merchants wanting easy money, on the one hand, or attacked as 'monetary dictatorship' from wage earners, on the other.[46]

The *Economist* was more frightened than Keynes about shining any light on the 'grandmother of Threadneedle Street', but it must be recalled that far from undermining the authority of the Bank of England or the Treasury, Keynes's plan called for giving both more discretion to manage the economy for the sake of price stability. As a result, he could still in 1923 describe the *Economist*, in the *Nation and Athenaeum,* as a 'gentle critic' and 'really with us on the main issue'.[47] That began to change only when Churchill announced his intention to return to gold at the pre-war parity of $4.86 on 28 April 1925 – a move Keynes attacked in the *Evening Standard,* and then in *The Economic Consequences of Mr. Churchill,* as premature. Keynes saw two problems with the approach: first, since prices remained about 10 per cent higher in Britain than in the US, the policy entailed more deflation, and could 'only attain its end by intensifying unemployment without limit, until the workers are ready to accept the necessary reduction of money wages under the pressure of hard facts'.[48] Second, as boom time America hoovered up most of the world's gold reserves, it meant, as he had argued earlier, 'inevitably, that we surrender the regulation of our price level and the handling of the credit cycle to the Federal Reserve Board of the United States'.[49]

## 1925: Keynes and the Economic 'Inconsequences' of Gold

If a cordial dialogue over the policies needed to return to gold had reigned hitherto, the return to gold at parity launched the conversation on a new and acrimonious course – as the assumption that industrial and finance capital had the same stake in the gold standard came under strain in clashes over free trade and foreign investment, culminating in the crisis of 1931. 'It is much to be deplored', replied the *Economist* to Keynes, in a leader entitled 'The Economic Inconsequences of Mr. Churchill', that 'distinguished economists should disturb the public mind by attributing far too much effect to our monetary policy as a cause of the depression'.[50] The fall in Britain's industrial output and employment was due above all to slackness in world trade, aggravated by other factors: abroad, currency depreciations; at home, higher wages and shorter hours, combining to raise costs of production, along with high municipal rates and a terminal decline in coal production. The rigours of gold would indeed pressure wages, but they would also propel industrial rationalization, amalgamation, modernization – business buzzwords of the era, aiming to restore the competitiveness of British firms in world markets.

When Keynes addressed the Federation of British Industries in Manchester, the paper professed to be shocked that so august an economist – in a style that 'could not have been excelled by Mr. Lloyd George himself' – would foster the idea that 'there are real divergences between "finance" and "industry"', or that monetary policy had been carried out in the sole interests of the former. All parties had endorsed a gradual return to the pre-war monetary setup, as outlined in the 1918 Cunliffe Report, while the Industrial Federation had implored Churchill to take the move a few short months before, assuming that gold would bring down costs and prices and restore stability of outlook. If banks were concerned only about their own profits, protested the *Economist* at the time of their annual shareholder meetings – which had come to play an 'important part in forming public opinion' since the war – they would have favoured a floating exchange, so as to bet on its fluctuations.[51]

The effects of the return to gold in 1925 were much as Keynes had predicted, and led to his most serious clash to date with the *Economist*. Organized labour resisted the wage squeeze, taking the unprecedented step of calling a general strike the next year. Britain, meanwhile, was hostage to a monetary system it no longer controlled: by 1928, the Wall Street boom not only stemmed the flow of dollars going abroad, it sucked foreign funds towards it – so that just when Britain needed cheap money, faced with a sharp rise in unemployment, it became dear, as interest rates rose to defend the reserves.[52] In these circumstances, the *Economist* admitted the need for cooperation between central banks to curb the deflation caused by this uneven distribution of gold – publishing a memo to this effect by Sir Henry Strakosch, the financier with whom Layton was then trying to buy the *Economist*. Along with Sir Arthur Salter, they lobbied the League to adopt a resolution to study the problem, putting them at odds with Bank governor Montagu Norman, as worried as ever that public scrutiny of any kind might force central banks to admit they 'could regulate prices through their gold and credit policies'.[53]

The belated shift to greater central bank coordination could not prevent a looming confrontation with Keynes, however, who in light of the same events began to ask fundamental questions not just about gold, but free trade – first, as it pertained to capital exports. The *Economist* had expected the rapid debt settlement with America and the return to gold at parity to jump-start foreign lending. In 1928, 'Our Export of Capital' posed two characteristic and related questions about the success of these measures: 'whether America is taking our place as a supplier of world capital' and 'the amount we can afford to lend abroad'. The surplus of income account, which it used to measure capital exports, was £181 million in 1913, or £270 million in 1927 prices; fifteen years later, it was still less than half this, at £96 million. Citing the Liberal Industrial Inquiry, which Layton chaired and whose report Keynes largely wrote, the paper even suggested the pre-war heights might never be regained, before concluding, optimistically, that though 'we shall irrigate the world with new capital on a somewhat smaller scale', the 'role of purveyor of capital is now shared by Great Britain with America'.[54] Nor was it concerned that even this new, shared role actually reflected a worrying trend for the City to finance long-term investments with 'hot money' from abroad; these short-term funds were simply 'filling the gap caused by the temporary disappearance of our available surplus'.[55] 'Is the Financier a Parasite?' No, the *Economist* replied.[56]

When Keynes attacked the 'timidities and mental confusions of so-called sound finance' in the *Evening Standard* in August 1928, he had in mind the deflationary torsions that first the return and then the maintenance of gold had forced on the Bank of England. The *Economist* dismissed his claim that such polices had 'reduced the wealth of Great Britain by no less than £500,000,000' over the past five years – demonstrating that, even as Layton joined with Keynes to advise Lloyd George in the upcoming election, sound finance remained a dividing line over what Liberals should aim to do in office. It was one thing to call for state action to build roads and telegraph wires or to speed industrial rational-ization to 'conquer unemployment', along with international accords to liberalize trade, repay debt, restore gold and create a world central bank. But Keynes went too far when he called for 'stimulating prosperity by a moderate measure of inflation', or suggesting this 'could have saved us' from post-war industrial readjustments, 'which would probably have been more severe if artificially postponed'.[57]

The debate grew even more heated as the general election cam-paign began in February 1929. Tory MP Carlyon Bellairs – a retired naval officer and ex-Liberal – wrote to the *Times* to argue that classical free trade theory, forged on nineteenth-century assumptions that capital was immobile, no longer applied, since capital could now move anywhere in search of the best return; protection was a way of concentrating capital at home instead of sending it to employ foreign labour. The *Economist* replied imme-diately and revealingly: 'Has the bottom fallen out of the Christian doctrine because circumstances changed since the days when the Gospels were written?' There was no evidence that a 'shortage of local capital is even a contributory factor in the troubles of our distressed industries'; besides, it added, capital exports 'stimulate commodity exports – a statement which will be supported by all, only with a variety of emphasis and qualification'.[58] Keynes seized on this last clause, relaunching a debate that had last flared up in the *Economist* in 1927 – when Layton had used it to publicize the World Economic Conference in Geneva, at which he and other businessmen and quasi-official experts had tried to reach the tariff-reduction agreements that eluded their governments.[59]

Posing his questions as humble points of clarification, Keynes began to write a series of letters to the *Economist,* asking it to explain the 'train of causation' linking capital and commodity exports. Railway loans of the Victorian era, subscribed in London and spent on British equipment, were a classic case, but such transactions probably accounted for no more than 20 per cent of loans today. What about the other 80? The *Economist* first replied that capital export increased the supply of sterling on world exchanges, making pounds cheaper and giving exports a fillip.[60] Greater supplies of sterling would lower its exchange value, Keynes agreed, but only if they were not hitched to a precious metal preventing its depreciation. 'Your argument does not make sense, unless your meaning is that foreign investment stimulates exports by driving us off the gold standard.'[61] The *Economist* switched tack, arguing that foreign lending encouraged gold outflows, raising the discount rate, which lowered domestic prices until they were more competitive.[62] Keynes affected surprise: 'I think that exporters (who have not been as grateful as, on your theory, they should have been) would like to have it explained in what way a higher Bank rate improves their competitive position in foreign markets.' He at last deigned to 'decipher' the *Economist's* muddle in its own pages: either high interest rates raised exports by compelling manufacturers, in despair, to sell at a loss; or, it lowered costs of production by curtailing credit and creating unemployment. 'Have I rightly interpreted your meaning?'

> If the next time you applaud the tendency of foreign lending to stimulate exports, you will add the explanatory words 'because it will make the maintenance of full employment impossible at the present level of wages, so that unemployment will continue until British wages are reduced, which will enhance our competitive power in foreign markets', then I will promise to write you no more letters![63]

The *Economist* apologized for the unusual step of devoting an article each to these letters, but it had little choice given the stakes. Keynes had gleefully laid traps for the *Economist* here and in the *Nation and Athenaeum,* in which he tried to show that industry and finance *could* be at odds, and that the management of the gold standard had needlessly deepened their divergence.[64] It must be stressed again, however, that Keynes criticized the 'mandarins' in the *Economist* as much for the harm they had done to the City as to Britain's industrial north: his support for 'tied lending' was meant to renew the virtuous mid-nineteenth century circle of foreign investment and exports – and to allow the City to compete with New York and Paris, which already engaged in similar breaches of free trade.[65] And while Keynes may have outwitted the *Economist,* it was the latter that prevailed on the level of policy. A glance at the memoranda of Treasury officials makes clear how closely they relied on the *Economist* to combat not just capital controls but – going back to James Wilson's writings on the 1840s railway mania, which still figured in the civil service exams – to loan-financed public works schemes in general, as 'crowding out' private investment.[66]

### 1929: Keynes, the Crash and Its Aftermath

It was the anvil of events, not superior cleverness, which eventually decided many of these issues in favour of Keynes, as the Wall Street bubble finally burst in 1929, precipitating the Great Depression. While this soon sent unemployment skyward, for a short time it relieved pressure on sterling, allowing the Bank rate to fall and easing credit; by May 1930, Britain was again losing gold, this time to France, resented for its undervalued currency and generally rosier outlook.[67] Labour, whose tenure in office since May 1929 had so far hardly been the disaster the Treasury officials had imagined, met this crisis with calls for retrenchment. Philip Snowden, the Labour Chancellor and until recently vice-president of the Free Trade Union, pressed in Cabinet and Parliament for measures to restore confidence in sterling at all costs, including cuts to escalating expenditure on unemployment insurance. At the turn of 1931, Labour set up the 'economy committee' the Liberals had proposed in Parliament, appointing a retired City insurance executive, Sir George May, to lead its 'non-partisan' mission.

Just before the May Report appeared in July 1931, another government-appointed body with a remit to investigate the causes of the economic slump issued the results of its two-year inquest. The City, revealed the Macmillan Committee, had indeed been using short-term inflows for loan operations, and was thus vulnerable to just the sort of crisis then unfolding in bank runs abroad. As panicked investors reacted in a rush to withdraw funds from London, the Bank raised rates two percentage points, to no avail: half the gold reserves vanished in two weeks; credit lines from the gold-besotted Federal Reserve and Bank of France came and went. By August 1931, Labour prime minister Ramsay MacDonald, ignoring the alternative of devaluation, sought another loan to back the currency – this time from the bankers at J. P. Morgan, to whom he secretly submitted a budget based on the May Report.[68] When his Cabinet balked at the cuts MacDonald wanted to unemployment benefit and public employee pay, he resigned along with Philip Snowden and J. H. Thomas to form a nominally all-party, but Conservative-dominated, National Government – the Labour Party soon expelled all three. An act to appease markets did the opposite when sailors in the Royal Navy affected by the pay cuts mutinied at Invergordon on 15 September. The stock market and sterling exchange crashed, forcing Britain off gold six days later; in addition to a virtual ban on foreign loans, the next year free trade went too, when preferential rates were adopted among the Commonwealth countries, as part of the 1932 Ottawa Agreements.

Keynes and Layton were not merely passive observers to this chain of crises; they actively shaped them. Their mirror reactions to 1931 said a great deal about their visions for liberalism: diverging over the parameters of sound finance, they continued to believe that the financial and mercantile resurgence of the City was a precondition for British survival as a great power, in a world system now in the inexpert, if not outright incompetent, hands of Americans.[69]

The *Economist* likened the summer of 1931 to that of 1914. But instead of sowing doubt as Hirst had, Layton projected calm, arguing the Macmillan Report showed short-term liabilities *decreasing* since 1928, from £302 to £254 million, while long-term investments of £4 billion would protect Britain against any 'sudden or prolonged call'. Had London 'deliberately placed itself in too vulnerable a position?' 'The answer to such criticism is that banking is one of our staple and most remunerative industries', and 'it is London's business to encourage the influx of foreign money.'[70] Such self-assurance bordered on denial, compounded by failure to foresee the approaching disaster. In May, Layton had authored a pamphlet reiterating that the City was holding its own in partnership with Wall Street, even as the Kreditanstalt bank failure in Vienna set off the crisis that would engulf it; in July, he was in Geneva on behalf of the League, trying to avert the Austro-German customs union with a hugely ambitious alternative for a tariff union of pan-European scale.[71]

Britain was like an eccentric millionaire without enough change to pay a taxi fare, the *Economist* explained: anyone would lend it pocket money once it showed it had the political will to balance budgets by eliminating 'extravagances' and defending gold convertibility, with the alternatives of a tariff or devaluation (Keynes favoured the former) ruled out.[72] The May Report 'aroused the whole country' to patriotic sacrifice, even if it erred in asking if 'democracy is to be shipwrecked on the hard rock of finance'. The 'real' question: 'Is sound finance to be shipwrecked upon the hard rock of democracy?'[73] The National Government was the 'swift, decisive and effective' response, and Ramsay MacDonald 'deserved well of his country' for casting aside his own Labour Party to lead it. 'Britain's centuries old position as a Great Power' was at stake; and it was not a naval mutiny but the 'stability of sterling' and 'maintenance of our credit abroad' that threatened it.[74]

The *Economist* thus announced 'The End of an Epoch' in late September with a thud, admitting the flight from gold had produced no bank runs, no riots, no crash, instead heralding an uptick in exports, consumer and business confidence. And yet the paper continued to view the situation as temporary. In 1932, it denounced as 'nauseating the symphony of imperial wind instruments' braying for imperial preference, and called on Liberals to resign from the National Government over the adoption of tariffs at the Ottawa conference, this 'mere piece of pettifogging political hoodwinking'.[75] Layton dispatched eight pages explaining free trade to prime minister MacDonald, who meekly apologized. And though he resigned from the planning of the London Economic Conference due the next year, Layton in fact played a key behind-the-scenes role, in part because this gathering would still be empowered to negotiate a return to gold, to which he and the *Economist* remained committed.[76]

Far from lamenting the 'end of an epoch', Keynes celebrated. Graham Hutton, *Economist* assistant editor, remembered him bursting into a *New Statesman and Nation* luncheon direct from the Treasury on 21 September 1931, 'rubbing his hands and chuckling like a boy who has just exploded a firework underneath someone he doesn't like'. 'At one stroke, Britain has resumed the financial hegemony of the world!', Keynes jubilantly informed the journalists.[77] The fact that twenty-five countries had followed Britain off gold was, Keynes added in a Treasury note, 'an exceptional opportunity for uniting the whole Empire on a reformed sterling standard', to be 'managed by the Bank of England and pivoted on London'.[78] His stress on imperial leadership at the moment of its apparent collapse is remarkable, especially as Keynes admitted the 'great advantage in purely national currencies managed solely in the interests of domestic stability and social peace'. Britain had another destiny, however, and much to gain from a wide currency union. A sterling standard based on 1929 wholesale prices would raise what imperial countries could charge for food and raw materials, increasing both their power to consume British goods and the City's income from equities held abroad – in other words, reconciling industry and finance along mid-nineteenth century lines, only now on the basis of 'Empire free trade'.[79]

For Keynes, that still very substantial alteration to the liberal creed was justified above all by the need to balance American power – which threatened to digest the British Empire, a danger he perceived as early as 1917, while scrounging for dollars at the Treasury.[80] Far from wishing to suppress or alter the structural

primacy of finance – beyond criticizing it on occasion for neglect-
ing home investment[81] – Keynes came to see that its recovery
would first have to pass through the real economy, on the back
of a trade surplus, and was far readier than Layton's *Economist*
to consider unorthodox solutions to do this, including tapping
the Empire. Sensing an opening in March 1931, as passage of the
Smoot-Hawley Tariff demonstrated US failure to assume a con-
structive global role, Keynes briefly argued for a revenue tariff and
for the gold exchange to be 'relentlessly defended, that we may
resume the vacant financial leadership of the world, which no one
else has the experience or public spirit to occupy'.[82] Five months
later, the same hope led him to the opposite conclusion, when he
toasted devaluation with Hutton.[83]

The *Economist* and the 'mandarins' who read it found this
inconsistency disturbing, but it must be borne in mind so as not to
misunderstand the postlude to these debates in 1936: the *General
Theory of Employment, Interest and Money* and its call to 'euth-
anize the rentier'. Despite the presence of many of his students
on its staff at this point, the *Economist* remained extremely cautious about the interventions Keynes proposed – agreeing on little
more than the need for low interest rates, which kept up stock and
housing prices in the pit of a now worldwide depression. When
the young Tory MP Harold Macmillan's *Reconstruction: A Plea
for National Unity* appeared three years prior, for example, the
paper harshly criticized its reliance on Keynes: overproduction
was impossible, while stripped of 'verbal embellishments', the
schemes to force reorganization in the cotton and coal industries
'amount in fact to Protection plus Monopoly!'[84]

Keynes's magnum opus was so explosive in the City in 1936
that Layton abandoned the practice of anonymity in asking Austin
Robinson, Keynes's student and colleague at Cambridge, to sign
his review of it. A row ensued with Robinson, who later spoke
about Layton's role in it:

> He was so able and in a way one of the early creators of quantitative
> economics. But he was at the same time curiously anti-intellectual.
> One of my most vivid memories of crossing swords with him was
> over the review in the *Economist* of Keynes's *General Theory*.

He and Geoffrey Crowther (who was potentially more able but in practice very obstinate and anti-intellectual) were terrified of seeming to praise the *General Theory* or to say that it was important. They not only made me sign the review when the *Economist* normally published unsigned reviews. They also cut out, without my agreement, the final paragraph in which I summed up the book. I never quite forgave Geoffrey Crowther, and I still think that Layton ought to have had a little more perception and courage. He was a great man but he had rather severe limitations.[85]

Layton and his deputy Geoffrey Crowther hedged their bets, censoring the part of the review that referred to supplementing monetary with fiscal action. During bouts of pessimism, in which the marginal efficiency of capital was low, Robinson was allowed to hint, it might be impossible to achieve a rate of interest high enough to induce lenders to lend or low enough to get borrowers to borrow and invest. In such cases, Keynes 'would wish to supplement private investment by public investment, or to increase the propensity to consume by social services or redistribution'.[86]

The *General Theory* was not just a theoretical rebuttal to the Treasury attacks on Lloyd George's plan to 'conquer unemployment' – which could, its officials had claimed in 1928, only crowd out private investment, with no cumulative economic benefit. Keynes's call for the 'euthanasia of the rentier' and the 'somewhat comprehensive socialisation of investment' in the final chapter of the *General Theory* was also a product of his clashes with City opinion more broadly since 1925, as embodied in the *Economist*. This would have been the more frustrating for Keynes insofar as the obstinacy he encountered from City circles was out of proportion to their disagreement.[87] Layton seemed just as ambivalent thirty years after the appearance of the *General Theory*, offering Keynes a belated, backhanded recognition. 'Since 1945 full employment and Keynesian policies have been an assumption of our public life, at times to a damaging degree.' 'The tragedy', Layton added, 'was that they won acceptance twenty years too late. Unemployment and slump left scars on the British working population that still cramp our ability to face the future.'[88]

## Sterling Thirties: Empire and Editorial Change, 1931–38

If Layton set the *Economist* against the tide of imperial and national self-sufficiency after 1931, the paper he ran nevertheless reflected the historic changes set in motion that year. The creation of the sterling currency area and the Ottawa system of imperial tariffs accelerated the trend of the decade before, with foreign investment falling as a share of national income, even as a larger part of it now flowed to the Empire.[89] In 1928, Layton visited India, the top destination for investment, as assessor to the Simon Commission. Layton's wife Dorothy joined him on the voyage, with both viewing it through the prism of Katherine Mayo's 1927 bestseller *Mother India* – a follow-up to *Isle of Fear*, her justification of US imperialism in the Philippines – which highlighted the cruelties of the Hindu caste system, in particular the practice of child marriage.[90] As the latest *Economist* editor to try to reform the Raj, Layton proposed a new federal system in which the central government in Delhi would raise and distribute tax revenues to the provinces, which would then spend the bulk of them – on sanitation, health, education and agriculture, much the same priorities as in the Liberal Yellow Book.[91] Indian nationalists rejected the very premise of the Simon Commission, with no Indian members among the authors of its report on the reform of Indian institutions, and not so much as a hint of Dominion status when it appeared in June 1930 amidst Gandhi's Salt Satyagraha.

The *Economist* received the three round table conferences that superseded it, and later the Government of India Act of 1935, as a victory for moderates on both sides, 'another step along the road to self-government' at a time 'when the accepted principles of parliamentary democracy are under challenge in so many countries'.[92]

India was not the only part of the Empire in which newly powerful nationalist movements contested the terms of British rule. In 1936, the Arab Revolt began in mandated Palestine after Jewish immigration into it more than doubled in five years: it took a force of 25,000 – the largest British overseas deployment since the Great War, and its most significant colonial intervention in the interwar period – to crush the uprising, alongside Jewish settler volunteers.[93] The *Economist* backed harsh repression to bring

Arab 'bandits' to heel, while pressing London and the League of Nations to implement the political solution that had proved itself in Ireland: partition. Fed up with British troops and police being a target of both Arab and Jewish attacks, and entrapped by the 'morally incompatible' promises made to each of them since the Balfour Declaration in 1917, the *Economist* came out in favour of a two-state solution in 1937.[94]

Starting in the late 1920s, the *Economist* experienced the first significant changes in its ownership, design and circulation – with Layton responsible, in his own painstaking way, for updating each aspect of the original edifice. As a result, the characters and arguments of owners, board members and editors, and even office politics, came into view with unusual sharpness.

The press was arguably subject to more insistent pressure to rationalize than any other industry in Britain, a process the war accelerated as mass circulation dailies edited in London edged out the provincial morning papers, while also fighting one another for readers.[95] The world of weekly political journals may have been slightly more genteel, but not by much. Layton, Keynes and other Liberal Summer Schoolers bought the *Nation and Athenaeum* from the Rowntrees in 1922, merging it with the Webbs' *New Statesman* in 1931 and the Courtauld-backed *Weekend Review* in 1933. Layton was convinced the *Economist* could achieve similar growth on its own, provided the descendants of James Wilson would sell their shares in it, ending a practice of 'distributing profits up to the hilt to the many family beneficiaries'. 'The need to plough back profits and expand the staff led me to approach some of my friends with a view to buying the paper and turning it into a private company.'[96] At the same time, Henry and Laurence Cadbury made Layton, a former tutor to Laurence, financial advisor to the family-owned *Daily News*. After helping to negotiate its merger with the *Westminster Gazette* and *Daily Chronicle*, in 1930 Layton became chairman of the combined *News Chronicle*, whose circulation of 1.4 million would enable it to compete with the giant tabloids – Rothermere's *Daily Mail* and Beaverbrook's *Daily Express* on the right, and Labour's *Daily Herald*.[97]

It was the *Economist* that presented the greater difficulties, however, when – after three years of negotiations – an unexpected rival appeared in 1928. This was Brendan Bracken, a twenty-seven-year-old mythomaniac, who claimed to be an Australian orphan (his mother lived in Ireland) and the illegitimate son of Winston Churchill, his political mentor. Bracken was the sort of person who instructed servants to interrupt dinner parties with imaginary messages – 'the prime minister is on the phone, sir' – and he provided rich material for the novelist Evelyn Waugh, who based his Canadian wheeler-dealer Rex Mottram on Bracken in *Brideshead Revisited*. Lanky, with thick glasses and crinkly red hair, Bracken had made a name converting the staid *Illustrated News* into *English Life,* a pageant of foxes, hounds, horses, homes and titles. He then turned to another gentlemanly pursuit, buying up business publications for the publishers Eyre and Spottiswoode: the *Banker* in 1926, the *Financial News, Economist* and *Investors Chronicle* in 1928, and the *Financial Times* in 1945.[98] Bracken made his first move for the *Economist* at a party with the society hostess Sibyl Colefax, Wilson's great-granddaughter. 'I suppose you are sentimentally attached to your holding', he remarked. 'Oh, no', she replied. 'I find it a very dull paper and feel no attachment to it at all.'[99]

Layton invoked the tradition of independent liberalism that risked being lost under Bracken, with his flamboyant links to the Tories, to launch his own bid. He managed to corral an impressive list of immensely wealthy liberal backers: Ernest Simon, John Simon, Laurence Cadbury, Walter Runciman and some of the grandest bankers in the City, including the Rothschilds, Schroders and Lazard brothers. His key ally in this was Henry Strakosch, an Austrian Jewish emigré to Britain who had risen to the chairmanship of the Union Corporation, the dominant player in South African gold mining. Like Layton, Strakosch was deeply engaged in trying to rebuild the free trade world order in the 1920s and '30s, as both a respected authority on the monetary system and a member of the financial committee of the League.[100] Notwithstanding this financial firepower, when bidding raised the *Economist*'s asking price from £60,000 to £100,000 – it made about £4,000 in profit annually – Layton baulked, and opted to cut a deal with Bracken. The latter agreed to a joint purchase, but also to a structure of ownership and control designed, as Layton put it, to allow 'the editor to run the paper as though it belonged to him'.[101] In a charter that went further than a similar scheme at the *Times,* the editor obtained power over policy, salaries, hiring and firing. For an added layer of insulation from business pressure, four trustees without financial stakes in the company would be needed to take on or dismiss the editor, approve share transfers or install a chairman. Bracken became managing director and took two board seats for Financial News Limited. But Layton held the balance, reflecting his sway with the trustees, and the fact that the City had intervened to buy half the paper at his urging. Strakosch became chairman of the board, with Layton and Runciman behind him, and Bracken and the banker Major Guy P. Dawnay holding the board seats allotted to the *Financial News.* Of the trustees, three were Layton's friends: Sir William Beveridge, Sir Josiah Stamp and the shipping magnate Sir Alan Anderson; Sir Lionel Halsey, retired vice-admiral and royal equerry, was in the fourth position.[102]

The most visible change in the wake of this handover was to the look of the *Economist* – a change Layton resisted, however, for another five years. (Keynes, in contrast, had revamped the *Nation* a full twelve years earlier in 1922.) Until 1934, the *Economist* looked more or less as it had a century before. The title ran across the top in heavy Gothic letters. The table of contents and money market news were crowded into a double column, along with bank and insurance advertisements, that sank to the bottom. This Victorian relic now got a facelift. Scrubbed clean, the new façade was neoclassical and imposing, like that of a bank. A single column banished all other material but the lead article and the contents to the back, and a clean serif font ran throughout, crafted by the team that had remade the typeface for the *Times* in 1932. As sober and unfussy as this was, it was a rude shock to Montagu Norman, the governor of the Bank of England, who complained bitterly of the change. Strakosch worried it might hurt circulation abroad. In fact, it signalled an opening to the world already underway: circulation increased steadily under Layton from 6,000 in 1930, passing 10,000 for the first time in 1938, with half that from overseas.[103]

## A New Generation of 'City Radicals' at the *Economist*

Layton hired editors, writers and foreign correspondents at the same time as this circulation surge, moving many into a much larger twenty-four-room office off Fleet Street – rented from *News of the World* on Bouverie Street, opposite the *Daily News* – in 1928. The new recruits represented a generational and ideological shift at the *Economist*. Among this fresh intake of students of Keynes at Cambridge, and Harold Laski at the London School of Economics, the most important were all 'self-confessed radicals' under thirty: Douglas Jay and Geoffrey Crowther, born in 1907, and Graham Hutton, born in 1904. Arriving at the paper in 1932–33, they pointed to a realignment that responded to the political landscape of the 1930s. With the Liberal Party weak and divided over the tariffs imposed after 1931, and the fascist right on the rise in Europe, could a younger and more radical staff push the *Economist*'s liberalism to the left?

Douglas Jay had kept liberal company as a classics student at New College, Oxford, where warden Herbert Fisher introduced him to Lloyd George and Jan Smuts, and at All Souls. It was as assistant editor in charge of foreign correspondence at the *Economist* that Jay emerged as a policymaker for the Labour Party, after Graham Hutton told the left-liberal political scientist Harold Laski that Jay should serve on the Labour National Executive's trade and finance committees.[104] Hutton was the *Economist*'s foreign editor, a specialist on Central Europe who had been Laski's student at the London School of Economics. Even Geoffrey Crowther, least adventurous of the lot, had studied at Cambridge under Keynes, who recommended him to Layton.[105] Together these three young men wrote and collated much of the *Economist*, along with Aylmer Vallance, the most bibulous and leftwing assistant editor ever to hold the job. (Vallance moved to the *News Chronicle* in 1933, then in 1936 to the *New Statesman and Nation*, where he advocated a popular front to include British Communists.)[106] Layton presided over Monday meetings and looked in on Wednesdays and Thursdays to correct proofs and approve leaders. But it was the historian Arnold Toynbee who did the most talking. In part, this reflected his seniority – born in

1889, he was over a decade older than the new editors – but it was also a question of style, both personal and professional. Toynbee wrote for the *Economist* on world politics in almost every issue from 1922 to 1939, substantially overlaying his annual surveys for the Royal Institute of International Affairs. Editors recalled his 'hand-written manuscript, perfectly legible, which required amendment of no syllable or comma'; and that, 'once started on his monologue' at meetings, 'he would never stop until he reached some dead end like the Falkland Islands. We listened to him spellbound'.[107]

In the 1930s, the progressive atmosphere spilled out from the office to the Mecklenburgh Square flat Graham Hutton shared with *New Statesman and Nation* editor Kingsley Martin. Parties at the flat often featured two young Hungarian economists: Thomas Balogh, who, armed with a letter from Joseph Schumpeter, was given a job at the London bank O. T. Falk & Co. in 1930, and the nickname 'Oxballs' by Keynes; and Nicholas Kaldor, a researcher and instructor at the London School of Economics since 1927.[108] Both men became key post-war advisors to Labour (later trying to press the *General Theory* into service under Harold Wilson as industrial and incomes policies aimed at boosting growth). Nicholas Davenport, a broker and a columnist at the *New Statesman and Nation,* was another 'City radical' swept into this milieu, seeing mainly to the money market and Stock Exchange sections at the *Economist*, along with Hargreaves Parkinson, Norman Crump and Henry Hodson (Hodson also moonlighted for the liberal imperialist journal *Round Table* as assistant editor, and on Ramsay MacDonald's Economic Advisory Committee).[109]

The 1930s *Economist* was packed with radicals, in other words, and was providing nearly as much brainpower to Labour as it had to the Liberals. How surprising was this development? The answer lies in the peculiar meaning of socialism for British intellectuals like these, and of a break to Labour among those of liberal bent hoping to achieve it after the debacles of 1931. Douglas Jay may have written *The Socialist Case* in 1937 while at the *Economist,* but chose that title to 'emphasize the extent to which Marx was a revisionist, whose dogmatism and stridency were not shared by earlier socialists such as Robert Owen'.[110]

Not only did Jay praise the social utility of the entrepreneur; his actual proposals for achieving equality – nationalizations limited to mines and utilities, the taxation of inherited incomes – would not have been out of place in a Liberal Party manifesto from 1906. Nicholas Davenport fussed about sacrificing his beliefs at the 'gates of Mammon', but during the 1926 General Strike saw no problem joining other stockbrokers in unloading docks, running buses and offering to chauffeur the police. 'My personal sympathies were with the miners who were having a raw deal, but as a responsible Keynesian and financial writer I could not support revolutionary action which might upset the economy and throw up a huge deficit on the balance of payments.'[111] (Layton took a similar line: having negotiated with the Miners Federation general secretary A. J. Cook to avoid a strike, he condemned it as 'unconstitutional'.)[112] Davenport's entry point to socialism was ethical and religious, like that of many other recruits to Labour: his father was a pious churchman who gave up a brewing business to preach to the downtrodden of Leicestershire. Graham Hutton, meanwhile, emerged from the London School of Economics in the late 1920s as an early market fundamentalist without renouncing the socialism of his teenage years – a stance he elaborated in *Burden of Plenty* in 1935. (In 1953, he and Geoffrey Crowther published *We Too Can Prosper*, a salute to US-style capitalism as an example to laggardly Britain, after which Hutton became involved with the neoliberal Institute for Economic Affairs.)[113]

On the rare occasions that Keynes came in for censure from these disciples in the 1930s, it was not on theoretical grounds, but for his decided chilliness towards the lower classes and their anointed party, which had not changed much since the Liberal Summer School in 1925. 'Above all, I do not believe that the intellectual elements in the Labour Party will ever exercise adequate control', Keynes had said, declaring his allegiance to the educated bourgeoisie. 'Too much will always be decided by those who do not know *at all* what they are talking about.'[114] By the 1930s, figures like Douglas Jay probably accepted Keynes's argument that governments could manage total effective demand so as to blunt the edges of the economic cycle, but they flinched from such overt displays of hauteur, especially given the Liberals' electoral decline. *Daily Herald* editor Francis Williams invited Jay to a meeting with Keynes in 1937, hoping to convince the economist to compromise with Labour and trade union leaders, to get them to adopt the *General Theory*'s main lessons. 'I never appreciated until today', said Jay afterwards, 'how much Keynes thinks like a rich man.' 'Not, of course, in his economic thinking', Williams commented, 'but in his attitude to the uneducated working classes among whom he was prepared to go slumming if need be but to whom he found it virtually impossible to make any concession of understanding.'[115]

## XYZ, or Making Labour Respectable

It was the socialism of stockbrokers that was making headway at the *Economist*, whose radical recruits aimed to supply Labour with men who *did* know what they were talking about. The Labour leadership was just as keen, and in 1932 a group of journalists and bankers formed the XYZ club to provide it with informal advice. Vaughan Berry, a bill-broker for the Union Discount Company, was looking for a place where, according to Nicholas Davenport, 'City men could meet the Labour leaders and instruct them in the mysteries of City finance so they would not make a hash of it when they came to power'.[116] The XYZ club held dinners above the Lamb, a pub on Mitre Street, and included the journalists Francis Williams, Davenport, Jay and the *Guardian* City Editor Cecil Sprigge; assorted bankers, brokers and company directors (several of whom were also MPs or local councillors); and the economists Hugh Quigley and Evan Durbin. Labour politicians played a prominent role from the start, and many went on to become senior members of the post-1945 government: Hugh Gaitskell was secretary, while Hugh Dalton, Clement Attlee, F. W. Pethick-Lawrence, Stafford Cripps and Herbert Morrison all attended regularly. A measure of the club's success was its change of address in 1945, when it moved to the House of Commons, and the impact of its ideas on the post-war Labour governments. Proposals to nationalize the Bank of

England and set up a National Investment Board and Industrial Finance Corporation were eventually implemented under Attlee and later Harold Wilson.

Memoirs left behind by the XYZ club's journalist participants are strikingly consistent. Nicholas Davenport called all the Labour politicians he met, except Sir Stafford Cripps, 'sublimely ignorant of the City and suspicious of its institutions, especially the Stock Exchange which they regarded as a casino'.[117] Douglas Jay saw XYZ as 'an effort to re-educate the Labour Party out of its 1931 failures'. Both Vaughan Berry and Francis Williams were convinced by 'the events of 1931' of the need for a new approach: Labour, though 'badly winded by the results of the 1931 General Election' and 'woefully short on expert knowledge', was 'passionately anxious to find a respectable alternative both to the economics of scarcity practiced by the National Government and Marxism'.[118] The embrace seemed mutually beneficial. Labour, seen as badly mishandling the crisis years of 1929–31, would burnish its image for economic competence, while the City gained assurances that any reforms it introduced would integrate finance into a mixed economy without endangering its largely private character. MacDonald and Snowden had shown incredible zeal on behalf of liberal economic principles. The XYZ club had no time for the defensive ignorance they had shown, pushing Labour to self-flagellating extremes in order to satisfy markets in 1931. They were at ease with Keynesianism.

The reason why this new politics did not translate into a clear shift in editorial line at the *Economist* was due to its editor, who systematically removed anything from it that might be controversial to the City, in part because of his dual role at the *News Chronicle*. 'Slow, academic and indecisive', recalled Nicholas Davenport – indecisive in every way, so that once on a trip to Strasbourg, Layton stood paralyzed in a hotel lobby, unable to choose between a room with a lavatory or one in the foyer, until Davenport decided for him.[119] His silences could last for minutes: Geoffrey Crowther claimed to take editorial decisions over the phone based on subtle variations in them. If Layton felt a leader was too emphatic, late on Thursday, 'he used to simply add the words at the end, "Time alone will show"'.[120]

In its caution, the *Economist* stood in contrast to the mass circulation daily, the *News Chronicle,* which, after Layton put Vallance in charge of it in 1933, began to promote a weak version of the Popular Front and attacked Oswald Mosley's Union of British Fascists, offering to join forces with Labour's *Daily Herald* on 'an advanced progressive policy' in 1934. Lloyd George agreed to invest in the project, deriding the Liberals at dinner with Layton as a 'complete washout', who 'ran away at the last election, surrendering everything, and leaving all the bag and baggage behind'.[121] The *News Chronicle* campaigned for the Peace Ballot in 1935 to rouse popular support for collective security and the League of Nations; from 1936 it gave space to William Forest and Arthur Koestler, who filed reports in favour of the republican side in the Spanish Civil War. Yet even this guarded form of progressive politics led to fallout. Vallance, who wanted a genuine popular front to comprise the entire left, communists included, was fired in 1935 after drunkenly cheering on the latest drubbing of the Samuelite Liberals (orthodox free traders, whose classical views allowed for little more than public works to combat the Depression) at an election eve party.[122] For the *Daily News* trustees, this was too much. Clive Pearson, the second son of Viscount Cowdray, who ran S. Pearson's global engineering and energy businesses, asked Layton for a statement of the line on Labour. 'Sympathy and support in matters where they are in agreement with Liberal ideas', but no backing for 'the party as it at present exists.'[123] By 1936, Layton was instructing the new editor, Gerald Barry, to avoid the phrase 'popular front' as too leftwing, in favour of 'Peace Alliance' – the sort of hedging that led the *Daily Worker* to mock a 'refained front … communists keep out', even as the *Daily Express* poked fun at Layton as a 'knitted woollen statue coming unravelled'.[124]

But it was the effect these scuffles had on Layton's position at the *Economist* that rankled him, as another Beaverbrook paper, the *Evening Standard,* pointed out at the same time:

> If Sir Walter Layton has taken the decision that the *News Chronicle* shall turn Socialist, then his own position becomes extremely interesting, for he is also editor of the *Economist*. The *Economist* is owned half by Financial Newspaper Proprietors Limited, and

half by leading financiers, including Sir Henry Strakosch, and it is
believed, Rothschild and Cowdray interests. There can be, therefore, no prospect of the *Economist* turning Socialist, so Sir Walter
Layton will have to ride two horses. It is a feat to which he is
accustomed.[125]

Fleet Street rivals were not the only ones who took note.
Strakosch was concerned enough about this moonlighting to ask
Vallance – a baffling idea: was he ignorant of Vallance's outlook? –
to take over from Layton in November 1932, on the grounds that
the *Economist* risked becoming a mouthpiece for a left Liberal
Party, like the *News Chronicle*. Vallance declined, in a reply he
copied to Layton, arguing the *Economist* benefited from the latter's public engagements, on which he acted as a kind of elite
salesman for it: no longer 'a staid and colourless City weekly', it
was 'a very definite organ of opinion associated throughout the
world with the name of an editor who is not so much a journalist
as an international public man'. Strakosch's fears were unfounded,
Vallance added, citing the diminished and divided Liberal parliamentary party. '*The Economist* is known as a "liberal" journal
and "Liberalism" is now so indeterminate, unattached a thing
that – to say nothing of the fact that Layton and I are both very
jealous of the traditions of the *Economist* – I can see little danger
of the *News Chronicle* being ever regarded as a party organ.'[126]
It is not clear here or later on, when Strakosch renewed his calls
for Layton to quit, the precise nature of his objections; Strakosch
certainly drifted to the Tories after 1931, becoming such a close
confidant of Churchill that when the future prime minister lost
a fortune on Wall Street in 1938, Strakosch bailed him out to
the tune of £18,000 – but on those grounds his preference for
Vallance, who was well to the left of Layton, is hard to explain.[127]

### Roosevelt, Stalin, Mussolini

In the 1930s, the great challenge for the *Economist*'s brand of
liberalism came less from political realignments at home, however
– where, as Vallance argued, the liberal creed could no longer

be confused with the party – than from abroad. Here, experiments, alternatives, and outright threats emerged, to which the *Economist* paid serious and sustained attention: the New Deal in America, the Five-Year plans in Soviet Russia, and the fascist programs in Italy and Germany. Differing in his assessments, Layton established a direct dialogue with each – in particular Rome and Berlin, where Mussolini and Hitler looked to the *Economist* as a conduit to the City, on which their own interwar economic and foreign policy aims to a great extent depended.

In 1936, the *Economist* published the most comprehensive survey of the New Deal to appear in Britain, framed as a sympathetic comparative assessment of efforts to combat the Depression.[128] On the eve of Roosevelt's re-election, 'it may be of assistance, especially to observers who have watched the New Deal from afar, to summarise what has been done and to point to the morals which appear to emerge from the record'. The morals it drew revealed as much about 'the vast experiment of the last three and a half years' in the US as it did about the paper under Layton. Cautious – claiming, for once, 'no absolute authority' – it was also ahead of the president, urging him on to systematic reforms, in the voice of the younger City radicals. Thus far his was a 'very moderate Liberalism', and 'if the criterion be Utopian, the achievements of the New Deal appear to be small'.[129] Of public works, there had been too little: average annual expenditure on public construction was still only 60 per cent of its pre-Depression level; in housing, a bailout had prevented perhaps a million home-owners from being evicted, but done nothing for slum-dwellers, and 'the slums of America are among the worst in the world', reaching 'their nadir in the coloured quarters'; industrial activity was anaemic, partly because the National Industrial Recovery Act had been a chaos of 'divergent economic and social theories' – taking positive steps to empower trade unions, for example, while also encouraging industrial cartels that raised prices and dampened demand.

Too timid in these areas, the New Deal had gone too far in others. After doing a masterful job to restore depositors' trust in banks on taking office, Roosevelt had pursued 'penal legislation' that enforced a 'complete divorce between banking functions and any form of security trading', while failing to provide any legal framework for a system of national branch banking, out of 'prejudice against bankers, especially big bankers'.[130] Nor could the *Economist* stomach Roosevelt's decision in 1933 to abandon the gold standard, which was ethically 'a dangerous precedent and an incitement to the insanity of competitive depreciation'. Nowhere was the paper's mixture of bold calls for experimentation and reluctance to depart from pre-war norms more striking, in this context, than in its treatment of Keynes, who went completely unmentioned. And yet, buried in the survey, the *Economist* had adopted most of his vocabulary, albeit safely, inside quotation marks: what recovery had occurred was due not 'to the theory of credit creation and cheap money' but to a 'rival theory' – that of 'deficit financing' which had expanded the 'stream of purchasing power' and 'primed the pump', citing research that 'the multiplier' had been two.

Layton had already steered the *Economist* towards a more thoughtful engagement with the Soviet Union around the time of Stalin's consolidation of power in Moscow, which brought with it the first Five-Year Plan in 1928. The paper was now less exclusively concerned with the repayment of bondholders and more curious about planning, especially as the economic malaise in the West deepened after the crash of 1929.[131] Layton had published a special report on Russia in 1927, praised by Ivan Maisky, the future Soviet ambassador to the Court of St James, who helped him put it together, 'as objective material as possible … an act of civic courage and political far-sightedness'.[132] In 1930 the paper carried 'An Impression of Russia', issued as a pamphlet, in which the country was said to be in the midst of a 'remarkable experiment', a nearly unprecedented drive to industrialize rapidly without substantial infusions of foreign capital; yet it held opportunities for investment so vast it could not be ignored, whatever the limits or risks involved.[133] 'Human nature being what it is, we have still to discover whether an attempt to create a completely new order of society based on a curious blend of Americanised hustle, idealistic propaganda and methods reminiscent of those of the tyrants of Syracuse, can be crowned with ultimate success.' That would hinge on the agricultural effects of the 'daring and fateful moving of the wheat belt up to the confines of Asia', collective farming, and village communism.[134]

Layton scribbled speaking notes on the pamphlet version of this report at the 'Society of Cultural Relations Between the Peoples of the British Commonwealth and the USSR' in 1931; asked to keep his remarks apolitical, he introduced Mr Gourevitch, a member of the Supreme Economic Council, whose talk was entitled 'The Third Year of the Five Year Plan'.[135] Reports continued to stream into the *Economist* during the decade. One from Kharkov in 1933 observed a 'cruel drain on energies and resources' and 'acute shortage of nearly all consumer goods', but also progress: 'new offices, new shops, new schools, new institutes, new hospitals, new crèches, new workers flats ... a new theatre to rival Moscow's.' Most important, there were new factories like the massive Kharkov Tractor Works. 'The Soviet boast that no loyal Soviet citizen need go idle is not an empty one, and it is true that the unemployment problem as we know it is non-existent in Russia.'[136] Layton's relationship with Maisky – who spent much of his time as Soviet ambassador to Britain cultivating City bankers and journalists – was such that by 1938 Layton could act as Maisky's go-between with the prime minister Neville Chamberlain.[137]

Nor were the Soviets the only wayward power to court the good opinion of the City through the *Economist* editor. In Italy, where Mussolini's march on Rome culminated in his appointment as prime minister in October 1922, the *Economist* returned the compliment, praising Il Duce – who took his lead from London in pledging to restore 'thrift, labour, discipline' to an economy racked by inflation and labour revolts – as 'passionate and full of vigour'. Here, the liberal economist and senator Luigi Einaudi – the *Economist*'s Italian correspondent from 1908 until 1946, shortly before he became Italy's president – justified the delegation of 'full powers' to the Fascists in 1922 as necessary to avoid 'Muscovite communism and barbarism', and to implement a package of budget cuts, indirect tax raises, public sector layoffs and privatizations.[138] Cheers greeted 'the renunciation by Parliament of all its powers', Einaudi wrote, for 'Italians were sick of talkers and of weak executives' and 'would accept a Czar for the sake of getting out of chaos'.[139] Like the shift to austerity in

Britain in 1921, such measures paved the way for a return to gold for Italy in 1927, after the 'battle of the lira' the year before and a secret conclave of central bankers in London had set convertibility at 92.46 lira to the pound.[140] From his base in Turin, Einaudi supplied the paper with a positive account of economic progress under Mussolini at least until 1937 – criticizing the regime almost exclusively for departing from economic orthodoxy during the Depression, when Mussolini raised tariffs, created new state monopolies, and took direct control of the foreign exchanges.[141] In February 1932, Layton met Mussolini, who appeared to be well aware of the importance of the *Economist* in shaping opinion in London and New York:

> On reflection, however, there is a doubt which of us did the interviewing. Mussolini started the conversation by asking me what I thought of 'the crisis'. I naturally asked to which of the many current crises (the devaluation of the pound, the reparations moratorium, disarmament, the Manchurian deadlock) he referred. So he made his question more specific and asked whether the *Economist* (of which he claimed to have been a regular reader) would support the disarmament plan which Signor Grandi had laid before the Disarmament Conference in Geneva two or three days previously. It was an interesting opening gambit which represented Mussolini himself as Europe's number one peace-loving statesman. The pose was a caricature, though our long talk was both frank and friendly.[142]

### The *Economist* and Hitler

Layton then moved on to Hitler – whose advisors were also eager to present the new chancellor in a good light – meeting him in March 1933, a month after the Reichstag fire, and in the midst of a boycott of Jewish businesses that the *Economist* and *News Chronicle* criticized.[143] Reichsbank president Hjalmar Schacht, reinstalled to reassure both domestic capitalists and foreign creditors about the Nazis' financial competence so that a stimulus to reduce unemployment and to rearm could begin, acted as Layton's translator with the Führer in Berlin.[144]

Short, thickset and clad in a russet-coloured suit, his face had lost the sharpness of outline which is noticeable in his early photographs; but the famous lock of hair over the forehead was in its place … I came away feeling that I had not discovered the source of his power. He rarely looked straight at me but closely followed Schacht who was on his left and doing most of the interpreting. The only sign of the familiar Hitler was that from time to time he raised his voice – and it was a fine resonant voice – as though addressing a public meeting for he answered most of my questions with little more than the ordinary phrases he had been using for years … I asked him questions under three heads: 1) economic questions and the Nazi idea of autarchy, 2) the boycott and internal repression, 3) international affairs. On the first he refused to be drawn: I was given to understand that I might refer to Schacht, though whether Schacht interpolated or whether Hitler actually said it, I do not know.

On the boycott Hitler, in effect, politely warned me off with the statement that it was an internal matter for Germany. He claimed – with justice – that the Nazi forces were well under control. This conclusion was prefaced by a short lecture on the history of the Nazi movement, and the struggle between two Germanys, one which had knuckled under the peace treaties, the other determined to uphold her pride. But the Nazi fight was not merely a German fight, it was also a war against communism. It was therefore a battle for other countries, England included. If we understood the true meaning of the communist movement we would be whole-heartedly supporting him.[145]

Schacht flattered Layton, assuring him the interview had 'gone better than any of the others', and 'Hitler always had difficulty in finding common ground with people familiar with international affairs and took refuge in his speeches.' But did Hitler understand finance, Layton asked? 'Yes, certainly. He has at least one idea and a very good one. It is to leave it to Schacht.' When Schacht heard that Layton had repeated this conversation to others during his tour of Germany that year – among them Goebbels, ex-chancellor Brüning, and Generals von Schleicher and von Hammerstein – he wrote asking him to kindly stop. 'My answer was and certainly meant that he would do, what I would do. That is to say, that he has as sound ideas about finance as I pretend to have.'[146]

But if Layton was disturbed by what he saw in Germany, he muted criticism of it in the *Economist,* in part because London had much to lose from a showdown harming economic links between it and Berlin. Not only did German trade depend on the City for short-term finance, Britain was also Germany's main export market and a source of hard currency, while the British Empire supplied Germany with vital raw materials.[147] An *Economist* leader based on Layton's visit predicted the German Nationalists' coalition with the Nazis would prove 'one of the great miscalculations of history', but also hoped that a shaky current account would force Hitler to compromise with his European neighbours, as had happened with Mussolini. When Schacht put an end to debt payments that June, however, the paper shrugged this off as inevitable, while it all but cheered the Anglo-German Payments Union sealed the next year.[148]

It was a Layton family vacation to Cornwall in late August that allowed Douglas Jay to slip in one of the *Economist*'s few open attacks on the regime – a review of *The Brown Book of the Hitler Terror,* which claimed that Nazis had started the Reichstag blaze to solidify their grip on power and purge their Communist opponents. With only Graham Hutton and Geoffrey Crowther in the office, the unfiltered leader ran, accusing the Third Reich of an 'orgy of barbarism and brutality', whose concentration camps, anti-Semitic killings and book burnings were 'the direct consequence of incitement by Nazi leaders' and 'bound to produce a shock of revulsion and horror throughout the civilized world'.[149] An indignant letter immediately arrived from the German finance minister, Count Schwerin von Krosigk. 'As you know, for many years I have had the highest admiration for you and your journal', he wrote, addressing Layton. 'It is therefore the more to be regretted that you have now thought fit to publish a one-sided judgment of the situation in Germany.' Layton replied that 'the attitude of the *Economist* in commenting on matters affecting Germany such as reparations, the war guilt question and disarmament, during the ten years of my editorship is, I hope, a sufficient guarantee that I would not willingly misinterpret the German situation.' Instead of an apology, though, Layton promised 'a full and unbiased report of the case for the prosecution at the forthcoming Leipzig trial', offering to attend it in person, and asking Jay for a weekly column on its progress when this was refused.[150]

It was not so much the domestic terror unleashed by fascists within Italy and Germany, however, as their quest to undo the Versailles settlement by force, outside and in defiance of the League of Nations, that undermined Layton's editorship. In his intervention, Jay had gone so far as to ask 'whether the right to equality of status among the nations' could be claimed by the Third Reich, hinting that force might be justified against a 'government which revenged itself on its own fellow-countrymen'. But in practice his threat only came down to the standard editorial line – not opposed to rearmament, but insisting that to be legitimate it had to be collective, pivoting on Geneva.[151] As the breakdown of the international order gathered pace during the second half of the 1930s, it put this position – on which Layton and the *Economist* had wagered so much – to a devastating series of tests.[152]

Mussolini's threatened invasion of Abyssinia at the start of 1935 was supposed to be an occasion for the League to demonstrate its effectiveness, when Emperor Haile Selassie asked it to arbitrate. Instead, the ensuing crisis erected an epitaph to it. After placing arms embargoes on both sides that left the Ethiopians exposed to a campaign of aerial gassing, the League bent to the Hoare-Laval Pact signed in secret between the foreign minister of Britain and the French premier – a 'polite way', alleged the *Economist* when news of it broke, 'of cloaking' Italy's 'virtual annexation' of the independent African nation. 'Completely at a loss to understand' how the Baldwin-led National Government in Britain, returned five weeks earlier on a pledge to uphold the League Covenant, if necessary by force, could commit such a volte-face, the paper looked to 'public opinion' to overturn it.[153]

Hitler's gamble to remilitarize the Rhineland the following March, on the other hand, was a clear violation of the Locarno pact. 'Yet, morally,' the *Economist* declared, 'to send German troops into the German Rhineland amid the acclamations of a German population is an act which has nothing at all in common with Signor Mussolini's invasion of a foreign country, a member

of the League, and his employment of all the devilries of mechan-
ical warfare against an unoffending and defenceless population.'
The paper asked Hitler to consider temporarily withdrawing
his troops, 'in exchange for an understanding that they shall be
allowed to return again as soon as a new European settlement
has been negotiated on the terms which Herr Hitler himself has
put forward'. [154] Layton and Arnold Toynbee delivered this article's message direct to Britain's prime minister Stanley Baldwin,
alongside much of the soon-to-be notorious Cliveden set with
whom they were weekending in Norfolk, after Toynbee's return
from Berlin to interview Hitler: 'Welcome Hitler's declarations
wholeheartedly ... condemn entry of German troops into forbidden zone ... [but] not to be taken tragically in view of the peace
proposals which accompany it ... Versailles is now a corpse and
should be buried ... Treat entrance to zone as ... demonstration of
recovered status of equality and not as act of aggression.'[155] A few
days earlier on 8 March, Toynbee had written a confidential memorandum to the prime minister and the foreign secretary, Anthony
Eden, arguing that Hitler desired the return of Germany's colonies, but in Europe only 'reuniting the whole German nation, but
not including anyone else'.[156] Layton agreed: a colonial revision in
favour of Nazi Germany, extending the League's mandate system
to it, could secure peace in Europe. Both Layton and Toynbee
pressed in the *Economist* for 'imperial economic disarmament',
removing the grievances of 'have-not' powers by revising the
Ottawa accords to allow for 'intermediate tariffs' between the
British Empire and foreign blocs.[157]

    With British assent, the Rhineland matter was buried in a
committee of the League, emboldening Hitler and Mussolini to
strike again – in Spain – where the men and materiel they supplied to the Fascist rebels tipped the scales in the civil war which
broke out that July. The *Economist* heaped scorn on Britain's
response: its policy of 'nonintervention' recalled Abyssinia, but
was worse, in that a vital imperial interest was at stake – control
of the Mediterranean.[158] And yet the paper's position was hardly
more forceful. Instead of lifting a trade embargo that, it admitted,
only hurt the republican side, it proposed that the embargo be
better-enforced. Tougher talk came in 1937 after the bombing of

Guernica, when it moved that if Germany persisted in such viola-
tions, 'we let Berlin know at once that we shall give our consent
to any countervailing action the French may choose to take'.[159]
Layton sounded bolder on the podium than in print, enjoining, at
the 1936 Liberal Summer School, 'a popular front for Britain', but
again with very striking limitations on it. He recommended that
there be no rearmament outside the League, and that Britain 'constantly ... make it clear to Germany we are anxious and willing'
to include it in a 'system of collective security' – by, inter alia,
ceding a share of colonies to it, and that 'indeed, we should expect
to see, an extension of German influence in Central Europe'.[160]

Hitler's *Anschluss* of Austria, which followed in March 1938,
brought a more sombre vision of a German-dominated *Mittel-
europa* – 'vast totalitarian Empire', anti-communist, anti-Semitic,
set to crush France and encircle Britain, like 'one gigantic rock
of Gibraltar' – yet, at the same time, the feeble hope that united
action might still 'compel Herr Hitler to give Czechoslovakia not
intolerable terms'.[161] The capitulation of France and Britain six
months later at Munich was thus foretold. If abandoning the
Czechs to their fate over the Sudetenland was a bitter pill, the
*Economist* swallowed it while uttering a 'prayer of thanksgiv-
ing' for being spared the 'hell of totalitarian war' on the night the
Munich Agreement was signed.[162]

Layton resigned as editor the same day, so it was Crowther,
chosen as his replacement, who wrote this prayer to peace.
Strakosch was behind the ouster, having renewed his calls for
Layton to quit that May – a fact Layton's biographer attributes
to the City, on edge at his newly confrontational tone towards
the Fascist powers. In fact, the opposite seems more probable:
the failure of appeasement, as judged by Strakosch with Bracken
as his boardroom ally, likely prompted the move. The confusion
stems in part from Strakosch himself, who kept his indictment of
Layton vague. 'An undue amount of space has been devoted to
foreign politics', he wrote in an internal memorandum, 'and the
tendency has been to present these subjects in a manner which
savours far too much of party politics.'[163] The timing of his call so
soon after *Anschluss* – and a record of passing secret intelligence
on Hitler's rearmament program to Churchill, from his business

contacts in Germany – suggests that Strakosch was in fact less cautious than Layton about confronting the Third Reich.[164]

The staff of the *Economist* and *News Chronicle* certainly had grounds for thinking so. Frustration at Layton's prevarications had reached a boiling point by 1938. Douglas Jay was already at his wits' end when he left the *Economist* in 1934. '"Will Hitler desist from further aggression?" we would ask. "Time alone will show", added Layton, altering the entire tone of the article.'[165] At the *News Chronicle*, Layton could not make up his mind what to publish as edition after edition went to press on the night of Munich, with editor Gerald Berry later complaining bitterly of a watered-down leader, ready by 3:30 a.m. Vernon Bartlett, the correspondent whose article Layton diluted, was more direct. After putting the paper to bed in London, Layton called him at his hotel in Prague to chat. 'Fuck you', Bartlett shouted into the receiver and hung up.[166] In his valedictory, Layton cited the 'deterioration of political relationships which has reduced the League of Nations to impotence', along with the failure to re-establish trade on a 'rational basis', to explain and bookend his years as editor. Starting out with 'high hopes of world appeasement inspired by a great practical measure of disarmament' at Washington in 1922, these had ended a 'hair's breadth' from world war in 1938.[167]

Layton struck a more defiant note in his internal response to Strakosch – a seventeen-page letter that broke down for the board of trustees the actual distribution of articles by theme, with 1935 as baseline: 58 per cent economic, 42 political; of which the majority were domestic, not foreign. If he missed the real accusations being levelled against him, however, Layton showed the firmer grasp of what set the *Economist* apart as a journal of opinion – that it provided political views to the business world, and had the ear of politicians for the mechanics of business. If foreign politics were now more visible in the paper, he claimed, that was because business was 'dominated by political events' and business readers looked to the *Economist* to understand their interrelationship. The proof? Circulation had gone from 6,000 in 1931 to over 10,000, half of this abroad, with strong growth in Europe, the Empire and America. The *Economist* was no longer limited to the role of 'spare chancellor' in Britain alone; its sights were trained on the horizon. 'Next to the *Times* it is more widely quoted by important American papers (e.g. *New York Times, Chicago Tribune*), than any English Newspaper'. More: 'A thousand words of summary are cabled every week by the American Embassy to the State Department and its readers include Roosevelt, Mussolini, Azaña and Brüning (when Chancellor).'[168]

# II

---

## TRANSLATIO IMPERII

# 6

## Extreme Centre

In 1914, the *Economist* had recoiled from war as a crime against economic sense, fatal to the flow of trade and credit that was both the greatest monument to British power and its one true security. Under Geoffrey Crowther, the paper saw the onset of war in 1939 in starkly different terms: less a sin against liberalism than a chance to revive liberalism as an instrument of policy after two frustrating decades of inaction and decline, based on a position he called the 'extreme centre'.[1] Whereas Francis Hirst had plunged the *Economist* into chaos when he broke with the Liberal government in August 1914, this time its editors acted from the start as advisors and appointees to government, crafting economic battle plans and post-war blueprints, whose shift leftward reflected the altered context of the new conflict. Abroad, Britain had no major allies after France's fall in June 1940; at home, a coalition drew Labour and Liberal remnants into a Conservative regime, and when international isolation lifted, relief took the shape of alliances with Soviet Russia, followed by Roosevelt's New Deal America. The need to sustain popular support under these circumstances was correspondingly greater, resulting in the Beveridge Report – a cradle-to-grave welfare scheme, whose publication to widespread acclaim in 1942 underscored the contrast. It would take more than vague promises of 'a land fit for heroes' to see Britain through the Second World War.

If two world wars made very different first impressions on the *Economist,* its proposals on how to pay for each were nevertheless an important bridge between them. Arguments Hartley

Withers had advanced in the paper from 1916 – vigorous controls to curb inflation, including high taxes on incomes, profits and luxuries to reduce borrowing, as well as strict supervision of production, consumption and trade – were readily and more rapidly implemented. Taxes covered 54 per cent of spending in 1940–45, as opposed to 32 per cent in 1914–18, with the price level only 30 per cent higher at its end as compared to doubling in the earlier period.[2] The impression of lessons learnt had a basis in fact. Whitehall saw the return of the most talented administrators of the earlier war, chief among them Liberals removed from the frontlines of power after it, whose plans for collective security and freer trade had often gone little further in the previous decade than the pages of Walter Layton's *Economist*. That changed once Neville Chamberlain made way for Winston Churchill as premier in the crisis of May 1940. Arthur Salter, William Beveridge, Layton and Keynes – between them responsible for shipping, food, munitions, employment and external finance during the First World War, and now largely in academic roles – along with the slightly younger economist Hubert Henderson, all went back to work; indeed, as self-styled 'ancient warlords', in September 1939 they were already exhorting the government to proceed with decisive measures of economic mobilization.[3]

Nor was this influx limited to the long in tooth. Douglas Jay became an assistant secretary under his old editor Layton at the Ministry of Supply, with many other current and former editors, including Geoffrey Crowther himself. The *Economist* thus came to function as both an arm of the wartime state, and an open line of communication between it and the City of London.[4] Nowhere was this dual role more in evidence than in the founding documents of the future welfare state. Not only did Crowther have a hand in the Beveridge Report, as well as its sequel *Full Employment and a Free Society* in 1944, he shaped the reception to them in financial circles, revealing the aims and strict limits baked into the post-war consensus as the *Economist* envisioned it.

## Geoffrey Crowther Going Up

Crowther sought to transform the *Economist,* often with singular ruthlessness, so that neither it nor its editor would be easy to ignore in the debates over economic planning that were sure to follow the Second World War. His route to the editor's chair was familiar: born in 1907 to a middle-class family in Yorkshire, where his father taught agricultural chemistry at the University of Leeds, he was a gifted student, obtaining a scholarship in modern languages to Clare College, Cambridge. In addition to the obligatory stint as president of the Union, he switched to studying economics, for which he gained a double first in 1928; less typically, he also won a Commonwealth Fellowship to Columbia and Yale, where he married law student Margaret Worth, and got to sample work on Wall Street. Keynes, Crowther's tutor at Cambridge, intervened repeatedly on his behalf after he returned home in 1932 – tipping him for posts as banking advisor to Ireland, and to Layton at the *Economist,* doing so again six years later when Brendan Bracken asked for Keynes's advice on a successor there.[5]

The faith Keynes and Layton placed in Crowther was amply justified over a career of three-odd decades as editor, managing director and chairman. Circulation rocketed, rising from 10,000 in 1938 to 55,000 in 1956. Over that span, the paper itself expanded, with a bevy of talented new journalists from across the political spectrum, among them many women – including Margaret Cruikshank, the editor of the new American Survey, inaugurated in January 1941. The page count roughly doubled, and two redesigns made it more inviting to readers and advertisers. The irreverent managing director Brendan Bracken urged the first of these in 1945: 'Don't you think that the lettering of the title of the *Economist* is more appropriate to an undertaker's journal than your lively paper?' 'I quite agree', replied Crowther. 'I am already talking to a typographer. Of course what we really need is a more attractive name, but I suppose nothing can be done about that after 101 years.'[6] Finally, as director, Crowther pushed to build a new headquarters, embodying the post-war synthesis he tried to effect intellectually: a bold modern design by avant-garde

'Team 10' architects Peter and Alison Smithson, made up of three Brutalist towers clad in Portsmouth stone – located in the London neighbourhood of St. James, a bolt-hole of the British gentlemanly elite, with its clubs, haberdashers, wine merchants, rifle stores, art dealers, and a royal palace. Alison Smithson found her clients 'very pretentious, as though they were the intellectual cream', but her design won their praise; Crowther compared the architects to Christopher Wren. As an investment, it returned handsomely. Rents tripled on the site after its completion in 1964, to the point where the *Economist* could sell it in 2016 to buy the half of the paper from Pearson that its shareholders did not already own.[7]

What was unusual about Crowther was his personality – sly, sarcastic, pushy – which stands out strongly from that of his shy and diffident predecessor. In photos, he is round with alert beady eyes and a cowlick-wisp of hair. Roland Bird, hired as stock-exchange assistant the same year as Crowther, described his 'stocky build, with small hands and dominating head'.[8] For Hugh Dalton, Labour's Chancellor of the Exchequer from 1945–47, with whom he rowed ferociously, he was 'a fat little pig'. Crowther may have been generous to editors but could also hector them, as he did at a dinner party where he enjoined one guest to point out and correct their notable flaws: Roland Bird, deputy business editor, 'intensely reliable, steady and sound' but 'one of those to whom your words on lucidity should be addressed'; Elizabeth Layton, book reviewer, 'clear and simple but rather slipshod and full of clichés'; Margaret Stewart, trade union correspondent, 'good reporter but has difficulty in being anything else'; Barbara Ward, foreign affairs, 'quite brilliant but a certain tendency to go overboard in support of her latest idea.'[9] Nor was he shy about reminding Layton, now chairman of the *Economist*, about the services he was rendering it. In 1944 Crowther asked for a raise. 'I do not aspire to more than reasonable bourgeois comfort. If I could educate my children, have a simple place in the country, do a certain amount of travel, buy the books I want and save something for my old age, I should be quite content.' But, he quickly added, 'with twentieth century taxation, this simple catalogue requires a great deal of money.' He promised not to turn into a 'Fleet Street *prima donna*' or to quit to become a CEO, at least not until he raised annual turnover to £100,000.[10] This done, he proceeded to do both – making the incredible demand that the new *Economist* offices be a tower, so that its top floor could serve as his penthouse; and ceaselessly accepting corporate jobs and directorships, distinguished mainly by the boardroom battles and botched mergers these precipitated.[11]

## Crowther and a Liberal Five-Year Plan

The *Economist* was to remain Crowther's cardinal achievement: to understand the outsize role it played under him during and after the war, however, requires a sense of his positions from the pre-war decade, when in response to the political impasse that blocked the way for progressive liberals after the financial crisis of 1931, he developed the idea of the extreme centre.

Crowther had been a lead author on the exemplary manifesto of 'middle opinion' in that period, *The Next Five Years* – an 'essay in political agreement', modelled on the Liberal Yellow Book of 1929, but appearing in a context of party fragmentation that by 1935 required a broader tent. To unite Labour, Liberals and Conservatives fed up with or left out of the National Government, it proposed planning (applying the term loosely to appeal to each political group): fiscal stimulus to even out the trade cycle, industrial boards to stoke business consolidation and raise profitability, regulation of natural monopolies in energy and transport as public utilities, and expansion of New Liberal social reforms such as unemployment benefit, old-age pensions and family means testing.[12] Crowther wrote the chapter on banking – with fellow Liberals Layton and Salter, and direction from Tory MP Harold Macmillan – that classed it too as a 'public concern'; defending the private character of the Bank of England and the joint stock banks, Crowther asked for greater transparency from them, in a tacit admission that lack of oversight had led to neglect of domestic for foreign investment.[13]

The *Next Five Years* had little impact on the 1935 election, however, in part because its authors had more parti pris than they cared to admit. Since almost all had backed the austerity budget

that gave birth to the 1931 coalition government, their contention that economic planning could easily be implemented by it
provoked hostile reactions from the bulk of the Labour Party
that had refused to follow Ramsay MacDonald, as well as the
Conservative-dominated government he fronted, for seeming
to side with its most virulently effective critic – still, at this late
date, Lloyd George, with his call for a New Deal and an electoral
Council of Action.[14]

Crowther learned from this failure, sharpening the edges of the
*Next Five Years* into something quite distinct from the middle
opinion it represented, both in the *Economist* and in popular
works under his name: 1936's *Ways and Means: A Study of
the Economic Structure of Great Britain Today,* adapted from
twelve BBC radio talks, and *Economics for Democrats* in 1939.
In outline the views they espoused were vintage New Liberal: a
folksy defence of the City and of the export strategies linked to
foreign investment ('it all sounds very learned, but it is really just
the same as schoolboys swapping penknives for conkers'), with
claims that both collectivist and capitalist aspirations could be
attained via steeper inheritance and income taxes.[15] But to these
Crowther added two notable departures: a Keynesian argument
that savings and investment could fall out of step, and that the
state had more direct means than the bank rate to bring them into
line, whether as public works or itself 'lending and borrowing for
capital purposes'; and secondly, a sense that, for now, depression
in the export industries required a low uniform tariff, alongside
development of a capital market for domestic investment of the
same high quality as for abroad.[16]

On the eve of his editorship, then, Crowther had found his way
to the 'extreme centre', imparting it to the *Economist* as three
enduring characteristics. The first was breezy pragmatism on economic matters: the debate over free trade versus protection was
now 'a religious quarrel', with 'the only politically realistic question at this hour' being 'what sort of protective tariff a nation like
Great Britain should have'.[17] The second was smug confidence,
distilled in his bons mots, for instance that the first rule of effective journalism was to 'simplify, then exaggerate'. But this had a
deeper meaning in the politics of the age, which convinced him

that both the Conservatives and Labour were sinners against economic good sense. The former peddled a 'new feudalism' – tariffs abroad plus monopolies at home – which in cases like the British Iron and Steel Federation had combined to raise prices, restrict output and enrich owners ('Under Conservative rule, the British community is more planned against than planning'); the latter confused profits with large incomes, wanting to tax both to death, when it ought to aim at raising profitability so that wages could rise in line with productivity.[18] Liberalism soared above these partisan creeds, surveying a political landscape in which the centre *could* be extreme. If a vain search for a coalition to carry out its program was an obvious weakness, it was also fundamental to its appeal, with Crowther articulating lofty goals that the hidebound parties could not – 'efficiency, adaptability, equity', or a cure for 'poverty, inequality, irregularity'.[19] Finally, there was Atlanticism. Crowther showed a positive enthusiasm for and understanding of America unlike any previous editor, convinced from his student days that the City had as much to learn from Wall Street as British industry from Ford.[20]

## The *Economist* at War

The tocsin of war was the emergency the middle way had waited for, and helps explain why some of the boldest, most prescriptive economic battle plans came from liberals. When Keynes issued *How to Pay for the War* in February of 1940, the *Economist* reviewed it positively, but for once stressed his timidity. A tax on workers (compulsory savings rebranded as deferred pay) and capital levy (in the future) might curb inflation in a fair and orderly way, but would hardly cover a year of expenditure, which Keynes conservatively budgeted at £2.85 billion. Other expedients were available: extensive rationing, industrial controls, interdiction of luxury goods, asking more of the middle class.[21] In July 1940, Crowther provided his own assessment in *Ways and Means of War*, which despite the fall of France, saw a clear path to victory based on 'more and more of the economic weight of the United States being thrown into the same scale', and the comparative advantage of the British Empire over Germany in 'manpower and material'.[22] Hayek reviewed this work, calling it a 'sane and balanced picture of the relative economic strength of the belligerents', and an uplifting one, for in addition to their developmental lead over the Reich, the British had the weapon of the naval blockade, which set 'limits to the economic efforts Germany can make'.[23]

The defeats that followed over the next two years may have pierced the confidence of these early prognostics. But in the atmosphere of wartime London – the *Economist* edited between air raids and sleepless nights, and in coffee shops after bombs flattened the office near Fleet Street in May 1941 – they also spurred leftwing ambitions. So did the Nazi onslaught on Russia a month later. This drew a great sigh of relief from the *Economist,* which acknowledged the epic resistance of the Red Army along the Eastern Front – going so far as to hire the Marxist historian and recent revolutionary Isaac Deutscher to interpret this enigmatic new ally for it in 1942.[24] A penniless refugee from Poland who had only learnt English after arriving in Britain three years earlier, Deutscher wrote over 650 articles for the paper, most before 1947. In addition to a regular 'Russia at War' column, Deutscher's pieces ranged widely over the Balkans, Greece, Switzerland, France, Finland, Algeria, Libya and Persia; and in 1945, he reported from occupied Germany, where he shared a camp room with the future author of *1984,* George Orwell, sensing in him a tendency to persecution mania.[25] Deutscher's first-hand knowledge of Eastern Europe and Soviet Russia – he was sent to Moscow in 1931 as a delegate of the outlawed Polish Communist Party, before being ejected from it for exhorting (with Trotsky) an active line against Hitler – has never been equalled at the *Economist* (the same is true of the *Times,* where a similar wartime transformation saw his friend E. H. Carr, 'the Red Professor of Printing House Square', promote the idea of a permanent post-war alliance between Britain and the Soviet Union).[26]

Closer to home, the *Economist* could also act as a forum for its resident 'City radical' Nicholas Davenport, whose *Vested Interests or Common Pool?* argued that labour and capital were 'rivals in crime' – the first for inflationary wage demands, the second for a psychological incapacity to raise output – that the state should bypass. Leasing all capital assets, the state could then pay out rent to owners and wages to workers from a common stock.[27] While Davenport's plan invited 'cautious scepticism', the *Economist* agreed to 'socialisation of all persons and all property, wherever the war effort requires'.[28] Meanwhile, the goal of post-war full employment was already being debated in its pages, with Labour economists Joan Robinson and Thomas Balogh writing to criticize the *Economist* in October 1942 for preferring private to public investment, and for seeing Keynesian demand management as an *alternative* to centralized planning and public ownership; without both, they argued, wage inflation and crises of confidence were bound to arise.[29]

The immediate pressure to extend planning within the war economy was always accompanied by longer views – looking forward to a post-war order of greater equality and efficiency, and also back to the past, with the extreme centre acting as the link between them. The Beveridge Report – penned by William Beveridge, the civil servant who helped to pioneer labour exchanges and unemployment insurance under the New Liberals at the Board of Trade before 1914 (only to watch in dismay as these turned into ad hoc schemes of outdoor relief for the mass unemployed of the Depression) – exemplified this duality.[30] The *Economist* had no difficulty endorsing 'one of the most remarkable state documents ever drafted' in December 1942, while arguing at the same time that all it did was 'rationalize' existing structures on the basis of this experience. 'All contingencies of life and livelihood, birth, marriage and death, age, unemployment, accident, illness and disease will be covered by a single, comprehensive system of contribution and benefit under state auspices.' Yet it was simply a tax plan to secure 'minimum levels of income' with a Keynesian aim of 'subsidising consumption' and 'preventing sharp falls in production and employment'.[31] The success of the entire project, which was 'not revolutionary', depended on a return to liberalism at home and abroad: never so loose as to 'lessen incentives to work and advancement', promoting 'full employment and the freest possible trade', and ensuring low and steady inflation, which Beveridge's plan secured by creating 'a greater class of rentiers than ever before' with a 'vested interest in the stability of the currency'.[32]

Crowther did a variety of war work while editor, from analyses of manpower deployment for the Cabinet, to US goodwill tours.[33] No job was more revealing, however, than his role in drafting the follow-up report from Beveridge in 1944, *Full Employment in a Free Society*. 'I am fully in agreement with the line you take, which is closely similar to that taken in the series of articles in *The Economist* a year ago', Crowther remarked in a detailed memorandum to Beveridge, followed up by in-person meetings, on the draft that emerged from the conference on international aspects of post-war employment policy at Nuffield College in September 1943. 'The comments I make below are in the nature of footnotes rather than dissent.'[34]

Yet these footnotes did make clear three important concerns Crowther harboured about a post-war world of welfare and full employment, which carried over from the pre-war decade, and set strict limits to it. First, any major change in social structure must be ruled out. Crowther poured scorn on economist E. F. Schumacher, who had remarked in the draft that full employment might be hard to achieve without tackling the issue of ownership of the means of production. 'No doubt it would be easier to achieve full employment if Control of Employment and the Essential Works Order remained in force in peacetime. No doubt it would also be easier if the whole of industry – or at least the large capital-using industries – were nationalised.' But Conservatives would not consent to the latter, nor Labour to the former. 'I must confess to being considerably irritated by people like Schumacher, who deliberately try to make it more difficult by raising very large general issues of the type best calculated to frighten the British electorate.'[35] Keynesianism must, in the second place, primarily be a strategy of capital investment. Britain required large injections in emulation of its two powerful allies: to close the gap in labour productivity with the American worker, what was needed was 'a long-term Stalinist policy of investment, on which the chief hope for a rapid rise in the standard of living depends'.[36] For Crowther, this excluded any deliberate attempt to restrict savings, and meant that consumption would have to be closely watched, lest stimulus of it lead to 'a shortage, not surfeit, of savings'. The third point is the most striking, for unlike the first two, it seems to have been the common assumption of all participants including Beveridge.[37] The main 'international implications of full employment' for Britain in the post-war world were that the country must work to prevent any repetition of the rising tariffs, currency devaluations and other moves to autarky of the inter-war period. Full employment in one country was impossible. For if others allowed their trade cycles to continue, leading to a crash and mass unemployment, they would again try to export their way out of trouble at the expense of trading partners, precipitating a global race to the bottom. In contemplating one international obstacle, however, the participants in the conference tellingly all but ignored another, arguably more salient one – that of finance capital, the free movement of which had repeatedly imperilled progressive social legislation in Britain, in a pattern that was set to recur: cries of capital flight and lost confidence in protest at the People's Budget in 1909, collapse of the second Labour government amidst a run on the pound in 1931.[38]

The war represented the finest hour for the extreme centre, giving its advocates a voice inside the state, while demonstrating that 'vested interests' still operated there to frustrate its boldest initiatives. It is significant in this respect that Beveridge introduced his plan only after Ernest Bevin, Labour's powerful wartime minister of labour, had banished him to what he hoped was an obscure committee; and that the coalition government sought to bury the sequel to it in 1944 with a waffling White Paper, compared unfavourably to the Beveridge Report by the *Economist*. While the White Paper was indeed a landmark that signalled the state's 'conscious assumption of responsibility and authority' for full employment, it was too ambivalent about the deficit spending this might entail, wrote the *Economist*: 'in economic policy, as in war, it would be nice to combine victory with a balanced budget but a deficit is better than a defeat.'[39] Beveridge himself became a trustee of the *Economist* after the war, exchanging letters with Crowther and his successor Donald Tyerman on everything from how to stop communist infiltration of trade unions and wage inflation to getting copies of the *Economist* into German hands under the occupation. ('As you know one of the most acute shortages in Germany at the moment is of English periodicals,' Beveridge wrote from Berlin in 1946.)[40]

But this ought not to obscure how careful were its wartime dilutions of free trade, in particular as this affected investment. In a book celebrating the *Economist*'s centenary in 1943, Crowther drew a direct line from the first editor James Wilson, whose sunken eyes stared grimly from the front page, to himself. Liberalism still aimed at the greatest freedom for the greatest number. But laissez-faire had in this respect turned out to have certain disadvantages: 'irregularity and inequality of the society it breeds', at a time when larger electorates insisted 'inequality and insecurity' rank 'equally with that abolition of poverty which seemed, a hundred years ago, to stand alone'. This was followed by an immediate qualification, however, for 'if events prove that restrictionism and monopoly are organically inseparable from Government intervention in the economic field, then it will be the duty of the *Economist* to that extent to swing back towards the purest individualism.'[41] Hayek, a devoted reader, gently mocked the idea of such an unbroken continuity with the Victorian era, wondering in a review whether Crowther wasn't himself a little doubtful about it.[42] The *Economist* for its part had only praise for the outspoken emigré at the London School of Economics when his polemic against planning, *The Road to Serfdom*, appeared a few months later. 'The state that is fully planned, that is democratic and that preserves the basic rights of individuals does not exist', it agreed, adding only that returning to pure laissez-faire could prove as oppressive for individuals as a command economy. 'The problem of this century is to find the most fruitful method of combining planning – the right kind and degree of planning – with freedom.'[43]

## The Empire Front: Writing Blank Cheques

Concessions to the working class, embodied in visions of welfare and full employment at home, had their complement abroad in 'the commonwealth at war' – the dominions, crown colonies and other dependencies being promised at one and the same time greater self-government and tighter economic integration, underwritten by capital investment from London.[44] After the fall of France in 1940, the *Economist* shifted focus from European to 'imperial defence, to see how best a world Empire can win a world war – if need be, alone'. Crowther rested much of his economic optimism on the imperial factor, which was not a question of 'summoning the Dominions, or India, or even the colonies to the aid of Britain', for now that 'aggression walks abroad in three continents, the war is their war'. Canadians, Australians, New Zealanders and South Africans had already enlisted in the services, while supplies from their countries were available to Britain wholesale: Canada's nickel, lead, zinc, timber, wheat, dairy and industrial plant; Australia and New Zealand's wool, meat and minerals; South Africa's gold; Rhodesia's chrome and asbestos. The dominions needed to cooperate more closely, as each took up a greater share of regional defence: to Cape Town – Kenya, the Gold Coast, Egypt; to Canberra – New Zealand, the Dutch East Indies, Singapore; to Ottawa the English Channel; while London handled logistics, provided most of the air and sea power, and general industrial capacity.

That left India, 'the next-Dominion-to-be, looking west to Africa and the Middle East and east to Australasia and the Pacific', producing not only jute, cotton, wool, hides, skins, timber, oilseeds, rubber, manganese and chrome, but a million tons of finished steel per year. 'India manufactures nine-tenths of her war requirements, rifles, machine guns, propellants, howitzers, ammunition.'[45] On closer inspection, however, this arsenal looked less secure. India's Congress Party was 'crazy' to refuse its full cooperation against the Nazis, or expect London to hand it a 'virtual dictatorship over the Moslem League' in exchange.[46] By 1942 India was itself a theatre of war, after Japan captured Malaya and Singapore in February and then struck at Java and Burma. 'The dispatch from Batavia in Tuesday's *Times* was the most terrifying document that has appeared in print for many years', ran a panicky *Economist* after the fall of the supposedly impregnable fortress of Singapore. This was the worst military defeat of the war for Britain, which surrendered 130,000 troops and a state-of-the-art naval base to the outnumbered Japanese in just over a week of fighting. 'Soft troops, un-enterprising commanders, outwitted strategists, an incompetent administration, an apathetic native population – these are not the signs of a gallant army betrayed by bad luck; they sound uncomfortably like the dissolution of an Empire.'[47]

The paper now argued for much larger concessions to Congress in India, urging the mission led by Sir Stafford Cripps in March to barter post-war independence for wartime cooperation.[48] Cripps's failure was a serious blow, and the paper reacted bitterly to the taunt from Gandhi accompanying it, that he had handed India 'a post-dated cheque on a crashing bank'. 'If the check was post-dated, it was also blank', protested the *Economist*. 'It imposed no government upon the Indians which they would not work out and accept for themselves. It was honest, generous, and backed by the whole British people. In time, if Indian Nationalism is built on more than sand, they will discover the chance they are spurning. The cheque will be cashed.'[49] Credit and liberal good faith had more than metaphorical connections, especially in light of the historic reversal of the relationship between City and subcontinent then underway. 'All Indian obligations, both direct and indirect, will have been liquidated before hostilities cease', observed the *Economist* in early 1942, in fact underestimating the size of sterling balances accruing to India (as forced loans from it to pay for wartime supplies) in London.[50]

In the end, the failure to secure a grand bargain in India troubled the *Economist* less in terms of defence – Nehru had promised to 'spare no expedient' in repelling the invaders – than as opening a vulnerable political flank to its US ally.[51] The need to present the Empire as an up-to-date and 'free association' stemmed in part from the efforts Britain had made to secure that alliance since 1940: the price of Lend-Lease aid from the Americans was an end to imperial preference and all other discrimination in trade and payments after the war, with the US intentionally keeping British dollar reserves at a low level to ensure compliance. The Ministry of Information sent Crowther to Washington, D.C., in 1943 to begin to plead for patience, at a time when growing sterling balances with India and Egypt showed that the Empire was valuable in part as a hedge against total dependence on this official drip of dollars. At the American Economics Association in Chicago, Crowther argued that even as Britain shared a sincere interest in freer trade and a multilateral payments system, in the short run it needed time to resurrect industrial exports and invisible income, with modest tariffs till then to prevent 'experiments' in full employment leading to an unbalanced surge of imports.[52] Crowther joined another editor, Graham Hutton, now director of British Information in Chicago, with the same public relations mission.[53]

Diplomatic overtures soured at the approach of victory, however, as the Roosevelt administration showed every sign of calling in US loans, leading the 'Americanophil' *Economist* suddenly to question the future of the transatlantic alliance. 'Is it right to surrender the means of safeguarding British interests, as Bretton Woods and the American commercial proposals would have us do, in the hope that American policy will be stable and sound?'[54] The paper pointed to hypocritical criticisms of British intervention in Greece as a portent of what London could expect if it traded away its free hand abroad to the US – and this from a 'country where both political parties were ready to promise in the hope of securing the electoral vote of New York State, that they would force a wholly Jewish State on the Arab minority in Palestine'. Arthur Salter's American wife added three exclamation points to this line in a furious note to Crowther, explaining, 'America is a vast continent, young, very generous, eager, sensitive, and critical', and putting the country 'in its place' had caused 'the greatest pain and consternation ... entirely insulting to all Americans of honor'.[55] Ethel Salter was not the only one shocked by this leader, which caused a sensation on both sides of the Atlantic. As Isaiah Berlin, monitoring the US press for the British ambassador in Washington, found out, its author was not Crowther – but Barbara Ward, the young foreign editor, whom Berlin called 'a hysterical and naïve girl'. She had, he wrote, 'shaken the reputation of the *Economist,* which is now regarded as an excusably but nevertheless markedly nationalist journal'. Even Roosevelt weighed in and 'gently pointed out that some things are better not stated' – a measure not just of who read the *Economist*, but that its pronouncements packed diplomatic punch, especially since it was considered 'a liberal, serious, fair-minded and, on the whole, pro-American publication'.[56]

Indeed, that was almost certainly the point in publishing this 'plain-spoken' piece in the *Economist*, in the midst of the tense Anglo-American negotiations over the shape of the post-war international economic order. The hostile reaction from the US press did not deter Crowther, who may have received quiet approval for these philippics from Brendan Bracken, then Minister of Information.[57] In a follow-up, the *Economist* wrote that the US would violate the spirit of the Atlantic Charter to interpret 'non-discrimination' too literally. This would restrict (rather than free) trade between war-ravaged countries, whose pent-up demand for US goods was so vast that the only post-war check on their export would be the availability of dollars – *not* the existence of a British sterling area.[58] Leo Amery, secretary of state for India and Burma, wrote volubly a few days later: 'Your article on American relations the other day created a great stir and I think provided a useful jolt to American self-satisfaction and criticism of everybody else.' Amery added: 'The Americans not only identify non-discrimination with the Most Favoured Nation but want to ram the latter down our throats, even to the extent of forcing us and the Dominions out of Imperial Preference.'[59]

But Washington's abrupt cancellation of Lend-Lease in August 1945 – a 'guillotine', the paper called it – brought Britain's position painfully home. Though a 'bitter pill', the *Economist* advised swallowing the Americans' new offer: another loan, to settle the outstanding Lend-Lease orders, and to secure a line of credit. Yet it denounced the terms attached as 'cruelly hard', and warned of disaster if they were enforced. Strong-arming Britain into free trade and convertibility within the Bretton Woods system in just two years' time risked repeating the debacle of 1925, when London prematurely returned to gold, a deflationary strait-jacket that had also left it vulnerable to swings in the US economy.[60] The parallel was more exact than Crowther realized. For in the convertibility crisis that arose as soon as the terms of the American loan were honoured in 1947, the paper swung back to 'sound finance' with attacks on Labour as in 1931.

## Strange Victory: Labour and the City, 1945–51

The surprise victory of Labour in July 1945, in the first general election in ten years, thus occurred under dark clouds, with the

*Economist* friendly to the new government for barely two years, until the next dollar crisis. That record is striking. For not only did the paper agree with Labour on the post-war objectives of social security and full employment at home, along with preservation of a liberal empire and commonwealth abroad; it also supplied the party with ideas on how to link these zones, centred 'above all on the provision of capital' to raise living standards and bind commonwealth and colonies more closely to Britain.[61] The XYZ alumni now at the top of the Labour Party proved in most respects highly deferential to the culture and customs of the City, whose investment activities had already shifted to the sterling area – the currency bloc formed after much of the Empire and key trading partners followed London off gold in the 1930s – making the City more central to the imperial project, even as its purely international standing declined. Labour's plans and City interests seemed to overlap, and the two to be set for cooperation after 1945.[62]

Crowther viewed the new prime minister, Clement Attlee, as sound on the subject of finance and empire, cheering his cabinet picks from Labour's right wing: Ernest Bevin, as foreign secretary, who backed keeping conscription in order to defend British assets in the Middle East and Asia; Herbert Morrison, deputy prime minister, given to describing Labour as 'great friends of the jolly old Empire'; Arthur Creech Jones, the colonial secretary, and Hugh Gaitskell, at fuel and power, who likewise saw colonial development in Africa as in Britain's 'enlightened self-interest'.[63] Their strategies turned to a large extent on the sterling area, where the Labour leaders hoped to lock in features of the wartime imperial economy after 1945. The sterling balances were a paradoxical advantage for London, which managed non-sterling purchases and currency flows for the whole bloc, while acting as its largest importer – re-exporting, in turn, dollar-earning commodities such as oil from the Middle East, rubber from Malaya, or minerals and cocoa from the Gold Coast and Northern Rhodesia. Sterling members submitted to this control since restoring convertibility too soon might result in a run on the pound, as happened in 1947, making the balances worthless and ruining most members' prime export market.[64]

On the back of this worldwide imperial division of labour, the City staged a remarkable recovery after 1947. In just two years after the advent of the Marshall Plan, it sent £1500 million, or 8 per cent of national income, abroad – even as rationing in Britain continued for bread.[65] No capital levy on financial profits made out of the war ever materialized. Nor was the *Economist* concerned about Labour's most visible sign of trespass into the Square Mile – its nationalization of the Bank of England in 1946. 'Business Notes' blandly reported that the Bank, though answerable to the Treasury, 'as now, is free to conduct its affairs according to its own judgment of what is in the national interest and will not be subjected to day-to-day interference'. The appointment of the Scottish businessman and banker Lord Catto as the Bank's governor, showed the 'government does not contemplate revolutionary changes' – with Crowther, in any event, having backed a form of public control of the central bank since 1935.[66]

Why, in light of all this, did the *Economist* turn so swiftly against Labour? A short answer would be Hugh Dalton. The paper engaged in one of its bitterest polemics with the Chancellor of the Exchequer, blaming him in startlingly personal terms for the economic crises that buffeted Britain. Nicholas Davenport, Crowther's *Economist* colleague in the 1930s, was also a close friend of Dalton's: the XYZ alumnus, LSE professor and Fabian socialist, who, after many years of thought, he hoped to see 'shake up' the City. 'Crowther was the fiercest critic of Hugh's cheap money policy and wrote blistering articles against it', Davenport recalled. 'Hugh hated him and used to call him "Little Piggy Crowther" because he looked at that time rather like a well-fed porker.'[67] An advocate of 'practical socialism' (which he had contrasted in the 1930s with the impractical or leftwing kind), Dalton sided with Attlee inside the cabinet on the need for scaling back defence spending, rapidly reducing the size of the British armed forces serving abroad, and accepting a smaller role in the Middle East – a stance that put him at odds with the majority of his colleagues, who agreed with Ernest Bevin and the chiefs of staff that Britain's great power status hinged on the region (the bombers based there could strike Russia) and was worth the costs even if they required belt-tightening elsewhere.[68]

Dalton was a target from the start. The *Economist* recommended he be fired from the Board of Trade and not promoted to the Treasury, and objected to his 'sneering denigration of his opponents'.[69] Dislike veered towards hatred as Dalton refused to check a small uptick in inflation in the standard way by raising interest rates. When he intervened in the gilt-edged market, 'oozing suave confidence', to convert 3 per cent local loans to 2.5 per cent undated Treasury stock – soon after monetizing part of the national war debt – he asked 'the investor to give a complete hostage to the policy of ultra-cheap money for more than a generation'.[70] In March 1947, scoffing that 'the song in Mr. Dalton's heart is wind on the national stomach', the *Economist* demanded a swift dose of deflation, two months after the 'Big Five' bank chairmen took up the same refrain.[71] By the time a run on sterling began in July, its patience was at an end. A belated attempt to slow the economy left it cold: raising taxation to an 'incentive-crushing' 40 per cent of national income while failing to eliminate costly food subsidies was 'illogical', 'uncourageous', 'irresponsible demagoguery'.[72] Dalton quit, with the *Economist* kicking 'the worst Chancellor of the Exchequer in modern times' as he exited. Stafford Cripps, his replacement, was suitable, but what could he achieve in 'a party that likes neither austerity, nor intellects'?[73] It was kinder to Cripps when he devalued the pound by 30 per cent two years later, but attributed his delay in doing so to the 'uncommon stubbornness' of socialists, and insisted that devaluation was not enough to overcome the 'rigidities' Labour had imposed on the economy.[74]

Dalton, for his part, was convinced the *Economist* had sabotaged his chancellorship, complaining bitterly that it refused to give him credit even when he had followed its prescriptions in his last supplemental budget. 'Little Piggy Crowther tells *statistical* lies ... his personal animosity towards me is such that he can't even get his arithmetic correct when I'm about.'[75] Dalton was not far off. Fourteen years later he still had a target on his back. Looking for a reviewer to savage the final volume of Dalton's (gossip-filled) memoirs, the *Economist*'s editor turned to Herbert Morrison, who declined, saying it 'would be paying an undue compliment to the muckraker' and it 'reads to me like the memoirs of a failure with the result that bitterness has entered his soul.'[76]

It was the occasion on which Dalton sparred directly with Crowther, however, that reveals the issues at stake in their quarrels – for it came just after the fall of the Labour government in 1951, between two self-professed Keynesians over how to interpret Keynesianism in a Britain bereft of Keynes. This great economist 'was extremely unfortunate in the moment of his death', observed Crowther in a review of the first full biography of Keynes by another former pupil, Roy Harrod.[77] For he left implementation of theories worked out in the inter-war years of mass unemployment to disciples without 'a readiness equal to his own to change their minds', so that already the post-war period was 'plagued by chronic inflation, by an excess of the wrong sort of planning and by an aversion from thrift'. Keynes was being pressed into the service of this 'New Illiberalism' despite having been a passionate liberal, argued Crowther, who seized on a now famous letter from Keynes praising Hayek's The Road to Serfdom: 'a grand book, morally and philosophically I find myself in agreement with virtually the whole of it, and not only in agreement with it but deeply moved agreement.' Dalton was the only person singled out by name for crimes against Keynesianism, with Crowther adding a knife-twist: 'His old Cambridge friend "Daddy" Dalton scattered to the winds, in a few months of roaring boom, the American credits which he [Keynes] literally gave his life to win for Britain.'[78]

'I write to you to supplement and to correct some false impressions on Maynard Keynes, at once my teacher, my friend and my advisor at the Treasury', Dalton replied to what he privately called the 'Editor of the Prig's Weekly'. 'Of course, much of his economic thought goes against the grain of the editorial policy of the Economist', while 'his teaching has certainly inspired and sustained the Left in British politics more than the Right'. Above all there was no reason for supposing that had he lived, Keynes 'would have moved your way'. 'In the last nine months of his life, when he was with me at the Treasury, he never wished, as you did and still do, to see money less cheap or employment less full.'[79] That year Crowther tilted the Economist to the Conservatives, with such fierce attacks on Labour that they even disconcerted loyal reader Harold Macmillan.[80]

~

The Labour government of 1945–51 has been criticized for failing to have a more robust plan to nationalize industries in line with its manifesto promises, but what was more striking was its lack of any plan at all so far as finance was concerned. Indeed, Labour adopted the export strategies of the City, hoping that the sterling area would allow Britain to continue to play a leading and independent role in world affairs. For its complacency, Labour received a rude shock as the most important journal of City opinion quickly rounded on it anyway. In one sense, this was not unlike 1931, when the *Economist* pressured the second Labour government to abandon reform and balance the books, or else see British hegemony vanish in a crisis of confidence. But in fact, the fallout between the *Economist* and Labour was much more profound in the post-war period than it had been after 1931. Contextual differences go some way to explaining this. In the wake of the Second World War, Britain faced a new sort of economic crisis, on three fronts at once: an acute dollar shortage; a decline in its invisible earnings, and so a growing trade deficit; and, exacerbating both, heavy foreign outflows. These stemmed partly from military commitments, with over half a million troops still overseas in 1947. But they also reflected high levels of capital export to the sterling area and beyond (at £1.5 billion, 'well in excess of receipts from the US loan'), adding to pressure on the balance of payments, which not even Labour's success in raising export of goods (up 75 per cent in the five years after 1945 over the five before) could overcome.[81]

Crowther's taunt that Dalton had wasted the dollar credits Keynes had died to obtain would have been especially galling in this light. Not just because Dalton had sided with Keynes in one of his last memoranda in February 1946, arguing for rapid reductions to the service budgets in order to avoid a balance of payments crisis – even if, as Keynes put it, that meant cutting less of a 'dash in the world'– but because one of the biggest dollar-drains came from this expenditure, along with foreign lending. The irony is that the City's renaissance not only undermined Crowther's desire to see 'Stalinist-levels' of inward investment, but also the possibility of mutual development inside the commonwealth. Either of these would have required deliberate planning (or 'somewhat

comprehensive socialisation') of investment far beyond anything
the *Economist* – or Labour – had ever seriously contemplated. In
reality, most capital export in these years went to white dominions
like Australia and South Africa, while Britain bought up colonial
resources at below market prices to earn dollars. During Labour's
years in power, investment in the colonies was just £40 million –
even as colonial sterling balances rose to £160 million.[82]

The *Economist* remained devoted to the ideal of a liberal
commonwealth ('as inspiring and full of hope in its economic
aspects as in the political') after the defeat of Labour, warning the
Conservatives in 1952 that while the sterling area could not be
relied on as a 'magic incantation', it could be the basis for rebuilding the national economy, until such time as it was strong enough
to restore free trade and convertibility. 'The other members are
attached to the United Kingdom by the market it provides for
their exports and by the capital it provides for their development',
the latter being the most important element. For though 'it may
not be true any longer that trade follows the flag, it is certain that
trade follows the loan.'[83] Dalton and Crowther clashed over the
constraints this system imposed on their ambitious plans for the
post-war British economy. But their inability to theorize an alternative had for each man very different consequences, something
captured in the lament of Davenport in August 1945, on the day
he drove Dalton to his first day at the Treasury:

> The silencer had broken down and the noise was deafening but
> Hugh did not appear to notice. He was in fine shouting form. He
> boomed away about his job and when we got to Great George
> Street he said to me: 'I have got your XYZ papers in my bag and
> I am going to put them on my desk, press the button for my new
> slaves and ask them why we should not put them into practice.'
> I knew that the slaves would soon become his masters. 'Come
> and see me,' he shouted, 'whenever you like'. But I knew that
> would be impossible: the monastery guards would bar the way.
> Agnostic as he was, Hugh before long would be taking the vows
> of an office whose high priests were ordained to worship the
> pound sterling and the Crown as the twin pillars of the British
> Establishment. Their worship of pound sterling in its convertible

holiness in August 1947 was to be the beginning of Hugh's downfall.[84]

The fallout from the convertibility crisis was even more dramatic than this suggests. In its wake, the US redrafted plans to stabilize the international capitalist order. Not only did it agree to easier terms for Britain, but for its other main allies in Western Europe, as the Cold War began in earnest. The significance of the Marshall Plan was not just that it provided dollars to these countries – with strings to purchase US goods, and remove leftists from office – but that it allowed them at the same time to discriminate *against* the US dollar in terms of trade and payments.[85] For Britain, this meant domestic economic expansion could continue at the same time as the imperial trade and currency union to which it was linked. The consequences of Marshall aid for the *politics* of post-war Britain were thus just as momentous as elsewhere in Europe, if less obvious. The *Economist* can tell us a great deal about them, in particular the way the centre of the extreme centre now shifted right.

As Marshall aid began to flow, the *Economist* called for dismantling the restrictive microeconomic policies that the Labour government had carried over from the war – food subsidies, rationing, rent controls and industrial quotas – and by 1950–51, it was telling readers to vote Conservative, in order to end these 'inflation-breeding' distortions. If Keynes remained its preferred guide to macroeconomics, the *Economist* rejected interpretations of him that went beyond demand management. Labour was not to be entrusted even with that much.[86] By 1955, Crowther was accusing Labour leaders of 'surrendering common sense to doctrinaire obstinacy' for refusing to admit the obvious wisdom of a shift in policy that Labour itself had initiated with health service charges and that the Conservatives had sensibly carried forward since 1951: the denationalization of steel, the lifting of price controls, and the rise in interest rates had all helped to tame inflation and plug holes in the balance of payments. The *Economist* again endorsed the Conservatives, appealing to all those who wished to 'keep their place in the world'.[87] Labour had acquired a powerful enemy, just as the growing circulation of the *Economist* was beginning to catch up to its Olympian tone. 'Many readers of the *Economist* look upon that paper as an oracle, and so do its editorial writers', Bracken teased in a *Financial Times* column in 1952. 'There is no subject on which they are unwilling to lay down the law.'[88]

## Extreme Centre Empire: Barbara Ward, 1939–50

Marshall aid seemed to secure Britain's place in the world. As a result, the *Economist* no longer fumed about American hypocrisy. Rather it emphasized the joint role the British Empire could play alongside the US in the struggle against Soviet communism. This readily dovetailed with the liberal mission the *Economist* had already elaborated during the war – of a commonwealth built on investment from the City, a free association of people, based on mutual aid and development. If most of the *Economist* staff leaned to one side or other of this ideology of imperial purpose, none synthesized them more completely – or showed how they evolved along with the Cold War better – than its foreign editor Barbara Ward.

Crowther hired the devoutly Catholic Ward in 1939 on the advice of Arnold Toynbee, her mentor at Oxford and then at the Ministry of Information. Ward's first book, *The International Share-Out,* had just appeared, which argued against appeasing Germany, Italy and Japan with a repartition of the existing empires. Instead, she proposed a 'colonial new deal' in which Britain embraced free trade (abandoned at Ottawa), racial equality (a rebuke to South Africa) and the free movement of people, as well as the handover of some of its own colonies to the League, where Germans, Italians and Japanese could help administer them as mandates.[89] Once war began, her *Economist* reports on Turkey and the Near East described the British Commonwealth as the 'antithesis' of fascist imperialism and exploitation, the only 'confederation in which the unity necessary for planning and the autonomy necessary for free national growth co-exist'.[90] By the summer of 1945, Ward was barnstorming for Labour with Herbert Morrison and Ernest Bevin, whom she moved to tears with her speech at Wandsworth on full employment. If that must be the goal in Britain, she declared, 'abroad success turns on Britain's ability to maintain a policy independent of both Russia and America and to associate with itself the like-minded nations of Europe and of the Commonwealth'.[91]

The idea of Britain suspended somewhere between America and Russia vanished in August 1947, however, as Ward moved in lockstep with Crowther to shore up support for the Marshall Plan. She exhorted Bevin in private and in the *Economist* to accept the aid, and appealed to the public in the US and Britain – the former wary that Attlee's government was 'pink' (on the contrary, 'nothing incongruous was found in the Archbishop of Canterbury opening a Labour Party Conference with a service of dedication and worship'), the latter that US dollars came with strings – by reminding both of the alternative: the Kremlin. In stark contrast to a year before, Soviet Russia was ready to 'exploit every weakness, every grievance, every economic disturbance to extend its own power and influence'.[92] This, according to Ward, explained most of the unrest that now flared across the Empire, where it was fine to parlay with nationalists, so long as they were 'reasonable' – meaning that they were willing to stay inside the 'liberal commonwealth', and were not communists.

How did Ward translate this position into the paper's coverage of colonial revolts from 1947, when it was often difficult to tell communists and 'reasonable' nationalists apart? In Greece, communist partisans who had fought the Nazis became for the *Economist* mere proxies for Stalin – out to sabotage European reconstruction, and overturn the royalist government that Britain had reinstalled by armed force in 1944. Amidst the economic crises of 1947, Attlee asked America to take over the role. In what became the Truman Doctrine, the US president asked Congress for funds to assist 'free people who are resisting attempted subjugation by armed minorities or by outside pressures'. The *Economist* cheered. But it wanted more: an 'unequivocal statement that maintenance of an independent Greece is a vital American interest', for which it was ready 'to clear out the rebels, not simply contain them' even 'if military action is involved'.[93] The paper looked for a similar way out in Palestine, where the British mandate was due to end in 1948. The only hope of avoiding an immediate Arab-Jewish war was for a joint Anglo-American agreement to retain troops in Palestine after 1948 – with the US 'to carry at least half the direct military burden and the lion's share of the economic cost' – until such time as Arabs and Jews were reconciled to a two-state partition or single federated system. This 'purely humane' stance, which 'recoils horrified from the possibility that the Jewish people, already decimated by the Nazis' should 'be exposed to new violence in a war they cannot win', was 'reinforced by the realisation that Palestine lies dangerously near the frontline between Russian and Western interests in the Middle East'. [94]

The passage to independence for the vast subcontinent of the Raj was a more exclusively British affair, if a grotesquely bungled one, issuing in a point-blank partition between Hindu and Muslim majority areas. Effected without any popular consultation, it created some 12 to 18 million refugees overnight, left at least a million dead, and – in colluding with Nehru's seizure of Muslim-majority Kashmir – bequeathed a festering conflict between the two successor states of India and Pakistan that has never ended. For the *Economist,* this was an 'honourable and dignified conclusion to a chapter of history', which became the occasion for a stream of self-congratulations over an imperial mission accomplished. 'The peace and order of the British Raj were 19th century India's Marshall Plan', and Nehru was a statesman of the carat of Burke. [95]

Many national movements did not meet the criteria set out by Ward. In Malaya, the biggest earner of dollars in the Empire, the *Economist* backed the declaration of a state of emergency in 1948, to give colonial authorities extraordinary powers to crush the communist 'bandits' attacking rubber plantations and tin mines. This was a struggle of 'overriding importance' for the entire East Asian region – and for Washington, the paper hinted, whose 'modest blessing' Britain needed to stay the course in this 'testing point' for 'free nations'.[96] Iran was another such testing point. Here the nationalization of the Anglo-Persian oil fields at Abadan – then the largest oil refinery in the world and the single biggest British overseas investment – took the *Economist* by surprise. From March 1951, it counselled a version of gunboat diplomacy straight out of the nineteenth-century paper. 'One or two naval vessels' sent to manoeuvre in the Gulf should suffice, since 'Persians like all Moslem peoples respect power and strength'. But RAF squadrons in Iraq should be reinforced just in case, for 'the nationalist virus spreads amazingly quickly in the Middle East'.[97] The elected prime minister of Iran, a genteel Qajar-descended jurist educated in France and Switzerland, was treated to hysterics. Mohammad Mossadegh was an 'extreme right-wing nationalist and dictator', 'stupid', 'surrounded by a gang of criminals, religious fanatics and adventurers' who had literally cowed Iranians into an assault on the rule of law at gunpoint, the sole beneficiaries of which would be the 'well-disciplined Communist Party [that] could, without doubt, organise a coup d'état'.[98] In fact, it was the CIA and MI6 who would organize a coup to overthrow Mossadegh in 1953, officers restoring the Shah for fear of their communist neighbours to the north, in what the *Economist* described as an 'explosion of public feeling'.[99]

In Guyana and Kenya, the British response to nationalist challengers was still harsher. But here the *Economist* wavered over the right mix of liberal reforms and military repression as effective solutions to them. In the small South American colony of Guyana, it hailed a new constitution handed down from London in 1953 as a model of orderly progress towards self-government, and was initially unruffled by the victory of the People's Progressive Party in the subsequent elections, on a platform to allow unions to set wages with the sugar planters on a nationwide basis. But once London decided (with a shove from the US, whose nationals owned most of the fields and mines) that communism was afoot, it acquiesced to the landing of troops, suspension of the constitution, and arrest of the party's leaders as the only course available.[100] Kenya experienced an actual rebellion from 1952, its Land Freedom Army demanding redistribution of the richest soil in a series of bold executions of white settlers on their highland estates. The paper advocated pitiless repression of 'Mau Mau terrorists' and guerrilla fighters, and the imprisonment of 'extremist' leaders like Jomo Kenyatta, and swallowed the government's line on the notorious detention camps it had set up in the colony – that these had 'rehabilitated' nearly 80,000 Mau Mau supporters.[101]

Of course, constitutional and land reforms were also needed to address local grievances, the paper conceded, as it covered the 'Kenyan emergency' for the next eight years, aware that the model of City-led colonial development depended partly on what happened there.[102] Growth in Kenya – a brisk 3 per cent on average from 1948 to 1960 – might neutralize racial discontent, which the paper saw as a by-product of population growth among the native Africans.[103]

The vision uniting these assessments of empire belonged to Ward, who reframed editorial coverage of it to fit the Cold War. In *Policy for the West* in 1951, drawn partly from her *Economist* leaders of the year before, she took a civilizational view. If nationalists were prepared to fight communism, independence might be granted them, without loss of power or prestige to Britain, as in India, Pakistan or Ceylon, which all 'freely decided to remain as Dominions within the fellowship of the Commonwealth'.[104] Wherever communists or left nationalists sought self-determination, however, the West should crush them. That meant doubling down in Malaya, Africa, and alongside allies engaged in similar operations. Thus Ward backed American intervention in China on the side of the nationalists as Japanese rule collapsed in 1945, since this left China 'a potential Greece of the Far East'. While Chinese communism might be less noxious than other varieties, it had to be fought. 'There cannot be any doubt that Communist victory in China would mean its alignment with the Soviet Union, with the same campaign against all Western influences, political, cultural or economic'.[105] France, meanwhile, deserved credit for holding the line against Ho Chi Minh in Indochina, and for evolving a new approach there based on the British model: Vietnam, Cambodia and Laos folded into a commonwealth à la Française in 1949, with a soupçon of home rule for the nationalists, to inoculate them against communism and build up the French puppet regime of Bao Dai.[106]

By far the biggest test, however, came with the Korean War in 1950. There Britain had a solemn duty to assist the Americans in blocking communist advance from the north into the south – in what was in effect a civil war in the peninsula, after half a century of Japanese colonization. The *Economist* was so agitated by the conflict it worried that Britain's massive rearmament – defence spending rising from 7 to 13 per cent of GDP in two years, with 100,000 British troops dispatched to the Korean peninsula at US behest – was a sign of *complacency*, 'ominously reminiscent of 1939-40'.[107] Remarkably, four years later in 1954, the *Economist* discerned a similar plot to overrun Central America from Guatemala, where no motive for modest agrarian reforms could be found besides international communism, despite the fact that one American company, United Fruit, owned 42 per cent of all the land. To stop this, it endorsed the CIA-mounted invasion of Guatemala from Honduras and El Salvador, followed by a coup against the elected leader, dismissing stories that cast 'President Arbenz in the role of an innocent victim of foreign aggression inspired by Wall Street' or blamed 'the greed of the United Fruit Company backed by old-fashioned US imperialism'. Its correspondent was gung-ho about the dictatorship, which would endure for over four decades, killing or disappearing hundreds of thousands: 'the government, the political parties, the labour unions, and the independent agencies dealing with such matters as social security and land reform had all been so thoroughly infiltrated by Communists that there was no alternative to starting all over again.'[108]

In contrast to Crowther, who was prepared to cut back social spending to pay for rearmament as the Cold War intensified, Ward saw butter for natives as the necessary complement to guns.[109] Going considerably further than the *Economist*, in her last book as foreign editor Ward called on Britain and America each to dedicate 15 per cent of their national income to defence, with an annual 3 per cent added on for a colonial Marshall Plan – providing a boost to full employment at home and a form of social democracy abroad, as part of a worldwide Keynesian stimulus.[110] At the end of 1950 Ward went abroad to test these theories, overseeing development projects with her Royal Navy officer husband, sending back reports to the *Economist* from India, Australia and the Gold Coast (where she grew close to Kwame Nkrumah).[111] By then Ward was a star, crisscrossing the globe to extol liberal capitalism as a test of 'faith and freedom' – and now to far more powerful audiences, US Democrats like Adlai Stevenson, John Kennedy and Lyndon Johnson.[112]

## Donald Tyerman and the Cold War News Room

Crowther may have moved the extreme centre to the right by 1950–51, but for the rest of the decade the newsroom he built was less narrow. The *Economist* itself became a field for Cold War conflicts over liberalism, with meeting-room rows, disputed stories and journalist spies who wished to do much more than report news. No one was more active in all this than Crowther, who retired in 1956, but on the condition that he continue to influence editorial policy, while making a great deal more money in the City. Crowther asked Layton, now Baron of Danehill, as chairman of the *Economist* to make Donald Tyerman the next editor, and to create a new post of managing director just for Crowther. 'Tyerman is fully capable of taking on the specifically editorial responsibilities, and I would be quite willing to divide my job in the conviction that we could work together intimately and fruitfully.' Roland Bird, the deputy editor, should be passed over, since 'to put him in as editor would be to exclude me from the paper far more than I wish or could stand.'[113] He told Tyerman that 'though it is entirely right the new editor should have the full authority of the position, and that his writ alone should run in the paper, I do not propose to disinterest myself in the editorial contents of the paper.'[114] Two years later, angling mendaciously for another lucrative billet in the City, Crowther could write to Siegmund Warburg, one of its most powerful merchant bankers, that as the *Economist*'s 'non-executive director', he was a 'free man'. While it 'would not be appropriate for me to become a director of a merchant banking house, as some people might think, however mistakenly, that this enabled some special influence to be exerted over the editorial comments of the paper', this 'would not apply to a directorship of another company in your group, such as Mercury Securities, since very few people would have the knowledge or the interest to trace a connection between it and the paper.'[115]

Donald Tyerman returned to the *Economist*, where he had started twenty years earlier at the same time as Crowther. Deputy editor during the lean years 1939–44, Tyerman had in effect put out the *Economist* with Ward, before joining the *Times* as assistant editor when Crowther returned full time. His popularity among younger writers at the *Economist* was due in part to a permissive style, which he captured best himself while reminiscing on what it was like to edit the paper during the Blitz. 'We did it over coffee in the Brettenham House cafe, after 8 Bouverie Street was destroyed in May, 1941. It was a sort of brainstorming. We talked in dozens ... then we went back with leaders to write ... we thought and felt and argued our way to what to say, Catholic or Marxist or Liberal, or what not.'[116] He showed courage to have made it that far: polio had left him paralyzed from the neck down at three, but he eventually recovered control of his limbs, and earned a scholarship to Brasenose, Oxford, where he excelled in modern history. Tyerman always walked with splints, and it is hard to miss, in Crowther's preference, a desire for physical control over him. Not only did Crowther initially sit in on weekly meetings – until, dominating them to such an embarrassing degree, even he realized the need to stay away – but later was 'constantly throwing in brilliant ideas from the chairman's office'. Crowther, 'the renowned former editor', wrote another staffer, 'continued to overshadow his unfortunate successor'.[117]

Tyerman was not a pushover, however. At the *Economist* he would display the same independent streak he had at the *Times* where he and E. H. Carr wrote fiery leaders in 1944 opposing the British military intervention in Greece which aimed to crush the main resistance movement that had fought the Nazis and restore a pliant monarch at the head of a conservative government in Athens. These articles rocked the coalition government in parliament, infuriated both Churchill and Bevin, and caused a diplomatic spat with Washington.[118] At the *Economist* his tolerance for different, contradictory views was the last hoorah for the kind of popular anti-fascist atmosphere that had inspired these articles on Greece.

That led to fights with Crowther almost from day one, with crises over the Suez canal, the Cuban Revolution, the defection of Kim Philby and the 1964 election – at which point Tyerman was eased out of the door. Tyerman did make a mark, recruiting talented public school graduates like John Midgley, former Bonn correspondent for the *Times*, as foreign editor, and Barbara Smith to assist him. He promoted Elizabeth Monroe to Middle East editor; Keith Kyle to political and parliamentary affairs editor in 1957; and the Polish Marxist Daniel Singer, on staff since 1948, to Paris correspondent in 1958. Still, most of the 'young Turks' were Crowther's hires. Many of the arguments that flared within the newsroom turned on liberalism and empire, and just how much anti-communism or the US alliance ought to shape editorial policy in these areas. Under Tyerman, the *Economist* asked probing questions, and sometimes came up with surprising answers about both. But in each case the dynamic was clear, as was the trend: angry blowback from the managing director's office, until Tyerman was replaced in 1964.

### Keith Kyle and the American Survey

Kyle became the *Economist*'s first full-time Washington correspondent when Crowther poached him from the BBC in 1953. The twenty-eight-year-old producer had impressed Crowther, who interviewed Kyle for a Commonwealth Fellowship. 'You may have noticed I was being rather hard on you at the interview', Crowther told him a few days later. 'That was deliberate, because I wanted you to fail.' Crowther decided Kyle should go to the US, but for the *Economist*.[119] The first in his family to go to public school and Oxford, where he became a passionate Liberal and member of the Union, Kyle developed a close relationship with his history tutor at Magdalen, A. J. P. Taylor.[120] In 1945, Kyle shipped out as a second lieutenant to India – an experience that left him so disillusioned about the white officers and civil servants who ran the British Raj that he strongly defended the move to independence on his return to Oxford at a Liberal-Tory debate in 1948. 'And what are your credentials for speaking on India?', challenged a Conservative in the audience. 'Scindia's Field Battery, 1st Indian Field', Kyle replied. As he recalled, 'from that moment I felt I had the audience in the palm of my hand and, filled with adrenalin, I poured out my convictions on the end of the Empire.'[121] 'I disbelieved in socialism, which I thought high-minded but unreal', Kyle wrote, describing his politics at the time, 'but I wanted passionately to ensure the immense let-down of those who had served in the First World War would not happen the second time around.'[122]

Until Kyle, the American Survey was edited from London. Margaret Cruikshank, a New Yorker married to the editor of the *News Chronicle*, was the first editor; she then worked jointly with the half-American Nancy 'Colonel' Balfour, a 'small, squat, animated spinster' and 'tetchy, highly intelligent boss', who collected contemporary British sculpture – Moore, Pope – in her spare time. The American Survey was a shoestring operation: phone calls were a luxury, not to be indulged in for more than a half hour once a month, with stories filed by airmail and short messages sent by telex, 'a primitive fax machine which spun like a crazy top and gave out strange sounds and odd puffs of smoke'. Kyle used writers rather like himself: on economic policy, Edwin L. Dale Jr.; on constitutional law, Adam Yarmolinsky; on defence, Adam Watson, a war correspondent for the *Baltimore Sun*. Paul Jacobs, a stringer hired for his perspective as a trade unionist, anti-nuclear and anti-war activist, who later founded *Mother Jones*, was further to the left.[123]

Washington was provincial but exciting. Kyle gained access to some of the most important people in it, such as the CIA director Allen Dulles, whose son – 'the most right-wing character I had ever met' – he had known at Oxford. In due course Lyndon Johnson manhandled Kyle while explaining the arcane rules of the Senate. John F. Kennedy, a rising star after the Democratic convention in 1956, asked if the *Economist* – to which his father Joseph, as US ambassador to London, had given him a lifetime subscription – was dumbing down by introducing line drawings. 'His temperament was rather more conservative than I had supposed.' Kyle was less impressed by other aspects of life in America. Washington, with its unrepresented black majority, was 'run like a colony, and a fairly primitive one'. In reporting on desegregation and the bus boycott in Montgomery, Alabama, he was far more impressed by the courage of Rosa Parks and Martin Luther King Jr. than the white officials he met – just as in India. McCarthyism was most disturbing of all. Kyle recalled a cocktail party where the *Economist* was attacked as everything the senator from Wisconsin was against; on his side there was little but contempt for the 'most notorious abuser of human rights in the name of anti-Communism'.[124] While none of this made Kyle an opponent of American foreign policy, it did place him at odds with a relay of rightwing editors in London that Crowther began to appoint at the same time, the first of whom was a shadowy young Australian named Brian Crozier.

## Brian Crozier and *Foreign Report*

Recruited as the *Economist*'s East Asia correspondent in 1954, Crozier also took control of its new 'confidential bulletin' called *Foreign Report*. Crozier seems to have landed the job through British secret service contacts picked up as a reporter for Reuters in Vietnam, Cambodia and Malaya, and he returned the favour – printing propaganda from MI6, the CIA and other Western spy agencies in this eight-page bulletin for the next decade: indeed, *Foreign Report* explicitly marketed itself to corporations, governments, news outlets and select individuals as containing information 'too hot' to go in the *Economist* itself, though in practice much of it did. Crozier's links to the Information Research Department, set up secretly in 1948 by the Labour government to lead the 'propaganda counter-offensive against Communism' from inside the Foreign Office, were very close. Andrew Boyd, an *Economist* colleague, introduced Crozier to his IRD contact over lunch at the Traveller's Club in 1955. Afterwards, around 20 to 30 per cent of each issue of *Foreign Report* came from the IRD.[125] As Crozier saw it, there was no conflict between this sourcing of stories and journalistic ethics. The Soviet Union was an evil so pure – an 'irredeemable obscenity of history, condemning humanity to inescapable enslavement' – that it had to be fought by any means necessary, and that meant using not just physical but psychological force. Crozier felt it his mission to rouse the West, whose 'timidity' in the Cold War thus far shocked and dismayed him. How else, in his opinion, to explain the Truman Doctrine and McCarthy trials? The former was limited to containment when the need was 'not simply to resist further encroachments, but to liberate countries that had fallen to the Soviet Empire'; the latter had allowed itself to be misperceived as 'hysterical' when 'there was indeed a vast network of Soviet spies in America'.[126] In this worldview, national movements for independence did not take place, and there was nothing inevitable about decolonization. There were only 'Moscow-directed insurgencies', which spread in one unscrupulous chain from East Asia to North Africa to the Middle East and on to Latin America.

Crozier's 'outside interests', which sent him on constant trips abroad, seem to have been an open secret at the *Economist*. 'I don't know who pays for Brian, you see', Tyerman joked.[127] On a flight back from an intelligence-gathering trip to Algiers, Crozier happened to sit next to Colonel Antoine Bonnemaison, of the Service de Documentation Extérieure de Contre-Espionnage, who became one of his important sources. Bonnemaison was reading a letter from General Salan, thanking him warmly for talks on 'psychological warfare' he had given to the French Army. 'On learning I was the editor of the *Economist*'s *Foreign Report* he told me he had long been a regular reader and admirer of "my" bulletin.' Crozier obtained a scoop – predicting in *Foreign Report* that General de Gaulle, popular among the demoralized French officer corps in Algeria, was about to have a 'second coming'.[128] On assignment for the *Economist* in Francophone Africa in 1961, Crozier hailed the ouster and murder of the first elected leader of the independent Congo, Patrice Lumumba, who 'had many Communist friends', and applauded Mobutu Sese Seko, who 'gave Communist embassies forty-eight hours to leave the country'.[129] The same year, Crozier worked up his field notes into *The Rebels* – on independence struggles in Palestine, Cyprus, Malaya, Indochina, Algeria and West Africa – which, he boasted, was soon the 'textbook on counter-insurgency' and 'stasiology' for security services in Israel, Greece, Lebanon, Taiwan, Columbia and the US. His only regret was that 'in deference to my connection with the *Economist*, I had written impartially'. Incredibly, some readers were not sure which side he was on: 'in future I would give priority to objectivity over impartiality'.[130]

Crozier led a busy life after leaving the *Economist* in 1964. He published a biography of Franco based on an interview with 'Spain's saviour' in 1967, questioning whether the Nazis had really bombed Guernica after all.[131] He ran two CIA-funded media mills, Forum World Features and the Institute for the Study of Conflict, which fought moves towards 'peaceful coexistence' and détente – with FWF sending stories to press outlets both abroad and at home, such as the *Sunday Times* and the *Guardian*, until 1975, when *Time Out* exposed it.[132] Undeterred, Crozier then 'closeted' himself with General Augusto Pinochet to draft a post-coup constitution for Chile; supplied juntas in Uruguay and Argentina with 'psychological techniques' to use on leftist dissidents; and later that decade founded Shield – a committee of experts to 'educate' the Conservative leader Margaret Thatcher on communist subversion, the 'political equivalent of AIDS', inside the Labour Party, trade unions, schools, universities, churches, media and local councils ('the site of a possible Marxist-Leninist coup'). In 1977 he set up a 'boutique' intelligence firm, 'the 61', to spy on the peaceniks and pink journalists these civil society groups contained, with a wink from nominally law-abiding Western governments.[133]

Crozier had a continuing impact on the *Economist*. Brian Beedham, the foreign editor from 1963 to 1989, was a friend and collaborator, who brought another Crozier protégé, Robert Moss, onto the paper in 1970. Four years later, Moss was editing *Foreign Report*, which at that point, fumed Barbara Smith, 'was being written by Mossad'.[134] The bulletin's vantage point on empire differed from that of Kyle or Ward. Crozier dismissed the idea of developing the commonwealth with British capital as 'a morass in which billions of pounds were sunk without a trace by Western banks', while decolonization failed to register, vanishing from a radar that only picked up the Cold War.[135] At times liberalism itself became a byword for blindness to this all-encompassing struggle. Those who opposed abridgments of civil liberties or nuclear arms were '*bien-pensant* liberals' and 'soft liberalism incarnate', while the Liberal Party – through which Crozier passed a 'regretted membership' of six months in 1962 – was filled with 'wets' and 'pacifists', had 'no understanding of the real issues and was unlikely to learn.'[136] Crozier and his allies clashed spectacularly with those they found too soft at the *Economist* in 1956, as a sudden crisis engulfed the paper and its new editor.

## The Suez Crisis

For the *Economist,* the Suez Crisis began in July 1956, when the US pulled its loan offer to build the Aswan Dam in Egypt. Britain was forced to follow suit, suggesting that London might now be unable to act alone as an investor; the same soon became clear about its military capacity. Of the first loan instalment, $200 million was to come from the World Bank, $56 million from the US and $14 million from Britain; when Dulles demurred, so did new prime minister Anthony Eden. One week later, the Egyptian president Abdel Nasser took over the Suez Canal. On 4 August, in 'Europe's Achilles Heel', the *Economist* advised calm, pointing out that Nasser was guilty of 'bad manners' for nationalizing the waterway, but had not restricted traffic through it; that by the terms of the concession, ownership would pass to Cairo anyway in 1968; and that an occupation would solve nothing. There were better options, some picked up from the earlier fight with Mossadegh over the Anglo-Persian Oil Company in Iran: diplomatic isolation, building a second canal and more pipelines, and above all threats to withhold capital, since Nasser had struck 'the severest possible blow to the principle of investment in under-developed countries'.[137]

It came as a complete shock to the editors when Eden instead launched an attack with France to retake the canal, on the pretext of breaking up a prearranged Israeli assault. News of the Anglo-French ultimatum to both 'sides' reached Keith Kyle at Washington's Press Club, where he had gone to find out the latest news on the Hungarian uprising. Stunned, he let telexes fly. First, to the Conservative Party central office, whose representative he was due to meet at the Mayflower Hotel two days later to discuss his joining a party of 'fine liberal fellows like Eden, Rab Butler and Iain Macleod'. 'I had seen, as if in a burning flash, just why I could never be a Conservative and why it had been a mistake to suppose I ever could have been.' He also sent messages to Labour leader Hugh Gaitskell, and to Tyerman, recounting an off-the-record discussion between the secretary of state John Foster Dulles and several journalists, in which Dulles fumed at the British government's ineptitude. Americans were just as committed to removing

Nasser, but 'the British had to have it by Christmas', and Dulles warned that Imre Nagy's announcement that Hungary would withdraw from the Warsaw Pact – eleven days before the Soviets intervened to stop this – meant 'the US would not need to defer so much as it had done to the colonialism of its NATO partners'.[138]

Back in the *Economist*'s London office, Barbara Cruikshank and Nancy Balfour pointed at Kyle's message to show that Britain was out on a dangerous limb. John Midgley seconded them, and Elizabeth Monroe, the Middle East editor, channelled their views into 'Splenetic Isolation' the next week. US reluctance to confront Nasser was indeed frustrating, Monroe granted, but acting alone, 'under cover of a smoke-screen of obfuscatory statements', France and Britain had done 'their worst to justify the "imperial" label they so much (and, as it seemed, so rightly) resented'. 'In the larger Asian world, they have supplied Soviet propagandists with enough anti-colonial material for a decade', in an operation with an improvised air about it, this 'strange union of cynicism and hysteria'.[139] Monroe returned later to what she and some of her colleagues felt was lost at Suez. 'The consequences of Eden's decision to the remainder of British power and influence in the Middle East were great and detrimental', she wrote in 1963's *Britain's Moment in the Middle East*. France and Israel could hate Nasser. 'Britain, beset by extraneous interests, could not'; it had to consider 'Commonwealth opinion, particularly Nehru's pacifist opinion' in India and 'think of the effect on their faithful ally, Nuri Pasha in Iraq'.[140]

Tyerman called on Eden to resign the next week, but added a new reason, evoking the intensity of the crisis. 'A British Prime Minister must not be alienated from the uncommitted countries and very much more, must not be at loggerheads with the leaders of America', especially given the opportunities this created for 'our real potential enemies'. Suez had already emboldened 'Russian imperialism', which 'ten days ago looked as if it might be drawing back' in Hungary.[141] Crowther expressed heartfelt agreement. 'Eden's worst crime was not using force', he wrote, emphasizing his own slant on the situation in a letter to Tyerman. 'It was endangering the Anglo-American alliance by disloyalty, fraud and deceit.' Repairing ties was impossible so long as the 'vain, petty, vindictive' Eden was in office. 'He must go.'[142] With only Brian Crozier opposed to caving to the Americans, Crowther's words were decanted directly into the leader of 17 November.[143] 'The great task of statesmanship now is to rebuild the alliance', it declared. 'We cannot go it alone, we must learn that we are not the Americans' equals now, and cannot be.'[144] This was also the first time the paper registered the magnitude of the run on sterling that had begun with Eden's ultimatum, as 'no ordinary crisis'. Having failed to predict the financial fallout, the Chancellor, Harold Macmillan, now exaggerated it, telling colleagues on 6 November that £100 million had gone – one-eighth of the reserves.[145] Faced with the break-up of the sterling area, devaluation, and a return to rationing, Eden halted the operation that morning; only then did the US allow Britain to draw on IMF funds to defend the exchange rate.[146]

If dissent was minimal within the newsroom, criticism rained down from outside the *Economist*. 'From a heavy postbag this week', ran a special letters section, 'we have selected a few from the large majority which take an opposite view from that expressed in our leading article "Splenetic Isolation".' For K. Clarence Smith of Surrey it 'dealt a shattering blow to the respect with which I have hitherto regarded your opinions'. 'As an old and regular reader of your paper, I write today for the first time to any paper to say how deplorable I think your leading article was', ran another. Many bristled at the idea that absolute deference should be shown Washington. 'I do not think the majority of our people would find that proposition acceptable.'[147] J. E. Simon, the Conservative MP from Middlesborough West attributed 'obsessional attacks' on Eden to 'a psychological malaise' at the *Economist*, which ignored 'the likelihood of a general war in the Middle East, Russian inter-vention leading to world war, loss of oil supplies' if Nasser had not been punished.[148] Kyle, just returned to London, recalled his chilly reception at the Oxford and Cambridge Club, where he and a friend joined a few young men gathered around a small coal fire, the one source of heat during the fuel shortage caused by Suez:

'Of course, I've cancelled my subscription to the *Observer*,' said one, amid murmurs of approval. 'It's such a shame about the list

of Oxford dons signing that letter to *The Times*,' said another.
'It means that I shan't be able to go to my tutor's sherry parties
ever again.' There was a general sigh of sympathy. 'And then,'
said a third man, 'there's the *Economist*.' The party then noticed
the two of us sitting silently by the fireplace. 'Do you read the
*Economist*?' I was asked. 'No,' I answered with studied venom, 'I
write it.' There was a stunned silence and then, slowly and sadly
the young men rose and without a word left the club.[149]

## From Liberal Commonwealth to Special Relationship

Suez was only the first salvo in a war of words over the future of
empire, as a subtle difference in emphasis between Crowther and
Tyerman gradually sharpened into a disagreement – not over the
'special relationship' ('much the most important thing' for both),
but whether this left room for independent policy with respect
to imperial and 'uncommitted countries' (a reference to the Non-
Aligned Movement announced at Bandung, Indonesia, in 1955).
'Though the paper accepted, in a general way, that European
empires had had their day', Barbara Smith wrote of her first
years at the *Economist*, which she joined in 1956 covering Latin
America, 'we argued heatedly over the timing and the pace of
Britain's departure from Cyprus, Aden, huge chunks of Africa.'[150]
Keen to 'witness the process of decolonisation in Africa', Kyle also
joined the fray, writing on Kenya starting in 1960, and meeting
Jomo Kenyatta, Tom Mboya and other leaders in London during
independence negotiations. Next year he flew to Tunis for the
All-African People's Conference. If decolonization in some form
was inevitable, at least Britain, he consoled himself, was better
at it than France: the 'pragmatism' of 'Africans from the English-
speaking colonies such as Chief Enahoro from Nigeria' impressed
him more than the French-speakers, who talked loftily and with
paranoia, he felt, of 'le néo-colonialisme' and 'la balkanization'.[151]
Indifferent to these larger questions, Kyle viewed decolonization in processual terms: in books on Kenya and Cyprus after
leaving the *Economist* – drawing on his work for it, the BBC in
East and Central Africa, and the Royal Institute of International

Affairs, Chatham House – there is little criticism of British statesmen (who, outside Suez, are seen to have carried out an orderly
end to empire), or those to whom they passed the baton in the
ex-colonies.[152] Editorials were therefore mainly cautious compromises, and not just because of pushback from Crowther. Smith
recounted her one 'nose-to-nose meeting' with the latter at around
this time in a painfully slow-moving office elevator, as decolonization sped up after 1960. 'Valiantly making conversation, I
suggested that the colonial secretary of the day was doing rather
well, but Crowther harrumphed, "Yes, if you want him to give the
whole damn lot away!".'

The notion that after 1945 the *Economist* accepted the end of
empire 'in a general way' is unsustainable. As Smith discovered,
arguments over 'pace and timing' were not mere technical details,
and turned on the preservation of property rights, resource-access,
strategic interests, and connecting these – the likely ideological
direction of the successor state; in other words, the very issues of
'neocolonialism' that Keith Kyle had so airily dismissed in Tunis.
What did arguments about 'the end of empire' look like in practice?

The *Economist* backed 'self-determination' for Cyprus after the
start of armed nationalist insurgencies there in 1955, but only if
British military bases remained. The Mediterranean stronghold,
acquired from the Ottomans in 1878, had a new purpose – as
Britain's imperial 'headquarters for the Middle East' and NATO's
'eastern flank'. In 1960, the paper endorsed a castrated version
of independence, which made the bases on Cyprus sovereign
enclaves, and severely restricted the freedom of its new government to direct or alter its affairs: a Treaty of Guarantee between
Britain, Turkey and Greece allowed all three powers to intervene
at will on the island, while constitutional 'safeguards' for the
Turkish Cypriot minority blocked Nicosia's exercise of legislative,
administrative, judicial or military power on a national basis.[153]
The same year also began with a special issue on Africa, where
Harold Macmillan embarked on a whistle-stop tour – set to meet
'the challenge of Black Africa in Ghana and Nigeria, and the obdu-
racy of White Africa in Salisbury and Cape Town'. The *Economist*
proposed speeches for the prime minister with the 'right clichés'
to satisfy a 'strong, liberal African lobby or crossbench' – about

free elections and a free press, with highlights on Cameroon, Nyasaland, Basutoland, Bechuanaland and Swaziland, which had all expressed a cross-racial preference to 'hold onto their connections with Britain'.[154] The paper read the actual 'winds of change' speech Macmillan gave in South Africa along the same lines as its own drafts: not a shift, but a restatement of the policy of gradually preparing colonies for self-government. Nigeria, in contrast to neighbouring Congo, was a shining example of this, moving 'with almost majestic calm and self-confidence towards its date with national destiny', when it would become 'Africa's greatest democratic state' thanks to a federal 'British-made constitution'. The Central African Federation offered similarly rosy prospects, if only black nationalists in Nyasaland would agree to set aside their 'neuroses' about union with Northern and Southern Rhodesia in exchange for guarantees of parity with whites during a five-year federalist trial period.[155]

Britain was not the only power to try to direct the winds of change abroad, and editorial decisions about gusts outside the empire and commonwealth could be just as contentious where they touched on the Cold War. The historian Hugh Brogan, then a young foreign section writer, recalled 'vigorous debates on decolonization' at Monday meetings in the 1960s, one of which he won: should the *Economist* continue to support the French war in Algeria, after revelations its soldiers there had massacred peaceful protestors? The argument ended in a decision to carry the rebel slogan 'Vive le FLN!' on the cover, and Tyerman asking Brogan to write a leader to go with it, 'Algeria's Cry', which declared 'the 114 Moslem civilians who were killed in Algiers and Oran achieved as much in their deaths as the scores of thousands who have died in the field during the past six years.'[156] Independence for the Congo inspired no similarly principled stand, however, in part because Brian Crozier was the correspondent on the spot in Leopoldville: equivocating about the crimes of the departing Belgians, including their role in the assassination of the first prime minister Patrice Lumumba, the paper did grant that his murder at the turn of 1961 – 'unstable and wildly unsuccessful' though Lumumba was – dealt a regrettable 'blow to moderates in the Congo and Africa'. How so? Insofar as it created a 'potent myth' in 'African minds' associating Lumumba with anti-colonialism, while allowing 'Mr Khrushchev' to accuse UN peacekeepers as well as Lumumba's torturers, President Kasavubu and General Mobutu, of being 'colonial puppets'.[157]

The Cuban Revolution was connected and still more consequential – a tipping point. Barbara Smith backed the bearded revolutionaries, tracking them from the hills of the Sierra Maestra all the way to Havana, which they entered on the heels of the fleeing dictator Fulgencio Batista on New Year's Day 1959. 'Visiting Cuba soon after Fidel Castro's revolution was eye-opening', she wrote, comparing festive scenes there to the US-backed dictatorships through which she had passed. 'People interviewed in the street actually liked their new young government.'[158] US attempts to throttle it by cutting sugar quotas, placing an embargo around the island, then invading it at the Bay of Pigs in 1961, increased her sympathy for the revolution. In the weeks leading up to the missile crisis the next year, the *Economist* was more worried about Kennedy's 'obsession with Cuba', objecting to bellicose editorials in *Time*, the *New York Herald Tribune* and the 'growth of extremist attitudes towards foreign policy in the United States'.[159] After a US spy plane snapped images of a Soviet missile base under construction on the island, on 27 October a leader headed 'Cyclone Cuba' urged negotiations at the UN, but still saw the US as the rasher power, forcing a 'showdown over the shipment of Russian arms to Cuba'.[160] The paper praised Kennedy the next week for obtaining a 'complete Russian retreat' but also Khrushchev for statesmanship, having secured US agreement not to invade Cuba again – as great a relief to the allies of the one as of the other.[161]

'Cyclone Cuba' so incensed Crowther that he insisted Tyerman have it rewritten. Midgley, its main author, had already tamped down hints from Smith and Alex Campbell, Washington correspondent, that fuzzy photos of the Soviet bases might be fakes. Brian Beedham, the future foreign editor, was tasked with softening its criticism of the US the morning the paper went to press. Crozier fumed, but even his friend Beedham at this point preferred compromise to nuclear war: 'The attitude of the *Economist* shocked me. It took the same line as the leftish *Guardian*, advising scepticism over the US evidence and caution in response. This was not the paper I had joined in the days of Geoffrey Crowther, who, I learned later, had been equally shocked and had let it be known that he would ask the board to replace Donald Tyerman as editor.'[162] A similar reaction set in after some light hand-wringing about the coup in Brazil in 1964. A lead article blaming the (elected) President Goulart for his own ouster provoked outrage, since it also criticized the 'anti-communism' of his rightwing opponents as 'a mask for unwillingness even to consider their country's major problems'. Subscribers in Brazil, shocked at this, pelted angry letters at the *Economist* for weeks, after which reporting on the new junta was left to a correspondent in Rio enthusiastic at its salutary economic policies.[163]

Perhaps the final nail for Tyerman was the defection of his soon-to-be infamous correspondent in the Middle East. Kim Philby was the suave former head of counter-espionage for MI6, who had come under suspicion as a Soviet double agent after the Second World War when he tipped off two of his fellow 'Cambridge Five' conspirators to flee to Moscow in 1951. He was forced to resign, but cleared for lack of evidence, and the SIS and Foreign Office eased him in 1956 onto the *Observer* and *Economist,* where MI6 expected to reactivate him from Beirut. In a testy exchange with Crowther after Philby defected in 1963, Tyerman insisted that the latter had approached the *Economist,* which took him on only after the *Observer* (it *had* unbeknownst to Tyerman gotten a request from the Foreign Office) agreed to share the cost.

> What *we* got from the FO was neither a request to employ him (which we would automatically have jibbed at) nor a permission to employ him (which we would never have asked for) but simply the 'assurance' from our various informal personal contacts, when we told them, (a) that there was no ground at all, politically, after his clearance by the Foreign Secretary, why he should not be employed and (b) that, on personal grounds, they were all glad that, after bad times, he was getting the break he deserved.
>
> *I have to confess that I have no bad conscience about this.* Hindsight now puts the question whether it is worse, both being bad, to employ a man at the FO's request (which I would never

do) or take on the man *now* 'admitted' *to be the* 'third man'. Then, of course, he was officially *not* the third man; his work for us in the first and longer part of his engagement was excellent and, as Elizabeth herself told the *Observer* on Sunday, properly impartial and judgematical. At the very end, he did flag, as we said in our piece, but for personal not political causes; and, when he went, we had for some time been wondering what to do about him, simply on journalistic grounds.[164]

From his father's house in Ajaltoun, Philby had sent back faultlessly anti-communist articles, the sort he thought would rhyme with British upper-class prejudices, on Iran, Iraq, Syria, Egypt and Yemen. When his output flagged, Tyerman sent down Midgley – Philby's friend from Cambridge, with him in Berlin in Easter 1933 when the Nazis came to power – to encourage him, as well as Barbara Smith; they got drunk instead at hotel bars, Smith chasing a baby fox around Philby's Beirut flat months before he disappeared in 1963. 'He was fun in an elusive way', she said.[165] For Crowther, Philby's exposure was another blow to the *Economist*'s reputation, further confirmation it had become too leftwing. But that was a misperception – not just because Philby had been the opposite of leftwing as a reporter, but because it was the rightwing Crozier and Moss who would use the *Economist* as their alibi for collecting and distributing anti-Soviet 'misinformation' for the rest of the Cold War. And if they were the most extreme, unethical cases, they were by no means alone. Among the editors with links to British intelligence going back to the war were Donald McLachlan, John Midgley, Elizabeth Monroe and Patrick Honey; by one account, more IRD-listed journalists served on the *Economist* than on any other London newspaper.[166] Still, it stung, not just because Philby had bilked these very agencies for so long, but because his scrapes with danger and bed-hopping were the stuff of real spies, not just storytelling. The goal of replacing Tyerman now shifted into high gear, leaving him just enough time to commit one final sin against the gospel as Crowther had laid it down, when the *Economist* endorsed Labour in 1964.

## Labour, 1964 and All That

The 1959 election had brought the expected verdict, with the *Economist* asking which politician had done more to redeem the sins of his party – 'Mr. Macmillan in discarding the false promises of Suez and prestige diplomacy, or Mr. Gaitskell in cutting back to sense the false promises of inflationary socialism?' The answer was Macmillan, who 'repaired the transatlantic alliance, which Suez broke, and rebuilt those Commonwealth bridges that were torn down'.[167] Labour, in contrast, was not to be trusted at home – expansion under it not worth the risk to 'a vulnerable pound again and rising prices and costs' and to 'the flow of credit', with 'guns unmasked ... against the City and all its works' – nor abroad, where its vision now seemed blurred by longings for 'missionary deeds of social and economic growth in the Commonwealth and among the underdeveloped millions of the world'.[168] Five years later, what altered this judgment? In 1964 the *Economist* betrayed almost as little enthusiasm for Labour as for the Conservatives, both culpable of 'woolliness and timidity'. If Labour was (just) preferable, this was less shocking than Crowther's angry reaction might indicate. After thirteen years in power, the Tories walked with a limp, stumbling badly in the period leading up to an election widely predicted to go against them.

Macmillan may have touted the level of national prosperity to voters as unprecedented during his second stint in office but, well aware of Britain's persistent international weakness – growth the lowest among the advanced economies in Europe, exports as a share of the world total in steady decline, the sterling area ineffective as a panacea for either – in 1961 he opened talks to join the European Economic Community in hopes of spurring modernization. The *Economist* vigorously backed him. When de Gaulle vetoed the application two years later, claiming that Britain wanted to have its cake and eat it – retaining commonwealth preferences while also gaining access to the common market – the paper railed at 'a new Bonaparte' plotting his return to 'the Europe of 1810, self-sufficient, Francocentric, door shut tight against the nation of shopkeepers, back turned upon the New World'. But it also admitted the government's economic plans now lay in tatters, with no clear alternative for effecting the 'vast productive reshuf-fling of resources, the revivalist change in mental attitudes' of the sort the French, German or Japanese were undergoing.[169] When the Profumo scandal struck at just this moment, it shocked the *Economist*. Not because the Minister of War and Russia's naval attaché were having an affair with the same lady – 'its rationalist and nonconformist tradition' disbarred it from looking into these 'salacious details' – but because 'a Prime Minister of Britain [was] about to be overthrown by a 21-year old trollop'.[170] The choice of Scottish aristocrat Sir Alec Douglas-Home to succeed Macmillan did little to reverse the Conservatives' slide.

Finally, that year Norman Macrae, the paper's economics editor, published *Sunshades in October,* an indictment of 'stop-go eco-nomics' under the Tories that joined a growing body of statistical research, political pamphlets, business and trade-union reports on the same theme. The thinking behind 'stop-go' began as a perfectly sane reaction to Labour's disastrous record from 1945 to 1951, he argued, as excessive demand became a grave economic crisis. The problem was that this continued to terrify economists even after it had ceased to be a problem, once the Conservative Chancellor R. A. Butler had dismantled 'the ration book economy', freeing up market forces to set the price of food, interest, raw materials and construction by 1954. Yet the currency and balance of payments crises that supervened were still seen through the same lens, requir-ing the same corrective as before: demand deflation. Macrae had been as guilty of this as anyone, urging governments to 'cut down demand very ruthlessly' if 'ever external economic events make it necessary' in his most famous (if often misunderstood) article, 'Mr Butskell's Dilemma' in 1954.[171] A decade later, however, he conceded that these periodic cutbacks had had the opposite of their intended effect. Instead of holding down costs per unit of labour and raising exports, restrictive policies had raised costs and reduced efficiency, above all in the new, high-tech industries on which the growth of British trade depended.[172] In a typical turn of phrase, Macrae mused that economists clinging to deflation on theoretical grounds as the only way (given full employment) to stop imports from rushing ahead of exports during a boom, were a bit like clever scientists who could prove it is 'impossible for a bumble-bee to fly, because its wings are too small for its body. As a bumble bee does fly, I have long felt that it is time for that latter theory to be re-examined.'[173]

In this context Harold Wilson was appealing, all 'freshness' and 'brisk resolution', whose hymns to the white heat of technology were what 'a country awaiting its economic miracle' needed. In its editorial of support for Labour, the *Economist* acknowledged most of its readers would vote Conservative anyhow, but out of fear, 'though the riskier choice, Labour – and Mr. Wilson – will be the better choice for voters to make on Thursday'. Macrae recalled that 'although Crowther and most of the rest of the board did not agree', a majority of the editors thought 'post-Gaitskell Labour should come back for a while into being a party of government because another spell of opposition during the 1960s could turn it into an old-time socialist party instead of a new-age responsible social democrat party.' The hope was Labour might be able to tame the trade unions, heading off wage inflation (the type that worried Macrae) while doing a better job than Conservatives at 'expanding the national income by all possible means'.[174]

## Labour and the End of the Line

Suez, Cuba, Philby, now Wilson: Crowther was furious and fed up. He refused to even consider the two candidates Tyerman favoured as his successors. Midgley and Macrae were too close to the editorial decisions he hated – on Cuba and Labour, respectively – to get a hearing. The chairman now looked for outsiders, hastily and somewhat unaccountably approaching Roy Jenkins, then a young Labour MP with intellectual chops as the biographer of Attlee, Dilke and Asquith, who favoured dropping public ownership from the party platform, and a policy of wage restraint from trade unions. When the board baulked at hiring even a liberal Labourite, Crowther pushed for Alastair Burnet, a former staff editor from 1958 to 1963, who had left to become a television news anchor on ITN. In his letter of recommendation to the board Crowther underlined two qualities which in his view made Burnet suitable, aside from his great personal charm: 'he is a liberal in the fairly exact sense of the word, without qualifying for the capital

L by having any attachment to the Liberal (or any other) party.' This was a typical untruth: Burnet may have been liberal, but he was attached to the Conservatives in the exact sense, as member and advisor. Second, in foreign affairs, 'he is a very firm believer in the policy of the North American Alliance, without any of the leanings towards neutralism which (to my regret) have sometimes been apparent in the *Economist* in recent years.'[175]

Tyerman betrayed no bitterness about his treatment, and later denied Crowther ever interfered in his editing. 'Nothing has made me despair more for human folly than the cries that still go up in this country', Tyerman wrote in his valedictory, 'catcalling Americans as a threat to peace when they have become in historic fact its saviour.' That did not mean, of course, the US was infallible: 'candid criticism there should be from good (but only good) allies.' Later, when Crowther died suddenly, a peer of the realm, eulogized in 1972 by the LSE's Lionel Robbins at Westminster Abbey, Tyerman recounted his own memories of the man. He stressed in *Encounter* that Crowther's friendship for Washington never saw him lapse into a reactive conservatism: 'never, crudely, a cold warrior', he 'admired Dean Acheson'. For him, 'the great issue in home affairs was not anti-socialism, any more than it was anti-communism abroad. It was positive not negative: liberty.'

The distance the *Economist* had travelled since Crowther became editor in 1939 on the eve of war was nevertheless extremely striking. By the end of his editorship, Crowther was reduced to ruminations on the special relationship, once telling the *New York Times*'s Cy Sulzberger, 'British relations with the United States ought to be as freely candid as Australian with Britain.'[176] In 1964 Tyerman simply added that at the same time Britain should seek out 'the closest dovetailing into Europe'.[177] Absent from either reflection was any mention of empire or commonwealth, nor the vision of world power that accompanied these after 1945, to be built upon foreign investment doled out by the City. Britain might need to accept a subsidiary role in upholding liberalism around the world in the next phases of the Cold War. Not the *Economist*: here a true partnership was possible, with the paper supplying the best intelligence to the new imperial power across the water, in a struggle to the bitter end with communism.

# III

PAX AMERICANA

# 7

## Liberal Cold Warriors

The appointment of Alastair Burnet was a watershed for the *Economist,* which began a sharp and permanent turn to the right, and to America, under him. The first ever paid-up Conservative to edit the paper, his tenure was marked by unconditional support for the war in Vietnam, where the US escalated its assault on the North just as he took over in 1964. The changes Burnet heralded were generational: from Bagehot to the younger Crowther, editors had looked to the Liberal Party as their central reference, as the institutionalization of liberalism; from Crowther's intake after 1938 to Tyerman's after 1956, most staff – Ward, Kyle, Midgley, Monroe, Smith – were formed by the Second World War, when the 'extreme centre' encompassed economic planning, the New Deal was held in high esteem, and Soviet Russia was still an ally, with all the mixture of attitudes that went with this short-lived parenthesis. The *Economist* since Burnet has been produced for the most part by pure products of the Cold War, without any adult experience of what preceded it. (Deputy editor Norman Macrae was the main exception, chronologically, but with childhood memories of 1930s Moscow that served as a premonition of the same mindset.) More than any single economic point of policy – and even as global capitalism changed dramatically over three decades, with post-war boom fading into long downturn before a neoliberal shock – the political struggle between liberalism and communism structured coverage at the *Economist.*

## The Burnet Show

'Few editors of the *Economist* have been famous faces', began the in-house obituary for Burnet, who passed away in 2012. A political reporter for ITN, as editor he continued to cover general elections and the monarchy, and in 1967 began to anchor the *News at Ten*. His small sleepy eyes sat beneath heaping eyebrows, which furrowed, implored, wheedled, or rose archly, depending on the subject, with the whole crowned by a slick bouffant of hair that greyed over time but never lost altitude. A colleague described him as a proto–Jeremy Paxman, the BBC journalist famous for flustering politicians and pop stars as well as helming patriotic documentaries that celebrate the quirky side of the British character. Burnet was even more reassuring than that; for Americans, something like a cross between Walter Cronkite and Barbara Walters. Like the former, he was portentous enough to call national elections six times from 1964 to 1987, and narrate the moon landing, albeit with less gravity: 'there it is, the old moon – the one the cow jumped over'. On the other hand, he basked in the warm glow of the royal family, chronicling their weddings, births, funerals and daily rituals in books and television specials, sometimes with embarrassing deference. On hand when Prince Charles wed Diana Spencer, as the latter descended the steps of St Paul's Cathedral with a twenty-five-foot train in tow, he exclaimed, 'If there is any heart that hasn't been won over by her today, it can kindly surrender now.' Sniffing at flowers on the ninetieth birthday of the Queen Mother, who observed it was a day in a million, Burnet was heard off-camera: 'She's made so many days in a million.' *Private Eye,* the satirical weekly, dubbed him 'Arslicker Burnet'. The TV show *Spitting Image* gave him his own puppet. In one segment, 'in private, in person, incredibly boring, a year in the life of Sir Alastair Burnet', his likeness prepares for a week of 'fawning and cringing, if he can fit it into his busy schedule of licking and slurping', as he clutches a canister of oil and toilet paper roll; in another, Charles and Diana walk up an endless red carpet that turns out to be his tongue.

His interest in what he called 'plain folk' notwithstanding, Burnet's background was standard for an editor: born in Sheffield in 1928 to Scottish parents, his father was an engineer, who nurtured hopes that his son would play cricket for Yorkshire. Burnet went to the Methodist Leys School in Cambridge, then on to Worcester College, Oxford, where he studied history but refused a second-class degree, believing he deserved a first. After a few years at the *Glasgow Herald,* he began his first stint on the *Economist* in 1958. Burnet did not take himself too seriously. One of his major impacts on the paper was that it no longer did either. He presided over meetings with a gin and tonic, did impersonations, and commissioned pieces on his favourite sports. Covers portrayed catchy visual-verbal gags, with captions and thought bubbles gently deflating world leaders, like *Private Eye* for the ruling class. There was Labour's Harold Wilson dressed as Santa Claus for Christmas in 1967: 'But I haven't got the sack'; the Tory leader Edward Heath on his sailboat: 'So what's my handicap for 1970?'; around New Year in 1972, Richard Nixon splashing through the surf: 'Hope I needn't walk on it this year'. Some even took principled stands. When British passport holders from East Africa of Asian descent were denied entry to Britain in 1968, it pictured a UK passport in a pile of garbage, 'If that's what it's worth'. Circulation rose along with jauntiness: 60 per cent in a decade, to 123,000. 'He *did* work hard', recalled one journalist, 'and from 6 p.m. to 1 a.m. he left to do TV. His private life suffered, but not the paper.'

Burnet was at the same time an active Conservative, who took on added stature within the party thanks to his editorship. When the National Union of Miners defied the government and went out on strike in February 1974, Burnet was one of those who advised the prime minister of the day, Edward Heath, to call elections, breakfasting with him every morning during the ensuing campaign. The title of his address to the Conservative Political Centre a year later registered his shock at the outcome: the question no longer '*who* governs' but '*Is* Britain Governable?' His answer was that of a moderate who thought two steps could save the situation: gathering a coalition to build consensus around sensible reforms, and forcing the trade unions to hold competitive elections, 'more important than any parliamentary by-election, and more important than most elections for the control of a city or a county'. He ended with a warning to those who favoured a more frontal assault on labour, already gathered at think tanks like the Institute of Economic Affairs or the Centre for Policy Studies, where Thatcher was imbibing much of the neoliberal program she brought to 10 Downing Street four years later:

> I believe it would be ruinous for the Conservative Party, in the decisive political battle of this generation, to adopt the policies of the study, to be tempted into an academic view of unemploy-ment ... People will accept much more if they can be sure the intention of a government is that real incomes are rising than they will if they suppose that monetarism ... is the only formula. We should not suppose that everyone in Britain is converted to the helpful doctrines of Dr. Milton Friedman, or that, even if they read *Newsweek*, they have ever heard of him.[1]

## Brian Beedham, Robert Moss and Vietnam

The moonlighting of a celebrity editor gave a great deal more freedom to his two deputies – Brian Beedham and Norman Macrae – each equally influential in their domains, both con-vinced liberal capitalism must fight communism to some final reckoning. How did the *Economist* represent the battlefields of the US Empire, which took that fight direct to the enemy, and what were the implications for democracy? From 1965 to 1989 the answers were given by the dour, domineering and articulate Brian 'Bomber' Beedham, whose author photos show him dressed like a retired US intelligence analyst in a natty sweater layered over a shirt and tie, wearing aviator glasses and a beard. Feared and respected – if never much liked, with two near misses at being editor to show for it – Beedham started out like much of the staff since Crowther: on a scholarship to Oxford in 1952 and then a Commonwealth Fellowship to the US. There he received his first lessons in Atlanticism in 1956, when he called the British mili-tary attaché in Washington to enlist for service in the assault on the Suez Canal. The attaché hung up, and the patriotic Beedham deduced two things from an expedition that ended almost as abruptly: London could no longer act abroad without leave from the US, but what it *could* do was awaken the latter to its responsibilities as the new policeman for the world.

So the next year Beedham instead reenlisted in the *Economist,* where Brian Crozier, the only other champion of Suez, welcomed him. Crozier left the paper in 1964, but continued to exert pull via Beedham, who also hired Crozier's twenty-three-year-old protégé Robert Moss as a correspondent in 1970. Crozier had been so impressed on meeting the young Australian the previous year that he had asked Moss to draft the inaugural report for his new Institute for the Study of Conflict (ISC), set up to 'expose' détente with the Soviet Union as a fraud and 'save the Western Alliance'.[2] At first glance Moss might have seemed an endearing contrast to his humourless mentor: pudgy face, ruffled beige trench coat, smoking cigars, mixing dry martinis; he 'liked the smell of cordite in the morning', he said, doing his best James Bond. Moss continued writing for Crozier's CIA-funded ISC (which also took money from multinationals like Shell and British Petroleum) and Forum World Features (a kind of Associated Press of 'misinformation') during his ten years at the *Economist,* often using both it and *Foreign Report* as covers for paid intelligence agency work and the planting of false stories.[3]

Beedham gave Moss free rein, with striking results. 'Foreign Report is unique in that it forecast almost to the day the coup d'état in Greece in 1967 and the coup in Chile in 1973', ran a boastful 1979 blurb for the magazine, described by two investigative journalists as a 'gossip column of the intelligence world'.[4] In 1980 Moss would leave the *Economist,* taking with him an aura of authority that only the paper could have provided. He became an advisor to Margaret Thatcher, who in her memoirs thanked 'the editor of the *Economist's* Foreign Report, an expert on security and strategic matters' for drafting her famous 'Iron Lady' speech warning of the 'Sovietization of Britain' in 1976. He was also, Thatcher noted warmly, 'destined to be a bestselling novelist', with a spy thriller that read just like his journalism for the *Economist* but with lashings of violence and pornographic sex (which she did not mention).[5] Moss suffered a nervous collapse a decade later at the end of the Cold War – today he is a 'dream

shaman' in upstate New York, advising people on how to visit
dead relatives and world leaders in their sleep – and his story captures some of that conflict's obsessive hold over the paper he and
Beedham had such a pivotal hand in editing.

No issue defined their approach more than Vietnam, where in
1954 the US began to take over the role of the defeated French –
funding a fragile, repressive client state in the South, while fighting
communists there and in the North, to prevent any reunification
of the country under Ho Chi Minh. For the staff writer and future
historian Hugh Brogan, *Economist* coverage of the war by the
early 1960s was 'pure CIA propaganda', which claimed South
Vietnam was thriving under Ngo Dinh Diem, its US-installed
premier. 'Rice can be exported once more. Farm taxes are down.
Education, sanitation and health have been greatly improved'
and 'the great mass of the people, neither hungry nor profoundly
interested in western concepts of philosophical liberalism and
parliamentary democracy, are non-communist.'⁶ 'But it's so
nice to have good news for once', sighed Barbara Cruikshank
when Brogan objected to such stories, in particular to their rosy
depiction of life in the 'strategic hamlets' – concentration camps,
rebranded – to which peasants were herded at gunpoint. Perhaps
these had 'defects in practice', the paper admitted in 1963, but
they could be fixed: fencing off farmers from communists (one
could not be both, in its view) was the right start, but Americans
ought to learn from 'the French here a decade ago and the British
in Malaya' how imperative it was for white men to keep out of
sight. 'They should provide the material and technical means of
winning the war, but leave the fighting to the Vietnamese', for
only 'they can merge with the population like a fish in water'.⁷

Articles sounded more like pep talks than dispassionate analyses. For Beedham, the Tet Offensive, launched from the North
and across the South in 1968, was 'an attempt, conducted with
brilliant tactical dash, to force a settlement before it is too late',
but doomed to failure. 'American opinion at home has hardened
in support of the war. The statistics are moving against the communists where it matters.'⁸ Two issues later, there was alarm when
the offensive appeared to rattle nerves instead, as 'Viet Cong'
breached the US Embassy in Saigon, and the death toll for US

# The Economist:

## OR

## THE POLITICAL, COMMERCIAL, AGRICULTURAL, AND FREE-TRADE JOURNAL.

**PRELIMINARY NUMBER]**     AUGUST, 1843.     **[AND PROSPECTUS.**

## CONTENTS.

INTRODUCTORY ARTICLE:—

| | |
|---|---|
| Free Trade | 3 |
| Restrictive System | 6 |
| Colonies | 7 |
| Sugar | 9 |
| Wool | 11 |
| Wheat | 12 |

PROSPECTUS:—

| | |
|---|---|
| Leading Articles | 13 |
| Parliamentary Reports | 14 |
| Free-Trade Movements | 15 |

PROSPECTUS CONTINUED:

| | |
|---|---|
| Summary of News | 15 |
| Commercial Report | " |
| Agricultural | " |
| Colonial and Foreign | " |
| Notices of Books | " |
| Gazette and Prices Current | " |
| Correspondence and Inquiries | " |
| Extra Monthly Statistical Number | " |
| Annual Index and Title Page | " |
| Concluding Remarks | " |

*If a writer be conscious that to gain a reception for his favourite doctrine he must contend with certain elements of opposition, in the taste, or the pride, or the indolence of those whom he is addressing, this will only serve to make him the more importunate. There is a difference between such truths as are merely of a speculative nature and such as are allied with practice and moral feeling. With the former all repetition may be often superfluous; with the latter it may just be by earnest repetition, that their influence comes to be thoroughly established over the mind of an inquirer.*—CHALMERS.

It is one of the most melancholy reflections of the present day, that while wealth and capital have been rapidly increasing, while science and art have been working the most surprising miracles in aid of the human family, and while morality, intelligence, and civilization have been rapidly extending on all hands;—that at this time, the great material interests of the higher and middle classes, and the physical condition of the labouring and industrial classes, are more and more marked by characters of uncertainty and insecurity. In vain has the hand of ART (led on and guided by a complete glare of SCIENCE, aided by INDUSTRY of unsurpassed intelligence and perseverance, nurtured and fertilized by CAPITAL almost without limit) developed the resources of the human mind and the material creation in a manner which has at once astonished and exalted the world;—in vain have all parts of the earth been brought nearer and nearer to us;—our Indian territory within forty days' journey, the great American continent within ten days' sail, our continental neighbours and every part of our own country separated only by a brief space of a few hours;—in vain the producers and consumers of the whole world, the administrators of mutual wants, the encouragers of mutual industries, have been brought in easy and close collision and contact, and thus facilitated the supply of every want, and the demand for every exertion of human skill and industry;—in vain do we acknowledge all these unequalled and unlooked for elements of national prosperity: for at this moment the whole country—every interest without exception—the owner and occupier of the soil, the holder of our great mineral world, the manufacturer who gives form, shape, and utility to the produce of nature, the artisan, the labourer of every description, the merchant and shipowner (the great links of ex-

change), and the capitalist who facilitates the operations of all,—every one of these interests stand at this moment CONFESSEDLY in a condition of the most unprecedented depression, anxiety, and uneasiness. And what rather adds to this anomaly than in any way accounts for it, is, that our population has been rapidly increasing, not only in numbers, but also in great skill and productive ability.

But while Art, Science, Intelligence, and Enterprise have been thus engaged the last half century in behalf of our country and the human race, in what manner has legislation been occupied? Let cool and calm deliberation determine this question. In the early part of that period the little time which could be spared by the legislature from the excitement of political strife, the struggle for political power and place, was occupied with the stirring events attendant on the long and continued wars in which we were engaged, and the principles of commercial and industrial legislation attracted little of its attention. Under such circumstances it was not difficult for those interests who possessed great political influence to obtain enactments which they supposed would be beneficial to themselves. Unfortunately, however, both governments, and classes, and individuals have been too apt to conclude that their benefit could be secured by a policy injurious to others; and too often the benefit proposed has even been measured by the injury to be inflicted: hence all the laws which were framed under this influence had a tendency to raise up barriers to intercourse, jealousies, animosities, and heartburnings between individuals and classes in this country, and again between this country and all others; and thus, under the plea of *protecting* individuals or classes against each other, and the whole against other countries, was the system of COMMERCIAL RESTRICTION completed by the enactment of the corn and provision laws, passed in 1815; amid the utter forgetfulness on the part of the legislature, that it had no power or privilege which could enable it to confer a favour or wealth on any one part of the community, without abstracting as much from others: in fact, that it possessed no inherent source of productiveness which could enable it to be generous.

The policy of England, always, but especially at this particular time, looked up to by all the world as the highway to greatness, was eagerly followed in her commercial regulations by other countries; navigation laws, hostile tariffs, prohibition of English manufactures, were resorted to by other governments, each in a way according to the notions they had of their own interest, in imitation of, or opposition to, the policy of England.

*The preliminary number and prospectus, August 1843*

*'Monetary Crisis', 8 August 1914: 'Since last week millions of men have been drawn from the factory to slay one another by order of the warlords of Europe. It is perhaps the greatest tragedy of human history.'*

*'Back to Gold', 31 March 1934*

Nixon on Vietnam, 8 November 1969

'The War for Asia', 17 April 1971

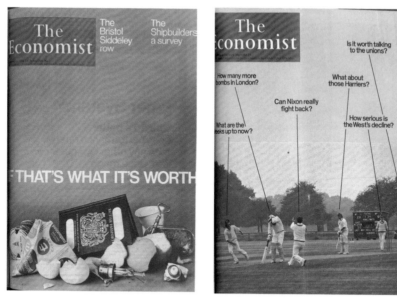

'If That's What It's Worth',
2 March 1968

The cricket team, 25 August 1973

'Britain under Siege', 20 January 1979

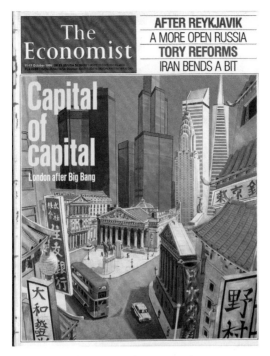

'Capital of Capital', 11 October 1986

'Save the City', 7 January 2012

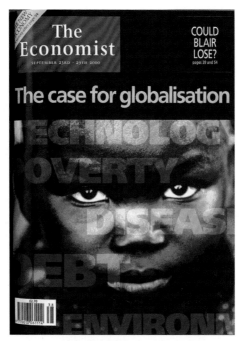

'The Case for Globalisation', 23 September 2000

'The Hopeless Continent', 13 May 2000: 'Does
Africa have some inherent character flaw that keeps
it backward and incapable of development?'

*'A Heart-Rending but Necessary War', 3 November 2001*

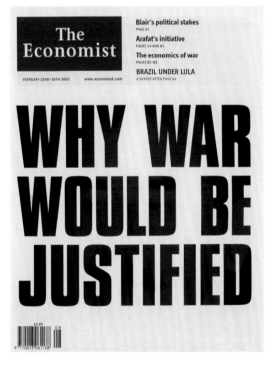

*'Why War Would Be Justified', 22 February 2003*

'The Weakened West', 21 September 2013

'Putin's War on the West', 14 February 2015

forces began its climb to 15,000 in a year: 'Americans would be admitting that they had been beaten by the technique of guerrilla war as applied by a minority of the population of one small Asian country. That would affect the way that men in Moscow make their plans for the future.'⁹ On the My Lai Massacre in retaliation for Tet, involving the murder of around 500 unarmed children, old men, and women (many of whom were also raped) by US marines: an isolated incident, 'minor variations on the general fallibility of men at war', and paeans to Western freedom of the press for bringing it all to light. 'The bloodiness of this war is undeniable. But it is hard to detect on the American side anything that could be called a policy of atrocity.'¹⁰

The Nixon administration's decision to target Cambodia in 1969 – carpet-bombing it on the same pretext as Laos (where five years of this had rendered large swathes uninhabitable and over a quarter of the population homeless), and then invading it – did give rise to tensions at the *Economist* ... with what result? 'No one wants to raise the spectre of a second Vietnam', it began in 1970. 'But if the new Cambodian government is threatened by a foreign army, as distinct from a local rebellion, Mr. Nixon, whatever his reluctance, will have to consider the consequences of failing to support it.'¹¹ That month, Nixon announced his 'Cambodian incursion'. The paper even sniped at Henry Kissinger – the chief architect of this scheme as the National Security Advisor – for mulling peace with the North Vietnamese in October 1972 on terms far too lax. It was an extraordinary thing to write about this peace plan, which Hanoi accepted after many concessions and millions dead, only to watch Nixon drop it till after the US election (betting, on a pollster's tip, this would win him more votes) while ordering the saturation bombing of Hanoi and Haiphong.¹² 'There is no reason a liberal should accept why the two Vietnams ought to be reunited until it has been shown that a majority of the people in both of them, or at least of those in the south, wish it to be so.' Until this was certain, let the bombs fall where they may.¹³

Beedham was just as relentless when it came to combatting criticism of the war, which increased as prospects for winning it faded. In Britain, he pressed Wilson's Labour government for 'clearer voiced practical support for the American position'.¹⁴

Wilson was in fact unwavering, offering not just moral encouragement to Lyndon Johnson, but also training, supplies, signal
intelligence and support from bases in Hong Kong and Malaya. If
he refused to say so in public, or to accede to pressure for British
boots on the ground, this was for fear of splitting Labour, whose
left wing urged him to condemn indiscriminate US bombings
of civilians in Northern towns and villages in June 1966, in a
move that infuriated the *Economist*.[15] 'If the British want to, they
can give up the attempt to influence American policy. They can
retire to the sidelines and blow raspberries.' Instead, they should
respect the special relationship, whose rules were simple: Britain
must 'go along with the main aims of American foreign policy
in return for the right to nudge the Americans back on course. It
is a fair exchange.'[16] It was silly to rant about 'US Imperialism'.
'How can anyone this side of lunacy suppose that the American
troops fighting in the paddy-fields of Vietnam can raise their real
gross national product back home by a single cent?' Americans
were the *real* victims, there for 'unselfish reasons'; 'the communists are the force on the move in the area'. Beedham could
not fathom how students 'should be tempted to scream abuse
in Grosvenor Square' at the US Embassy, where huge Vietnam
Solidarity Campaign marches converged in 1968.[17] And when the
Pentagon Papers were published by the *New York Times* in 1971,
he lumped it in with the same sort of student truants. Temporizing
about the presidential lies running from Truman to Johnson that
the Pentagon Papers revealed, Beedham maintained that these did
not alter the merits of the Vietnam War, and in fact necessitated
them. 'There are powerful reasons democratic governments are
seldom particularly open with their people on the brink of war.'
The most powerful of these? A 'liberal intelligentsia' that 'prefers
not to bring itself to face the possibility of war until it sees the
knife at its own throat' – pacifists, appeasers, the sort of people
who had lain supine before the Kaiser and Hitler.[18]

  The idea that it might be justified to lie to citizens now informed
not just the content but also the sourcing and editing of foreign
news at the *Economist*. 'Vietnam just wasn't debated at Monday
meetings', recalled Johnny Grimond. 'Beedham simply had too
much control, so the invasion of Cambodia might come up, but

never the war itself.'[19] Nor was this confined to Southeast Asia, just one front in a vaster war, as Beedham explained in a special debate with foreign editors of the Polish weekly *Polityka* in 1965. 'If we in the West accept the existence of a line in Europe beyond which there is no poaching, then you must accept a similar line in Asia.' For 'if in the name of "wars of national liberation", you support the use of violence to change the regime in South Vietnam, how can we appeal to other people to refrain from violence in the pursuit of "liberation" elsewhere: Pakistanis over Kashmir, the Austrians over South Tyrol – in the end, maybe, the west Germans over east Germany?'[20]

## Enemies: Suharto to Allende

The *Economist* applied Beedham's implacable Cold War logic to cover the entire earth. In Indonesia, the stakes were high, and so was the need for secrecy about Western involvement: in this case, 54,000 British troops fighting for Malaysia, a federal entity whose borders London had drawn in 1963, provoking immediate clashes with Jakarta over them. Beedham sought a physical and psychological war to 'check' Sukarno – the independent-minded first president of Indonesia, whose grip on power rested in part on the national communist party (PKI) – explaining as much to the *Salt Lake Tribune* at the height of the 'Konfrontasi' in 1964. A guerrilla campaign in the jungles of northern Borneo directed against the former British territories of Sarawak and Sabah was serious, but one that a modest escalation – say, 'infiltration of British-trained guerrillas into Sumatra' to 'remind Sukarno that two can play the guerrilla game' – could solve, 'for there are signs President Johnson and Secretary Dean Rusk are as worried as the British about Dr. Sukarno'.[21] Beedham, of course, was in the psychological war business himself – writing stories with help from Crozier and the Information Research Department. In 1965, he accused Sukarno 'of trying to appease the Indonesian communists, even to bequeath the succession to them'. On this pretext, General Suharto ousted Sukarno that year, rounding up and killing half a million communists and suspected communists; the British and Americans supplied a list of names and other assistance to Suharto, as a bloody curtain descended on Indonesian democracy for three decades. For the next thirty years, the paper consistently extolled Suharto and whitewashed his crimes – minimizing student protests against his 'postponement' of elections and praising his reform of the army into a 'fast-moving, police-action force' in 1968–69, justifying his invasion of East Timor in 1975, legitimizing his Golkar party's victory in 1987 as 'relatively peaceful' and 'convincing', and commending his economic management.[22]

The *Economist* refrained from criticizing US interventions even on the rare occasions when these violated its low bar for the respect of democratic niceties. In 1965, Johnson sent 42,000 marines to the Dominican Republic, in what the paper called a 'reflexive move', but then excused as a pardonable misunderstanding from 'the most internationally responsible country in the world'. Most rebel officers in Santo Domingo were not Castroite communists, it admitted, but supporters of the 'democratic leftist' Juan Bosch, chafing under a corrupt military junta that had removed him from the presidency two years earlier.[23] In Greece, it deplored the 'colonels' coup' as a 'tragic stupidity' before elections slated for April 1967, but denied the CIA had any hand in plotting it – even as *Foreign Report* wrote quite candidly on its aims in doing so: to keep the Papandreou-led Centre Union from winning the elections by installing General Papadopoulos, a former Nazi collaborator and current CIA agent, and associated generals, instead.[24] That May, in a different register, the paper cheered a 'glittering victory' for Israel over Egypt in the Six-Day War – finally 'teaching a lesson' to Nasser, a 'would-be Bismarck' with dreams of uniting the Arabs, and Russians, behind him.[25] By the time Egypt launched a counter-attack in 1973 – a huge last-minute airlift of US tanks and aircraft turning the tide for Israel – the *Economist* line on the Middle East was more or less fixed. Peace would come when Arabs and Jews desired it, not from outside interference, ensuring that Israel – as the largest single recipient of just such external help from Washington – has seen little need to compromise with its neighbours, let alone the Palestinians under its thumb.[26]

Perhaps the most significant breach of democratic practice and journalistic ethics in the line of imperial duty came with the coup in Chile in 1973. Beedham delegated this dossier to Robert Moss, who was not content merely to criticize the leftwing physician Salvador Allende – elected president of Chile in 1970 promising a 'peaceful road to socialism' – but worked actively to prepare opinion for his forcible removal. Nixon had personally ordered the CIA to foment a coup before Allende even took the oath of office, with instructions to spare no expense and 'make the economy scream'.[27] Crozier, for whom Moss was already writing ISC Conflict Studies while travelling across Latin America for the *Economist,* tipped his protégé to help carry out this mission.[28] 'The next move from my CIA friends was to suggest the need for a book on Chile. The author I proposed to commission was Robert Moss, whose qualifications were ideal.'[29]

'In the Chilean summer, it is hard to imagine civil war', began a special *Economist* report from 1972, signed by Moss. 'Yachts bob out in the Pacific at Algarrobo, beautiful girls sip pisco sours in the Grand Hotel at Zapallar.'[30] To show how vulnerable this society really was – or at least the part of it drinking cocktails at hotel bars – the paper ran negative stories on Allende almost every week: his warm embrace of 'Cuban terrorists'; economic shortages caused by his land reforms and nationalizations, so that Chinese restaurants in Santiago now served 'sweet-and-sour turkey'; or dismissing revelations that the US was funding his opponents in the media, the political parties and the trade unions through an International Telephone and Telegraph subsidiary.[31] Filing these stories still left Moss enough time to lecture and write for the Institute of General Studies (IGS), a CIA think tank that met inside the US Embassy in Santiago, aiming to connect military officers with free-market economists; and to write for *SEPA,* a magazine for the same officer cohort, which splashed an article of his on its cover six months before the coup: 'An English Recipe for Chile - Military Control'.[32] At the same time, Moss readied his book, which instead of fertilizing the ground for the coup, had to be revised as a post-hoc justification of it, when Chile's generals launched an all-out assault on Allende's government at the start of September in 1973.

*Chile's Marxist Experiment* was distinguished by two compulsions, the first of which was bragging, so that Moss could not help crediting smooth coordination among top brass during the coup to 'reports prepared by a group of independent and opposition economists who had been meeting on a weekly basis since January' – that is, to himself and the IGS.[33] The other was sniggering: the 'irony' that Allende used a gun Fidel Castro gave him to commit suicide as tanks and jets pounded the presidential palace, which, as he refused 'four separate offers for safe conduct' was nothing but vain heroics – 'maybe he felt that death was preferable to a retirement divided between a villa in Havana and speech-making over fashionable dinner-tables.'[34] Citing sloppily fabricated 'evidence' of an imminent communist 'night of the long knives', Moss maintained that the army had acted in self-defence: 'Chile's generals reached the conclusion that democracy does not have the right to commit suicide.'[35] As a token of appreciation, the generals bought 9,750 copies, distributed through Chilean embassies; a member of the IGS, now running the state publishing house, printed another 15,000 in Spanish.[36]

When news of Allende's death reached him in London, Moss danced down the corridors of the *Economist* chanting, 'My enemy is dead!' He returned in haste to finish his book while officially on assignment for the *Economist*, producing a special report for it on the coup in October. In it, he praised the new junta for holding public trials of suspected leftists, and for allowing foreign journalists and the Red Cross to visit the 5,000 or so people being held at the national football stadium in Santiago – where Moss somehow missed gruesome scenes of torture and summary executions, along with the disappearances that came to mark the Pinochet regime. He ended with a simple endorsement: 'The events of September 11 were not a typical Latin American coup but the culmination of a long (and broad-based) public campaign against a minority government that was suspected, probably rightly, of preparing to perpetuate itself as a dictatorship.'[37] Bagehot, writing in 1851, had worked harder than this to justify the coup in France. The larger point is that Moss operated openly, and for seven more years after this dance of death, during which time his profile did not get any lower. Brazenly overlapping with studies for Crozier's ISC, his *Economist* articles spread the alarm about supposed communist threats in Spain, Portugal, Northern Ireland, Iran, South Africa and Nicaragua.[38] In all this, he showed that, in the free world, it was possible to do well by doing good: free trips from the Shah; quid-pro-quos for a cheery gloss on apartheid South Africa's invasion of Angola; a £20,000 salary to edit *VISION*, a magazine owned by the Nicaraguan dictator Anastasio Somoza.[39] Moss left the *Economist* in 1980, using contacts he had made there to publish his first novel, *The Spike*. Here the hero is journalist Robert Hockney, ex-Berkeley radical turned anti-communist crusader, whose erotic adventures are rendered in as much graphic detail as his quest to expose media outlets and think tanks as thinly disguised KGB fronts.[40]

## Macrae-economics: Considering Japan and West Germany

Norman Macrae was the mirror image of Beedham and Moss, complementing their geopolitical engagements with his own take on global capitalism.[41] His manner was quite different, however. Macrae dressed in a standard-issue suit and tie, looking like he had slept in them for weeks, while correcting copy at his desk. At meetings he stammered out his points and burst into giggles at inappropriate moments, his large boxy frame heaving up and down. No one could read his handwriting, or his corrections, except a devoted secretary, who was said to enter a trance to decipher it (this before computers, which he touted but never used). Though admired as a brilliant, original mind, he too was passed over for the editorship, three times. As a former section editor put it: 'the chap cut his own hair', and 'even then the editor had to be vaguely representable in public, you know, for visitors, on TV'. Andrew Knight would call him 'warm-hearted and good and very eccentric'. Rupert Pennant-Rea remembered that 'many of his spoken sentences began with the words "the thing is" and then rather tailed away'; 'let him write about the subject, however, and words flowed beautifully, without a single "the thing is".'

Separated by bearing, united by worldview – Beedham and Macrae agreed the greatest threat to it lay due east, in the Soviet Union. Macrae was born in Konigsberg in 1923, his father a high-ranking diplomat, who ended up as British Consul to Moscow at the height of Stalin's purges from 1935 to 1938. Joining his family for school holidays as a teenager, Macrae said he could never forget the maids who seemed to vanish suddenly from the corridors of the embassy. (Later, he took his own children on summer trips, not to the beach or museum, but to Eastern Europe, 'to teach them the difference between freedom and tyranny'.[42]) But, as with Beedham, it was disappointment with the weakness and hypocrisy of *his* side that came as the true call to action. A bomber navigator for the RAF ('a public sector job with public sector productivity') during the Second World War, he descended to earth in Germany in 1945, 'just as the Russians were coming in from the other side':

> All the politicians, including Churchill and Roosevelt, told us these were fine liberating democrats. And of course I knew from those school summer holidays so briefly before that those were astonishing lies. That has given me one advantage in my 40 years as a newspaperman. I have never since then believed a word either politicians or public-relations officers have said.[43]

After demobilization, he went to Cambridge, of which he was not fond: 'More intellectual, my left foot.' 'Sub-polytechnic Marxism' was more like it: some students actually thought it a good idea to give 'the secret of how to make an atom bomb to Marshall Stalin, who was clinically insane'. Macrae nevertheless found his home at a paper populated by graduates from the same social milieu, if not the same politics, becoming *the* driving force on economics at the *Economist*. Statistically dense, stylistically buoyant, many of his surveys turned into books and pamphlets – on capital markets, housing, industrial, trade and monetary policy, inventors, inventions and the near and not-so-near future.[44] Writing from a comparative perspective, he set the post-war performance of British capitalism against the more miraculous experiences of its rivals, in special reports on Germany, France, America and Japan – this last the subject of ground-breaking work, with 'Consider Japan' in 1962, 'The Risen Sun' in 1967 and 'The Pacific Century' in 1975, all published in Japanese translation. His obituary called him an 'unacknowledged giant of postwar Britain', one of the few journalists to rank with Milton Friedman, Daniel Bell and Peter Drucker. But Macrae was not exactly unknown. In 1988 Emperor Hirohito recognized him with the Order of the Rising Sun. Like many whose star first rose in the West, he was simply big in Japan.[45]

If the nineteenth century the *Economist* had looked for investment outlets in the East, by the mid-twentieth it went in search of lessons. The parallels between Britain and Japan, two island nations 'with very similar import structures and a tendency to run into import deficit at one stage of the internal trade cycle', captivated Macrae. He was aghast that some Japanese policymakers he met in the 1960s thought it 'time to learn respectable economics from the British and slow down their rate of growth'. One reason for coming to Japan, he told his hosts, was on the contrary to find an escape route for Britain, whose post-war economy seemed caught in a cycle of 'stop-go' – periods of expansion in which imports quickly raced ahead of exports, precipitating a balance of payments crisis, at which point government intervened to restrain demand, deflating the economy. The result? British industrial production had grown by 28 per cent, exports by 44 per cent, from 1953 to 1961; over this period, Japan increased its respective totals by 217 and 237 per cent. In 1955 Japan's GDP was £8.2 billion against Britain's £17 billion. By 1967 it was expected to be £40 billion, 18 per cent larger than Britain's at about £34 billion.

In trying to explain the divergence, Macrae rejected explanations based on race or culture. Japanese 'were not nowadays naturally servile to authority, or so silly as to actively enjoy hard work', and 'the inbred collectivism of the Japanese people' was not unlike 'the atmosphere in the heartier English public schools'. Macrae paid attention to government policies instead, which turned out to be inimical to standard practice in Britain and the US. American businessmen landed in Tokyo expecting 'the great new successful free enterprise community of our time, created in America's own image'. He prepared them for disappointment: 'Japan, even more than France, is the land of indicative economic planning à outrance.' Five years on, he was even more emphatic: 'Ultimate responsibility for industrial planning, for deciding in which new directions Japan's burgeoning industrial effort should try to go, and for fostering and protecting business, lies with the government.'[46]

On his first trip to Japan, Macrae emphasized the way that planning worked for budgets and banks. The former were relentlessly expansionary, combining fiscal stimulus and tax cuts, year after year. The latter were even more peculiar: virtually insolvent, with a deposit-to-loan ratio of less than 3 per cent, banks relied on the central bank for liquidity and responded to its instructions on when to tighten credit and investment. If fiscal policy acted as accelerator, monetary policy was the brake. When Britain overheated, by contrast, the Treasury simply depressed demand across the economy, hurting growing firms far more than old and inefficient ones. For this reason its top three exports to Japan in 1961 were liquor, sweets and textiles. 'The vision of the average Japanese is that Britain today is a non-developing country; filled no doubt with whisky stills, children's bonbons, skilled at making up material from old sheep; but not a dynamic country capable of producing anything expansive and new.'[47] On his next visit, corporate culture caught his eye. The Japanese miracle perplexed Americans and Europeans, who demanded it 'liberalise its rules about capital inflow' and permit foreigners to buy up its businesses. Macrae was sceptical of their chances. On returning to his Tokyo hotel at night, he encountered 'American businessmen reviving themselves in the bar with moans and martinis'. 'The society's rotten with fornication and your English Scotch [sic]', one drawled at him. 'OK, so I'm no puritan myself ... But I don't buy me a prostitute every night with my shareholders' money, and I don't suppose the London *Economist* buys you one either, huh?'[48]

Capitalism worked differently in Japan. Employees enjoyed lifetime job security, top income tax rates on executive pay were more than 10 per cent greater than in Britain, and if corporate income as a percentage of GDP was higher than in the West, gross capital profit rates were lower. Far from condemning its methods as unorthodox, Macrae was enamoured by them. Beneath the boom of his bar mates, he was forced to mutter, 'economic miracle ... remarkable planning techniques ... record of growth'. To help explain these achievements he returned to the financial system, which now carried an implicit criticism of Wall Street and the City of London. Banks' control over investment funds in Japan, instead of the stock market, 'had overcome one of the weaknesses of the normal western free enterprise system – which is that the total of investment that seems profitable to individual profit-seeking firms is unfortunately almost invariably smaller than a dynamic economy should require'. Capital investment between 1956 and 1963 averaged 34 per cent in Japan as compared to 17 per cent in the US and Britain. Average annual growth was 10.1 per cent in the former, just 2.6 to 2.8 per cent in the latter. In 1975 he was still optimistic about Japan as it began to export its development model to its neighbours.[49]

West Germany was another reason to reassess the so-called English disease. In 1966 its record of growth was second only to Japan, averaging upwards of 6 per cent for over a decade; while its share of industrial exports had doubled since 1950, largely at the expense of Britain, whose share had fallen from 21 to 13 per cent. Again, Macrae was more impressed with economic policies than 'nonsense about national temperaments'. German trade unions and management structures could easily be emulated in Britain. The former were fewer (16), more democratic ('secret ballots'), richer ('regular dues'), more professional ('trained left-of-centre economists'). They were also less likely to strike or walk out based on the introduction of new equipment, since they shared in management decisions, and, though paid slightly lower wages, had seen these rise by 130 per cent (against 80 per cent in Britain) since 1955. Managers, on the other hand, could enrich themselves as well as their companies – with a lower top income tax, higher capital taxes geared to investment and activist banks, which kept track of business efficiency.[50]

### The City and the EEC: In Search of a British Miracle

How did Britain compare to these countries? Macrae raised that question in every foreign report, even as his answer changed in response to events at home. In 1964, Harold Wilson had promised to replicate the German and Japanese miracles, with a state-led modernization of the economy that harnessed science, technology and efficient management. But that project failed. Once in power, Wilson deflated the economy, sidelining the Department of

Economic Affairs and abandoning his National Plan, in order to protect sterling, for yet more Treasury- and City-inspired stop-go. In 1970, his successor, Edward Heath, came to office pledging a dose of free-market rigour – no more subsidies for 'lame duck' industries – and legislation to bring the trade unions to heel. But this too had come to naught. Heath backtracked as soon as unemployment hit 1 million, before miners brought down his government. By then, a world crisis had overtaken the national one that Macrae had hoped to solve in his studies abroad.

At this juncture, the deputy editor gave his verdict on the political, economic, social and cultural institutions that had long made his country the odd man out, in a 1973 survey that also signalled a bitter turn in narratives of national decline. 'Britain entered the postwar era as the richest country in northwest Europe except Sweden. Because our economic growth rate since then has been about half that of our neighbours we are now the poorest except Ireland.' In 1964, Macrae had pushed the *Economist* to back Wilson, in the hopes of unleashing economic growth. Instead, what Britain got was 'government by inferiority complex', as Labour 'solemnly deflated the economy into ever greater unemployment and stagnation, in order to save an exchange rate which almost everybody outside Whitehall knew it was both undesirable and impossible to save anyway'. This episode led Macrae to conclude that Britain was not ruled by parliament, but a 'bureaucratic oligarchy' of about 3,000 administrative civil servants – which might have been fine, if these were younger, less risk-shy, and more like their French or Japanese brethren. From 1970, Edward Heath and the Tories offered another lesson, when their attack on the unions' legal immunities was handily defeated. If this stood, more electrical blackouts could be expected, descending the country into a literal dark age of social disorder, even a 'Latin American situation'.

Declinist, not defeatist, Macrae advocated a raft of measures to contain this looming crisis – as significant for the neoliberal elements these already contained as for the ways in which they differed with the ideas gaining traction among intellectuals who would be close to Thatcher. Macrae called for a long overdue showdown with organized labour (perhaps through a 'shock legal action' as in the 1901 Taff Vale case), and for reversing the 'Attlee nationalizations' of 1945–51. This version of nationalized industry – 'narrow, monopoly production in certain rigidly defined fields' like coal, railways, power utilities, steel – had always been doomed, not just because public corporations were kept from moving between product lines as did all private firms (Imperial Tobacco now made crisps as well as cigarettes), but because they in turn produced monopoly unions, and cost-push inflation. 'The crucial point for any reform is not that ownership of particular plants should be wrested from the state but that there should be competition to make the products of nationalized industries.' No 'forced sale' then, but the extension of competition to 'all municipal or other public services' – from libraries to trash pickup to prisons – on a performance contract basis.[51] Still, it was difficult to be crudely anti-statist in light of the last thirty years, which suggested that Britain did not have *adequate* planning. In Tokyo, a civil servant at the Ministry of Economy, Trade and Industry once apologized to Macrae for handing over a report brimming with mathematical jargon. 'There must presumably be something else, if not mathematics, of which those in charge of British economic policy tend to be excessively fond', ventured the civil servant. 'Moralising', replied Macrae.[52]

What remained almost unthinkable was that monetary methods could or should be the main means of lifting the malaise. Here was the bedrock, as it were, of the weak Keynesian consensus at the *Economist,* where several reasons spoke against the manipulation of interest rates to increase unemployment or shake out inefficient firms. For Macrae, there were not just the memories of the Depression, as well as the experience of the post-war decades of 'stop-go', but overlaying both the logic of the Cold War: near-full employment as the price of democratic legitimacy in Western liberalism's struggle with the Soviet Union. Amidst the miracle years of post-war capitalism, the bias was for expansion, and against constriction. As if to highlight the gap this left between the *Economist* and the neoliberal program, Macrae's survey of the economy in 1973 brought a reply from Arthur Seldon, joint head of the pioneering think tank the Institute of Economic Affairs, who 'agreed with 90 percent' of it, but wished Macrae had followed 'his analysis to its conclusions' and called for denationalization of the 'two state services that account for a high proportion of government: education and medical care'.[53]

Macrae's frustration with the 'stop' in stop-go economics led to overlap with neoliberals like Seldon, however, on an important issue. To avoid the deflationary effects of defending the pound sterling at a fixed exchange rate, Macrae had backed a float since the late 1950s, irrespective of the City's sterling area ties. More exciting opportunities now beckoned, at the interconnection between Europe and America, whose sluice was the growing Eurodollar market. Starting in the late 1950s, some of the City's leading merchant bankers joined Treasury and Bank regulators to encourage American, Asian and other multinational banks and corporations to come to London to tap these liquid markets in 'offshore' dollars – whose chief attraction was their unregulated status, operating outside Federal Reserve and Treasury oversight and capital controls established under Bretton Woods.[54] Since Macrae was neither uncritical of the banks nor a conventional neoliberal, it is all the more striking that he too looked for a partial solution to British difficulties in the speculative innovations of London's financial hub.

Indeed, as Macrae contemplated the advantages of British membership of the European Economic Community (EEC), it was the prospects for the City that stood out: the end of fixed exchange rates and sterling area capital controls – which EEC entry demanded – meant that as 'northern Europe starts exporting its manufacturing industries to the poor south and communist east', British banks would boom, organizing the flexible holding, licensing and other investment and ownership strategies and structures of the post-industrial world.[55] *Britain into Europe*, a collection of writings from the *Economist* staff, made the case for entry from this perspective in 1971 – arguing that it was high time for the City to abandon sterling's reserve status (with the 'awful record' of 'two devaluations, ten grisly postwar sterling crises, ten occasions on which Britain suffered a sharp drain on its gold and foreign exchange reserves') and most commonwealth preferences in goods.[56] The City should instead look to the 'dollar and Eurocurrency markets' of the future, becoming 'the banking centre of the community, where the working dollar balances of Europe are kept – a new, more desired, very much more fruitful European version of the sterling balances used by Britain to finance its profitable investment abroad'. The City would act as a hinge between two eras of political economy, with Britain pivoting to the global currency markets of the future.[57]

If Keynesian demand management remained a relevant tool in the liberal policy mix, this had as much to do with the US – which Macrae visited for the paper in 1958, 1969, 1975, 1978 and 1980, more than any place else, outdoing even Beedham in his devotion to it. While enthusiasm for the 'greatest country on earth', and its mission, 'to be at once political sedative, social healer and the leader of mankind's last important economic advance', never wavered, fears arose that its social and racial conflicts might plunge it into chaos, and then migrate to Britain. 'Negros have swarmed into rotting ghettos', Macrae reported in shock in 1969 – that year a turning point in his perception of the inner city – plagued by unemployment and crime, which have 'sprouted a large charade cast of tough so-called "black power" leaders'. Many whites suffered from 'feelings of insecurity and terror', and some in Washington told him they carried guns, 'just in case'. 'White Americans fear (probably rightly) that "black power" ideology may make some Negro youths feel that robberies and assaults on white women are almost a noble act of black revolution.' White students egging on black comrades at protests, as well as the 'temporary tolerance of violence by many American white liberals', particularly incensed him. Stimulus was needed on a scale unimagined even by Johnson's War on Poverty, to head off 'mortal peril'. America 'would be wise to give almost overstrained priority to maximum economic growth, even though this will mean tolerating more inflation than its middle classes will like'.[58] But just as important was reassuring those middle classes by empowering police and suppressing locally elected community action programs, to 'encourage an exodus from the ghettos at all deliberate speed'.[59]

Macrae's strong feelings about law, order and local democracy in the US had a personal element, which he disclosed towards the end of the survey. Invited to speak at a university symposium on South Africa, he was heckled by students for being a 'wicked honky', who, in the *Economist*, had opposed the immediate implementation of black majority rule. 'Dreamy, liberal intellectuals in Washington still held some idealistic notions of what a planned disturbance of this kind would be like', he scoffed. 'What I found was the dreariest old Nazism ... the cult of violence, the cult of youth, the cult of proclaiming that one is ruled by a plutocracy ... anyone over the age of 45 knows when and where in Europe youth was last asked to bathe in these emotions.' Students roamed the hallways carrying buckets 'into which obviously non-revolutionary middle-aged gentleman were requested to put entirely unaudited dollars "to finance the South African revolution"'. Macrae was petrified. First he tried to run. Then he pretended to be a friendly journalist asking sincere-sounding questions about Vietnam, which the students, he felt, answered stupidly. Later, at an assembly, he saw 'black-power-uniformed thugs seize [the university president] by the scruff of the neck as a band of black drummers beat an accompaniment'. 'A man of decency and international eminence' surrounded by a black drum circle – his overwrought memory of this scene never left him.[60]

By the turn of the 1970s, Macrae could not hide his contempt for anything that smacked of counter-culture – from the Beatles to black radicals, hippies, feminists, environmentalists, the New Left and gays (he once proposed an *Economist* leader on a spray to 'cure' homosexuals by reversing their aversion to the smell of their mothers). These people were not just enemies but lightweights, who well-meaning liberals mistakenly wished to engage in dialogue. In the end, his economic position dovetailed with Beedham's politics: in a backward country like Brazil or Chile, or in a poor black neighbourhood in America or Britain, democracy could easily become the enemy of liberal capitalism. Richard Nixon, with scant respect for the former, received barely a slap on the wrist over Watergate. The *Economist* viewed the affair as a mildly amusing intrigue almost up to the day the president resigned.[61] Macrae, at any rate, looking to escape from the corset of fixed exchange, praised Nixon for dismantling Bretton Woods between 1971 and 1973.[62]

**Andrew Knight: Special Relationships, 1974–86**

The *Economist* may have applauded the delinking of the dollar from gold and the effective end of the Bretton Woods system of fixed exchange in 1973. But this drastic step also pointed to a deep, rumbling crisis of the liberal capitalist order that America had built after 1945. In one sense, this was a testament to its success, in particular in Germany and Japan. Two decades after their wartime defeat, newer, lower-cost industries in both countries – making everything from cars to consumer electronics – began to capture market share from American firms abroad and at home. For the first time in the twentieth century, the US recorded a trade deficit in 1971. The decline in profitability suffered by US manufacturers soon engulfed their foreign rivals too, while attempts to restore profit rates unleashed trade union militancy across the advanced economies. The problem was not just economic, but political and imperial. Mired in Vietnam, Washington had little to show for its efforts there besides monetary chaos. In the context of low interest rates, dollars spent on 'butter and guns' sloshed through the global economy, joining huge pools already 'offshored' in the City of London, where investors used them (among other things) to bet against the US currency. Nixon's devaluation in 1973 was a defensive strike, meant to wind up a long, losing battle to maintain confidence in the gold convertibility of the dollar, and restore competitive capacity against German and Japanese exporters. As a means of reviving the world economy, it came to grief immediately. The oil price quadrupled after the Yom Kippur War, and a new word was coined to describe the effects this had down the decade: stagflation. Perhaps most alarming of all, these very developments seemed to strengthen the Soviet Union, which gained hard currency from surging oil prices and a freer hand abroad after America's geopolitical setback in Southeast Asia.[63]

At this moment of apparent crisis for the American-led liberal world order, Andrew Knight became editor of the *Economist*. In contrast to past occupants of this position, Knight found it more difficult to get hired in the first place than to obtain the top job. On his second try in 1964, Brian Beedham thought him 'brooding' but 'with the large advantage of not being a smooth young man', and 'worth bearing in mind'. Two years later Fred Hirsch, the intellectually distinguished finance editor, was about to end a third interview, dismissing a bungled explanation of monetary policy with, 'I don't think much of that', when Knight rejoined, 'Well, what do you expect for £1250 a year?'[64] Quick wits won him a spot covering investing. But he had a bumpy ride. The business editor, Mary Goldring, criticized his knowledge of the money markets, and foisted him on the American Survey in 1968. Knight enjoyed this – too much for his superiors John Midgley and Nancy Balfour, who wanted less socializing and more business articles; he was recalled from Washington after just two years. On top of this, Knight was 'basically illiterate', according to one section editor, 'his command of grammar left something to be desired'.

Yet two chances appeared and Knight seized them. The first was an opening in Europe, which he began to write about in 1970 as an assistant editor – lobbying for British membership of the EEC as well as a separate section devoted to it, to be edited by him from Brussels. There in 1973, his address book swelled: Valéry Giscard d'Estaing, the French presidential hopeful, was just one of the illustrious friends he made in the bureaucratic capital of Europe. Knight's second break came that year when Burnet opted to leave and caused an uproar by pushing Beedham as his successor. 'There was a strong feeling among younger members of staff that it would be nice to have someone more accessible and less right-wing', recalled Johnny Grimond.[65] Balfour and Mary Goldring protested to the board of directors, though in opposing Beedham, none had in mind the alternative of Knight, with Goldring resigning at the prospect. During this row, Knight crossed the Channel to make his case – most forcefully to the new chairman, the financier Evelyn de Rothschild, as well as to the board member and grocery magnate John Sainsbury, and assistant editor David Gordon. Knight's pitch? He would conquer America, a challenge for which his two years of hobnobbing in Washington now seemed an asset. 'The American Survey had given us a great reputation in the US. I could go to the White House anytime I wanted', Knight told them. 'The *Economist* could fulfil a unique function: analytical, opinionated, with distance'. It offered 'something *Newsweek* and *Time* couldn't'. Rothschild agreed that 'exposing the *Economist*, at the risk of loss, to the American market was worth a shot'; Sainsbury, 'the most prestigious board member', clinched the consent of the rest of this 'mildly obstructionist' group.

At age thirty-four, Knight became the second youngest person ever to edit the *Economist*. Despite serious scepticism from many staff, he was uniquely suited to the mission he had set himself: transforming the *Economist* from a fellow traveller into an active participant in the political and economic debates that mattered in America. What had prepared him for this role? Though born in New Zealand, Knight was bundled off to England as a child. His father, an air force officer, chose Ampleforth, the elite Catholic public school, where Knight rose to head boy and became a favourite of his housemaster Cardinal Basil Hume. At Balliol, Oxford, he took a second in Modern History, before being sent, again by his father, to a merchant bank in the City. Knight did not like being a banker and tried a lateral move to what seemed the more exciting world of financial journalism. In 1964, he joined the *Investors Chronicle*, before stepping up and up: editor of the *Economist*, chief executive of the *Daily Telegraph*, the chairman of News International. If the *Economist* greatly enhanced Knight's standing, this reflected his success in raising its profile, too.

In every written account of Knight, the word 'ambition' appears repeatedly – almost as if it were a physical attribute, to be noted along with his height or eye colour. 'Written in neon', said a former section editor. 'He even worked funeral services.' Profiles tend to place him behind closed doors, partly obscured, amidst padded leather and polished wood. The journalist and military historian Max Hastings recalled their first meeting in 1985 at Brooks, a private club in Saint James. 'A man of striking pale, ascetic good looks ... he had long ago shed any evidence of his family roots in New Zealand ... and could have been mistaken for a youthful ambassador or Whitehall permanent secretary.' Hastings observed Knight carefully as they changed parlours. 'He acquired an almost oriental look when his eyes narrowed as he smiled. His meticulous courtesy also held a touch of the East. He had always possessed the ability to make the mighty feel

safe in his hands.'[66] Andrew Neil, another journalist who served
under Knight at the *Economist* and then at News International,
called him 'an accomplished courtier to the rich and powerful,
especially outsiders who needed help with the British establishment'.[67] These included Canadian mogul Conrad Black, whom
Knight advised to buy the *Daily Telegraph* in 1986, in a deal
Evelyn de Rothschild underwrote, and all three toasted atop the
Economist tower (asked who he intended to make managing
director of the *Telegraph*, Black replied, 'Our genial host, Andrew
S. B. Knight, Esquire, peerage anticipated'); and Rupert Murdoch,
the Australian who purchased the *Sunday Times* in 1983, briefly
making Knight chairman of his growing media empire in 1989.[68]

At the *Economist,* Knight turned a transatlantic love affair into a
new business model. The strategy rolled out in 1977 when Clive
Greaves, head of advertising, went to New York to 'spend money'.
'There was no market research, just intuition based on my years
in Washington. I get and deserve credit for getting into America.'
Greaves consulted advertisers with a goal to double circulation
in time for the 1980 presidential election, at the same time hiring
subscriber acquisition mailings expert Beth O'Rorke.[69] In 1987,
Abbott Mead Vickers BBDO devised a white-on-red ad campaign
that began to appear in taxis, buses, subways and airports in cities
in Europe and North America: 'Would you like to sit next to you
at dinner?'; 'Protects against foot-in-mouth disease'; 'World domination without the laser death ray master plan'. 'We lost money
for six months when we expected losses for the first two years',
Knight recalled with pride, '27,500 subscribers were there when
I started. That was 125,000 when I left.' Today more than half of
all circulation flows through the US and Canada, about 850,000
copies. But making it in America was not just about sales; it also
affected the layout (the American Survey moved ahead of Britain)
and the outlook of the paper. On taking over, Knight assured
Beedham that 'I basically agreed with him' and 'history bore him
out, if not on Vietnam, certainly on the need to resist the Soviets'.
For Moss he had the highest regard, entrusting him for the next
seven years with some of the highest profile leaders on foreign
affairs.[70]

## The *Economist* against Détente

What then was the view of the American empire at the *Economist* – from now on not just devoted, but increasingly sold to the people running it, at the height of the Cold War? The first indication came with the Portuguese Revolution in 1974. The *Economist* was intensely worried by the sudden collapse of the Estado Novo dictatorship in Lisbon, and the land seizures, factory occupations and street protests that broke out in popular revolt against it; in particular, it feared the influence of radical socialist and communist elements among officers in the Movimento das Forças Armadas, many of whom had refused to go on with the regime's brutal colonial wars in Angola, Guinea and Mozambique. Portugal may have been poor and undemocratic, but it was also a member of NATO of global importance, as a still extant imperial power in Africa and Asia. The paper's choice to take this volatile situation in hand was the aristocratic, monocled General Spínola: considered a moderate, Spínola had served as a volunteer under Franco and as an observer with Hitler's armies, before experiencing a de Gaulle–like epiphany about the need for 'reforms' as military governor of Guinea. After Spínola was pushed out of the provisional government, launched a failed coup and fled in March 1975, the *Economist* denounced the direction of the Carnation Revolution in purple prose: 'completely controlled by Marxists', it was using Nazi 'Reichstag fire techniques' to erect a 'totalitarian state', with 'wider repercussions' than 'the failed Marxist experiment in Chile' that could lead to the break-up of NATO.[71]

Moss was the unmistakable author of these lines. Months later, he wrote in the same alarmist tones about 'the southern flank' of the NATO alliance. In July, the Greek junta launched a coup against the leader of Cyprus, Archbishop Makarios III. Long a thorn in the side of the British, who retained huge sovereign military bases on the island, Makarios had fought for national self-determination against them: first as *Enosis,* or union with Greece, backed by 96 per cent of Greek Cypriots in a referendum in 1950; and then for independence, which arrived in neutered form ten years later, when Makarios became the first elected president. The *Economist* not only justified his ouster, reminding readers that

Makarios had been a pest – ruling with AKEL, the Communist Party, while pursuing a non-aligned foreign policy (under him Cyprus was one of only four non-Communist states to trade with North Vietnam), outside NATO. It also glossed over the bloody consequences: Turkey's invasion of Cyprus, with the connivance of Kissinger as well as Wilson and Callaghan in London, which in addition to 4,000 dead and 12,000 wounded, drove 180,000 Greek Cypriots from their homes, amidst similar reprisals against the Turkish community.[72] The paper even attributed the collapse of the junta in Athens to deft American diplomacy – which had 'presided over a radical change for the better in the politics of the eastern Mediterranean', and hoped for more decisiveness of this sort going forward. If not, Spain and Italy could be next in line for subversion, 'providing the greatest opportunity for the westward spread of communist governments in Europe' since 1945.[73]

Outside Europe, the Portuguese Empire rapidly disintegrated, posing immediate questions for US policymakers about what should – and should not – replace it. In December 1975, they gave their answer in East Timor. Hours after getting the green light from Ford and Kissinger in person, on a layover in Jakarta, the Indonesian dictator Suharto invaded the island, which had just proclaimed independence from Lisbon under the banner of the leftwing Front for the Liberation of East Timor. The *Economist* not only refused to criticize Indonesia's annexation, but turned a blind eye to the genocidal death toll of some 100,000 in eighteen months, roughly a sixth of the Timorese population.[74] In Angola, Kissinger tried to prevent the Marxist-inspired MPLA from taking over as the date set for independence approached, by sending money, weapons and advisors to its two smaller rivals, the FNLA and UNITA. In October, mere weeks before the Portuguese were due to leave, South Africa took a more direct approach – invading from the south at the same time as a coordinated assault from Zaire to the north, converging on Luanda. Only Cuban troops – ferried from Havana at the last moment on ageing Britannia turbo props, without prior consultation with Moscow – allowed the MPLA to hold out and then to win.[75] As the *Economist* warned, however, this was not the end of the story. South Africa could not allow a victory for black radicalism to go unchecked, threatening its hold over Namibia, and the apartheid regime itself in Pretoria. Nor could the US tolerate the defeat of its clients. The *Economist* suggested several possible chess moves to American leaders: sweetened aid to Angola if it kicked out the Soviets, a 'total naval blockade' of Cuba, mining its main ports. Plans to bomb and invade the island could also be prepared, though might be 'slow to take effect' and 'arouse anti-Americanism'.[76]

From this swashbuckling perspective, the election of Jimmy Carter in 1976 seemed like the start of a strategic unravelling, given the new president's naïve pursuit of arms control and misty rhetoric about human rights. For the *Economist*, Carter showed just how dangerously inept he was in his handling of the Iranian Revolution. By 1979, this mass mobilization had forced out the Shah, whose family had reigned for twenty-six years at the pleasure of Washington. To anti-imperialism, the new leader, Shiah cleric Ruholla Khomeini, added religious fundamentalism. In November, students overran and took hostage the US embassy. The *Economist* called for swift retribution: capture the islets of Abu Musa and the Tumbs; embargo food; if nothing else worked, invade.[77] Instead, the hostage crisis dragged on for over a year, during which the Soviets sent troops into Afghanistan. Seeking to prop up a teetering communist regime in Kabul, Moscow intervened after the murder of President Taraki by his second, Hafizullah Amin, who it feared might defect to the American camp; and just as the Iranian revolution unleashed a potent new form of Islamic radicalism, which threatened to spread to Muslim republics inside the Soviet Union.[78] At this the *Economist* exploded, seeing proof of a total loss of nerve. 'Who invited 40,000 Russian soldiers complete with their Quisling [Babrak Karmal] into Afghanistan? Answer: President Carter, the American congress and American opinion – and those American allies who have not believed, and have done little to remedy or reverse a crumbling of America's willingness to exercise power.' At a minimum, the US and NATO must arm the holy warriors, or mujahedin, who were resisting Soviet forces, with the latest tank-busting missiles.[79]

This excoriation of American fumbling from the right carried over with a vengeance to Central America, where that same year Sandinista guerrillas drove the brutal Somoza dynasty from power in Nicaragua. The paper did not advise direct intervention to prop up this US client, bombing its citizens in the slums of the capital city of Managua for the world to see. But that could change. 'If Cuban silhouettes do emerge through the murk in Nicaragua, the Americans will have to act.'[80] Nor did it apply to the leftwing revolts sparked in neighbouring El Salvador and Guatemala, where 'American arms will be required to uphold democracy', as bodies piled up from the rightwing death squads in each.[81] Soon it did not apply to Nicaragua either. Ronald Reagan had begun to orchestrate a covert war against the Sandinistas there in 1981, eventually arming more than 15,000 Contras in Honduras and Costa Rica to harry the new regime. Five years later, the Iran-Contra scandal exposed the money-laundering operation, violating American law itself, that was used to finance this – tragic news for the *Economist*, less because it implicated the president and his advisors in a criminal conspiracy, than for endangering congressional funding for counter-insurgency efforts.[82] In the meantime, the *Economist* had backed an outright invasion of tiny Grenada in 1983, and the toppling of its revolutionary government. In 'Licensed to Kill', it airily defended this act, on the grounds that 'adversaries of the west should live in a state of uncertainty', while brushing off critics in Britain, troubled by US treatment of a commonwealth member. 'Superpowers do not need allies', it told them, 'only cheerleaders.'[83]

What they needed was the *Economist*. By 1983 it was not a proponent so much as a pillar of the special relationship, which Knight carefully erected out of his friendships with veterans of the Nixon administration. None was more important than Kissinger, who became a sort of informal housemaster; so at ease, he did a playful TV spot for the *Economist* in 1996, in which an airline passenger, Mr Burnside, in suspenders and French cuffs, drinks champagne serenely until someone takes the seat next to him. 'Hey, it's Henry Kissinger! Ready for a good chat?' Mr Burnside looks queasy; having failed to read the *Economist* he is unprepared for the most fateful small talk of his life. In 1979, the tone was graver. That February, the former US secretary of state sat down with Knight for a two-part exclusive interview about the second strategic arms limitation treaty; the discussion also roamed widely over the Cold War. Who would emerge in better shape after a nuclear show-down? The US. How many civilian deaths could be expected? '100m', Kissinger replied, 'but it will nevertheless leave us politi-cally paralyzed.' 'Or could do so ... ', Knight interjected hopefully. 'Probably would do so.' Kissinger dismissed the idea that treaties could usher in world peace; if the West did not raise its 'coun-terforce capabilities', it 'could be entering a period of maximum peril'. Should the ratification of SALT-II, the arms control treaty, be linked to 'good behaviour' from Moscow? Yes, Kissinger replied:

> Look at what has happened since 1975, in the space of a little more than four years: we have had Cuban troops in Angola, Cuban troops in Ethiopia, two invasions of Zaire, a communist coup in Afghanistan, a communist coup in South Yemen, and the occupation of Cambodia by Vietnam, all achieved by Soviet arms, with Soviet encouragement and in several cases protected by Soviet veto in the United Nations. In addition Soviet advanced aircraft piloted by Soviet personnel are protecting Cuba – presum-ably against us – so that Cuban pilots and aircraft are operating all round Africa – also presumably against us. That cannot go on and have Salt survive.[84]

Soon after this call for ending détente, the *Economist* ran a savagely hostile review of *Sideshow: Kissinger, Nixon and the Destruction of Cambodia*, which accused its author William Shawcross of writing a 'sleazy and distasteful' piece of 'propa-ganda' blaming Kissinger for 'destroying that beautiful country, Cambodia'. Shawcross wrote an angry letter, to which Kissinger wrote a long, angrier reply, denying one of the central claims of the book – that he had any hand in the coup against Prince Sihanouk in 1970 which eventually brought the Khmer Rouge to power in Phnom Penh. It 'took us completely by surprise; at first I even thought he had engineered it himself in order to stage a dramatic comeback'.[85] Samuel Thornton, a naval intelligence officer in Saigon at that time, then wrote a letter to the *Economist* in which he described his own part in planning the coup with the full approval of the White House. Knight refused to publish it,

privately assuring Thornton that he had investigated these alle-
gations and found them untrue. The investigation seems to have
consisted of asking the former director of the CIA Richard Helms,
two admirals and Kissinger himself. 'If all journalists used Knight's
method of asking those at the very top about their possible misdeeds', Seymour Hersh observed, 'none of the major investigative
stories of the past two decades would have become public.'[86]

Clubbiness is the appropriate term to describe these relationships, which worked in both directions, in ways large and small.
Kissinger might have been the biggest fish. But George Shultz was
of greater practical importance, as both a Labour and Treasury
Secretary under Nixon; he resigned in time to take over the Bechtel
conglomerate in 1974 and a post at Stanford, where he acted as
conduit to Reagan. It was on Knight's visit to California in 1978
to attend the exclusive, all-male Bohemian Grove retreat that
Shultz convinced him that 'Reagan was an intelligent, viable alternative to Carter, who I hated in almost every respect.' Four years
later, Shultz was having dinner with Knight in London. 'Andrew
said, "What's new?" I said "I'll tell you at 6 o'clock."' At half
past seven Knight's phone rang. 'He came back and said, "That
was the *Economist* reporter in Washington breathlessly telling
me you had been named Secretary of State." And I said, "Well,
what did you do, tell him you were having dinner with me?" He
said, "No, I didn't want to one-up him that badly."'[87] Shultz regularly consulted the *Economist* during his seven years at the US
State Department – taking heart from its position on Iran-Contra,
mulling over its advice on his Middle East peace initiative.[88]


### Late to Neoliberalism?

Since the 1960s, the *Economist* had played a key role in debates
over British economic decline via Norman Macrae, who set relatively disappointing figures for output, productivity and growth
in a global and comparative context. But his treks abroad aimed
to find solutions to these shortfalls, in optimistic and eclectic
admixtures – of Japanese banking, German industrial relations,
American entrepreneurialism or French indicative planning. In

the 1970s, the onset of a worldwide economic downturn and the crises of Vietnam and Watergate changed the tenor of *Economist* coverage, which became much darker. Macrae's frantic accounts of Columbia student protestors, or the unruly poverty of black neighbourhoods in New York and Washington, DC, were illustrations of this mood. In Britain, the ongoing confrontation between trade unions and the Heath government, and the trail of uncollected trash and candlelit offices and homes it left behind in 1974, also drew dire warnings; indeed, that 'Britannia's dream of apocalypse is now horribly near to coming true', with inflation soon to reach Weimar levels.[89] But for just these reasons, Macrae was reluctant to embrace what became the standard neoliberal solutions to the crises of profitability and inflation that swept the advanced Western economies – and at first neither he nor many other *Economist* editors thought that Margaret Thatcher and Ronald Reagan were the best leaders to see liberalism through this turmoil. Given that the *Economist* has become a byword for the neoliberal revolution these two politicians embodied, why was the paper so late to rally to it?

Although gaining ground, in the 70s neoliberalism was not yet the hegemonic system of thought it would become by the century's end. Weakest post-war in the universities, its adherents had long gathered outside of these to spread their message in think tanks and 'thought collectives' – nowhere more successfully than in Britain. This reflected the strength of classical liberalism in its world historic home, from which neoliberals had always derived inspiration. In the 30s, the stiffest resistance to Keynes had after all come from the LSE, where before departing for the US, Hayek wrote *The Road to Serfdom* as a call to reject 'foreign ideas' about the state, and return to the classical conceptions of Smith and Mill; and the economics department had ties from its inception to the most important international association of neoliberal thinkers, the Mont Pelerin Society in Switzerland, founded in 1947.[90] The launch in 1955 of the Institute for Economic Affairs further cemented these connections. Arthur Seldon and Ralph Harris developed the IEA into a powerful corporate fundraiser in Britain, inviting leading US academics to give talks, and publishing pamphlets to win those whom Hayek deemed 'second-hand

dealers in ideas' – teachers, journalists, doctors, lecturers, politicians and businessmen – to its principles.[91] By 1974, many were
converts. That year Keith Joseph and Margaret Thatcher founded
the Centre for Policy Studies inside the Conservative Party, in
order to convert it to 'rigorous free-market ideas' and policies.
Five years later the Adam Smith Institute relocated from the US to
London, where it exerted pressure from outside the formal party
structures.[92]

Through these and other transnational channels, the neoliberals
had crafted a broad philosophical account of individual liberty,
the state and the law in relation to markets – and fought against
the trammelling of these by socialists of all shades.[93] But it was on
a far narrower point that much of the argument was carried in the
run-up Thatcher's election in 1979: the doctrine of monetarism
– which posited monetary growth as the cause of inflation, one
that governments could measure and should restrict – as the key
to restoring order to the economies of the West. It was this belief
that the *Economist* resisted, amidst a broader shift in ideological
sentiment towards the IEA that it had done much to bring about.
A long-time critic of the post-1945 consensus when it came to
welfare and nationalizations, Macrae did accept one pillar of it:
full employment. This made him hesitant to endorse the deflationary shock that a tight money policy and balanced budgets
might induce, unless mitigated by other forms of government
intervention. It also made him and the paper a target of Milton
Friedman – the televisual neoliberal economist at the University
of Chicago, whose 'standard lecture' in the 1970s (according to
Macrae) included the quip, 'The *Economist* as a newspaper has
practically every virtue, except that it believes in incomes policies.'
Macrae explained why in a dialogue with Friedman in 1974, when
the latter was in Britain at the behest of the IEA for the October
general election. 'There is not a very great difference between
the money supply policies favoured by Mr. Friedman and by the
*Economist*', Macrae began. 'And almost all economists now accept
one part of Mr. Friedman's teaching: that when governments
are trying to restimulate demand they habitually and erratically
expand money supply by too much.' The 'main difference between
Mr. Friedman and us is over the alternative to much higher rates

of unemployment, which we think is incomes policy'.[94] Four years on, Macrae made another attempt to meet the 'prophet of monetarism' partway, in 'Towards a Keynesian Friedmanism'. This macroeconomic hybrid would have three gear shifts: Keynesian demand management 'one year in five'; interest rate adjustments to control the money supply every year; and 'instant bank rate monetarism', to direct the flow of credit on the model of the nineteenth century Bank of England, or twentieth century Bank of Japan.[95] But the present crisis just 'could not be cured by monetarist discipline' alone, and 'monetarists are cheating when they say that "only rises in money supply can cause inflation"'.

The issue was not just whether monetarism could tame inflation, but how much unemployment it would produce. For Macrae, employment was not so much a moral good or even an economic, demand-sustaining necessity, as the literal cost of doing business in post-war democracies. Such a justification was contingent: when Thatcher won again in 1983, despite unemployment rates unseen since the Depression, the calculus changed. A year later, with growth at 3 per cent, 'something in the British economy is defying Keynesian convention, and it is time for Keynesians to accept that'.[96] The shift in economic policy was not simply about convincing arguments, however. As in the 1930s, it came with a shove from concatenated national and international crises.

## Thatcher and Reagan

Britain had felt the effects of the oil price spike and sputtering global growth with special force in the 1970s. Balance of payment and currency crises battered the country again in 1976, now with annualized inflation at around 24 per cent, leading the Wilson-Callaghan government to seek an IMF bailout. While spending cuts attached to the IMF loan (then the largest ever made) helped bring down the rate of inflation, this was also due to the acceptance by workers of pay caps – an incomes policy that collapsed two years later, when public sector unions struck against another round of real-term wage cuts. Inflation shot up, unemployment climbed above a million, and growth fell to a post-war low. The 'winter of discontent' ended in a narrow election win for the Conservatives under Margaret Thatcher – who campaigned on the promise that monetarist medicine could cure the economy of inflation by restricting the money supply. Ronald Reagan captured the White House in 1980, with similar plans to restore 'morning in America', as the swing to the right picked up speed across the OECD. Here the *Economist* hesitated, with the newsroom divided about the best – the most liberal – solution to the crisis.

While Thatcher's program of lower direct taxes, smaller government and weaker trade unions was precisely what the paper wanted, that was not 'reason by itself to vote for her' in 1979. 'Visceral', 'unreflective', 'frightening', her rhetoric seemed to promise a repeat in office of Edward Heath: provoke the trade unions, lose, then hand the reins to 'a perfectly awful Labour government by 1984 – one far worse than the respectable alternative available today, a house-trained party gone rabid again in the kennels of opposition'. The good dog in this metaphor? The current occupant of Number 10, James Callaghan, who had already moved Labour away from Keynesianism by 1976, soliciting the IMF loan in exchange for budget cuts of 20 per cent, while informing his party that governments could no longer 'spend their way' to full employment.[97] The *Economist* worried that his defeat risked moving Labour in the wrong direction, towards the 'loony' far left represented by MPs like Tony Benn or Michael Foot. Truly to 'switch emphasis back to private wealth creation and private choice' in Britain, the Conservatives must win not one but two or three elections in a row against Labour, turning it into a well-behaved opposition of the centre-left; but for that, a Tory leader had to show 'continuity, dare we say a sense of national consensus'. In effect, the paper wanted what would become the hegemonic project of Thatcherism, without being sure that Thatcher was the right leader to offer it. 'There is a chance that office will temper her convictions', but 'all this is to be proved. None of it yet can be proved. We are not confident that it will be proved, but we would like to see it tried.' For those confused by what this meant, it added, '*The Economist* votes for Mrs. Thatcher being given her chance.'[98]

Reagan formed a partial contrast. In 1980 the paper gave him more decided backing, focusing on the issue that mattered most to it: foreign policy. On that score, Jimmy Carter was so 'dangerously second rate' that 'an ally trembles at the prospect of his return'.[99] Reagan would be the better president when it came to showing 'firmness with Russia', unleashing 'American arms-making resources in full' and exposing Soviet economic and political frailties. Yet on other scores the *Economist* had some doubts. Reagan had a crude view of government in which all regulations and taxes formed a hindrance to innovation, as if its duties were simply 'to balance the budget – otherwise inflation results – and to hold back the excessive demands of abortionists, drug addicts, homosexuals and women'. But it took 'an act of Lafferesque faith in buoyant tax revenues to believe that the American economy could simultaneously withstand a 30 per cent tax cut, a large increase in defence spending and a balanced budget'; while the old-fashioned conservatism of Reagan's Supreme Court choices risked 'making America a less liberal society'.[100]

On one level, the paper's conflict of emotions may seem surprising. After all, the *Economist* had in many ways prepared the ground for Reagan and Thatcher. In both the US and Britain, it had worked hard to undermine détente, offering a platform for Kissinger to preach 'unilateral rearmament' during the Carter years. In Chile, Robert Moss had discovered how American power could do more than score propaganda points against Moscow; it could eradicate a left with no links to it, whose socialism had previously constituted a legitimate political opposition. Indeed, Moss honed this point over many years on the *Economist*, repeatedly invoking the danger that democracy posed to the economy, the rule of law and individual liberty, in a formula intentionally open-ended – so as to apply to Britain. 'What has happened in Chile under Sr. Allende's government suggests that, in the long term, political democracy is inconceivable without economic pluralism', he wrote in 1972.[101] A year later he added, 'the Allende government's programme of nationalisation cannot be regarded as "reform" in an economic sense, since it did not result in better management, higher productivity, the introduction of new technology, or imaginative new investment.'[102] By 1975, in *The Collapse of Democracy*, Moss was explicit about the lessons Chile held for Britain ('a singularly depressing example of the

abuse of democratic institutions by the enemies of a free society'),
whose decay could only be halted by 'reasserting the rule of law in
industrial relations', stiffening the backbones of government and
business, where 'every major economic decision was being taken
*in fear of the trade unions'*, and shrinking the state, except 'in the
realm of defence'. This was published by the National Association
for Freedom (NAFF), which Moss helped to found, and then
talked up in the *Economist*.[103] Given the creeping 'Sovietization
of Britain' – Moss had a good word for authoritarianism: 'in the
event a democratic society breaks down irretrievably', it was preferable to 'totalitarian rule'.[104] Three years later, Thatcher brought
this Chilean baggage with her to 10 Downing Street: not just Moss
and Crozier, but Hayek and Friedman, the economists invited to
clean up Allende's 'Marxist experiment'. Once in office, one historian has remarked, Thatcher quickly sidelined Moss and her
other 'eccentric' advisers on 'counter-subversion'.[105] But this mis-
characterizes their impact. What they had done in the *Economist*
and elsewhere was to heighten ideological tensions through constant intimations of disaster and campaigns of misinformation,
creating a climate in which authoritarian solutions to disarm the
left became respectable. Liberals, they hammered home, had to
accept the need for a political reckoning with the trade unions
and the Soviets, in a combined assault at home and abroad. Less
significant than their missed chance to exercise power was their
powerful justification of the neoliberal turn up to 1979.

## Divided Counsels: Newsroom Shakeouts

While Brian Beedham exercised near-complete control at the
foreign desk, beyond it *Economist* journalists were divided
about the right response to the crises of the 1970s. In this, the
newsroom reflected a larger breakdown of consensus, helping to
explain the strange hesitance of tone in the political endorsements
of Thatcher and Reagan on their first outings: neither the foreign
editor nor Andrew Knight could exercise full control on these
questions, and other voices made themselves heard. Editors like
Edmund Fawcett, Johnny Grimond and Barbara Smith all clashed

with Knight, who in turn recalled a series of brave stands against them. 'I can remember horrid weeks of isolation over Angola, as an early disbeliever in Carter; in the first Reagan election; over the Falklands and Grenada ... on all of which I can now feel quite smugly comfortable that I was right not to give into the first wave of lemmings declaring the world should jump over the precipice in an orgy of despairing condemnation.'[106] Though 'far more suspicious of Thatcher than Reagan', Knight regretted the ambivalent notes he was forced to insert in his praise of the latter. 'I was lobbied so hard by Grimond and Fawcett, I had to hedge'. Barbara Smith, leading the Washington bureau, also pushed back, and Edmund Fawcett, the correspondent there, remembered, 'I called Knight up and argued with him – Why was the *Economist* endorsing a candidate in a foreign election? – but I lost.' Their efforts explain the question mark appended to what was meant to be a bold cover declaration: 'Anyone but Carter?'

Knight need not have worried. Reagan invited him to dinner promptly after the election. 'Reagan wanted to thank me. He thought the endorsement of this respectable English publication, which came at a difficult moment in the campaign, had been a big deal in getting him elected.' All the guests at this memorable repast, including the conservative columnist George Will and Carter's outgoing trade representative, Robert Strauss, were invited to ask a question. Knight held his until dessert.[107] 'Whereas I know we have to take on the Soviets, and show them that Vietnam hasn't diminished us, and what to do on the economy, reducing government', Knight remembered Reagan saying in reply to his question on Israel-Palestine, 'I don't know what to do on the Middle East because I think they're both right.' Knight commented, 'This impressed me tremendously.' Edmund Fawcett and his *Economist* colleague Tony Thomas – unable to insert more than a few caveats in the endorsement of Reagan, and unconvinced by his declarations of impartiality on Israel-Palestine – published *The American Condition* in 1980, expanding on their doubtful impressions of 'middle-aged America' outside the paper.[108]

Back in London, the newsroom saw similar shakeouts. Dick Leonard, assistant editor, was a link to the liberal, free-trade socialists of the 1930s, when the likes of Douglas Jay wrote for the paper; indeed, as a Labour MP from 1970–74 and personal private secretary to Anthony Crosland (author of *The Future of Socialism,* the revisionist classic), Leonard was a lineal descendent of this tradition on the right of Labour. Knight offered Leonard the Britain section of the paper in 1974 after a boundary redrawing cost him his parliamentary seat – a bridge to the Wilson government formed that year. Leonard was unsure if he could take a job at a publication that had been so close to Edward Heath and the Tories under Burnet. 'Nonsense! I'm going to bring it back to the centre', Knight told him. 'But after two or three years', Leonard recalled, 'the paper drifted insidiously to the right. Knight got closer and closer to Thatcher, and I found myself writing fewer and fewer political leaders'. One was a signed tribute to Anthony Crosland, who died suddenly in 1977, 'the first time people found out I worked there'.[109] Pro-European, Leonard was then eased into the Brussels bureau; a section downsized two years after he left it in 1985, with no full-time correspondent for seven years, Beedham insisting on priority for America. Leonard's eventual replacement as editor of the Britain section captures the rightward shift of the *Economist* in these years.

Andrew Neil, a Burnet hire in 1973, played several roles at the *Economist* at the start – reporting on the Troubles in Northern Ireland, the House of Commons, and on the trade unions. He also appeared on TV, where his truculence and distinctive haircut earned him the nickname 'Brillo' from the satirical weekly *Private Eye*. In 1979 Knight sent him to the US, a three-year sojourn that changed him profoundly. 'I revelled in its dynamic, can-do culture, the ease with which new technology was introduced and exploited and the free and fast social mobility between the classes.'[110] He grew close to Irwin Stelzer, a free-market economist and consultant, who argued deregulation was the wave of the future – first in airlines, then being divvied up under Carter. No fan of Thatcher when he left – 'I had not voted for her: she had yet to discover her radical-right market economics (as had I)' and seemed 'an unsavoury amalgam of bourgeois prejudices and simplistic monetarism from the reactionary right' – all had changed on his return. As Britain editor, 'I was now seeing our ills through a strong free-market prism', urging 'privatization and deregulation and exposés of expensive and debilitating state intervention'. Rupert Murdoch was impressed and lured him away to edit the *Sunday Times* in 1983.[111] A pushy, ambitious man, Neil was a significant voice, whose departure says a lot about the paper when he left. He titled his final report on the TUC conference in Blackpool, 'The Unions Don't Know Where They Go Now – Except Down'. Predicting that unionized employment in Britain, still at roughly 50 per cent, would follow the lead of the US – where it had fallen from 34 per cent in 1965 to less than 20 – he quipped that nobody had phoned in a bomb threat at this year's conference: 'now that's a real sign of lost status'.[112] Knight solemnly announced his departure to a packed meeting. 'We are losing Neil.' 'Everyone applauded', recalled one *Economist* editor of the relief that swept the room. 'Neil thought we were congratulating him!'

Notwithstanding a degree of personal loathing for Neil, the *Economist* as a whole was moving in his direction. By 1982, the paper was swept up in patriotic euphoria over the Falklands War, in which 'Britain has said something to itself', the 'free world' and 'the old men of the Kremlin'. Long in need of 'its own sort of cultural revolution', Britain had dispelled the 'malaise' of the post–Second World War and post-Vietnam generations that saw 'military values and men as out-of-date jokes'. 'A younger generation' had witnessed 'an affair of principle' and soldiers 'a bit more handsome and heroic than Mr. David Bowie'.[113] Such sentiments helped to turn a possible election defeat into a second, larger victory for Thatcher in 1983, which had been uncertain before the war with Argentina, in the wake of a severe recession provoked by her government's ratcheting up of interest rates to a historic high. After four years, inflation fell back to roughly 4 per cent, but at a terrible cost, eviscerating manufacturing in the north of England and Scotland, and raising unemployment above 3 million.[114] 'This newspaper, which had difficulty in coming down narrowly against Mr. Callaghan's government four years ago, has no hesitation in condemning Labour today', it wrote. 'As to who should win this election, we have no doubt: we favour the return of Mrs. Thatcher to Downing Street.' Her manner was not always genial, but her policies were realistic and if there was a strain of 'economic masochism' in her, 'she is buying the chance of future tolerance in British society by forcing it to endure her economic intolerance today.'[115]

If some doubters remained, they had less and less influence over editorial policy. Emma Duncan, later deputy editor, recalled that Neil almost got her fired when she started at the paper in the early 1980s – 'furious' that she had failed to produce a piece that 'said that every truck and every car in the British rail network ought to be sold off in one go'. Remarkably, Seumas Milne – much later to serve as chief strategist for Jeremy Corbyn – was on staff at the same time. He recalled editorial meetings between 1981 and 1984 in which Beedham expressed 'suspicion of monetarism, neo-liberalism and the like' because he 'wanted the working class to stay strong and contented, if only to fight the Cold War'.

But the most vocal critic of Thatcher at editorial meetings was Simon Jenkins, hired by Knight as the *Economist*'s political editor in 1979 after the *Evening Standard* fired him. Reliably Conservative up to then, Jenkins was one of several editors to back the alliance between a new Social Democratic Party – breakaway challenger to Labour on the centre left – and the Liberals, as the choice most consistent with *Economist* tradition. For this reason, the *Economist* ran a small article on 'anti-Tory tactical voting', designed to benefit the alliance.[116] Jenkins also criticized Thatcher's decision to fight Argentina over a 'few rocks' in the South Atlantic, which Britain had been preparing to return, as a foolish act of imperialism. Knight kept both criticisms from this 'brilliant, eccentric journalist' out of lead articles, however, while allowing him to fire shots elsewhere. For the 1982 Christmas issue, Jenkins wrote a mock Shakespearean history play in which Thatcher storms against her ministers and allies – telling her to 'forget, forgive, conclude and be agreed' – as spineless.[117] When Jenkins's book with Max Hastings, *The Battle for the Falklands,* appeared the next year, Knight reviewed it himself in the *Economist*. 'The Falkland Islands are not about "colonial Britain" – despite what Mr Jenkins, Mr Hastings and others keep saying. There are no Red, Mayan, Aztec or subcontinental Indian masses being subjugated, no African tribes, no imported slave races, no debauched Polynesians or Aborigines.' Rather, in a moral tone borrowed from Thatcher, it was 'a dispute over international principle in which right vanquished wrong'.[118]

## Rupert Pennant-Rea: Cold War on a High Note, 1986–1993

Under Rupert Pennant-Rea the *Economist*, no longer a half-hearted convert to neoliberalism, became one of its advance guards. As a former Bank of England economist, Pennant-Rea was well aware of the deregulatory dynamics that had made the City of London an offshore haven for foreign money and foreign banks since the late 1950s. This training also distinguished him from his predecessors, who made no secret of their innumeracy: Burnet had hired the first economics editor at the *Economist*, Brian Reading; next came Sarah Hogg, who with Macrae often 'inserted the economic spine' into leaders written by Knight; and after Pennant-Rea left this post to become editor, the influential Clive Crook took up the position. Like Knight, Pennant-Rea was born to an aviator father beyond the British Isles, in the colony of Rhodesia. In 1934 Peter Pennant-Rea had moved from Britain to South Africa, and then on to Rhodesia to work as an aircraft engineer for the British firm de Havilland, returning briefly to England to fly for the RAF in 1943. As Rhodesia's director of civil aviation, he refused to recognize Ian Smith's unilateral declaration of independence in 1965, which ignited a fourteen-year war between the white minority regime in Salisbury and the black majority.[119] Pennant-Rea was a teenager when the family returned to Britain. Bypassing Oxbridge for Trinity College in Dublin and Manchester University, he went to work for a trade union and a business lobby. In 1973, he joined Britain's central bank as a junior economist, just as the collapse of Bretton Woods and the surge in Middle East oil revenues sent fresh waves of capital pouring into London. Four years on, Sarah Hogg made him economics correspondent for the *Economist*. By the time he succeeded her in 1981, Pennant-Rea had turned from the centre-left into an 'anti-government, anti-inflation zealot', and in his own estimation the paper as a whole was not far behind.[120] In 1986, he beat out three rivals in the contest to replace Knight: his mentor Sarah Hogg, the political editor Simon Jenkins, and Nico Colchester, then foreign editor of the *Financial Times,* whom he made his deputy at the *Economist*.

If this was an unusual path to the editorship, it was also a different character walking it. 'Rangy, goofy-looking, with a dead-pan demeanor, pre-fashionable sideburns' and a comb-over, Pennant-Rea reminded one profiler of Monty Python's John Cleese – but serious, opinionated, speaking in a 'nasal drawl' with 'notes of Rhodesia and Dublin'.[121] Pennant-Rea had even found time to write an economics thriller in 1978, the novel *Gold Foil*. In it, the US and the Soviet Union hatch plots to corner the market on bullion in South Africa (the former to tame inflation by returning to the gold standard, the latter to pay for imported grain). Financial journalist Caroline Manning, 'endowed with beauty and brains', a taste for 'Vidal Sassoon' and 'Fifth Avenue clothes', and a bit of a leftist, senses a story. James Glendinning, charming but oafish advisor to the Bank of England's chief cashier, is charged with implementing the secret gold plan, liaising with the Bank of South Africa, the IMF and the State Department. After some chasing, Glendinning accidentally leaks the scheme to Manning during a night of extramarital bliss in Johannesburg. Her story makes the *Guardian* front page, halting geopolitical connivances of West and East, and pushing black and white South Africans into a power-sharing agreement.[122] A Danish book club adopted it, but otherwise *Gold Foil* 'sank without a trace, probably deservedly', said Pennant-Rea modestly. The book was a response to opponents of apartheid he met in Britain, who failed to distinguish Afrikaners from English-speaking whites, 'their roots in Africa (including mine) being much shallower. I imagined the day when white Afrikaners and black South Africans could reach a rapprochement, irrespective of the rest of the world ... as things turned out, my sense was pretty accurate.'[123]

Truth proved almost as strange as fiction on Pennant-Rea's departure from the *Economist*. In 1993, he followed Sarah Hogg into the Conservative government of John Major, who in 1990 had made her head of his Policy Unit. At her urging, Norman Lamont, the Chancellor of the Exchequer, gave Pennant-Rea the job of deputy governor of the Bank of England. The two now occupied the highest political posts of any editors since the first, James Wilson – a testament to the immense prestige of the *Economist,* and its deep historic relationship to City and state. For Pennant-Rea, however, life behind the pink-liveried doormen of Threadneedle Street was cut short. In 1995, the financial journalist Mary Ellen Synon revealed that she and 'Roo' had been having an affair on the premises. Coming at a moment of crisis for one of the City's oldest private investment houses, Barings – as acting governor he refused to bail it out – Pennant-Rea was forced to resign.[124] Public service may have ended on a sour note, but private affairs flourished. He began a career in the City, and based in part on his success in raising revenue and readership as editor, became non-executive chairman of the Economist Group in 2009. Today, he works from one of the glass towers that ring the north edge of the Square Mile, non-existent before the burst of financial liberalization he strongly backed during his first months as editor.

## Big Bang: Finance, Innovation, Integration

Pennant-Rea made a number of changes to the paper – expanding its coverage of finance, starting a new Asia section, and creating new, more personalized columns, such as Lexington on American life and Bagehot on British politics. His most important editorial contribution related to finance and in particular to Big Bang – the name given to the moment on 27 October 1986 when rules governing financial transactions in Britain were torn up, with the aim of increasing the volume, variety and value of market trading done in the City. That included eliminating fixed brokerage commissions and barriers to foreign entrants, looser ownership rules, still laxer regulation, and screen-based trading – moving and expanding the centre of exchange out from the trading floor of the Stock Exchange.[125] The *Economist* hailed the event, seeing its significance in terms of the domestic and international standing of the City. London was already an attractive place to do business, of course. Investment banking had never been divided from commercial or retail banking, as in Japan or the US; time zones and language were right for the twenty-four-hour trading cycle that now ran between Tokyo and New York; and it possessed 400 years of international expertise and lax taxation. All it needed was to offer a welcome mat for newcomers and make markets for them even bigger and more liquid – achieved by removing what barriers remained between London's gilt and share markets (1985 turnover, $476 billion) from 'the much larger and wonderfully competitive Euro-equity markets (1985 turnover, $2,250 billion)'. While this might 'crack the cake' of domestic custom and upset the ancient guild-like structures and personal relationships that still dominated these sectors – British financial firms were smaller than foreign counterparts, and even hallowed names would fail when challenged on home ground – 'British authorities must let most of them, even quasi-banks, go under.' 'Lombard Street, Wall Street, or Patrice Lumumba Street, Timbuktu', it now mattered much less where the head office was: 'what really matters for Britain is that the City expands its financial resources, financial knowhow and financial jobs.' This would reduce the gentility of the place, and the personal power of the Bank of England governor. But what was the alternative? Japan's Nomura had a stock market capitalization of $30 billion, the US bank Solomon $6 billion, compared with way under $1 billion for prestigious old City investment and merchant banks like Warburg, Kleinwort Benson, Hill Samuel, Hambro. Even before Big Bang, the paper pointed out, only eight of twenty top brokerage firms were still in British hands.[126] This insistence that the City must also feel the chill draught of the global market, come what may for its national brands, linked finance to the overall Thatcherite project. Like British industry and public services, British banking would be subject to the fortifying effects of competition. Combined with minimal oversight – who supervised banking and who securities could be worked out later – the City was set to be transformed.[127]

Pennant-Rea wrote three books on economics along the road to Big Bang, which supplied simple theoretical arguments for it: *Who Runs the Economy?* in 1979, *The Pocket Economist* in 1983, and *The Economist Economics* in 1986. Each one gave greater weight to the free market, with the second pair – co-authored with Bill Emmott and Clive Crook, respectively – so fervent that they received testy reviews in the *Economist* itself. 'They identify the dead hand of restrictive practices and market distortion everywhere', wrote Howard Davies in 1983. 'But even the best of causes can suffer from overstatement.' Of the sequel, Rudiger Dornbusch wrote, its authors went 'beyond intuition, and occasionally even beyond prejudice ("trust markets, overrule them at your peril")'.

He cited a breezy dismissal of Keynesianism from the conclusion: 'Few economists now believe that government can or should "fine-tune" demand. That way of thinking is dead, its death a tribute to the power of the rational-expectations approach.' But, Dornbusch interjected, 'that thinking surely is not dead, as any chancellor of the exchequer, six months from an election, can attest.'[128] Neither outside reviewer – Davies, future deputy governor of the Bank of England; Dornbusch, a Chicago-trained economist – were particularly leftwing.

No matter: with regulatory bonfires ablaze, the Thatcher Revolution was said to be delivering at last. GDP growth rose to 4 per cent in 1986 and 4.5 in 1987 and 1988, as inflation dropped to 2.5 per cent. Unemployment remained high at 11 per cent, but rising real income for those still in work, as well as 'gains' from privatization – more homeowners, given the chance to buy council flats by taking out mortgages; more shareholders (5.5 million), offered shares as the state sold off profitable public utilities like British Telecom – meant 'more money, more security, more independence for ordinary Britons'.[129] In 1992, the *Economist* backed Thatcher's handpicked successor on this record, after a party revolt over Europe toppled her as leader. If it worried John Major was 'too relaxed about spending and borrowing', this tacitly acknowledged the difficulties Thatcher had left him: inflation was back at 8 per cent and rising in 1988, interest rates touched 15 per cent in 1989, recession set in by 1990.

Far from questioning the policies of the last decade, for the *Economist* this simply demonstrated the need to press ahead – in particular for Britain to join the European Exchange Rate Mechanism. Pegging sterling to the Deutschmark, the paper argued, would oblige British governments to defend the pound sterling on the open market, placing strict limits on the level of inflation it could tolerate. Thatcher only agreed to try it in 1990; in the event, recession and high interest rates (again touching 15 per cent to defend parity) forced a humiliating exit and devaluation five months after Major's election in 1992. Black Wednesday was not the fault of deregulation or the lifting of the last barriers to capital mobility, the *Economist* insisted, which were like genies that could not be put back in their bottles. 'Rebuilding capital controls is beyond the wit of governments, and even if it could be done, the cost in misallocation of resources would be huge.'[130] For this stalwart backing of John Major's exchange rate policy, some journalists groused, Pennant-Rea was 'rewarded' with the Bank of England job the next year.[131]

### Ends of the Cold War: Interpreting Liberalism's Triumph

By then another revolution was underway in Eastern Europe, which turbocharged the neoliberal dynamic at the *Economist*, and seemed to stamp it with an almost providential seal. The collapse of the Soviet Union and its satellites took place with breathtaking speed between 1989 and 1991, opening up new vistas for capital overnight. The 1980s had been a decade of reversals for Moscow, which saw a crash in oil prices and thus its export earnings, squeezing imports of basic goods as well as the technology needed to modernize production; at the same time Reagan threatened it with a new arms race, even as it strained to spend more than twice what the US did on defence as a share of GDP, with half its per capita income. In this context, the arrival of a younger, idealistic reformer in the Kremlin, pledged to economic and political liberalization and dialogue, should have been music to the ears of the *Economist*. Not so: wary of Mikhail Gorbachev, it enjoined Reagan and his 'overcautious' understudy George Bush Sr. not to compromise with him, even as his chaotic management of glasnost and perestroika set the disintegration of the Soviet system in motion.

If the paper greeted all signs of this with glee – 'we just sat back and enjoyed the ride', according to Pennant-Rea – it also brought a characteristic ferociousness to its coverage of events, closing out the Cold War as it had waged it. For peacefully dismantling the Warsaw Pact and pulling the Red Army out of Europe, Gorbachev deserved nothing. No new Marshall Plan: 'it has to change itself fundamentally before it can be helped'. No strategic reciprocity: the US should leave its armed forces and missile bases in Western Europe, and expand NATO east at top speed, for the alliance 'had woven itself into the fabric of European stability'.[132] In 1990, with American 'freedom of regional manoeuvre greatly enhanced', the

*Economist* called for a war in the Persian Gulf before Bush did – as an unbeatable chance for America to lead 'the world into a time of real peace and economic progress.'[133] One journalist called the office a hothouse with no debate. 'In a crucial meeting we spent our time arguing about fish quotas, not war.' For Gorbachev, however, this meant the end of the line: he had been 'immensely helpful in building up the coalition against Saddam Hussein', but 'not indispensable' and 'when the fighting is over, will not be needed … the west should be looking for a better man.' By the turn of 1991, that was Boris Yeltsin, who promised not to reform communism but to hasten its breakdown at the centre by raising the same cry for Russian national sovereignty as the Baltic, Caucasian and East European states had done.[134]

The *Economist* did more than comment or give advice on these events. It supplied philosophical reflections on the meaning of liberalism's victory, with Beedham and Macrae offering panoramic views of its past, present and future on the eve of their retirements. Beedham started out cautiously in the summer of 1989, peeking behind the Iron Curtain in 'Long Live Spring'. Predicting the consequences of perestroika, in particular its reduction of imports from Eastern Europe, he explained how to push reform further: as step one, privatize and split up state enterprises, end subsidies, and force them to compete with one another; allow the market to set prices, even if runaway inflation resulted; found private banks to lend money based on expected return, not planning targets; start stock markets; solicit Western investment through debt swaps and joint ventures. Unleashing economic freedom – at a minimum the legal right to own, protect and pass on private property – was a precondition for rolling back totalitarianism, which was looking far more vulnerable than he anticipated. Stalin's henchmen had not 'found a way to stay on top forever', he decided, 'happy liberals are declaring that Hannah Arendt must have been wrong after all' and 'Leninism can finally be lowered into the grave.' How long would this take? Based on interviews with Politburo members in Poland, Hungary and Yugoslavia, Beedham guessed that Gorbachev was unlikely to intervene as they moved from economic reform to multi-party elections, effectively giving up

Communist control. If Bush bargained hard, most Soviet satellites might be allowed to leave the Warsaw Pact – though this also risked provoking a coup to oust the pliable 'Gorby'. But by then it might not matter: its armies withdrawn, economy in tatters, an ethnic crisis or two on its hands in the south, and the Russians would be too vulnerable to turn back the tide. 'The case for drastic change is strong, and the chances of getting away with it not bad.'[135]

Beedham became even bolder as the disarray in Moscow mounted, Gorbachev refusing to intervene to prop up embattled regimes anywhere, apparently just as in thrall to liberal ideals as the apparatchiks in Poland or Hungary. Four months later, Beedham wrote a valedictory that read like Herodotus on speed, his vision of world history punctuated by a dozen 'really top-ranking' dates. 'One of history's biggest mistakes began to be rubbed out ... and this makes 1989 even better than 1945, when Hitlerism was erased' (though neither year made the list, since in great years 'something new is written in the human ledger'). Ranging from 457 BC, when 'Pericles got Athenian democracy firmly on its feet', to 1775 when America gave us 'liberal democracy, plus self-determination', he admitted to a distorted timeline. But 'no apology is needed for the fact that most are Euro-American dates'. Was any needed for imperialism? Empire received just one mention, and that was to the civilized manner in which it was wound up. 'The post-1945 freeing of the colonial empires was carried out in the name of self-determination and liberal democracy, though it achieved little of the second.' America's record since was as a beacon of liberty. 'In 1989 yet another echo from Lexington has been crashing, this time more efficiently, round Eastern Europe.' In rejecting one form of historical causation, Beedham praised another, Whiggishly optimistic about human progress, inflected by Christianity. The death of Christ was crucial, for 'people who have been told that God became one of them, and let himself be crucified to help them, feel rather better about the human condition afterwards.'[136] The religious leitmotif grew even stronger after the Soviet Union disappeared from the map, with a survey on 'Islam and the West' in 1994 shocking even his friend Samuel Huntington for its simplistic view of cultural and religious difference.[137]

Yet the foreign editor also revealed a kind of nostalgia for a fading world, as source for a satisfying argument. In one survey, he 'stitched together' five conversations with communist leaders who in 1989 admitted to seeing history roughly as he did. 'Despite the lying and brutality of the past 40 years, this region still has some of the world's most attractive politician-intellectuals', he suddenly announced. What, he asked his composite communist, did socialism really mean? 'The attempt to create a society, maybe several hundred years from now, in which people can be prosperous, free and equal.' Was there still a big difference between this and capitalism? 'Not all that much, especially if you take the social-democratic version of the Western system.' Then what was distinctive about Marxism? 'Marxism is one part of a long tradition, which goes back to the Bible, the Reformation, the French Revolution.' Had it accomplished anything? 'It may have stirred capitalism into becoming more civilized.'[138] Beedham might as well have had this conversation with himself, so closely did it hew to thirty years of advice served up to his foes. By having surprisingly reasonable communists confess to their own errors, he consummated his victory over them in the realm that mattered most – ideas.

A strange upshot of his argument was that positive changes were not being made by dissidents, but by the national communist parties themselves. Even in Poland, where trade union opposition to its rule was fiercest, the party 'was probably still strong enough to suppress any opposition ... if there is to be change it will be because the party has grown tired of refusing.' This hardly matched the rhetoric about totalitarianism. Nor did he suspect his adversaries of being quite as spineless as his dialogue with some of them suggested. Beedham worried that Gorbachev was trying to dislodge West Germany from NATO, balancing out disintegration in his half of Europe. 'If he succeeded, "the West" would no longer mean what it has meant for the last 40 years'; while the DDR in East Germany, its economy 'long the best in the region', its Politburo (whose members, implicitly, refused to talk to him) most in tune with its leader, Erich Honecker, 'looks as if it could go on forever'.[139] Less than six months off, he never imagined the fall of the Berlin Wall. Even after it crumbled, a sense of disorientation

pervaded his articles. Rejecting the idea that history was at an
end, as Francis Fukuyama first opined in 1989, Beedham pointed
to real threats – from terrorism to Iraq to Russia – but without
his trademark enthusiasm. 'Perhaps history got its timing wrong',
he mused in 1990. 'A generation later, the countries of democratic
Europe might have been cohesive enough to cope with the consequences' of the collapse of communism in Europe.[140] Could the
West retain its edge with no competitors? 'The old war of principle, the contest between grand ideas, is over. The new politics
is full of dull detail.' Perhaps direct democracy could revitalize
it, plebiscites counteracting apathy among voters in the new age
of ideological vacuum, while fending off the armies of lobbyists,
'freebooters of the modern political world', 'literally corrupting'
since 'the many are harder to diddle or bribe than the few'.[141] By
1993, his mood had darkened. Could it be that victory was purchased at the price of a decline in civic energies, and a descent into
complacency and corruption?

Macrae was free from these gloomy afterthoughts, in part because
the technological trends which interested him showed every sign
of accelerating after 1989. Not for him the cloak and dagger of
geopolitics or the millennial lifecycle of civilizations. History
interested him less than the future, and it was as a frenetic prophet
of progress that he skipped through the pages of the *Economist*.
He too took personal delight in being on the winning side of a
long, strenuous argument. 'During the brief civilian working lives
of us returning soldiers from the second world war', he wrote in
1988, 'we have added seven times as much to the world's producing power as was added during all the previous millennia of
*Homo sapiens*' existence.'[142] Given how unlikely that seemed on
his joining the paper in 1949, he wondered how anyone younger
could 'dare to sound pessimistic'. As Beedham basked in the disgrace of communism, so Macrae gave notice to its feeble Western
imitators.

'A Future History of Privatisation, 1992–2022' claimed co-
credit for coining the term thirty years earlier, when, everywhere
but in the *Economist*, privatisation seemed a 'hopeless crusade'.
In the 1960s, 'it was hard to persuade even sensible people how

wrong were those like Galbraith, who told eager politicians that the interests of the poor could be served best by spending much more of GDP through politician-dictated monopolies instead of market-leading common sense.' In a normal enterprise, if a middle manager found his boss was 'making a horlicks of his job', he could leave and start a new firm; under state ownership in Britain, he could file a piece of paper and never be promoted; 'in Russia he got shot'. In council houses, 'life deteriorated into drugs, hopeless-ness, squats' – a 'vicious circle of hell'; state schools in poor areas turned kids into 'drug-addicted delinquents'; welfare created 'ille-gitimacy, dependency, lack of neighbourliness, crime, drugs, riot so as to loot'.[143] Like Beedham, Macrae also proposed a timeline of important dates, but his stretched into the future: in a few years all but three coal pits would close; in five, the railways would be sold off, including the safety and signal controls, making them safer and more efficient, 'rather like an airport'; the same went for power plants and the electric grid, whose new owners would innovate by 'discovering ever cheaper ways of releasing energy from storage in matter'; telephones and TVs 'will leave the public sector' and in 'tones similar to today's lessons about 19th century child labour, sociologists will tell with horror of the exploiting classes' device named the BBC'. Schools and health care would be privatized next, but in 'some disguised form of the "voucher" system'. Between 2000 and 2010, prisons and police would also go private; the former paid more if their inmates did not re-commit crimes, the latter permitted to release criminal records in order 'to throw them open to investigation by many competitors'. Computers would replace expensive lawyers and error-prone judges, and companies would race each other to punish criminals, with the goal of preventing recidivism at attractive rates. In 2010, local elections would have 'multinational corporations appear on the ballot', campaign promises transformed into legal contracts.[144]

The possibilities for privatization were as varied as the human experience. By 2015, children and the old, sick, or disabled would take out insurance on their 'conditions'; charity would be replaced by 'bidding for contracts to try to help "endangered people"'. War could use rationalizing too. Southeast Asia was a lesson in what didn't work: 'the inefficiency of state spending was shown when the mighty United States began to lose a war to slightly ridiculous North Vietnam.' The Gulf War was instruction in what did: a coalition, using automated, precision-guided rockets. By 2020 this alliance would fold together NATO and the former Warsaw Pact, import cheap bombs from Japan, vet arms sales to the global south, and recruit soldiers from 'the cheapest high-quality markets: Gurkhas, Britain's SAS, sons of old soldiers from villages with fighting in their blood'.[145] Some of these musings read like reworked science fiction narratives, only cheerful, and without a shred of social critique – as if the 1987 film *Robocop* were told from the perspective of the corporation that built cyborgs to police Detroit. In fact, Macrae's predictions have mostly come true, or look like they will.

If the new era caused him fewer pangs than Beedham, Macrae too showed signs of being out of step with it. Asking famous minds to assess 'Mrs. Thatcher's place in history' in 1989, the paper carried a revealing note from him. (In strangely appropriate proximity to Anthony Burgess, author of *A Clockwork Orange*, who dismissed 'ten years of a middle-class lady with an affected accent who chills the heart'.) 'Margaret Thatcher and Ernie Bevin are the only two I have known', Macrae wrote warmly, 'who have always in government simply asked: "which decision do I think will have the best effects?" That is why they are most intensely disliked by exactly the same sad sorts of people.'[146] An eccentric vantage-point on a half-century: praise for a rightwing trade unionist boss and Labour bully at the time Macrae joined the *Economist* in 1949, and the union-busting leader of the Conservatives when he left it. By 1990, Macrae even had unflattering things to say about banks, whose irresponsible behaviour was to blame for an upsurge in financial crises in the past decade – over-investing in Latin American debt, then corporate buyouts, now property loans. 'For bankers', he predicted, who were sure to be overexposed when the latest real estate bubble burst, 'the future has to look bleak'. Their coming unemployment would be wholly salutary, reducing risky bets (abetted by national deposit insurance schemes), and downsizing the global financial sector – at 10 per cent of world GDP, grown too big for its own good. 'In the 1980s bright graduates streamed on that conveyor belt into banking and financial services. Their prospects, by the time they retire, seem on par with those of 1950s coalminers.'[147] This prediction was not just at odds with the editorial bottom line, but spectacularly wrong. Endorsing fresh-faced Bill Clinton in 1992, 'standard-bearer of a new Democratic party: fiscally responsible, socially hard-headed' – and set to fatten the Wall Street banks with repeal of the Depression-era Glass-Steagall Act and thin the welfare rolls – the new generation of *Economist* journalists were all aboard for the new world order.[148]

# 8

## Globalization and Its Contents

The *Economist* reached the last years of the twentieth century on a high. The money pouring into finance seemed to vindicate its stance on Big Bang at home, while the fall of communism did the same for its long slog on behalf of Western liberalism abroad. At the same time, it rapidly gained readers and influence in the US, which became its home away from home. Pennant-Rea stepped down in 1993 just as the 'new economy' of the Clinton years got underway – to its boosters a break from all precedent, as information technology unleashed investment and growth alongside low inflation, low unemployment and near-constant productivity gains, which were bound to attenuate or even eliminate the business cycle itself.[1] Since then, three points have connected the constellation of liberal ideas at the *Economist*: the planetary primacy of finance, vast enough to be shared out between Wall Street and the City of London; the American Empire, as both policeman and journalistic training ground; and globalization, its precondition the prior two, as cornucopia for former colonies and satellites. In all these years, no other publication articulated these points with greater authority, passion or geographical range.

Financial deregulation, and the boom in equities it fuelled, was the unmistakable leitmotif of this period. Global stock markets soared in value from under $3 trillion in 1982 to over $30 trillion in 2000. As the boom gained pace on Wall Street, financial profits rose threefold in the five years to 2000, reaching $21 billion. In some of the riskiest, most profitable lines, London outpaced New York – dominating not just foreign exchanges, but with 43 per cent of over-the-counter derivatives markets, 20 per cent of the hedge fund market and 57 per cent of European private equity business by 2006.[2] In a pattern of divergence dating back to the turn of the twentieth century, interest and exchange rates stoked this speculative frenzy even as industrial production sank yet further. Britain lost 4.1 million manufacturing jobs between 1979 and 2011: from 26 to 22 per cent of total output during Thatcher's reign to 18 per cent under Major to just 11 per cent at the end of New Labour.[3] The City, in stark contrast, added over 70,000 well-paying jobs up to 2008, as the financial sector went from 7 to nearly 10 per cent of GDP. Equity market turnover, roughly equal to the national product in 1997, was three times greater a decade later.[4]

The City had not enjoyed this kind of prominence since 1914. Geography alone made it relevant to the new world order, with a trading day that straddled time zones in the US and Asia, while its berth in Europe made it a capital market of choice for states 'transitioning' from communism in the east. The *Economist* could not have ignored these developments if it tried. Hedge funds set up shop in St James and Mayfair, pulling up West End office prices to the highest in the world. Fund managers flapped through Economist Plaza, and some moved into its tower. A Japanese concept restaurant opened up on the premises, co-owned by a Russian oligarch's son, the perfect spot to do a deal over smoky plum negronis.[5] In an attempt to reach the same class of people, and advertisers, Economist Group executives launched *Intelligent Life,* since rebranded *1843,* a luxury lifestyle effort to show '*The Economist* in evening dress, on holiday, and at leisure'.

The stature of the *Economist* rose along with that of finance, enmeshed in its central nervous system as never before. Editors departed to join banks, as others arrived from government bodies meant to regulate them. Rupert Pennant-Rea renewed the 'community of interest' between the paper and Bank of England, becoming its deputy governor in 1993; when the Bank was freed to set rates five years later, the paper cheered. Clive Crook, then the paper's powerful deputy editor, had started his career at the Treasury writing speeches for ministers and senior civil servants. Experience of finance was, and remains, all but required to be a contender for the top job – whether at a private bank or multilateral lending institution, in Tokyo, London or New York. Though not as well-paid as their banking peers, the editor-in-chief can aspire to perks few other journalists can match – with lucrative stock options, bonuses and pensions, but also speaking fees, board memberships, book deals, reverential TV appearances, prime billing on the global forum circuit, the odd secret society invitation.[6]

Despite the new cosmopolitanism of the City, at least one aspect of its gentlemanly capitalist social character remained: the presence of the ancient universities. Graduates of Oxford and Cambridge were more numerous than ever at the *Economist*. From the latter, deputy editor Ed Carr, and ex-Europe head Gideon Rachman, now a *Financial Times* columnist, were vetted for the top job in 2006. Many others would continue to rise through the ranks – from the US editor John Prideaux (Cambridge) to Washington bureau chief James Astill (Oxford) to the former New York bureau chief Patrick Foulis (Cambridge), to younger recruits such as Jeremy Cliffe (Oxford) and Emma Hogan (Cambridge). But this cloistered cross-sample actually overstates the academic diversity of the staff. Just one Oxford college (out of thirty-eight), enrolling no more than 600 students (out of some 22,000), has churned out a hugely disproportionate share of the most important *Economist* editors.

An informal agreement between a fellow of Magdalen, the historian R. W. Johnson, and Andrew Knight, had transformed that college into a sort of *Economist* prep. 'Knight called me in 1970 to help him recruit talent.' 'If they're really good, let's take them straight away instead of sending them to the provinces first', Knight told Johnson, who 'only gave him really top flight people' like David Lipsey, Stephen Milligan and Chris Huhne – respectively becoming a Labour life peer, Tory MP and Liberal Democrat Cabinet minister. It got so packed with them, a joke circulated about a possible candidate for editor in 1993. 'Don't worry', one *Economist* staffer said to another, 'she only went to Wadham.'[7] Former Magdalen men included the Mid-East and Africa editor Chris Lockwood (one of two *Economist* journalists that Prime Minister David Cameron named under oath as friends and advisers at the Leveson Inquiry into press standards), and Matt Ridley.[8]

The 5th Viscount Ridley and Baron Wensleydale, as Ridley is also known, made a splash as science editor from 1983 to 1992 – and continued to do so later from the House of Lords, with popular non-fiction titles purveying feel-good social Darwinism for the *Economist* audience.[9] Most striking of all was the record at the top, with the last editor but one, his nearest rival as deputy editor, and the editor before that all members of the 'Magdalen mafia': John Micklethwait, Clive Crook, and Bill Emmott.

## Bill Emmott and the Modern Greats

Emmott was born into fairly humble circumstances in 1956. His father was a public accountant, whose family had owned a sweet shop in Lancashire, and who met his mother while working for a local council at the end of the Second World War. Raised in London, he went to Latymer Upper in Hammersmith, at the time a selective grammar school, after which he won a spot at Magdalen to study the standard *cursus* for future editors – Philosophy, Politics and Economics. At Oxford's Nuffield graduate college in 1978, as part of 'a cunning plan to combine an academic career with freelance writing', he began a dissertation inspired by current events in France, where an alliance between the Socialist and Communist Parties, the *Union de la gauche,* seemed on the cusp of victory at the polls; prodded by R. W. Johnson, then working on his *Long March of the French Left,* Emmott delved into the French Communists' previous spell in government from 1944 to 1947 in search of clues as to its future behaviour.[10]

Johnson also passed his name to Knight, who recalled their first interview: 'Emmott was a very nice, smart chap, just not particularly ebullient.' Johnson remembered a more severe judgment: 'He's useless, no spark, no spirit!' Johnson insisted, and Knight finally relented – just as Emmott was due to leave for the Paris archives in 1980.[11] Chris Huhne, two years Emmott's senior at Magdalen (and at the start of a lucrative career in finance and politics, ultimately cut short by matrimonial lies about a speeding ticket), was leaving for the *Guardian*, and Dick Leonard proposed Emmott take over the European desk. Giving up the doctorate,

Emmott changed his ticket for Brussels, where he covered the European Economic Community (EEC) until 1982. After a stint as economics correspondent in London, in 1983 he set off for Japan on an assignment that altered his life and outlook.

## Land of the Rising Pun: Japanese Lessons in Finance

By then, Japan was no longer an undiscovered country. After stuttering at the start of the 1980s, its industrial engine roared back to life, promising to add another decade to its thirty miraculous years of growth since the war. In large part because of the turn to deficit finance under Reagan, Japanese exports increased at the average rate of 9.5 per cent from 1979 to 1985, and to the US alone at 23 per cent per annum. More striking were the current account surpluses these generated, which made Japan for the first time the largest creditor to the Americans.[12]

Emmott, arriving at this historic juncture, took note of the policy changes that had allowed Japan to harness this capital globally, and advised other states to follow suit: the abolition of exchange controls in 1980; the erosion of barriers between banking and brokerage; in 1984, a concerted opening that invited foreign banks into currency and government bond markets, with more reforms promised – of the sort the City undertook 'after a long and gruelling battle with vested interests' in 1986.[13] Emmott found the doors of Japan Inc. wide open to him as a correspondent for the *Economist,* whose profile Norman Macrae had raised among the country's ministerial and commercial elites. The famed *Economist* deputy editor was therefore an essential reference for Emmott, present in his attention to details of Japanese daily life, and how they had changed. On average, people were older, families smaller, farmers fewer, and a new group of pleasure-seeking youngsters had emerged, *shinjinrui.* Emmott pitched his analysis of Japan as a challenge to Macrae, however, in a book that would help him win the editorship, *The Sun Also Sets: Why Japan Will Not be Number One,* in 1989.

Emmott came out against the widely held view that Japan was about to overtake the US as both an economic and a political

superpower – singling out Macrae for criticism. 'Every risen economic power', Macrae had argued in the *Economist* the year
before, 'seeks eventually to mould its era.'[14] Macrae had welcomed the prospect, arguing that the Japanese might emerge as
more 'progressive top bankers' than either the British under the
first Duke of Wellington, 'who opposed railways on the grounds
that they would enable the working classes to move about', or the
Americans, 'who thought that slavery was a peculiar social and
economic institution that could endure'.[15] In *The Sun Also Sets*,
which Emmott drafted in London in 1988, he conceded 'Japan is
Asia's natural leader', but only America – with its unique mix of
'free enterprise, open markets, individual initiative' and inflow of
driven young immigrants – could lead the world.[16] And whereas
Macrae had credited civil servants in Tokyo with almost heroic
professionalism and creativity, Emmott scorned them as obso-
lete. Deprived of much of their power by market deregulation,
the Ministry of Finance and 'infamous' Ministry of Trade and
Technology were fighting 'a losing battle', he contended; 'the trend
is firmly set toward freedom and a more open system.'[17]

When the Tokyo stock market crashed just after the book
appeared, leading to a 'lost decade' of economic growth and
ending all talk of a *Pax Nipponica,* Emmott looked like an oracle.
But that was somewhat misleading, for it was precisely the
unshackling of finance that had led to the crisis which Emmott
had celebrated as the harbinger of renewal and modernity. 'The
idea of Japan as a superpower is based primarily on the country's
huge exports of capital and on its sudden emergence as the world's
largest net creditor.'[18] And when a rising yen threatened to staunch
this flow after 1985, the stock market bubble that pumped it back
up bedazzled him. From 1986 to 1989, residential and commercial property prices doubled. Foreign exchange and government
bond futures markets – back in 1980 'long on exotic names and
bewildering regulations and short on business volume, innovation
and freely flowing cash' – leapt ahead of those in Western countries. With nine of the ten largest commercial banks, the four top
Eurobond underwriters and the four largest investment banks,
'these command the same mixture of fear, admiration and hate
as do Japanese car or video manufacturers'. By 1988, Tokyo's

market capitalization was 50 per cent greater than New York's, and even ordinary Japanese were getting in on the act – buying 'Roni Wrinkle' condoms, as 'gleaming white' BMWs clogged the streets, housewives bought gold and shorted futures, and 'money fever' took hold.[19]

In 1989, there were clear signs pointing to a Japanese bubble. Average price to earnings ratios on the Nikkei index had risen past 60. Land prices were so high that the grounds of the imperial palace in central Tokyo were worth more than the state of California. But even if a bubble did exist, it was 'convenient' and 'there might never be a crash' and if there were, 'Japan could, and almost certainly would, recover.'[20] The stock market sank like a stone a few months later, losing half its value in a year, and Japan began two decades of deflation with low or negative growth. But it would have been easy to miss that in Emmott's next books, *Japan's Global Reach* in 1992 and *Japanophobia* in 1993. 'The sunset of 1990–1993, first in finance but then in the real economy, has made life appear dark.' But long-term prospects 'are bright and warm' and 'the macroeconomic picture in Japan looks very healthy'.[21] Since then, no crisis – however big – has dented his belief in the rationality of financial-market exuberance.

Emmott was just as blasé about a wave of savings and loan failures in the US in a special survey on banking for the *Economist* in 1988 – urging financiers to seize this chance to demand repeal of Glass-Steagall, which barred commercial banks from underwriting or trading securities. At the same time, he dismissed the *Economist*'s own Wall Street correspondent Christopher Wood, who predicted that soaring asset prices in New York, London and Tokyo were driven by unsustainable levels of private debt, and would soon lead to a major depression. Emmott called him 'emotional', a 'doomster' and argued that the 'industrialized countries are chugging merrily along, apparently oblivious to the crash' that had briefly spooked them in October 1987.[22] In 1989 Michael Milken, the 'king of junk bonds' at Drexel Burnham Lambert, bankrupted the fifth largest US investment bank and went to jail. 'There is nothing wrong, in principle, with junk bonds', Emmott wrote. He bridled at caricatures of Wall Street as a 'den of greed and chance', which was a 'harsh judgment to make of the freest-flowing and most sophisticated financial markets the world has ever known'.[23] Made business affairs editor in 1989, Emmott surveyed the landscape from atop St James with optimism. A Labour voter when he joined the paper in 1980, he was now a devotee of Thatcher. Even if it required another decade of her monetarist disciplines – 'it may even take a generation before British business has recovered fully from its conditions in the 1970s' – the country could look forward to 'again becoming the workshop of Europe', as foreign direct investment flowed to Midlands factories, gleaming shopping malls opened in Newcastle, and financial firms rushed to open in London.[24]

### The Tweed Jungle: 'Free Minds, Free Markets, Free-for-All'

Back in Britain, Emmott also had time to pursue a hobby – planning to be editor when Pennant-Rea stepped down, a contest that turned out to be as cutthroat as the hostile takeovers he covered as business affairs editor, with ten colleagues (out of about fifty) duelling for the job. In *Vanity Fair,* Jacob Weisberg described a 'bitter power struggle' to replace Pennant-Rea turning 'the chummy corridors of the world's most prestigious financial weekly' and 'a place staffers have fondly compared to an Oxford common room' into 'a kind of Euro trading pit – Barbarians at the Gate in Tweed'.

In a gruelling seven-week competition that reached a 'fever pitch of anxiety and neurosis', what counted was age, class – and floor. The thirteenth floor, housing domestic and foreign writers, produced the most candidates, including Nico Colchester, deputy editor, formerly at the *Financial Times*; Matt Ridley, returning from Blagdon, his family's 9,000-acre estate in Northumberland; and Mike Elliott, the gregarious, foul-mouthed Washington bureau chief. Floor twelve, where business writers worked, sent forth economics editor Clive Crook, and Emmott. 'The 13th is more British. The 12th is more American', Weisberg reported. 'The 12s view the 13s as woolly-headed liberal academics who don't understand economics. 13s stereotype the 12s as bloodless techno-heads and libertarian ideologues.' Taking bets on the outcome, the associate editor David Lipsey gave odds to the two floors' eventual finalists,

Colchester and Emmott. Both men had to make it past a committee composed of the management guru Sir John Harvey-Jones,
the chocolatier Sir Adrian Cadbury and Pearson's director, Frank
Barlow, before their fate was decided by the whole board 'over a
breakfast of kippers at the Savoy' – a process some editors likened
to a 'setup', and which left Colchester 'unable to talk about it
without choking up'.[25]

Emmott had a less bloodstained account: his advantage was
neither youth nor his books so much as his secondment to be editorial director of the Economist Intelligence Unit in 1992, where he
got to know board members and executives (displaying 'an Attila
the Hun style of management', according to Weisberg) – above
all Marjorie Scardino, there after running the North American
business, and who rose during the same period to lead the entire
Economist Group.

Emmott was something of an ideas man among the *Economist*'s
later editors – not only in his 'Sphinxlike' bearing, but in range:
articles on Japan carried haikus, stock market surveys digressed
into Dickens, laments about Italian backwardness were introduced by Dante. Like Bagehot, he wrote widely under his own
name, his voice merging with the paper, even as his name tran-
scended it. Three books and a documentary film have arrived
since he stepped down, and his musings can be read hourly – on
Twitter, where his sobriquet is '#bill_emmott: scarlet pimpernel,
agent provocateur', and in print in most major time zones, including the US, Britain, Italy, Japan and India. He is paid to share his
thoughts at Alpine business retreats, and on corporate and non-
profit boards.

Emmott's task as editor, he later told the *Financial Times,* was
'to get readers and make them addicted to the paper'.[26] He was
successful. Circulation exploded from 500,000 to over a million
in thirteen years under his reign, with the greatest rise coming in
North America. He modernized the paper, hiring more foreign
correspondents and implementing a rigorous fact-checking operation. But Emmott also displayed an interest in the traditions of
the paper, and the history of liberalism continuous with it. On a
trip to open a bureau in Kolkata, India, in 1999, he stopped at a
Scottish cemetery for a 'little ancestor worship'. The first editor,

James Wilson, was buried there, having died ten months into his job as India's finance minister in 1860. Tracking down his overgrown grave, Emmott happily observed the ledger inscription, 'Wilson, the right Hon'ble James, who was expressly sent from England to restore order to the finances of India.'[27] In 2006, his farewell was similarly mindful of his forebears. 'What is striking is how strongly this period has fitted Wilson's original view, how it made his principles feel more relevant than ever.' For 'the economic and political impact of the liberalisation of domestic and international markets for goods, services, technology and capital – globalisation ... would bring delight to Wilson's eyes.'[28]

## The British Model: 'Thatcher and Sons'

When Emmott became editor in 1993 in the aftermath of Thatcher's revolution, Britishness itself had a new valence for him and other editors. The very harshness of the medicine Thatcher had meted out – double-digit interest rates, sweeping privatizations of the telecom, gas, airline and other state-owned industries, slashing of top income tax rates in half, undoing of labour regulations, enforcement of pit and plant closures amidst high levels of unemployment – now allowed the *Economist* to position itself at the cutting edge of change. By the time the New Economy boom arrived, the country appeared to have turned a corner; at home and abroad, the paper was once again in the enviable position of giving lessons, not taking them.

Full of confidence, Emmott and his deputies took one contrarian stance after another – eager to restore the *Economist*'s reputation for radicalism. In 1994, the paper came out against the monarchy as an 'idea whose time has passed', suddenly wishing to replace it, pending a referendum, with a republic. Bagehot, 'the finest and most influential writer ever to have been editor', had, it recognized, defended this 'dignified' part of the constitution back in 1867, saying 'we must not let daylight in upon magic'. But much had changed, including the notion that loutish uneducated masses could not understand or even vote for a representative assembly. Bagehot, the leader added, had also said, 'Among a cultivated population, a population capable of abstract ideas, it would not be necessary.'[29]

*Economist* board members, all members of the Order of the British Empire, grumbled. When asked, Knight called it shocking, 'not at all in keeping with the traditions of the *Economist*'. Indeed, the paper had strong ties to the aristocracy and the royal family, not just by way of the royal-watcher Alastair Burnet, but also in Norman St John-Stevas. Sedulous courtier of the House of Windsor, swathed in downy shades of Tyrian purple ('crushed cardinal', he called it), who owned a framed pair of Queen Victoria's stockings, St John-Stevas had been parliamentary correspondent from 1954 to 1967. After being elected a Tory MP for Chelmsford, St John-Stevas continued to write and pass information to the *Economist*.[30] That helped at the start of the Thatcher era, when he advised the prime minister in his role as leader of the House of Commons until she sacked him as a tongue-wagging 'wet' in 1981. He called Thatcher 'Blessed Margaret ... she who must be obeyed ... the leaderene ... Attila the Hen' and TINA (for 'there is no alternative'), sometimes in her presence, and she later wrote: 'I was sorry to lose Norman but he made his own departure inevitable. He turned indiscretion into a political principle.' Royals sometimes returned the attention. Prince Charles disclosed his political frustrations to the *Economist* in 1986 in an interview with Simon Jenkins, who called it 'the manifesto of a social democratic prince'.[31]

Emmott, for his part, had long held the monarchy in disdain, though not out of deeply republican convictions. Commenting on a picture of Charles and Diana rambling through a Balmoral wheat field, he once lamented 'the Royal family sets a tone that remains anti-business'. The Queen was past hope, showing more interest in her corgis than any form of commerce. He encouraged her eldest son to act like a true role model, not a country squire, and 'to promote interest in business of every sort, as much as places to work as a way to get rich'.[32] In 1994, he observed 'the crown even has a certain, though not inevitable, bias against capitalism'.[33]

This contrarian posture was effective optically even when it was wide of the mark. In 1997, the paper attacked New Labour on the eve of its landslide, since on economic policy its 'basic instincts are illiberal' – a misread of the party Tony Blair and Gordon Brown had pushed to the right in opposition, by dropping demands for public ownership and accepting the fiscal and monetary strictures Thatcher had laid down. For David Lipsey, now political editor and Bagehot columnist, this was the 'one sour note of my tenure' at the *Economist*, since Emmott 'came to his decision in private, without discussing it face to face with me'. Emmott's fear that 'there was a hidden Old Labour wishing to get out from under the New Labour exterior' proved 'as wrong as could be' – something Lipsey was in a position to know. Long on the Labour right – he had started out as an advisor to Anthony Crosland and James Callaghan, before turning to journalism in 1979 – the Bagehot columnist was so 'carried away with excitement as Tony Blair threw away the baggage of Old Labour, as I had been urging' that he 'surreptitiously rejoined' the party.[34] As the Blair-Brown duumvirate pushed neoliberalism further than Thatcher had dared, in particular in the City – devising new 'light-touch' regulations, slashing capital gains from 40 to 10 per cent on long-term assets, granting the Bank of England full independence to set rates – Emmott backtracked. 'Tiresome as third-way nonsense is to curmudgeons such as *The Economist*, its success as a marketing device is not in doubt.' Downing Street spin-doctors, 'reconciling Britain to the Thatcher revolution, consolidating it, extending it' meant 'voters are happy, leading-thinkers are happy, everyone except the bewildered souls who believed in Old Labour are happy.'[35] Never a favourite, always shown grinning dementedly for no reason, in 2001 and 2005 Blair got the *Economist*'s blessing: superimposing his smiling face onto Thatcher's head – lipstick, earrings, coiffure – it advised readers, 'Vote conservative'.[36]

## Pushing Buttons Abroad

Each tartly-worded leader and irreverent cover raised the circulation of the *Economist*, as well as its profile as intellectual maverick – above all in the US, where social issues became an index of its liberalism as such. In 1996 the paper came out for gay marriage, inflaming the religious right, though its reasons had little to do with romantic love: 'single people were more likely to fall into the arms of the welfare state', and marriage was a 'great social stabiliser of men'.[37] It repeatedly called for stricter gun laws, especially after the Columbine shooting in 1999, earning it the ire of America's second amendment enthusiasts.[38] Even 'hard' drugs ought to be legalized, it explained in 2001, with reference to the US, where one in four prisoners was locked up for minor drug offences. Had not John Stuart Mill written: 'Over himself, over his own body and mind, the individual is sovereign'?[39] If it took safer lines on the death penalty and euthanasia, there was nothing circumspect about its political interventions. After endorsing Bill Clinton in 1992, four years later it opted for Bob Dole; even more scandalous, judging by the letters that poured in from readers, it demanded Clinton resign as president in 1998 over his mendacity about an extramarital affair with an intern in the Oval Office, citing 'deceit', 'moral weakness', 'bankruptcy', 'sleaziness', 'self-pitying paralysis', 'reckless risk-taking', 'broken trust', 'disgraced office'. It was not the 'sexual dalliance' itself that irked the paper – it had endorsed Clinton back in 1992, 'knowing full well he was a bit of a rogue and a risk-taker' – but the 'flagrant lying', 'unworthy of a president'. (Later, it said Donald Rumsfeld should hand in his badge over torture at Abu Ghraib in Iraq.)[40]

There was a great deal of tough love to go around. Emmott claimed to 'flinch a little' when he remembered meetings with Bill Gates, co-founder of Microsoft, 'a self-confessed devoted reader of *The Economist*', who 'would berate the publication's then-editor-in chief for its support for the antitrust action against him and his company' from 1998–2001. For fun, Emmott would tease Jon Corzine, CEO of Goldman Sachs.[41] And Emmott fired shots across the bow of Japan. One article on the state tobacco monopoly's unfair competition with foreign cigarette-makers, 'Marlboro Country', prompted the Japanese company to summon him to a boardroom where each of his sentences was cut out, pasted on a board and refuted. After a cover of a samurai tripping over himself in 1998, 'Japan's Amazing Ability to Disappoint', the embassy in London issued a 'petulant protest' and Motoo Shiina, a Diet member, personally chided Emmott.[42]

The Italian prime minister had more than petulant words for the paper. 'Why Silvio Berlusconi Is Unfit to Lead Italy' in 2001 – on his legal problems and links to organized crime, which appeared just before the spring elections – sparked a bitter row with the tanned media mogul turned politician. Berlusconi sued for libel, twice, and *Il Giornale,* a Milan newspaper owned by his brother Paolo, derided '*The E-Communist*' and compared its goateed editor to Lenin. Away when the decision to run this material was taken, Emmott came to own it – obscuring the fact that Clive Crook chose it, Tim Laxton and David Lane researched it, and Xan Smiley wrote it. Much of Emmott's career since 2006 has nevertheless been devoted to sparring with Berlusconi, as well as browbeating the country into market reforms: a 2012 documentary, *Girlfriend in a Coma,* shows Emmott doing his best Michael Moore, accosting Berlusconi in a crowded salon of 'elites'.[43]

### Finance and Globalization

The *Economist* did not ignore the financial bubbles that punctuated the New Economy years – in sovereign debt, dotcom stocks and housing – up to 2008, but it minimized them as relatively small bumps on the road to globalized capitalism. Mexico, East Asia and Russia were among the hardest hit by interlinked currency and debt crises. When Moscow defaulted in 1998, triggering the collapse of Long Term Capital Management – the heavily exposed hedge fund that lost $4.6 billion in four months – the paper defended the computer wizards whose models had failed to foresee this: 'it is pleasant to mock the Nobel Laureates who helped found LTCM, but much of this mockery clouds the truth', for 'the question arises whether recent events are ever likely to be repeated.'[44] But it also went on the attack against any who used such examples of 'market failure' to criticize, question or hold up globalization, with deputy editor Clive Crook leading the charge.[45]

Crook was thirty-eight in 1993, but looked 'more like a teenager in the grey flannel slacks, white oxford-cloth shirt, and blue pullover sweater that are his only known costume'.[46] 'Fearsomely brilliant', 'arguing for Free Trade in this gruff Lancashire accent', he was 'the Manchester School come to life'; others called him the 'intellectual Godfather', with Emmott by turns 'enthralled' and 'intimidated', as editors asked (on points of doctrine), 'Is Clive ok with this?' Penning the feistiest articles in favour of trade liberalization, Crook sensed that 1999 was the moment to 'come out fighting' at the World Trade Organization summit in Seattle. Holding high the banner of the WTO, the *Economist* exhorted the national governments gathered there to make a better sales pitch to citizens whose 'support for free trade is weak at best'. Trade reform 'was not irreversible', after all, and the last round in Uruguay in 1994 urgently needed updating to cover farming, services, finance, telecoms, computing and transport. 'Anti-globo' protestors, meanwhile – over a hundred thousand of whom took to the streets, from environmentalists to organized labour – should be ashamed.[47]

One cover showed a nameless Indian girl clutching a blanket, her glistening eyes raised in accusation, under the title 'The Real Losers from Seattle'. Five billion poor people in the developing world would suffer if greens, trade unions and anarchists got their way. India, 'home of our cover child', showed how growth and welfare had improved in tandem after the country rejected 'decades of socialist anti-globalisation'. To demand that trade agreements include labour standards or child welfare safeguards or environmental protections was totally misguided. These would 'not give that Indian child a better life', and 'tying trade to rules that forbid her from working will not help her either: that way lies greater poverty, not a better education.'[48] In a sign of how concerned Crook and other editors were about the growth of anti-globalization sentiment in these years (a fact obsured by what came after), on 11 September 2001 – the day two planes crashed into the World Trade Center in Manhattan – the *Economist* on newsstands had nothing to do with Middle Eastern terrorists. In red, white and black, the cover read 'Pro Logo', and savaged the Canadian activist Naomi Klein for her 'utterly wrong-headed' *No Logo* (1999), the best-selling 'bible of the anti-globalisation movement'.[49]

For his part, Emmott spied untrammelled vistas for financial innovation until the end. In his last signed piece in 2006, he hailed US banks for entering sectors served only by payday lenders and pawnbrokers. Citibank signed an agreement with 7-Eleven to put cash machines in 5,500 stores, while credit card companies 'targeted the unbanked and under-banked' – poor minorities and immigrants, who stood to gain from access to cheaper credit. (Banks anticipated culling $9 billion in fees from them, and that was 'before any cross-selling of other products'.) The subprime mortgage crisis hit the next year. Among the community banks Emmott cited as paragons, just one limped into 2012.[50] Yet the crash barely checked his stride. In 2008 'Crisis, What Crisis? Enough Kerfuffle, It's Just a Slowdown' appeared in the *Guardian*. Five months went by before a retraction, and as the title suggests, this was no standard mea culpa: 'I Wasn't Right. But That's OK.' A sense of civic duty had led him to 'overly optimistic economic predictions', he explained, in an attempt 'to argue that we risked *talking* ourselves into recession'.[51]

## America's New World Order

Emmott had predicted a 'golden age' of peace and prosperity when he took over the *Economist* soon after the collapse of the Soviet Union. 'US defence spending will fall to 3 percent of GDP', freeing up $125 billion a year to spend on health, education, debt repayment. 'American troops will be withdrawn from virtually all overseas bases', with foreign investment doing the rest – in a 'world of three billion new capitalists, workers, managers, inventors, investors and traders'.[52] A year on, he still saw the Pax Americana as uniquely consensual. Proof of its success, he argued in 1994 before the Trilateral Commission – a 'discussion forum' for business and political elites in the US, Europe and Japan, set up in 1973 – was the spread of 'globalisation, by choice' based on 'voluntary decisions of governments.'[53] Butter, not guns, was the order of the day.

In the event, Emmott's editorship witnessed nonstop American interventions abroad, which flew in the face of his forecast, and

led to a falling out with his foreign editor Johnny Grimond. Until
1989 Grimond edited the American Survey, as perhaps the strongest and most vocal opponent of Beedham on staff when the
latter retired. Grimond was also one of the few journalists with
ties to the political party whose history was intertwined with the
*Economist*: his father, Jo Grimond, led the Liberals from 1956
to 1967; his grandmother, Lady Violet Bonham Carter, was president of the Liberal Party; Asquith was a great-grandfather. A
graduate of Eton and Oxford, who stood for parliament himself
in 1970, Grimond was a careful guardian of the house style, and
seemed well attuned to Emmott. In 1993, both signed off on
the US mission to Somalia and after some hesitation to Rwanda
in 1994.[54]

But by far the most significant military actions of the period
came against the former communist federation of Yugoslavia,
as it fractured along ethnic lines; at least at first, the *Economist*
was not just hesitant, but critical of the aerial bombings NATO
led in 1993 and 1999, a stance almost without precedent and
so far without repetition. In both cases, Grimond wrote the
main leaders. Bosnia was not a genocide but a civil war between
Muslims, Serbs and Croats, he wrote, on whom outsiders 'could
impose a peace, if at all, only with resources of soldiers and will-
power they do not have'. Better to send food and medicine but
peacekeepers only 'where there is peace to keep'. 'Serbs, brutal as
they are, are not exterminating Muslims as Nazis exterminated
Jews.'[55] Six years later, Grimond doubted the legality as well as
strategic sense behind the more intensive bombardment of Serbia,
whose rationale was to stop the genocide of Albanians in Kosovo.
'NATO's first unambiguous attack on a sovereign state could set
an awkward precedent.'[56] Did China have the right to attack India
to protect Muslims in Janmu or Kashmir? What about Russia,
whose rampage in Chechnya was so horrific? 'So far, the West's war
against Serbia has been a shambles. The humanitarian catastrophe it was designed to avert has merely been intensified' while,
'dazzled by technology and obsessed with avoiding casualties of
their own, the allies seem unable to hurt, let alone destroy, Serbia's
army. Meanwhile, the list of accidents – innocents bombed, aircraft lost – grows longer.'[57] Over time, this position softened: 'the

West was not wrong in principle to intervene, whatever the legal position', reasoned the *Economist* by April, though it still insisted the bombing was doing more harm than good.[58]

Emmott had deferred to his more experienced foreign editor during the conflict, but doubts set in soon after, as the glow of victory cast it in a new light – and senior British and American officials pelted the paper with angry letters, stunned by its uncharacteristic criticism. By July, Emmott had reconsidered his foreign policy. 'The post-communist, post-Kosovo world now taking shape will not be an end-of-history sort of place in which all good democrats can put their feet up. It will be a world of clashing interests and outrageous atrocities, in which democrats will have to get involved.'[59] Emmott then demoted Grimond to lead the Britain section, and gave the Bagehot columnist his job. For a world that must be made safe for democracy, Peter David was a better fit: passionate Zionist, whose Lithuanian Jewish parents moved to England from South Africa as critics of apartheid in 1960, Beedham had hired him to cover the Middle East in 1984. David felt so strongly about the part America played in the region, he dedicated a coffee-table book to the glories of the first Gulf War in 1991, *Triumph in the Desert,* prefaced by General Colin Powell, with photos of smiling marines hugging grateful Kuwaitis.[60] It was David who set the tone of foreign coverage after 11 September 2001.

Reacting to the terrorist attacks that day with intense patriotic feeling, *Economist* covers depicted jets, helicopters, tanks and other military hardware against smoke, sand and billowing flags for the next three weeks, as titles grew larger and more guttural: from 15 September on, 'The Day the World Changed', 'The Battle Ahead', 'Closing In'. Articles spoke of 'lost innocence', 'implacable evil', an attack more infamous than Pearl Harbor, and asked if 'anything will ever be the same?' On 22 September it called for war, without yet knowing where, or who, it would strike. 'It will be long. It will cause anguish and arguments. It will involve more casualties. It is as hard to define the exact objective as to tell whether or when that objective has been achieved.' The US-led Western alliance would prove its worth beyond doubt by sending ground troops to wherever that ground turned out to be:

'America's allies in NATO have proclaimed their willingness to stand up and be counted by invoking for the first time its Article 5 on mutual defence.' 'America must demand, and receive, the tangible support it implies.'[61]

When Afghanistan emerged as the target, the paper ran with apple-cheeked Afghans staring up from headlines, as if the *Economist* were a charity solemnly asking donors to save the children by blowing them up. It pressed President George W. Bush not to stop at al-Qaeda there, but to bring down the Taliban too, a case of regime change in which 'permanent obligations need not be incurred'.[62] Seventeen years later, the US was still at war in Afghanistan, with no end to its mission in sight, unable to secure the garrisoned capital of Kabul and losing ground to the Pathan rebels outside it. Before Operation Enduring Freedom was even underway, however, the Bush White House had begun planning for the second Gulf War.

The *Economist* backed each stage of the build-up to it – applauding Bush's 'axis of evil' speech in 2002 as 'remarkable' and 'brave', stirring up fears that Saddam Hussein had weapons of mass destruction ('aggressive, cruel and reckless ... remove Mr. Hussein before he gets his bomb'), and then rationalizing the failure to discover any afterwards ('both at the time, and in retrospect, the decision to go to war rather than to wait was justified').[63] In the newsroom, Crook backed David at meetings and in the editorial process, inserting as much flammable material into articles as possible. Another recalled David referring to 'classified CIA material' he had seen – provided by Russia, and claiming Iraqis had supposedly visited Moscow to buy nuclear technology and rocket launchers. 'It was very convincing stuff.' Outside St James, these same editors somehow interpreted the millions of anti-war protestors in New York, London and elsewhere as, 'if anything, even keener on "regime change" than the British or American governments'.[64]

Emmott denied there had been no debate. He organized special discussions between editors to get disagreements 'out in the open' – estimating the overall tally for and against at '60–40', with senior editors Crook, David, Smiley, Micklethwait and Edwina Moreton, diplomatic and deputy foreign editor, in favour of the war; Barbara Smith, Grimond and Max Rodenbeck, Middle East bureau chief, spoke out against. Still, Emmott acknowledged that these debates took place with the expectation the answer 'was already there', and that 'I and Peter and Clive would endorse an invasion'. [65]

In fact, Emmott had already vaulted past his subordinates, producing a blanket justification for all imperial actions on the part of the US now and in the future – perhaps in psychological overcompensation for his dereliction during the Balkan wars. Its title a reprise of Dean Acheson's triumphalist account of his role in constructing the American world order in the launch to the Cold War, 'Present at the Creation' was Emmott's twenty-eight-page survey in June 2002 making the case for a pre-emptive strike in Iraq, in which he reimagined the decade since the end of the Cold War as one of 'hesitance', 'declining interest in foreign affairs', Americans acting by 'improvisation, with no clear sense of purpose or coherent strategy, and a rather short attention span'. Then 9/11 intervened, forcing the US to recognize tasks as Herculean as any in 1945: after 'happy victories in Afghanistan', there were 'rogue states developing weapons of mass destruction', 'violent militancy in Central Asia', the need for 'nation-building in Iraq', 'pressure on Iran and Pakistan', 'encouraging China to toe the line', keeping 'one eye on Indonesia', 'training armies and police forces ... in the more than 60 countries where al-Qaeda is said to have cells'.[66] Instead of bringing home its 250,000 soldiers and closing its 725 overseas bases, the US needed more of both. Since 'America's special national interest' was the 'closest match to a world interest', providing 'more trade, more investment, more security, more democracy', its continued presence overseas would be welcome. The long arc of globalization still bent towards peace, he believed, even when it looked like it might be taking a detour. Free trade 'answered the criticisms of country building: it is a way of helping countries help themselves', while multilateral bodies like an international court of justice 'can usefully supplement such police actions as well as reduce their costs'.[67]

Emmott thanked the leading historians of grand strategy and international relations Paul Kennedy, John Lewis Gaddis and Graham Allison for feedback on this manifesto, and listed a bibliography of foreign policy mandarins with ties to the White House and the State Department: Dean Acheson, Henry Kissinger, Walter Russell Meade, Donald Kagan, Richard Haass, Joseph Nye, Adam Joffe, John Bolton, Samantha Power. Emmott outdid his sages, however. Both more optimistic and more ambitious about the potential for America to remake the world in its image, he predicted invading Iraq would yield peace between Israel and Palestine, bring moderates to power in Iran, and give 'a new start for America with the rest of the Arab world'. A 'radically warmer relationship with Russia' was already evident, and in exchange for 'more western investment in oil and gas', it would hunt down jihadis, share intelligence, sign arms treaties, back a missile defence shield, and 'make America's military access to Central Asia [bases in Uzbekistan and Kyrgyzstan] permanent'. Moscow was also prepared to help out on the UN Security Council, where the US needed its cooperation on authorization votes and weapons inspectors. In a suitably cynical conclusion to this effusion of goodwill, he admitted this was for show, to speed up the timetable for war. 'There will be a multilateral process. It will fail. And then America will invade.'[68] For thirty-two weeks after this, the paper dutifully repeated the demand UN inspectors be given a chance.

If victory in Iraq was even more spectacular than in Afghanistan – the Baathist regime crushed in three weeks of shock and awe – so was the insurgency and civil war that followed. The failure of both invasions to yield secure, stable democracies never caused Emmott to question the fundamental morality of American power – 'its ultimately self-denying purpose', its 'blend of opportunity, knowledge and freedom'.[69] Afghanistan and Iraq were success stories. The US was 'not a true hegemon', nor 'a true policeman'. 'It is like a giant elder brother, a source of reassurance, trust and stability for weaker members of the family, and nervousness and uncertainty for any budding bullies.'[70] Only after stepping down did he criticize this sibling, who had turned out to be rather troubled. 'Few of his contemporaries think of George Walker Bush as a visionary American president, unless they are using the term to imply a touch of madness', he wrote in 2008 about the man he once put in heroic profile on the cover of the *Economist*. Even then, Emmott was nostalgic about Bush's 'grandest of grand foreign-policy strategies, seeking nothing less than a transformation of the Middle East and Central Asia', with 'democracy, or at least accountability, replacing dictatorship. But it collapsed in ruins.'[71] For all his hand-wringing, and casting about for new champions of globalization in India or China, however, Emmott saw no alternative: 'America is the one country from whom an intervention or retaliation would be feared', he reasoned, now about Asia. 'Even after the Iraqi disaster, America should be seen as a stabilizing force.'[72]

## Exit Stage Right

In the aftermath of the Iraq invasion, there was more bickering inside the *Economist* – albeit with US foreign policy a side show to the main event: jockeying to replace Emmott. Even at the start of his tenure, there had been rows. After convincing Crook and Emmott to send an office email announcing a 'triumvirate' in 1994, Asia editor (and ardent admirer of Singapore's Lee Kuan Yew) Jim Rohwer quit in a storm when Crook got cold feet. In 1997, there was the fallout over Emmott's secretive decision to back the Conservatives over New Labour. In 1999, Sebastian Mallaby, the Washington bureau chief, resigned after Emmott spiked his American politics survey, which argued that the checks and balances of the US constitution actually hampered effective government. Pressing Emmott to punish this 'illiberal' heresy and banish Mallaby to Berlin, Crook emerged one rival down for the editorship when Mallaby left.[73] But it soon became clear that Emmott was determined to stay past the usual ten years. In 2005, it was Crook's turn to leave in frustration for the *Atlantic Monthly*. By then the board of directors was putting pressure on Emmott, concerned that top talent was fleeing the paper because of his determination to stay. When Emmott replaced Crook with Emma Duncan as deputy editor, viewed as unlikely to challenge him, John Micklethwait did so instead – bringing the board a job offer from the rightwing British weekly the *Spectator* that forced Emmott to depart suddenly in March 2006.

## Dukes of Moral Hazard: Micklethwait and Wooldridge

The appointment of John Micklethwait as the sixteenth editor was announced with great fanfare in 2006. 'In his tailored suit and polished shoes', the *Guardian* found him 'poised, unmistakably upmarket ... the essence of a well-educated English gentleman editor, charming, a touch self-deprecating, but to the point.' The *Independent* caught up with the new forty-three-year-old head of 'one of Britain's greatest media brands', 'blood relative of the Duke of Norfolk, tall, straight-backed with a thick mop of hair, a clipped English accent and a desk that looks out across the royal parks'.[74] Micklethwait was cool, polite, experienced; having spent the 90s in New York and Los Angeles – the two fastest growing urban markets in the fastest growing national market for the *Economist* – he told the board he could double circulation again to 2 million inside a decade.[75] The first person to move directly from editing the American section to editing the paper, his experience gave him an edge over the other finalists, business editor Ed Carr and deputy editor Emma Duncan.

A practising Catholic, Micklethwait attended Ampleforth, the same school as Knight, a mentor who brought him along to Bilderberg conclaves, where he became a well-connected note-taker. Like Emmott, he went to Magdalen, though he studied history, not PPE. In personality, Micklethwait was a combination of the two men – at meetings, 'vague, diffident, easy to underestimate', but with a class profile and worldly ambitions cut from much the same cloth as Knight. After university he got a job at Chase Manhattan Bank in New York. 'I was not a terribly successful banker', he confessed later, joking that his first investment was in Eurotunnel, which lost £925 million in its first year and later went bankrupt.[76] His next job was at the *Economist* as finance and business editor in London, before his posting to Los Angeles.

During and after his sojourn in America, much of the intellectual thrust came from his colleague and writing partner, Adrian Wooldridge, described as a 'Norman Macrae-like figure – clever, if rather kooky'. 'When I first arrived he terrified me, because he seemed so posh, always dressed in very stripy Jermyn Street shirts and nodding emphatically in meetings.' Wooldridge came to the paper in 1988 – after Balliol and All Souls, Oxford, and a Harkness Fellowship to Berkeley, in pursuit of modern history – developing a distinctly wry and assertive writing style, as Washington bureau chief from 2000–10, and in a series of columns, as Lexington, Schumpeter and, presently, Bagehot.

## The Liberalism of Frequent Flyer Miles:
## Redeeming Globalization

Micklethwait and Wooldridge spent well over a decade in the US working and raising families, feeling so at ease in New York, Los Angeles and everywhere in between – from authentic Texas to suburban Illinois – they began to write with a curious Oxbridge-on-the-Mississippi twang: conservatives were not just mad or proud but 'pig-wrestling mad', 'damned proud', 'country-club Yankees' being 'just the sort who get up Joe Sixpack's nose'.[77] Emmott had raised the bar for future editors, penning three books before, and one during, his tenure (not to mention several in Japanese translation). Acting together, Micklethwait and Wooldridge wrote even more, with five books on discoveries made in America – examining its business consultants in *The Witch Doctors* in 1996; leadership of globalization in *A Future Perfect* in 2000; spirited innovations in *The Company* in 2003; politics in *The Right Nation* in 2004 (accurately predicting Bush's victory and helping to secure Micklethwait the editorship); and its peculiar religiosity in *God Is Back* in 2009.

This body of work, closely overlapping with their articles for the *Economist*, displayed levels of giddiness about American-style capitalism that surpassed Emmott's.[78] Nowhere was the breathless tone more apparent than in *The Future Perfect*, written after the East Asian financial crisis and WTO protests in 1998–99, 'to make the intellectual case for globalization'. That case rested in large part on a group they dubbed the 'cosmocrats' – a perplexing neologism, evoking a Soviet-era space program, instead of the global race of yuppies they had in mind – ordering 'loups de mer' for dinner, while 'forever eliminating barriers, overcoming limits, removing rigidities'. A 'broadening class of people who

have benefited from globalization', cosmocrats might just be 'the
most meritocratic ruling class the world has ever seen'.[79]

The cosmocrats were everywhere, if you knew how to look.
There were relative unknowns like Patrick Wang in Hong Kong,
scion of an industrial family, 'his suit exquisitely tailored, his thick
black hair neatly combed, and he speaks impeccable Harvard
Business School English'. Or Jang Ha-sung, economist and activist shareholder in Seoul, 'preppie-looking in a blue blazer, club
tie and button-down shirt, a former student of finance at the
Wharton school', feet up at home, as 'opera burbles in the background'. Western countries also had some: in Bolton, England,
Marcus de Ferranti, Eton graduate, electronics heir, fighter pilot,
who emerged from aristocratic torpor to found a virtual telephone exchange; in Johannesburg, Lyn Van Haght, 'tall, blond
Californian', who ran a heavily-fortified testing centre for private
education company Sylvain, 'creating the black middle class that
the continent needs so desperately'.[80]

Some looked strange: Steven Hirsch, an LA pornography studio
chief, 'tanned and aerobicized' but oddly 'sounds as if he has graduated from a high-powered business school' or Jackson Thubela
in Soweto, a 'gold toothed twenty year old who often wears an
Adidas tracksuit' and ran a phone stand. Others looked just as
you might expect: Jack Welch, the legendary CEO of 'boundary-
less' General Electric, or Bill Gates, who was not just a brilliant
businessman but a daring philanthropist, 'imaginative enough to
solve problems that have flummoxed the public sector' with a
'relentlessly curious and competitive brain'.[81]

Wooldridge and Micklethwait brushed past some less appealing
signposts of globalization along the way. An appointment with a
toy wholesaler in downtown LA was punctuated by a shocking
scene along Fifth Street, 'dingy and dilapidated, host to denizens
of the lowest rungs of the underclass', among them 'amputees
delivering drug-crazed lectures to the sidewalk, beggars begging
from each other'.[82] Other 'losers from globalization' had a pica-
resque dignity, ranked and sorted as 'has-beens', 'storm damage',
and 'non-starters'. Dwight Bobo, a worker on strike at a GM
stamping factory in Flint, Michigan, was a has-been. 'Perhaps the
saddest thing about Bobo is the fact that he is a decent man who

must surrender to the inevitable.' They added, 'a bit like the deer that he hunts', he 'is simply being culled'.[83] But this trailed off: 'We must be careful not to take the hand-wringing too far.' To show 'the human race is, in general, advancing', they travelled to Brazil where 'the crapshoot that Bobo resents is helping to change the life of Marcos Andrade', machine operator at a stamping facility GE had built in Sao Caetano do Sul, who 'whistles when he hears how much workers in Flint are paid'. The two authors marvelled with him as bathos for Bobo turned to Schumpeterian shrug: 'the creative destruction continues'.[84]

Even Thomas Friedman got an earful for his naïve thesis in 1999's *Lexus and the Olive Tree,* that globalization was as inevitable as the dawn. 'Given the carnage it has caused', they wrote, before adding, '(or is said to have caused)', advancing it would require political leadership. Here was a mission for the cosmocrats, if only they chose to accept it. The very tawdriness of politics 'seems to put them off'. If there is ever 'a great battle about globalization, then the people one might have expected to form the heart of the defense will probably be on a plane somewhere'.[85]

In the meantime, Micklethwait and Wooldridge made the case for globalization on their behalf. In *Future Perfect*, the advance of industrial production was 'surely not the root cause' of pollution in places like China, 'and may well prove part of the solution'.[86] *The Company* celebrated a revolutionary idea gifted to posterity by two Victorian Liberals, who established that companies had the same legal rights as human beings, and that investors had limited liability on the capital placed in them. All efforts since then to put limits on companies was misguided: the 1991 US Civil Rights Act resulted in 'more red tape and more lawsuits' and the 2002 Sarbanes-Oxley legislation that set tougher rules on corporate auditing, accounting and reporting was an 'overreaction' to fraud at Enron, Tyco and WorldCom.[87] They even decried calls for corporate social responsibility *from* corporations. For 'in general, companies have become more ethical: more honest, more humane, more socially responsible'. From Quaker candy makers to Hewlett-Packard, from IBM to Johnson & Johnson, 'they pillage the Third World less than they used to, and they offer more opportunities to women and minorities', especially compared to before, 'when the initials of the Royal African Company were branded on the chests of thousands of slaves'.[88]

*The Right Nation* and *God Is Back* were more substantial, unearthing positive elements for their cosmocratic liberalism, albeit from two unlikely sources. The first stemmed from a fascination with rightwing American intellectuals: William Buckley at *National Review,* Milton Friedman and the Chicago boys, and the neoconservatives, including Irving Kristol, Daniel Bell, Seymour Lipset and Nathan Glazer. Aside from the admirable 'cutting edge' they gave to US foreign policy, the neocons were also 'muckrakers of the Right', 'discrediting government' by exposing affirmative action and welfare dependency. In fact, they were quite close to the philosophical traditions of the *Economist.* 'As they grew older, neocons embraced old-fashioned liberalism – the liberalism of meritocratic values, reverence for high culture and a vigorous mixed economy.' Looking past the misleading label, 'America's conservatism is an exceptional conservatism: the conservatism of a forward-looking commercial republic rather than the reactionary Toryism of old Europe.' They cited an exchange in which Max Beloff, a British peer, incredulously asked Irving Kristol how he dared call himself conservative, since without deference to tradition, including those threatened by 'the abuses of capitalism, it is only the old Manchester School [of classical liberalism].'[89]

There remained a difference between the 'old-fashioned liberalism' of Europe and the 'exceptional conservatism' of America, however – though, on closer inspection, the latter turned out to be a great improvement. In alliance with the evangelical right, neocons not only showed great tactical nous. They demonstrated how religious observance went hand in hand with wealth creation, in a kind of generalized ethic of capitalism. *Future Perfect* opened in New York at a Bruderhof retreat, a community which embraced global supply chains and the internet for its toy business – proof that 'if the modern marketplace can do the devil's work, it can also do the Lord's.'[90] America was not just economically and militarily dominant ('superpower is too weak a word'), crucially it was also the most devout state in the West. This explained the productivity gains of the New Economy. 'Today the triumph of secularization in Europe seems to be going hand in hand with the decline of the work ethic, just as the survival of religion in the United States is going hand in hand with the survival of the work ethic.'

This went beyond Max Weber's theory about the origins of capitalism in Protestant Europe. It hinted that industriousness was elastic, rising or falling with changes in the religious sentiment giving rise to it. Europeans 'liked to think of themselves as rational heirs to the Enlightenment', but they suffered from a consequent competitive disadvantage when it came to God.[91] Later, in Shanghai, Micklethwait and Wooldridge sat in on a Bible study group composed of young professionals, all convinced that Christianity was behind American greatness. In full agreement, the authors pointed out that the US supplied not only missionaries to China, but also a 'gospel of pluralism' in the form of the first amendment – engineered by 'the genius' of the founding fathers as much to keep the state out of religion as the other way around.[92]

If spirituality increased material wellbeing, a great deal sprinkled over the earth would increase it by a large amount. 'Religion is being driven by the same two things that have driven the success of market capitalism: competition and choice.' The cosmocrats had found the ultimate consumer durable: God. The Shanghai Bible study group had 'biotechnologists, a prominent academic, a Chinese-American doctor, successful entrepreneurs, two ballet dancers' and 'BMWs parked in front'. 'In much of the world it is exactly the sort of upwardly mobile, educated middle classes that Marx and Weber presumed would shed such superstitions who are driving the explosion of faith.' The millenarian element in the *Economist*'s free trade manifesto of 1843 had returned as a form of religious sociability. More than faith, this was a sign of US dominance 'so omnipresent that everyone has, as it were, a virtual America buried inside their brains'.[93]

## 2008: Saving the System

On becoming editor in 2006, Micklethwait said his goal was to make the *Economist* 'the user's handbook for globalization', tackling 'the big issues'.[94] 'Whenever there is dissent within the office,

argument always comes round to the question, "What would be
the liberal approach?"' A return to first principles – pivoting on
economic freedom and suspicion of the Leviathan state – should
not be confused with pro-business bias, he patiently explained.
'We do not treat business people with slavish idolatry or put them
on the cover playing golf.' The stakes were far higher. 'We'd rather
be seen as pro-capitalism.'[95] Just two years on, that stance was
put to the test, as the biggest crisis since the Great Depression
engulfed the global capitalist system.

The *Economist* did not see that crisis coming: indeed, its market
analyses (suffused by efficient market theory) ruled it out. In 2006,
as US real estate prices began to fall, setting off a reaction in the
repo markets in housing debt – on which big banks and other
financial institutions had come to rely for short term-funding –
the horizon was cloudless, at least for the financial system. The
*Economist* recognized that as housing prices 'flatten off', the US
economy – driven by consumer spending and residential construction, abetted by low interest rates – would slow down. But
that needn't result in a crash. On 24 March 2007, 'Cracks in the
Façade' considered what the rise in delinquencies and defaults
on subprime mortgages, and the cost of insuring against these,
might mean for markets and the wider economy; the 'biggest risk'
was that 'politicians rewrite the rules ham-fistedly'.[96] By 2008,
when this securitized, supposedly safe debt turned toxic, banks
holding it as loan collateral rushed to cover their losses, and
panic selling swept markets (even those unrelated to mortgages),
exposing highly leveraged banks as illiquid, when not insolvent.[97]
Lehman Brothers collapsed in September, brought down by the
credit squeeze, with state authorities everywhere stepping in to
avert more failures.

As Lehman sent shockwaves through world markets, the
*Economist* – hurricanes, cliffs, ruins, free-falling globes on the
cover – suddenly declared it 'time to put dogma and politics to
one side and concentrate on pragmatic answers'.[98] There was no
such thing as laissez-faire in a foxhole, for 'when global finance
stops only governments can start it again', clearing banks of bad
assets, guaranteeing their liabilities, dowsing them in liquidity. The
Troubled Asset Relief Plan (TARP) was the first step to restoring

confidence in the financial system, and the paper saluted former Goldman Sachs executive Hank Paulson at the US Treasury for pledging $700 billion to the effort ('a number plucked out of thin air', he later revealed).[99]

Still, the administration of George W. Bush had taken too long to summon this courage, and should never have let Lehman fail (especially after bailing out the mortgage lenders Fannie Mae and Freddie Mac). Lamenting that 'Conservative America needs to recover its vim', in November 2008 the *Economist* endorsed Democrat Barack Obama as the best man to restore 'America's self-confidence' and re-launch its global brand – 'reselling economic and political freedom to a world that too quickly associates American capitalism with Lehman Brothers and American justice with Guantanamo Bay'.[100] In Britain, Gordon Brown's 'bold and comprehensive' handling of the crisis earned him the belated approval of the *Economist*. As he recapitalized the banks, provided £1 trillion in guarantees, and the Bank of England pumped £200 billion into government bonds and kept interest rates at zero, Bagehot mused, 'How did Britain's hapless Prime Minister become saviour of the Universe?'[101]

## Not a Step Back: Liberalism and the Crisis at the *Economist*

Some financial journalists reconsidered their positions in the aftermath of this calamity, chastened by their blindness to it, and writing bold think-pieces announcing the death of neoliberalism, the revenge of Keynes, even of Marx.[102] Not the *Economist*. Steadfast, it acted as a kind of automatic stabilizer for a liberal ideological order suddenly racked with self-doubt – which helps explain why neoliberal policies that caused the crash were prescribed as the only cure for its aftereffects, amidst persistent stagnation in the world economy a decade later.

Not only did the *Economist* demand that governments bail out banks, warning of utter disaster on the scale of 1929 if they did not – 'no country or industry would be spared from the equivalent of a financial heart attack' – it pushed aggressively for the austerity that flowed from this, in order to pay down the debts that states had taken off banks' balance sheets. The crisis thus became a powerful rationale for urging cherished reforms, advocated long before 2008. In 'Capitalism at Bay', the paper advised liberals to keep calm and carry on. 'All the signs are pointing in the same direction, a larger role for the state, and a smaller and more constrained private sector. This newspaper hopes profoundly that this will not happen.' But, 'in the longer term a lot depends on how blame for this catastrophe is allocated. This is where an important intellectual battle could and should be won.'[103] The *Economist* suited up for battle. As the credit crunch turned into a global recession, it argued nothing much was wrong with the real economy, still less capitalism; and if the causes of the crisis were technical – 'dodgy lending', 'cheap money from emerging economies, outdated regulation, government distortions and poor supervision', 'dangerous incentives and the reckless use of mathematical models' – so were the solutions: 'smaller, better regulated, more conservative' banks, and more oversight.

In point of fact, the *Economist* pushed back against proposals to attach conditions to the bailouts, or restrict banks' freedom: 'wholesale nationalizations' would 'undermine property rights', sap the entrepreneurial spirit, and foment cronyism. Breaking up the banks or returning them to Glass-Steagall rules, which had once kept investment and depository banks separate, was ill-advised. Even oversight could go too far, for 'liberalisation had good consequences as well: by making it easier for households and businesses to get credit, deregulation contributed to economic growth.'[104] With concessions as footling as these in the pit of the crisis, the paper clambered out in no time. Deregulation was back on the agenda by 2010. In 2012, the front cover evoked the London Blitz under the banner 'Save the City', signalling finance had been unfairly attacked.[105]

Having demanded a bailout for Wall Street, the *Economist* refused to countenance the same for the US car industry or the millions it employed. 'Banks qualify for help because the entire economy depends upon their services. They are vulnerable to sudden collapses in confidence that can spread to other banks that are perfectly solvent.' Detroit 'employs a network of suppliers, which would suffer if production shuts down', and yet, 'nothing would sap a recovery and job-creating enterprise like locking up badly used resources in poorly performing companies.'[106] And even as monetary policy grew increasingly unorthodox, with central banks buying up public and private assets and keeping interest rates at or near zero, the *Economist* took up the battle hymn of a doctrinaire deflation ('growth friendly fiscal consolidation') in country after country by the turn of 2010, from Portugal, Ireland and Spain to Italy and France – but nowhere more lustily than in Britain itself, which could once again become an economic model unto the world.[107]

Enthralled by the Liberal-Conservative coalition that came to power there in 2010, the *Economist* hailed its legislative agenda as 'revolutionary': cuts of a quarter to most state departments, higher consumer taxes, student tuition fees raised from £3,200 to £9,000, a public sector pay freeze and 330,000 layoffs in four years, spending cuts to bring deficits down 6.3 per cent by 2014–15.[108] This was just the start. Why should the 'bloated' National Health Service be off-limits? 'Tories should have used their disastrous inheritance as an excuse to break their promise to maintain NHS spending.' In welfare, means-testing child benefit and eliminating winter fuel payments and bus passes for the elderly could yield savings. David Cameron appeared on the cover in a Union Jack Mohawk, 'Radical Britain: The West's Most Daring Government'.[109] If that was not clear enough, Wooldridge spelled it out under his own name in the *Times* in 2012: 'Stop the war on wealth, we need these rich few.'[110] A year later, Margaret Thatcher's death was treated like the martyring of an insurgent, rifles pointed skywards, spent ammo clanking to the ground. 'Freedom Fighter', blared the *Economist* in black and white.[111]

## Bestirring the 'Weakened West'

Though he acknowledged past mistakes in Afghanistan and Iraq, Micklethwait showed neither remorse nor reticence about urging on further American wars. On this score, the *Economist* did not always give Barack Obama the credit he deserved, grumbling that he was too hesitant to use the hard power at his disposal. In

Libya, all went well. When Arab Spring protests gave way to an armed rebellion against Muammar Qaddafi in February 2011, the paper called for a NATO-enforced no-fly zone from the start. Soon it was demanding aerial bombardments, a naval blockade and regime change – to guard 'against the threat of butchery in Benghazi' and give 'a region of 350 million Arabs stuck in poverty and dysfunctional politics' a 'chance to come alive'. Such an attack was 'unarguably legal', based on a 'helpfully elastic' UN resolution 'endorsing "all necessary measures" to protect civilian life', opposed only by 'the pacifist brigade'.[112] Some 17,000 air sorties later, it was 'a good war' for NATO: admirably restrained, its pilots 'keeping collateral damage to a minimum', and with Europe supposedly in the lead of an operation essentially conducted by the US, a 'template for future operations'.[113]

Concerning Syria, however, the president was a disappointment. There, in a bloody civil war in the aftermath of the Arab Spring, where Obama was funding and arming Islamist rebels, it called for partition in 2012: a Turkish run 'safe-haven' in the north-west, funded by NATO and Arab League countries, to train the Free Syrian Army fighting against forces loyal to President Bashar al-Assad.[114] A year later, it called on Obama to strike at Assad for using chemical weapons: 'hit him hard', it urged. Let a 'week of missiles rain down on the dictator's "command and control" centres, including his palaces' to 'deter him from ever using WMD again'. Should this fail, show him 'as little mercy as he has shown to the people he claims to govern. If an American missile then hits Mr Assad himself, so be it'.[115] When Obama asked Congress to authorize the attack he had readied, and settled for mediation by Putin, the paper was aghast at this blow to presidential power (which must be 'quick and agile', 'take hard and unpopular decisions'), to 'the credibility of US foreign policy' (creating expectations this might be 'subject to the vagaries of congressional sound bites' in future), and to all those 'who cherish freedom' and 'put their faith' in the West (represented on the cover as a lame and toothless lion, casting a forlorn look at Syria from across the Mediterranean).[116]

This overwrought language about the fate of the free world was reminiscent of the Cold War for a reason. Under Micklethwait, the *Economist* once again spied a Russian behind every setback for the West; a narrative that took shape in 2008 after Moscow trounced Georgia in a dispute over South Ossetia and Abkhazia in the Caucasus. This, argued the paper matter-of-factly, was a setback for the West, 'which has been trying to prise away countries on Russia's western borders and turn them democratic, market-oriented and friendly.'[117] Six years later, such prising provoked a new conflict, when pro-Western protestors toppled Viktor Yanukovych in Kiev, and Putin reacted by backing pro-Russian separatists in east Ukraine and annexing Crimea, home of Russia's Black Sea Fleet and a Russian majority population. For the *Economist,* this was quite simply the end of 'the existing world order'. Crimea was a new Sudetenland, Putin another Hitler, 'armed with a self-proclaimed mission to rebuild the Russian Empire' from 'Central Asia to the Baltic'. Anything less than sanctions against him was 'appeasement': a 'fundamentally antagonistic' state, Russia should be 'cut off from dollars, euros and sterling', finance and trade, with a total embargo on its oil and gas.[118]

The editor most responsible for this feverish coverage was Edward Lucas, who came of age as the Cold War ended. His father John Lucas – a philosopher who hosted dissidents at Oxford and smuggled Plato and the Greek New Testament into communist Czechoslovakia – raised him to fight in the closing act of that conflict. At the LSE, he campaigned for Solidarity in Poland, before setting off to Berlin, Prague and Krakow as an activist-cum-journalist in 1988. Expelled from Lithuania after he arrived to show 'symbolic support' for its anti-Soviet regime in 1990, he started an 'intentionally provocative' English-language weekly in Estonia in 1993 with a column, Troopwatch, that 'monitored the occupation forces' misbehaviour'.[119] As Moscow bureau chief at the *Economist* from 1998 to 2002, he formed a view of Russia that differed from the prevailing optimism about the post-Soviet transition to liberal democracy and capitalism.

In 2008, Lucas's *The New Cold War: How the Kremlin Menaces Both Russia and the West* barely glanced at the decade of economic chaos and decline that followed the fall of the Soviet Union. 'Never in Russian history have so many Russians lived so

well and so freely', he observed, with a growing middle class able
to buy property, travel abroad and send their children to boarding
school.[120] But if Moscow now accepted the rules of the game so
far as capitalism was concerned, it remained unreconciled to the
geopolitical order governing it – with the same gnawing hunger
for power as before. 'Once it was the communist trade unions that
undermined the West at the Kremlin's behest. Now pro-Kremlin
bankers and politicians betray their countries for thirty silver
roubles.' Long before the standoff over Ukraine, Lucas pushed
for a confrontational line on Russia. 'Until we make it clear we
believe in our own values, we cannot defend ourselves against the
subversion and corruption leaking into our citadels of power.'[121]
In 2012, *Deception: Spies, Lies and How Russia Dupes the West*
arrived to reinforce that point.

In style and outlook, Lucas was a link to the Crozier-Moss-
Beedham tradition at the *Economist*: amiably bedraggled, with
a wry sense of humour and the air of an MI6 man – like those
he 'rubbed shoulders and clinked glasses' with as a young man,
but refused to join, because 'I reckoned I could do more good on
the outside' – and with similar extracurriculars. Senior vice president at the Center for European Policy Analysis, a Washington
and Warsaw-based think tank with a list of donors that includes
the US State Department and arms companies, Lucas runs its
stratcom [i.e. propaganda] program, euphemistically described
as an 'on the ground effort to monitor, collate, analyze, rebut and
expose Russian disinformation' in 'central and eastern Europe'.[122]

Given this outlook, it is hardly surprising that revelations about
the reach of the US security and surveillance state since 2008
should not have perturbed the *Economist*. Obama's unprecedented
use of drones to assassinate suspected terrorists on his 'kill lists' –
in Yemen, Somalia or Pakistan, where America was not at war,
and without judicial oversight even when the targets were its own
citizens – 'do not undermine the rules of war', though more could
be done to 'adapt' a 'potent new weapon' to the constitution.[123]
When the US Army private then named Bradley Manning leaked
hundreds of thousands of secret government documents related
partly to the wars in Iraq and Afghanistan in 2010, exposing war
crimes committed by US mercenaries, the *Economist* insisted that

both he and the 'digital Jacobins' at Wikileaks to whom Manning confided this cache be punished. Julian Assange should be extradited, though in the meantime the paper found 'some consolation' that his revelations actually offered 'a largely flattering picture of America's diplomats: conscientious, cool-headed, well-informed, and on occasion eloquent'.[124] Three years later Edward Snowden, a private analyst for the National Security Agency, exposed the staggering extent of its illegal surveillance of US citizens and foreigners, including such staunch allies of the US as German chancellor Angela Merkel. Disagreement between Lucas and other editors resulted in a toothless verdict on the American security empire – 'our point is not that American spies are doing the wrong things' – and a vindictive one on the traitor who had exposed it: Snowden, who had fled to Moscow must return to face US justice.[125] Lucas, writing under his own name, was less equivocal. He denied the NSA had done anything illegal and strongly insinuated Snowden was a Russian agent in a 2014 e-book, *The Snowden Operation: Inside the West's Greatest Intelligence Disaster.*

### The Rise of ZMB and the Keynes-Hayek Divide

In 2015, Michael Bloomberg hired Micklethwait to restructure the news side of his data terminal business in New York. Of the three finalists competing to replace him in London – Ed Carr, Tom Standage and Zanny Minton Beddoes – the last was a long-running favourite with both staff and management, in possession of all the prerequisites to be editor: PPE at St Hilda's College, Oxford, MPA from Harvard's Kennedy School and time spent in America, where she had lived since 1996. In due course appointed, she became the first woman to occupy the role, after 172 years – well-known from television and radio, elegant in brightly coloured suits and patterned dresses, a prized guest on panels and at global gatherings from the Davos Forum to Bilderberg. Sharp and eloquent, she was also refreshingly willing to listen and debate with her interlocutors. Born in Shropshire to an Army officer father and a German mother, she went to Moreton Hall, a public girls' school near her home.

In her first summer at Harvard, Beddoes travelled to Poland with her professor Jeffrey Sachs, working as an intern in an old Soviet Ministry building, 'writing policy memos designed to help Poland's reformers to build a market economy'. In 1992, she turned down a job from Goldman Sachs to pursue similar work as a junior economist at the IMF, first in Senegal and Mali and then in Kyrgyzstan. 'This meant basic things, like figuring out national income, which had never been done before. In Kyrgyzstan, I'd go to the train station and literally count trains to see what they were sending out.' Opting to pursue journalism after two years of this, she wavered between the *Economist* and the *Financial Times* – with Harvard classmates Clive Crook and John Heilemann at the first, and New Labour's Ed Balls at the second. '*Economist* editorials have more heft', she decided, perhaps with the example of Sachs in mind, who had launched 'shock therapy' in Yugoslavia, Poland and Russia in a signed piece for the paper in 1990, urging a 'transition to a private-sector market economy in one year'.[126] Emmott hired her for the new post of emerging markets correspondent in 1994 and two years later promoted her to be economics editor, based in Washington, D.C.

In that post until 2007, Beddoes enthusiastically backed globalization, explaining the role that regional and global financial markets played in it: private pension schemes in Latin America in 1995, copper, uranium, cotton, oil and natural gas in Central Asia and the Caucasus in 1998, global banking and regulations after the Russian default in 1999, rebalancing of the world economy away from US households in 2003 and towards Asians and Europeans in 2005.[127] But the 2008 crisis altered the landscape at the *Economist,* and her place within it, as fault lines emerged over how to respond to the Great Recession. Named business editor just as the crisis hit, Beddoes convened the section editors and invited two outside economists to offer critiques. 'We saw mistakes we had made in the 1960s and 70s – corporatism, industrial policy, state subsidies, high taxes.' But there were other historical missteps – in the 1920s and 30s, when laissez-faire needlessly prolonged a depression: 'this also bolstered my position, which you might call small-government Keynesianism'. In contrast to Micklethwait, Beddoes defended a bailout of Detroit automakers at the time – doing so again in a heated exchange on the Bill Maher show in 2012, pointing out that if they had filed for bankruptcy 'in the midst of this huge financial crisis, they would have been liquidated, with hundreds of thousands of jobs lost throughout the Midwest.'

This mild-mannered, post-2008 'Keynesianism' put her at odds with two wily old operators at the *Economist*, Ed Lucas and the capital markets editor and Buttonwood columnist (on finance), Philip Coggan. 'There is a kind of divide, yes, between the Keynesians and the Hayekians', Lucas explained in 2011. Beddoes was a 'fierce Keynesian ... on what to do about the Eurozone, on US stimulus'. 'I think she is wrong. But she is very, very smart and articulate.' On the other side were Coggan and himself: 'I'm the most Austrian of all the Austrians' and 'we want to save capitalism from itself', giving it a supple yet strong regulatory framework – clawing back some ground from the financiers, their tax breaks and offshore wealth havens. (Neither fiscal stimulus nor monetary easing would work – since, they argued with Hayek, after a certain threshold, lower interest rates had deflationary effects, encouraging people to save and not to spend.)[128]

For a moment, he and Coggan seemed to have the upper hand. After three years of recession, and with the spectre of a sovereign debt crisis hanging over Europe, young *indignados* took to the streets in Madrid to protest austerity in May 2011, kicking off a global 'movement of the squares' that reached New York by September. In October, the *Economist* cover featured a young man with a twenty-dollar bill taped to his mouth, American flag grazing his cheek, at the Occupy Wall Street encampment. 'Rage against the Machine: Capitalism and Its Critics' seemed, after the requisite jokes about hygiene among the campers, to side with its critics. That was Coggan, who argued for taking their 'deep-seated grievances' seriously – with youth unemployment at 21 and 17 per cent in Europe and the US respectively, real wages falling for the middle class, and inflation eroding the savings of the elderly, as bankers raked in bonuses. He contrasted the Occupy movement with the 'selfish' protests in Seattle in 1999, 'easy for economic liberals to dismiss' as 'an attempt to impoverish the emerging world through protectionism'. Lucas was slightly cooler. For without organized labour, argued a second piece written largely by him, the occupations in Berlin, London, Madrid, New York and Rome would struggle to be heard. 'Protestors can occupy the world's financial markets physically, but they have not shown they can spook them.'

In fact, it was the incoherence of Occupy's demands that interested Coggan and Lucas, allowing them to invent some. Closing tax loopholes, lowering marginal rates, and moving '"to Basel 3 and higher capital requirements" is not a catchy slogan, but it would do far more to shrink bonuses on Wall Street than most of the ideas echoing across from Zuccotti Park.' In his Buttonwood column, Coggan mooted reforms of this kind after 2008, urging readers dissatisfied with efficient market theory to look at Hayek and his teacher Ludwig von Mises – whose theories of the business cycle helped to explain the crisis as one of low interest rates leading to a credit boom, followed by misallocation of resources and a protracted slump.[129] *Paper Promises: Money, Debt, and the New World Order* in 2011 suggested the Austrian school offered the best solutions as well: 'there is nothing to be done except to let prices and wages fall to adjust to the new reality.'[130] Coggan and Lucas were more extreme, or simply more rigorous, than their colleagues; but the goal of deepening austerity they had in common with them. If states must curb the power of bankers, it was so as to pare back what waged workers could expect too: for the US to 'reduce its debt burden, it must tackle its cherished entitlement programs', retirement, pensions, health care, social security.[131]

Beddoes, for her part, did not see a serious divide between Hayek and Keynes at the *Economist* in the years leading up to her appointment. 'Ed Lucas may think my economic views are crazy. A few are sceptical of quantitative easing or fiscal stimulus. But not many', she said in 2012. For her, the crisis simply required 'pragmatic short-term acceptance of demand stimulus, without abandoning small state micro-economic policies, and with a path to balanced budgets'. The survey she wrote in October 2012, 'True Progressivism', was in fact a kind of synthesis of the two positions, incorporating the Coggan critique of finance within it. 'That cover had a huge effect and met with almost no internal dissent.'[132] It was also an intellectual manifesto, as important for making her case to be editor as books had been for Emmott and Micklethwait.

In it Beddoes acknowledged the problem of inequality, which had seen the richest 1 per cent in the US double their share of national income since 1980, while the top .01 per cent (around 16,000 families) had quadrupled their take. And that trend towards greater inequality was not confined to America; measured by Gini coefficients it had risen in China, India, Russia, Sweden and almost everywhere else that had chosen 'openness' and 'reform' in the last three decades. In addition to the populist dangers this bred, a growing body of literature suggested too large an underclass 'slows growth, causes financial crises and weakens demand'.[133] Up top, financiers should pay their share of income tax, and the 'implicit subsidy' to banks too big to fail (around $30 billion in lower borrowing costs) should end; ditto cronyism, in communist China as in the capitalist US, where private money flowed without legal limit into politics. Moving towards the middle, the state should stop subsidizing mortgages in the form of interest deductions. At the bottom, better access to health care and education was essential.

But the small print involved much the same entitlement cuts Coggan wanted. Sweden was the upmarket model cited for tax reform and budget discipline. It was true, she granted, that income inequality had leapt by 25 per cent there since 1980. But the Swedes were still among the most equal of peoples, in part because market reforms had boosted growth without sacrificing services (improved, in their turn, by charter schools and private health providers). Latin America, on the other hand, was a bargain option. Inequality was also falling in (most) countries there, thanks to 'targeted' spending on primary schools for the poor, while its conditional cash transfers offered a more 'cost-effective' welfare system (less than .4 per cent of GDP in Brazil) that also produced good behaviour in terms of school attendance and job hunting. Globalization had winners and losers, just as Micklethwait and Wooldridge had shown; but for Beddoes, at least, it was not enough to lament the has-beens this scattered on the roadside of progress. For the rich world to 'live within its means' while becoming fairer still involved trade-offs – which she preferred to see as 'whether to invest in poorer kids or continue to pay generous pensions to richer older people'.[134] Liberalism should aim for equality of opportunity, not outcome, which meant a new round of reforms based less on class conflict than the intergenerational kind.


## New Offices, New Progressivism

After seven turbulent years, 2015 looked like a relatively auspicious time to take up the reins of the *Economist*. The global economy remained anaemic, but stability had returned to the developed bits of it, in part because of falling commodity prices. Beddoes started out on the same path as her predecessor. In Britain, she backed David Cameron's Conservatives in April, citing their 'energetic and promising reforms' since 2010: government spending cut from 45.7 per cent of GDP to 40.7 per cent, even as 'public satisfaction with the police and other public services has gone up'; a million public sector workers laid off, but unemployment at a record low.[135] Labour, then under Ed Miliband, was a threat to all this progress – for, despite a commitment to carry on with austerity, it also had plans to raise the top rate of tax by 5 per cent, collect a 'mansion tax' on houses worth over £2 million, and cap rent rises, zero-hour contracts and household energy bills. Not only did these timid gestures 'risk chasing away the most enterprising, particularly the footloose global talent that London attracts', they betrayed an 'ill-founded faith in the wisdom of government'.[136] When a sincere leftist emerged to lead Labour after the defeat Miliband duly suffered at the polls, the *Economist* was caught between disbelief and disdain. Lost in a 'political timewarp', Jeremy Corbyn had 'nothing to offer but the exhausted, hollow formulas which his predecessors abandoned for the very good reason that they failed' – dooming Labour to 'electoral oblivion' until the day he quit, which was sure to be soon.[137]

Across the Atlantic, America looked more inspiring than ever – or at least its outgoing president did; in October 2016, Obama became the first one to contribute a signed piece to the *Economist*, showing how complete was the ideological marriage between them, in which he warned of the dangers of populism, declared capitalism 'the greatest driver of prosperity and opportunity the world has ever known', and pitched the upcoming election as a choice to 'retreat into old, closed-off economies or press forward, acknowledging the inequality that can come with globalisation while committing ourselves to making the global economy work better for all people'.[138] As the curtain descended on Obama's time in office, the *Economist* signed off on his last military adventure abroad, the orchestration of Saudi Arabia's assault on Yemen. Later – after Riyadh's imposition of an economic blockade and two years of pummelling the country by land, sea, and air had provoked the worst humanitarian crisis anywhere in the world – the paper finally asked if a moral issue might be at stake: 'How can the West denounce the carnage in Syria when its own ally is bombing civilians in Yemen?' In fact, quite easily; the two wars were different. 'The West should stay close to the Saudis, uncomfortable though this may be', seeking only to 'restrain the damage of their air campaign, and ultimately bring it to an end'.[139] What its coverage downplayed was not just the suffering inflicted by the Saudi-led strikes, over 60 per cent of which hit non-military targets – weddings and funerals, farms and fisheries – but the direct culpability of the US in supplying the warplanes, bombs, intelligence, targeting and refuelling, to carry them out.[140]

Beddoes's first year or so was less about controversy than tone. 'Mind-stretching journalism' was the order of the day, built on life-cycle issues and served up with lashings of new technology. The *Economist* peered into the future of autism, clones, drones, longevity, millennials, assisted suicide, viral resistance, microchips, robots, artificial intelligence, driverless cars, gene editing and quantum mechanics. 'We don't want to be the grandpa at the disco', she told the *Guardian* in 2016, which pointed to the eight social media staffers she had hired, as well as the Twitter-storm of articles designed to convert millions of social media followers into paying subscribers, and with more resources devoted to Economist Radio, TV and now Film.[141] Months after her elevation, the *Economist* itself changed hands, when Pearson decided to sell its 50 per cent stake in the company shortly after it offloaded the *Financial Times* in a deal with Japan's financial news giant Nikkei. Here, because of its unusual charter, the *Economist* could put together its own all-cash offer for £469 million – with Exor Investments, the Agnelli family vehicle that controls entities as diverse as Fiat, Juventus and *La Stampa*, taking a 43.4 per cent stake in the Economist Group while accepting a 20 per cent voting cap. To finance the deal, the paper agreed to sell its historic tower in St James for around £130 million; at the end of 2017, about 200 staff moved into custom-built offices – fit for a '21st century media organization', as Beddoes put it – close to the premises it had occupied in the late nineteenth century, on the bustling Strand.

# Conclusion

## Liberalism's Progress

Any sense that 'true progressivism' had a clear path in front of it vanished in June 2016, as the first in a series of hammer blows struck the *Economist*. Brexit, which David Cameron had pledged to put to the British people as a simple in-out vote on remaining in the European Union, returned a shocking verdict when a majority opted to leave – against the advice of economists, all the major party leaders, and personal warnings from President Obama, the heads of the IMF, NATO and JP Morgan. In the rather more diverse and competitive media landscape in Britain, no outlet was more clearly pro-Remain than the *Economist,* with an anti-Brexit cover on the eve of the referendum its best performing in years, a newsstand sell-out.[1]

That edition warned against the 'illusion' promoted by 'liberal Leavers' that Britain could become a 'Singapore on steroids' outside the EU: half of all exports went to the European single market, which was also vital to the City, in the form of passporting rights for its foreign-owned banks. The last point loomed largest, as it had ever since the *Economist* first made the case for turning towards Europe and away from the sterling area: the American, Japanese, Swiss and other non-EU financial firms based in the City, gaining access to customers in all twenty-seven member states, had made London supreme – with 70 per cent of the market for euro-denominated interest-rate derivatives and 90 per cent of the prime brokerage market servicing hedge funds. Nor would free trade suddenly take a step forward, since 'the slow, grinding history of trade liberalisation shows that mercantilists tend to have the upper hand'; besides, 'obstacles to growth' had less to do with Brussels bureaucrats than Britain, with 'too few new houses, poor infrastructure and a skills gap'.[2] A week on, the outcome was 'a senseless, self-inflicted blow' and 'tragic split' – 'the tumbling of the pound' presaging a recession, 'a permanently less vibrant economy', 'extra austerity', and the potential breakup of the EU as well as the UK. Stiffening its upper lip, the paper called for a second referendum to approve the terms of Brexit, preferably on the Norwegian model guaranteeing full single market access (which 'might be easier to win than seems possible today' as 'the economy will suffer and immigration will fall of its own accord'). To contain a similar backlash elsewhere, the EU must boost growth by 'completing the single market in, say, digital services and capital markets' and creating a 'proper banking union'.[3]

In the US, the 'truly terrifying' Donald Trump was quick to see the parallels between his own presidential bid and Brexit – hailing the latter as a 'great thing' on a visit to his golf course in Scotland that June. The *Economist* had asked Republicans to steer clear of the real estate mogul since the primaries in 2015 with little success. It did not warm to him afterwards: in one interview, a bewildered New York bureau chief surveyed Trump in his office, an 'Aladdin's cave of celebrity puff', desk stacked with magazines like a 'dentist's waiting room', a 'mound of Trump-covered copies of *The Economist*' and the assurance, 'I put you up front'.[4] Above all, it objected to his pessimism as unworthy of Reagan (a man he professed to admire) and a 'caricature' of America – which was neither as hateful nor as badly-off as he made out, 'and on most measures is more prosperous, more peaceful and less racist than ever before'. The economic recovery was 'now the fourth-longest on record, the stock market is at an all-time high, unemployment is below 5% and real median wages are at last starting to rise'.[5]

If race and economics were ruled out, what was wrong with America? Trump himself, 'who has done most to stoke national rage', with his Muslim ban, Mexican wall, anti-China tariffs, NATO-bashing – all to chants of 'lock up' Hillary Clinton.[6] In a fulsome endorsement of her in November, the paper portrayed Clinton as a canny incrementalist, who could shepherd bills on parental leave or sentencing reform through congress and show 'that ordinary politics works for ordinary people'; in foreign affairs, she had the right 'judgment and experience', as exemplified by her early support for US involvement in Syria. Trump, in contrast, was 'horribly unsuited' to lead 'the nation that the rest of the democratic world looks to for leadership', or to be 'commander-in-chief of the world's most powerful armed forces and the person who controls America's nuclear deterrent'. With so much at stake, the 'choice is not hard', a point it drove home, declaring, 'We would sooner have endorsed Richard Nixon – even had we known how he would later come to grief.'[7] (In fact, it did support Nixon.) Chastened by the result, a week later the *Economist* wondered aloud if it had misunderstood the whole arc of history since the fall of the Berlin Wall. 'The election of Mr Trump is a rebuff to all liberals, including this newspaper.'[8]

Despite this moment of introspection, however, the shocks continued for the *Economist*, which was no more far-seeing after Brexit and Trump than before. In Britain, it welcomed the 2017 snap election called by the new prime minister, Theresa May, to 'strengthen her hand' as savvy – freeing her to pursue a softer Brexit, and to annihilate Labour, which opinion polls showed her trouncing by over 20 points in April. In lockstep with the rest of the British media, it was certain that Jeremy Corbyn – 'witless', a 'loony leftist', 'soft' on Putin, Chávez and terrorism – would suffer a crushing defeat, making way for a sensible Labour leader in the mould of Tony Blair. That left it to guess at the scale of the impending rout: more like 1983, when Labour won only 209 seats under its leftwing leader Michael Foot, or 1935, when it held just 154?[9] In fact, Corbyn steered his party to the biggest electoral swing in its favour since 1945, eliminating the Conservative majority, to deliver a hung parliament. To cling to power, May would have to rely on the tiny, far-right Democratic Unionist Party from Northern Ireland. Corbyn achieved this, moreover, on the back of a manifesto promising to renationalize the rail, water and postal services, raise the minimum wage, revive collective bargaining, increase taxes on wealthy individuals and businesses, and make university free again – each of which the *Economist* vehemently opposed as 'backward-looking' and 'dangerous'.[10]

This latest assault on liberalism was the final straw, provoking unusual signs of fissiparity and fracture at the paper. As May's 'strong and stable leadership' campaign faltered, the *Economist* switched horses in mid-stream, advising a vote for the Liberal Democrats that June as a 'down-payment' on a future 'party of the radical centre' – à la France, where Emmanuel Macron had demolished old left-right oppositions with En Marche, inspiring 'France, Europe and centrists everywhere.'[11] At one moment 'Bagehot' bitterly compared Britain's political class to a second-rate cricket team whose best batter was 'a crypto-communist who has never run anything but his own mouth'; the next, he paid Corbyn a compliment, saluting him as a disruptive innovator.[12] Months earlier in Italy, a similar schizophrenia was on display. When Prime Minister Matteo Renzi, a devotee of Blair's third way, submitted constitutional changes designed to entrench him in power, the *Economist* came out against them. This provoked consternation from its own correspondent in Rome, who ventilated it off the record to *La Repubblica*. Fuming at this 'brutal anti-Renzi affidavit' and 'slap in the face', the liberal Italian daily ran it as a front-page story, reporting the decision had split the *Economist* staff, with Beddoes and younger editors against backing the constitution, the Europe section in favour. 'We supported Remain and Hillary', explained its unnamed source. To back Renzi's referendum when it too risked going down in defeat, as it subsequently did, 'could have been considered the kiss of death'. This at least was the view of John Hooper, the leaker of these tidbits, who then wrote in favour of Renzi's reforms in *The World in 2017*.[13]

Observing these tergiversations, a former senior editor called it a moment of identity crisis for the paper. 'The *Economist* believes in free trade capitalism, sure, but it also believes in America.' What to do when both are stumbling? 'Since Knight, the editor's role has been to pull a center, or even center-left staff, to the right' – think of Knight and Reagan, Pennant-Rea and the First Gulf War, Emmott and Iraq, Micklethwait and the neo-cons and religious right. That worked, so long as the paper was out in front of the neoliberal wave, coasting it, or on the offensive. But now, in the age of Trump? 'In the past, the *Economist* would have tried to shock respectable opinion, to somehow support him ... but it's been forced to take the same line as the *New York Times*. For thirty years it captured the zeitgeist but the zeitgeist seems to have moved on.' Another, old-guard editor still at the paper complained that meetings had descended into a millennial farce of trigger warnings, gender-neutral bathrooms and #MeToo.

And then there are the circulation figures, which no longer defy gravity. Print circulation has fallen to 1.25 million – though 300,000 digital subscribers have steadied readership at about 1.5 million.[14] Much of the loss stems, executives claim, from weeding out discount and bulk subscriptions to lounges and clubs, as part of a focus on premium readers that included a 20 per cent price hike in 2016; as a result, a new metric – of revenue per copy – has risen, even as print advertising collapses, accounting for just 18 per cent of Economist Group sales in 2016, down from more than 40 per cent in 2009 (though at £35 million it still outpaces digital ad revenue at £23 million).[15] This is why Micklethwait took to describing premium pay TV-services like HBO and Sky as models; and it is the rationale for pumping millions into acquiring new subscribers – peddling insect ice cream and civet faeces coffee from food trucks on city street corners, and beaming into Snapchat, Twitter, Facebook and Apple News, with podcasts and a virtual reality app, to grab the attention of '72 million globally curious' potential readers. Whether the *Economist* can withstand that degree of curiosity, while preserving its special identity, is another story.

## Liberalism, a Love Story

As if to underscore the sense that liberalism itself is at a crossroads, an *Economist* journalist produced a serious historical study of it for the first time in 2014. Edmund Fawcett, a former correspondent in Washington, Paris and Berlin, who also edited the European and books sections, set out to write a 'biographically-led, non-specialist chronicle', drawing on his own three decades of service to what he terms – in contrast to communism - the 'God that succeeded'. In range and erudition, *Liberalism: The Life of an Idea* is an intellectual cut above any previous book by a post-war

*Economist* staffer. Yet it is also clearly the work of one, marked by wit, brio and a rough-and-tumble feel for events. Its author sets thinkers alongside politicians and theory next to practice, to sketch liberalism 'naturalistically, as a norm-governed adaptation to historical circumstances', defined by four 'broad ideas': acceptance of inescapable ethical-material conflict; distrust of power; faith in human progress; and civic respect for others, whatever they think, as a 'democratic seed in an otherwise undemocratic creed'. Their combination is, Fawcett maintains, what sets liberalism apart from socialism and conservatism, communism and fascism, competitive authoritarianism, national populism and Islamic theocracy.[16]

From this starting point, Fawcett departs from convention in two important ways. First, in a break with Anglophone parochialism, he sketches the defining traits of liberalism across a four-fold grid of Britain, France, Germany and America. Though the exclusion of Italy – given the eminence of Benedetto Croce as a philosopher, Guido De Ruggiero as a historian, and Luigi Einaudi as a practitioner of liberalism – is conspicuous and the grid is stretched to cover minor figures in France and Germany to maintain its consistency, the scale of the enterprise is impressive. Second, in Fawcett's account, liberalism was born not with seventeenth century political theory or eighteenth century economic thought, but with early nineteenth century capitalism, and as a reaction to it. Nor were its first significant progenitors British. Neither John Locke nor Adam Smith set this story of liberalism going, but two continentals – Alexander von Humboldt and Benjamin Constant – and its ensuing impetus comes less from originating notions of liberty than an ongoing need to manage industrial change after 1815. Liberalism then moves through three distinct historical phases: from the confidence of its youth in 1830–80, through difficulties and setbacks in the time of its maturity in 1880–1945, to recovery and triumph in the epoch from 1945 to 1989.

In the first of these, liberals stood firm against absolutist rule on the one hand, and plebeian masses on the other, defending the rights of the propertied and the educated against both. In France, François Guizot and Alexis de Tocqueville personified the vigorous youthful unity of this liberalism, as major thinkers and politicians. Guizot, a historian at the Sorbonne and 'liberal of the first rank', who argued for 'the radical illegitimacy of all absolute power', served as the dominant prime minister of the constitutional monarchy of Louis Philippe after 1830, making sure it was not weakened by extending the vote to those incapable of using it responsibly: the only acceptable sovereigns in politics were law, justice and reason. Tocqueville, author of the sociological classic *Democracy in America*, who served as foreign minister under the Second Republic, developed the idea of voluntary associations of civil society as a counterweight to both a despotic state power and popular democracy. In Germany, Hermann Schulze-Delitzsch, a judge and legislator, popularized mutual banks and cooperatives, so that workers might help themselves to rise into the golden middle ranks of society. Britain had an abundance of comparable figures – poor law and sanitary reformer Edwin Chadwick, free trade tribune Richard Cobden, self-help adviser Samuel Smiles, and above all, the political philosopher, economist and MP for Westminster John Stuart Mill, who combined the finest liberal values of the period better than anyone, cherishing them all, but recognizing the 'dangers and complexities' of each.[17] Towering over this landscape were the two greatest statesman of the time – Abraham Lincoln, who gave immortal expression to the aims and ideals of American liberalism at Gettysburg, and William Gladstone, champion of free trade and frugal budgets, whose language of rights and sympathy, international decency and self-determination, gave moral focus to liberals in England and beyond.

In a second phase, liberalism groped towards 'an economic compromise with democracy to save capitalism', marking a passage to adulthood that was far from easy, since most liberals dreaded democracy. As Guizot put it in 1851: 'You can put down a riot with soldiers and secure an election with peasants', but to govern, 'you need the support of the higher classes, who are naturally the governing classes.'[18] But as time went on, pressure for expansion of the franchise grew steadily, and rejection of it increasingly impolitic, with liberal opposition to a wider suffrage becoming 'at most a holding operation'. Liberal parties might suffer, for various reasons, from the rise of mass politics, but 'as liberalism conceded to democracy, democracy conceded to liberalism'. In this give-and-take, 'liberalism stood to gain in one large way more than it lost. For at the heart of the historic compromise was a commitment to compromise itself.' With liberalism's triumph, 'the idea of politics as total control was pushed to the margins', protecting society from socialist longings and conservative resentments.[19]

Not simply a wider suffrage, but some shielding from hardship was part of the bargain. In finding a 'common roof for the House of Have and the House of Want', France was first with its democratic republicanism after 1870, followed by Germany with its welfare provisions under Bismarck, and then the arrival of New Liberalism in Britain and Progressivism in the US. Social reform was the hallmark of each; and here, Germany was most liberal, with sickness and old-age insurance and industrial accident coverage by 1889. Liberal thinkers worked to justify the new responsibilities of the state. In Britain, philosopher T. H. Green moved beyond laissez-faire, arguing that public authorities should not just protect the negative freedom of individuals from arbitrary power or interference with their lives, but foster the positive conditions of freedom to act according to their worth. In France, Radical Prime Minister Léon Bourgeois adapted the leftwing term 'solidarity' to describe the debt each citizen owed society, to be acquitted by paying income tax. In the US, Herbert Croly pursued a similar line as founding editor of the *New Republic*, exhorting vigorous intervention from Washington to promote science, efficiency and social justice.

The First World War came as a shock to the progressive liberalism of this time. But by 1917 it had produced a trio of 'outstanding leaders' – Lloyd George, Clemenceau and Wilson – who proved capable of winning the war for the better side. This setback overcome, worse was to follow. The Great Depression was the most acute disappointment yet for liberals, who struggled to diagnose its causes or prescribe its cures. Keynes at Cambridge, Fischer at Yale and Hayek at the LSE differed in their attempts at each – underconsumption, to be countered by pump-priming; debt-deflation, corrected by central bank action to raise prices; over-investment, leaving markets to clear – but at a deeper level they were united in seeking liberal solutions to the crisis of the epoch.[20] So too, in testing these ideas by trial and error, Hoover and Roosevelt were both liberals, if Roosevelt with much greater success as the better politician. His New Deal inspired alarm at its infringement of the principles of the free market among thinkers who gathered in Paris in 1938 to honour the journalist Walter Lipmann. The reaction produced a powerful, if overstated antidote, with Hayek's *The Road to Serfdom* in 1944, 'a noir classic' in which 'a misunderstood liberal walks the mean streets of a collectivized world'. But in practice it supplied an exemplary case of the 'piecemeal social engineering' upheld as the antidote to communism by Karl Popper in his complementary classic *The Open Society and Its Enemies* a year later.[21]

Liberalism's third period after 1945 would draw from each of these opposite reactions to the inter-war crisis, in successive phases. For three decades, it leant far more towards Keynes than to Lipmann and his circle, as Western societies transformed themselves into fully-fledged democracies based on universal suffrage and mass consumption, deploying the counter-cyclical instruments of fiscal and monetary policy he had urged, to secure full employment and high wages. Consumer spending now represented the economic side of liberalism's compromise with democracy, in a more equal sharing of wealth, while in Britain the no less liberal William Beveridge pioneered a modern welfare state, with interlocking forms of insurance, and a National Health Service at its core. Politically, too, liberalism rebuilt itself on a firmer foundation of rights. The 1948 Universal Declaration of Human Rights, on which Fawcett's father worked for the British Foreign Office, was inspirational; civic associations like Amnesty International, founded by Peter Benenson in 1961, strove to ensure it was respected. In Germany, another legal pillar of the post-war order was laid with the Grundgesetz of 1949, 'liberal democracy's exemplary charter', approved without need of any direct or popular vote.[22] In the wings, the philosophers Michael Oakeshott and Isaiah Berlin were eloquent exponents of the quiet virtues of negative liberty and a diversity of ends, while John Rawls upheld rights rather than consequences as a standard of value for liberals, stimulating countless like-minded responses.

In these years, in Fawcett's account, a set of pragmatic liberal politicians plied their trade with admirable post-ideological skill and determination to bore through hard boards, just as Max Weber had recommended. In France, Pierre Mendès-France was a passionate 'liberal centrist'. Next door, Willy Brandt persuaded the German Social Democrats to discard the pretence they were socialists rather than liberals, which paid off at the polls by 1969. In the US, Lyndon Johnson championed civil rights legislation and enacted sweeping social reforms to create a Great Society. But by the late seventies, a reaction had set in, as stagnation and inflation showed there were limits to Keynesian recipes for growth. Since the Second World War, and a deepening division of social labour, liberalism had become professionalized into separate branches. Politicians were no longer thinkers, while thinkers rarely became politicians. But ideas still counted, and those who developed them included a set of theorists, heirs of Lippman and his colleagues, whose arguments now had a notable practical impact on politics. In the US, the public choice economist James Buchanan pushed for legal limits on taxes and spending, while Milton Friedman led the charge for deregulation and privatization. Broader and more encompassing than either was the post-war body of work produced by Hayek, linking political, epistemological and economic arguments against state intervention into the operation of free markets and the distribution of incomes in a compelling, if in the end overly utilitarian, synthesis.

In grappling with the novel problems of stagflation, liberal politicians took heed of the counsel of these liberal thinkers. By 1979, a group of outstanding leaders began to act on their visions. With Hayek in her handbag, Thatcher showed great courage and charisma in restoring free market vigour to British society, although paradoxically concentrating political power in Whitehall and economic power in big business.[23] The next year, Reagan rode to office on the disappointed liberalism of Democratic voters and, slashing taxes and red tape, restored buoyancy and prosperity to America. In France, Mitterrand was elected as a socialist, but confronted with the realities of the European Community in the eighties, ruled out any Albanian-style isolationism to become the first liberal president of the Fifth Republic. In Germany, Helmut

Kohl pulled off the unification of his country, a historic achievement of rare political imagination and decisiveness. In sum, 'credit to the captains', who 'learnt from past mistakes, made liberalism universal not just Western, embedded liberalism in fairer institutions, accepted social rights but corrected their subsequent costs, conquered inflation, and brought peace and unity to a fratricidal continent'. If liberal thinkers of the period 'left lessons in what not to do and what not to think', the politicians 'left strong results. They created a globalized world'. By 1989, 'liberal confidence had returned'.[24] With the final collapse of the God that failed, there could be no shadow of doubt which God had succeeded.

Though the mood for liberalism has darkened since, Fawcett sees little reason for despondency. The anti-Western attack on the Twin Towers in 2001 and the financial crash of 2008 were certainly, each in their different ways, sobering events. But liberals should bear in mind that liberal self-confidence has always had its ups and downs, and that its strength lay in its proven capacity for self-criticism. With plenty of that today, its underlying vitality seems assured. The growth of income inequality and fiscal overstretch are also worrying problems, which need to be addressed. But it would be a mistake for liberals to abandon their values in the face of them. A seductive belief in spontaneous economic order, or reliance on providential narratives of the end of history, should be avoided. Rather, politics remains the priority – which means managing contingency and chance, as liberals have always done. In the West, there may be a touch of melancholy in wondering what more is to be accomplished, but that is not true of Brazil, China, India or Iran, where liberals 'can afford to be more forward-looking and zestful. They have work for many life-times.'[25]

*Liberalism: The Life of an Idea* stands out in the literature on its subject, mostly thin philosophical musings of intellectually provincial scope, as a historically informed and comparatively executed account of what has become the ruling political idiom of the West. It starts out on a fresh note, avoiding customary Anglophone clichés, and is not short of critical asides. Yet despite these virtues, it remains an exercise in the higher apologetics. Conceptually, the weaknesses of the ensuing construction stem from the loose, all-purpose definition of liberalism presiding over it – acceptance of inescapable ethical-material conflict; distrust of power; faith in human progress; and civic respect for the opinions of others: a quartet of pieties that represents few if any of the figures arrayed in the book. Did Humboldt or Constant believe conflict inescapable? Did Guizot or Weber distrust power? Bagehot respect the opinions of others? Tocqueville firmly believe in progress? Simply to pose such questions is to be reminded how poorly most of Fawcett's practitioners embodied his precepts, however impressionistic.

A merit of this definition of liberalism, nevertheless, is that it does not include the term democracy. On this, Fawcett is clear: historically, democracy and liberalism were distinct. In 2014, now retired, he wrote a letter to the *Economist* chiding it for equating them. 'Liberalism is about how people are to be shielded from undue power', he rebuked it, whereas 'democracy is about who belongs in that happy circle', adding that liberals like Schumpeter and Hayek understood 'voter democracy was commonly at odds with economic prosperity'.[26] But although the two are never equated in his own writing, liberal attitudes and policies toward democracy are consistently euphemized. At worst, liberals 'dragged their feet' over extensions of the franchise, or were not 'natural', 'born' or 'electoral' democrats, so tacitly rank as some other, meta- or crypto- kind. Symptomatically, no alternative political force that actually pushed for democracy, as distinct from reluctantly adjusting to it, is ever specified: the labour movement is blanked out. What liberalism pushed for, on the other hand, is made clear enough. For Fawcett, liberalism's great achievement and grounds for congratulation was to force democracy to accept capitalism. After all, he writes, 'if the few were to share with the many, the many should accept the existence of the few'.[27] What could be fairer? Just what the sharing was in this bargain, and why liberals even felt it necessary, are left discreetly unspecified. For explanation, the internal dynamics of liberal reason and respect for others suffice. What counts is that 'capitalism was here to stay'. As for the century or so since the advent of manhood suffrage (votes for women or blacks don't detain the narrative), Fawcett notes that liberals 'consented with little question to the claims of the national security state', a formulation suggesting they were not themselves responsible for it.[28] From the passage by the Wilson administration of the US Espionage and Sedition Acts of 1917–18 to the Patriot Act in the time of Bush and surveillance under Obama, this secret world now comprises some seventeen agencies with an annual budget over $60 billion. Fawcett's distinction between liberalism and democracy might account for this enormous expansion of the security state, but he never criticizes it even as a violation of his fundamental liberal 'right to be left alone'.[29]

If democracy has its place in the narrative, empire is predictably confined to the margins. On the rare occasions it figures in the years of confidence, it is minimized or excused in the profiles of his leading liberals. Tocqueville's zealotry in the conquest of Algeria goes unmentioned. In twelve pages on Mill, his stance on British rule in India gets two half-sentences – a 'temporary imposition to teach Indians to govern themselves' and 'masters might be needed for a time in order to teach self-mastery'; and of Mill's support for colonial repression in Ireland, not a word.[30] Gladstone is in favour of the self-determination of peoples, but 'accepts' the seizure of Egypt, as if he were a mere spectator of it, not British prime minister. Vice versa Cobden, who was a resolute foe of all Britain's imperial wars, but is nevertheless enlisted by Fawcett in the cause of 'humanitarian intervention', an unctuous hypocrisy he would have detested.[31] As it becomes adult, liberalism is allowed some traffic with imperialism, and opportunistic responses to jingoism, but its record is downplayed by selecting two failures – Chamberlain and Bassermann, whose schemes came to nothing – to illustrate it, rather than the far more consequential likes of Jules Ferry, Theodore Roosevelt or Winston Churchill. After partitioning the planet in a fit of absent-mindedness up to 1914, the Great War naturally came as a surprise to those who had taken their spoils for granted. 'It shocked liberals that such a war could be fought at all', since 'warfare was a liberal nightmare at its blackest'.[32] What liberals were these? Lloyd George and Clemenceau, pledged to fight to the last man, and Wilson – spared any blushes for his record on colonialism, race or red-baiting – were hardly among them.[33]

Fawcett makes no attempt to account for the outbreak of the First World War, declaring: 'In 1914 came an unexpected and inexplicable world war', and remarking that for liberals 'it was all very puzzling'. For him the puzzle lies in its consequences, not its causes, even if liberals had some vague – never specified – part in its origins. 'A terrible war that liberalism largely brought upon itself contributed to a great expansion of that liberal bugbear, unchallenged state power.'[34] The war, then, was an enigma: it had nothing to do with empires. Liberals created or extended these in the nineteenth century, to be sure, but not in a deliberate sense. Empire was a 'happenstance creation of missionaries, teachers, buccaneering adventurers, and capitalists no doubt' – not soldiers or gunboats, thankfully. Though, once acquired, 'ruthless force' might be used to hold them, empires were almost always better than what came before them in darkest Africa and Asia, where 'precolonial masters were commonly crueler, more exploitative and more domineering than the imperialists.' Later, doubts arose about 'the obviousness of the moral claim that the great benefits for the many outweighed the grievous or terminal harm to a few', and after 1945 liberals abandoned their overseas possessions 'out of overstretch and exhaustion'. But the empires they had built brought benefits often welcomed by colonial peoples: progress and modernity, rule of law and property rights.[35]

With a view of modern imperialism as rosy as this, Fawcett logically pays little attention to the struggles of the colonized peoples for their independence, and can remark briskly of the Western powers repressing them that they were 'not running global charities'. It was a pity that the career of Mendès-France as prime minister, father of liberal centrism in modern France, was cut short in 1955 when the war in Algeria caught him 'unawares', obliging him to react with a mixture of coercion and conciliation. In the US, the war in Vietnam rates one sentence, to absolve Lyndon Johnson, 'unfairly' denied credit for his domestic achievements by this foreign entanglement – which 'the American left blamed him for continuing, the right for losing, and Wall Street for fighting without raising taxes'. In the new century, Bush's good intentions were also unjustly criticized, for America 'waged wars in Afghanistan and Iraq against a genuine but elusive foe, extreme

Islamism', even if operations in Iraq were unhappily less well informed and prepared than in Afghanistan.[36]

As an economic doctrine, liberalism is scarcely less sanitized. In the nineteenth century, laissez-faire is dismissed as an urban legend, without mention of Jean-Baptiste Say, Thomas Malthus or James Wilson, let alone the famines in Ireland or India that its doctrines justified. Rather, Liberals were eminently practical arbiters of the mutable borders between the state and the market, rivals that also needed one another – resisting the supremacy of either, viewing both as variable instruments to be used according to the changing needs of 'human betterment', and by the mid-twentieth century getting the balance right. The effect of this retouched group portrait is to leave key economic debates and turning points unexplained. When the interwar slump hits, no statesmen or set of ideas is responsible for it. Like the Great War, the Depression falls like a meteorite in the liberal cosmos, whose origins are no concern of this historian. Keynes argues in a vacuum, transfigured into an advocate of 'worker's democracy' because he emphasized effective demand, though Hayek was still more of an economic democrat, since – less of an aesthete – he celebrated shopping. Post-1945, liberal democracy achieved an equilibrium between state and market forces of unprecedented success. But thirty years later, as mysteriously as the onset of the slump, it fell out of whack, at which point Hayek and Friedman – respectively 'wholesaler' and 'retailer' of ideas – had the right remedies. After another quarter-century, these too were adrift amid growing instability and inequality. The answer? Certainly, among other things, a dose of austerity – fiscal retrenchment to rein in state spending. Keynesianism and Neo-Liberalism are thus imperturbably underwritten, their guiding thinkers at one in seeking 'to limit capitalism's disruptive instabilities without injuring liberal principles'.[37] Whatever that might mean, the realm of finance and its crises are nowhere to be found in this story of liberalism as artful balancing act.

The closer to the present, the more jarring this papering over of intellectual disagreement becomes: by the 1960s, almost no Western ruler or thinker is left out of Fawcett's omnium gatherum of liberalism, with results bordering on parody. 'Most liberals have called themselves something else', he confesses at the outset.[38] Indeed. Thus not only Hoover and Roosevelt, Nixon and Johnson, Brandt and Thatcher, Reagan and Mitterrand, not to speak of Kohl – only Andreotti and Blair are missing – but the Hegelian Oakeshott and the Kantian Berlin (who could not abide each other), the anti-communist Orwell and the pro-communist Sartre, the catholicizing Alasdair MacIntyre and the enlightener Eric Hobsbawm, all become liberals *malgré–soi* – with 'forgotten', 'hidden', 'closet', 'centrist', 'Marxist' and other qualifiers to rope them in. The inflation of the term is a self-undoing: liberalism becomes such a catch-all, it ends up as little more than a stand-in for the West and all that is good and varied about it. In this sense, even one of the *Economist*'s most independent minds of recent years is unable to shake off the paper's impregnable self-satisfaction.

Four years later, the current editor drew on Fawcett's history in her own 'manifesto for renewing liberalism' in the *Economist*'s 175th-year anniversary issue – in a striking indication of the paths open to the magazine under her, for now 'championing a creed on the defensive'. Two features of her prospectus stand out. First, the word 'capitalism' has all but vanished. 'Liberalism' is instead ubiquitously substituted for it, with only two shyly euphemistic references to 'the rougher edges of capitalism' – a hint not just of the reputational damage the latter has suffered since 2008, but a possible way of coping with this, by downplaying the centrality of capital in the political formation and forward march of the liberal creed. Second is the unshakable permanence of the imperial core of the *Economist* outlook, which has not budged even semantically. If the invasions of Afghanistan and Iraq are now deemed 'misguided', the real danger is Americans drawing the wrong lessons from them, retreating behind their borders, and the 'astonishing' fact that so few millennials think it 'important for America to maintain its military superiority'. As an antidote, the manifesto calls for a 'League of Democracies', invoking the neoconservative historian of international relations Robert Kagan and the late senator John McCain as authorities: 'it will always be easier and wiser for liberals to trust America to do the right thing in the end.' Perhaps unsurprisingly, this *Economist* moved briskly past the less sightly landmarks that might have explained the need for liberalism's resuscitation.[39]

## Actually Existing Liberalism

Since 1843, the *Economist*, viewed as a continuous and unified project, illuminates a different history of liberalism – dispelling some of the mellow mists that normally surround it. Bracingly direct, with James Wilson adamant that *his* journal would aim for the 'landed and monied' and be 'nothing but pure *principles*', the paper had what one of its later writers saw as an enlightening candour in addressing its readers: you opened it, he observed, to 'hear the bourgeoisie talking to itself, and it could talk quite frankly'.[40] A powerful fraction of that class, which Marx called the 'aristocracy of finance', has indeed spoken through the *Economist,* first in Britain, and then also in America – not as the only, or purest, expression of liberalism, but as the *dominant* one, with the greatest global impact for 175 years.

Liberalism has, of course, always come in different strands and hues. Fawcett's indiscriminate expansion of the term to cover anything useful for his purpose obscures these, and the need – ignored not only by him – for an adequate taxonomy. Economic liberals, political liberals and social liberals are distinct species, but hybrids have been common enough. Finer distinctions abound. At one end, there was long a liberalism that gravitated towards socialism, of which the most striking case is that of Mill – who reversed his judgment in *Principles of Political Economy* that schemes to abolish private property were 'chimerical' just a year after he published it, in the wake of the 1848 revolutions. 'The social problem of the future we now considered', wrote Mill in his *Autobiography*, was 'how to unite the greatest individual liberty of action with a common ownership in the raw materials of the globe'.[41] In the second half of the twentieth century, the gamut of liberalism has run from a mild social-democratic reformism all the way to a hard-boiled libertarian hostility to the state verging on anarchism – of late, Rawls versus Nozick. In the space between jostle free-market zealots (Bastiat to Tullock), apostles of civil society (Tocqueville to Bellah), tutors of moral sensibility (Arnold to Trilling), guardians of law and order (Porfirio Díaz to Giolitti), dreamers of perpetual peace (Angell to Habermas), each with their own intellectual genealogies and political tics. Across the public sphere today, much of the media articulates a *bien–pensant* consensus, posted as progressive, that is generally regarded as liberal. In political clarity, coherence and throw weight, the *Economist* stands above this ruck. As in classical composition, subdominants recur beneath the dominant, in a tonal balance that distinguishes the *Economist* with respect to the rest of the liberal press. From centre-left to centre-right, few of the weeklies or dailies approach it, simply in terms of print circulation: not the *Nation,* with around 100,000, or the *Guardian*, with 150,000; not *Le Monde* or the *New York Times,* with 330,000 and 590,000; not the *New Republic* at 50,000, the *Atlantic* at 500,000, or the *New York Review of Books* at 135,000. (Often, the *Economist* circulates as widely in print as these journals *outside* its Anglo-American home base, with close to 150,000 in Europe, 90,000 in the Asia Pacific and 15,000 in the Middle East and Africa region.) Even when digital viewership is added – making the *Times* and *Guardian* among the most popular on the planet – or if the *New Yorker* with its 1.2 million readers is thrown in – the contest is not close, and each falls short of the *Economist* by measures other than circulation. Likewise, individual writers may have greater wattage than any at the *Economist*, and express some of the same ideas: David Runciman, in the *London Review of Books*, praising the muddled middle, and lamenting deviations from it, in Corbyn, Brexit or Trump; Stephen Holmes, denouncing 'Putinism' in *Foreign Policy;* Timothy Garton Ash, fighting populism from a perch at the *New York Review of Books.* Yet none of these journals or thinkers, on their own, can match the *Economist* – with its longer, deeper history, closer connection to power, and far greater global presence and reach.

In considering that success, ideas have mattered most. If the *Economist* never became the 'grave de fortune' of which Cobden warned (in garbled French), this was because it addressed three questions left unanswered by classical liberalism, but which proved decisive to its spread in the age of global capitalism: how could liberals navigate democratic challenges from the industrial working class at home, imperial rivalries and rule abroad, and the ascendency of finance within an economic order once focused on agriculture, trade and industry? No other paper has offered up such a 'precious collection of facts, doctrine and experience', as Bastiat put it, to guide liberals through these shoals – allowing the historian to extrapolate dominant themes of the dominant liberalism from it. These did not come unadulterated at all stages of its career. As we have seen, there were episodes when other strands – Cobdenite pacifism under Hirst at the outbreak of the First World War, Durbinite reformism during the Second World War under Crowther, blips of Anglo-legalism under Tyerman, or sporadic criticism of US actions during and after the Cold War, from Midgley, Smith and Grimond – deflected it from a perfectly consistent path. But such divagations were brief, each followed by resolute course correction. Swiftly reasserting itself, the dominant was always a liberalism whose lodestars were two: the universal virtues of capital and, where they arose, the particular necessities of empire. The most enduring embodiment of the former was finance; the most important of the latter, Britain and then the United States. Other considerations had to be taken into account; among them, in due course, the will of the people. But, where they conflicted, that will was not to stand in the way.

So democracy: for the whole length of the nineteenth century, the *Economist* resisted it. Bagehot was adamant, writing extensively on 'what securities against democracy we *can* create' in the reform bills that popular pressure was pushing the House of Commons to consider: multiple votes for the propertied, with variable franchises depending on town or borough size, were the barest safeguards.[42] 'True liberalism' was simply opposed to the 'superstitious reverence for the equality of all Englishmen as electors' – which absurdly claimed 'the lowest peasant and mechanic are the measure of the electoral capacity of the most educated man in the land.'[43] If you still had doubts, chat to your footman; this would confirm what Bagehot knew for a fact – that ten thousand educated, propertied men alone were fit to vote, the rest as 'narrow-minded, unintelligent and incurious' as two millennia ago.[44]

After 1877, the tone changed, since the Reform Acts of 1866 and 1884 were so far from enacting that 'pure democracy' Bagehot feared. But the underlying hostility to the vote as a natural right, as opposed to a privilege tied to property and education, remained: till 1907, payment of MPs and one-man-one-vote were 'inexpedient' and Home Rule in Ireland was anathema, while under Hirst some of the old fire against the franchise returned – this time directed at the 'virago' suffragettes, who were too irrational to be entrusted with the political powers they demanded. After the war, which had forced the issue of universal male suffrage, the problem of democracy remained, but took a new form, as a question of economic control. This was a very serious matter, since the new mass electorate coincided with the mass unemployment of the Depression. With the barbarians at the gate, the gold standard and Bank of England were barriers to politicizing currency and credit; in 1931, Layton made it clear that in the crisis confronting the Labour government, 'sound finance' must and would win out over democracy.[45] Since then, the question of sound finance versus democratic will has recurred again and again.

After 1945, it was joined by another development: the national security state, which the *Economist* did more than endorse. From the onset of the Cold War, it was an energetic side-car of that secret state in the battle against Soviet communism – with editors routinely accepting material from the Information Research Department, set up covertly for propaganda purposes out of the British Foreign Office in 1948. Between 1954 and 1980, Brian Crozier and Robert Moss spread 'disinformation' from a still wider array of sources, including MI6 and the CIA – not just in the intelligence gossip sheet they ran, *Foreign Report,* but directly in the *Economist*. Along with Brian Beedham, they attacked those – congressmen, journalists, whistle-blowers – who dared shine a light on the national security apparatus. 'There are powerful reasons democratic governments are seldom particularly open with their people on the brink of war', it explained on the publication of the Pentagon Papers.[46]

So empire: the *Economist* has supplied a consistent, case-by-case justification of liberal imperialism, from the nineteenth century to the present. That run began with the Crimean War in 1854, when

Wilson broke with Cobden and Bright over the issue of free trade and peace – which, until then, all three saw as mutually reinforcing. But as French and British soldiers laid siege to Sevastopol, and with Wilson at the Treasury, the *Economist* turned against this notion with a vengeance, as a 'hideous and shallow doctrine'. Cobden was a 'demagogue', Bright 'a tool and sycophant of the Czar', and war against 'Muscovy' was for 'human rights, civil liberty, enlightened progress' and 'freedom of trade, freedom of movement, freedom of thought and freedom of worship'.[47] 'We may regret war', mused the paper in 1857, in an article that urged the use of force to pry open China to trade, but 'we cannot deny that great advantages have followed in its wake'.[48]

The *Economist* rarely looked back – from the bombardments of Canton, Kagoshima and Alexandria to the campaigns in India, Afghanistan, Zululand, Sudan or Burma, on to the Second Boer War. Only once did it veer seriously off-script: in August 1914, when Francis Hirst channelled the traditions of Cobden to criticize the government for its secret diplomacy and the financial press for docility, and campaigned for a negotiated peace. But this lasted two years; and so discordant was it that even Walter Layton, one of his successors – committed to collective security through the post-war League of Nations – temporarily quit the paper in disgust. After 1916, the litany in favour of the liberal empire resumed, continuing past even decolonization from emergencies in Malaya, Kenya and Cyprus on to the Falklands in 1982.

The difference in the second half of the twentieth century has been the focus on the US version of liberal imperialism – with a wink and a nod from its leading practitioners and theorists. Under the banner of anti-communism, the paper provided a running rationalization for interventions as far afield as Greece and Korea, Guatemala and Iran, Vietnam and Laos, Chile and Indonesia, Angola and Ethiopia, Nicaragua and Grenada. It greeted the end of the Cold War with huzzahs to the new world order, and calls for bombers for the Balkans, invasions of Afghanistan and Iraq, and for NATO to expand to the borders of Russia – all on a fresh gust of democratic optimism. Internationalism of the sort espoused by Hirst or Layton went silent, with a few editors left to make that case as best they could. In a rollicking account of life at the

*Economist* since 1956, Barbara Smith admitted that she had often disagreed with its policies – 'when we supported third-world anti-communist monsters', during Vietnam, or 'when, as at present, we seem too closely identified with official America'. Did she or the other dissenters resign over these disagreements? 'We did not. Shameful that, I agree.'[49] In 2012, Johnny Grimond gave a speech at his retirement party announcing that in all his time there, the *Economist* 'never saw a war it didn't like' – a memorable barb, eliciting nervous laughter from his colleagues and a riposte from Bill Emmott.[50]

So, finally, to finance. A 'friend to the investor' since the railway mania of the 1840s, the paper has made some of its most storied contributions of all to this field. Wilson championed unlimited and unregulated competition in banking, including when it came to the printing of notes. Bagehot, a banker before he was a journalist, tamped down this celebration of unbridled competition – pointing out that what was wanted in the currency was *fixity* of value, not competition, especially in the event of commercial crises, when many of these rival notes would turn out to be worthless. Under him, the *Economist* came around to central banking, as crucial to a complex financial sector, laying down practical rules for its conduct, and shifting the focus to foreign flotations and loans. In subsequent years, it never lost sight of these flows of investment, becoming at times itself indispensable in resolving crises occasioned by the City's global role: as editor at the fin-de-siècle, Johnstone was the bondholders' advocate in Egypt, whose 'assistance was secured in straightening out affairs after the Argentine crisis' when Baring Brothers went bust in 1890.[51]

In the twentieth century, even when bankers came in for criticism under Hirst, 'free trade finance' continued to be the motor of peace, prosperity and reform, with the hegemony of the City as 'the banking and financial center of the world' jealously defended. And once Hirst was out of the way in 1916, this self-identification took a more straightforward turn: Withers's emphasis on the heroic sacrifices of the City during the First World War, and the rejection of any capital levy on profits from it; or Layton's efforts to restore confidence in the pound with a return to gold in the interwar years. After 1945, the standing of sterling as international and imperial currency and British power were even more closely linked – with Labour, according to the paper under Crowther, culpable for the fragility of both, 'its guns unmasked against the City and all its works'. The loosening of what restrictions there were on finance capital came gradually in the post-war years, through the pooling of offshore Eurodollars in London from the late 1950s, then in a rush with the collapse of Bretton Woods in the early 1970s and finally with a Big Bang in 1986 – hailed by Pennant-Rea as a shot in the arm for financial services, before he left for the Bank of England in 1993. Under Emmott and Micklethwait, the neoliberal drive for the insulation, light regulation, privatization and globalization of markets, reached its apogee – culminating in the crash of 2008, and the editors' breathtakingly unrepentant response to it.

A long way from the wishful images of popular parlance in Europe or philosophical discourse in America, this is the record of actually existing liberalism, at its most powerful. Averting their gaze, liberals have scratched their heads at the political volatility of the present, unable to recognize their handiwork. The tripartite structure is intact – with democratic dissatisfactions, imperial conflicts and debt-fuelled financialized capitalism as far as the eye can see. It is rare for a 'newspaper' that describes the world to shape its possibilities, but for over 175 years such has been the case of the *Economist*.

# Acknowledgments

Without help I could not have written this book, and I wish to express my gratitude to just a few of the many people who have had a hand in it. I would like to thank my teachers at UCLA, Lynn Hunt and Perry Anderson, along with my classmates Jacob Collins and Naomi Taback, for intellectual inspiration and comradeship. For their friendship in Los Angeles and beyond, my thanks to Rachel Kushner, Laura Owens, Asha Schechter, Patricia Lennox-Boyd and Jamie Stevens, and the other artists who welcomed me; and to my cousins, Lois Brodax and the Kremens. My colleagues at the City University of New York have supported my research, as have grants from the Professional Staff Congress and Amiel and Melburn Trust. For suggesting I explore this topic in the first place, credit is due to Serge Halimi and the editors at *Le Monde Diplomatique*, and for help during the research, Patrick Weil.

I am grateful to the outside readers of the manuscript, whose criticisms, queries and suggestions vastly improved it – in particular Thomas Meaney and Kelly Burdick; as well as to my colleagues at the *New Left Review*, especially Susan Watkins and Tony Wood. At Verso, Tom Hazeldine has graciously and intelligently worked to refine the text, while Jake Stevens and Mark Martin have done an excellent job of producing it. I also wish to thank Amana Fontanella-Khan, for her sage advice on the finished work.

Last but not least, I owe much to the unfailing courtesy and candour of the *Economist* editors who shared their stories and their views – often at variance to mine – with me. My special thanks go to Bill Emmott, Andrew Knight, John Micklethwait, Zanny Minton Beddoes and Rupert Pennant-Rae, but many others who have worked for the paper were equally helpful.

On a more personal note, my gratitude goes to my family, whose love and support have over many years made this possible – especially my parents Jack and Iris, to whom I dedicate this book.

# Notes

## Abbreviations

BL: British Library
BLOU: Bodleian Library, Oxford University
CAIB: Covert Action Information Bulletin
CHAR: Churchill Archive
CUL: Cambridge University Library
CW: Collected Works
HC Deb: House of Commons debate
HIA: Hoover Institution Archives
LMA: London Metropolitan Archive
LSE: London School of Economics
MCL: Manchester Central Library
ODNB: Oxford Dictionary of National Biography
SN: Standard Note
TCC: Trinity College, Cambridge

## Introduction

1. Frank Langfitt, '"Economist" Magazine Wins American Readers', National Public Radio, 8 March 2006.
2. 'The Economist Group Media Information', 21 October 2013.
3. Christine Haughney, 'Magazine Newsstand Sales Plummet, but Digital Editions Thrive', *New York Times*, 6 August 2013. For recent chronicles of its rise, amidst the generalized fall of the printed press, see David Shaw, 'The Economist Takes the High Road to Global Success', *Los Angeles Times*, 20 July 2003; Stephen Hugh-Jones, 'So What's the Secret of "The Economist"?', *The Independent*, 26 February 2006; Stephen Brook, 'Let the Bad Times Roll', *The Guardian*, 25 February 2008; Matt Pressman, 'Why *Time* and *Newsweek* Will Never Be *The Economist*', *Vanity Fair*, 20 April 2009; Noah Davis, 'Why *The Economist* Is Winning', *Business Insider*, 21 July 2011.

4. Jeremy W. Peters, 'The *Economist* Tends Its Sophisticate Garden', *New York Times*, 8 August 2010. For a defence of the *Economist* against its jealous detractors, see Ryan Chittum, 'The Economist's Success Is Not a Marketing Story', *Columbia Journalism Review*, 9 August 2010.

5. James Fallows, 'The Economics of the Colonial Cringe', 6 October 1991. 'The audience for this is not people who care about the world, but people who believe it is important to care about the world': Tom Scocca, 'Everyone Copies It, but Does Anyone Translate It?', *New York Observer*, 19 March 2007.

6. Economist annual reports 2007 and 2017. According to its research, *Economist* readers were among the richest in the US in 2009 – with a median household income of $166,626 compared to $156,162 for the *Wall Street Journal* – and around the world, 'where every third reader is a millionaire'. Twenty per cent confessed to owning 'a cellar of vintage wines'. 'Audience Advertising Categories', 2 April 2009.

7. Examples, in order: 25 October 2014; 20 September 2014; 11 October 2014; 4 October 2014; 13 September 2014; Mark Sweney, 'Merkel Listens to the Economist's Audio App', 16 November 2014.

8. Anthony Powell, *A Dance to the Music of Time: First Movement*, Chicago 1995, Vol I, pp. 76–77, 83, 86–87, 104.

9. Michael Kinsley, quoted in Fallows, 'The Economics of the Colonial Cringe', *Washington Post*, 6 October 1991.

10. 'Hendrik Coetzee', 29 December 2010.

11. 'Because every story is attributable only to the paper, every story is also the responsibility of the paper ... co-operation replaces competition and – rather contrary to *Economist* editorial philosophy – it turns out that co-operation can produce a better product than competition', argued former political editor David Lipsey, *In the Corridors of Power: An Autobiography*, London 2012, p. 171. Blogs have modified, without undoing, the editorial cloak of invisibility. Self-promotion on social media and TV are greater threats.

12. Michael Reid, *Forgotten Continent: The Battle for Latin America's Soul*, New Haven 2007, p. 159; 'Brazil: Lula's Leap', *The Economist*, 2 March 2006; 'Brazil's Foreign Policy: Lula's World', 2 March 2006; 'The Moderates Fight Back', 19 July 2014.

13. The *Economist* described internal cabinet battles over spending cuts in 1984 as spilling 'old blood on the carpet', after being personally briefed about them by the deputy prime minister, Willie Whitelaw. 'Old blood on the carpet, old blood in the cabinet', 7 September 1985; Kiran Stacey and Emily Cadman, 'Archives 1984: Thatcher's Struggles Provide Lesson for Cameron', *Financial Times*, 2 January 2014. Lunch takes place on Wednesday, the day after the budget is presented in the Commons, allowing, as one former editor put it, for a 'deeper conversation'.

14. Barbara Smith, 'Not So Hard Labour', *Economist*, 20 December 2003.

15. Richard Cobden writing to James Wilson, 22 June 1843, Wilson Papers, MCL; Norman McCord, *The Anti-Corn Law League: 1838–1846*, London 1958, pp. 182–84.

16. *The Times*, 5 August 1859. Emilie Barrington, *Life of Walter Bagehot*, London 1914, p. 286; 'The Bankers' Gazette', *The Economist*, 9 October 1852; Zhaojin Ji, *A History of Modern Shanghai Banking: The Rise and Decline of China's Finance Capitalism*, Armonk 2003, p. 43.

17. Karl Marx, *The Eighteenth Brumaire of Louis Bonaparte*, New York 1963, p. 103.

18. Raymond Streat, *Lancashire and Whitehall: The Diary of Sir Raymond Streat*, ed. Marguerite Dupree, Manchester 1987, Vol II, pp. 143–45. Streat left a snapshot of the 1943 celebration at the Connaught Rooms. The Bank of England governor Montagu Norman gave a toast. 'He traced the community of interest over 100 years between the *Economist* and the Bank of England, both privately owned but both, he thought, rather the better able on that account to serve the public interest.' Feasting on 'rare bounties in war time' and 'excellent claret and a real Havana cigar', at a top table sat Chancellor Kingsley Wood; Labour's Home Secretary, Herbert Morrison; John Maynard Keynes; 'Lord Portal, Stanley Bruce and sundry ambassadors and foreign ministers.' 'The company below the salt was very distinguished. On one side was Lord Wardington, Chairman of Lloyds Bank; on the other Sir William Moore, E. H. Lever, Robert Barlow, Ashley Cooper of Hudson's Bay Company, Sir Robert Sinclair, Head of Ministry of Production. Elsewhere I saw Barrington-Ward, Editor of *The Times*, Professor Robbins, Sir Armond Overton, Holland-Martin, old Sir George Paish, Paul Cadbury, Sir Alan Anderson ... only other Manchester face was Sir Noton Barclay, Chairman of the District Bank.'

19. 'A Manifesto', 15 September 2018.

20. 'I often feel very annoyed and frustrated by the use of the word liberal. It's gotten completely, hopelessly messed up in America', then editor John Micklethwait told Harry Kreisler in 'Globalization and the Conservative Movement in the US', University of California Television, 6 February 2007.

21. Alan Ryan, *The Making of Modern Liberalism*, Princeton 2012, pp. 22, 41. Ryan acknowledges flaws in modern liberal democracies, but is clear they are superior to anything that came before and any present alternative, and would be seen as a 'triumph' by 'most political thinkers in the past two and half millennia': Alan Ryan, *On Politics: A History of Political Thought from Herodotus to the Present*, London 2012, Vol II, pp. 905, 941–45, 948, 972–73, 976–77.

22. Berlin was upfront about which side he took. Pluralism, 'a recognition that human goals are many ... and the negative liberty it entails, seems to me a truer and more humane ideal than the goals of those who seek in the great disciplined, authoritarian structures the 'ideal' of positive

self-mastery by classes, or peoples, or the whole of mankind.' This was an error, a 'metaphysical chimaera', inspiring 'the nationalist, communist, authoritarian and totalitarian creeds of our day': Isaiah Berlin, *Four Essays on Liberty*, Oxford 1982, pp. 124, 131, 141, 144, 171.

23. There 'is certainly no necessary connection between the negative view of liberty and liberalism'. In fact, the two 'most uncompromising exponents' of negative liberty – Hobbes and Bentham – were not liberals at all, according to John Gray, *Isaiah Berlin*, London 1995, p. 21. Gray's own work has become sufficiently unmoored from historical context to posit a chain of equivalence linking Saddam Hussein, Joseph Stalin, Baader-Meinhof, al-Qaeda, French Jacobins and American neocons on the basis that each was inspired by 'secular faiths of the Enlightenment'. Gray, *Heresies: Against Progress and Other Illusions*, London 2004.

24. In the most sophisticated recent attempt at a comprehensive, contextual definition of liberalism, Duncan Bell argues that the conflation of liberalism and the Western tradition, and the elevation of Locke as its central thinker, dates to the third decade of the twentieth century: part of an ideological contest with 'totalitarianism' that began to gain traction in the US and Britain between the 1930s and 1950s. The implication that liberalism might be disentangled from such Cold War imbrications, however, begs the question about Bell's own 'summative conception': why could liberalism, and not another 'ism', be sent to do battle with communism? Duncan Bell, 'What Is Liberalism?', *Political Theory*, June 2014, pp. 682–715.

25. The best wide-angle account – juxtaposing English, French, German and Italian variants of liberalism in nineteenth-century Europe – remains Guido de Ruggiero's work, written nearly a century ago. Writing under the influence of Giovanni Gentile and Benedetto Croce, and in response to the rise of Italian Fascism, Ruggiero's history was Hegelian, having as its goal a higher unity – the Liberal State – which would soon subsume the illiberal threats of Fascism on the right and socialism on the left. This outcome required revitalized Liberal parties, however, and an effort to recall 'the middle classes to a sense of the reflective and critical value of their own activity and a recognition of the universal character of their historical mission': *The History of European Liberalism*, London 1927 (Italian original 1925), pp. 343, 440–43. For an impressive recent study ranging over some of this terrain, see Jörn Leonhard, *Liberalismus: Zur historischen Semantik eines europäischen Deutungsmusters*, München 2012. Recent work on the outward dimensions of liberal thought do not transcend national boundaries: *Victorian Visions of Global Order: Empire and International Relations in Nineteenth Century Political Thought*, ed. Duncan Bell, Cambridge 2007; Gregory Claeys, *Imperial Skeptics: British Critics of Empire, 1850–1920*, Cambridge 2010; Georgios Varouxakis, *Liberty Abroad: J. S. Mill on International Relations*, Cambridge 2013.

26. If, by the fifteenth century, the word 'liberty' was associated with freedom, it was not until the late eighteenth that 'liberal' was used to affirm individual freedoms. Raymond Williams, *Keywords: A Vocabulary of Culture and Society*, New York 1985, pp. 179–81.

27. Charles J. Esdaile, *Spain in the Liberal Age: From Constitution to Civil War, 1808–1939*, Oxford 2000, pp. 31–34; Richard Herr, 'The Constitution of 1812 and the Spanish Road to Parliamentary Monarchy', in *Revolution and the Meanings of Freedom in the Nineteenth Century*, ed. Isser Woloch, Stanford 1996, pp. 85–88; Richard Herr, *An Historical Essay on Modern Spain*, Berkeley 1971, pp. 73–74; Stanley G. Payne, *Spain: A Unique History*, Madison 2011, pp. 141–45.

28. G. de Bertier de Sauvigny, 'Liberalism, Nationalism and Socialism: The Birth of Three Words', *The Review of Politics*, April 1970, pp. 147–166; Pamela Pilbeam, 'The Growth of Liberalism and the Crisis of the Bourbon Restoration, 1827–1830', *The Historical Journal*, June 1982, pp. 351–66; Aurelian Craiutu, *Liberalism under Siege: The Political Thought of the French Doctrinaires*, Lanham 2003, pp. 112, 290, 287–88; *French Liberalism from Montesquieu to the Present Day*, eds. Raf Geenens and Helena Rosenblatt, Cambridge 2012.

29. Thomas P. Neill, *The Rise and Decline of Liberalism*, Milwaukee 1953, pp. 72–75, 112, 115. Liberal pamphleteers began to urge gradual reforms under a constitutional monarch, rejecting both ultra-royalists and 'Napoléonistes' as extremists, several years into the reign of Louis XVIII. See *Avis aux libéraux, par un liberal*, Paris 1818; *Examen du libéralisme. Par un liberal*, Paris 1819. Guizot and Constant used papers to spread '*idées libérales*', the latter signing a letter listing these as 'practical knowledge, the development of industry, destruction of prejudice … and hastening the constitutional education of France': Etienne Aignan, Benjamin Constant, Évariste Dumoulin, A. Jay, E. Jouy, Pierre Louis de Lacretelle, and Pierre-François Tissot, *La Minerve française*, Paris 1818, p. 4.

30. Richard Whatmore, 'The Politics of Political Economy in France from Rousseau to Constant', in *Markets in Historical Contexts*, eds. Mark Bevir and Frank Trentmann, Cambridge 2004, pp. 46–50, 65–69; Ruggiero, *European Liberalism*, pp. 172, 204; Dean Russell, 'Frederic Bastiat and the Free Trade Movement in France and England, 1840–1850' (PhD diss., Université de Genève 1959), pp. 25–26, 62–64, 91–93; David Todd, *L'identité Économique de la France: Libre-Échange et Protectionnisme, 1814–1851*, Paris 2008, pp. 331–51, 416.

31. Smith invoked the term in *The Wealth of Nations* in 1776 to describe certain professions, or generous wages; he also referred to a 'liberal plan of equality, liberty and justice', that is, 'allowing every man to pursue his own interest in his own way', and also, in a digression on the Corn Laws, to a 'liberal system', by which he meant 'freedom of the corn trade'. Adam Smith, *The Wealth of Nations*, ed. Edwin Cannan, New York 2003, pp. 509, 681–82.

32. José Luis Abellán, *Historia Crítica del Pensamiento Español*, Madrid 1984, Vol IV, pp. 58, 78–82; Jörn Leonhard, 'From European Liberalism to the Language of Liberalisms: The Semantics of Liberalism in European Comparison', in *Redescriptions*, 2004, pp. 17–31; Leonhard, *Liberalismus*, pp. 329–32, 347, 410–12, 416, 494.

33. In a letter from 1831, Mill opposed the 'speculative Toryism' of Wordsworth, Southey or Coleridge, 'a reverence for government in the abstract ... duly sensible that it is good for man to be ruled; to submit his body and mind to the guidance of a higher intelligence and virtue', to lower case liberalism, 'which is for making every man his own guide and sovereign master, and letting him think for himself and do exactly as he judges best for himself, giving other men leave to persuade him if they can by evidence, but forbidding him to give way to authority; and still less allowing them to constrain him more than the existence & tolerable security of every man's person and property renders indispensably necessary': Mill to John Sterling, 20 October 1831, in *Collected Works*, ed. Francis Ethelbert Louis Priestley, Michigan 1964, Vol XII, p. 84. It was not until the late 1850s, however, that he began to refer to a movement of which the 'advanced Liberals' in parliament were the vanguard. Retrospectively, Mill dated his adherence to 'Liberalism' from his first trip to France in 1821 when he was just fifteen. 'The chief fruit which I carried away from the society I saw, was a strong and permanent interest in Continental Liberalism, of which I ever afterwards kept myself au courant ... a thing not at all usual in those days with Englishmen, and which had a very salutary influence on my development, keeping me free from the error always prevalent in England, and from which even my father with all his superiority to prejudice was not exempt, of judging universal questions by a merely English standard': Mill, 'Autobiography', in *CW*, Vol I, p. 63.

34. For contrast, see Alex Tyrell, 'La Ligue Française, The Anti-Corn Law League and the Campaign for Economic Liberalism in France During the Last Days of the July Monarchy', in *Rethinking Nineteenth-Century Liberalism*, eds. Anthony Howe and Simon Morgan, Aldershot 2006, pp. 99–116.

35. Karl Polanyi, *The Great Transformation: The Political and Economic Origins of Our Time*, Boston 2001, pp. 141–57; Walter Bagehot, 'Postulates of Political Economy', in *The Collected Works of Walter Bagehot*, Vol XI, p. 222.

36. Eric Voegelin, *On the Form of the American Mind: The Collected Works of Eric Voegelin*, eds. Jürgen Gebhardt and Barry Cooper, Baton Rouge 1995, Vol I; Louis Hartz, *The Liberal Tradition in America: An Interpretation of American Political Thought Since the Revolution*, New York 1955.

37. Herbert Hoover objected to their 'perversion' of the term, as did Walter Lippmann in his book *The Good Society* of 1936. For this history, see Ronald D. Rotunda, *The Politics of Language: Liberalism as Word*

*and Symbol*, Iowa City 1986, pp. 14–17, 33–40, 58–60, 62–64, 70, 74; Hartz, *Liberal Tradition*, pp. 259–66, 270; David Green, *Shaping Political Consciousness: The Language of Politics in America from McKinley to Reagan*, Ithaca 1987, pp. 79–84; Barry D. Riccio, *Walter Lippmann: Odyssey of a Liberal*, New Brunswick 1994, pp. 128–33.

38. Norberto Bobbio, *Liberalism and Democracy*, London 1990. For Kahan, a limited suffrage based on intellectual capacity defined liberalism in nineteenth century France, Germany and England – the latter thus much the most successful branch, since it enjoyed one of the least democratic franchises in Western Europe in 1914: Alan S. Kahan, *Liberalism in Nineteenth Century Europe*, London 2003, pp. 133–35, 139–41, 191.

39. See Uday Mehta, *Liberalism and Empire: A Study in Nineteenth-century British Liberal Thought*, Chicago 1999; Sankar Muthu, *Enlightenment Against Empire*, Princeton 2003, pp. 3–6; Jennifer Pitts, *A Turn to Empire: The Rise of Imperial Liberalism in Britain and France*, Princeton 2005. Contrasting Smith, Burke and Bentham with the Mills and Tocqueville, Pitts maintains that 'no explanation that rests on some set of basic theoretical assumptions in the liberal tradition can possibly explain such flexibility on the question of empire', concluding that 'liberalism does not lead ineluctably either to imperialism or anti-imperialism' – claims that rest partly on the notion that liberalism already existed in the eighteenth century and can be elided with thinkers in the nineteenth century: *A Turn to Empire*, pp. 1, 4. For a different sense of Smith's 'anti-imperialism', see Donald Winch, *Adam Smith's Politics*, Cambridge 1978, pp. 140, 151, 180.

40. Kynaston has written a comprehensive survey. David Kynaston, *City of London*. 4 vols, London, 1994–2001. For caution in ascribing coherent policy interests to the City, see *The British Government and the City of London in the Twentieth Century*, eds. Ronald Michie and Philip Williamson, Cambridge 2004, pp. 11–12.

41. *The Economist, 1843–1943: A Centenary Volume* was a 'modest memorial' comprising a slim collection of essays published two years after the offices, printers, library and records burned in the Blitz. The next two works appeared for the sesquicentennial in 1993. In *The Economist: America, 1843–1993*, the former editor Alastair Burnet narrated '150 Years of Reporting the American Connection', while Ruth Dudley Edwards, a freelance journalist, produced what was meant to be the more comprehensive work. 'I was so hard up at the time that if they had asked me to write the book in iambic pentameters and set it to music I would probably have consented', Edwards told the *Independent*. Last-minute interventions from many staff hands resulted in an impenetrable 948-page tome, despite the omission of the ten years up to 1993 – a turning point, as Thatcher and Reagan remade the state, the Cold War ended, and the *Economist*'s circulation took off. 'I did not intend to write much about the last decade or so', she told chief executive David Gordon. 'While you are actually

in your jobs it would hardly be helpful to start analysing your defi-
ciencies.' With such obliging manners, her efforts were unlikely to be
particularly revealing. Ruth Dudley Edwards, *The Pursuit of Reason:
The Economist, 1843–1993*, London, 1993, pp xi–xix; 'History saved
from bombs and bin-liners', *The Independent*, 2 Sept 1993.

## 1. Free Trade Empire

1. The Reform Bill did not include radical demands for manhood suffrage, annual parliaments, or a secret ballot. Nor did it address the
   imbalance between counties and boroughs, or south and north. It
   added about 300,000 to the rolls; after 1832 a seventh of all adult
   males could vote. The extent to which this altered the social property
   relations on which political power was traditionally based is indicated
   by census figures from 1872, five years after passage of the Second
   Reform Act. Four-fifths of the land in England, Scotland, Wales and
   Ireland was still owned by fewer than 7,000 people. Norman Gash,
   *Aristocracy and People: Britain, 1815–1865*, Cambridge, Mass 1979,
   pp. 17, 145–55.
2. Gash, *Aristocracy and People*, pp. 200–209; E. J. Hobsbawm, *Industry
   and Empire: From 1750 to the Present Day*, London 1976, pp. 71–78.
3. 'There is no employer of labour in this country who gives employment
   to 5,000 people and upwards who is not a member of the council of
   the League', boasted League chairman George Wilson, though himself
   owner of a smaller-scale starch plant, in 1846. Paul A. Pickering and
   Alex Tyrell, *The People's Bread: A History of the Anti-Corn Law
   League*, London 2000, pp. 22–33, 199–212, 228.
4. Ibid., 91; Marc-William Palen, *The 'Conspiracy' of Free Trade: The
   Anglo American Struggle over Empire and Economic Globalisation*,
   Cambridge 2016, pp. xxv, 11–15; Boyd Hilton, *The Age of Atonement: The Influence of Evangelicalism on Social and Economic
   Thought*, Oxford 1988; C. P. Kindleberger, 'The Rise of Free Trade
   in Western Europe, 1820–1875', *The Journal of Economic History*,
   March 1975, pp. 31–32, 51.
5. For an excellent account of the unique centrality of free trade to the
   political, economic and intellectual history of Britain from repeal
   onwards, see Anthony Howe, *Free Trade and Liberal England,
   1846–1946*, Oxford 1997. For 'Free Trade' as a 'genuine national and
   democratic culture' that shaped Britain's 'civil society' and 'national
   mission', see Frank Trentmann, *Free Trade Nation: Commerce, Consumption, and Civil Society in Modern Britain*, Oxford 2008, pp.
   4–10.
6. And of the losses to be sustained in bad times: at £20,000, the firm lost
   almost as much the following year. Miles Taylor, 'Cobden, Richard
   (1804–1865)', *Oxford Dictionary of National Biography*, 2004.

7. 'Corn laws are a part only of a system in which Whig and Tory aristocracy have about an equal interest.' Cobden to Thomas Dick, 7 October 1836, in Richard Cobden, *The Political Writings of Richard Cobden*, London 1886, p. 2.

8. In reply to a 'reader of the Economist, Hawick', Wilson produced a list of the 'best books on Political Economy': 'Smith's *Wealth of Nations*, McCulloch's edition; the Works of Mons J. B. Say; Ricardo's *Principles of Political Economy and Taxation*; Mill's *Political Economy*; Tooke's *History of Prices*, and Porter's *Progress of the Nation*. Smith's *Wealth of Nations* as fixing fundamental principles; Tooke's *History of Prices*, and Porter's *Progress of the Nation*, as the most interesting, entertaining, and instructive practical applications of those principles, are most strongly recommended as the best books for the common student.' 'Correspondence and Answers to Inquiries', *Economist*, 11 Nov 1843.

9. Bagehot, 'Memoir of the Right Honourable James Wilson', in CW, Vol III, p. 324.

10. Ibid., 326–28.

11. James Wilson, *Influences of the Corn Laws as Affecting All Classes of the Community, and Particularly the Landed Interests*, London 1839, p. 5. A similar work appeared the same year from G. R. Porter, head of the statistical department of the Board of Trade, author of *Progress of the Nation*, and Wilson's close personal friend and neighbour at Dulwich.

12. Bagehot, 'Memoir of the Right Honourable James Wilson', in CW, Vol. III, p. 333.

13. Cobden to Wilson, 3 May 1839, in Emilie Barrington, *The Servant of All: Pages from the Family, Social and Political Life of My Father, James Wilson: Twenty Years of mid-Victorian Life*, London 1927, Vol. I, p. 27.

14. *League Circular*, No. 7, July 1839, p. 6.

15. J. R. McCulloch, *The Literature of Political Economy: A Classified Catalogue*, London 1845, p. 80.

16. 'How few of us there were, who, five years ago, believed that, in seeking repeal, we were also seeking the benefit of the agriculturalists!' Richard Cobden, *Speeches on Questions of Public Policy*, London 1870, Vol. II, p. 98.

17. Wilson, *Influences of the Corn Laws*, p. 95.

18. David Ricardo, *Works of David Ricardo*, eds. Pierro Sraffa and M. H. Dobb, Vol. IV, Cambridge 1951, p. 197.

19. Ibid., 17–18, 37. There was a religious, millenarian dimension to Wilson's conception of free trade. Its optimism about economic growth, however, was a departure from evangelical expectations: see Hilton, *The Age of Atonement*, pp. 54, 69, 246–47.

20. Wilson sympathized. 'Sweets once tasted, advantages once enjoyed, are not easy to relinquish.' In some districts, things had progressed to the point where oatmeal or barley had been substituted by wheat-flour, 'as

being at the moment from unnatural causes as cheap'. Is it any surprise that riots break out – 'murderous scenes, which have disgraced our manufacturing districts?' Or that workers are pushed to extremes, 'otherwise distinguished for their patient, persevering industry and ingenuity, and which have won England triumphs more glorious, territories more extended, and influence more respected, than she ever obtained by her most dazzling military achievements'? Wilson, *Influences of the Corn Laws*, pp. 47–48, 108.

21. 'In his plain business-like way Mr. Wilson demolished Lord Monteagle's fallacy about a fixed duty of 5s being paid, not by the British consumer, but by the foreign grower of wheat, and went on with a number of statistical proofs of the injury inflicted by "protection" not only without wearying his audience but manifestly to their high gratification.' Archibald Prentice, *History of the Anti-Corn-Law League*, London 1853, p. 58.

22. Cobden was an exception, noted Wilson's daughter, though 'he naturally viewed the doings of the League, which was his own child so to speak, with more tolerance than did my father and his friends. Cobden even did not entirely scout the Chartists' creeds and doings, but to my father they seemed little less than criminal and most baneful to any real progress.' Barrington, *The Servant of All*, pp. 30, 41.

23. Ibid., 16–23.

24. Ronald K. Huch, *The Radical Lord Radnor: The Public Life of Viscount Folkestone, Third Earl of Radnor, 1779–1869*, Minneapolis 1977, pp. 7–9, 151.

25. Tocqueville attributed the English radicals' focus on political demands for parliamentary reform to the desire of its middle classes to emulate the aristocracy socially and accumulate great fortunes. He looked forward to meeting Radnor, he told a correspondent, 'who unites these rare qualities of being a member of the highest aristocracy and at the same time of the radical party, two seemingly incompatible things, but which sometimes coexist in this country.' At Longford he was treated with 'perfect grace', his sleeping quarters the size of a ballroom, with four or five giant washbasins, and a hunting expedition, revealing a castle and grounds combining grandeur and comfort 'surpassing the most beautiful chateaux in France'. Tocqueville to his father, 24 August 1833, OC, Vol XIV, pp. 173–74; Tocqueville to Marie, 27 August 1833, OC, Vol XIV, pp. 391–94.

26. James Wilson, *Fluctuations of Currency, Commerce, and Manufactures: Referable to the Corn Laws*, London 1840, pp. 100–101; James Wilson, *The Revenue; Or, What Should the Chancellor Do?*, London 1841, pp. 9, 21. Wilson waded into numerous controversies. For a summary of his economic tracts on currency and trade, see Robert G. Link, *English Theories of Economic Fluctuation 1815–1848*, New York 1959, pp. 102–26.

27. Barrington, *The Servant of All*, p. 68.

28. Cobden to Wilson, 22 June 1843, Wilson Papers, MCL.

29. Cobden urged that these be distributed to 'all the leading Tories in Manchester and neighbourhood ... and to Ashton, Stockport, Bolton, Preston, Salford and Oldham'. Norman McCord, *The Anti-Corn Law League: 1838–1846*, London 1958, pp. 182–84.

30. Anthony Howe, *Free Trade and Liberal England, 1846–1946*, Oxford 1997, p. 14.

31. Barrington, *Servant of All*, p. 69. After the first two years, when Cobden may have bailed it out to the tune of £600, the *Economist* has been profitable. McCord, *Anti-Corn Law League*, p. 184.

32. Barrington, *Servant of All*, p. 68.

33. Scott Gordon, 'The London Economist and the High Tide of Laissez Faire', *Journal of Political Economy*, December 1955, p. 484.

34. Herbert Spencer, *An Autobiography*, London 1904, p. 379.

35. S. Leon Levy, *Nassau W Senior: The Prophet of Modern Capitalism*, Boston 1943, p. 279.

36. Thomas Hodgskin, *Labour Defended Against the Claims of Capital, or the Unproductiveness of Capital Proved*, London 1825. He was considered so extreme an advocate for the working class and such a severe critic of all laws that it is surprising his Benthamite friends did not begin to avoid him sooner, or that his post at the *Morning Chronicle*, obtained for him by James Mill in 1822, was not endangered earlier. Mill wrote to Lord Brougham in 1832 to complain of the 'mad nonsense of our friend Hodgskin about the rights of the labourer to the whole produce of the country, wages, profits and rents, all included. These opinions, if they were to spread, would be the subversion of civilized society; worse than the overwhelming deluge of the Huns and Tartars.' Mill to Brougham, September 3, 1833, in Alexander Bain, *James Mill: A Biography*, London 1882, p. 364.

37. This pamphlet probably brought Hodgskin to the attention of Wilson. But it also hinted that its author was already familiar with Wilson's work. 'The time will come, I believe it is not far off, when reason, truth, and justice will prevail, and when even the landlords will help us to abolish these laws.' Thomas Hodgskin, *A Lecture on Free Trade in Connexion with the Corn Laws: Delivered at the White Conduit House on January 31, 1843*, London, 1843, pp. 22–23.

38. Thomas Hodgskin, *Natural and Artificial Rights of Property Contrasted*, London 1832, p. 101.

39. Elie Halévy, *Thomas Hodgskin*, London 1956, pp. 131–65.

40. Herbert Spencer, *The Proper Sphere of Government*, London 1843, p. 5.

41. For his time at the *Economist*, see, Herbert Spencer, *An Autobiography*, London 1904, pp. 329–30, 333, 341–43; David Duncan, *The Life and Letters of Herbert Spencer*, London 1908, pp. 56–62.

42. Herbert Spencer, *Social Statics: Or, The Conditions Essential to Human Happiness Specified, and the First of Them Developed*, London 1851, pp. 286, 294.

43. 'Literature', *Economist*, 8 February 1851.

44. Bernard Semmel, *Imperialism and Social Reform; English Social-Imperial Thought, 1895–1914*, London 1960, pp. 29–31; Geoffrey Hawthorn, *Enlightenment and Despair: A History of Social Theory*, Cambridge 1987, p. 91.

45. William R. Greg, *Enigmas of Life*, London 1891, vii–xliv; John Morley, *Critical Miscellanies*, London 1886, Vol III, pp. 213–56. In the arena of Victorian eccentricities and ailments Spencer was not to be outdone. His hypochondria was comprehensive, lamenting chronic headaches, heart strain, insomnia and checking his and other people's' pulses constantly. Mark Francis, *Herbert Spencer and the Invention of Modern Life*, Chesham 2007, p. 55.

46. George Eliot, *The George Eliot Letters*, New Haven 1954, Vol. II, pp. 21, 66. His popularity with Eliot is unlikely to have been increased by the opinion he expressed in 1859. 'There are vast numbers of lady novelists for the same reason that there are vast numbers of lady seamstresses. Thousands of women have nothing to do.' 'False Morality of Lady Novelists', *National Review*, January 1859, pp. 144–67. For Greg's extension of Darwinism to race, nation and sex see, 'The Doom of the Negro Race', *Fraser's Magazine*, March 1866, pp. 277–305; 'On the Failure of "Natural Selection" in the Case of Man', *Fraser's Magazine*, September 1868, pp. 353–62; 'Realities of Irish Life', *Quarterly Review*, January 1869, p 78.

47. Harriet Martineau, *The Collected Letters of Harriet Martineau*, ed. Deborah Anna Logan, London 2007, Vol IV, p. 260; Martineau, *Collected Letters*, London 2007, Vol V, pp. 233–35.

48. 'Donc, en attendant une autre définition, voici la mienne. L'Etat, c'est la grande fiction à travers laquelle tout le monde s'efforce de vivre aux dépens de tout le monde.' 'L'État', *Journals de Debats*, September 1848; Dean Russell, *Frederic Bastiat: Ideas and Influence*, Irvington-on-Hudson 1965, p. 33.

49. *The Economist, 1843–1943: A Centenary Volume*, London 1943, p. 30.

50. 'M. Bastiat and his Works', *Economist*, 15 May 1852.

51. 'Preliminary Number and Prospectus', *Economist*, 1 August 1843.

52. James A. Monsure, 'James Wilson and the Economist, 1805–1860' (PhD thesis, Columbia, 1960), pp. 13–15.

53. *Economist*, 1 August 1843.

54. 'Our Brazilian Trade and the Anti-Slavery Party', *Economist*, 16 September 1843; 'Superior Value of Free over Slave Labour,' *Economist*, 30 December 1844. To label the *Economist* 'generally a strong opponent of slavery' is a mischaracterization. Sven Beckert, 'Emancipation and Empire: Reconstructing the World Wide Web of Cotton Production in the Age of the American Civil War', *American Historical Review*, December 2004, p. 1419.

55. 'Mr. Gladstone's Railway Bill', *Economist*, 6 July 1844.

56. 'The Inconsistencies of the Late Debates,' *Economist*, 30 March 1844; 'Protection to Labour', *Economist*, 6 April 1844.

57. Lord Ashley was 'well-meaning, but mistaken; philanthropic, but

unwise'. 'Should the Capitalists Be Blamed?', *Economist*, 28 November 1846.

58. Monsure, 'James Wilson and the Economist', p. 138; *Economist*: 3 January 1852; 15 July 1854; 10 March 1855; 1 March 1856.

59. Karl Marx, *Capital: A Critique of Political Economy Volume One*, London 1990, 11n, 336–38n. Marx attacked Senior and Wilson, citing the *Economist* of 15 April 1848. He also paid tribute to Leonard Horner, chief factory inspector until 1859, who 'rendered undying service to the English working class'. Horner and his semi-annual factory reports were routinely condemned as biased in the *Economist*, with Wilson reaching his wits' end in 1855 when he wrote, 'it was as dangerous to employ men like Mr. Horner to carry the Factory Acts into execution as to employ inefficient commissaries and storekeepers and captains at the port of Balaklava'. 'Factories-Owners and Inspectors', *Economist*, 10 March 1855.

60. *Economist*: 'Right of Property in Inventions', 1 February 1851; 'Right of Property in Expression', 28 April 1855; 'What Shall We Know?', 25 August 1855; 'Why Companies are Now Necessary', 19 July 1856.

61. 'Knowledge versus Dictation, the New Board of Health', *Economist*, 10 April 1847.

62. 'Regulation of the Supply of Water', *Economist*, 19 January 1850; 'The Metropolitan Supply of Water', *Economist*, 23 November 1850.

63. 'Chambers's Papers for the People', *Economist*, 13 July 1850.

64. This ended with a rhyme in honour of scavenging, rag-picking, and other supposedly lowly occupations: 'Then let every toil be hallowed/ That man performs for man,/ And have its share of honour/ As part of one great plan.' 'The Disposal of Refuse', *Economist*, 13 September 1856.

65. 'The Board of Health', *Economist*, 5 August 1854. 'This was during the Crimean War, and the full flavor of the article can perhaps be indicated by saying that a comparable suggestion in 1943 would have been that Sir William Beveridge was really a bureaucratic despot at heart and his spiritual home was Nazi Germany.' Gordon, 'The London Economist,' p. 485.

66. 'Ragged Schools and Emigration', *Economist*, 10 June 1848; 'Ragged Schools and Charity', *Economist*, 24 June 1848.

67. 'National Education', *Economist*, 1 February 1851. Gradually, in the aftermath of the Crimean War, it gave way to the idea of strictly limited state grants to schools, provided that all parents pay some tuition, and purely on grounds of national economic utility, that England could thereby maintain her economic leadership of the world.

68. *Economist*: 'Definitions in Political Economy', 26 November 1853; 'A Manual of Political Economy for Schools', 7 April 1855; 'On the Methods of Reasoning and Observation in Politics', 27 November 1852.

69. George Jacob Holyoake, *Sixty Years of an Agitator's Life*, London 1906, p. 229.

70. Charles Read argues that the response to the famine had little to do with laissez-faire ideology. Instead, a financial crisis forced the British Government to cut relief to Ireland in 1847, in obedience to economic laws (no longer Malthusian, but an up-to-date 'macroeconomic policy trilemma'). Read thus tries to minimize 'the strong laissez-faire beliefs' of Wilson, whose 'influence on government in the famine period was limited'. Read, 'Laissez-faire, the Irish Famine, and British Financial Crisis', *Economic History Review*, May 2016, p. 430. The notion that Wilson had scant influence, or that economic and ideological factors are easily disentangled in the crisis, is hard to square with the evidence. See Trevelyan to Wood, 26 July 1847, Hickleton Papers, CUL, CUL-Microfilm–1499.

71. Aware that free trade and state aid might be seen as complimentary policies, given the scale of the blight, the paper noted, 'it is questionable whether this would actually bring us a positively increased supply – whether government brought home 1,500,000 quarters, merchants would bring so much less.' It had no doubt what was about to happen in Ireland, 'famine unquestionably impends', but it once again questioned the wisdom of ignorant interventionists. 'We do not know a more frightful spectacle than that of a number of people rushing to do good.' 'Charity as a Remedy in Case of Famine', *Economist*, 29 November 1845.

72. Cormac Ó Gráda, *Black '47' and Beyond: The Great Irish Famine in History, Economy, and Memory*, Princeton 1999, pp. 4, 77–83.

73. Russell was praised for his sober reflections on the failure of Peel's policies. 'We do not propose', Russell was quoted, 'to interfere with the regular trade by which Indian corn and other food is brought into the country (Hear, hear). We propose to leave that as much at liberty as possible, thinking the market is best supplied in that manner without government interference.' His chief secretary for Ireland, Mr Labouchere, was also given plaudits for criticizing the manner in which Indian meal was 'sold indiscriminately 20 per cent below prime cost', which, the paper put in, 'ruined and calumniated a useful class of honest and industrious retail traders', was a 'confiscation of property', and vitiated 'the utility to society of high prices when supplies are scanty'. The new Whig ministers did not go far enough in condemning the previous administration, whose scheme of buying corn, cooked up by Peel and Deputy Commissary General Hewetson, 'a theoretical political economist', might be suitable for 'a pastoral tribe or an army' but was 'folly … in a complicated commercial society'. 'Measures for Ireland', *Economist*, 22 August, 1846.

74. 'The Food Crisis', *Economist*, 19 December 1846.

75. 'Ireland', *Economist*, 27 February 1847. The *Economist* published extracts from these letters. For context, see Cecil Woodham Smith, *The Great Hunger: Ireland 1845–1849*, New York 1962, pp. 54, 120, 132–33, 148.

76. 'Should the State Employ the Irish', *Economist*, 26 December 1846;

'The True Cure for Ireland', 28 August 1847. Public works – 'pauperism and slavery combined' – instilled a culture of helplessness in Ireland. Worse, the wage fund theory showed how taxes, spent in this fashion, 'diminish the funds for the employment of labour, and ultimately aggravate the evil'. To those who sought food for the Irish whatever the cost, it replied, 'We thought that this had been so clearly demonstrated by Mr. Malthus to be an impossibility that we feel only astonishment at its being proposed.' 'Feeding the Irish', *Economist*, 21 March 1846.

77. Clarendon to Wilson on 29 July 1847, 30 August 1847 and 22 December 1847, in Barrington, *Servant of All*, pp. 122–23, 129–30. Wilson also warned Clarendon about the effects of relief on the London money market. Peter Gray, *Famine, Land and Politics: British Government and Irish Society, 1843–1850*, Dublin 1999, pp. 76–77, 251.

78. 'Ireland', *Economist*, 27 February 1847; 'Irish Coercion Bill', 18 December 1847.

79. Frederick Engels, 'The Coercion Bill for Ireland and the Chartists', *La Réforme*, 8 January 1848.

80. Clarendon to Wilson, 7 June 1848, in Barrington, *Servant of All*, p. 139.

81. Christine Kinealy, *A Death-Dealing Famine: The Great Hunger in Ireland*, London 1997, p. 127.

82. 'The Obrien Insurrection', *Economist*, 5 August 1848; 'Ireland's Necessity, England's Opportunity', *Economist*, 2 September 1848. The latter would appear to be the work of Greg. The Oxford scholar Benjamin Jowett reported of *Economist* contributor Nassau Senior; 'I have always had a certain horror of political economists since I heard one of them say that he feared the famine of 1848 in Ireland would not kill more than a million people, and that would scarcely be enough to do much good.' Woodham-Smith, *Great Hunger*, pp. 375–76.

83. Clarendon to Wilson, 26 September 1848, in Barrington, *The Servant of All*, pp. 139–40. Clarendon called for a state loan to fund relief. 'Surely this is a state of things to justify you asking the House of Commons for an advance, for I don't think there is another legislature in Europe that would disregard such suffering as now exists in the west of Ireland, or coldly persist in a policy of extermination.' Clarendon to Russell, 26 April 1849, in Kinealy, *A Death-Dealing Famine*, p. 138.

84. 'The Saxon, the Celt and the Gaul', *Economist*, 29 April 1848; 'Household Suffrage', 8 July 1848; 'New Reform Agitation', 27 May 1848. Cobden objected to this rabid hostility to any widening of the suffrage. After being taunted by the Chartist leader Fergus O'Connor for his association with the *Economist*, he wrote to Wilson that 'no person has a right to identify you with liberal politics because you are a Free-Trader. But I still regret as much as ever the view you take ... upon the danger to property consequent upon giving working people the suffrage – because I find, in the inevitable tendency of democratic principles it places you in an unfavorable position in the eyes of a class

which must exercise more and more power in the legislation.' Cobden to Wilson, September 1843, in Barrington, *The Servant of All*, p. 71.

85. 'The Fermentation of Europe', *Economist*, 1 April 1848. Grey and Lansdowne wrote to congratulate Wilson on this leader, which seems to have been written by Greg. Wilson confided his disdain for France to Cornewall Lewis after visiting Paris in December 1848: Barrington, *The Servant of All*, pp. 142–44.

86. Barrington, *The Servant of All*, pp. 156, 199; Bagehot, *CW*, Vol. III, p. 332.

87. Barrington, *The Servant of All*, pp. 88, 204–5, 209.

88. 'The Bankers' Gazette: Bank Returns and Money Market', *Economist*, 9 October 1852. In the subscription contract of 1852, Wilson is listed as a shareholder with 1,000 shares, among the four or five largest, along with the other founders: Joseph Robert Morrison, Lindsay William Shaw, Robert Lowe MP, John Gladstone (Stockwell Lodge, Surrey), John Bagshaw, Peter Bell, George Bowrings Carr and William Book. Chartered Bank of India, Australia and China Subscription Contract, 16 November 1852, Standard Chartered Bank, LMA, CLC/b/207/CH02/ 01/001.

89. Compton Mackenzie, *Realms of Silver*, New York 2005, pp. 4–9.

90. Wilson to Gladstone, 17 May 1853, Gladstone Papers, BL, Add. MS 44346, ff. 15–30.

91. Monsure, 'James Wilson and the Economist', p. 115.

92. Justin McCarthy, *Short History of Our Own Times: From the Accession of Queen Victoria to the General Election of 1880*, London 1887, p. 164.

93. Barrington, *The Servant of All*, p. 268.

94. Cobden was right to attack empire's 'grasping disposition', entailing 'responsibility, care, trouble and expense without any corresponding advantages'. Citing recent examples of British prickliness in China, Switzerland, Uruguay and Brazil, 'we are apt to go a little further than Mr. Cobden' and replace all diplomats with merchants. 'We are sensible of the necessity of protecting trade, but we believe that trade is better able to protect itself without than with the help of the State; the interference of the State with other states, ostensibly for the protection of commerce, more frequently injures than serves it. Commercial men … come, we are afraid, to rely too much on men-of-war to procure those results which can only be procured by their own fair dealing, civility, and assiduity in their business.' 'Our Diplomacy', *Economist*, 25 December 1847.

95. *Economist*: 'War with a Despot', 31 December 1853; 'Eastern Question', 26 March 1853.

96. 'The Turkish Crisis', *Economist*, 6 August 1853. Tsar Nicolas, alleged defender of the more than 10 million Christians living under Ottoman rule, could lend his territorial ambitions a religious halo that was denied the British and French: the fact that their ally was a Muslim state spurred them to find liberal justifications for the Crimean War.

97. 'The Cloud in the East', *Economist*, 24 September 1853.
98. Orlando Figes, *Crimea: The Last Crusade*, London 2010, p. 176.
99. 'Our Gallant Army in the Crimea', *Economist*, 14 October 1854.
100. 'True Purpose of the War', *Economist*, 2 December 1854.
101. 'War or Peace?', *Economist*, 19 May 1855; 'A New Way to Peace', 2 June 1855.
102. 'Let us reflect with the deepest gratitude, but also with a wholesome terror, what would have been our fate, if these startling revelations … had surprised us in the midst of a struggle on our own shores instead of at the distance of 3,000 miles, and with the French as assailants instead of as allies!' 'The Practical Good to Be Educed from Our Disasters', *Economist*, 27 January 1855.
103. 'The Balance Sheet', *Economist*, 9 February 1856.
104. F. D. Munsell, 'Crimean War', in *Victorian Britain: An Encyclopedia*, ed. Sally Mitchell, London 2011, pp. 202–3; Figes, *Crimea*, pp. 483, 488.
105. Wilson used the *Economist* to promote the government line on the war, as well as the policies favoured by allies in it. At Lord Clarendon's urging, he ran a leader arguing that the British blockade of Russia should give way to a total trade embargo, before circulating a Treasury memorandum to the same effect. 'Our War Commercial Policy: can it be continued?', 30 September 1854. Wilson played down the cost of the war, and the fact that debt financed the largest share of it. 'The Balance Sheet', *Economist*, 9 February 1856. Astronomically more than the £2,840,000 budgeted in 1854, it cost closer to £76 million – two thirds from loans. Olive Anderson, *A Liberal State at War: English Politics and Economics During the Crimean War*, New York 1967, pp. 201–6, 261–63.
106. For the *Economist* on wartime budgets, loans and banking, respectively, see 'The War Budget and Its Principles', 11 March 1854; 'The Money Market, the Rate of Interest, and the War', 8 September 1855; 'The Banks of England and France', 22 September 1855. For political gossip, see the 'Foreign Correspondence' column from 1855 to 1856. For social and political activities of Wilson and Greg, see Barrington, *The Servant of All*, pp. 272–82, 252, 293.
107. The *Economist* had prior disagreements with Cobden. But perhaps because of their relatively small scale they did not lead to a falling out, or to revisionism. In the Don Pacifico Affair, for example, Britain claimed to send warships to Greece on behalf of a Jewish merchant born in Gibraltar, whose house was sacked during a riot in Athens in 1847. The lesson of the episode, according to the *Economist*, was the 'proud fact that however humble the condition of the man, be he but an English subject … the authority and power of England are at hand to secure him certain justice against undeserved outrages and loses … It is a conviction that gives confidence to the English merchant and success to his enterprise; and secures for him respect and safety wherever he goes.' 'The Greek Claims', 15 June 1850.

Cobden attacked this attitude in the House of Commons a week later as sham liberalism. Cobden, *Speeches on Questions of Public Policy*, p. 227.

108. Cobden wished to dispute the idea then widespread that Britain should intervene to protect the Poles from the Russians. His pamphlet ranged widely, asking how Britain could think to intervene on such a basis with the plight of Ireland on its doorstep. The entire empire was 'planting, supporting and governing countries', he added. And 'so grateful to our national pride has been the spectacle, that we have never for once paused to inquire if our interests were advanced by so much nominal greatness. Three hundred millions of permanent debt – millions of direct taxation are annually levied – restrictions and prohibitions upon our trade in all quarters of the world; and for what?' Cobden, *The Political Writings of Richard Cobden*, pp. 21, 36.

109. Richard Cobden, *The Letters: 1815–1847*, ed. Anthony Howe, Oxford 2007, Vol. I, p. 452; Cobden to Frederick Cobden, May 1853, in *The Life of Richard Cobden*, ed. John Morley, London 1906, p. 613.

110. J. A. Hobson, *Richard Cobden: The International Man*, London 1919, p. 105.

111. Cobden to Joseph Parkes, 18 December 1855, in *Letters of Richard Cobden*, eds. Anthony Howe and Simon Morgan, Oxford 2012, Vol. III, p. 174.

112. Cobden to John Bright, 11 August 1856, in Hobson, *Richard Cobden*, p. 226.

113. 'Mr. Cobden's Letter and the Russian War', *Economist*, 10 November 1855.

114. 'Literature', *Economist*, 6 August 1853; 'Mr. Cobden's What Next – and Next?', 12 January 1856.

115. *Economist*: 'Nicholas and His Apologists', 9 December 1854; 'The Tactics of the Opposition and the Interests of the Country', 6 October 1855; 'The Beauties of Bright', 2 February 1856.

116. 139 Parl. Deb. (3rd Ser.) (1855) 1283–1287.

117. Ibid., 1287–1290.

118. McCarthy, *Short History*, p. 164.

119. J. Y. Wong, *Deadly Dreams: Opium, Imperialism, and the Arrow War in China*, Cambridge 1998, pp. 9–10, 335–65, 411–12; Carl A. Trocki, *Opium, Empire and the Global Political Economy*, London 1999.

120. 144 Parl. Deb. (3rd Ser.) (1857) 1155–1245.

121. John Newsinger, 'Elgin in China,' *New Left Review*, no. 15, June 2002, 119–40, much the best treatment of the connection between liberalism and imperialism on display during the Second Opium War.

122. Cobden to Richard, 13 April 1857, in Hobson, *Richard Cobden*, p. 210.

123. The *Illustrated London News* described Bowring as 'one of the reform philosophers of the age, a gentleman who has given his life to

languages and liberalism; a traveller; a commercialist; a Benthamite'
in 1842. As an MP he had opposed the opium trade. He changed his
mind in no small part because by 1856 he was indebted to, and his
son employed by, one of the world's largest opium dealers, Jardine
Matheson: G. F. Bartle, *An Old Radical and His Brood*, London
1994, pp. 11, 36, 58–9, 90.

124.  Bowring had earlier been hailed for negotiating a treaty with Siam
in 1855, 'which throws open the whole of that rich country to European enterprise ... The old system of monopoly has been abolished,
and a duty of only 3 per cent is to be collected on all articles. British
subjects are to be allowed to settle in the country, erect dwellings,
cultivate soil, and buy and sell without restriction.' *Economist*, 25
August 1855. Opium was also to be freely admitted.

125.  'The Chinese Debate and Its Issue', *Economist*, 7 March 1857.

126.  'Our Prospects and Our Difficulties', *Economist*, 14 March 1857.
See also, 'Peace the Result of Free Trade', 9 May 1857.

127.  McCarthy, *A Short History*, pp. 166–67.

128.  'Results of the Elections', *Economist*, 4 April 1857; 'Mr. Bright and
His Retiring Address', 18 April 1857.

129.  Cobden to Parkes, 9 August 1857, in Morley, *Life of Richard
Cobden*, p. 663.

130.  Cobden to Mr Richard, 16 June 1857, in Hobson, *Richard Cobden*,
pp. 218–19. 'A lively, brief, touch-and-go style of showing up these
people is best', assured Cobden, who intended some of this material
for the *Morning Star*.

131.  James L. Sturgis, *John Bright and the Empire*, London 1969, p. 40.

132.  Cobden to Bright, 17 October 1858, in E. D. Steele, *Palmerston and
Liberalism, 1855–1865*, Cambridge 1991, p. 121.

133.  Bright on 29 October 1858 in Birmingham in *Speeches on Questions
of Public Policy*, Vol. II, pp. 373–99.

134.  Wilson to Lewis, 17 December 1858, in Barrington, *Servant of
All*, Vol II, pp. 103–7; Steele, *Palmerston and Liberalism*, p. 122.
Wilson had indicated his desire for a rapprochement after Bright
was returned to the Commons, but before his incendiary speech,
welcoming Bright back for past services 'to commercial and individual freedom', even as Wilson anticipated that if 'India remain
anxious and agitated Mr. Bright's advice to that country may differ
very materially from our own'. See 'Mr. Bright's Return for Birmingham', *Economist*, 22 August 1857.

135.  Saul David, *The Indian Mutiny: 1857*, London 2002, pp. 9, 19,
28–31; Eric Stokes, *The Peasant Armed: The Indian Revolt of 1857*,
ed. C. A. Bayly, Oxford 1986, pp. 1–16.

136.  'The Indian Army', *Economist*, 4 July 1857.

137.  'India', *Economist*, 18 July 1857; 'Mind of the Mutiny', *Economist*,
19 September 1857; 'Delhi, Moghul and British Civilization', *Economist*, 31 October 1857.

138.  'The Indian Sufferers', *Economist*, 29 August 1857.

139. 'The Bright Side of the Picture', *Economist*, 26 September 1857.

140. 'The Indian Crisis of the Past Year', *Economist*, 2 January 1858.

141. 'The Treatment of the Sepoy Mutineers', *Economist*, 27 February 1858; 'The Military Policy of Lord Canning's Proclamation', 15 May 1858.

142. Tim Dyson, *A Population History of India: From the First Modern People to the Present Day*, Oxford 2014, p. 95.

143. *The Times*, 5 August 1859.

144. *The Times*, 5 October 1859 and 29 September 1859.

145. Barrington, *Life of Walter Bagehot*, London 1914, p. 286.

146. Barrington, *The Servant of All*, p. 145.

147. The *Economist* welcomed what was in effect the nationalization of the East India Company on precisely these grounds. Total net revenue was, it estimated, £22,000,000 in 1857, after debt interest payments. It assured holders of East India Company stocks and bonds (returning anywhere from 4 to 10 per cent per annum) that its obligations would now be counted as Indian Government debt – in line with Australia or Canada, and thus just as secure. 'The Financial Obligations of the East India Company', 2 January 1858.

148. Bagehot, *CW*, Vol. III, p. 344. While Wilson backed a state guarantee for the railway companies, he opposed a general guarantee on Indian debt. His opposition to the latter was based on the fiscal laxity such a guarantee might encourage in India. In practice, the reforms he had imposed, along with the direct political control now exercised by Britain, were sufficient – evidenced by the investment that flowed into India over the next two decades. See, V. G. Kale, *Dawn of Modern Finance in India*, Poona 1922, p. 51.

149. This exception to the rule of laissez-faire in the case of peoples considered primitive occurs throughout the work of Mill – thematically and chronologically, from political economy to politics. John Stuart Mill, *Principles of Political Economy*, London 1848, p. 366; John Stuart Mill, 'Considerations on Representative Government', in *On Liberty*, London 1861, p. 217. See Pitts, *A Turn to Empire*, pp. 123–60.

150. Bagehot, *CW*, Vol. III, p. 345.

151. *The Times*, 5 October 1859.

152. Bagehot, *CW*, Vol. III, p. 357.

153. Sabyasachi Battacharya, *Financial Foundations of the British Raj*, Simla 1971, pp. 4, 204–6; James Wilson, *Financial Statement*, Calcutta 1860, p. 9.

154. Bagehot, *CW*, Vol. III, p. 359.

155. Zhaojin Ji, *A History of Modern Shanghai Banking: The Rise and Decline of China's Finance Capitalism*, Armonk 2003, p. 43.

156. Cain and Hopkins, *British Imperialism*, p. 330; B. R. Tomlinson, 'India and the British Empire, 1880–1935', in *Indian Economic and Social History Review*, October 1975, pp. 337–80.

157. Cain and Hopkins, *British Imperialism*, pp. 338, 341, 342. For an

account of the Home Charges, see James Foreman-Peck, 'Foreign Investment and Imperial Exploitation: Balance of Payments Reconstruction for Nineteenth-Century Britain and India', *The Economic History Review*, August 1989, pp. 354–74.

158. Bagehot, *CW*, Vol. III, p. 359.
159. Wilson to Bagehot, 19 July 1860, in Ibid., pp. 358–59.
160. 'Sir Charles Trevelyan's Minute on Mr. Wilson's Budget', *Economist*, 12 May 1860; Indian Finance and the Madras Protest', 2 June 1860.
161. Class snobbery pervades Trevelyan's comments about Wilson. Humphrey Trevelyan, *The India We Left: Charles Trevelyan, 1826–65, Humphrey Trevelyan, 1929–47*, London 1972, pp. 78–87.
162. Bagehot, *CW*, Vol. III, pp. 354, 360–62.

## 2. Walter Bagehot's Dashed Doubts

1. W. David Clinton, *Tocqueville, Lieber, and Bagehot: Liberalism Confronts the World*, New York 2003, p. 2.
2. S. A. M. Westwater, 'Walter Bagehot: A Reassessment', *Antioch Review*, January 1977, p. 39; *CW*, Vol. XV, pp. 68–81.
3. J. M. Keynes, 'The Works of Bagehot', *Economic Journal*, September 1915, p. 369.
4. Wilson's *Congressional Government* (1885) made ample use of Bagehot's *English Constitution* to argue that the US suffered from a weak executive, which cabinet government on the English model might remedy. 'My desire and ambition are to treat the American Constitution as Mr. Bagehot … has treated the English Constitution. His book has inspired my whole study of our government', he confided to Ellen Axson in 1884. 'He brings to the work a fresh and original method which has made the British system much more intelligible to ordinary men than it was before, and which, if it could be successfully applied to the exposition of our federal constitution, would result in something like a revelation to those who are still reading *The Federalist* as an authoritative constitutional manual.' Ray S. Baker, *Woodrow Wilson: Life and Letters*, New York 1946, Vol. I, pp. 213–14. Though Wilson came to see the president as a more powerful office vis-à-vis Congress, he remained just as admiring of Bagehot, calling him a 'wit as well as a seer' in the *Atlantic* in 1898. For the *Atlantic* articles, see *CW*, Vol. XV, pp. 150–88; Mrs. Russell Barrington, *The Life of Walter Bagehot*, London 1914, p. 3.
5. *CW*, Vol. XV, pp. 216–19.
6. 'Times change, even the *Economist* changes a little', Macmillan reflected. 'Its format surprised me when it began. I used to remember it as rather a dull looking professorial paper that always rebuked me. Every article began, "Mr. Macmillan has now, in the last effort of this year, destroyed the British economy for ever." But it didn't seem to

matter very much. Now, however, I read it to get news about all parts of the world and it has become what is called "a very readable paper." Brilliantly edited and magnificently produced. When I was coming up today from Sussex I just wondered what Bagehot would have thought of it. I think on the whole he'd have liked it because it suits the age, it suits the time. It's practical, it's modern, it's objective, it's up to date. That's what he liked.' *CW*, Vol. XV, pp. 219–22.

7. Ferdinand Mount, *The British Constitution Now*, London 2011, p. 41.

8. Ferdinand Mount, 'All the Sad Sages', *London Review of Books*, February 2014, pp. 9–11.

9. Biographers include Richard Hutton, Bagehot's friend, in 1878; Emilie Barrington, his sister-in-law, in 1914; the *Economist* staffer Alastair Buchan in 1958; and official *Economist* historian Ruth Dudley Edwards in 1993. The only critical appraisal came from the poet and civil servant C. H. Sisson in 1972. Bagehot was, Sisson wrote in execration, the quintessential 'man of affairs', hateful of all that was artistic, primitive, rural or spiritual – 'a good laugh at the monarchy, a series of little jeers at the historical Church, a jealous look at the gentry'. In arts and letters, praise for Shakespeare's wise investments; aspersions on Coleridge, who was peculiar, 'walked around, talked to undergraduates or women, but did not do anything noticeable such as running a bank'. C. H. Sisson, *The Case of Walter Bagehot*, London 1972, pp. 127, 37.

10. Edith had 'attacks of delirium', thinking she was mute and smashing the bank windows. Bagehot could calm and amuse her and his half-brother, Vincent Estlin. 'Every trouble in life is a joke compared to madness', he once said. Alastair Buchan, *The Spare Chancellor: The Life of Walter Bagehot*, London 1959, p. 23; *CW*, Vol. XII, pp. 341–42.

11. Other students may have found Bagehot priggish for informing his landlord that two lodgers were skipping classes and Sunday services to consort with women. Norman St John-Stevas, 'Walter Bagehot: A Short Biography', in *CW*, Vol. I, pp. 39, 41–42.

12. A Covent Garden meeting in 1844 was memorable for O'Connell's voice, its 'higher tones very dignified and impressive, and the lower ones very sweet', his fiery attack on slavery, and his linking the cause of Free Trade and Irish Freedom. James Wilson, also present, was remarkable to Bagehot at this time for being visibly annoyed by the cheers for O'Connell that kept interrupting his own speech. Barrington, *Life of Walter Bagehot*, pp. 11, 122.

13. Barrington, *Life of Walter Bagehot*, p. 177.

14. *CW*, Vol. XII, pp. 274–75.

15. Jonathan Sperber, *The European Revolutions, 1848–51*, Cambridge 2005.

16. The coup was illegal. But 'no legal or constitutional act could have given an equal confidence', and elections, due in May, would have

been violent if 'preceded by six months' famine among the starvable classes'. *CW*, Vol. IV, pp. 30–36.

17. Bagehot, wrote Hutton, 'not only eulogized the Catholic Church, but supported the Prince-President's military violence, attacked the Freedom of the Press in France, maintained that the country was wholly unfit for Parliamentary government – and worst of all perhaps – insinuated a panegyric on Louis Napoleon himself, asserting that he had been far better prepared for the duties of a statesmen by gambling on the turf, than he would have been by poring over the historical and political dissertations of the wise and the good.' *CW*, Vol. XV, pp. 106–7.

18. *CW*, Vol. XII, p. 329.

19. 'The spirit of generalisation, which, John Mill tells us, honourably distinguishes the French mind has come to this, that every Parisian wants his head tapped in order to get the formulae and nonsense out of it.' Ibid., p. 328. To his father, he boasted of breakfasting in the Palais Royal, after climbing the railings, and reminding himself not to run: 'it is a bad habit to run in a Revolution, somebody may think you are the "other side" and shoot you.' 'I am pleased', he concluded wearily, 'to have had an opportunity of seeing it *once* but once is enough, as there is, I take it, a touch of sameness in this kind of sight.' Barrington, *Life of Walter Bagehot*, pp. 194–96. His mother received a delighted confession: 'I am in short what they would call a *réactionnaire*'. 'And I think I am with the majority – a healthy habit for a young man to contract.' 'I wish for the President decidedly myself as against M. Thiers and his set in the Parliamentary World; even *I* can't believe in a Government of barristers and newspaper editors, and also as against the Red party, who though not insincere, are too abstruse and theoretical for a plain man.' *CW*, Vol. XII, p. 326.

20. Barrington, *Life of Walter Bagehot*, pp. 56–57.

21. Bagehot to Killigrew Wait, 5 January 1853, in Barrington, *Life of Walter Bagehot*, pp. 211–12.

22. Ibid., pp. 62, 357. If, in addition, a 'genius' ventured an opinion on political economy, he received a swat. Ruskin earned his share, as the title of an *Economist* article Bagehot devoted to him attests: 'Aesthetic Twaddle versus Political Economy', 18 August 1860.

23. *CW*, Vol. I, pp. 189–90, 213, 406–8. At times playing both sides of the street, or what he called, after St Paul, his 'divided nature', weighed on Bagehot. 'Taken as a whole, the universe is absurd', he declared during these years, struck by the incongruity between the human mind and its employments. 'How can a *soul* be a merchant? What relation to an immortal being have the price of linseed, the fall of butter, the tare on tallow, or the brokerage on hemp? Can an undying creature debit "petty expenses", and charge for "carriage paid"?' Gertrude Himmelfarb, *Victorian Minds*, New York 1968, p. 222; 'The First Edinburgh Reviews', in *CW*, Vol. I, p. 338.

24. Barrington, *Life of Walter Bagehot*, pp. 225–28.

25. Ibid.

26. CW, Vol. XIII, p. 547.
27. Barrington, *Life of Walter Bagehot*, pp. 231–33.
28. Ibid., pp. 391–92.
29. Sisson, *Case of Walter Bagehot*, pp. 48–55. Bagehot confided the torment he continued to feel over his defeat to the Metaphysical Society during a dinner at the Grosvenor Hotel in 1870, reprinted in the *Contemporary Review* as 'On the Emotion of Conviction'. For years after his defeat, no matter how hard he reasoned, 'I had the deepest conviction that I should be "Member for *Bridgwater*"', he told the assembled members. 'Even still, if I allow my mind to dwell on the contest, if I think of the hours I was ahead in the morning, and the rush of votes at two o'clock by which I was defeated, – and even more, if I call up the image of the nomination day, with all the people's hands outstretched, and all their excited faces looking the more different on account of their identity in posture, the old feeling almost comes back upon me, and for a moment I believe that I shall be Member for Bridgwater.' *The Contemporary Review*, London 1871, p. 33.
30. Bagehot had a high opinion of Gladstone. He nevertheless made constructive criticisms from time to time, urging the necessity of defence spending, for example. Bagehot also wanted to make income tax permanent – another point against Bright, who preferred to abolish the income tax along with tariffs and replace both with a property tax. On starting out as director Bagehot wrote to Gladstone, informing him that Wilson 'used to write the economical and financial articles in the paper mainly himself as well as direct its general policy; and both these departments have in some sort fallen to me'. Since 'the *Economist* has a certain influence over men of business whose opinions are not without importance on financial subjects', Bagehot was ready 'to call on you if there were anything which you thought the paper might discuss with advantage'. After Bagehot's death Gladstone wrote to his widow, Eliza, 'During the time when I was Chancellor of the Exchequer, I had the advantage of frequent and free communication with him on all matters of finance and currency.' CW, Vol. XIII, pp. 553–56.
31. 'For the first time in nearly thirty years there is the prospect of a Conservative majority in the House of Commons. It requires more thought than we have as yet had time to give to realize a state of things so new and so different from that to which we have been so long accustomed': 'The Conservative Majority', *Economist*, 7 February 1874.
32. Trustees should resist chasing after glossy advertisements as a source of revenue, 'always obtained by papers of good reputation and good sale'. CW, XIV, p. 426.
33. CW, XIV, London 1986, p. 424.
34. 'Nassau Senior', in CW, Vol. II, p. 379.
35. This was Bagehot's first published article. 'The Currency Monopoly', in CW, Vol. IX, p. 236.
36. Wilson had just released a pamphlet taken from his *Economist* leaders that opposed – along with Tooke and other representatives of the

'Banking School'– any interference in the financial sector, including the Bank Act of 1844. Bagehot quoted Wilson, in *Capital, Currency and Banking*, as having 'never been able to discover any good ground for the objections of a portion of even the most uncompromising free traders, against the application of the same principles to banking and especially to notes payable on demand.' Bagehot countered, 'the chief utility of unlimited competition is its quality of reducing the cost of production to the minimum which nature admits of ... but improvements in the process of coining brought about by the competition of individual coiners would have a different and less beneficial effect. What is wanted in money is *fixity* of value.' To Wilson he addressed another argument: 'If new banks of issue had been allowed to spring up during the railway mania, who can doubt that a large number of insolvent concerns would have come into existence, and have gone down at the first appearance of depression, leaving the holders of their notes with papers not only inconvertible, but valueless?' CW, Vol. IX, pp. 244, 247.

37. Ibid., p. 235. At least in this early article laissez-faire is almost completely redefined. Bagehot says it must meet certain moral and political criteria before it can be applied. For Wilson laissez-faire was the force tending automatically to realize these goals and could never contradict them.

38. 'Who indeed will be bold enough to say that without some such tax the higher classes of this country would pay their fair contribution to the public revenue?' 'Equalisation of the Income Tax', 23 February 1861.

39. 'We believe there is no worse blunder as to the scope of political economy than that which would represent it as contrary to its laws thus to interfere with the natural working of the principle of supply and demand. The principle on which the whole science is based is that, when men know their own interest, and are left free to act as they please, they may be trusted to pursue it far more efficiently for themselves than by the State or any other power can pursue it for them. But children do not know their own interest, and if they did, are not free to act as they please.' Nor were the interests of parents and children identical. 'It was one of the greatest blunders economists ever made', Bagehot reiterated, 'to prejudice people against a true science by pushing it beyond its natural limits.' 'Government Protection for Children', 21 May 1864.

40. 'Advantages of State Ownership of Railways', 7 January 1865.

41. Bagehot put the trade union phenomenon in perspective: in some cases a little resistance on their part prevented wages from sinking below subsistence level, and at least they were not as bad as the Luddites, who 'years ago kept Nottinghamshire in terror'. Legal unions, new laws against intimidation, and the 'useful selfishness' natural to man would take care of the threat posed by these combinations. 'It was because the guilds were legal that they perished, not because they were

prohibited.' So 'allow new combinations to start easily, and they will be numerous enough, and competitive enough, to keep up the natural progress of society.' 'The Work of Trades Unions', 27 April 1867; 'The Effect of Trade Unions upon Wages and Prices', 13 July 1867. Bagehot urged that trade unions be given the status not of 'friendly societies' but of London clubs like the Athenaeum. 'The Trades Union Bill', 10 July 1869.

42. 'We need scarcely say a word as to his claim for the extension of the suffrage to all adult women', he wrote in 'Mill's Address to the Electors of Westminster' on 29 April 1865. 'No party, and scarcely any individual politician save himself, holds this theory.' Bagehot's view of the lower classes also applied to the women in their ranks. 'Out of the two or three million of women whom he [Mill] would thus endow – including half-a-million maid-servants – not above ten thousand would have any political opinions at all, or any *political* preferences for one candidate over another; and that in consequence to give them votes would merely be giving extra votes vicariously to their fathers, their husbands, their masters, their lovers, or their priests.' Even if women were as 'enlightened and rational' as Mill thought them – something Bagehot doubted – 'conceive the position of an unhappy woman, embracing his views, to whom an "advanced Liberal," a Radical of Mr Bright's school, stood in any of the relations we have specified! How she would be snubbed by her father, boudé by her husband, deserted by her lover, bullied by her master, and excommunicated by her priest!' See also, 'Women's Claim to Registration', *Economist*, 19 September 1868; 'Suffrage for Women', 7 May 1870.

43. 'Postulates of Political Economy' appeared in the *Fortnightly Review* in February and May 1876. *CW*, Vol. XI, p. 222.

44. Classical theorists, from Smith to Ricardo – with supplements from James Mill, Senior, Torrens, McCulloch and John Stuart Mill – were more instructive than either the German or neo-classical newcomers. *CW*, Vol. XI, p. 234.

45. Michael Edelstein, 'Foreign Investment and Accumulation 1860–1914', in *The Economic History of Britain since 1700*, eds. Roderick Floud and Deirdre McCloskey, Cambridge 1994, Vol. II, pp. 173–76.

46. *CW*, Vol. XI, p. 233.

47. Ibid., p. 230. English political economy was still imperfect, Bagehot admitted. As in his first texts, a criticism of the unbridled laissez-faire he found in the *Economist* of the 1840s is evident. Its laws did not apply everywhere or at all times, though increasingly they would, as one country after another began to imitate England. 'A similar money market, a similar competing trade based on large capital, gradually tends to arise in all countries.' He also claimed to scale back its pretensions. 'Our political economy does not profess to prove this growing world to be a good world – far less, to be the best. Abroad the necessity of contesting socialism has made some writers use the conclusions

brought out by our English science for that object. But the aim of that science is far more humble; it says these and these forces produce these and these effects, and there it stops. It does not profess to give a moral judgment on either; it leaves it for a higher science, and one yet more difficult, to pronounce what ought and what ought not to be.' Ibid., p. 238.

48. Barrington, *Life of Walter Bagehot*, pp. 373–76.

49. Ibid., p.23.

50. Ibid., p. 399; Gladstone Papers, BL, Add. MS 44410, ff 154, 204–5. Overend, Gurney & Co. made its name in the bills of exchange business before plunging into financial investment, and the longer-term lending required for railways and shipyards. Short-term deposits were being used to finance long-term investments in overpriced assets, inflated by a stock market boom; when the market crashed, depositors rushed to withdraw, and the bank was exposed as insolvent. For the *Economist* on the crisis, see 'Overend, Gurney and Co', 15 July 1865; 'What a Panic Is and How It Might Be Mitigated', 12 May 1866; 'The Practical Effect of the Act of 1844', 26 May 1866; 'Overend, Gurney and Co., Limited and Unlimited', 16 June 1866.

51. *Lombard Street* in CW, IX, London 1978, p. 147.

52. Ibid., pp. 64–65. Ashworth characterizes *Lombard Street* as 'ramming home' that the Bank had 'the responsibility of maintaining a reserve big enough to meet the needs of all England'. After its publication, 'both in theory and practice no one doubted that England was a country with one single reserve for its whole financial system.' William Ashworth, *An Economic History of England, 1870–1939*, London 1960, pp. 165, 170.

53. *Lombard Street*, p. 55.

54. Ibid., p. 82.

55. Ibid., pp. 214, 81.

56. Ibid., p.155.

57. Ibid., p. 167.

58. Edelstein, 'Foreign Investment', in *Economic History of Britain since 1700*, p. 173; Eric Hobsbawm, *Age of Capital*, London 1976, pp. 190–94; Larry Allen, *The Global Financial System 1750–2000*, London 2001, pp. 176–78.

59. *The English Constitution* in CW, Vol. V, p. 206.

60. 'The mass of Englishmen are not fit for an elective government; if they knew how near they were to it, they would be surprised, and almost tremble.' CW, Vol. V, pp. 240, 379–80. Cobden had earlier used similar language. In an 1838 letter to his brother from Prussia, Cobden praised its government, comparing it to the 'English constitution – a thing of monopolies, and Church-craft, and sinecures, armorial hocus pocus, primogeniture and pageantry'. What tickled Bagehot appalled Cobden, however: Wendy Hinde, *Richard Cobden: A Victorian Outsider*, New Haven 1987, p. 55. The same sort of analysis – with inverted judgment – is to be found in Marx. What the

author of *Capital* derisively called the 'executive committee of the bourgeoisie' was, for Bagehot, the very best feature of parliamentary government in England.

61. *CW*, Vol. XV, p. 81.

62. In 1859, Bagehot fretted that the reform bills beginning to snake their way through the Commons might – even accidentally – enfranchise a substantial number of workers. To guard against 'ultra-democracy' he proposed a complex, varying franchise, in which ratepayers in the largest towns (above 75,000) could vote. This meant only the top layer of workers, 'self-taught artisans', who merited 'special representation' because of their 'active intellects' and 'self-sufficient dispositions'. The unskilled masses and smaller town dwellers did not count, while farm workers, 'with low wages and little knowledge, have no views and no sentiments which admit of parliamentary expression'. In this way, the lower orders would gain no more than 50 MPs out of a total of 658. *CW*, Vol. VI, pp. 196, 203, 226–27.

63. 'Conservative Criticism of Liberal Politics', 25 February 1860; 'Plurality of Votes: The True Principle of a Reform Bill', 24 March 1860.

64. 'Considerations on Representative Government', 11 May 1861. The Labour politician Richard Crossman noted the overlap between Mill and Bagehot in his introduction to a 1963 edition of the *English Constitution*, while observing some resentment on the part of the latter over the 'ascendency' of the former. For Crossman, Bagehot was partly justified in this: he had gone beyond the 'paper description' of the constitution offered up by Mill in *Representative Government*, thanks to 'the role he [Bagehot] allots to the Cabinet ... a new central authority which could manage the state'. Mill relied on 'the old-fashioned notion of a division of power between the executive and the legislature'. Crossman, 'Introduction', in Walter Bagehot, *The English Constitution*, London 1963, pp. 8–9.

65. 'Plurality of Votes', 24 March 1860. Indignant at this swipe from the *Daily News*, Bagehot ended: 'Now, which is the true Liberalism – the Liberalism which contends that the true ideal of Parliament is to have the largest number of really organic interests and ideas meeting together in the representative assembly, to try each other's strength and weakness – or that which deprecates such a true representation of the intellect of the nation on the ground that if a particular class *happens* to be the largest in every constituency, it is the "natural" or even "Providential" arrangement to let the voice of no other class be heard at all?' 'True Liberalism and Reform', 27 January 1866.

66. 'Experience and Reform', 5 May 1860.

67. 'The Defeat of the Ministry and the Prospects of Reform', 2 April 1859; 'The Practical Difficulties of Secret Voting', 2 September 1859.

68. 'There *only* lower the franchise', he wrote. Even there, lest this 'throw the most intelligent part of the country into the exclusive power of the least intelligent inhabitants,' there should be three members with each voter given three votes, ensuring 'the rich and cultivated one

member at least; for they would always be a large minority, and any minority greater than a fourth is by this sure of a vote'. 'A Simple Plan of Reform', 24 December 1864.

69. 'I prefer to cite the following article, stating the same plan, which appeared in *The Economist*', Bagehot wrote of his practical 'scheme of Reform'. At the end he added, sensing perhaps that the tide of public opinion and the moods of both the Liberal and Conservatives had shifted, 'I do not know whether such a scheme as this is now possible. Perhaps the passions of men have become too excited, and a far more commonplace plan is all which can now be hoped for. But I am sure it was possible when the above article was written, and that it would have saved us from many evils.' *CW*, Vol. VI, p. 351.

70. Crossman erred when he suggested that Bagehot, unlike Mill, thought it was possible to do without electoral reform. He probably ignored his output for the *Economist*. Crossman, 'Introduction', *The English Constitution*, pp. 9–10.

71. *CW*, Vol. V, pp. 208, 299.

72. 'A permanent combination of them would make them (now that so many of them have the suffrage) supreme in the country. So long as they are not taught to act together, there is a chance of this being averted, and it can only be averted by the greatest wisdom and the greatest foresight in the higher classes.' Ibid., pp. 173–74.

73. 'The New Reform Bill', 2 March 1867

74. 'It is plain that what we used to call our public opinion upon the constitution of the House of Commons, was not an opinion based on proof and due to inquiry, but only a chance impression', he wrote in April 1867. 'The extreme weakness and moveableness of what we thought rooted opinions, has been concealed from us for many years, because the questions most eagerly discussed have been questions of foreign policy, and upon these where the data are so difficult to learn and change from day to day, it is no dishonour to change an opinion quickly and rapidly. A fixed judgment on changing facts is, as men of business know, the most dangerous thing in the world. But here at home, and upon a much discussed question like Reform, there ought to have been no room for change.' 'The Painful Moral of Present Politics', 20 April 1867.

75. 'Why has the "Settlement" of 1832 So Easily Melted Away?', 1 June 1867.

76. Queen Victoria was not amused by this attitude to her person, much less her constitutional powers (reduced by Bagehot to consultation, encouragement, warning, and acting as camouflage for the cabinet). George V recalled that she was 'quite displeased' that he had been reading 'such a radical writer': Daniel Craig, 'Bagehot's Republicanism', in *The Monarchy and the British Nation, 1780 to the Present*, ed. Andrzej Olechnowicz, Cambridge 2007, p. 139.

77. 'The Lords will pass the great coming change, and the Queen will ratify it without a substantial doubt, and without material amendment. The

elaborate checks on the power of the House of Commons, on which Blackstone and others so often insist, have now – just when they were wanted, if ever – ceased to act, and been unheard of.' These were the main reasons 'why this great revolution – a greater revolution, probably than that of 1832 – has been so noiseless and so silent. Let us hope that its results may be as quiet and unnoticed, for then, perhaps, they will be good.' 'Why has the "Settlement" of 1832 So Easily Melted Away?', 1 June 1867.

78. 'The most essential mental quality for a free people, whose liberty is to be progressive, permanent, and on a large scale ... is much *stupidity*. I need not say that, in real sound stupidity, the English are unrivalled.' Bagehot asked readers to imagine a House of Commons composed only of witty *litterateurs* like Disraeli. 'It would be what M. Proudhon said of some French assemblies, "a box of matches".' 'Letters on the French Coup d'État', in *CW*, Vol. IV, pp. 50–51.

79. *CW*, Vol. IV, p. 81. The link between national character and political structure remained crucial for Bagehot. The idea that there were certain rights, or one form of government, which ought to obtain at all times and places was an error that confused politics with ethics – as if you had 'no more right to deprive a Dyak of his vote in a "possible" Polynesian assembly, than you have to steal his mat.' 'There are breeds in animal man just as in the animal dog'. 'When you hunt with greyhounds and course with beagles, then, and not till then, may you expect the inbred habits of a thousand years to pass away, that Hindoos can be free, or that Englishmen will be slaves.' Ibid., pp. 48–52.

80. There is scant evidence for Varouxakis's claim that Bagehot – 'the best that Victorian political thought had to offer on French politics during the Second Empire' – reconsidered his position on the Second Empire in the 1860s. Georgios Varouxakis, *Victorian Political Thought on France and the French*, New York 2002, pp. 90, 170.

81. 'The Mercantile Evils of Imperialism', 31 August 1867.

82. Bagehot scorned these clever men on the hunt for a 'despot to work out their ideas'; if ever their utopias were enacted they stood a better chance of being hung. 'Any despot will do what he himself likes, and will root out new ideas ninety-nine times for once that he introduces them.' Even Matthew Arnold was guilty of Francophilia, and thus of trying to slip 'a yoke upon our minds and styles'. *CW*, Vol. VII, pp. 50–51.

83. 'France or England', 5 September 1863; 'The Emperor of the French', 5 December 1863.

84. 'The Gravity and Difficulty of Affairs in France', 7 August 1869. France could not enjoy English-style liberty, because it had a national character without deference, and hated its bourgeoisie as much as its nobility: 'Her passion for equality is so great that she will sacrifice everything to it. Free government involves privilege, because it requires that more power should be given to the instructed than the

uninstructed: there is no method by which men can be both free and equal.' 'France or England', 5 September 1863.

85. 'The Emperor of the French', 5 December 1863.

86. 'Caesareanism as It Now Exists', 4 March 1865.

87. 'The Mercantile Evils of Imperialism', 31 August 1867.

88. 'Caesareanism as It Now Exists', 4 March 1865.

89. 'The Mercantile Evils of Imperialism', 31 August 1867. 'She cannot distribute the savings of France to the activity of France as London distributes our savings to our merchants': 'France and the Money Market', 14 December 1867. Bagehot was well aware of the French banking innovation, the *Crédit Mobilier*, but while impressed with its profits, he did not think its model of realizing them – playing the bourse with a limited amount of capital – would allow it to invest in infrastructural projects (aside from railways) on a very large scale. See, 'The Credit Mobilier and Banking Companies in France', *National Review*, January 1857, Vol. IV, in *CW*, Vol. X, pp. 341–71.

90. 'His position is too great to be lightly risked. He takes infinite pains to avert all chance of failure.' 'The Emperor of the French', 28 November 1863.

91. 'The times are changed since eager rulers dragged reluctant peoples into war. Now, it is the people who are ready to fight, and monarchs and ministers who hold them back.' For 'we believe that both Count Bismarck and Napoleon are anxious to avoid a rupture ... and will do all that can be done to avert it.' 'Continental Alarms', 5 October 1867; 'France and the Money Market', 14 December 1867.

92. 'The Emperor's Letter', 26 March 1870.

93. 'To account for such conduct we have to abandon all recent ideas ... and forget our experience of him as an important statesman and as for years one of the conservators and guardians of peace in Europe.' 'The Declaration of War by France', 16 July 1870.

94. Bagehot attributed the shocking collapse of the French army, considered the most potent fighting force on the continent, to the reluctance of the French peasants to fight, shifting his admiration to the victors of the moment. King Wilhelm IV, who officered his army with nobles – 'a strong guarantee for *esprit de corps*' – represented a more efficient regime type; one that, for all its atavistic qualities, had the support, said Bagehot, of the right sort. 'An hereditary king, strong in the affection of an aristocracy near his throne, and of a middle class that shows an educated preference for the old dynasty, has no need to fear the displeasure of the lowest among the population.' 'The Collapse of Caesarism', 20 August 1870.

95. 'The Emperor Napoleon', 11 January 1873.

96. 'The Lessons of the Plebiscite', 14 May 1870. The year before, he urged moderation on grounds that a revolution in France was bound to be a setback for the liberal cause in Europe. 'A defeat of French Liberals is not their defeat only; it is a defeat of *all Liberals*.' 'The Gravity and Difficulty of Affairs in France', 7 August 1869.

97. Popular political apathy, 'a blind popular feeling once fairly on the wane', along with a monarch bound by liberal principles, was 'the best conceivable cement for a political system'. 'That is what we have in England. The liberals of France will do well to avail themselves of the advantages offered by the present situation to secure a similar combination of political advantages for France.' 'The Liberals and the Emperor', 21 May 1870.

98. Much of this piece was directed against the 'defenders of the Commune in England'. 'The Destruction in Paris of What the World Goes to See at Paris', 27 May 1871.

99. Bagehot lampooned the radical republican members of the Commune like a banker rejecting a loan applicant with no collateral: *their* republic was 'associated with absurdly superstitious hopes', arising from a 'sort of belief among the reds that the proclamation of a Republic was a mystical expiation which would save Paris', 'screamed and wept over from balconies', worshipped as if it were 'a feminine deity', or as if on hearing its name 'enemies would sheathe their swords, and the proletariat in great European capitals would rise in their might, and forbid further bloodshed'. Thiers seemed the man to 'shake off all delirium, and face the alarming facts of conquest and an empty Exchequer'. 'Constitutional Tendencies in France', 14 September 1872.

100. Ibid. Thiers was hailed again the next year, on semantic grounds, for his 'astute policy of gradually accustoming France to associate order and strength, and a certain limited amount of liberty, with the name and form of a republic.' 'The Imperialist Manifesto', 25 January 1873.

101. 'Why an English Liberal May Look without Disapproval on the Progress of Imperialism in France', 6 June 1874. Bagehot tried to impress upon Liberals in England the necessity of what seemed illiberal measures in France, where the constant threat of a redistributive revolution was nipping the latest wave of capitalist development in the bud. 'In England we have always had a secure government, and we find it difficult to bring home to our imaginations the evil of wanting it. But if we lost it, no people would suffer half so much. The whole industrial life of England is based in an unexampled degree on credit and confidence, and that credit and confidence the faintest idea of a revolution would at once destroy. It would be worse than a mercantile panic many times over. If our system of credit is so delicate as to be shaken by the failure of Overend, Gurney & Co., it would collapse into ruins at the fall of Queen Victoria. We must imagine Lombard street to be for months in possession of the roughs, and then we shall understand what it is which Frenchmen fear.' 'The Prospects of Bonapartism in France', 30 May 1874.

102. 'French Politics', 20 June 1874. The French, he granted, were a little too discerning to fall for the royal ruse that kept power in England in the hands of the middle and aristocratic classes. '"A king who

reigns but does not govern" is a sort of logical nondescript.' 'The only monarchy possible in France is the Empire, and that is one not based on English ideas but on the very opposite of English ideas. A French copy of the English Constitution must not be one of its exterior but one of its interior'. 'A Suggestion for the Future Government of France', 15 August 1874.

103. 'The Conservative Republic', 6 March 1875. Pierre Rosanvallon has praised Bagehot as one of the few modern thinkers to attempt a positive definition of Caesarism. *La Democratie inachevée: Histoire de la Souveraineté du Peuple en France*, Paris 2000, p. 219.

104. 'Limits of the Principle of Nationalities', 18 June 1864. The Austro-Hungarian Empire was an exception, incapable of a 'national life' in a liberal age in which 'unity is all but necessary', because the peoples within it had no common feeling, different rights, and 'did not understand each other'. Switzerland was another exception, albeit in the opposite sense, showing that a heterogeneous state 'may maintain a free life, though three languages are spoken in its Parliament, and though more than three races make up its population', but only under the extreme threat of external enemies. 'The Gains of the World by the Two Last Wars in Europe', 18 August 1866.

105. 'The Influence of Foreign Anxieties upon the Money Market', 24 August 1867.

106. 'M. Mazzini's Manifesto', 11 October 1862. At the time of Mazzini's death, Bagehot paid tribute to a 'political force' whose talents, though used 'for impossible, and therefore anarchic ends', had 'revivified the political life of Italy and furnished the raw materials of which the great political strategy of Count Cavour was able to make such wonderful use'. Despite his flaws Mazzini 'was by no means like Garibaldi'. 'He was a half-way house between the "inspired idiot" of Caprera and the wily diplomatist of Turin.' 'Mazzini', 16 March 1872.

107. 'Prince Bismarck's Foreign Policy', 10 April 1875.

108. The influx of capital into Egypt, India and elsewhere went hand in hand with a more competitive imperial order – seeking to ensure reliable cotton supplies, and pushing peasants into cultivating it – according to Sven Beckert, *Empire of Cotton: A Global History*, New York 2014, pp. 243, 247–49.

109. 'The Probability of an American War', 14 December 1861.

110. 'The True Attitude of the Government of This Country Towards the Federal States', 25 April 1863. One member of his entourage did receive praise, the financial architect of the war, Treasury Secretary Salmon P. Chase. 'If the American war closed now, history could only say that Mr. Lincoln was a vulgar man with some respectability and a little humour, and that Mr. Chase had got much money under great political difficulties and with very little taxation.' 'Mr. Chase's Resignation', 23 July 1864.

111. 'Mr. Lincoln's Re-Election', 26 November 1864.

112. 'English Opinion as Distinguished from English Action on American Questions', 31 October 1863. After his re-election Bagehot described Lincoln as 'a person whose words are mean even when his actions are important'.

113. The electoral process was one of the worst sources of constitutional inefficiency exposed by the Civil War. In order to stand a chance of winning the Electoral College, each party 'selects at a preliminary caucus the most unexceptional member whom they can find'. 'If the wit of man had devised a system specially adapted to bring to the head of affairs an incompetent man at a pressing crisis, it could not have devised one more fit': 'The Practical Operation of the American Constitution at Present Extreme Crisis', 1 June 1861. Once elected, the president had to wait months to take office, which had given the rebels time to plan, while Lincoln fretted over 'petty details of patronage'. The entire system turned on the presidential cycle. 'Great questions, public duties, political efficiency, are secondary' to these contests, where, every four years, 'every political office, large and small, changes hands' and 'the whole patronage of the country is turned into one great bribe': 'The Practical Operation of the American Constitution at Present Extreme Crisis', 1 June 1861.

114. 'The Last Probabilities of War and Peace', 21 December 1861.

115. 'The Practical Operation of the American Constitution at Present Extreme Crisis', 1 June 1861. Laws and manners had degenerated. Whereas leaders 'in Washington's time were gentlemen and men of education' and 'institutions were free, but not democratic', now 'dirtier and rougher men' had taken over, who 'truckled and temporized and cajoled and cringed and fawned upon the mob' to get elected. 'The constitution has become an almost unmitigated *ochlocracy*.' 'What May Be in America', 17 August 1861.

116. 'Presidential and Ministerial Governments Compared', 13 December 1862. Not only was a parliament better at choosing leaders than the masses – the 'Commons sees Lord Palmerston every day; the American people never saw Mr. Lincoln at all' – it was very easily rid of them. 'If Lord Palmerston should be unequal to a sudden exigency, we can seek elsewhere.' A large, modern nation such as America could not ask voters to weigh in constantly. 'The mass of the people are occupied in their own affairs, busy with their own trade, their profession, or their idleness.' 'The nation *en masse* is indifferent ... the popular mind is at sea; it cannot elect for itself; and it falls into the guidance of professional electors (President-maker is the American word)': 'The Defect of America', 6 December 1862.

117. A prime minister, in contrast, was a 'tenant-at-will'. This was preferable since in four years 'a Crimean war or an Indian mutiny may introduce on a sudden elements of incalculable force which no one could anticipate': 'The Last Probabilities of War and Peace', 21 December 1861. 'The worst defect of a presidential government is, that it *leases* for a stated term the supremacy to a single man,

without the possibility of knowing beforehand whether he will be fit to control and master the unforeseen': 'The Defect of America', 6 December 1862.

118. 'Presidential and Ministerial Governments Compared', 13 December 1862.

119. Congress could not even stage a vote of want of confidence, nor could the president or members of his cabinet face their critics there. 'Those who act cannot speak, and those who speak cannot act.' As a result, Lincoln was unaccountable for his inept war policies. The indecisive conduct of the Civil War on the Northern side had revealed 'what was for the most part unknown in Europe, – the *bureaucratic* character of the American people': 'The Invasion of the Federal States', 11 July 1863.

120. 'The trifling disasters of the English before Sebastopol excited more rage in England than the gigantic defeats of the Northern armies have excited in America': see 'The Federal Constitution Responsible for Federal Apathy', 10 January 1863. Bagehot later elaborated on 'the terrible waste of the highest educating capacity' in presidential forms of government, citing as an example a battle between then Secretary of the Treasury, Hugh McCulloch, 'a man of remarkable knowledge and ability', who held sound views on currency ('for example, that government can no more create money by its bare fiat than it can create coals or tallow') and Congress, which did not. See, 'The Refusal to Impeach President Johnson', 14 December 1867.

121. The need for a 'dictatorship' extended past the present crisis. Bagehot wondered how even mundane tasks – the dismissal of a popular general, overriding 'crotchety states' – would work in the absence of this unique moral force, this 'good and benevolent, but restless temporary despot', 'who really reverenced civil liberty and could tolerate venomous opposition' and whose authority could thus 'never be directed to ends wholly disapproved by the ways of those who conferred it': 'The Assassination of Mr. Lincoln', 29 April 1865.

122. 'The Disruption of the Union, as It Would Affect England', 19 January 1861.

123. 'America', 8 June 1861.

124. 'Recognition or Mediation', 18 October 1862. The impossibility of conquering the South was a constant refrain. 'We *know* that a restoration of real union, of voluntary union by arms is impossible': 'America', 1 August 1863.

125. 'Fall of Richmond and Its Affect upon English Commerce', 22 April 1865.

126. 'What May Be in America', 17 August 1861.

127. 'Our Duty', 30 November 1861.

128. 'Will There Be an American War?', 7 December 1861. In happier days they were already 'the most punctilious, overbearing, and contentious government which the world has ever seen'; now, 'in the

false shame of humiliated pride', they were becoming unbearable. 'Mercantile Difficulties of the American Civil War', 25 May 1861.

129. 'Shall the Blockade Be Respected', 25 January 1862.

130. 'English Feeling Toward America', 28 September 1861.

131. In 1853 Bagehot wrote Hutton, then in the West Indies, 'Have you seen anything of the blacks? It can't be a pretty study, but it may be an instructive one. People are quite wild here again about slavery, as strong as they ever were when there was a *bona fide* agitation in this country on the point. I should like to know accurately what comes from emancipation, taking it as a question of sacrifices. I can imagine many cases in which slavery is good for a population, but none or not many in which *traders* can be trusted to be slave owners. It may answer in rural villages where they only supply their own demand, and where the notion of the slaves being "capital" is extremely secondary, but never in a mercantile community where that notion is the main one and the notion of moral and personal dependence extremely faint': *CW*, Vol. XII, p. 30. Bagehot took a similar line in 'The American Constitution at the Present Crisis', a long essay in the *National Review* in October 1861. (*CW*, Vol. IV, p. 295). But both there and in *Physics and Politics*, first published serially in the *Fortnightly Review* from 1867 to 1872, he also saw the merits of slavery at given times and places. 'The evils which we have endured from slavery in recent ages must not blind us to, or make us forget, the great services that slavery rendered in early ages', he wrote, citing Aristotle, Wakefield, and the Bible in support. 'Refinement is only possible when leisure is possible; and slavery first makes it possible.' Though such fine feelings have 'no market value in the early bidding of nations', their result, 'originality in war', did. 'Slave-owning nations, having time to think, are likely to be more shrewd in policy, and more crafty in strategy': *CW*, Vol. VII, pp. 58–59.

132. General Lee's failed invasion of the North in 1863 was regrettable for it could have forced it to come to terms. 'Though we wish the South to be independent, we wish it to be weak': 'Shall the Blockade Be Respected?', 25 January 1862.

133. 'America', 1 August 1863.

134. 'The Disruption of the Union as It Would Affect England', 19 January 1861.

135. 'American Complaints Against England', 14 September 1861.

136. 'English Opinion as Distinguished from English Action on American Questions', 31 October 1863.

137. Marx cited the *Economist* frequently in his journalism, criticizing it in 1861 and 1862 for back-pedalling on the Emancipation Proclamation ('all cant') and stoking patriotic hysteria in Britain over the Trent Affair. He also relied on it for facts and figures on US cotton and wheat imports, and for glimpses of ideological clarity ('the cloven foot peeps out'). Karl Marx, *The Civil War in the United States*, New York 1961, pp. 5, 12–13, 42–43, 128, 145–46.

138. 'The Monroe Doctrine in 1823 and 1863', 14 November 1863.
139. 'Negotiations for Peace', 18 February 1865.
140. 'Abandonment of Transportation', 25 February 1865.
141. 'Mr. Gladstone on Home Rule for Ireland', 30 September 1871.
142. 'The Conservative Majority', 7 February 1874.
143. 'The Irish Viceroyalty', 21 October 1876. David Clinton paints a misleading picture of Bagehot as 'anticolonial', in part by ignoring Ireland, but also because he focuses so exclusively on Bagehot's opposition to British intervention in the 'Eastern Question' in the last two years of his life. While this lends some support to the idea that Bagehot was wary of armed meddling in European affairs, it leaves out his attitude to the Empire, and all that came before 1875. His vehemence from this point on has more to do with hostility to a Conservative government led by Disraeli, whom he despised, than Clinton allows. Clinton, *Tocqueville, Lieber, and Bagehot*, pp. 76, 96–97, 100–102.
144. In championing 'a purely muscular morality', Carlyle and his intellectual allies, including John Ruskin and Charles Dickens, were behaving irresponsibly. 'It is far more painful to witness their serious errors – because they ought to know better – than to read of the crimes and blunders of the poor coloured folk of Jamaica, whose very inferiority should have secured them the justest treatment.' 'Mr. Carlyle on Mr. Eyre', 15 September 1866.
145. 'It is probably the destiny, it is even now the function, it is certainly the interest of the European, and more particularly of the English family of mankind to guide and urge and control the industrial enterprises of all Asia, of all Africa, and of those portions of America settled by African, Asiatic, or hybrid races.' The 'scientific organization' of labour to achieve maximum result at minimum of cost, 'without strikes or quarrels' was 'secured, it must freely be acknowledged, by slavery' but this had 'moral and social consequences which are not beneficial'. 'Economic Value of Justice to the Dark Races', 9 December 1865; 'The Insurrection in Jamaica', 18 December 1865. See Bernard Semmel, *The Governor Eyre Controversy*, London 1962, pp. 115, 141, and Thomas C. Holt, *The Problem of Freedom: Race, Labor, and Politics in Jamaica and Britain 1832–1938*, Baltimore 1992, pp. 318–23.
146. 'Japan', 24 October 1863.
147. 'Japanese Offenses and British Retaliation', 7 November 1863. William Watson, 'The Namamugi Incident, 1862', *History Today*, May 1964, p. 325.
148. 'The Financial Effect of the Suez Canal Purchase', 27 November 1875; 'The Political Effect of the Suez Canal Purchase', 27 November 1875.
149. 'The Indian Viceroyalty', 5 December 1863. Did Bagehot once remark to Hutton, as the latter claimed, that 'he would have been glad to find a fair excuse for giving up India, for throwing the Colonies on

their own resources, and for persuading the English people to accept deliberately the place of a fourth or fifth rate European power?' Possibly, as dinner-table paradox. But there is nothing in his published writings, or private letters, to suggest he seriously held these views. CW, Vol. XV, p 119.

150. 'The New Mexican Empire', 22 August 1863. Buchan describes the *Economist*'s attitude to 'Napoleon's Mexican adventure' as being so critical that 'it is believed the British government put private pressure on Bagehot to modify its tone lest Anglo-French relations, which were then bad, became irretrievably embittered.' This seems very unlikely, and is based perhaps on a citation of Hutton's essay in the centenary volume. *The Economist 1843–1943*, p. 84.

151. CW, Vol. VII, pp. 64–72, 40. For more on race and national character in Bagehot, see Edward Beasley, *The Victorian Reinvention of Race: New Racisms and the Problem of Grouping in the Human Sciences*, New York 2010, pp. 78–80.

152. Sisson, *Case of Walter Bagehot*, p. 111.

153. For the rich, Harrison argued, political science attained 'absolute perfection' when it left their comfort alone, 'whilst parading a resultless activity under the name of self-government, freedom and progress. To such a one the grand glory of Parliament is that it does nothing – and does that nothing in a highly patriotic and constitutional manner.' 'Our Venetian Constitution', *Fortnightly Review*, March 1867, pp. 266, 270–71.

154. 'Mr. Gladstone', *National Review*, July 1860, in CW, Vol. III, pp. 429, 432, 438–39.

155. 'Very rarely, if ever in history, has a man achieved so much by his words – been victor in what was thought at the time to be a class-struggle – and yet spoken so little evil.' 'Mr Cobden', 8 April 1865.

156. 'Bolingbroke as a statesman', *National Review*, April 1863, in CW, Vol. IV, p. 160. Bagehot's 1863 pamphlet *Count Your Enemies and Economise Your Expenditure* singled out Cobden's *Three Panics* of the previous year: 'ever since we can remember he has objected to the magnitude of our armaments. He objected as much when they cost sixteen millions as now when they cost twenty-eight millions. Common sense tells us at once that there is something wrong here.' CW, Vol. IV, p. 48.

157. 'Principles of Political Economy', *Progressive Review*, 1848, in CW, Vol. XI, p. 193.

158. John Stuart Mill, 'French Affairs', *Daily News*, 6 August 1848, in *Collected Works of John Stuart Mill*, Vol. XV, Toronto 1986, pp. 1110–112. Mill's Parisian correspondents included not just Tocqueville, a critic of the revolution, but Louis Blanc, one of its leaders. Alan Ryan, *J. S. Mill*, London 1974, p. 183.

159. John Stuart Mill, *Principles of Political Economy*, in CW, Toronto 1965, Vol. III, pp. 775–76.

160. 'The crimes of the *parti de l'ordre* are atrocious, even supposing that

they are in revenge for those generally attributed to the Commune':
Mill to Frederic Harrison, [May?] 1871, in *The Later Letters of
John Stuart Mill 1849–1873*, eds. Francis E. Mineka and Dwight N.
Lindley, Toronto 1973, p. 1816.

161. 'On Representative Government', *Economist*, 18 May 1861. 'We
can agree with him on everything, except in the degree.' 'Mr. Mill's
Address to the Electors of Westminster', *Economist*, 29 April 1865.

162. 'Despotism is a legitimate mode of government in dealing with barbarians, provided the end be their improvement': John Stuart Mill,
*On Liberty*, London 1859, p. 23; 'Of the Government of Dependencies by a Free State', in *On Representative Government*, London
1861, pp. 313–40. For a thorough assessment of empire in Mill's
thought, see Jennifer Pitts, *A Turn to Empire: The Rise of Imperial
Liberalism in Britain and France*, Princeton 2005, pp. 138–60.

163. J. S. Mill, *England and Ireland*, London 1868, p. 37. 'Assessing Mill's
response to Fenianism involves entering an attitudinal labyrinth. He
disapproved of both the ends and means of Fenianism': Bruce L.
Kinzer, *England's Disgrace: J. S. Mill and the Irish Question*, Toronto
2001, pp. 169, 178, 181.

164. 'Mr. Mill on Ireland', *Economist*, 22 February 1968. Three years
earlier, the *Economist* published a series of letters from the economist
John Elliott Cairnes, who proposed to encourage peasant proprietor-
ship in Ireland with a bill to compensate tenants for improvements.
Mill wrote to Cairnes in January 1866: 'I have read several of your
letters in the *Economist* and admire them greatly', but as a remedy
this 'seems to fall far short of your premises': Kinzer, *England's Disgrace*, p. 182; 'Letters', *Economist*, September–November 1865.

165. Bagehot, 'Senior's Journals', *Fortnightly Review*, August 1871, in
*CW*, Vol. VII, p. 300.

166. See Alan S. Kahan, *Aristocratic Liberalism: The Social and Political
Thought of Jacob Burckhardt, John Stuart Mill, and Alexis De Tocqueville*, New York 1992, pp. 4, 156.

167. Desjobert was a disciple of Jean-Baptiste Say and one of a small
group of deputies to consistently oppose France's imperial designs in
Algeria. Alexis de Tocqueville, *Writings on Empire and Slavery*, ed.
Jennifer Pitts, Baltimore 2001, pp. xxiv, 5.

168. Alexis de Tocqueville, *Recollections*, New York 1970, pp. 39–40.

169. Alexis de Tocqueville, *Selected Letters on Politics and Society*, Berkeley 1985, p. 228.

170. Alexis de Tocqueville, *Democracy in America*, eds. Harvey Mansfield
and Delba Winthrop, Chicago 2000, p. 7. For a post–1848 shift, see
Domenico Losurdo, *Liberalism: A Counter-History*, London 2011,
p. 263.

171. 'The Crédit Mobilier and Banking Companies in France', January
1857, *CW* X, pp. 356–57; 'One Difference between France and
England', 12 September 1868; Buchan, *The Spare Chancellor*, p. 99;
Barrington, *Life of Walter Bagehot*, p. 235.

### 3. Edward Johnstone and the Aristocracy of Finance

1. David McLellan, *Karl Marx: A Biography*, Basingstoke 2006, p. 224.
2. Karl Marx, *The Eighteenth Brumaire of Louis Bonaparte*, New York 1963, p. 103.
3. Ibid., p. 101.
4. Ibid., p. 67.
5. 'Bagehot's Memorandum on the *Economist*, 1873' in *CW*, Vol. XIV, p. 424. The 'incalculable sums' London was ready to invest abroad by the 1870s needed tracking, for 'no incipient and no arrested civilisations ever had this facility before. What will be the effect on such civilisations now, no untutored mind can say.' 'Postulates of Political Economy', in *CW*, XI, p. 230. Bagehot's stress on the City's international role here, in 1876, represents a noticeable shift from his assessment of Lombard Street in 1873 as the conduit between 'the quiet saving districts of the country and the active employing districts.' 'Lombard Street', *CW*, IX, p. 53.
6. Lathbury wrote for a string of publications before the *Economist*, including the *Daily News*, the *Saturday Review*, and two connected with his friend Lord Acton, the *Home and Foreign Review* and the *Chronicle*. He remained a contributor after leaving, going on to edit the *Guardian*, the Church of England weekly, and eventually published the *Correspondence on Church and Religion of W.E. Gladstone* in 1910. 'Lathbury, Thomas (1798–1865)', Peter B. Nockles in *ODNB*, 2004; *Guardian*, 16 June 1922; *Times*, 15 June 1922.
7. Lewis Edwards, 'A Remarkable Family: The Palgraves', in *Remember the Days: Essays on Anglo-Jewish History*, ed. John M. Shaftesley, London 1966, pp. 303–22; 'Robert Harry Inglis Palgrave, Esq.', in *Bankers' Magazine*, Vol. XLVII, January to December 1887, pp. 35–38.
8. R. H. Inglis Palgrave, 'The Country Banker', *Quarterly Review*, January 1886, pp. 148–49. After resigning his editorship, Palgrave began a decades-long quest of the kind Bagehot had begun in *Economic Studies*, compiling a national dictionary of political economy published in three volumes between 1894 and 1899. 'Palgrave, Sir (Robert Harry) Inglis (1827–1919)', A. C. Howe in *ODNB*, 2004.
9. The *Times*'s City editor, Marmaduke B. Sampson, was a director of the Rothschilds' São Paulo Railway, and boosted Brazilian and Russian stocks, until 1874. Leland Hamilton Jenks, *The Migration of British Capital to 1875*, New York 1921, pp. 254–55, 399.
10. This sort of career path was common. Palgrave edited the *Bankers Almanack* until 1919. A. J. Wilson, his number two, started the *Investor's Review* in 1891. William Newmarch, the statistician who compiled the first price index under Bagehot, in collaboration with Tooke and Jevons, continued with journalism, and went into banking. *The Economist 1843–1943*, pp. 20–21, 33.
11. Edwards, *Pursuit of Reason*, pp. 325, 328, 333, 357.

12. 'The Retiring Editor of the "Economist"', *The Bankers' Magazine*, London 1907, Vol. LXXXIV, pp. 149–51.

13. John St Loe Strachey, *The Adventure of Living: A Subjective Autobiography*, London 1922, p. 180.

14. 'Mr Edward Johnstone', 13 December 1913.

15. Ibid.; Wayne Parsons, *The Power of the Financial Press*, Aldershot 1989, pp. 35–39.

16. David Landes, *The Unbound Prometheus*, Cambridge 1969, pp. 240–43.

17. P. J. Cain and A. G. Hopkins, *British Imperialism*, London 1993, pp. 173–79; Michael Edelstein, *Overseas Investment in the Age of High Imperialism*, New York 1982, p. 3. Overseas investment rates were cyclical and volatile, reaching as low as .6 per cent in 1877 and as high as 8.5 per cent in 1913. On whether capital was pushed out by falling returns at home, pulled out by high returns abroad, reflected inadequate domestic aggregate demand, or a combination of factors, see Edelstein, 'Foreign Investment and Accumulation 1860–1914', in *The Economic History of Britain since 1700*, eds. Roderick Floud and Deirdre McCloskey, Cambridge 1994, Vol. II, pp. 181–96.

18. Some have questioned how much Britain invested abroad, and whether doing so was profitable. For a downward revision, see D. C. M. Platt, 'British Portfolio Investment Overseas before 1870: Some Doubts', *Economic History Review*, February 1980, pp. 1–16. For claims that the Empire offered returns below those available in Britain after 1885 (based on the accounting records of 482 British firms), and burdened taxpayers with military costs two and a half times higher than in Germany or France, see Lance E. Davis and Robert A. Huttenback, *Mammon and the Pursuit of Empire: The Political Economy of British Imperialism, 1860–1912*, Cambridge 1986. George Paish relied on the *Economist* and the *Statist*, where he worked under Giffen, to lay 'the statistical and interpretive groundwork for all future research in this area' from 1909 to 1914. 'Paish, Sir George (1867–1957)', Roger Middleton in *ODNB*, 2004. More recently, Feinstein rejected Platt's 'doubts', in favour of the higher figures adduced by Paish, and the *Economist*. Charles Feinstein, 'Britain's Overseas Investments in 1913', *The Economic History Review*, May 1990, pp. 288–95. Edelstein used a sample of 566 equity, preference, and debenture securities in the *Economist*'s *Investors Monthly Manual* to compare domestic, foreign, and colonial 'realized rates of return' from 1870 to 1913. He finds an average 4.6 per cent for domestic and 5.7 per cent for overseas, a 1.1 per cent differential, rising to 1.58 when 'adjusted for risk'. Edelstein, *Overseas Investment*, pp. 16, 126, 140.

19. P. J. Cain, 'Economics and Empire: The Metropolitan Context', in *The Oxford History of the British Empire*, ed. Andrew Porter, Vol. III, Oxford 1999, pp. 47–50; ibid., *Hobson and Imperialism*, Oxford 2002, pp. 243–47. Pollard puts the number of British investors in 1914 at 300,000. But this includes small-time participants. Probate registers

reveal that about half of stock exchange securities held at death were part of fortunes over £50,000, and weighted to foreign assets. Sidney Pollard, 'Capital Exports, 1870–1914: Harmful or Beneficial?', *The Economic History Review*, November 1985, pp. 498–99. O'Brien judges the Empire 'neither sufficient nor necessary to the growth of the economy', but concedes, 'benefits accrued disproportionately' to white settlers in the dominions and colonies, and 'to those at the top end of the income and social scales in British society'. Up to 1906 the latter, defined as those making over £1,000 a year, paid less than 8 per cent of their incomes to the state, accounting for just 11 per cent of total tax revenue, while receiving 40–45 per cent of national income. Benefits included military, diplomatic, and civil service posts, and subsidies to investment that mitigated risks from default. Patrick K. O'Brien, 'The Costs and Benefits of British Imperialism 1846–1914', *Past and Present*, August 1988, pp. 180, 194–95, 200.

20. 'The Extent of our Colonial Investments', 16 February 1884.
21. 'Why There is Stagnation in the Stock Exchange', 24 November 1883.
22. 'The Imperial Ottoman Bank', 30 June 1883.
23. Hobsbawm, *Industry and Empire*, p. 126.
24. 'The Deficits of Brazil', 31 May 1884; 'The Position of Uruguay', 17 October 1885.
25. 'The Future of Mexico', 20 January 1883.
26. 'Priority Claims on Peruvian Bat Guano', 13 October 1883.
27. 'The Trade and Finance of the Argentine Republic', 5 May 1883.
28. Philip Ziegler, *The Sixth Great Power: Barings 1762–1929*, London 1988, p. 237. Argentina's share of total investment was more than double Brazil's by 1890: £157 million to £69 million, with Mexico at £60 million, and Uruguay, Cuba and Chile some distance behind. Hobsbawm, *Industry and Empire*, p. 126. Roca's 'Conquest of the Desert' brutally established Argentine control over Patagonia, killing and forcibly uprooting indigenous peoples to make way for European-descended settler agriculture.
29. For a sense that inflationary pressures might lead to a stock market crash, though not a sovereign debt crisis, see 'Argentine Borrowings', 24 November 1888; 'The State of Affairs in Argentina', 30 November 1889; 'The State of Affairs in Buenos Aires', 21 December 1889. The *Economist* seems to have hired its own correspondent only in 1890. He tamped down talk of financial revival with warnings about political chaos – '"Those fools in London," is now a common expression on the Bolsa' – and stalled debt renegotiation. 'Argentine Affairs', 21 November 1891.
30. The guarantee fund was equal to 1.2 per cent of 1890 GDP. John D. Turner, *Banking in Crisis: The Rise and Fall of British Banking Stability, 1800 to the Present*, Cambridge 2014, pp. 154–57. In just four years, between 1886 and 1890, Barings raised almost £18 million for Argentina. The Barings Crisis that followed may have been minor compared to Overend, Gurney, & Co. in the City, as the *Economist*

noted, but its external impact was wide-ranging, including a 10 per cent plunge in Argentina's GDP in 1890–1891. 'Liquidation of the Barings', 22 November 1890; Ziegler, *Sixth Great Power*, pp. 237–42; H. S. Ferns, 'Investment and Trade Between Britain and Argentina in the Nineteenth Century', *Economic History Review*, May 1950, pp. 203–18.

31. 'Under almost irresistible pressure his [Johnstone's] assistance was secured in straightening out affairs after the Argentine crisis': 'Retiring Editor', *The Bankers' Magazine*, p. 150.

32. Cain and Hopkins, *British Imperialism*, pp. 248–50; Edelstein, *Overseas Investment*, pp. 250–51.

33. 'Intense ignorance of the real facts about mines and mining' from the 'Cabinet downwards' was 'fostered by the press', and kept shareholders 'in the dark as to the hundreds of wildcat ventures ... incomparably more dishonest' even than in the Transvaal. 'The Gold Mines of West Australia', 16 July 1898; 'Mr Scott Lings and the *Economist*', 11 November 1899.

34. Bagehot, *Economic Studies*, CW, Vol. XI, p. 279.

35. 'Our Investments in South America', 8 December 1883.

36. For direct forms of investment, see Mira Wilkins, 'The Free-Standing Company, 1870–1914: An Important Type of British Foreign Direct Investment', *Economic History Review*, May 1988, pp. 259–82.

37. Disraeli, by 'a little overshooting the mark', risked decreasing 'the liking of the masses for the throne'. 'The New Title of the Queen', 18 March 1876.

38. The *Economist* interpreted the agreements that issued from Berlin in very broad terms for British power. Ottoman foreign policy would henceforward be 'directed from London, not Constantinople', with England also becoming the 'rising sun' and 'ultimate source of honour and prosperity' internally, since 'Orientals are never slow to discover where the true centre of power lies'. 'What the Convention with Turkey Means', 13 July 1878. Occupation of Cyprus was necessary but insufficient, a sign 'we persist in the insane fiction of treating the rulers of Turkey as equals'. 'Turkey and the Convention', 24 August 1878.

39. 'Earl Grey on the Afghan Difficulty', 12 October 1878. The amir had 'publicly and ostentatiously concluded a preferential alliance with Russia', and was 'a menace to British India.' It replied to Sir John Lawrence, viceroy of India from 1864 to 1869, who objected to the Second Afghan War on legal grounds, that the pertinence of 'international jurisprudence' to Oriental states was 'extremely doubtful'. 'We are only surprised that no one has proposed to call in the Czar as arbitrator.' 'The Afghan Difficulty', 26 October 1878.

40. Annexations benefited Boers, British settlers, and natives alike. The aim in South Africa was a federation on the model of Canada. 'The Transvaal', 12 May 1877. The paper criticized incompetence, especially in local officials, but with the goal of winning wars underway rather than debating their merits. 'Responsibility for the Disaster in

Zululand', 22 February 1879; 'End of the Zulu War', 26 July 1879; 'The Next Step in South Africa', 2 August 1879; 'The War with the Transvaal', 5 March 1881; Porter, *The Lion's Share*, London 1996, pp. 94–101.

41. 'Our Colonies and Possessions', 28 April 1883.

42. 'The Expansion of the Empire', 13 December 1884.

43. A. G. Hopkins, 'The Victorians and Africa: A Reconsideration of the Occupation of Egypt, 1882', *Journal of African History*, 1986, pp. 377–78, 380.

44. The 250 or so other victims were Egyptians. Donald Reid, 'The Urabi Revolution and the British Conquest, 1879–1882', in *The Cambridge History of Egypt*, Vol II, ed. W. M. Daly, Cambridge 1998, p. 231.

45. Certain Liberals had claimed that these men were legitimate nationalists, and that Britain selfishly 'sought to thwart the efforts of the Egyptian people to establish a government more in harmony with their national sentiments'. 'The Situation in Egypt', 15 July 1882. Liberals in favour of intervention needed to do a better job of explaining that it was neither for the sake of bondholders, who must assume their own risks, nor for trade, which might alarm other states that ought to be ready for peaceful penetration by Britain: 'What surer way could there be of deterring such countries as China, or even Turkey, from admitting British capital with the freedom we wish to see than to tell them that if they allow our traders to gain a footing within their boundaries they open the door for armed interference on our part with their affairs?' 'British Interests in Egypt', 29 July 1882.

46. 'Our Policy in Egypt', 1 July 1882. Delays in putting troops on the ground – due to French indecision – did have a welcome effect, showing the world that Britain 'sought not only to safeguard our own interests, but also to secure for the people of Egypt a larger amount of freedom and of self-government than they have yet enjoyed'. 'Egypt', 22 July 1882. War was 'compatible with the liberties' of the Egyptians, saving them from the Turks. The more 'autonomous Egypt becomes, the more absolutely independent of foreign dictation ... the better we shall be pleased'. 'Egypt', 26 August 1882.

47. 'Europe and the Egyptian Crisis', 8 July 1882; 'Attitude of the Powers', 16 September 1882.

48. 'Financial Control in Egypt', 13 January 1883. 'Our expedition to Egypt was neither a humanitarian crusade nor buccaneering adventure.' 'We went because we had definite interests ... the success of Arabi would have driven European capital and industry out of the country, revived the direct control of the Sultan, and permanently endangered the high road to the East.' 'Mr. Gladstone on Egypt', 11 August 1883.

49. 'It is no doubt to be desired that Egypt should continue to regulate its finances in accordance with Western methods; but that the Khedive himself can see to.' 'Egypt and Financial Control', 30 September 1882; see also Darwin, *The Empire Project*, pp. 70–72.

50. 'The Fall of Khartoum', 7 February 1885.

51. 'The campaign should be one river battle, a month of confused expeditions, and then tranquility.' 'Upper Burmah', 24 October 1885.

52. To Randolph Churchill, secretary of state for India, Lord Dufferin called his ultimatum to King Thibaw 'a very friendly proposal for the settlement of the dispute between his Government and the Bengal Burma Trading Association'. Ernest Chew, 'The Fall of the Burmese Kingdom in 1885: Review and Reconsideration', *Journal of Southeast Asian Studies*, September 1979, p. 378; 'Upper Burmah', 24 October 1885. The British burned, uprooted and moved whole villages in their effort to kill and isolate guerrillas who continued to resist after the annexation.

53. It was 'inappropriate' for British Chambers of Commerce to 'glory' in this war. 'Mr Bright on the Probable War with Burmah', 7 November 1885. But, 'so long as civilised and uncivilised races are brought into contact by the industrial and commercial activity of the Western world, operations such as those in which we are reluctantly engaged on the Irrawaddy must from time to time be inevitable. Arbitration is out of the question with a barbarous despot', while 'no state can permit its subjects, engaged in legitimate pursuit of trade and exercising rights given to them by contract, to be plundered at pleasure'. 'England and the East', 21 November 1885. There was 'no need for alarm' after a guerrilla war sprang up. General Macpherson could 'subdue Burmah with an army of 30,000' in dry season. 'Burmese Difficulties', 21 August 1886.

54. 'The Congo and the Niger', 18 October 1884.

55. 'If he wanted an Australia, he should have looked to South America', or 'if he desired an India he should have found one in Asia'. But he had preferred '"plantations" often chosen, as in the Cameroons, and perhaps Zanzibar, with little reference to conditions of either climate or of soil.' 'New View of Prince Bismarck', 29 September 1888.

56. Russia respected firmness. During the Pendjeh crisis the paper threatened to retaliate – 'there are occasions which compel a country to choose between war and national dishonour' – for Russian sorties beyond the River Kushk into Afghanistan. 'The Battle on the Kushk', 11 April 1885.

57. 'The French Expedition to Tonquin', 5 May 1883; 'M. Ferry's Speech at Havre', 20 October 1883.

58. Other than perhaps to distract the country from the Dreyfus affair. 'The Fashoda Affair', 24 September 1898. France itself 'chose to sever her connection with Egypt, and put an end to Dual Control' in 1882. Britain, obliged to 'build up prosperity and order' alone – and defend it from a 'turbulent foe to the South', building up an army and 'great railway system' – would never give way to a 'Power which deliberately declined to take any part in the civilising process'. 'Question of Fashoda', 1 October 1898; 'Temper of the Country About France', 15 October 1898.

59. P. M. Holt, *The Mahdist State in the Sudan 1881–1898*, Oxford 1958, p. 222; Porter, *Lion's Share*, p. 167.

60. 'Continental Criticism of England', 30 September 1899.

61. This was addressed to France, whose investors owned a large share of Spain's debt. 'United States and Spain', 12 March 1898. 'America and the Philippines', 5 November 1898. See too V. G. Kiernan, *America: The New Imperialism: From White Settlement to World Hegemony*, London 1978, pp. 100–104. Panama was an 'American Egypt'. 'The Panama Canal Again', 7 November 1903.

62. Such liberties were 'considered so vital to American well-being', after the Civil War, 'Congress enfranchised the whole negro population, giving them (on paper, at least) equal rights with the whites' since 'it was dangerous for a Republic founded on the doctrine of human equality to contain within its bounds a nation of helots.' 'If that were true of negroes at home', it was even more so of 'half-breeds and of degraded people like those who mostly make up the population of the Philippines thousands of miles beyond the sea.' While they 'theoretically share the "rights" of American citizens', they were 'ludicrously unfit' for them. 'A policy of annexation introduces a conflict of principle into the Republic.' Other consequences included a 'practical renunciation of the Monroe Doctrine, on the intelligible ground that one cannot eat one's cake and have it'. It also meant greater taxation, and centralization of power, to support a large standing army and navy. 'The Parting of the Ways in America', 9 July 1898.

63. T. G. Otte, *The China Question: Great Power Rivalry and British Isolation, 1894–1905*, Oxford 2007, pp. 2, 17. 'If the corpse, so rotten and so vast, does not infect the whole world, the world will be unusually fortunate.' 'The Disintegration of China', 11 March 1899. For new, urgently needed markets – within eight months US textile mills produced enough for twelve – America looked 'mainly in the Far East, and especially China' where a 'spirited foreign policy' was based on 'fear of the Chinese market being closed to them by the action of Germany, Russia and France'. 'The Parting of the Ways in America', 9 July 1898; 'The United States and The Open Door', 6 January 1900.

64. Punishment had to be severe to 'maintain proper respect for the representatives of Western peoples' in future, but without 'demoralising' state authorities, and preferably exacted by them – to 'maintain China intact against Western greed and intrigue'. 'Chinese Problem', 29 September 1900. This was compatible with regime change. To leave the empress in power would be a 'denial of justice'. 'If impunity for murder is to be the first result of the federation of the world, then the world had better remain unfederated.' 'First Duty of Europe in China', 15 September 1900. When 'justice' turned into looting, the paper condemned it, not out of 'rigid morality', but for 'impairing efficiency by impairing character'. 'Loot', 7 December 1901. It failed to note that British officers, far from 'winking at' pillage, organized it at daily auctions. James Hevia, 'Looting and Its Discontents: Moral

Discourse and the Plunder of Beijing, 1900–1901', in *The Boxers, China, and the World*, eds. Robert Bickers and R. G. Tiedemann, New York 2007, pp. 96–97.

65. 'The Chinese Indemnity', 30 March 1901. The partition of China among many powers would lead each to demand privileges like 'setting up banks, and above all exclusive rights of making loans, and protecting their bondholders by European management of the finances pledged for the interest'. 'The Problem of China', 23 June 1900; 'China and the Concert of Europe', 29 December 1901; 'The Foreign Secretary on China', 25 May 1901.

66. Uday Mehta, *Liberalism and Empire: A Study in Nineteenth-Century British Liberal Thought*, Chicago 1999, p. 20; Karuna Mantena, *Alibis of Empire: Henry Maine and the Ends of Liberal Imperialism*, pp. 21–55; Frederick Cooper, *Colonialism in Question: Theory, Knowledge, History*, Berkeley 2005, p. 6. For overviews of, as well as interventions in, the scholarly literature on liberalism and empire, see Jennifer Pitts, 'Political Theory of Empire and Imperialism', *The Annual Review of Political Science*, 2010, p 211–35; Andrew Sartori, 'The British Empire and Its Liberal Mission', *The Journal of Modern History*, September 2006, pp. 623–42.

67. Even recent scholarship that disputes this motive concedes the Transvaal's new economic clout (after gold finds in 1868) threatened to pull other South African states towards it, and away from Britain's Cape Colony. By 1898 it was the largest producer of gold, accounting for 27 per cent of the world total. Britain was responsible for half of the £75 million invested there by 1899, and two-thirds of its trade. Christopher Saunders and Iain R. Smith, 'Southern Africa, 1795–1910', in *The Oxford History of the British Empire*, ed. Andrew Porter, Oxford 1999, Vol. III, pp. 609–10.

68. Forgetting itself for a moment, the *Economist* deplored 'the disturbing, revolutionary effect caused by the sudden growth of an enormously aggressive capitalism in a heretofore stagnant and conservative community', 'the evolution of giant monopolies', which had left 'society, all institutions … hypnotised': 'England and the Transvaal', 10 June 1899.

69. 'Chamberlain is supposed to be an adherent of what is called the new diplomacy, which, like the new journalism, the new women, and many other novelties, is not altogether an improvement on the old.' 'The Transvaal and the New Diplomacy', 2 September 1899.

70. 'Just as the British and Dutch were fused in the earlier history of New York': 'Mr Chamberlain's Deliverance', 3 April 1897. Boers were white, an economic and cultural argument against fighting them, since they were capable of instituting the proper kind of political economy. Englishmen 'will sometimes fight dark peoples on ill-understood or uncertain grounds' for their own good. 'With white people they prefer to be sure they have a good plea': 'Transvaal Negotiations', 15 July 1899.

71. It was unwise to link 'the fate of the British Empire' to 'whether a certain number of capitalists and miners on the Rand are to qualify to vote in seven years or five'. 'Boer and Briton', 26 August 1899.

72. 'The Transvaal Issue', 7 October 1899. Instead of three months, the war lasted almost three years, cost £230 million, and sucked in 450,000 British and imperial troops. About 22,000 died on the British side, 34,000 Boer soldiers and civilians, and 'not less' than 14,000 Africans. Saunders and Smith, 'Southern Africa', pp. 609–10.

73. 'Motives of the Boers', 14 October 1899.

74. 'Some Reflections on the War', 16 December 1899; 'The Military Proposals', 17 February 1900; 'The Elections', 22 September 1900. Criticisms from opposition Liberals were unwelcome. 'It is the time of the general, not of the politician': 'Political Opinion and the War', 23 December 1899. For a contemporary report on the concentration camps – an institution and term invented by the Spanish general Valeriano Weyler in Cuba in 1896–98, and seamlessly adopted by the British in 1900 – see Emily Hobhouse, *Report on a Visit to the Camps*, London 1901.

75. The paper spilt a lot of ink to disprove their liberal-sounding claim that if 'every nation has a right to regulate its own internal affairs', that included Egypt. 'The Situation in Egypt', 15 July 1882.

76. 'Bright on the Probable War with Burmah', 7 November 1885.

77. 'The Soudan Expedition', 6 June 1896. John Morley's loyalty to Gladstone over Home Rule also cost him: formerly a 'clear-sighted' and 'judicious editor of the *Fortnightly Review*' with a talent for 'speaking out', he was now a 'party hack'. 'Mr Morley and the Gladstonian Muzzle', 1 February 1890.

78. For a dramatic change of view before and after his conversion to Home Rule, see 'Mr Gladstone's Letter', 4 July 1885; 'Mr Gladstone's Scheme', 10 April 1886; 'Mr Chamberlain's Position', 12 June 1886; 'Immediate Result of the Election', 26 June 1886; 'Government and the Liberal Unionists', 31 July 1886.

79. 'Round Table Conference', 8 January 1887; 'Shifting of Parties', 18 June 1887; 'Mr Gladstone's Disclosure', 2 July 1892; 'Justification of the Unionists', 18 February 1893; 'Home Rule and Experience of History', 25 February 1893; 'Imperial Federation and Home Rule', 15 April 1893; 'Second Reading', 21 April 1893; 'The House of Lords will not lose an atom of popularity by rejecting this ill-considered and ill-ominous measure': 'Third Reading', 2 September 1893; 'Mr Gladstone and the Lords', 16 September 1893. See the chronology posited by John D. Fair, 'Liberal to Conservative: The Flight of the Liberal Unionists after 1886', *Victorian Studies*, Winter 1986, pp. 294, 314; and T. W. Heyck, 'Home Rule, Radicalism, and the Liberal Party, 1886–1895', *Journal of British Studies*, May 1974, pp. 66–91.

80. 'Lord Beaconsfield', 23 April 1881.

81. 'Lord Salisbury', 29 July 1899; 'The Old Ministry and the New', 19 July 1902.

82. 'Mr Balfour's Aims', 21 November 1903; 'Mr Balfour', 26 December 1903. Before his premiership, Balfour had been a 'firm and imperturbable' Chief Secretary of Ireland from 1887 to 1891 – especially after the Mitchelstown Massacre, which earned him the nickname 'Bloody Balfour'. 'The New Irish Demand', 'The Session', 17 September 1887.
83. 'The Elections', 22 September 1899.
84. Campbell-Bannerman's 'methods of barbarism' outburst about the Boer War was 'not becoming in a politician of his position'. 'Real Reason for Keeping Present Government', 30 November 1901. If Lord Rosebery 'puts aside, or triumphs over the influences' which the paper thought had 'availed to paralyse him as an effective political force – no limit can be easily set to the part which he may yet play'. 'Two Conceptions of Empire', 17 October 1903. Lord Rosebery represented middle ground – between the 'insane imperialism' of Chamberlain, especially after he came out for imperial preference in 1903 – and idealistic pacifism lingering among advanced Liberals.
85. 'Unionist Service to Home Rule', 13 January 1906. Once the size of the Liberal victory became known, the paper advised the Unionists to ditch Chamberlain and tariff reform without delay, and unite behind Balfour – now 'one of the finest intellects applied to modern politics' – to lead an effective opposition. It hoped that 'the Liberals of the City' would graciously see that Balfour was returned 'at once'. 'General Reflections', 27 January 1906
86. Roy Jenkins, *Asquith*, London 1964, pp. 32–33; J. A. Spender and Cyril Asquith, *Life of Lord Oxford and Asquith*, London 1932, Vol. I, pp. 45–46. Articles such as 'The English extreme left' in *The Spectator*, 12 August 1876), made Asquith a good fit for the *Economist*. See, 'Asquith, Herbert Henry (1852–1928)', H. C. G. Matthew in *ODNB*, 2004.
87. 'The New Radicalism', 20 January 1883.
88. Asquith helped Spencer compile material for a book on the 'synthetic philosophy' of English political institutions. He found the 'old philosopher' rather absurd, but added, 'it is not for the unemployed to be over-fastidious on such a point.' For Spencer, Liberalism had grown 'more coercive in its legislation' as it got 'more into power'. 'What', Asquith asked, 'would he have said if he had lived to see a Liberal Government introducing Old Age Pensions and National Insurance?' H. H. Asquith, *Memories and Reflections, 1852–1927*, Boston 1928, Vol. I, pp. 49–52.
89. So long as much of this state action was devolved to the municipal level, along lines championed by Chamberlain in Birmingham, it added, in a significant qualification. 'The New Radicalism', 20 January 1883.
90. 'The Passing of the Franchise Bill', 21 June 1884; 'The Folly of the Peers', 12 July 1884; 'The Compromise', 22 November 1884. The paper estimated that 2 million more (or 5 out of 7 million) males 'capable of bearing arms will be voters'. 'A Retrospect', 27 December 1884. For a reassessment of the scope of pre-1918 democracy, see

H. C. G. Matthew, R. I. McKibbin and J. A. Kay, 'The Franchise Factor in the Rise of the Labour Party', *English Historical Review*, October 1976, pp. 724, 726.

91. The Manchester school had little to show on the score of peace – with the partial exception of America and France, where more liberal commerce had led to better relations. 'The Change in Radicalism', 1 March 1884.

92. Ruth Dudley Edwards wrote of Asquith, astonishingly, that 'the civil liberties issue concerned him deeply', and he supported 'renewal of the Coercion Act only as a regrettable temporary expedient' and 'sought and examined alternatives'. Edwards, *Pursuit of Reason*, pp. 349–51. Asquith wrote that coercion 'should be made vastly more stringent': 'Irish Protection Bill', 29 January 1881; 'Chamberlain on the Irish Agitation', 31 December 1881; 'Substitutes for Coercion', 8 April 1882.

93. 'The Irish tenant farmer is not the victim of injustice or wrongdoing' and the law was more favourable to him than in England, Scotland or France. 'It is sometimes argued that the present generation of Irish landlords may fairly be made to suffer for the sins, real or supposed, of some former generation of Irish landlords – that, in fact, the landlords of today may be robbed, if it is found convenient, because the Irish tenants, say, of Cromwell's day, were robbed.' No English government would ever act on this principle. 'If the possession of land for two centuries, and its peaceful descent from father to son, or from vendor to purchaser, does not confer an indispensable title, there can be no such thing to be had.' 'Notes on the Irish Land Question', 19 March 1881. The Land League's proposal to induce 'a run on the Bank of Ireland', a rush to exchange currency for gold at the 'enemies' bank', was based on a similarly irrelevant argument that 'the £3,000,000 capital of the bank was "borrowed" – i.e. taken by the British government during the war with the French Republic.' 'Bank of Ireland and the Land League', 22 October 1881.

94. 'More Notes on the Irish Land Question', 26 March 1881.

95. A complex society, the *Economist* wrote after the Mitchelstown Massacre – when police fired on a public meeting of Irish nationalists – 'must be controlled by laws; and if laws are to exist, those who break them, whether by non-payment of debt, or by meeting in defiance of them, or by inciting to crime, must be reduced to obedience by suffering pain. Debts must be collected, even if defaulting debtors thereby lose their homes, as in England all bankrupts do. Seditious meetings, when formidable, must be dispersed, even if it is needful to use soldiers, or to take the lives endangered by a volley on a mob.' 'The New Liberal Lever', 1 October 1887.

96. As the *Spectator*'s editor and proprietor after 1898, Strachey later broke with the Unionists too, over Tariff Reform, which might be acceptable for 'national security' reasons, but never on economic grounds. John St Loe Strachey, *Adventure of Living*, pp. 9–10, 179, 298–99, 307–8.

97. 'If, under such circumstances, it is inconsistent with the principles of Liberalism to resort to force, there is, as Mr Chamberlain points out, no escape from the conclusion that "Liberalism cannot defend the freedom which it is its object to establish, and is powerless to protect the majority against the anarchy and disorder which are fostered by an irreconcilable minority."' 'Mr Chamberlain on the Irish Agitation', 31 December 1881.
98. H. C. G. Matthew, *The Liberal Imperialists: Ideas and Politics of a Post-Gladstonian Elite*, Oxford 1973, p. 143.

## 4. Landslide Liberalism

1. Or 145 seats. H. V. Emy, *Liberals, Radicals and Social Politics 1892–1914*, Cambridge 1973, p. 85.
2. In 1905 Campbell-Bannerman held off Herbert Henry Asquith, Richard Haldane and Edward Grey – the Liberal Imperialist triumvirate led by the erratic Earl of Rosebery, the ex-premier who argued that Liberals needed to be as militantly patriotic in foreign and colonial policy as Conservatives. Their 'Relugas Compact' tried to force Campbell-Bannerman into the Lords. H. C. G. Matthew, *The Liberal Imperialists*, pp. 110–19; Peter Rowland, *The Last Liberal Governments 1905–1910*, New York, 1968, pp. 9–18.
3. Sugar, coal and corn duties, reintroduced to help finance the Second Boer War, were also unpopular. Anthony Howe, *Free Trade and Liberal England 1846–1946*, Oxford 1997, pp. 225–26.
4. Balfour and his 'little piggers' went halfway, endorsing retaliatory tariffs. The scenes Bagehot had recalled from the 1840s, when 'excited masses of men and women hung on the words of one talking political economy', had returned, but under conditions in which Britain's industrial lead looked less secure. Bagehot, 'Mr Cobden', *CW*, Vol. III, pp. 223–24.
5. A. K. Russell, *Liberal Landslide: The General Election of 1906*, Newton Abbott 1973, pp. 69, 107–8, 160–64.
6. The 'franchise represented a theory of property rather than individual rights' – extending from 'fancy borough' to 'broader household, occupation, and lodger franchises'. Multi-occupant homes and rooms, lodgers, recent removals, most soldiers, sailors, and seamen, and all poor relief recipients were excluded. Until 1918, the top 11 per cent had far greater 'voting power' than the bottom 89 per cent. Ibid., pp. 15–21. Russell estimates workers already made up two-thirds of the electorate; around 60 per cent is more likely according to H. C. G. Matthew, R. I. McKibbin and J. A. Kay, 'The Franchise Factor in the Rise of the Labour Party', *English Historical Review*, October 1976, pp. 733–35.
7. The LRC had a £100,000 election fund. F. Bealey and H. Pelling,

*Labour and Politics 1900–1906*, London 1958, pp. 143–46, 158. The result was a breakthrough: 53 Labour MPs (29 under the LRC, 24 allied to Liberals) compared to 2 in 1900. Russell, *Liberal Landslide*, pp. 70–74.

8. Especially after the army's performance in the Boer War seemed to reveal the enfeebled state of British soldiers. Bernard Semmel, *Imperialism and Social Reform*, London 1960, passim.

9. Chamberlain played this role before and after 1886, famously speaking of the 'ransom' property should pay for the 'security' the state afforded it. For his part in tariff reform, see Julian Amery, *Joseph Chamberlain and the Tariff Reform Campaign*, London 1969, pp. v–vi; E. H. H. Green, *The Crisis of Conservatism: The Politics, Economics and Ideology of the British Conservative Party, 1880–1914*, London 1995, pp. 242–53.

10. The state's moral purpose was set in a familiar frame: the 'removal of obstacles' to individual fulfilment – as in compulsory education. T. H. Green, *Lectures on the Principles of Political Obligation*, eds. Paul Harris and John Morrow, Cambridge 1986, p. 161; Melvin Richter, *The Politics of Conscience, T. H. Green and His Age*, Cambridge 1964, p. 341. For the importance of Hegel – even if, after A. J. P. Taylor, of an 'oddly transposed variety' – to the 'Liberal Idealists', see Jeanne Morefield, *Covenants Without Swords: Idealist Liberalism and the Spirit of Empire*, Princeton 2004, pp. 8, 25.

11. Mill also backed a land tax, another idea central to New Liberals, but with an older pedigree, found in Ricardo and Malthus, and Cobden's demand for free trade in land. Michael Freeden, *The New Liberalism: An Ideology of Social Reform*, Oxford 1979, pp. 12–18, 43, 55–58; Bruce K. Murray, *The People's Budget 1909/10: Lloyd George and Liberal Politics*, Oxford 1980, pp. 34, 95–97; Stefan Collini, *Liberalism and sociology: L. T. Hobhouse and political argument in England, 1880–1914*, Cambridge 1979, pp. 171–84; Sandra Den Otter, *British Idealism and Social Explanation: A Study in Late Victorian Thought*, Oxford 1996, p 89, 108–11 and *passim*.

12. Francis W. Hirst, *In the Golden Days*, London 1947, pp. 111–13.

13. Ibid., pp. 113, 131–32.

14. Edgeworth, an ethicist turned economist who learned his craft from Jevons, could be practical too – going over 'the whole ground of the science' from Mill's *Political Economy*, introducing Hirst to Marshall on currency, and to statistical analysis. An essay Hirst wrote on monopolies under his influence won the Cobden Prize in 1899. Ibid., pp. 133–36. For his classical learning, which inspired 'an Aristophanic skit on Oscar Wilde', see L. C. M. S. Amery, F. W. Hirst, H. A. A. Cruso, *Aristophanes at Oxford*, Oxford 1894; Hirst, *Golden Days*, p. 147.

15. Hilaire Belloc in *Essays in Liberalism*, London 1897, pp. 3–4, 19–20, 25, 155.

16. Workers had benefited most. 'Wages, like incomes, have doubled in real value in thirty-six years.' *Essays*, pp. 53, 59, 62.

17. He condoned regulation or control of natural (as opposed to arti-ficial) monopolies – 'coinage, sanitation, water, gas, tramways' – as exceptions that proved the rule, applying only where competition 'is difficult or impossible'. A graduated income tax was an 'encourage-ment rather than a menace to private property', a 'check on huge swellings of wealth'. But there were limits. Raising taxes too high could lead to capital flight, or, 'more loathsome', a 'corrupt desire among the poorer part of the electorate for increased expenditure'. Hirst felt, at this stage, that old-age pensions were such a 'bribe'. Ibid., pp. 69, 82–83, 89,

18. Asquith did not find himself in 'substantial disagreement', however. Hirst, *Golden Days*, p. 157; *Essays*, x.

19. For the debate, and the reaction of *Chronicle* editor H. W. Massing-ham, see, Freeden, *New Liberalism*, pp. 62–64.

20. S. Ball, 'Socialism and Individualism: A Challenge and an Eirenicon', *Economic Review*, October 1897, pp. 490–520. In a subsequent exchange, Ball was 'surprised' to see Hirst invoke economic man 'in all his naked and primitive simplicity' – 'not even brought up to the date of Marshall', who at least conceded the growing importance of 'motives to collective action' within capitalist industry itself. See, 'Individualism and Socialism I, II', *Economic Review*, April 1898, pp. 225–35.

21. They won the backing of the *Speaker*'s owner, Liberal MP and chemi-cal baron Sir John Brunner, and that of Sir William McEwan, owner of the *Edinburgh Evening News*. The *Speaker* had originally been founded to compete with the *Spectator*, run by Hutton and Townsend, after that paper defected from the Liberals over Irish Home Rule in 1886.

22. On 'foreign and home politics', Hirst observed of Hobhouse and himself, 'both of us have moved, but he, I think, the most'. Hirst, *Golden Days*, pp. 174, 193, 205, 214. Hirst records that Ball, his socialist critic, left the Fabians over their racial and economic justi-fications of the war: 'in a sense this is more of a truth because it is incorrect.' Peter Clarke, *Liberals and Social Democrats*, Cambridge 1978, p. 77.

23. D. A. Hamer, *John Morley: Liberal Intellectual in Politics*, Oxford 1968, p. 333. For Hammond, Hobhouse, Hirst, Hobson and others on the *Speaker*, see *Towards a Social Policy: Or Suggestions for Con-structive Reform*, ed. J. L. Hammond, London 1905.

24. P. J. Cain, *Hobson and Imperialism: Radicalism, New Liberalism, and Finance 1887–1938*, Oxford 2002, p. 96; Francis W. Hirst, Gilbert Murray, and J. L. Hammond, *Liberalism and Empire*, London 1900, p. 54; Hirst, *Golden Days*, p. 185; J. A. Hobson, *The War in South Africa: Its Causes and Effects*, London 1900.

25. The 'barren and intoxicating splendour' of the Sudan conquest was a precedent. Murray wrote on 'the exploitation of inferior races' in ancient and modern empires; Hammond on nationality and morality

as the hallmarks of liberal statesmanship, which had made England the 'guardian of European civilization': *Liberalism and Empire*, xvi.

26. Ibid., p. 72

27. Ibid., pp. 63, 75.

28. Ibid., p. 114.

29. Hobson and Hirst made taxation of land values central to combatting imperialism, but Hobson added a theoretical bent with the 'unearned increment'. J. A. Hobson, *Imperialism: A Study*, London 1902, pp. 54, 64. Hirst also used a root metaphor. 'What is this giant upas tree that has to be cut down?' *Liberalism and Empire*, p. 4.

30. A 'great future awaits that portion of the Liberal Party' which repudiated the 'wasteful excesses of aggressive imperialism' and conscription, while maintaining 'the superiority of our fleet at the proportions fixed by tradition and reason'. Not only was this a winning electoral strategy in Britain, it was also the first step to reducing imperial rivalries 'for it is our expenditure which forces the pace ... upon a reluctant Czar, a recalcitrant Reichstag, and an unwilling Chamber of Deputies'. Ibid., 32, 113–14. 'We wish we could discover a single reason for prefixing the epithet Liberal to the new type of Imperialism.' Hirst, 'Pitt the Youngest', *Speaker*, 4 November 1899.

31. *The Arbiter in Council*, London, 1906, pp. 350, 507. Reid asked Hirst to write a blue book on reforming maritime law for Cabinet circulation, hoping to convince Grey to back it at the Foreign Office, and the Hague. 'But Grey and the Admiralty were obdurate, holding that as we were the greatest naval power we ought not to abandon for the sake of protecting our own commerce the right as belligerents of destroying the enemy's and cutting off all his imports': *Golden Days*, pp. 238–40. See also Francis Hirst, *Commerce and Property in Naval Warfare*, London 1906, and the indignant exchange in the *Times*, 'Private Property at Sea', 11 November 1913.

32. Hirst, *Golden Days*, pp. 136, 228–29; *F. W. Hirst by His Friends*, pp. 63–73. Hirst and Hoover seem to have met in the context of Hirst's agitation for a negotiated peace in 1915, when Hoover was leading relief efforts in Belgium, and the two discovered they shared their enthusiasm for classical liberalism. An ailing Hirst visited Hoover just before the stock market crash in October 1929, and was examined by the White House doctor. 'Medical Notes of Dr. J. T. Boone', 17 December 1929. Hirst Papers, BLOU, Box 13.

33. Hirst met the statistician and former assistant editor at the club. *Centennial Volume*, p. 71.

34. Cain, *Hobson and Imperialism*, p. 97; as 'non-interventionist', see Clarke, *Liberals and Social Democrats*, p. 78; a 'committed pacifist' with a 'completely closed mind', Edwards, *Pursuit of Reason*, pp. 398, 465, 525.

35. 'Pitt the Youngest', *Speaker*, 4 November 1899; *Liberalism and Empire*, pp. xv, xvii. 'I have never been able to agree with the Quakers', he reflected. A 'clearly aggressive attack on one nation by another – e.g.

that of Soviet Russia on Finland, or of Germany on Holland – should be resisted unless resistance is hopeless'. Hirst, *Golden Days*, pp. 233, 256, 258.

36. Party leaders were praised for learning to work for 'relative adaptations'. 'Eclipse of Socialism', 16 March 1907.

37. Edwards, *Pursuit of Reason*, pp. 495–97, 498. Like Walter Layton, Reid was Cambridge-educated; he left the paper over its anti-war stance, returning after as assistant editor. In 1932, he joined the *Daily Telegraph* as City Editor. *Accountant*, 5 November 1938; *Spectator*, 28 October 1938.

38. '*Laissez-faire*, for him, is a religion; his door-mat at home carried instead of the conventional "Welcome", the words "Peace, Free Trade and Goodwill."' Hamilton had points in common with Hirst. She was sympathetic to Germany, studying in Kiel before attending Newnham College at Cambridge. There, she read classics and economics, influenced by G. Lowes Dickenson and Alfred Marshall, and honed her debating skills in defence of free trade and opposition to the Boer War. Ibid., pp. 41, 80.

39. See the recollection of labour historian and Wadham alumnus, A. F. Thompson, in *Hirst by His Friends*, p. 37.

40. 'Enmity of Germany to Great Britain', 5 December 1896; 'Latest Manifesto of the German Emperor', 28 April 1900; 'The Powers and Morocco', 10 June 1905; 'The Conciliatory Chancellor', 7 October 1905; 'Armaments', 28 July 1906.

41. 'The Prime Minister's Character and Policy', 12 October 1907. His personality traits in another idiom: 'an elderly and rich Presbyterian whose three passions in life were his wife, the French nation and his collection of walking sticks.' George Dangerfield, *The Strange Death of Liberal England*, New York 1935, p. 29.

42. Asquith had brilliantly undermined Tariff Reformers, who wanted to tax items such as sugar to pay for pensions. 'A Great Budget', 9 May 1908. The *Daily Mail* called Hirst's article 'exalted nonsense'. He replied: 'They certainly showed no solicitude for the taxpayer or the debt in the years preceding the Boer War, or during the Boer War, or after the Boer War'. 'Second Thoughts on the Budget and the National Debt', 16 May 1908.

43. Rowland, *Last Liberal Governments*, pp. 143, 150–53.

44. A 'super tax' on incomes of £3,000 to £5,000, rising from 1s to 1s. 2d, could 'hardly be called unreasonable'. Higher rates had prevailed during the Napoleonic, Crimean and Boer Wars. 'The Budget', 1 May 1909.

45. The estimated cost of health insurance when fully operational in 1915 was £24,500,000: £11,000,000 would come from workers, £9,000,000 from employers, the remainder from the state. 'National Insurance Scheme', 6 May 1911.

46. Lloyd George's was 'the most successful Budget from the revenue producing point of view which the financial historian of this, or, perhaps,

any other, country can recall in times of peace'. 'Budget of 1911', 20 May 1911.

47. 'Rejection of the Budget', December 4 1909.

48. Links between the City and Liberals had frayed since the Unionist split under Gladstone in the 1880s. David Kynaston, *The City of London: Golden Years 1890–1914*, London 1995, Vol II, pp. 494–502. For 'Bankers' Clearing House' petition, see 'Bankers and the Budget', 15 May 1909.

49. R. H. I. Palgrave, 'The Influence of the Taxation of Capital upon the Welfare of a Country', *Bankers' Magazine*, December 1909, 728–30.

50. 'Free Trade in Being', 13 March 1909.

51. 'The Word Socialism', 9 October 1909. 'Our own extraordinary record of the new capital raised in London during the last six months' showed that 'if the rich can save at such a rate ... even a super-tax and highly graduated death duties are hardly felt in times of peace and prosperity.' 'The Budget', 2 July 1910. City aversion to reform was magnified by the People's Budget, but predated it. 'We have no doubt that the introduction of old-age pensions for the poor will be regarded with a good deal of disfavour in the City, which is apprehensive just now about anything that may be thought socialistic.' 'A Great Budget', 9 May 1908.

52. Avner Offer, 'Empire and Social Reform: British Overseas Investment and Social Reform, 1908–1914', *Historical Journal*, March 1983, pp. 123, 131. See their joint report on national credit, foreign lending and trade to the US Senate Monetary Commission – set up after the 1907 crash, in part to study European financial centres, leading to the Federal Reserve Act in 1913: Francis Hirst and George F. Paish, 'The Credit of Nations' and 'The Trade Balance of the US', Washington 1910.

53. Hirst feared 'the damage which an inevitable Liberal defeat would do to the free-trade cause'. He unsuccessfully stood elsewhere in 1910 and 1929. Anthony Howe, 'The Liberals and the City 1900–1931', in *The British Government and the City of London*, ed. Ronald Michie et al., Cambridge 2004, p. 142–43; Youssef Cassis, *City Bankers, 1890–1914*, Cambridge 1994, p. 21.

54. 12 December 1908.

55. 1 February 1913; 10 May 1913. 'I first knew them at the time she was a suffragette; and far from being suppressed by him, he seemed to be a little afraid of her breaking loose on the subject, and asked us not to refer to it at a dinner he was giving.' Charles C. Burlingham to Henry L. Stimson, 6 December 1939, in George Martin, *CCB: The Life and Times of Charles C. Burlingham, First Citizen of New York*, New York 2005, pp. 639–40. On Hirst's parting of ways with the Hammonds, Hobhouses, and Murrays on female suffrage, see Clarke, *Liberals and Social Democrats*, pp. 80–81. For conflict between Liberalism and 'early feminism', despite 'ideological affinities', see Martin Pugh, 'The Limits of Liberalism: Liberals and Women's Suffrage,

1867–1914', in *Citizenship and Community: Liberals, Radicals and Collective Identities in the British Isles, 1865–31*, ed. Eugenio F. Biagini, Cambridge 1996, pp. 45–65. Helena may have been inspired by her prominent suffragette relations, Jane Catherine Cobden Unwin and Anne Cobden-Sanderson.

56. Hamilton, *Good Friends*, p. 82. Hirst circulated a letter to oppose attempts 'by certain persons belonging principally to the Independent Labour Party to convert us into a Committee for promoting Women Suffrage'. Hobson returned it to Hirst with a 'No' to mark this sentence, and a note that began, 'you make too much of this', 23 January 1906, Hirst Papers, BLOU, Box 13.

57. Reductions would avoid the kind of 'war crisis' likely to further damage trade and employment. Hirst to Campbell-Bannerman, 9 November 1907, Campbell-Bannerman Papers, BL, Add. MSS 41238–41240.

58. Hirst to Asquith, 30 January 1906; Asquith to Hirst, 9 May 1908, in Howe, *British Government and the City*, pp. 139–40.

59. Lead articles often did both. Hirst praised Asquith for reducing the naval budget, while noting it remained over double the pre–Boer War figure. Still: 'We tremble to think what might have happened to the banking and mercantile houses of London and the provinces had the prodigal system of his predecessors continued a little longer, and if there had been no purchases of Consols by the Government broker.' Although a majority of the rich were, 'for social reasons', Conservative, 'we have reason to know that very many of the most intelligent and influential persons in the City recognize, and frankly own in private, what a tower of strength the Government's financial policy has been to them … The contrast between the British Sinking Fund and the German Loan marks and explains a great part of the difference between the financial security of London and the financial disquiet of Berlin,' 16 May 1908.

60. Even if Britain's naval superiority over Germany had not been so complete, building such big ships was a blunder, given the advent of submarines, torpedoes and mines. 'The Dreadnought will be marked down by the recording angel as a double offence against the British nation and against the human race. But for this "invention" most of the slums in our great towns could have been cleared away without any addition to rates or taxes.' Francis Hirst, *The Six Panics*, London 1913, pp. 61, 65–68, 72, 91.

61. In ten years, Britain had spent £300 million to Germany's £108; in 1909, £34 million to its £17–18; with total tonnage at 1,852,000 to its 628,000. 'The German Navy and the British Navy', 'The Political Fog', 6 February 1909.

62. Hirst to Brunner, 15 July 1912, in Stephen Koss, *Asquith*, London 1976, pp. 149–50. Hirst took this step after he and Brunner failed to get even a list of Liberal Federation officers in England, Scotland and Wales from the Whips. 'Fancy refusing the request of the President. It is a regular caucus for the pulling of wires and not for the

translation of principles into practice'. Hirst to Brunner, 29 December 1911, in Morris, *Abolition of War*, p. 304. For possible placement of the leak, see 'The Naval Scare of 1909', 8 June 1912; 'The Orgy of Armaments', 6 July 1912.

63. 'The Political Fog', 9 February 1909.

64. A National Liberal Club send-off included representatives from the *Liverpool Post, Yorkshire Observer, Sheffield Independent, Darlington Echo, South Wales Daily News, Aberdeen Free Press, Dundee Advertiser* – with Hirst hoping to sign up the *Western Daily Mercury, Eastern Morning News, Manchester Guardian, Daily News* and *Daily Chronicle*. Hirst to Brunner, 5 December 1911 in Koss, *Sir John Brunner, Radical Plutocrat*, London 1970, p. 247.

65. Murray, *People's Budget*, pp. 129–30. Churchill outdid them after being made First Lord of the Admiralty. At a meeting of the Committee for the Reduction of Expenditure on Armaments on 16 January 1914, Hirst compared him to Dryden's Zimri: 'A man so various that he seem'd to be; Not one, but all mankind's epitome:/ Stiff in opinions, always in the wrong;/ Was everything by starts and nothing long.' Koss, *Brunner*, p. 267.

66. 'In Aid of Turkey', 21 March 1908.

67. 'The Colonies and the Empire', 13 April 1907. The 'invisible' income from commercial and financial services in the City was making up for a growing trade deficit in commodities. Hobsbawm, *Age of Empire*, pp. 39, 51.

68. Bernard Semmel, *Imperialism and Social Reform*, New York 1968, pp. 89–90, 147

69. As an authoritative source only the *Statist* under Paish came close, making a major case for unrestricted capital export in part to reverse the rise in food prices to which he attributed working class unrest: Offer, *Empire and Social Reform*, p. 125. Giffen, who founded the *Statist* in 1878, was in contrast, attacking Liberals as socialists by 1909, and favoured an 'expansive imperialism'. R. S. Mason, 'Robert Giffen and the Tariff Reform Campaign, 1865–1910', *Journal of European Economic History*, Spring 1996, p.176; 'Sir Robert Giffen', *Economist*, 16 April 1910.

70. Still listed separately, the Transvaal and Orange River, Cape Colony, and Natal together took £338 million. Its estimate of £79,560,116 of total interest received was surely too low, given the 'natural disinclination of British investors to disclose the extent of their foreign and colonial investments' – a tacit acknowledgement that investing abroad was also a means to widespread tax evasion. 'Our Investments Abroad', 20 February 1909.

71. 'The reservoir would not overflow unless it were full': 'Free Trade in Being', 13 March 1909.

72. 'When a profitable opportunity for investment occurs in Birmingham, Bristol, Leeds, Manchester, Liverpool, Newcastle, Glasgow ... the last thing that the people think of is to go to London.' It did not consider

if this was itself a problem. 'British Capital at Home and Abroad', 20 November 1909.

73. 'Lord Revelstoke's Maiden Speech', 27 November 1909; J. A. Hobson, 'Do Foreign Investments Benefit the Working Classes?', *Financial Review of Reviews*, March 1909, pp. 22–31; George Paish, 'The Export of Capital and the Cost of Living', *Statist*, 14 September 1914, quoted in Offer, *Empire and Social Reform*, p. 126. It was 'the old system of Protection and colonial preference', before repeal of the Corn Laws that had sent British capitalists scrambling to set up textile mills on the continent. 'British Capital At Home and Abroad', 20 November 1909.

74. 'Bagehot's Lombard Street', 23 July 1910.

75. London was 'the capital city of banking and investment', Wall Street 'the home of speculation': Francis Hirst, *The Stock Exchange: A Short Study of Investment and Speculation*, London 1911, p. 243. He was ebullient on a trip to the US at the turn of 1911, writing a glowing prospectus of Liberal England in the *New York Times*, where Unionists were cowed over tariffs, industry was flourishing, and capital export soaring to new heights: 'British Finance in 1910', 11 January 1911.

76. Hirst, *Stock Exchange*, Ibid., pp. 15–17.

77. For Radicals' 'whistling in the dark', see A. Morris, *Radicalism Against War, 1906–1914: The Advocacy of Peace and Retrenchment*, London 1972, passim.

78. It hoped in future for a 'satisfactory and permanent settlement of the native question'. Blacks showed 'aptitude for education', trade and the professions, and as the majority, 'cannot be safely excluded from all share in government'. Holding up Cuba and the US as extremes of race feeling, 'we imagine that in South Africa a tolerable compromise will be found'. 'Union of South Africa', 31 July 1909.

79. Barbara Metcalf and Thomas Metcalf, *A Concise History of Modern India*, Cambridge 2001, pp. 155–62. Morley had no time for either 'the bureaucratic illusion that all troubles can be easily disposed of by the suppression of a few newspapers and demagogues … or the more dangerous illusion of certain Liberals that India is now ripe for self-government.' For the *Economist*, a 'philosopher and statesman', democrat and Irish Home Ruler, Morley 'cannot be accused of any lack of sympathy with popular aspirations'. 'Unsettlement in India', 25 May 1907; 'Constitutional Reform', 14 November 1908.

80. For those who regarded the Empire 'with the critical and anxious eye of a true patriotism, there has been one great event' – Morley's arrival in India. 'We are there to keep the peace among these peoples, to remove the grinding poverty which became chronic under native rule, to save them from internecine warfare, from the oppression of Eastern conquerors, and from the rivalries of other Western nations, who, however little we may know the native mind, assuredly know much less. We must persevere with our burden, maintain order, providing

as many safety-valves for discontent as is consistent with that aim: 'Empire of India', 29 May 1909; 'Indian Reforms', 29 November 1909.

81. In 1907, imperial preference would hurt India if 'retaliatory tariffs excluded the staple products of India from the markets of continental Europe'. By 1909, it would hurt Britain, since 'the moment protection is applied to England ... it will be the duty of the India Office to protect India against Lancashire.' 'Unsettlement in India', 25 May 1907; 'Empire of India', 29 May 1909.

82. Hamer, *John Morley*, p. 346.

83. Keith Wilson, 'The Agadir Crisis, the Mansion House Speech, and the Double-Edgedness of Agreements', *Historical Journal*, September 1972, p. 520.

84. 'This language naturally caused alarm, and evoked from the Press of both London and Berlin a warlike chorus, which shows that the Fleet Streets of Europe are full of inflammable material.' The majority of the speech was about peace and finance, the rest a 'passing mood'. 'British Interests and the Moroccan Dispute', 29 July 1911. Wilson in part agrees, but shows it was sanctioned by the Cabinet: Germans, wrote Churchill, 'sent their Panther to Agadir and we sent our little Panther to the Mansion House'. Wilson, 'Agadir Crisis', pp. 519–21.

85. 'British Interests and the Moroccan Dispute', 29 July 1911; 'Morocco and the Powers', 21 July 1911.

86. Jonathan Kirshner, *Currency and Coercion: The Political Economy of International Monetary Power*, Princeton 1995, pp. 83–85.

87. 'The Financial Influence of Paris in Berlin', 29 July 1911.

88. 'German Securities and the Paris Bourse', 5 August 1911.

89. The concessions Grey had made to Russia in Persia also came to light, inspiring a similar reaction. 'It would not be difficult to smash Grey if there were a Cobden or a Bright in the House', Hirst wrote, before adding 'I'm not sure we want to ... if pressure is steadily applied we may get what we want.' Hirst to Brunner, 5 December 1911, in Koss, *Brunner*, p. 249. Grey, undeterred, sealed a secret pact with France the next year, releasing the French navy to patrol the Mediterranean while the British fleet guarded the Channel. For Hirst's criticisms of Grey, and the need for a 'business understanding with Germany', putting 'an end to all our financial troubles', see 'What Is Our Foreign Policy?', 4 November 1911; 'Morocco Settlement and Anglo-German Relations', 11 November 1911; 'New Chapter', 25 November 1911; 'Debates', 2 December 1911.

90. 'Rejection of the Budget', 4 December 1909; 'Ireland and the Constitution', 15 July 1911.

91. A Conservative government had initiated this land repurchase scheme in Ireland. 'The Third Home Rule Bill', 13 April 1912.

92. Ex-Liberal MP Samuel Storey, a champion of Home Rule before Gladstone, mocked the 'fancy picture' Hirst had painted of Liberals' steadfast commitment to the issue since 1886. 'In 1894 the new

Liberal leader, Lord Rosebery, announced that Home Rule must cease to be a living part of the Liberal policy', a stance Asquith, Grey, and Haldane 'not merely acquiesced in, but actively assented to'. 'All that the pages of history can truly record of them [the Liberals] seems to be this: for eight years, under the impulsion of a great and resolute leader, they fought for Home Rule; that then for 11 years, under his punier successors, they shirked Home Rule; that not until 1910 when they were dependent upon the Irish party for power and place, did they re-discover the principle.' 'Letters', 6 June 1914.

93. 'Moral Issues of Home Rule', 30 May 1914. As the crisis finally hit, the paper called the suspension of Home Rule for the duration of war 'a wise course of action'. 'The Dublin Affray', 1 August 1914; 'Home Rule Bill', 14 September 1914.

94. Mary Agnes Hamilton, *Remembering My Good Friends*, London 1944, 65.

95. 'The War and the Panic', 1 August 1914.

96. Hirst served on several committees for the Carnegie Endowment, including one devoted to publicity chaired by Norman Angell. Hirst was among the senators, professors and journalists who composed a *Report of the International Commission to Inquire into the Causes and Conduct of the Balkan Wars* (1914). At Lucerne he was to meet with the Economic History and Research Division, whose eminent members ranged from Paul Reinsch, former US ambassador to China, to the ex-Japanese finance minister and Tokyo mayor, Baron Sakatani, to the likes of Hirst and Paish. Those who made it spent the first days of the war in a surreal atmosphere, drawing up study plans on how to prevent it: the laws of capture at sea and on land since Grotius, the effects of the Hundred Years War on Panama, the feasibility of an international chamber of commerce. Above all, it called for studies into the influence of stock exchanges, bankers, financiers, and concessions to foreign corporations – on the presumption that all of the above tended to promote peace. *Carnegie Endowment for International Peace: Year Book 1915*, Washington 1915, pp. 60, 64, 73, 92–96.

97. 'The War and the Panic', 1 August 1914.

98. Douglas Newton, *Darkest Days: The Truth Behind Britain's Rush to War*, London 2014, *passim*.

99. Hirst, *Golden Days*, 238.

100. Morley to Hirst, 5 August 1914 and 7 August 1914, Hirst papers, BLOU, Box 36.

101. Cabinet Memorandum, 27 July 1914, quoted in Newton, *Darkest Days*, pp. 194–97, 279–80.

102. Ibid., pp. 279–80.

103. 'The Germans, both in Austria and the Empire, are a brave and resolute people. They are now surrounded and outnumbered, but they will fight with a desperate energy which forbids us to be certain of success.' 'The War', 8 August 1914.

104. 'The Moratorium', 8 August 1914; 'Some Effects of the War at Home and Abroad', 15 August 1914.

105. 'Cabinet Crisis and Perplexities of Faith', 1 July 1916.

106. 'Atrocity and Chivalry', 5 September 1914; 'The Progress of the War and the Prospects of Peace', 12 December 1914.

107. Unionists had offered a coalition to the Liberals in 1914, before 'the question of Belgium arose'. 'Why, then, should they not come in now and conduct the war as responsible ministers?' 'The War and the Coalition', 15 May 1915; 'Coalition Government and Progress of the War', 29 May 1915; 'Mr Lloyd George and the War', 5 June 1915.

108. Hirst to Scott, 21 May 1915, in *The Political Diaries of C.P. Scott, 1911–1928*, ed. Trevor Wilson, London 1970, pp 124–25.

109. Hirst to Scott, 28 May 1915, Ibid., p. 126.

110. 'Liberal Principles and the Composition of the Government', 22 January 1916; 'The Economics of Compulsion and the Irish Disturbances', 29 April 1916; 'Ireland and Peace', 13 May 1916. If Asquith introduced compulsion, Hirst wrote privately, it would be a 'landmark' and 'culmination of Liberal imperialism – the furthest point in reaction to which imperialism can drag liberalism'. As for his leading warmonger colleague: 'Lloyd George is not exactly a Liberal imperialist. He is really a politician who has conducted operations upon the principle of serving out a judicious mixture of socialism and jingoism.' 29 December 1915, Hirst Papers, BLOU, Box 13.

111. 'The Cabinet Crisis and Perplexities of Faith', 1 July 1916.

112. Clarke, *Liberals and Social Democrats*, pp. 166–69, 173–74.

113. 'Possible Guarantees of Peace', 12 December 1914. For Russell's praise of the Carnegie Endowment inquiry into the Balkans, on which Hirst worked, see Bertrand Russell to Ottoline Morrell, 14 October 1914, in *Selected Letters of Bertrand Russell: The Public Years, 1914–1970*, ed. Nicholas Griffin, London 2001, p. 15. The *New Statesmen* refused to publish Russell's article about the inquiry, which in light of the onset of the war linked peace to socialism: Sidney and Beatrice Webb wished to avoid all mention of the war, which they called 'one of those huge catastrophes when evil thoughts prevail'. Bertrand Russell, *Prophecy and Dissent, 1914–1916*, ed. Richard A. Rempel, London 2000, pp. 105–12; Bertrand Russell, *Pacifism and Revolution, 1916–1918*, ed. Richard A. Rempel, London 1995, pp. 393–94.

114. 'An Apology for Peace Makers', 5 March 1919, Hirst Papers, BLOU, Box 13; Catherine Merridale, *Lenin on a Train*, New York 2017, p. 84.

115. 'Service for All', *The Times*, 31 May 1915.

116. 'Through German Eyes', *The Times*, 16 March 1916.

117. 'Through German Eyes: The British Radical Press', *The Times*, 2 June 1916.

118. 'City Notes', *The Times*, 28 June 1916.

119. 'The Cabinet Crisis and Perplexities of Faith', 1 July 1916. Hirst kept this 'letter bag', which included messages from George Shaw-Lefevre, Thomas Ashton, Annie Besant, E. D. Morel, C. P. Scott, and Emily Hobhouse. From Italy, letters came from Edoardo Giretti and Luigi Einaudi, two liberal journalists and politicians, who contributed to the *Economist*; and from New York, Oswald Garrison Villard, *Evening Post* president, and publisher and editor of the *Nation*, and National City Bank executive George E. Roberts. Charles Burlingham wrote, 'but the *Economist* has a great name and influence and the necessity of considering the prejudices of your City readers has only served to make you weigh your words and make them weightier.' Burlingham to Hirst, 6 July 1916, Hirst Papers, BLOU, Box 42.

120. 'Your friends will have very much noticed the paragraph in City Notes of yesterday's *Times*. But I suppose in these times one has only to expect prejudice and offensiveness.' Keynes to Hirst, 29 June 1916, Hirst Papers, BLOU, Box 13.

121. 'Valedictory', 8 July 1916. That June, Hirst published letters from Lord Brassey, Loreburn, Beauchamp and Farrer.

122. Hamilton joined *Common Sense*, describing its office as 'a very odd assortment of persons – Lords Buckmaster and Beauchamp, Lady Barlow, Lady Askwith, Philip and Ethel Snowden, Ramsay Mac-Donald, Sidney Arnold, Richard Lambert, Robert Smillie ... Arthur Ransome among others.' Hamilton, *Good Friends*, pp. 85, 76–78. For Hirst's rapprochement with Lansdowne, the marquess who had negotiated the Entente with France, but favoured an early end to the war by 1917, see Keith Robbins, *The Abolition of War: The Peace Movement in Britain, 1914–1919*, London 1976, pp. 151, 157. For Hirst's retrospect on *Common Sense* and his time as secretary of the Lansdowne Committee, see 'An Apology for Peace Makers', 5 March 1919, Hirst Papers, BLOU, Box 13.

123. Elizabeth Bagehot to Hirst, July 1916, Hirst Papers, BLOU, Box 42.

124. Walter Layton, *Dorothy*, London 1961, pp. 57–58.

125. Hamilton, *My Good Friends*, p. 79.

126. This description is from a colleague, who reckoned that from 1904 onwards he, Withers and A. W. Kiddy 'held a grip upon financial journalism as strong as that of the famous professional triumvirate over golf championships'. Despite being unknown to the public (such journalism was still largely anonymous), 'any daily paper of standing in London which wanted a financial editor used to turn to one of us'. Frederick Harcourt Kitchin, *The London 'Times' Under the Managership of Moberly Bell*, London 1925, pp. 91–93.

127. 'City Notes', *The Times*, June 28, 1916.

128. 'Withers, Hartley (1867–1950)', Dilwyn Porter in *ODNB*, 2004.

129. 'It is unreasonable to expect the Boers to give full political powers to Englishmen', handing 'the country over to the Imperial Government or the Chartered Company.' No taxation without representation, a slogan of the Outlander cause, was sound, but 'not part of the

scheme of the universe'. Boers 'can point across their borders to Rhodesia, where British subjects live under an unqualified despotism'. Hartley Withers, *The English and the Dutch in South Africa*, London 1896, pp. 212–13.

130. Liberal fiscal policies were having an effect on investment abroad, but even a change of ministry would not do much on its own to alter that. 'For as new countries grow in wealth and population', investing in them 'will naturally and rightly attain to a relatively greater value.' Hartley Withers, *Stocks and Shares*, London 1910, pp. 294–302. See also, Hartley Withers, *Money Changing*, London 1913, pp. 47–69, 175–80.

131. Hartley Withers, *Our Money and the State*, London 1917, pp. 105–19.

132. See, alongside Hobson and Hobhouse, his 'Commerce and Finance as International Forces', in *The Unity of Western Civilization*, ed. F. S. Marvin, London 1915, pp. 198–221. In a collected volume endorsing the League of Nations, to which Sir Edward Grey lent his name, Withers argued that without such a body to keep the peace, each nation would strive for autarky, sapping trade, as fears of insecurity hobbled finance. Withers, 'The League of Nations: Its Economic Aspect', in *The League of Nations*, London 1919, pp. 87–100.

133. Here his answer to the 'social question' was at odds both with the Unionists – who favoured tariffs to protect home and imperial markets, and redirect capital to domestic investment – and most Liberals, who saw a role for government in taxing surplus income, and in welfare or social investment. 'Let us leave the question of national extravagance to statesmen. Individual extravagance is a matter that each of us can deal with himself.' Withers, *Poverty and Waste*, London 1914, p. 172. 'It is appalling to think of a world in which war and armaments are left to the unchecked will of irresponsible rulers and experts', replied the *Economist*. 'Luxuries and Thrift', 8 August 1914.

134. The contrast Withers formed with Angell, Hirst, Paish or Hobson is marked: if the latter now gave too much weight to finance as a force for peace, in the past they had exaggerated its role in war. 'Why did we go to war in South Africa? Finance played its part behind the scenes, but it never could have brought the war about if most of us had not wanted to wipe out the memory of Majuba, or paint the map of South Africa red.' Withers, *Poverty and Waste*, pp. 154–55.

135. 'Lombard Street is certainly entitled to congratulate itself.' Withers, *War and Lombard Street*, London 1915, pp. 99, 123. For July-August 1914 as a successful episode of crisis-management, and parallels with 2008 as seen by then Bank of England governor Mervyn King, see Richard Roberts, *Saving the City: The Great Financial Crisis of 1914*, Oxford 2013.

136. More scandalous were loans to insolvent governments, such as were raised for Honduras, Paraguay, Costa Rica, or Santo Domingo in the

1860s and '70s: Hartley Withers, *International Finance*, New York 1916, pp. 94, 111.

137. Withers, *International Finance*, pp. 104, 167, 39, 41.

138. 'After Two Years', 5 August 1916.

139. 'Financial Heroism', 6 October 1917.

140. 'Peace Talk and War Measures', 16 December 1916.

141. 'Meanwhile, the Allies will fight on with their confidence confirmed and gladdened by the proofs that Germany has given that she has shot her bolt.' 'The President and Peace', 30 December 1916.

142. 'Enemy Aliens', 4 November 1916.

143. As for war profiteering, it cited the case of investment trust companies, which had lost net revenue each year since the beginning of the war: £1,432,405 in 1913 had shrunk by 23 per cent to £1,104,631 in 1916. 'At the Front and at Home', 24 November 1917.

144. 'Peace Talk and War Measures', 16 December 1916.

145. 'After Two Years', 5 August 1916.

146. P. F. Clarke, *Hope and Glory: Britain 1900–1990*, London 1996, p. 96. Government spending peaked at 38.7 per cent of GDP in 1917; Broadberry and Howlett, 'The United Kingdom during World War I', pp. 210, 230.

147. Self-denial required borrowing at least as much as one expected to save for the year: 'borrow from his bank to pay the instalments as they mature, and save as fast as he can to pay off his banker.' 'The War Loan', 13 January 1917.

148. Ibid.

149. It criticized the 'hesitant' wartime record of the Asquith administrations, which had stoked currency inflation, let wartime profits accumulate untaxed, and failed to take full control of consumption and production. Yet it allowed that he and his ministers were 'tired men', who had put in 'great work' as 'constitutional reformers', and done their best in a pinch. Under Lloyd George, it expected 'vigorous government' – 'higher taxation of excess profits, with a prohibition of any distribution of profits above the pre-war level, a higher income tax, special taxation of all who are exempt from military service, sterner restriction of unnecessary imports, higher postal charges, travelling charges, higher taxation of all luxuries – alcohol, tobacco, picture palaces': 'The Political Crisis', 9 December 1917.

150. 'Achievement and Promise', 23 November 1918; 'Politics and Problems', 7 December 1918; 'Effort or Imagination', 18 January 1919. In contrast to Keynes's proposal that all inter-Allied war debts be mutually forgiven, the *Economist* under Withers argued that Britain should first cancel debts owed to it by weaker allies, then ask the US to 'fund our debt to them into a forty or fifty year loan', explaining that 'we still prefer this solution to Mr. Keynes's, for we believe that we can afford it if we work hard and reduce extravagance, and it is in accordance with our proud financial traditions': 'Turn of the Year' and 'The Peace Treaty', 27 December 1919.

151. The February Revolution looked to it like good news at first, both for the war effort and raising revenue. 'The Russian Revolution and War Finance', 17 March 1917; 'The Russian Kaleidoscope' 22 December 1917; 'Russia's Economic Position', 5 January 1918. 'These debts will undoubtedly be recognized', wrote its Wall Street correspondent, in the aftermath of October, 'as soon as the All-Russian Government formally takes its place among the Powers' –i.e. the Whites, backed by French, British, American and seven other expeditionary forces, won the Civil War. 'Russian Default', 19 July 1919; 'Soviet Russia', 13 December 1919. The paper soon abandoned this hope. 'The Results of Bolshevism', 28 May 1921. See also Keith Neilson, *Strategy and Supply: The Anglo-Russian Alliance, 1914–1917*, London 1984, p. 316; Hew Strachan, *Financing the First World War*, Oxford 2004, pp. 179–81.

152. 'Back to Sanity', 2 November 1918. For Withers's criticisms of wartime finance, and confidence the Bank Governor's plan would see off rivals to the City, see his *Wartime Financial Problems*, London 1919.

153. The only headline articles on the war in Ireland appeared after Withers had left, as a peace agreement was being negotiated – a policy shift the paper now supported. 'Policy and Principle', 5 November 1921.

154. The classic account is George Dangerfield, *The Strange Death of Liberal England*, London 1935.

155. 'Answers to the perennial question about the causes of collapse of the Liberal party cannot relate to the quality of the ideology available to it'. For it was 'better equipped than any other ideological force to handle the pressing social problems that had at last secured the political limelight': Freeden, *New Liberalism*, pp. 21–22, 225.

156. Packer emphasizes the admirable adaptability of liberalism to twentieth-century responsibilities, in this case 'fighting a modern, total war'. Even the abrogation of free trade, or conscription, failed to split the party. It had no 'deep-seated issues' and 'the government did not dissolve because it was tortured by Liberal principles, but because of an unforeseen political crisis'. Packer, *Liberal Government and Politics*, pp. 177–80. See also, Cameron Hazlehurst, *Politicians at War, July 1914 to May 1915*, New York 1971, p. 264. Soutou provides a powerful antidote to such benign explanations, arguing that the division of the Cabinet between those who feared dependence on the US and favoured a negotiated peace to avoid this, and those ready to fight on regardless, pitted finance against industry, in a battle which the former lost. Georges-Henri Soutou, *L'or et le sang: le but de guerre économique de la Première Guerre mondiale*, Paris 1989, pp. 364–72. On this, caution is required. As Hirst's ouster at almost the same time as Asquith indicates, it is debatable if the City opposed the end of 'business as usual' by 1916.

157. Lord Rosebery, who impressed the importance of continuity on his followers, was outdone by Grey, a still more ardent imperialist – embarrassing even the former with his calls for seizing the entire Nile valley and Uganda in 1894. Grey arrived at the Foreign Office with an idée fixe that Germany was Britain's 'worst enemy and greatest danger'. Grey to Henry Newbolt in January 1903, in Keith Robbins, *Sir Edward Grey*, London 1971, p. 131. For the evolution away from Salisbury's 'splendid isolation' by the turn of the century, see George W Monger, *The End of Isolation, British Foreign Policy, 1900–1907*, London 1963, pp. 1–20; Keith Wilson, *The Policy of the Entente: Essays on the Determinants of British Foreign Policy 1904–1914*, Cambridge 1985, pp. 5–6 and passim.

158. For the shortcomings of the Radicals, and the degree to which Grey was insulated from them – at a Foreign Office distinguished for its 'social exclusiveness', which viewed 'arbitrationists' and 'reductionists' as 'meddlesome busybodies' and 'amateur diplomatists', see Zara Steiner and Keith Neilson, *Britain and the Origins of the First World War*, London 1988, pp. 136–81, 184.

159. L. T. Hobhouse to E. Hobhouse, 24 December 1914, in Clarke, *Liberals and Social Democrats*, p.168.

160. Newton, *Darkest Days*, pp. 267–68; Asquith to Stanley, 4 August 1914, in Asquith, *Letters to Venetia Stanley*, Oxford 1982, p.150; Frances Stevenson, *The Years That Are Past*, London 1967, pp. 73–74.

161. Grey also played on the idea of an inexpensive naval war. 'For us, with a powerful fleet, which we believe able to protect our commerce, to protect our shores, and to protect our interests, if we are engaged in war, we shall suffer but little more than we shall suffer even if we stand aside.' HC Deb 3 August 1914, Vol. 65, col. 1823.

162. Hirst was no less enthusiastic than his predecessor about Japan, though under him the paper did caution that 'so startling a growth' in its foreign debt – '£115,000,000 as compared to something like £7,000,000 previous to the war' with Russia – 'even though occasioned by happenings which have raised the borrower into the foremost rank of nations, cannot be lightly regarded'. There was, nevertheless, 'everything to inspire confidence' – maritime pluck, a sinking fund, cash balances held abroad. It saw great promise in railway securities designed to open up Manchuria, Korea, Taiwan. 'Japan as a Borrower', 20 July 1907. For Masuda Takashi, then in London as head of the mercantile branch of Mitsui, 'the Rothschilds of Japan', see 9 November 1907; 5 January 1908.

163. Japan used an 1895 war indemnity from Peking (230 million silver taels deposited at the Bank of England) to move to a gold standard in 1897, the precondition for its borrowing binge. The £82 million China borrowed over the same period – to pay 'for its own subjugation' to Europeans and Japanese – must also be included in the City's total. Mark Metzler, *Lever of Empire: The International Gold*

*Standard and the Crisis of Liberalism in Prewar Japan*, Berkeley 2011, pp. 3, 258. The City, in this way, profited from both ends of the imperial redivision in Asia.

164. 'It has not been sufficiently appreciated how much the chancellor's domestic policy relied on sustaining the flow of capital export.' Offer, *Empire and Social Reform*, p. 128. Lloyd George's ties to the City extended to his insider dealings in Marconi shares in 1912, and to his bailout of the financial sector in July–August 1914 (see below).

165. In an introduction to Morley's letter of resignation in 1914, published a decade after the armistice, Hirst noted that Morley had criticized the Crewe Memorandum in 1907 – a secret Foreign Office report arguing that the rise of Germany posed a mortal threat to preservation of the British Empire, that would have to be met with all necessary measures. Morley saw it as too hostile to Berlin, and too focused on 'balance of power', but agreed on two points. Hirst approved of both as basic tenets of his own liberalism. First, 'that England was the natural enemy of any country threatening the independence of others and the natural protector of the weaker communities'. Second, that 'nations have always cherished the right of free intercourse and trade in the world's markets, and in proportion as England champions the principle of the largest measure of general freedom of commerce she undoubtedly strengthens her hold on the interested friendship of other nations, at least to the extent of making them feel less apprehensive of naval supremacy in the hands of a Free Trade England than they would in the face of a predominant protectionist Power. This is an aspect of the Free Trade question that is apt to be overlooked.' John Morley, *Memorandum on Resignation, August 1914*, New York 1928, pp. xxvii–xviii.

166. For Liberalism's 'democratic promise' to reign in 'cosmopolitan finance', see Howe, *British Government and the City*, pp. 136–38, 140; 'Policy did not reflect the dominance of one particular interest group, for that would threaten the assumption that the state was disinterested. Fairness was more than a rhetorical device; it had to be seen to be done': Martin Daunton, *Trusting Leviathan: The Politics of Taxation in Britain, 1799–1914*, Cambridge 2007, p. 388.

167. 'The strength of New Liberalism lay not in its transcendence of Cobdenism', but in 'its ability to dissociate free trade from laissez-faire': Howe, *Free Trade*, pp. 192–93; 268–72. The City's hostile reaction to New Liberal budgets, which Howe details, must qualify this conclusion somewhat: in effect, it chose between what must have been seen as two different types of interference with free trade – opting against direct taxation, and for protection.

168. Lloyd George put the eventual cost of the government 'cold storage' scheme, which guaranteed the purchase of unmarketable bills by the Bank, at £50 million: Roberts, *Saving the City*, pp. 5, 158, 237. Hirst put it at £200 million in case of a long war: 'The War, Trade and Finance', 22 August 1914. His *Economist* had the consistency to

oppose, or lament, moves like the stock exchange closure, remarking in a review of Withers's book, 'It is difficult to understand why a Government so versed in secret diplomacy had made no secret financial preparations for the great war to which its military and naval conversations are now known to have pointed.' 6 February 1915.

169. Bruce K. Murray relies in part on figures Herbert Samuel compiled and presented to the Royal Statistical Society in 1919, 'The Taxation of the Various Classes of the People'. Murray, *People's Budget*, pp. 290–96; 310–11.

170. Or about $44 billion in 1913 prices. Stephen Broadberry and Mark Harrison, 'Introduction', in *The Economics of World War I*, eds. Stephen Broadberry and Mark Harrison, Cambridge 2006, p. 23.

171. A. J. P. Taylor, *Essays in English History*, London 1976, p. 233. For a contrasting view of how much Britain truly left behind 'the benefits of a liberal market economy' in wartime, see Stephen Broadberry and Peter Howlett, 'The United Kingdom during World War I: Business as Usual?', in *The Economics of World War I*, pp. 206–34.

## 5. Own Gold

1. So L. S. Amery, whom Viscount Milner brought into Lloyd George's government, described it to the Imperial War Cabinet in 1917. John Gallagher, 'Nationalisms and the Crisis of Empire, 1919–1922', *Modern Asian Studies*, 1981, p. 356.

2. Alfred Draper, *Amritsar: Massacre That Ended the Raj*, London 1981, p. 96; John Darwin, *Britain, Egypt and the Middle East*, New York 1981, pp. 66–79.

3. They supplemented the Royal Irish Constabulary and regular troops. Charles Townshend, *The British Campaign in Ireland 1919–1921: The Development of Political and Military Policies*, Oxford 1975, pp. 25, 43, 110. Jon Lawrence, 'Forging a Peaceable Kingdom: War, Violence, and Fear of Brutalization in Post-First World War Britain', *Journal of Modern History*, September 2003, pp. 557–89.

4. Taxes raised the rest. In 1914, Lloyd George had shocked with a £200 million budget; as premier in 1919, his first in peacetime was over £2,500 billion – remarkable even with a near trebling of prices. Stephen Broadberry and Peter Howlett, 'The United Kingdom during World War I', in *The Economics of World War I*, eds. Stephen Broadberry and Mark Harrison, Cambridge 2005, pp. 217–22.

5. Unpegging the pound in 1919 was intended as a step preparatory to a return to gold, giving the Bank of England time to regain control of markets and retain gold reserves without restricting credit during demobilization. Donald Winch, *Economics and Policy*, London 1969, p. 79.

6. Barry Eichengreen, 'The British Economy between the Wars', in *The*

*Cambridge Economic History of Modern Britain*, eds. Roderick Floud and Paul Johnson, Cambridge 2004, Vol. II, p. 323.

7.  Japan and India also began to seriously compete with Lancashire. Robert Skidelsky, 'Retreat from Leadership', in *Balance of Power or Hegemony*, ed. Benjamin M. Rowland, New York 1976, pp. 165, 173, 175–77.

8.  For its secretary, Maurice Hankey, the Supreme War Council was the 'germ of the real League of Nations'. Peter J. Yearwood, *Guarantee of Peace: The League of Nations in British Policy, 1914–1925*, Oxford 2009, pp. 48, 56.

9.  11 December 1918, *The Papers of Woodrow Wilson*, ed. Arthur S. Link, Princeton 1986, Vol. 53, p. 366. For Bolshevism as both threat and spur to Wilson's conception of 'self-determination', see Arno J. Mayer, *Political Origins of the New Diplomacy 1917–1918*, New Haven 1959, pp. 329–67; David Foglesong, *America's Secret War Against Bolshevism*, Chapel Hill 1995, pp. 249–52. Britain played on such fears to secure US recognition of its protectorate over Egypt: Erez Manela, *The Wilsonian Moment*, Oxford 2007, pp. 145–47. Wilson's visit to Manchester's Free Trade Hall richly evoked his debt to its radical builders: Charles T. Thompson, *The Peace Conference Day by Day*, New York 1920, pp. 59–61.

10. Jan Smuts, *The League of Nations, A Practical Suggestion*, London 1918, p. 11. George Curry, 'Woodrow Wilson, Jan Smuts, and the Versailles Settlement', *American Historical Review*, July 1961, pp. 968–86; Mark Mazower, *No Enchanted Palace*, Princeton 2009, pp. 30–38. For Wilson, the racial hierarchy that placed white men above black at home extended outwards, and was one justification for his interventions in Mexico, Haiti, the Dominican Republic and the Philippines. His entente with Smuts in Paris had a firm basis: Manela, *Wilsonian Moment*, pp. 19–34.

11. Susan Pedersen, *The Guardians: The League of Nations and the Crisis of Empire*, Oxford 2015, pp. 40–41. In 1919, Britain secured the Afghan-Indian border using aerial bombing. Churchill had high hopes for it in Arabia and everywhere else. See David Fromkin, *A Peace to End All Peace*, New York 1989, pp. 422, 500; David Edgerton, 'Liberal Militarism and the British State', *New Left Review* no. 185, January 1991, pp. 138–69. At the War Office, Churchill authorized the Royal Air Force to use chemical weapons against 'recalcitrant Arabs as an experiment' in Iraq, writing that he did not understand 'squeamishness about the use of gas'; against 'uncivilised tribes ... gasses can be used that would cause great inconvenience and would spread a lively terror and yet would leave no serious permanent effects on most of those affected.' This was 'the application of western science to modern warfare': Alexander Cockburn, *The Golden Age Is in Us*, London 1994, p. 191.

12. A. J. P. Taylor, *English History*, p. 41.

13. Lloyd George was conscious of the parallel. *Lloyd George Liberal*

*Magazine,* 1920–1923, London 1973, p. 473; Peter Rowland, *David Lloyd George: A Biography*, London 1976, pp. 506–7. Days lost to industrial actions soared as boom went bust: from the already high 27 million in 1920 to 85.9 million in 1921, surpassed only in 1926, the year of the General Strike: Sean Glynn and John Oxborrow, *Interwar Britain: A Social and Economic History*, London 1976, p. 168.

14. This, more than nostalgia, explains why bankers on the Cunliffe Committee in 1918 idealized the gold standard as seamlessly adjusting rates and prices in line with gold flows. In reality, the pre-war standard had been a gold-sterling one, depending on wide availability of the latter and requiring increasingly frequent interventions from the Bank of England to maintain. De Cecco, *Money and Empire*, pp. 76–102; Geoffrey Ingham, *Capitalism Divided? The City and Industry in British Social Development*, New York 1984, pp. 176–79.

15. As Chancellor, Austen Chamberlain slashed spending by 75 per cent between 1918 and 1920: Eichengreen, *British Economy*, p 323; D. E. Moggridge, *The Return to Gold: The Formulation of Economic Policy and Its Critics*, Cambridge 1969, p. 15.

16. Bank and Treasury worked in tandem. To restore the former's control of money markets, impaired by the volume of Treasury bills on it, debt reduction was crucial. The demand for budgetary discipline, meanwhile, made the Treasury into the chief disciplinarian, its Permanent Secretary becoming Head of the Civil Service in 1919. Ingham, *Capitalism Divided*, pp. 176, 181.

17. Philip Snowden, Labour's Chancellor, quietly dropped the proposed levy in 1923, a signal his was a 'responsible', 'constitutional' party of government. Derek Aldcroft, *The Inter-War Economy: Britain, 1919–1939*, London 1970, pp. 329–30; Winch, *Economic Policy*, p. 97. Deflation reduced the cost of loans from the US, 'but increased the value of the much larger domestic debt and the income from them': David Edgerton, *The Rise and Fall of the British Nation: A Twentieth Century History*, London 2018, p. 122.

18. Ross McKibbin, *Parties and People: England 1914–51*, Oxford 2010, pp. 18–20. An influx of Liberals critical of the war increased Labour's reliance on them: Hugh Dalton, Frederick Pethick-Lawrence, F. B. Lees-Smith, Sydney Arnold all played major economic roles after 1914: Boyce, *British Capitalism at the Crossroads, 1919–1932*, pp. 14–18. Philip Snowden admonished not only Labour's rank and file – monetary matters 'must be kept free from political influences' – but even Churchill, his Liberal predecessor, for fiscal bloat: 'a well balanced budget is not a luxury which is to be avoided; it is a necessity which is to be provided for', he chided: Ingham, *Capitalism Divided*, pp. 183, 287; Winch, *Economic Policy*, pp. 92–93.

19. There were dissenting views about deflation and gold inside the major parties. But until 1931 – the Liberals in 1929 partially excepted – neither adopted them. Robert Skidelsky, *Politicians and the Slump*, London 1967, pp. 167–89.

20. David Hubback, *No Ordinary Press Baron*, London 1985, pp. 12–21.

21. Keynes, Marshall and Hirst helped prepare the oft-republished work: Walter Layton, *An Introduction to the Study of Prices*, London 1912, vi.

22. Walter Layton, *Dorothy*, London 1961, p. 58.

23. Stamp, who devised the excess profit duty while at the Board of Trade; Salter and Monnet on the Allied Maritime Transport Council; Drummond as private secretary to Asquith, Grey and Balfour at the Foreign Office. Yearwood, *Guarantee of Peace*, pp. 48, 56; Josiah Stamp, *Taxation During the War*, London 1931; Salter, *Allied Shipping Control: An Experiment in International Cooperation*, Oxford 1921. Along with Layton at Munitions, all played major and interlocking roles in the service of post-war liberal internationalism in conferences and at the League.

24. Francis Hackett, 'War Experts', *The New Republic*, 19 May 1917. Layton impressed Lloyd George for pointing out that Russia's request for 13.5 million tons of munitions in a few weeks could not travel over the Russian rails capable of a quarter that much a year – and for anticipating a revolution that Lord Milner failed to see coming: Hubback, *No Ordinary*, p. 42; Lloyd George, *War Memoirs*, London 1934, Vol. III, p. 1587.

25. In May 1918, Churchill made Layton chair of the 'Clamping Committee', tasked with co-ordinating efforts among the 12,000 officials inside the sprawling Ministry of Munitions: Geoffrey Best, *Churchill and War*, London 2006, p. 81. Layton stood unsuccessfully as a Liberal for Burnley in 1922, Cardiff South in 1923, and London University in 1929.

26. Labour made Layton a peer in 1947; Churchill insisted he stand as vice-president of the Consultative Assembly of the intergovernmental Council of Europe, established in 1949.

27. Readers of the *Economist* were, in other words, just the sort of men the new Economics Tripos were meant to train: Marshall to Layton, 2 December 1910, in *The Correspondence of Alfred Marshall, Economist*, ed. John K. Whitaker, Cambridge 1996, Vol. III, p. 274.

28. 'Memoirs', Layton Papers, TCC, Box 147, p. 25.

29. 'The Way of Peace', *Economist*, 19 November 1921.

30. 'The War after the War', *Economist*, 9 September 1922; 'Downing Street and the Dardanelles', *Economist*, 23 September 1922. These were likely written by Arnold Toynbee, then sending dispatches to the *Manchester Guardian* from Greece and Turkey, resulting in *The Western Question in Greece and Turkey: A Study in the Contact of Civilizations* (1922). For the controversy aroused by his criticisms of the Greek invasion of Anatolia, see Richard Clogg, *Politics and the Academy: Arnold Toynbee and the Koraes Chair*, London 1986.

31. 'The contingency of a purely Labour government is so remote that it is not worth further consideration', even if business circles were bound

to be astonished 'by the bourgeois character' of Labour in office. 'The Passing of the Coalition', *Economist*, 21 October 1922. Layton never broke more than briefly with Lloyd George, whom he saw as a main force in any Liberal-Labour or centre party of the future. In 1920, Layton declined to join Philip Kerr as political secretary to Lloyd George, but a few months later was consulting Lloyd George as well as Robert Cecil and Keynes on Eric Drummond's offer to direct the League's financial work. In 1924, Layton drew Lloyd George into the Liberal Summer Schools, which were initially meant to exclude him when begun in 1921. Hubback, *No Ordinary*, pp. 51, 54, 68.

32. 'The City suffered from the foolish egocentricity of the fly on the rim that thought it made the wheel go round.' Yet its 'prosperity was always based, ultimately, on Britain's industrial strength, and not the other way about': Sydney Pollard, *The Gold Standard and Employment Policies Between the Wars*, London 1970, p. 16. Although in principle the paper always denied that it put the City first, in practice it typically exemplified Pollard's image.

33. Wayne Parsons contends that Keynesianism 'captured' the *Economist* in the early 1930s, when 'an interventionist and managerialist consensus virtually replace the old laissez-faire, free-market principles'. The paper thus 'ensured that the Keynesian belief in managing the market economy' was 'incorporated into a form of discourse acceptable to the post-war financial community'. *The Power of the Financial Press*, New Brunswick 1990, pp. 84–85. It must, however, be added that this *form* affected the *substance* of its Keynesianism.

34. John Maynard Keynes, *The Economic Consequences of the Peace*, London 1919, p. 6.

35. Robert Skidelsky, *John Maynard Keynes: Hopes Betrayed*, London 1983, Vol. I, p. 207.

36. Hubback, *No Ordinary*, p. 83; note from 8 September 1955, Layton Papers, TCC, Box 82.116; Skidelsky, *Keynes*, Vol. I, p. 293. Keynes's first leader for the *Economist* was on 'Shippers, Bankers and Brokers', 6 February 1909.

37. 'Position of the Banks', *Economist*, 29 August 1914. This set off a firestorm, with one banker accusing Keynes of preaching from a 'comfortable academic armchair': 'Gold and the Banks', 5 September 1914. Hirst intervened to defend the bankers, in line with his view the City could not and should not facilitate the war. 'Policy of the Banks', 5 September 1914. Keynes replied to both in 'Gold and the Banks', 12 September 1914.

38. For the dissociation of laissez-faire and free trade as a defining trait of New Liberalism, see A. E. Howe, *Free Trade and Liberal England, 1846–1946*, Oxford 1997, p. 228; Hirst, *Hirst by His Friends*, p. 17. For Hirst's shift to an exclusively negative view of the state by the 1930s, see *Gladstone as Financier and Economist* (1931), *The Consequences of the War to Britain* (1934), *Liberty and Tyranny* (1935). Keynes told an audience at the Liberal Summer School in 1925 (the

third Layton and Ramsay Muir ran) that only New Liberalism – in contrast to outmoded creeds like socialism or laissez-faire, or modern scourges like Fascism or Bolshevism – was capable of 'directing economic forces in the interests of social justice and social stability'. Keynes, 'Am I a Liberal?', *Essays in Persuasion*, London 1932, p. 335.

39. 'The Peace Treaty', *Economist*, 27 December 1919.

40. 'A Solution to the Reparations Problem', 11 February 1922. Keynes pursued this further: the US needed 'to buy more and sell less' – lower tariffs and forgive debt – or else would be obliged to make 'an annual present' to cover the Europeans' account deficits. John Maynard Keynes, *A Revision of the Treaty*, London 1922, p. 175.

41. 'A Lost Opportunity', 5 August 1922.

42. Keynes and the *Economist* both thought magnanimity might predispose the US to a more favourable debt settlement. 'Beating About the Bush', 12 August 1922. Keynes added that Britain should abandon claims to pension and separation payments from Germany to encourage the French to moderation. Robert Cecil et. al., *Essays in Liberalism*, London 1922, pp. 51, 58.

43. D. E. Moggridge, *Maynard Keynes: An Economist's Biography*, London 1992, p. 389. For the pressure on Law to accept, particularly from Baldwin and Bank governor Montagu Norman, see Robert Self, *Britain, America and the War Debt Controversy: The Economic Diplomacy of an Unspecial Relationship, 1917–1941*, London 2006, pp. 45–53.

44. France and Italy waited to settle until 1926, paying 40 and 26 cents on the dollar respectively. Liaquat Ahamed, *Lords of Finance: The Bankers Who Broke the World*, New York 2009, p. 144. 'London's financial community' had 'long ago' decided it 'would and could pay the debt in full': 'Funding the American Debt', *Economist*, 3 February 1923.

45. 'Our Monetary Policy', 15 December 1923. Keynes talked of a 'monetary revolution', with gold demoted from 'despot' to 'constitutional monarch': Skidelsky, *Keynes*, Vol. II, p. 192. Yet Keynes still favoured giving central bankers great leeway. The Bank of England was 'one of our heaven-sent institutions', he told *The Times* on 25 March 1925, 'with no interests but the public good, yet detached from the wayward influence of politics'. 'The Return to Gold and Foreign Lending', in *The Collected Writings of John Maynard Keynes*, eds. Elizabeth Johnson and Donald Moggridge, London 1978, Vol. XIX, pp. 347–48.

46. Layton's main concern at this stage seems to have been that handing explicit control over policy to a 'small group of men' would provide those who wished to politicize their decisions with a clear target: 'Our Monetary Policy', 15 December 1923. A managed currency was inadvisable given the 'likelihood of many changes of Government' and the 'contingency the Government in power may not possess the whole-hearted confidence of a majority of the nation': Walter Layton et. al., *Is Unemployment Inevitable*, London 1924, p. 44.

47. 'As long as unemployment is a matter of general political importance, it is impossible that Bank rate should be regarded, as it used to be, as the secret *peculium* of the Pope and Cardinals of the City': *The Nation and Athenaeum*, 21 July 1923. Keynes wanted to remove the peculium, not the Pope or the Cardinals.

48. John Maynard Keynes, *Essays in Persuasion*, New York 1932, p. 257.

49. The US showed no sign of being a proficient or willing manager of the world economy, and Keynes unfavourably contrasted it with British *noblesse oblige*. 'Alternative Aims in Monetary Policy (1923)', 'Speeches of the Bank Chairmen, February (1925)' in ibid., pp. 210, 235; CW, Vol. IV, pp. 139–40; CW, Vol. IX, pp. 181, 199.

50. 8 August 1925.

51. Another factor was fear the Dominions might defect to the dollar. 'Finance or Industry', 17 October 1925. McKenna, ex-Chancellor, was chastised for 'grudging acceptance of gold ... calculated to strengthen the feeling among the less well-informed sections of this country that the operation has been manoeuvered by the bankers in their own interests, and that it has been contrary to the interests of British industry': 'The Bankers' Chautauqua', 30 January 1926. Keynes also used annual meetings to 'deliver homilies on the economic condition of the nation and the world' as a board member with Layton of the National Mutual Society. Keynes, *Essays in Persuasion*, pp. 220–43.

52. France's move to stabilize the franc on a gold basis at this moment only added to the pressure on sterling, to the intense frustration of the Bank of England, which accused the French of hoarding. By 1930, America held 50 and France 20 per cent of the world's gold reserves: Skidelsky, 'International Monetary System', pp. 171–73.

53. 'Monetary Stability and the Gold Standard', 10 November 1928. Norman and the other governors actively hampered the League's financial committee from appointing a Gold Delegation: Boyce, *British Capitalism*, pp. 167–72. After the Young Committee met the next year, Norman asked Layton to draft a charter with Sir Charles Addis for a proposed Bank of International Settlements, choosing 'words that would place the bank beyond the reach of governments'. For Layton this was impossible, since 'ultimately' and 'in the last resort' central banks had to have 'at least the tacit concurrence of the Government of the day'. Norman wrote Layton a few days after their interview, 'enigmatically and skittishly', 'Was it not Cardinal Newman who said that the will of God is perfect freedom?': Andrew Boyle, *Montagu Norman: A Biography*, London 1967, p. 247; 'Reparations Bank', 15 June 1929; 6 July 1929.

54. *Britain's Industrial Future: Report of the Liberal Industrial Inquiry*, London 1928; Lloyd George gave £10,000 to finance it and hosted its meetings at his country house at Churt. Hubback, *No Ordinary*, pp. 77–80.

55. 'Our Export of Capital', 11 February 1928.

56. 'Is the Financier a Parasite?' 14 July 1928; Boyce, *British Capitalism*, p. 172.

57. 'Monetary Policy and Prosperity', 18 August 1928; 1 September 1928; 'Mr Lloyd George's Pledge', 9 March 1929. Keynes, 'How to Organize a Wave of Prosperity', *Evening Standard*, 31 July 1928. Layton had made a similar point about *fiscal* policy in spring 1924 in the *Nation and Athenaeum*, in which Keynes accused him of wishing to 'sit by smiling' and wait for unemployment figures to 'cure themselves'. Keynes, *CW*, Vol. XIX, p. 218; Robert Dimand, *The Origins of Keynesian Revolution*, Stanford 1988, p. 89. Layton generally backed public works, while cautioning against monetary experiments. See, *The Third Winter of Unemployment*, ed. Walter Layton, London 1923, pp. 81–82; *Is Unemployment Inevitable? An Analysis and a Forecast*, ed. Walter Layton, London 1924, pp. 80–81, 83–84, 165–85; *Britain's Industrial Future: Liberal Industrial Inquiry*, London 1928.

58. 'A Protectionist's Mare's Nest', 23 February 1929.

59. The semi-official conference, hatched in 1925 at Belgium's third International Chamber of Commerce, gathered 194 delegates and 226 experts from fifty countries; Layton tried to leverage Britain's position as the world's largest importer to obtain pledges to lower tariffs. The *Economist* called it 'a landmark in economic history': 28 May 1927; see Boyce, *British Capitalism*, pp. 116–22. For a tariff on the grounds that modern capital mobility undermined the classical case for pure free trade from the likes of Douglas Graham, see the *Economist* 3 November 1928; 26 January 1929; 23 February 1929; *The Truth At Last About Free Trade and Protection*, London 1928.

60. 'The Effects of Foreign Lending' and 'Note of the Week', 9 March 1929.

61. Since this was probably not what the editors had in mind, 'I still await an answer to my question': 16 March 1929.

62. 'The Effect of Foreign Loans', 23 March 1929.

63. 'The Effect of Foreign Loans', 6 April 1929.

64. At this stage Keynes was optimistic about the City holding its own amidst the Wall Street boom. 'Bank rate: Five and a Half Per Cent', *Nation and Athenaeum*, 16–23 February 1929. Much of these exchanges appeared in *A Treatise on Money* in 1930, with general conclusions about foreign and home investment in an 'old country'. Keynes, *CW*, Vol. V, p. 312.

65. For 'mandarins', see Keynes to Churchill, 13 May 1928, in *CW*, Vol. XIX, p. 749. Keynes backed 'tied' lending in the *Nation and Athenaeum* and managed to insert it, presumably over Layton's objections, in the *Liberal Yellow Book*; it received support from left as well as right – in the *Empire Review*, *Morning Post*, *National Review* – and from the Foreign Office: Boyce, *British Capitalism*, pp. 175–76, 302.

66. *Keynes and His Critics: Treasury Responses to the Keynesian Revolution, 1925–1946*, ed. G. C. Peden, Vol. XXXVI, Oxford 2004, pp. 58, 69, 77.

67. And for what seemed selfish policies of hoarding meant to enfeeble Britain, according to the *Banker, Observer, Daily Herald* and *Financial News* – though not the *Economist*: Boyce, *British Capitalism*, p. 291.

68. Charles P. Kindleberger, *A Financial History of Western Europe*, London 1984, pp. 378–79.

69. Even in the Macmillan Report, Keynes rejected devaluation and defended the honour of the City, which up to 1914 had provided the flow of investment capital, trade finance, insurance and other services the world economy needed; New York and Paris had joined London as financial centres as a result of the post-war reparations and debt payments, but were lending 'only spasmodically', leading to liquidity crises: Boyce, *British Capitalism*, p. 331.

70. Though not if the assets were frozen abroad. 'Exchange Crisis', 8 August 1931. The report 'grossly underestimated' foreign claims on London, which were probably closer to £640 million, according to Kindleberger, *Financial History*, p. 378.

71. Walter Layton, *The Economic Situation of Great Britain*, London 1931, p. 35. The failure to foresee trouble on the horizon is striking given that the chairman of the *Economist*'s board, Henry Strakosch, was also a board member of Kreditanstalt, an important conduit for English capital into Austria. Boyce, *British Capitalism*, pp. 306–31. Appointed to the Committee of Enquiry for European Union, Layton was 'convinced a great opportunity had been missed' in the summer of 1931. Layton later claimed that after personally winning agreement from Austria, Germany, France, Italy and Sweden to lower tariffs to a maximum of 10 per cent, first Snowden and Samuel ('self-righteous all-out Free Traders'), and then Chamberlain blocked the deal. Raymond Streat, *Lancashire and Whitehall: The Diary of Sir Raymond Streat*, Manchester 1987, Vol. I, p. 162.

72. 'The British "Crisis"', 22 August 1931.

73. 'Democracy and Economy', 15 August 1931. Even if the May Report exaggerated the budget shortfall, such was the need for economy, it was acceptable 'to make the public's flesh creep': 'A New Axe', 8 August 1931.

74. 'The Government and Its Tasks', 29 August 1931. The mutiny at Invergordon was described as 'reports of insubordination in the Navy'. 'The End of an Epoch', 26 September 1931.

75. 'Harvest of Ottawa', 27 August 1932; 'Ottawa and the Loaf'; 'Liberal Ministers', 17 September 1932. For the split between Samuelite and National Liberals over tariffs, see David Dutton, '1932: A Neglected Date in the History of the Decline of the British Liberal Party', *Twentieth Century British History*, March 2003, pp. 43–60. Hirst, now head of the Free Trade Defence Committee, was more adamant: 'the Tariff of Abominations, the worst since Waterloo … it is now the turn of the colonies to control the mother country's taxes!': Frank Trentmann, *Free Trade Nation: Commerce, Consumption, and Civil Society in Modern Britain*, Oxford 2008, pp. 331–32.

76. Layton to MacDonald, 27 September 1933, Layton Papers, TCC. 'I assure you that I desire with all my heart that you will not lose touch with me but that whenever you want to say or write something, access remains as free as ever': MacDonald to Layton in Hubback, *No Ordinary*, p. 123. MacDonald appointed Layton along with Keynes, Stamp, Salter and others to his Advisory Committee on Financial Questions just after the gold rout in 1931. Roosevelt put paid to the 'goldbug' plan, refusing to attend the London conference, then devaluing the dollar while it met. For a perplexing claim the *Economist* drew 'sanguine' lessons about democracy from the London Conference, see David Runciman, *The Confidence Trap*, Princeton 2013, pp. 109–10; 'A World Adrift', *Economist*, 4 June 1932.

77. C. H. Rolph, *Kingsley: The Life, Letters and Diaries of Kingsley Martin*, London 1973, p. 164.

78. Keynes sent 'Notes on the Currency Question' to Leith Ross, Montagu Norman and Hubert Henderson on 16 November 1931 after a speech to the Political Economy Club on the same theme. Keynes, CW, XXI, p. 17.

79. Ibid., pp. 24–6.

80. Skidelsky, *Keynes*, Vol. I, pp. 309, 340–44.

81. See *The Nation and Athenaeum*, 31 May, 7 June, 9 August 1924; Winch, *Economics and Policy*, pp. 108, 155–56.

82. 'Proposals for a Revenue Tariff', *New Statesman and Nation*, 7 March 1931. The *Economist* pointed to the effects on the cost of living. 'Inconsequences of Mr. Keynes', 14 March 1931. 'Crocodile tears', Keynes jeered, citing its own call for reducing wages by 10–15 per cent. Keynes, CW, Vol. XX, pp. 499–500. Layton responded, along with Beveridge, Lionel Robbins and other LSE economists, in *Tariffs: The Case Examined*, ed. W. E. Beveridge, London 1931, pp. 76–92.

83. 'Out of the ashes the City of London will rise with undiminished honour ... for she has played the game up to the limits of quixotry, even at the risk of driving British trade almost to a standstill. No banker could do more': Keynes, 'The Future of the World', *Sunday Express*, 27 September 1931.

84. Nodding selectively at Keynes, it pointed to a disequilibrium between savings and investment, which adjustments to monetary demand alone could correct: 'Planning', 13 January 1934; for Macmillan's reply, 10 March 1934. See E. H. Green, *Ideologies of Conservatism: Conservative Political Ideas in the Twentieth Century*, Oxford 2002, pp. 158–62.

85. Hubback, *No Ordinary*, pp. 95–96. Douglas Jay's contention that the *Economist* vigorously supported reflation and began to use the term 'full employment' without reservation, 'helping in no small way to make the idea respectable', is exaggerated: D. W. Parsons, *Power of the Financial Press*, New Brunswick 1990, p. 69.

86. 'Mr. Keynes on Money', 29 February 1936.

87. This is the sense of Keynes's famous remark in 'Am I a Liberal?', a

1925 talk at a Layton-organized Liberal Summer School: 'The difficulty is that the Capitalist leaders in the City and in parliament are
incapable of distinguishing novel measures for safeguarding Capitalism from what they call Bolshevism': Keynes, *Essays in Persuasion*,
New York 1932, p. 327. For Keynes's ambiguous and shifting use of
the term 'rentier', which must qualify the radical conclusion of the
*General Theory* calling for the 'euthanasia of the rentier', see Ross
McKibbin, *English Historical Review*, February 2013, p. 99.

88. 'Memoirs', Layton Papers, TCC, Box 147, p. 250.

89. From 8 per cent in 1913 to 2.5 per cent in 1925; by 1930, £500
million or 12 per cent of overseas investment was in India. Atkin,
*British Overseas Investment*, pp. 13–16. For the failure of the 'imperial option', based on the decline of income on invisibles from £365
million in 1929 to £230 million in 1938, see Skidelsky in *Balance of
Power*, p. 184.

90. Katherine Mayo, *Mother India*, New York 1927; Layton, *Dorothy*,
p. 104. Layton's assistant was Benegal Rama Rau, later ambassador
to Washington and governor of the Bank of India. See Hubback, *No
Ordinary*, pp. 103–11; Ganesh Bhaskar Jathar and Shridhar Govind
Beri, *Indian Economics, a Comprehensive and Critical Survey of the
Economic Problems of India*, Vol. II, Oxford 1931, pp. 489, 531.

91. 'Indian Finance', 5 July 1930; 'Federalism in the British Empire',
9 August 1930.

92. Indians gained provincial self-government and the majority of seats
in parliament, but London kept tight control of finance, defence and
foreign affairs, with Dominion status deferred. The *Economist* criticized Gandhi's so-called non-cooperation movement as violent and
for refusing to concede representation for minority Muslim, Sikh and
lower caste Indians. See 'India', 24 May 1930; 'Indian Developments',
7 June 1930; 'Round Table Conference', 9 July 1930; 'Outlook in
India', 13 September 1930; 'The Crux for the Conference', 27 December 1930; 'Indian Truce', 14 March 1931; 'British Policy and India', 28
November 1931; 'The Lothian Report', 11 June 1932. 'Constitution-
making on a stupendous scale' called forth a nineteen-page supplement
on the history of the Raj from Layton on 2 February 1935.

93. Tom Segev, *One Palestine, Complete: Jews and Arabs under the British
Mandate*, New York 2000, p. 415.

94. Was Palestine another Ireland, the Arabs Sinn Fein? 'Are we going to
crush them in the ruthless fashion in which Mussolini has crushed the
Amharas? Or are we going to betray our Zionist protégés?': 'Palestine in Ferment', 30 May 1936; 'Uproar in Palestine', 13 June 1936;
'Turning the Screw in Palestine', 20 June 1936. Britain should retain
a mandate over the Holy Places, acting as a buffer between the two
communities, and impose a free trade treaty on both states: 'Partition
of Palestine', 10 July 1937; 'Geneva and Palestine', 7 August 1937;
'Mandate Commission', 28 August 1937; 'The Arab World', 11 June
1938; 'No Change in Palestine', 20 May 1939.

95. Clarke, *Hope and Glory*, p. 116.

96. 'Memoirs', Layton Papers, TCC, Box 147, p 206; 8 September 1955, Box 82.116.

97. Lloyd George acquired a majority of shares in the *Daily Chronicle* through his political fund in 1918, selling them on in 1926 to Sir David Yule, Sir Thomas Catto and the ex-viceroy Lord Reading; it was resold to Henry Harrison, the paper magnate, soon after. Lord Cowdry bought the *Westminster Gazette* in 1921. Taylor, *English History*, p. 118; 'Yule Family', Iain F. Russell in *ODNB*, 2004; Kathleen Burk, *Morgan Grenfell, 1838–1988: The Biography of a Merchant Bank*, London 1989, p. 82.

98. Charles Lysaght, *Brendan Bracken*, London 1979, pp. 82, 62. Evelyn Waugh on the Bracken-inspired Rex Mottram: 'His seniors thought him a pushful cad', but Lady Julia, 'recognized the unmistakable chic – the flavour of "Max" and "F.E." and the Prince of Wales, of the big table in the Sporting Club, the second magnum and the fourth cigar, of the chauffeur kept waiting hour after hour without compunction'. 'He wasn't a complete human being at all. He was a tiny bit of one unnaturally developed; something in a bottle, an organ kept alive in a laboratory. I thought he was a sort of primitive savage, but he was something absolutely modern and up-to-date that only this ghastly age could produce': *Brideshead Revisited*, London 1945, pp. 162, 177.

99. Lysaght, *Brendan Bracken*, p. 99.

100. Strakosch started as a foreign exchange dealer for the Anglo-Austrian Bank in London, where he moved in 1891 from his birthplace in Hohenau, Austria, before rising to oversee the Union Corporation. Along the way, he became a confidant of Montagu Norman and the Rothschilds, and an expert on the global monetary system – travelling to nearly as many conferences as Layton to try to repair it in the interwar period, for the League and as advisor to South Africa and India: H. Strakosch, *The Value of Gold in Our Economic System*, London 1918; Boyce, *British Capitalism*, pp. 42, 167; Russell Ally, *Gold and Empire: The Bank of England and South Africa's Gold Producers, 1886–1926*, Johannesburg 1994; C. E. Temperley, 'Strakosch, Sir Henry Edouard (1871–1943)', Maryna Fraser in *ODNB*, 2004. Strakosch criticized Keynes for 'The Economic Consequences of Mr. Churchill' in the *Times* of 31 July 1925. For his views in favour of stabilizing the price level by keeping gold but managing its distribution through the League and the Bank for International Settlements, see the *Economist* 10 November 1928 and 5 July 1930.

101. Hubback, *No Ordinary*, p. 87.

102. The largest individual shareholders were: Lord Cowdray of Pearson, an international construction firm converting itself into a financial and publishing business, which controlled Lazard Brothers, 7,500 shares; W. W. Greg, who was Julia Wilson and W. R. Greg's son, 7,000; at 5,000 each, Laurence Cadbury, Lionel Nathan de

Rothschild and Anthony Gustav de Rothschild, Walter Runciman and Baron Bruno Schroder; at 3,000, Henry Strakosch and Joseph Kitchin, both of Union Corporation; at 2,000 R. H. Brand of Lazard Brothers; 1,500 for Ernest Simon and Henry Graham White; 1,250 to Layton; 500 to Sir Laurence Halsey; 250 to D. E. W. Gibb. See Edwards, *Pursuit of Reason*, p. 620.

103. Stanley Morrison and Beatrice Warde of the Monotype Corporation, along with the chief compositor of Eyre and Spottiswoode. Warde had remarked to Hutton, who pushed the change: '*The Times* is pulling up its socks. Hadn't you better pull yours up?': Edwards, *Pursuit of Reason*, pp. 717–18, 736; Hubback, *No Ordinary*, pp. 85–86. Layton then targeted a circulation of 20,000. Layton to Strakosch, May–July 1938, Layton Papers, TCC, Box 81.62.

104. Jay claimed to have been converted to Labour in 1926 during the General Strike, while still at Winchester. Douglas Jay, *Change and Fortune: A Political Record*, London 1980, p. 22. Jay left the *Economist* in 1937, the year *The Socialist Case* appeared. Tom Dalyell, 'Lord Jay', *The Independent*, 6 March 1996.

105. Hutton was the brother-in-law of Evan Durbin, another young Labour economist trained at New College, Oxford, under Lionel Robbins. Durbin moved with Robbins to the LSE, becoming a personal assistant to Clement Attlee in 1942. See *Isaiah Berlin: Letters, 1928–1946*, London 2012, Vol. I, p. 433; Elizabeth Durbin, *New Jerusalems: The Labour Party and the Economics of Democratic Socialism*, London 1985, pp. 112, 253–54.

106. Martin Gilbert, *Winston Churchill*, London 1966, Vol. V, pp. 541, 605, 616; Hugh Purcell, *A Very Private Celebrity: The Nine Lives of John Freeman*, London 2015. Ian Mackay, interviewing for the industrial correspondent job at the *News Chronicle* in 1934, is supposed to have told Vallance he would take it if there were no objections to his politics: 'What are they?' 'I regard Stalin and Trotsky as a couple of crusted old Tories.' 'You'll do', replied Vallance. George Glenton and William Pattinson, *The Last Chronicles of Bouverie Street*, London 1963, p. 52.

107. Jay, *Change and Fortune*, p. 52; Nicholas Davenport, *Memoirs of a City Radical*, London 1974, p. 111. Layton may have met Toynbee through Gilbert Murray, his Greek tutor at Oxford. Toynbee's surveys for the Royal Institute appeared from 1925 to 1938. William H. McNeil, *Arnold J. Toynbee: A Life*, New York 1989, p. 132.

108. Balogh arrived after stints as a researcher at the French, German and US central banks, with Keynes interested in his then orthodox views on gold flows between these banks and the Bank of England. Keynes and the Second World War changed Balogh: 'the palpable impotence of the respectable ... when confronted with the collapse of the social framework and political stability of Central Europe, cured me of my childhood bogey of inflation': Paul Streeten, 'Thomas Balogh', in *A Biographical Dictionary of Dissenting Economists*, eds. Philip

Arestis and Malcolm C. Sawyer, Cheltenham 1992, pp. 28–35.
Parsons, *Power of the Financial Press*, p. 69; 'I mistrust everything
he says', a wary Leonard Woolf told Kingsley Martin: see Leonard
Woolf, *Letters*, ed. Frederic Spotts, London 1989, pp. 437–39, 452.
Nicholas Kaldor 'converted' to Keynesianism while on a fellow-
ship to the US in 1934–35, away from the LSE: Angus Burgin, *The
Great Persuasion: Reinventing Free Markets since the Depression*,
Cambridge, Mass, 2012, p. 29.

109. Hodson seems to have been recruited to the *Economist* through
Lionel Robbins, his economics tutor at Oxford, in 1928 – to find 'the
statistics he needed to complete his thesis on overseas investment':
Hubback, *No Ordinary*, p. 88. Hodson left to edit the *Round Table*
in 1934, spent part of the war in India working on constitutional
reform for Leo Amery, and from 1950–61 was the *Sunday Times*
editor. For other staff writers, see Edwards, *Pursuit of Reason*, pp.
687–88, 732–33.

110. *The Socialist Case*'s object was to counter the 'flood of quasi-Marxist
volumes pouring forth from Gollancz's Left Book Club': Jay, *Change
and Fortune*, pp. 62–63.

111. Jay liked Kingsley Martin when he was dropping marbles down the
actress Deborah Kerr's bosom but could not understand how he
could think Britain was suited to a 'centralised communist economy'
leading to 'concentration camps or lunatic asylums of which he
would be the first inmate': Davenport, *Memoirs of a City Radical*,
pp. 30, 109.

112. In the *Economist*, Layton also criticized Baldwin for breaking off
talks with the miners, and employers for threats to penalize sympathy strikers. 'How the Strike Came About', *Economist*, 8 May 1926;
'Cost of the Strike', 8 May 1926; 'Restoring Peace', 15 May 1926.

113. *Burden of Plenty?*, ed. Graham Hutton, London 1935, p. 133; *We
Too Can Prosper*, London 1953; *Rebirth of Britain: A Symposium
of Essays by Eighteen Writers*, ed. Arthur Seldon, London 1964,
pp. 14–15, put out with the Institute for Economic Affairs. For a
profile, see 'A Good Friend', *Economist*, 22 October 1988, and for
the nineteenth-century liberal outlook of some of Labour's leading
thinkers, see Stefan Collini, 'Moral Mind: R. H. Tawney', in *English
Pasts: Essays in History and Culture*, Oxford 1999, pp. 177–94.

114. Skidelsky, *John Maynard Keynes*, London 1992, Vol. II, p. 569; John
Maynard Keynes, 'Am I a Liberal?', in *Essays in Persuasion*, p. 324.

115. Francis Williams, *Nothing So Strange: An Autobiography*, London
1970, pp. 109–10. This criticism of Keynes did not prevent Jay from
issuing the notorious dictum: 'In the case of nutrition and health, just
as in the case of education, the gentleman in Whitehall really does
know better what is good for people than the people themselves':
*The Socialist Case*, London 1937, p. 317.

116. Davenport, *Memoirs of a City Radical*, p. 76.

117. Ibid., p. 77.

118. Jay, *Change and Fortune*, p. 60; Williams, *Nothing So Strange*, pp. 112–13.

119. Davenport chose the lavatory, fearing the effects of the local seafood. Davenport, *Memoirs*, London 1974, p. 44.

120. Jay, *Change and Fortune*, p. 50.

121. Stevenson, *Lloyd George*, p. 260.

122. James Thomas, *Popular Newspapers, the Labour Party and British Politics*, Abingdon 2005, pp. 13–14.

123. Surely the *Chronicle* would take a stand against nationalization of industry? 'The line between state ownership and control or unfettered private enterprise is a matter of expediency rather than principle', Layton wrote, echoing the middle course charted in the Liberal Industrial Inquiry. Hubback, *No Ordinary*, p. 155.

124. Hubback, *No Ordinary*, pp. 90, 188, 155.

125. 'No newspaper has attacked the National Government more fiercely than the "News Chronicle", but no man has been happier than Sir Walter Layton on occasions when the Prime Minister happened to consult him.' Ibid., p. 137.

126. Aylmer Vallance to Henry Strakosch, 27 December 1932, Layton Papers, TCC, Box 81.16.

127. 'As agreed between us I shall carry this position for three years, you giving me full discretion to sell or vary the holdings at any time, but on the understanding that you incur no further liability.' Martin Gilbert, *Winston S. Churchill*, London 1976, Vol. V, p. 920. When Strakosch died in 1943, he left Churchill £20,000 – along with the earlier debts taken over from his stockbroker, gifts amounting to about £2 million in today's money.

128. John Dizikes, 'Britain, Roosevelt and the New Deal: British Opinion, 1932–1938' (PhD diss., Harvard University 1979), p. 266.

129. 'But if the New Deal be compared, not with the absolute standard of Utopia, but with the achievements of other Governments, the former adverse judgement must be modified. If it be compared with either the performance or the promise of its rivals, it comes out well. If its achievement be compared with the situation which confronted it in March 1933, it is a striking success. Mr Roosevelt may have given the wrong answer to many of his problems. But he is at least the first President of modern America who has asked the right questions.' 'The New Deal', 3 October 1936.

130. Praising the Federal Deposit Insurance Corporation, it still had 'serious doubts' about it as a permanent system, since it amounted to a 'penalisation of sound banks' and 'endowment of imprudent banking'. Ibid. For more on the paper's favourable attitude to Roosevelt, and mixed reaction to his New Deal over time, see Alastair Burnet, *America: 1843–1993: 150 Years of Reporting the American Connection*, London 1993, pp. 114–22.

131. 'Russian Trade Agreement', 9 October 1920. Most Labour voters couldn't even pronounce Bolshevik, scoffed a piece dismissing the

alleged links between the two parties. 'The theory of Bolshevism may be good or bad, but in fairness to Lenin and Trotsky it ought to be said that it has no more to do with murder and other atrocities than the British Constitution has with the exploits of the Black and Tans': 'Labour and Communism', 30 July 1921. It found little to fear from Bolshevik influence on Labour, even during the red-baiting 1924 election: 'Defeat of the Communists', 11 October 1924. Nor was the paper opposed to diplomatic dialogue. If it criticized the first drafts of Labour's Anglo-Russian treaty, this was not due to the clauses about trade or fisheries, but because conditions attached to a new British loan were far too vague. This was 'bad morality and bad business': 'A Bad Treaty', 16 August 1924.

132. 'Russian Supplement', 19 March 1927; Hubback, *No Ordinary*, p. 86.

133. The *Economist* pointed out that by 1928, UK trade with the Soviet Union was second only to Germany and not by much: in 1927–28, it amounted to £150 million as compared to £186.2 million with Germany; in 1928–29, the figure was £192.5 million compared to £208.5 million with Germany. 1 November 1930.

134. Collectivization would depend on building enough machines and inducing the peasants to use them; establishing 'village communism' was more daunting and 'cannot take place as the result of sheer relentless compulsion ... [still] the idea of a new life has been awakened among the active members of the younger generation'. 'An Impression of Russia', 17 November 1931; Layton Papers, TCC, Box 81.10.

135. Ibid., Layton Papers, TCC, Box 81.10.

136. 'Russia Revisited I', 3 June 1933. The *Economist* under Layton provided more neutral and detailed coverage of Russia than did Keynes, or the *New Statesman and Nation* or the *Guardian*. See, 'A Short View of Russia' (1925) in Keynes, *Essays in Persuasion*.

137. Maisky's diaries reveal two visits to the Soviet embassy: during the Munich crisis on 18 September 1938, when Layton sent Arthur Cummings, *News Chronicle* political editor, to check a Cabinet rumour that the Soviets planned to do nothing, even if 'France came out to protect Czechoslovakia with arms in hand', which Maisky denied; and on 17 April 1939 from Layton, at the behest – so Maisky speculated – of Chamberlain, to indicate a last minute 'radical change' in public opinion in favour of a 'new course' to 'repel aggression and achieve agreement and cooperation with the USSR'. Maisky cultivated the British press, particularly in the City, 'which he assumed controlled British politics'. See his exchanges with Bracken, *The Maisky Diaries: Red Ambassador to the Court of St James's, 1932–43*, ed. Gabriel Gorodetsky, New Haven 2015, pp. 41, 45–46, 402, 499–500, passim.

138. Of Mussolini: 'For the moment, he has uttered at Naples only one economic sentence: "Italy needs at the helm a man capable of saying

*No* to all requests of new expenditure." So far, so good.' 'Will the new party have the will and the power to redress the awkward financial situation of the State, which is the only true cause of the present unfavourable movement of exchanges and prices?' Einaudi worried that the Fascists – like the Catholics and Socialists, who 'cater for the vote of multitudes crying always after State aid' – 'would hesitate before the task'. 'Italy – The Fascisti and their Program', 28 October 1922. I am grateful to Clara Mattei for bringing the extent of Einaudi's support for fascist austerity policies in the 1920s to my attention. See, Clara E. Mattei, 'Austerity and Repressive Politics: Italian Economists in the Early Years of the Fascist Government', Laboratory of Economics and Management Working Paper, Pisa 2015. Articles attributed to Einaudi are in *From Our Italian Correspondent: Luigi Einaudi's Articles in the Economist, 1908–1946*, ed. Roberto Marchionatti, Vol. I–II, Florence 2000.

139. Einaudi harshly criticized the post-war governments of Giovanni Giolitti and Francesco Nitti for raising taxes and tariffs, and as too susceptible to popular pressure in favour of welfare spending, and for not intervening more forcefully against striking workers, in occupation of factories, and the Communists. He welcomed the arrival of 'youths of the middle class, returned men and officers in indignation' that 'grouped themselves into "fasci"' with the result that 'the communists are everywhere defeated ... this renewed feeling of hope in the future of our country is not the least important cause of the better tone in foreign exchanges'. 'Italy – Passing of the Communist Peril', 16 April 1921. Reforms included independence to the Bank of Italy, and an end to what Einaudi called 'the demagogic persecution of savings and capital' – 'it was high time from the government bench that a voice should be raised against the frenzied finance of the Bolshevist after-armistice period': 'Absolute Government in Italy', 27 November 1922.

140. Industrial securities rose 10 per cent on average the week after stabilization, disproving critics who said it overvalued the currency. 'Stabilisation of the Lira', 31 December 1927; Roland Sarti, 'Mussolini and the Italian Industrial Leadership in the Battle of the Lira 1925–1927', *Past and Present*, May 1970, pp. 97–112.

141. Einaudi was generally supportive of Mussolini's fiscal and monetary policies, and generally critical of corporatist moves or state intervention (a notable exception being the bank bailouts in 1931–33). *From Our Italian Correspondent*, XXVIII, XLI. London editors, 'free from the risk of Fascist repression', may have been more critical, as Marchionatti argues, but not by much ('Nemesis of Fascism', 24 June 1924; 'New Crisis in Italy', 10 January 1925), or else qualified their criticisms. A free press, political parties, fair elections, an independent civil service and judiciary – all had been suppressed with 'deplorable methods', for none 'were needed to achieve the great results which admittedly have been accomplished since the new

*régime* took office': 'Italy Under Fascism', 25 September 1926. There is little to support the claim Layton later made that Einaudi's pieces were 'a thorn in the flesh of the Fascisti': Speech to the 'Instituto Italiano di Cultura', London, February 20, 1962, Layton Papers, TCC.

142. Layton, *Dorothy*, p. 90. At the time, however, the *Economist* applauded Mussolini's foreign minister Dino Grandi, whose call for the abolition of submarines and chemical and biological warfare as well as heavy artillery and tanks, 'rightly gave his country the moral initiative at Geneva': 'The Disarmament Conference', 13 February 1932.

143. On free trade and humanitarian grounds. 'Germany and Jewry', 1 April 1933. 'Germany's Boycott', 8 April 1933.

144. Hitler returned Schacht to his former role with these factors in mind, as the following exchange between them, in anticipation of the Nazis' arrival in office indicates. 'What would happen if *we* – or rather, a National Socialist Reichsbank president – were to begin with our way of financing employment the moment we take over the government?' Hitler asked. 'The international financial world would stand on its head and attack our currency with all the means at its command': Alan Milward, 'The Nazi Miracle', *London Review of Books*, 23 January 1986.

145. 'Memoirs', Layton Papers, TCC, Box 147.

146. Hubback, *No Ordinary*, p. 142.

147. Adam Tooze, *The Wages of Destruction: The Making and Breaking of the Nazi Economy*, New York 2006, pp. 70–71.

148. 'Outlook in Germany', 15 April 1933; 'Dr Schacht's Declarations', 10 June 1933; 'Guaranteeing Export Trade', 22 December 1934; Layton published 'The New Germany as I Saw It' in the *News Chronicle* on 5, 7, 10 April 1933. On the importance of the Anglo-German Payments Union, see Tooze, *Wages of Destruction*, p. 87.

149. 'The Hitler Terror', 2 September 1933.

150. Layton to Schwerin von Krosigk, 23 September 1933, Layton Papers, TCC, Box 81.17; 'The German Government and the Economist', 23 September 1933.

151. Jay wrote that honouring treaty obligations meant being willing to use force when these were violated: 'Pacifism' 2 December 1933. On Germany's withdrawal from the League, see 'Hitler Shows his Hand', 21 October 1933.

152. Japan's onslaught on Manchuria (which began with the Mukden Incident in September 1931), its refusal to abide by League resolutions ordering it to leave, and its withdrawal from Geneva in February 1933 were major blows to the League's prestige, but not yet fatal ones. The *Economist* devoted an article to these events almost every week from the time the Chinese referred the matter to the League in October 1931: 'The League and Manchuria', 17 October 1931; 'The Lytton Report', 8 October 1932; 'The League Makes Up Its Mind', 18 February 1933.

153. 'The Paris Blunder', 14 December 1935; 'Triumph of Public Opinion', 'Back to the League', 21 December 1935. Layton and his wife Dorothy campaigned vigorously for the 'Peace Ballot', organized by the League of Nations Union, in 1934–35. Layton interpreted the vote, with nearly 12 million participants, as a strong indication the public was prepared 'to take action to resist aggression' collectively – by economic (87 per cent) and military means (58.6 per cent). Layton, *Dorothy*, pp. 92–95.

154. 'Peace on the Razor's Edge', 14 March 1936.

155. This account of the telephone message to Baldwin is from Thomas Jones, appointed first assistant to the cabinet by Lloyd George in 1916, and its powerful deputy secretary until 1930. The weekend in question was at the estate of Lord Lothian (Philip Kerr), who was Lloyd George's former private secretary. Alfred F. Havinghurst, *Britain in Transition: The Twentieth Century*, Chicago 1985, p. 253.

156. 'I want England's friendship', Hitler told Toynbee, who interjected, 'I have the very strong conviction that in this vital point, Hitler was quite sincere in what he said to me': William McNeill, *Arnold Toynbee: A Life*, Oxford 1989, p. 172.

157. Walter Layton et al, *The Challenge of Democracy: A Popular Front for Britain*, London 1936; 'The Empire and the World', 1 May 1937. For the support colonial revisionism enjoyed among British liberals, see Pedersen, *The Guardians*, pp. 331–47.

158. 'Politics and Defence', 21 November 1936; 'The Silences of Mr. Eden', 28 November 1936; 'Spain and Britain', 22 August 1936; 'English Ships and Spain', 5 December 1936; 'Spain and Europe', 8 May 1937.

159. The *Economist* deplored the 'extreme bitterness, fanaticism and cruelty displayed by both sides', adding, 'if the Spaniards had been left to fight it out and Franco had won, Britain would certainly not have intervened against him': 'Storm over Spain', 26 June 1937. Bold warnings to Eden in 1936 – 'indulgence' over Manchuria, Abyssinia and Spain could lead to conquest of the British Empire by Japan, Italy and Germany 'without a fight' – gave way to advising Chamberlain to do his best to ensure the 'territorial integrity and independence of Spain' under General Franco in 1938. See 'The Silences of Mr. Eden' in 1936 and 'Cabinet and Spain', 25 June 1938.

160. For his address to the Liberal Summer School in 1936, see Layton et al, *The Challenge of Democracy*, pp. 18–21.

161. 'We must do what Mr. Churchill is calling for', the paper suddenly declared: uphold the Covenant, build alliances around Britain and France, 'inscribe our first "No" on the face of Spain': 'The Shadow of the Sword', 19 March 1938. The mixture of defiance and resignation resembles Toynbee's 'After Munich' essay for Chatham House, which it refused to publish, as a 'dangerous encouragement to Hitler'. In September 1939, he contemplated surrender for 'the world is in such desperate need of political unification' it might be

'worth paying the price of falling under the worst tyranny'. McNeill, *Arnold Toynbee*, pp. 171–74.

162. 'Eleventh-Hour Reprieve', 1 October 1938.

163. Layton Papers, TCC, Box 81.62.

164. Churchill Papers, Churchill Archive, 2/244/50–52 (4 November 1935); CHAR 2/244/53–59 (1 November 1935); CHAR 2/244/67–68 (7 November 1935); Churchill based several speeches in the House exhorting rearmament on reports from Strakosch; on 13 April 1936, he copied one to the MP Eleanor Rathbone, concluding, 'We really are in great danger'. CHAR 2/274/12–13.

165. Jay, *Change and Fortune*, p. 50.

166. Layton declined to publish the 'Henlein pamphlet', which purported to show the timetable for Germany's conquest of Europe on 29 September, instead dropping it in the mailbox of 10 Downing Street for Chamberlain, 'in case it might cause him embarrassment at a critical moment'. Hubback, *No Ordinary*, pp. 157, 163.

167. The subtext was criticism of France: the failure of the League was due to its animus against Germany, its devaluation of the franc against sterling that had rendered the return to gold unworkable, and its veto of the Austro-German Customs Union: 'From Washington to Munich', 22 October 1938.

168. Layton to Strakosch, May–July 1938, Layton Papers, TCC, Box 81.62.

## 6. Extreme Centre

1. For a larger shift in classical liberal thought about war, from economically destructive to potentially productive, see Alan Milward, *The Economic Effects of the Two World Wars on Britain*, London 1984.

2. Robert Skidelsky, *Britain Since 1900: A Success Story?*, London 2014, p. 244.

3. Keynes, *CW*, Vol. XXII, pp. 15–29.

4. Churchill sent Layton to the Ministry of Supply as Director General of Programmes, the Joint War Planning Staff, then on to head the Ministry of Production in 1942. Alec Cairncross, 'Economists in Wartime', *Contemporary European History*, March 1995, pp. 20, 27, 34.

5. Crowther authored a 'Report on the Irish Banking and Currency System' for the Irish Banks' Standing Committee, which recommended branch closures to increase profitability in the sector and to offer depositors a higher rate of interest, amidst the Depression. Cormac Ó Gráda, *Ireland: A New Economic History, 1780–1939*, Oxford 1994, p. 371.

6. Lysaght, *Brendan Bracken*, p. 256.

7. The Smithsons described it as 'a didactic building, a dry building'. It stands as both a rebuke and affirmation of the surrounding

neighbourhood: Helena Webster, *Modernism without Rhetoric: Essays on the Work of Alison and Peter Smithson*, London 1997, p. 60; Irénée Scalbert, 'The Smithsons and the Economist Building Plaza', *AA Files*, Autumn 1995, p.19; 'The Economist Bids Farewell to a Formative Home', *Economist*, 24 December 2016.

8. 'Crowther, Geoffrey, Baron Crowther (1907–1972)', Roland Bird in *ODNB*, 2004.

9. Crowther Letter, 8 December 1947, Layton Papers, TCC, Box 82.53.

10. Crowther to Layton, 9 July 1944, Layton Papers, TCC, Box 81.9. 'The rapid growth in circulation during the last three years puts us into a position to show what we can do in the post-war years.' Crowther to Layton, 1938, Layton Papers, TCC, Box 81.X.

11. This dictated the scale of the project, requiring purchase of over forty adjacent lots on the St. James site – mainly on favourable terms from the Crown Estates – to generate enough floor area. According to Peter Dallas Smith, one of the paper's two business managers and in charge of the project, Crowther 'saw himself as a tycoon in the making': Scalbert, 'The Smithsons and the Economist Building Plaza', p.19. Crowther briefly became chairman of the largest hotel group in Britain after the ill-fated merger of Trust Houses and Forte Holdings: *The Times*, 7 February 1972. See Edwards, *Pursuit of Reason*, p. 867.

12. The term 'planning' masked disagreements between the 153 signatories of *The Next Five Years*, especially as to whether it constituted socialism or was a capitalist alternative to it. See Daniel Ritschel, *The Politics of Planning: The Debate on Economic Planning in Britain in the 1930s*, Oxford 1997, pp. 232–79.

13. *The Next Five Years: An Essay in Political Agreement*, London 1935, pp. 97–124.

14. Crowther did not wish it to seem 'L.G's book': Ritschel, *Politics of Planning*, pp. 242, 249, 253, 266–73. Peter Sloman notes that despite the dominance of upper- and lower-case liberals in it, the Liberal Party diverged from the group on protection and industrial self-government: *The Liberal Party and the Economy*, Oxford 2016, pp. 113–17.

15. Geoffrey Crowther, *Ways and Means: A Study of the Economic Structure of Great Britain Today*, London 1936, pp. 179–87; *Economics for Democrats*, London 1939, p. 33.

16. *Next Five Years*, pp. 117–19. Crowther was vague about how to achieve higher levels of domestic investment; he did not suggest it should happen by restricting what the City sent abroad. After rejecting criticisms of foreign lending, he concluded, 'So we might as well make up our minds to a continuance of foreign lending as soon as the present world crisis is past': *Ways and Means*, pp. 154–56, 185–89.

17. Ibid., p. 75.

18. 'It is fully possible to maintain profits, and yet to impose such heavy taxation on the rich that all large incomes are severely reduced'; to 'allow profits to arise and then tax high incomes is a policy of levelling incomes *up*':' Ibid., pp. 75, 115.

19. Crowther, *Ways and Means*, p. 13; *Economics for Democrats*, p. 30. In the end, what was more liberal – in the sense of claiming to fairly represent all classes of the community, not just sectional interests in it – than an ideology without a party able (on its own) to put it into effect.

20. Ibid., pp. 140, 191.

21. 'The Keynes Plan', 2 March 1940.

22. Provided 'we prevent the enemy from overrunning our industrial areas or bombing them out of existence', those material advantages over Germany – including a higher national income overall, access to cheap raw materials and food, the ability to scale up civilian production for war – would turn into 'actual military superiority': Crowther, *Ways and Means*, p. vi; David Edgerton, *Warfare State Britain, 1920–1970*, Cambridge 2006, pp. 56–57.

23. Crowther's only flaws were 'too much faith in rationing' and a 'too optimistic ... vision of the post-war world': F. A. Hayek, 'How We Can Do It', *The Spectator*, 6 September 1940.

24. 'Most of the free world is opposed to communism' – and rightly so. But ideology was less important now, for 'the conquest of Russia is not an end in itself, but a means, an incident in the struggle with Britain and America for the domination of the world': 'Right About Turn', 28 June 1941.

25. For a few of his *Economist* pieces, see *Isaac Deutscher: The Man and His Work*, ed. David Horowitz, London 1971, pp. 233, 243–47. Orwell informed Deutscher that Churchill, Roosevelt and Stalin were plotting to divide the world permanently between themselves at Yalta. Deutscher pointed out that major conflicts between the Big Three were already rising to the surface. So incredulous was Orwell that he related their conversation in his column in the *Tribune*. Later, Orwell placed Deutscher's name on his blacklist of 'crypto-Communists and fellow travellers', as a 'sympathiser only', which he handed to the UK's Information Research Department in 1949. Isaac Deutscher, 'The Mysticism of Cruelty', in *Marxism, Wars and Revolution: Essays from Four Decades*, ed. Tamara Deutscher, London 1985, pp. 69–70; Andrew Rubin, *Archives of Authority: Empire, Culture, and the Cold War*, Princeton 2012, p. 29; Phillip Deery, 'Confronting the Cominform: George Orwell and the Cold War Offensive of the Information Research Department, 1948–50', *Labour History*, November 1997, p. 220.

26. *E. H. Carr: A Critical Appraisal*, ed. Michael Cox, New York, 2000, p. 129; *Capital and its Discontents*, ed. Sasha Lilley, Oakland 2011, p. 205.

27. Nicholas Davenport, *Vested Interests or Common Pool*, London 1942, p. 11.

28. 'The New Socialism?', 8 August 1942; 'In the Balance', 15 August 1942.

29. See leaders from 3, 10, 17 October 1942; and 'Letters to the Editor', 28 November 1942.

30. Jose Harris, *William Beveridge: A Biography*, Oxford 1977, pp.

97–98, 101. For Beveridge's late, partial 'conversion' from classical to Keynesian-style liberalism, see Winch, *Economics and Policy*, London 1969, pp. 196–97, 273.

31. Crowther blamed the element of income redistribution in the Beveridge plan on Balogh. Instead of stimulating consumption, Crowther favoured what he called 'the investment approach': 'Social Priorities', 5 December 1942.

32. Still, welfare must never be so generous as to 'lessen incentives to work and advancement'. Ibid.

33. For examples of his war work on machine tool and raw material needs, productivity, tapping labour of married and unmarried women, see 'The brake on our war effort due to the shortage of man-power in the war industries', 8 May 1940, Beveridge Papers, LSE, 8/15/5, and 'The Practicability of Present Programs', 8 May 1942, Beveridge Papers, LSE Piercy 7/34.

34. 15 November 1943, Beveridge Papers, LSE, 9A/15/17.

35. 'If the problem of Full Employment is to be solved within the framework of political democracy, it will have to be solved by the next Parliament – that is, by one or other of the two existing parties, or by both in coalition.' Ibid.

36. Stalin was the ultimate Keynesian, the 'greatest living practitioner of the investment approach', wrote Crowther half-facetiously. 'The rate at which national income expands is an almost direct function of capital investment (as witness Russia). Man increases his productivity partly by getting cleverer; but mainly by increasing the ratio of horse-power per head. The achievements of the aircraft factories during the war have shown that the Englishman can have a productivity equal to, or even in excess of, the American, if he is given the proper equipment. Yet in industry as a whole, his productivity is barely half that of the American, and, in spite of lower wages, labour costs in this country are a higher proportion of total costs than in America ... as long as there is any country in the world where mechanization, and with it the productivity per head, are higher than they are here, I refuse to admit that there is a case for deliberately restricting Investment or the Saving that makes it possible.' Ibid. One striking paradox of Crowther's enthusiasm for a Stalinist investment policy was that he wedded it to a defence of *private* investment.

37. Beveridge rejected a number of Crowther's points, including his hard distinction between structural and frictional unemployment, and the Soviet parallel. 'The argument from Stalin does not appear to me strong. The investment approach was natural, indeed inevitable, in Russia in order to industrialise an agricultural and arm an unarmed country. This has no relevance to the United States or Britain; we shall end the war excessively industrialised and fully armed.' Beveridge to Crowther, 1 December 1943, Beveridge Papers, LSE, 9A/15/17.

38. Beveridge Papers, LSE, 9A/13, Folders 3–4. 'Control of capital movements' was broached in the finished text, but for only two paragraphs

in a work of several hundred pages. *Full Employment in a Free Society*, London 1944, pp. 237–39.

39. 'Employment: The White Paper', 3 June 1944; Winch, *Economics and Policy*, p. 271.

40. Tyerman interviewed Beveridge in *The Listener*: 'War in the Workshop', 6 June 1940; 'Getting the Job Done', 13 June 1940. For exchanges after, see Beveridge Papers, LSE, (1944) 9A/24; (1946) 11/60; (1948) 2/B/48/1; (1956) 7/91.

41. *The Economist, 1843–1943: a Centenary Volume*, London 1943, pp. 15–16.

42. Hayek, 'The Economist, 1843–1943. A Centenary Volume', *Economica*, February 1944, p. 51.

43. 'Road to Serfdom?', 13 May 1944.

44. The Delhi Conference in October 1940 set up a single 'Economic War Council', which was 'probably far more needed than the looser Imperial War Cabinet so often asked for; and its institution would be another landmark in the development of free cooperation within the Commonwealth': 'Imperial War Economy', 2 November 1940.

45. 'The Commonwealth at War', 17 August 1940.

46. 'Salvation for India', 22 June 1940. The Bengal and Punjab, two Muslim majority provinces, were central to the war effort: the former contained more than half of India's industrial capacity, while the latter was the main recruiting ground for the Indian Army.

47. 'National Unity', 21 February 1942.

48. 'It would be hypocritical to deny that the expediency of the moment has given British policy the air of a death-bed repentance.' Still, 'no nation has shown more tangibly than the British its recognition of the truth of Aristotle's contention that a democracy cannot maintain an autocratic Empire without being corrupted and enfeebled': 'Message to India', 14 March 1942.

49. 'India at Stake', 18 April 1942.

50. 'Sterling balances, mainly from India and Egypt, totalled £3,500 million by 1945': 'End of an Era', 3 January 1942.

51. 'India at Stake', 18 April 1942.

52. 'Discussion', *The American Economic Review*, March 1943, pp. 332–33, 458.

53. Crowther gave a lecture at Harvard in August 1941 while on a 'confidential mission for his government'. 'English Economist Envisages Advanced Post-war Britain', *The Christian Science Monitor*, 8 August 1941. In 1946 Hutton published *Midwest at Noon* based on his time there since 1940, which carried as subtitle 'America's Maturing Inland Empire – As Seen through the Eyes of a Modern Bryce'.

54. 'Some very plain speaking is long overdue,' wrote the *Economist*, 'if only to act as a safety valve, and prevent worse happening.' To hear Americans tell it, 'Britain is imperialist, reactionary, selfish, exclusive, restrictive', and was not doing its share of the fighting. 'What makes the American criticisms so intolerable is not merely that they

are unjust, but that they come from a source that has done so little to earn the right to postures of superiority. To be told by anyone that the British people are slacking in their war effort would be insufferable enough to a people struggling through their sixth winter of black-out and blockade and bombs, of queues and rations and coldness – but when the criticism comes from a nation that was practicing Cash-and-Carry during the Battle of Britain, whose consumption has risen through the war years, which is still without a national service act – then it is not to be borne.' 'With every outburst of moral indignation in America, the ordinary Englishman gets one degree more cynical about America's real intentions about active collaboration, and one degree more ready to believe that the only reliable helping hand is in Soviet Russia': 'Noble Negatives', 30 December 1944.

55. Ethel Salter to Geoffrey Crowther, 2 January 1945, Layton Papers, TCC, Box 81.137–138.

56. Isaiah Berlin, 7 January 1945, in *Washington Despatches, 1941–45: Weekly Political Reports from the British Embassy*, ed. H. G. Nicholas, Chicago 1981, pp. 493–94; Isaiah Berlin, 1 February 1945, in *Flourishing: Letters 1928–1946*, London 2004, p. 528.

57. Peter Clarke, *The Last Thousand Days of the British Empire: Churchill, Roosevelt and the Birth of the Pax Americana*, London 2008, pp. 146–48.

58. There was, in other words, no reason for the US to reject certain currency controls, or bilateral clearing schemes of the sort Britain had just signed with Belgium – a 'miniature Keynes Plan', designed to smooth payment imbalances between surplus and deficit countries, which the US rejected at Bretton Woods. Such controls would expand 'the sum total of world trade', as opposed to the bad kind of discrimination, which simply transferred 'markets from one supplier to another': 'Peacetime Mutual Aid', 13 December 1945. For Britain's weak (and wishful) negotiating posture at Bretton Woods, and the acrimony it and the loan terms generated, see Benn Steil, *The Battle of Bretton Woods: John Maynard Keynes, Harry Dexter White and the Making of a New World Order*, Princeton 2013.

59. Leo Amery to Layton, 23 January 1945, Layton Papers, TCC, Box 81.137–138.

60. This advice was given 'against our better judgment'. 'Our present need' for dollars was nothing to be ashamed of, but a 'consequence of the fact that we fought earliest, that we fought longest, and that we fought hardest. In moral terms we are creditors; and for that we shall pay $140 million a year for the rest of the twentieth century': 'Dollar Loan', 8 December 1945. See also 'Lend Lease Guillotine', 25 August 1945; 'Dollar Crisis', 1 September 1945.

61. A few weeks before Labour's landslide, the *Economist* released its own electoral manifesto, underscoring a distrust of the two main parties unchanged since the 1930s. One section was on 'national efficiency', addressing Labour, which needed from the outset to secure a

treaty with the trade unions that pledged them to end all restrictive labour practices in exchange for the bulk of productivity rises going to wages. But it also made less expected points, for example that direct public ownership – of coal pits or shipyards – was generally preferable to public 'control', since the former approach kept control and responsibility in the same hands. 'Election Manifesto', 30 June 1945.

62. As a result of two world wars, foreign income as a share of national product in Britain may have fallen continuously since 1914. But the importance of the Empire within the makeup of overseas investment only grew. By 1936 sterling area holdings represented over 60 per cent of the total. 'Foreign investment is the nation's single greatest industry', the *Economist* declared in 1937. Interest and dividends from abroad had declined, but still accounted for one-twentieth of the national income: 'British Capital Abroad' 6 August 1938. For a recent study of the limits that City-oriented growth placed on what social democratic policy options existed after 1945, see Aled Davies, *The City of London and Social Democracy: The Political Economy of Finance in Britain, 1959–1979*, Oxford 2017.

63. Stephen Howe, *Anticolonialism in British Politics: The Left and the End of Empire, 1918–1964*, Oxford 1993, p. 144. For the social democratic ideology of empire promoted by Labour – Bevin, in particular – and its economic and geopolitical underpinnings, see John Darwin, *The Empire Project: The Rise and Fall of the British World System, 1830–1970*, London 2009, pp. 544–47 and passim.

64. Philip W. Bell, *The Sterling Area in the Post-war World: Internal Mechanism and Cohesion, 1946–1952*, Oxford 1956, pp. 316–17. For almost four-fifths of sterling area exports the British home market was 50 per cent larger than the US market. Darwin, *Empire Project*, pp. 582–83, 543, 547; Susan Strange, *Sterling and British Policy: A Political Study of an International Currency in Decline*, London 1971, pp. 4–5.

65. Alec Cairncross, *Years of Recovery: British Economic Policy, 1941–51*, London 1985, p. 153.

66. 13 October 1945; *The Next Five Years*, p. 100.

67. Davenport, *Memoirs of a City Radical*, 157.

68. Jim Tomlinson, 'The Attlee Government and the Balance of Payments, 1945–1951', *Twentieth Century British History*, January 1991, pp. 52–53, 59. Dalton formulated his 'practical socialism' at the same time as Crowther his 'extreme centre', the latter noting their affinities in the *Economist* of 24 April 1934. Dalton was interventionist, but not necessarily on the left: contemptuous of the 'thin, theoretical, tinny tintinnabulations' of Harold Laski, he mentored Labour liberals like Evan Durbin, Douglas Jay and Hugh Gaitskell: Ben Pimlott, *Hugh Dalton*, London 1985, p. 398.

69. 'Labour Landslide', 18 July 1945; 'First Twelve Months', 10 August 1946; 'Taxation of Rich', 16 January 1946. Pimlott, *Hugh Dalton*, pp. 401–7.

70. Dalton alluded to 'several journals' in his Mansion House speech that had questioned these moves, intending both the *Economist* and the *Banker*: 'Cheap Money', 7 September 1946; 'Repayment of Local Loans', 19 October 1946.

71. 'The Case for Deflation', 1 March 1947. See letters from Austin Robinson, Ralph Hawtrey and Frank Paish, among others, over the issue of 'suppressed inflation' in 8, 15, 22 March 1947; Pimlott, *Hugh Dalton*, p. 474.

72. 'Moral Crisis', 16 August 1947; 'Inconvertible Again', 23 August 1947; 'Side-stepping the Issue', 15 November 1947.

73. 'Mr. Dalton's Resignation', 22 November 1947.

74. 'Defeat or Opportunity', 24 September 1949.

75. Davenport, *Memoirs of a City Radical*, p. 177.

76. Hugh Dalton, *Memoirs: Call Back Yesterday 1887–1931*, Vol. I, London 1953; Hugh Dalton, *The Fateful Years: Memoirs 1931–1945*, Vol II, London 1957; Hugh Dalton, *High Tide and After: Memoirs 1945–1960*, Vol III, London 1962; Tyerman to Morrison 8 June; Morrison to Tyerman 13 June 1961, Morrison Papers, LSE, 8/21.

77. Roy Harrod, *The Life of John Maynard Keynes*, London 1951.

78. Ibid., p. 436; 'John Maynard Keynes', 27 January 1951.

79. 'John Maynard Keynes', 3 February 1951.

80. Macmillan diary, 30 Aug. 1951, quoted in E. H. H. Green, *Ideologies of Conservatism*, Oxford 2002, p.187.

81. Milward, *Economic Effects*, p. 72; Tomlinson, 'The Attlee Government', p. 59.

82. Tomlinson, 'The Attlee Government', pp. 59, 63–64; Allister E. Hinds, 'Imperial Policy and Colonial Sterling Balances 1943–56', *The Journal of Imperial and Commonwealth History*, July 2008, pp. 36–38.

83. 'Commonwealth with Solvency', 1 March 1952.

84. Davenport, *Memoirs of a City Radical*, p. 150.

85. Milward, *Economic Effects*, p. 72.

86. 'John Maynard Keynes', 27 January 1951; 'The Real Issues', 13 October 1951; 'The Next Government', 20 October 1951.

87. Extreme centre got a new, vaguer definition ('moderate and catholic in its aims, but audacious in their pursuit'), perhaps because to endorse a party went against its original premise: 'In the Sign of the Balance', 26 May 1955.

88. Lysaght, *Brendan Bracken*, p. 256.

89. Barbara Ward, *The International Share-out*, London 1938, pp. 69, 173–74.

90. 'Turks know that a powerful Britain is no menace to their independence; on the contrary, their chief complaint is that Britain has not been powerful enough.' Barbara Ward, *Turkey*, London 1942, pp. 112–14.

91. Planning need not coincide with totalitarianism. Britain might in this way correct both allies' excesses: too much free trade in the US, too little freedom in the USSR: Barbara Ward, *Democracy, East and West*, London 1947, p. 52.

92. Until 1947, liberalism was not above reproach, and even bore some blame for the rise of fascism: 'The defence of private property and free enterprise helped to produce 19th century parliamentary democracy in the West. But it also induced the German middle classes to support Hitler's anti-Bolshevik crusade, and this gave the West the infinite horrors of Nazism.' After 1947, it was a heroic rampart against communism. Ibid., p. 47; Jean Gartlan, *Barbara Ward: Her Life and Letters*, London 2010, p. 22; 'Mr. Marshall's Challenge', 14 June 1947; 'Initiative in Europe', 21 June 1947; Barbara Ward, *The West at Bay*, New York 1948, p. 143.

93. Though it found the Greek king's ministers 'slippery', better to defend them, so as to 'widen and liberalise' the regime later; perhaps with a technocrat like former central bank head Kyriakos Varvaressos, 'to create a responsible tax-paying business community': 'Strategy for Greece', 3 January 1948; 'American Responsibility', 11 December 1948.

94. 'Final Settlement for Palestine?', 26 August 1946. The *Economist* did not hold out much hope for this deal. Americans were unlikely to send troops nor, for domestic electoral reasons, to respect Arab objections to unlimited Jewish immigration: 'Realities in Palestine', 27 March 1948.

95. 'New Era in India', 16 August 1947; see also 'Black Flags in India', 7 September 1946. 'Scramble for Power in India', 10 May 1947; 'Is It Well with India?', 19 July 1947; 'Farewell to India: The Heritage', 17 January 1948; 'India's Mountbatten Year', 26 June 1948.

96. 'Test Point in Malaya', 12 November 1949; 'Sideshow in Malaya?', 25 March 1950; 'Struggle in Malaya', 6 January 1951.

97. 'Britain, Persia and Oil', 23 March 1951; 'Persia's Road to Ruin', 5 May 1951;

98. 'Persia's Road to Ruin', 5 May 1951.

99. Searching in vain for a firm commitment from Truman to remove Mossadegh from the very start, the paper had some of its sharpest words for Washington since 1945. 'If the Americans deserted the British in the first real test of their relationship in the Middle East, then the North Atlantic alliance will have suffered a blow from which it might never recover.' Ibid. In the meantime, it backed those measures Britain could take, removing Persia from the sterling area and blockading the oil it had 'expropriated': 'Persians and Foreigners', 29 August 1953.

100. 'British Guiana and Self-Government', 27 October 1951; PPP. leaders 'must realise British Guiana needs foreign capital, which will not be forthcoming in a Communist state'. 'Troops for Guiana', 10 October 1953; 'Doubts on Guiana', 24 October 1953; 'Implications of Guiana', 31 October 1953.

101. The British enclosed 800 or more Kikuyu villages as well as running a camp system, in which torture was officially sanctioned and routine, for a total detainee population of 1.5 million: Caroline

Elkins, *Imperial Reckoning: The Untold Story of Britain's Gulag in Kenya*, New York 2005, pp. xii, xvi, 344.

102. See 'Kilawara, Kikuyu and Kenya', 29 November 1952; 'Kenya's Future', 8 August 1953; 'More Liberalism', 21 November 1953; 'Life in Kenya', 21 March 1953. Much later: 'Disquiet over Kenya', 9 June 1956; 'Fair Play for Mau Mau', 28 February 1959; 'Censure on Whom?', 20 June 1959; 'Hola Verdict', 1 August 1959.

103. For the central place of Kenya in British plans for colonial development, and their effects on the shift from settler to plantation agriculture controlled by expatriate capital, see Gary Wasserman, *The Politics of Decolonization, Kenya, Europeans and the Land Issue, 1960–65*, Cambridge 1976; and of the Colonial Development Corporation in getting multinationals like Shell, Unilever, and Imperial Chemical to invest: Robert L. Tignor, *Capitalism and Nationalism at the End of Empire*, Princeton 1989, pp. 293–386.

104. Ward despaired 'of finding any modus vivendi with a power which claims everything and gives nothing', or with a people who mixed 'arrogance and fear, contempt and distrust, scorn and inferiority': Barbara Ward, *Policy for the West*, New York 1951, pp. 89–93.

105. 'Divided China', 13 January 1945; 'China's Tepid War', 20 December 1947. By 1948 the *Economist* was considering partition, with the Communists getting Manchuria: 'China without Chiang', 20 March 1948. The leader on 28 May 1949, 'South East Asia', was a call to remain vigilant, even as the Communists' victory over the Kuomintang looked inevitable.

106. 'French Fears in Indochina', 12 November 1949. Progress had been in part due to 'moral support from the British base in Singapore': 'Paris Views Indochina', 7 July 1951.

107. 'Strength with Speed', 8 July 1950; 'Cost of Defence', 29 July 1950; 'Tithe for Safety', 5 August 1950; 'Questions for Stalin', 25 November 1950; see also, 'Arms and Diplomacy', 20 January 1951; 'Cold Class War', 4 August 1951.

108. 'War through the Looking Glass', 26 June 1954; 'Guatemalans Take Stock', 24 July 1954. See also 'Guns for Guatemala', 29 May 1954 and 'Banana Split', 10 July 1954.

109. A stick with no carrot had led to the 'debacle' of the Chinese Revolution, where Chiang Kai-shek's Kuomintang had 'lost the support of the people because its economic and social outlook was too conservative and static': 'Policy for Asia?' 15 April 1950.

110. And to head off the capitalist crisis to which the Soviets so looked forward: Ward, *Policy for the West*, pp. 89–93.

111. In Accra, she saw a model in which investment empowered 'reasonable nationalists' like Kwame Nkrumah, the first prime minister at independence, with whom she used to chat for hours as the Volta River Project got underway. He was 'very intuitive, very sensitive, with many sound and wise instincts, and under tremendous pressure

from the extreme wing of his own party': Gartlan, *Barbara Ward*, pp. 65, 92–93, 117.

112. Ibid., pp. 92–93, 117; Barbara Ward, *Faith and Freedom*, London 1954, pp. 189, 231–33, 269; Alastair Burnet, 'After Ten Years', 26 October 1974.

113. Crowther to Layton, 28 June 1955, Layton Papers, TCC, Box 82.127.

114. Crowther to Layton, 15 August 1955, Layton Papers, TCC, Box 82.131.

115. Crowther to Warburg, 21 July 1958, Warburg Papers, LSE, /11/13: Mercury Securities was the holding company through which Warburg maintained his family's control over the merchant bank S. G. Warburg & Co. He was also instrumental in pushing the Treasury and the Bank of England to expand the City's Euromarkets business: Niall Ferguson, *High Financier: The Life and Times of Siegmund Warburg*, New York 2010, pp. 216–18, 259.

116. 'Barbara Ward', 6 June 1981.

117. 'Tyerman, Donald (1908–1981)', Norman Macrae in *ODNB;* Hugh Brogan, interviewed by the author, November 2011; Barbara Smith, 'Not So Hard Labour', *Economist*, 20 December 2003.

118. Charles Jones, '"An Active Danger": E. H. Carr at the *Times*, 1940–46,' in *E. H. Carr: A Critical Appraisal*, ed. Michael Cox, New York 2000, pp. 68, 76. In the *Times*, Tyerman rejected Churchill's assertion that the EAM in Greece were 'a gang of communists and bandits'. Rather it encompassed 'the whole range of opinion from centre to extreme left'. Any provisional government 'must be built around the active and mostly turbulent resistance movement which has kept the flame of nationhood alight under enemy occupation, privation and terror': John Sakkas, '*The Times* and the British Intervention in Greece in December 1944', *Balkan Studies*, 2012, pp. 32–33.

119. Keith Kyle, *Reporting the World*, London 2009, pp. 88–89.

120. Taylor set an example for unpredictability: 'notoriously on the left', but as likely to defend the pretender to the French throne as to criticize Soviet fiction. 'It was not necessary to agree with Alan politically – indeed, as a Liberal, I belonged to the party he most despised – to enjoy his company.' Kyle, *Reporting the World*, pp. 18–21.

121. Ibid., p. 53.

122. Ibid., p. 21.

123. Kyle, *Reporting the World*, 95; Irvin Molotsky, 'Edwin Dale Jr., Reporter and an Expert in Economics', *New York Times*, 11 May 1999; Neil A. Lewis, 'Adam Yarmolinsky Dies at 77; Led Revamping of Government', 7 January 2000. Watson's daughter, Susan Barnes, married Labour frontbencher Tony Crosland in 1964: Julia Langdon, 'Susan Crosland', *The Guardian*, 28 February 2011.

124. Kyle, *Reporting the World*, p. 94.

125. Paul Lashmar and James Oliver, *Britain's Secret Propaganda War*, Phoenix Mill 1998, pp. 117–18.

126. Ibid., pp. 9, 13, 16. For the IRD in the wider context of Western liberal propaganda, see Frances Stonor Saunders, *The Cultural Cold War: The CIA and the World of Arts and Letters*, New York pp. 49–50, 139 and passim.

127. Hugh Brogan, interviewed by the author.

128. Communist subversion remained the ultimate threat for Crozier: 'His specific target was Leninism. "What about Marxism?" I asked. He looked grave. "Marxism is a philosophy. It has a right to existence. Leninism is activism and a threat to the State." I owed much to Bonnemaison': Crozier, *Free Agent*, pp. 28, 33. Salan, the commander of French forces in Algeria, had tipped off Bonnemaison to de Gaulle's intentions in 1958.

129. Ibid., p. 39.

130. *Neo-colonialism* (1964), based on a 'thick folder of IRD documents', *South-East Asia in Turmoil* (1965) and *The Struggle for the Third World* (1966) followed. Ibid., pp. 36, 51.

131. 'It is by no means certain that the Germans bombed Guernica at all': Brian Crozier, *Franco*, Boston 1967, p. 247.

132. Forum World Features began as the media offshoot of the CIA's Congress for Cultural Freedom. Crozier took it over in 1965: Lashmar and Oliver, *Britain's Secret Propaganda War*, p. 134. Crozier kept a meticulous record of the scandal that ensued after *Time Out*'s revelation, defending himself there and elsewhere. See 'Conflicting Accounts', *Time Out*, 29 Aug–4 September 1975 and Brian Crozier Papers, HIA, Box 1, Folder 3 and Box 6, Folder 1.

133. Western governments had been hamstrung since 1972 when, 'egged on by unelected "investigative" journalists' in the aftermath of Watergate, the US Congress passed Privacy and Freedom of Information Acts, which 'destroyed US intelligence gathering capacity' and 'protected terrorists and political subversives'. Ibid., pp. 111, 126, 257.

134. Barbara Smith, interviewed by the author; see also 'The Life of Brian', 31 July 1993.

135. Crozier, *Free Agent*, p. 294.

136. Ibid., pp. 36, 74, 149.

137. Midgley wrote this leader. 'Europe's Achilles Heel', *Economist*, 4 August 1956.

138. Kyle, *Reporting the World*, pp. 111–12.

139. 'French ministers stung to fury by Egyptian support for the Algerian rebels are not the best councillors for a British Prime Minister smarting at his betrayal by an Egyptian president whose advocate he once was.' 'Splenetic Isolation', 3 November 1956.

140. Elizabeth Monroe, *Britain's Moment in the Middle East, 1914–1956*, Baltimore 1963, pp. 197–201.

141. 'The Prime Minister', 10 November 1956.

142. Crowther to Tyerman, 13 November 1956, Layton Papers, TCC.

143. Crozier thought the US could be naïve: mistakenly backing Nasser in

1952, they now halted a brilliant military campaign by their allies, which would have kept Egypt from falling to the Soviets. Crozier, *Free Agent*, pp. 24–26.

144. 'The Alliance', 17 November 1956.

145. The run began in late October. The first week of November saw £31.7 million depart: Keith Kyle, *Suez: Britain's End of Empire in the Middle East*, London 2003, pp. 464–65.

146. Ward had argued that 15 per cent of GDP should be devoted to defence, with 3 per cent for development. In the event, 9 per cent was too much, especially absent US support: Nicholas Mayhew, *Sterling: The Rise and Fall of a Currency*, London 1999, pp. 246–47.

147. 10 November 1956.

148. 24 November 1956.

149. Kyle, *Reporting the World*, p. 116.

150. Smith, 20 December 2003.

151. Kyle, *Reporting the World*, pp. 146–47.

152. See Keith Kyle, *Cyprus: In Search of Peace*, London 1997, p. 36; and on Kenyatta and the camps, *The Politics of the Independence of Kenya*, London 1999, pp. 46–47, 61. From 1974 to 1990, Kyle convened Chatham House's Middle East Research Group, issuing a book on Israel's internal politics during Rabin's premiership, by a group of Anglo-Israeli scholars: *Whither Israel? The Domestic Challenges*, eds. Keith Kyle and Joel Peters, London 1993.

153. At no point did the *Economist* consider abandoning the bases. 'Half measures in Cyprus', 21 July 1956; 'Cyprus After the Storm', 1957; 'Tragic Twist in Cyprus', 1 February 1958; 'Cyprus Confronts Its Future', 31 October 1959; 'An Independent Cyprus?', 14 February 1959; 'Cyprus' 28 February 1959; 'An Independent Cyprus', 16 July 1960.

154. 'What to Say in Africa', 9 January 1960.

155. 'White Africans', 15 October 1960; it eventually accepted dissolution of the federation, given intransigence of white and black leaders, into present-day Zimbabwe, Zambia and Malawi – 'Parity of Abuse', 25 February 1961; 'Nyasaland's Choice', 12 August 1961; 'Who Will Rule Nigeria?', 9 July 1960.

156. *Algerie française* was now a myth. 'Without that myth, or some form of it, the French position in Algeria is untenable': 'Algeria's Cry', 17 December 1960. For the diplomatic and moral victories of the FLN, see Matthew Connelly, *A Diplomatic Revolution: Algeria's Fight for Independence*, Oxford 2002, p. 134 and passim.

157. 'Congo Express', 25 June 1960; 'Congo Express Derailed', 'Ordeal in Leo', 16 July 1960; 'Black Man's Burden', 21 January 1961; 'After Lumumba', 18 February 1961.

158. 20 December 2003.

159. Cuba, like any other nation, had the right to trade, choose its own form of government and even make alliances with the Soviet Union: 'Obsessed by Cuba', 6 October 1962.

160. 'In his sensibly worded message to Lord Bertrand Russell on Wednesday, [Khrushchev] has shown a keen awareness of the dangers the world is running, and an apparent willingness to negotiate with Mr. Kennedy': 'Cyclone Cuba', 27 October 1962.

161. 'After Cuba', 3 November 1952.

162. 'It grieves me to say this, as Tyerman – a brave man who had overcome the handicap of legs crippled by polio had been invariably kind to me, despite our political divergences.' Crozier, *Free Agent*, p. 47.

163. Goulart was a reckless populist, guilty of advocating nationalizations and votes for the illiterate, to distract from inflation, and of 'sterile anti-Americanism': 'Brazil Cracks', 4 April 1964. Most letters, including from the British and Commonwealth Chamber of Commerce, expressed gratitude to the generals for saving Brazil from turning into a 'second Cuba': 18 April, 9 May, 6 June 1964. For positive evaluation of the new regime, and its reforms – 'prepared discreetly, without the demagogic publicity that characterised the unfulfilled promises of the previous regime' – see 'Roses for the Generals', 11 April 1964; 'Shipshape, Army Style?', 18 April 1964; 'Gorillas or Reformers?' 30 May 1964.

164. Donald Tyerman to Geoffrey Crowther, 10 July 1963, Layton Papers, TCC, Box 83.137.

165. Smith, 'Not so Hard Labour', 20 December 2003.

166. There were six *Economist* staffers on the IRD journalist list up to 1977, or one more than at either the *Times* or the *Telegraph*, according to David Leigh in 'Death of the Department that Never Was', *Guardian*, 27 January 1978; 'Tim Milne, *Kim Philby: A Story of Friendship and Betrayal*, London 2014; Kim Philby, *My Silent War*, New York 1968, p. 262. Midgley 'was in military intelligence during the war, trying to figure out German intentions'. 'Obituary', *Economist*, 4 June 2001. McLachlan, co-foreign editor with Ward from 1947–54, had worked on 'black propaganda' during the Second World War for the Foreign Office. Monroe was ex-director of the Middle East division of the Ministry of Information. Honey, who worked in the foreign section, was close to Crozier and the IRD. Lashmar and Oliver, *Britain's Secret Propaganda War*, pp. 118, 115. Elizabeth Monroe, *Philby of Arabia*, London 1973, p. 288.

167. Of criticisms levelled against the Conservatives over Suez, or repression in Cyprus, Nyasaland and in Kenya, only the last 'seem to lack any mitigation at all': 'Thursday's Child', 3 October 1959.

168. Ibid.

169. 'Roads to Rome', 17 June 1961; 'Engagement Announced', 30 September 1961; 'Back to Bonapartism', 19 January 1963.

170. 'Smut without Fire', 30 March 1963; 'After Mr Profumo', 8 June 1963; 'Prime Minister's Crisis', 15 June 1963; 'Implications', 26 October 1963.

171. 'Mr Butskell's Dilemma', 13 February 1954. This composite Chancellor – blending the Conservatives' R. A. Butler and Labour's Hugh

Gaitskell – has passed into legend as a symbol of the post-war consensus between the two main parties on macroeconomic policy. Neil Rollings, 'Poor Mr Butskell: A Short Life, Wrecked by Schizophrenia', *Twentieth Century British History*, January 1994, pp. 186–87, 196, 199. Macrae's use of the term supports this, but only in part. On the one hand, Macrae welcomed the moderating influence of 'Mr Butskell' on the wilder elements in both parties – in particular Labour and its 'graver irresponsibilities'. On the other, he coined the term in 1954 precisely to point out a character flaw in this consensual figure – his tendency to 'run away' under 'political pressures' when 'external economic events' required unpopular decisions, to restore confidence in sterling or right the trade balance. From the start therefore 'Butskellism' was also about the *limits* of consensus, and carried a tinge of political cowardice – putting off the raising of bank rate, large spending cuts, suppression of wage demands, or the floating of the pound.

172. He postulated that these high growth, high-tech industries had 'very significantly higher marginal productivity per factor employed than the average of other industries' so that it had become, in current conditions, 'economically profitable to inflate marginal demand up to a distinctly higher point than it used to be'. Norman Macrae, *Sunshades in October*, London 1963, pp. 17, 25.

173. Ibid., p. 28.

174. 'Tyerman, Donald (1908–1981)', Norman Macrae in *ODNB*. In governing, Labour might also abandon antiquated ideas about planning and nationalization: 'The Domestic Choice', 3 October 1964; 'A Vote of No Confidence', 10 October 1964.

175. Memorandum by Geoffrey Crowther, July 1964, Layton Papers, TCC.

176. Donald Tyerman, 'Crowther and the Great Issues', *Encounter*, May 1972.

177. Donald Tyerman, 'As We Move: 1956–65,' *Economist*, 17 April 1965.

## 7. Liberal Cold Warriors

1. In characteristic fashion, his analysis began with jokes about 'the coming to power of Mr. Paul Foot, Miss Vanessa Redgrave, or Messrs Eric Tomlinson and Des Warren', and ended with a children's poem by Ogden Nash, its final line, 'let's not despair'. Alastair Burnet, *Is Britain Governable?*, London 1975, pp. 21–22.

2. Beedham joined the *Economist* from the *Yorkshire Post* in 1955, but was only there for a few months before he left for the US. In 1958, he became Washington correspondent. 'Brian Beedham: The Pipe Smoking Warrior', 16 May 2015. Crozier cited an 'amusing letter from Brian Beedham' referring 'to charges that BC worked for British

intelligence' in 14 January 1969, Brian Crozier Papers, HIA, Box 2, Folder 2. Moss had a letter of introduction from his father-in-law, Geoffrey Fairbairn, a founding member with Crozier of the Institute for the Study of Conflict and a lecturer at the Australian National University. Moss, by his own account, was a prodigy with an academic post in ancient history; frustrated with 'teutonisms, complicated language and footnotes', he decided to come to London in search of more excitement: Crozier, *Free Agent*, p. 98.

3. Russell Warren Howe, 'Asset Unwitting: Covering the World for the CIA', *MORE*, May 1978; 'The CIA's "Students" of Conflict', *Embassy Magazine*, October 1976; Andy Weir and Jonathan Bloch, 'Robert Moss', *Covert Action Information Bulletin*, December 1979, p. 13.

4. Weir and Bloch, 'Robert Moss', p. 13.

5. Thatcher wanted to strongly denounce the Soviet Union, in light of what she saw as insufficient US support for 'anti-communist forces' in Angola. She found a draft speech from her own shadow foreign secretary, Reginald Maudling, 'so weak it wouldn't pull the skin off a rice pudding'. Her political secretary Richard Ryder, later vice-chairman of the BBC, sent her to Moss, who 'turned out to be an ideal choice': Margaret Thatcher, *The Path to Power*, London 1995, p. 361; Charles Moore, *Margaret Thatcher: The Authorized Biography: Not For Turning*, London 2013, p. 134.

6. 'Mr. Diem's Critics Speak Out', 7 May 1960.

7. Guerrilla tactics, cod citations from Mao, racial distinctions – all point to Crozier: 'Vietnam's Lessons', 9 November 1963. As late as 1966, a special correspondent praised the 'rehabilitated hamlets', where 'Buddhists work with Buddhists', and 'eager young American platoon-leaders' try to 'communicate with eager young South Vietnamese hamlet leaders': 'Hope for the Hamlets', 18 June 1966.

8. 'This Is It', 3 February 1968.

9. 'If He Gets to Saigon', 17 February 1968.

10. 'The Only Innocents', 29 November 1969.

11. 'Even Neutrals Need Guns', 4 April 1970.

12. Marilyn Young, *The Vietnam Wars 1945–1990*, New York 1991, pp. 274, 268.

13. 'Although he is not going to make it his policy to bomb them back to the stone age – that brutal phrase used years ago by one foolish American general, and so often put into other Americans' mouths since – he can cause a great deal of damage to North Vietnam. They have their calculations to make': 'The Peace that Wasn't', 23 December 1972; See also, 'It Is a Real Issue', 19 August 1972; 'The Ritual Becomes Real', 15 July 1973.

14. Washington was doing the same good work London had in the 1950s in Malaya: 'to demonstrate to countries momentarily intoxicated with their own power and revolutionary afflatus that there is a point at which their actions will meet resistance': 'The Narrow Channel' 8 August 1964; 'In the Face of Adversity', 9 January 1965.

15. Rhiannon Vickers, 'Harold Wilson, the British Labour Party, and the War in Vietnam', *Journal of Cold War Studies*, October 2008, pp. 47–50.

16. 'How Not to Influence the Americans', 9 July 1966.

17. 'Who Whom?', 28 October 1967.

18. To be clear about the parallels: 'It was people like this who on August 3, 1914 heard Sir Edward Grey spell out the argument for war ... and could still believe, even then, that Germany was prepared to respect the integrity of Belgium and that the real trouble was Britain's "mad desire" to maintain the balance of power. It was the same body of opinion which delayed rearmament in the 1930s until it was within a few weeks of being too late, and which then made Chamberlain jump through the Munich hoop': 'The Way We Go to War', 26 June 1971; 'Voices', 10 July 1971.

19. The paper backed the war long after almost every other major London news outlet had given it up as a lost cause. For many, this happened in 1965 when the US began to heavily bomb the North, including with napalm and CS gas.

20. 'Vietnam: An Argument with the Poles', 11 December 1965. The first letter the next week stated 'any impartial reader of your argument with the Poles must conclude the Poles come out best'. The second felt the *Economist* had given too much ground to *Polityka*, by conceding South Vietnam was not in fact a democracy. 'You say the South Vietnamese government broke its undertaking to hold elections in 1956. It made no such undertaking, was not a party to the Geneva agreements of 1954, and indeed strongly dissociated itself from them at the time.' This was signed, 'yours faithfully, Brian Crozier': 18 December 1965.

21. Brian Beedham, 'The Economist on Today's World: Sukarno Must Be Checked to Prevent Worse Trouble', *Salt Lake Tribune*, 18 January 1964. 'For anyone who first discovered the area through the stories of Joseph Conrad and Somerset Maugham, it is hard to realize that the tangle of islands we now solemnly call Indonesia and Malaysia is the scene of some very dangerous developments.' Sukarno was an even bigger threat than Nasser and might provoke a new Suez Crisis; whereas Washington had been right to oppose that 'melodramatic' adventure – this time, Britain could lead a 'low-level' war, with the same basic goals as the US in nearby Vietnam.

22. The *Economist* calculated the chances of Sukarno's removal by 'more responsible' politicians and soldiers as high, so long as Britain helped Malaya: 'In the Face of Adversity', 9 January 1965; 'Sukarno Confronted', 25 December 1965. For subversion efforts, see Paul Lashmar and James Oliver, *Britain's Secret Propaganda War*, pp. 1–10; William Roger Louis, *Ends of British Imperialism: The Scramble for Empire, Suez, and Decolonization*, London 2006, pp. 569–71. For representative coverage of Suharto: 'Low Posture for Asean, High Posture for Suharto', 23 March 1968; 'Suharto Reshapes his Army', 8 March 1969; 'Choreography by Suharto', 18 October 1975; 'Suharto and

the Reins of Power', 17 March 1990. Only in 1998 did the *Economist* call on him to stand down: his 'rigidity and autocracy' had been necessary to make Indonesia 'a prosperous regional power', but continued growth now required 'flexibility and democracy'. 'Stand Down Suharto', 17 January 1998.

23. 'Left with Castroism', 12 January 1963; 'Too Damned Equal', 28 September 1963; 'Safety First in the Caribbean', 8 May 1965. In 1963, Bosch became the first elected president of the Dominican Republic since the fall of General Trujillo. US intervention in 1965 ensured Trujillo's protégé, General Balaguer, became president in 1966 – to whom the *Economist* quickly rallied on grounds of economic good management. 'When the Peacemen Fly Away', 27 August 1966.

24. 'How to Stay Democratic Without Actually Cheating', 8 April 1967; 'New Nemesis', 29 April 1967; 'Marching Back to the Good Old Days', 13 May 1967.

25. 'Nasser Does It', 27 May 1967; 'Two Days' Work', 'Americans Play It Cool', 10 June 1967; 'Most of Israel says the Arabs had to be taught a lesson; it says it with sadness more than anything else.' They 'want to keep the Old City but hate the idea of capturing everything up to the west bank of the Jordan'. 'Will Israel's success go too much to its head? One doubts it: this is a very levelheaded people.' 'Teach Them a Lesson', 10 June 1967, and passim.

26. 'Israel Fearless', 13 October 1973; 'No Good Result', 13 October 1973; 'No More Doves', 27 October 1973. After the Six-Day War, US aid increased from $63 million to $102 million annually, reaching $634.5 million in 1971, quintupling after the Yom Kippur War in 1973 to make Israel the largest recipient of US foreign aid since 1976. John J. Mearsheimer and Stephen M. Walt, *The Israel Lobby and US Foreign Policy*, New York 2007, pp. 2–3.

27. 'Worth spending /not concerned risks involved /no involvement of embassy /$10,000,000 available, more if necessary/ best men we have/ game plan/ make the economy scream/ 48 hours for plan of action': CIA director Richard Helms took these notes during a meeting with Nixon, Kissinger and others on 15 September 1970. At this stage, their plot led to the murder (by extremist officers) of René Schneider, the Chief of the Chilean General Staff, known to be against military intervention in the electoral process – but not to the hoped-for coup. See Jonathan Haslam, *The Nixon Administration and the Death of Allende's Chile*, London 2005, p. 67.

28. 'Urban Guerrillas in Latin America' in 1970, 'Uruguay: Terrorism vs. Democracy' in 1971, *The War for the Cities* in 1972 – all retailed the idea that Che Guevara's failure to raise a peasant revolt in Bolivia in 1967 prefigured a shift in tactics and terrain for left subversives from the countryside to the city: Robert Moss, *The War for the Cities*, New York 1972, pp. 7, 27, 241–48.

29. Crozier, *Free Agent*, p. 110.

30. 'Birth of a Civil War', 11 March 1972.

31. 'Come off ITT', 1 April 1972; 'Who's for Sweet-and-Sour Turkey', 5 August 1972; 'Ticket to Cuba', 2 September 1972.

32. Fred Landis, 'Robert Moss, Arnaud de Borchgrave, Right-Wing Disinformation', *CAIB*, August 1980, p. 38.

33. Robert Moss, *Chile's Marxist Experiment*, New York 1974, p. 190.

34. Ibid., p. i.

35. For the way Moss used CIA-invented stories while denying CIA involvement, a representative sentence: 'The full extent of these preparations was not accurately known until after the September coup, when the military junta claimed it had discovered – in a safe in the office of the Communist under-secretary for the interior, Daniel Vergara – detailed plans for the assassination of hundreds of opposition leaders, senior officers, conservative journalists and businessmen.' Ibid., pp. 188–89, vi; Tanya Harmer, *Allende's Chile and the Inter-American Cold War*, Chapel Hill 2011, p. 61.

36. Peter Chippindale and Martin Walker, 'Tory's Book Funded by CIA', 'Only the Views We Want You to Read', *Guardian*, 20 December 1976.

37. 'Chile After Allende', 13 October 1973.

38. For examples of overlap, see Robert Moss, 'The Making of Europe's Cuba', *National Review* 11 April 1975 and 'Don't Do a Cuba on Portugal', *Economist* 12 April 1975; Robert Moss, 'Moscow's Next Target in Africa', *Daily Telegraph* 20 February 1977 and 'Podgorny Goes South', *Economist*, 8 January 1977. For ISC reports, see Iain Hamilton and Robert Moss, *The Spreading Irish Conflict*, London 1971; Robert Moss, *Revolutionary Challenges in Spain*, London 1974; Robert Moss, *The Campaign to Destabilise Iran*, London 1978.

39. New York Times News Service, London, 18 November 1979, quoted in Landis, 'Robert Moss, Arnaud de Borchgrave, and Right-Wing Disinformation', *CAIB*, August 1980, p. 37. When scant attention was paid to a propaganda piece by Moss in the *Daily Telegraph* – 'Moscow's Next Target in Africa', 20 February 1977 – Pretoria had it reprinted as a full-page ad in the *Guardian* and *Washington Post*. In November 1978 Crozier arranged for 'the top civilian in the SAVAK hierarchy to be closeted with Robert Moss for a whole week with a pile of secret reports in Farsi ... evidence of Soviet involvement with the Shah's enemies'. The result was the ISC's *Campaign to Destabilise Iran*. 'Shortly after the study had appeared the Iranian chargé d'affaires informed me that the Shah had authorised a first annual payment of £1 million to The 61': Crozier, *Free Agent*, p. 161.

40. Arnaud de Borchgrave, a *Newsweek* editor known to keep 'intelligence files' on fellow journalists, became Moss's co-author. The two met when de Borchgrave was hiding out in the English countryside – convinced his life was in danger after some threatening calls – at the estate of his cousin, *Economist* chairman Evelyn de Rothschild. 'We eventually realized that between us we knew most of the intelligence

directors in the Western world', de Borchgrave told the *New York Times*. 'We decided to pool these assets to gain access to the major defectors from Soviet intelligence, to see what they could tell us about disinformation and manipulating the media.' Rather than something that 'read like a PhD thesis', he and Moss decided to write novels. All were devoted to the idea that liberal bastions in media and government were swarming with KGB moles, working to dampen Western resolve to fight communism. *The Spike* posited this as the path to the takeover of the US in five years' time; in 1981, the danger was a *Death Beam* (originally *Death Star* until Lucasfilm threatened to sue); in 1983 in *Monimbo*, it was Fidel Castro, who planned to foment a race war in the US via the Black Panthers. Edwin McDowell, 'Behind the Bestsellers', *New York Times*, 22 June 1980. Marketed as containing news too explosive to be published in the mainstream press, the only truly distinguishing feature of the novels was gratuitous sex. *Death Beam* – featuring Vadim Krylov, KGB head, sloshing around with the prepubescent children of dissidents in a marble bathtub in East Berlin – was feted at its launch party in Washington by virtually the entire Reagan administration, including James Baker, Richard Allen, Edwin Meese and CIA director William Casey. Morgan Mason, the director of political affairs Reagan brought with him from Hollywood, told the *Washington Post*, 'Arnaud and Robert are good guys, and they're known to be on our side, so to speak. They are philosophically attuned to the administration, and we want to embrace them.' 'Beams All Around: Turning out for Robert Moss' Book Party', *Washington Post*, 11 November 1981. In 1985 de Borchgrave became editor of the *Post*'s rightwing competitor, the *Washington Times*, whose owner Sun Myung Moon was a Korean cult leader, presiding over mass wedding ceremonies. Moss went on an even more circuitous journey. Reacting to the collapse of the Soviet Union between 1989 and 1991 with the same intensity he had brought to fighting it, Moss had a breakdown, divorced his wife, moved to a barn in upstate New York, and took the time to look within. What he found there was a Native American woman, 'a clan mother and powerful healer', a friendly red-tailed hawk, a warrior shaman and an alter ego, Sir William Johnstone, 'who flourished in the 1700s as both the King's Superintendent of Indians, an adopted Mohawk war chief, and a redoubtable ladies' man'. Through them and a number of other birds of prey, Moss learned to re-evaluate 'previous ambitions and definitions of success', which he defined rather untruthfully as 'the commercial fast track in New York and London'. A group of Iroquois, helping him to interpret the archaic Mohawk dialect spoken in his dreams, led him to his new vocation. Moss has since published nine guides to 'active dreaming' and runs workshops where the spiritually curious can learn how to use 'dreams to understand your past, shape your future, get in touch with your deepest desires, and be guided by your higher self'. The man who once jumped for joy at the death of Allende now runs a website, blog and Twitter feed on healing through dreams. One blog post shows a picture of the toy hawk he rubs against workshop participants to activate their 'child selves' and remind them 'they can fly'. Robert Moss, *Conscious Dreaming: A Spiritual Path for Everyday Life*, New York 1996, pp. 12, 15, and back cover.

41. On returning from Brazil in 1965, Macrae contemplated the political commitments he shared with Crozier, Moss and Beedham. 'Editing the proofs of this survey in *The Economist* offices in St James's one is struck by an awkward thought', he interjected. 'If there was an organisation like this newspaper in Brazil – with a large staff of graduates from the national universities, communist activists would make a dead set at it. Down there in the canteen there would be a lot of smooth-faced men wielding large rolls of dirty banknotes.' He realized 'with some shock, that if he had been born in intellectual circles in Brazil, some of his very best friends would probably be communists'. Thankfully, 'nearly all of his best new friends in Brazil are, to a man, and probably rightly, supporters of the Castelo Branco coup d'état.' 'No Christ on the Andes', 25 September 1965.

42. 'The Unacknowledged Giant', 17 June 2010.

43. 'The Next Ages of Man', 24 December 1988.

44. Norman Macrae, *The London Capital Market, Its Structure, Strains, and Management*, London 1955; Macrae, *To Let?: A Study of the Expedient Pledge on Rents Included in the Conservative Election Manifesto in October*, London 1959; Macrae, *Sunshades in October: An Analysis of the Main Mistakes in British Economic Policy Since the Mid Nineteen-fifties*, London 1963; Macrae, *Homes for the People*, London 1967; Macrae, *The Neurotic Trillionaire; A Survey of Mr. Nixon's America*, New York 1970; Macrae, *The 2025 Report: A Concise History of the Future, 1975–2025*, New York 1984; Macrae, *The Hobart Century*, London 1984; Macrae, *John von Neumann: The Scientific Genius Who Pioneered the Modern Computer, Game Theory, Nuclear Deterrence, and Much More*, Providence, RI 1999.

45. 'The Unacknowledged Giant', 17 June 2010.

46. 'The Risen Sun', 27 May 1967; 'Consider Japan', 1 September 1962.

47. 'Consider Japan', 1 September 1962.

48. 'The Risen Sun', 27 May 1967.

49. 'The Pacific Century', 4 January 1975.

50. 'The German Lesson,' 15 October 1966.

51. 'De-socialize production, socialize markets', was the slogan Macrae used to describe the competitive principle he thought would – always with the help of computers – lead not only to more efficient services, but ones that could better serve poorer regions by offering salary incentives – for example, to teachers to teach there – practices blocked by the trade unions: 'The People We Have Become', 28 April 1973.

52. 'The Risen Sun', 27 May 1967. The 'burying' of the Department of Economic Affairs and George Brown's 1965 National Plan was another black mark for the civil service: 'The People We Have Become'.

53. 'Experience in state welfare has influenced academic thinking and public policy in America more than in Britain', lamented Seldon, who cited Milton Friedman and Edward Banfield as cases of the former, Senator Daniel Moynihan of the latter: 'Letters', 12 May 1973. See Keith Tribe, 'Liberalism and Neoliberalism in Britain, 1930–1980', in *The Road from Mount Pèlerin*, eds. Philip Mirowski and Dieter Plehwe, Cambridge 2009, p. 89.

54. Eurocurrency markets undermined the Bretton Woods system, since they operated without reference to the official, gold-backed value of the US dollar. For the competitive deregulatory pressures they exerted on policymakers, and their role in the formation of a transatlantic 'City-Bank-Treasury' – 'Federal Reserve-Wall Street-Treasury' nexus, see J. Green, 'Anglo-American Development, the Euromarkets, and the Deeper Origins of Neoliberal Deregulation', *Review of International Studies*, July 2016, pp. 9–14; Eric Helleiner, *States and the Reemergence of Global Finance, From Bretton Woods to the 1990s*, Ithaca 1994, pp. 15–16. For the slow 'divorce' between the City and sterling, in favour of alternative strategies after 1967, see Gary Burn, *The Re-Emergence of Global Finance*, London 2006, pp. 93–98, 184–85. In 1958 the *Economist* welcomed the policy of full convertibility of non-residents' sterling accounts into dollars, and initiated a debate on the implications of further exchange liberalization with Roy Harrod, Thomas Balogh and other leading Keynesian economists. 'Letters', 4 January 1958, 29 March 1958; 'Convertibility?', 27 September 1958.

55. 'Float Free and Low', 'Floating into Europe', 'Floating the Humpty Dumpty Commonwealth', 1 July 1972. Banking in this broad sense might even supplant the 'rigid' multinational corporation: 'The People We Have Become', 28 April 1973.

56. The City was less dependent on the global standing of sterling than before: world reserves of sterling were declining along with its role in trade, and there was little fresh borrowing from commonwealth countries. Marjorie Deane, Sarah Hogg, Pat Norton, Dudley Fishburn, Stephen Milligan and Alan Parker contributed alongside Macrae. Andrew Knight, *Britain into Europe*, pp. 14, 16, 17.

57. Ibid., pp. 14, 16, 17. The merchant banker Siegmund Warburg, Crowther's confidant, was an early promoter of the turn towards Eurodollar and Eurobond markets. He built his case precisely on the role the City could play in European integration, liberalizing and linking currency and capital markets as a prelude to Britain joining – and leading – the common market, with the support of the US. Ferguson: *High Financier*, pp. 208–13.

58. 'The Neurotic Trillionaire', 10 May 1969. The *Economist* supported Johnson's Great Society ('Richer for Poorer', 15 August 1964), and reiterated that in the case of the US, it was possible to produce guns and butter at the same time. 'The war is costing $25,000 million a year; but that is only about half of what the Americans will be adding

to their gross national product ... the United States can fight the Vietnam war and go on raising its standard of living at the same time. That is the measure of its economic power': 'The Impatient Ones', 19 August 1967.

59. 'The Neurotic Trillionaire', 10 May 1969.

60. Ibid.

61. Watergate received ample *news* coverage, but there was no editorial censure of the president, with whom it shared so much, from law and order to foreign policy. 'Watergate affair apart, the Nixon Administration is applying itself with increasing confidence to America's responsibilities in the world': 'The Ideas of Gerald Ford', 26 January 1973.

62. Macrae guessed this could mean big business for the City, as the leading market in foreign exchange. 'Come on, it's Fine', 21 August 1973.

63. Robert Brenner, *The Economics of Global Turbulence: The Advanced Capitalist Economies from Long Boom to Long Downturn, 1945–2005*, London 2006, pp. 99–101, 122–29; Giovanni Arrighi, 'The World Economy and the Cold War, 1970–1990,' in *Cambridge History of the Cold War*, eds. Leffler and Westad, Vol III, pp. 26–31; Barry Eichengreen, *Globalizing Capital*, Princeton 1996, pp. 128–35.

64. Hirsch was *Economist* finance editor from 1963 to 1966, and wrote for it earlier while also at the *Banker*. A socialist, he sometimes wrote letters to the editor as Fred Stag (the translation of Hirsch from German) – notably in response to the *Economist*'s savage review of John Kenneth Galbraith's critique of mid-twentieth century capitalism, *The Affluent Society*, in 1958. 'The unchallenged absurdities of advanced economics cited by Professor Galbraith', Hirsch wrote, 'stem from an attitude of mind which begins to become dangerous at quite a modest level of affluence. Perhaps the level at which the cream of a country's brains begins to be sucked into its advertising agencies': 20–27 September 1958. Hirsch quit shortly after the arrival of Burnet. But his time at the *Economist* shaped his critical appraisal of politics, society and economics in Britain. In 1965 he took detailed notes for a book to be titled *Is Leftwing Government Possible?*, and published *The Pound Sterling: A Polemic*; after he left, he developed themes from his defence of Galbraith in *Newspaper Money: Fleet Street and the Search for the Affluent Reader* with David Gordon in 1975, *The Social Limits of Growth* in 1977 and *The Political Economy of Inflation* in 1978. My thanks to Donald Hirsch and David Gordon for these references.

65. Andrew Knight, interviewed by the author.

66. Max Hastings, *Editor: An Inside Story of Newspapers*, London 2002, pp. 1–2.

67. Andrew Neil, *Full Disclosure*, London 1996, p. 191; One interviewer literally found him 'behind walnut veneered doors ... remaining motionless': Catherine Bennett, 'Mr Murdoch's Mixed-up Kid',

*Guardian*, 18 January 1993; Roger Cohen, 'Rupert Murdoch's Biggest Gamble', *New York Times Magazine*, 21 October 1990.

68. Conrad Black, *A Life in Progress*, Toronto 1993, p. 342. Knight and Black fell out three years later, when Knight quit as managing director to become the chairman of News International, with '£14 million worth of free Telegraph stock' in a move, wrote a furious Black, that 'raises substantial ethical questions'. Black later did time in a federal prison in Florida for obstruction of justice and fraud.

69. Denny Hatch, 'Direct Marketer of the Year: Beth O'Rorke, COO and Vice President, The Economist', *Target Marketing*, 1 October 2004.

70. Moss was 'a powerful force on the paper', remembered Knight, who shared an office with him before becoming editor in 1974. Interview with the author.

71. 'Straying to the Left', 11 May 1974; 'Kerensky with a Monocle', 5 October 1974. Moss wrote these and other alarmist pieces; compare his 'Making of Europe's Cuba', *National Review*, 11 April 1975 to 'Don't Do a Cuba on Portugal', *Economist*, 12 April 1975. For praise of Spínola, see 'War Hero Who Sees No Victory', 2 March 1974; 'Unendurable Burden', 27 April 1974; for the discrediting of an historic election (before and after), with 91 per cent participation, see 'Keen Voters', 26 April 1975; 'Lovely Election but No More', 3 May 1975. For context: Ronald H. Chilcote, *The Portuguese Revolution: State and Class in the Transition to Democracy*, Lanham 2010, p. 123.

72. Perry Anderson, *The New Old World*, London 2009, pp. 355–91.

73. 'Makarios's position as head of the church and head of state was becoming an anachronism': 'Cyprus: The Makarios Years', 20 July 1974. Makarios 'will not be the best person to preside over the new structure', for 'after the past fortnight he evokes many enmities', and was 'too dependent on the communists', so 'there are a lot of counts against him now'. 'Welcome Back', 27 July 1974; 'Why Would They?', 7 September 1974; 'The Price of an Island', 30 November 1974, 'Battle for Southern Europe', 10 August 1974.

74. In violation of federal law, the Ford administration secretly supplied arms to Suharto for this purpose. Christopher Hitchens, *The Trial of Henry Kissinger*, London 2001, p 90–107. For the *Economist*, 'a left-wing Timor, which could serve as a base for communist subversion and arms smuggling', was 'intolerable'. 'The spectre of another mini-Angola, combined with the evident impossibility of measuring opinion among the 650,000 largely primitive people of Timor, have kept most foreign governments quiet'; Jakarta's 'real worry is about reactions in Washington, from which it was hoping to get $43 million in military aid', etc. 'Indonesia Tidies the Map', 13 December 1975.

75. By late December, the tide had turned for the MPLA in Angola, with assistance from 3,500 to 4,000 Cubans. Piero Gleijeses, *Conflicting Missions, Havana, Washington, and Africa, 1959–1976*, Chapel Hill 2002, pp. 305–27.

76. 'It Wasn't Ready', 19 July 1975; 'Unrecognisable', 18 October 1975;

'War Is Won, Not Over', 14 February 1976; 'From the Angolan Rubble', 21 February 1976; 'Do It with Mines', 3 April 1976. The *Economist* frequently argued that Angolan rebels strengthened apartheid in South Africa, preventing the 'moderate deal' Pretoria had wanted with 'black Africa'.

77. In the event, the US did not have to invade Iran: Iraq did, with its assistance, in 1980. Saddam Hussein's war was just comeuppance, so long as it did not advance far beyond Khuzestan. 'Blood in the Oil', 27 September 1980. On the hostages: 'It is the right of the blackmailed to respond with low blows, cunning and deceit' – 'the affair is a matter of terrorism, not of religion, culture or anything else': 'Confronting a Cliché', 1 December 1979.

78. Odd Arne Westad, *The Global Cold War: Third World Interventions and the Making of Our Times*, Cambridge 2007, pp. 316, 323.

79. 'America Gone Soft', 5 January 1980. The potent Stinger missiles: 'Sams for the Love of Allah', 5 July 1980; 'Don't Forget Afghanistan', 25 October 1980.

80. 'Nicaragua: The Revolution Cuba Might Have Been?', 29 September 1979; 'Another Crisis for Carter', 30 June 1979.

81. 'The United States would be supine indeed if it refused to arm its friends, albeit unattractive, against an even more unpopular bunch brandishing Russian supplied weapons'; it was a 'do-gooder, not a bloodthirsty meddler'. 'The Savagery in Salvador', 28 February 1981. Reject peace on terms offered by the guerrillas in 1983, it advised: 'There Is an Alternative', 19 February 1983. As a result, the wars continued. In El Salvador, the death toll was 70,000; in Nicaragua, 30,000 died (relative to population, more than the US lost in the Civil War, First and Second World Wars, Korea and Vietnam, combined): Westad, *Global Cold War*, p. 347.

82. Iran-Contra showed weakness by indirectly paying a ransom for hostages in Lebanon and would 'rile a Congress that had insisted on cutting the Contras' aid': Burnet, *America*, pp. 243–45; the *Economist* pleaded passionately for continuing such aid, 'sparing Nicaragua from a less budgeable dictatorship than Somoza's': 'Contra Cut-off', 27 April 1985; 'Why the Contras', 6 September 1986; 'Lordy Me', 13 December 1986; 'Carry a Big Stick', 26 March 1988.

83. *Economist*, 5 November 1983. Predictably, the paper also applauded the bombing of Libya in 1986: unless Qaddafi stopped sponsoring terrorists, 'the time will come when it will be right to use more force and, if necessary, to overthrow him'. 'Appointment in Tripoli', 19 April 1986.

84. 'Kissinger's Critique', 3 February 1979.

85. 'Sideswipe', 4 August 1979; 'Letters: Cambodia and Kissinger', 8 September 1979.

86. Francis Wheen, 'Being Economist with the Truth', *Guardian*, 2 October 1996; George M. Kahin, *Southeast Asia: A Testament*, London 2003, p. 285.

87. 'Interview with George P. Shultz', *Miller Center*, University of Virginia, 18 December 2002.

88. Shultz thanked Knight for help with his memoirs: George Pratt Shultz, *Turmoil and Triumph: My Years as Secretary of State*, New York 1993, pp. 828–29, 1033.

89. In 1975, deep cuts in public spending, a real wages freeze, and a bigger devaluation of the pound could still avert catastrophe – defined as the rise to power of 'an anti-democrat party led by Mr Benn or some other left-wing prophet': 'No Need for Apocalypse', 17 May 1975. See for the period *Understanding Decline, Perceptions and Realities of British Economic Performance*, eds. Peter Clarke and Clive Trebilcock, Cambridge 1997, and for a reappraisal of the decade, Andy Beckett, *When the Lights Went Out: Britain in the Seventies*, London 2009.

90. Keith Tribe, 'Liberalism and Neo-liberalism in Britain, 1930–80', in Mirowski and Plehwe, *Road*, pp. 71, 86–87.

91. Ben Jackson, 'The Think-Tank Archipelago: Thatcherism and Neoliberalism', in *Making Thatcher's Britain*, eds. Ben Jackson and Robert Saunders, Cambridge 2012, pp. 46–49, 50–56. For more on the IEA, see Richard Cockett, *Thinking the Unthinkable: Think-Tanks and the Economic Counter Revolution, 1931–1983*, London 1994, pp. 122–99.

92. Radikha Desai, 'Second-Hand Dealers in Ideas: Think Tanks and Thatcherite Hegemony', *New Left Review*, no. 203, January 1994, pp. 29–31; Wayne Parsons, *The Power of the Financial Press: Journalism and Economic Opinion in Britain and America*, London 1989, pp. 172–99.

93. For an excellent recent archaeology of neoliberalism, see Quinn Slobodian, *The Globalists: The End of Empire and the Birth of Neoliberalism*, Cambridge 2018. See also Corey Robin, 'Wealth and the Intellectuals: Nietzsche, Hayek and the Austrian School of Economics', in *Hayek: A Collaborative Biography: Part Five, Hayek's Great Society of Free Men*, ed. R. Leeson, London 2015, pp. 112–58.

94. Friedman replied that he was 'pleased to learn the extent of our agreement'. But he pointed to one misunderstanding. While excessive government control over the economy was 'the most serious threat to the maintenance of a free society', it did not, as Macrae had implied, cause inflation; neither did trade unions. 'I have been dismayed, even in my few days in London, at the widespread support of "union-bashing" as a way to attack inflation.' For 'unions do much harm', but 'they do not and cannot produce inflation' – 'on the contrary, one of the unfortunate effects of inflation has been to strengthen unions'. Keith Joseph wrote to the paper testily to say that the *Economist* had inaccurately called him a 'follower' of Friedman, and that he owed his own recent 'conversion' to free market principles to him. 'You are in a position to know better': 'Paradise Regained', 21–28 September 1974. For context, see Jim Tomlinson, 'Thatcher, Monetarism and the Politics of Inflation', in *Making Thatcher's Britain*, Cambridge 2012,

pp. 62–94 and Jim Bulpitt, 'The Discipline of the New Democracy: Mrs Thatcher's Domestic Statecraft', *Political Studies*, March 1986, pp. 19–39; Daniel Stedman Jones, *Masters of the Universe: Hayek, Friedman and the Birth of Neoliberal Politics*, Princeton 2012, pp. 201–14.

95. 'Towards a Keynesian Friedmanism', 17 June 1978.

96. 'UnKeynesian Britain', 4 February 1984.

97. For the extent to which monetarism had been accepted by Labour's leadership during the 1976 IMF crisis, see Mark Wickham-Jones, *Economic Strategy and the Labour Party: Politics and Policy-Making 1970–83*, Basingstoke 1996, pp. 98–100; Noel Thompson, *Political Economy and the Labour Party: The Economics of Democratic Socialism, 1884–1995*, London 1995, pp. 222–25; Stedman Jones, *Masters*, pp. 241–54.

98. Callaghan might turn out to be the 'best practitioner of Tory policy', but the *Economist* doubted if he could bring along 'Labour's lethargic laggards' – who wanted bailouts for bankrupt firms and an incentive-crushing wealth tax. 'Only One Prime Minister' and 'Labour's Conservative', 28 April 1979. At the time, on the left Stuart Hall perceived more clearly the 'hegemonic thrust' of Thatcherism in his *Marxism Today* pieces, many of which appear in *The Hard Road to Renewal: Thatcherism and the Crisis of the Left*, London 1988.

99. 'Anybody but Carter?', 18 October 1980.

100. Reagan's one foreign policy blemish was Israel: 'Mr. Reagan is a simple-minded Zionist whose views will have to be reconstructed by going to the Middle East.' Ibid.

101. 'Can We Learn from Chile?', 17 June 1972.

102. Moss, *Chile's Marxist Experiment*, p. 79.

103. Robert Moss, *The Collapse of Democracy*, London 1975, pp. 8, 12; 'National Association for Freedom: Into Its Stride', *Economist*, 28 August 1976. In 1974 Thatcher spoke at the first fundraiser for the NAFF, whose house magazine *Free Nation* focused on confronting trade unions, and often suggested the Army 'intervene' to restore order to British politics: see Andy Beckett, *Pinochet in Piccadilly: Britain and Chile's Hidden History*, London 2002, p. 188. The NAFF shot to prominence when one of its twin millionaire founders, Ross McWhirter, was assassinated by the IRA. McWhirter had authored a pamphlet, 'How to Stop the Bombers', which offered £50,000 for the capture of IRA members. As an example of the NAFF finding its way into the *Economist* via Moss, see 'Quis custodiet?', 22 January 1977. This argued against the right of British postal workers to boycott communications with South Africa as part of an international labour protest against apartheid. Not just because 'anybody who thinks it is in the nastiest 10 [governments] is conveniently ignoring how other tyrannies treat *all* their peoples'. It also hailed an unnamed 'libertarian group' (NAFF), which saw that this could be the wedge for a wider struggle against the trade unions. 'At a time when there is

some threat to democracy in Britain (or at least when many serious
people think there is), when government elected by minorities of
the electorate sit through full parliamentary terms ... when measures of federal devolution are in the air, when over half of national
income passes through the hands of the state, it will be better to
become rather more American ... In some other democracies these
actions against freedom of employment and against freedom of
speech would be regarded as infringements of inalienable human
rights. It is time to move towards the installation of such rights in
Britain.'

104. A democracy in death throes had '*two* alternatives to anarchy, not
one ... authoritarian or totalitarian rule'. Despite 'semantic confusion characteristic of much public debate', the former left 'certain
areas' of social, intellectual and economic life alone. Ibid., 10–13.
Brian Crozier, then crisscrossing Britain to give lectures on this
very issue to army officers and cadets, congratulated Moss. Moss
replied to Crozier: 'Whatever is said for or against this book, it
cannot equal praise from the man who has taught me more about
the central challenge of our times than anyone else. I have often felt
that I was following in your footsteps. I now feel that we are joined
in a common cause.' Moss to Crozier, 21 November 1975, Crozier
Papers, HIA, Box 2.

105. Richard Vinen, *Thatcher's Britain: The Politics and Social Upheaval
of the Thatcher Era*, London 2009, p. 84.

106. Hastings, *Editor*, p. 68.

107. Tom Bower, *Outrageous Fortune: The Rise and Ruin of Conrad and
Lady Black*, New York 2006, p. 58.

108. Edmund Fawcett and Tony Thomas, *The American Condition*, New
York 1982, pp. 2, 6.

109. Other Labour profiles included James Callaghan's in 1979, 'Labour's
Conservative', 28 April 1979; Leonard, interviewed by the author.

110. Neil, *Full Disclosure*, p. 20.

111. Neil and Stelzer formed a consultancy firm, a version of Stelzer's
National Economic Research Associates, with the aim of ending the
BBC broadcast monopoly ('British TV was ready for a multi-channel
revolution'). Writing articles in favour of US-style deregulation of
the airwaves while running a business devoted to the same did not
strike him as a conflict of interest. Ibid., p. 21.

112. 'The Unions Don't Know Where They Go Now – Except Down', 10
September 1981.

113. 'At the End of the Day', 19 June 1982.

114. Peter Clarke, *A Question of Leadership: From Gladstone to
Thatcher*, London 1992, p. 304. When 364 academic economists
signed a letter to the *Times* in 1981 protesting a budget that slashed
spending in a recession, the *Economist* advised patience – waiting
six more months for signs of economic turnaround. 'Britain's Recession', 4 April 1981.

115. 'Thatcher's Britain', 4 June 1983.

116. Simon Jenkins, *Thatcher and Sons: A Revolution in Three Acts*, London 2006, p. 27; 'An Anti-Tory Tactical Voters Guide', 4 June 1983. Seumas Milne and Simon Jenkins, interviewed by the author.

117. 'Queen Margaret or Shakespeare Goes to the Falklands', 25 December 1982.

118. Andrew Knight, 'The War of April Fools' Night', 19 February 1983.

119. 'Peter Pennant-Rea', *The Times*, 12 March 2007.

120. 'From 1977 to 1986, I think you will see the paper's economic coverage and approach changed significantly.' As for Macrae, 'I think he felt he could leave the economics coverage to Sarah and me, and then to me and Clive. He was changing his own views, not least because he could see that many of the supply-side measures taken by Thatcher were having a positive effect on growth, without the need for a Keynesian fiscal stimulus.' Rupert Pennant-Rea, interviewed by the author. A glance at his signed articles, surveys, and co-authored books partly confirms this. Reports from East Asia, India, Sri Lanka, Britain, Brazil and Zimbabwe had new focus after 1979: the market was by and large the best way to move people off farms and into cities and factories, not state-led investment or planning, while selling off state-owned assets, creating export zones or lowering trade barriers made a place attractive to foreign investors; Hogg took the same line in Israel, Austria, Britain and West Germany.

121. Jacob Weisberg, 'The Tweed Jungle', *Vanity Fair*, June 1993.

122. Sample dialogue: '"Bastards," she said aloud, still thinking of the South African strikes. "Parasites on society." She found it very easy to slip into the quasi-Marxist jargon of her student days. But then wasn't she a leech as well?' Rupert Pennant-Rea, *Gold Foil*, London 1978, pp. 124, 91, 156, 159, 100, 185.

123. Interview with the author.

124. Richard Stevenson, 'Sex and Bank of England: Downfall for No. 2 Official', *New York Times*, 22 March 1995. Alexander Cockburn provides some context to these events in his memoirs. Alexander Cockburn, *A Colossal Wreck: A Road Trip through Political Scandal, Corruption, and American Culture*, London 2013.

125. Though much copied and expanded since, London's Big Bang remained 'the most rapid and complete regulatory reform of any market.' John Plender, 'London's Big Bang in International Context', *International Affairs*, 63, no. 1, 1 December 1986, p. 40; Eric K. Clemons and Bruce W. Weber, 'London's Big Bang: A Case Study of Information Technology, Competitive Impact, and Organizational Change', *Journal of Management Information Systems* 6, no. 4, 1 April 1990, p. 42.

126. 'Capital of Capital', 11 October 1986. On the 'pre-Big Bang scramble', see David Kynaston, *The City of London: A Club No More*, London 2002, Vol IV, pp. 715–20.

127. 'Capital of Capital', 11 October 1986. See also, Philip Augar, *The*

*Death of Gentlemanly Capitalism: The Rise and Fall of London's Investment Banks*, London 2000.

128. 'Guided Tour', 8 October 1983; 'Lemon Aid', 3 January 1987.
129. 'June's Choice', 6 June 1987.
130. 'May the Worst Lot Lose', 4 April 1992; 'Mayhem', 19 September 1992. Major's government spent £6 billion propping up the pound, and George Soros gained £1 billion betting against it – itself a case study in misallocated resources.
131. Weisberg, 'The Tweed Jungle', *Vanity Fair*, June 1993.
132. In searching for a historic parallel, the Marshall Plan had little resonance – a much closer fit was the concept of unconditional surrender: Burnet, *America*, p. 257; 'Yankee Stay On', 10 February 1990; 'As the Tanks Rumble Away', 1 September 1990; 'Doing Well by Doing Good', 15 June 1991.
133. 'If it comes to a choice between fudge without war and victory with war, Mr Bush should go to war.' 'Saying No', 11 August 1990; 'The Man with No Illusions', 25 August 1990.
134. 'Blood on His Hands', 19 January 1991.
135. Brian Beedham, 'Niech zyje wiosna: Long Live Spring', 12 August 1989.
136. Brian Beedham, '1989, and All That', 23 December 1989.
137. 'Beedham criticises me for arguing that seven or possibly eight civilisations now exist and says there are really only three: Western, Confucian and Muslim. I can think of no scholar of civilisations, dead or alive, who would agree with him.' Brian Beedham, 'Islam and the West', 6 August 1994; 'Letters', 3 September 1994.
138. '1989, and All That', 23 December 1989.
139. Ibid.
140. Brian Beedham, 'As the Tanks Rumble Away', 1 September 1990.
141. Brian Beedham, 'A Better Way to Vote', 11 September 1993.
142. Norman Macrae, 'The Next Ages of Man', 24 December 1988.
143. Norman Macrae, 'Future Privatisations', 21 December 1991.
144. Ibid., p. 19.
145. 'Future Privatisations', 21 December 1991.
146. 'Mrs Thatcher's Place in History', 29 April, 1989.
147. 'Banks in Trouble: Sweaty Brows, Slippery Fingers', 8 September 1990.
148. 'Time to Choose', 31 October 1992; 'Getting His Way', 7 November 1992.

## 8. Globalization and Its Contents

1. As Federal Reserve chairman, Alan Greenspan was the most eloquent spokesperson for the new economy, which his loose money policies from early 1995 to mid-1999 helped sustain – boosting stock market

valuations, and creating a 'wealth effect' that fuelled corporate and household borrowing. The *Economist* lauded him – 'Man of the New Year', 7 January 1989; 'Prosperity Not Politics', 27 August 1995; 'Almighty Alan Greenspan', 8 January 2008 – with one short hiccup along the way, when it suggested he might honourably step down to make way for someone younger in 'A Bias towards Change', 26 April 2003.

2. Philip Augar, *Chasing Alpha: How Reckless Growth and Unchecked Ambition Ruined the City's Golden Decade*, London 2009, pp. 119, 105, 34, 10–11; Lucinda Maer and Nida Broughton (2012), 'Financial Services: Contribution to the UK Economy', House of Commons Standard Note, SN/EP/06193.

3. Brian Groom, 'Manufacturers Remain Divided over Legacy of Thatcher Policies', *Financial Times*, 12 April 2013.

4. Augar, *Chasing Alpha*, pp. 10–11. Outward signs of decline could become a paradoxical source of strength: proof that, freed from fixed exchange rates and imperial currency commitments or controls, the City could float above the dwindling industrial economy.

5. Angela Monaghan, 'London's West End Is Most Expensive Office Location', *Daily Telegraph*, 19 February 2013; 'Opening of Sake No Hana', *Tatler*, 1 December 2007.

6. Over nine years, John Micklethwait earned above £500,000 per year on average, and though Zanny Minton Beddoes is on track to earn less, she made five times an ordinary section editor in her first year as editor: The Economist Group 2016 Annual Report.

7. R. W. Johnson, interviewed by the author. See also, R. W. Johnson, *Look Back in Laughter: Oxford's Postwar Golden Age*, Newbury 2015, pp. 118–19.

8. Cameron's other close contact was Xan de Crespigny Smiley, who went to New College, Oxford. David de Crespigny Smiley, his father, was a race car driver, food critic, baronet and spy – who swept through Arabia in a cloud of camels, tanks and planes in the Second World War; parachuted behind enemy lines in Albania in 1944 and then served in East Asia. David Smiley, *Arabian Assignment*, London 1975; David Smiley, *Irregular Regular*, Norwich 1994; 'Colonel David Smiley', *The Telegraph*, 9 January 2009. Lisa O'Carroll and John Plunkett, 'David Cameron Admits Close Friendships with Journalists', *The Guardian*, 14 June 2012. Cameron appointed Lockwood to his Policy Unit in 2013.

9. In 2010, the *Economist* praised Ridley's bestselling *Rational Optimist* for claiming 'exchange is to cultural evolution as sex is to biological evolution', with markets the 100,000-year-old fluid of transmission for innovation. The book also called climate fears overblown: just look at the Chernobyl nuclear disaster, which killed only 4,000 humans and indirectly benefited local wildlife: *The Rational Optimist*, London 2010, pp. 5–7. After his departure from the paper, Ridley was often cited – on evolution ('Story of Man', 20 December 2005), fossil fuels

('Engine Trouble', 21 October 2010), climate change ('Americans and Global Warming', 16 February 2011), and gender imbalance at work ('Too Many Suits', 26 November 2011). In a review of the *Rational Optimist*, even the *Economist* thought him 'slightly unfair to government', which could do some things, like 'enact a carbon tax, and cut payroll taxes': 'Getting Better All the Time', 13 May 2010. It was left to Bill Gates to criticize Ridley's proposals to abolish 'top-down aid' in favour of an internet marketplace for 'bidding' on it. Bill Gates, 'Africa Needs Aid, Not Flawed Theories', *The Wall Street Journal*, 30 November 2010.

10. Emiko Terazono, 'Lunch with the FT: Perfectly Pitched', *Financial Times*, 10 March 2006.

11. After a second meeting went no better, R. W. Johnson rang Knight and said 'Andrew, you're a snob! You only like Magdalen boys who went to Eton!' Johnson, interviewed by the author.

12. By 1986, almost 40 per cent of all its exports were bound for the US, where the relative strength of the dollar was a major boon. Brenner, *The Boom and the Bubble: The US in the World Economy*, London 2002, p. 105.

13. Bill Emmott, *The Sun Also Sets: Why Japan Will Not Be Number One*, London 1989, p. 95.

14. Emmott, *Sun Also Sets*, pp. 8, 37.

15. 'The Post-Hirohito Century', 17 October 1987.

16. Emmott, *Sun Also Sets*, pp. 271–73.

17. Calls for a 'federal industrial policy' in the US in imitation of the Japanese – which might grow louder, if budget cuts and tax rises took place under Bush Sr., – were dangerous, in that 'America will learn from the wrong Japanese example, will emulate something Japan has in fact abandoned.' Ibid., pp. 93, 95, 97, 100, 271.

18. Net exports of long-term capital were $65 billion in 1985 and $137 billion in 1987, roughly equalling the GNP of Sweden or Switzerland. Emmott, *Sun Also Sets*, p. 17; 'The London of Asia', 8 December 1984.

19. Ibid., pp. 34, 67, 87, 89, 127. In the City, Nomura was 'for a time, the largest private recruiter of new graduates from Oxford and Cambridge': Bill Emmott, *Japan's Global Reach: The Influences, Strategies, and Weaknesses of Japan's Multinational Companies*, London 1991, pp. 151–52.

20. Emmott, *Sun Also Sets*, pp. 126–28.

21. Emmott, *Japanophobia: The Myth of the Invincible Japanese*, New York 1993, p. 222; Emmott, *Japan's Global Reach*, pp. 177–78, 189. The reason for his uncanny serenity? Bank consolidations, better ratings of investment risk and, above all, a rebound in stock prices stimulated by government policy.

22. 'International Banking: Survival of the Fittest', 26 March 1988; 'Apocalypse When?', 15 October 1988. Christopher Wood, *Boom and Bust: The Rise and Fall of the World's Financial Markets*, London 1988, pp. 5, 22, 145.

23. Taking on debt for tax purposes using leverage to fund mergers and acquisitions was in accordance with the 'sound principles of finance'. 'International Finance', 27 April 1991.

24. Amidst his optimism, he did note criticisms of the 'productivity miracle'; and that, after a decade of Thatcher, inflation and current-account deficits were rising: 'Business in Britain', 20 May 1989.

25. The other contenders in 1993 were Jim Rohwer, Hong Kong chief; Frances Cairncross, environment editor, Daniel Franklin, Britain editor; Johnny Grimond, foreign editor, and David Lipsey, writing for the Britain section. See Jacob Weisberg, 'The Tweed Jungle', *Vanity Fair*, June 1993.

26. Ibid.

27. Bill Emmott, *Rivals*, London 2008, pp. 123–24.

28. Bill Emmott, 'The Long Goodbye', 30 April 2006.

29. 'An Idea Whose Time Has Passed', 22 October 1994. Letters poured in from across the globe, almost without exception hostile to this republican turn: the Monarchist League in London, New Zealand Young Nationals in Auckland; the peer Lord Ampthill; a patriot in Nova Scotia; a royalist from Denmark; a New Mexican tourist. 'Long to Reign over Us', letters to the editor, *Economist*, 5 November 1994.

30. Jenkins, *Thatcher and Sons*, pp. 57–58. 'A Wit May Also Be Wise: In Praise of an Unconventional Democrat and Scholar of Walter Bagehot', 10 March 2012.

31. 'Politics and the Prince of Wales: All Dressed up and Nowhere to Go', 19 July 1986. According to Andrew Neil, Queen Elizabeth sent her son to the *Economist* to be interviewed, wishing to indirectly distance herself from Thatcher, who – Neil claimed – she reportedly considered uncaring and insufficiently critical of apartheid. Neil, *Full Disclosure*, p. 202. But the piece was not exactly dictated by her, relaying the Prince's complaints about being kept on a short leash by his mother's minders.

32. Why else did only 22 per cent of Cambridge graduates still go into business, he asked, opposing this noble pursuit to useless paths in the professions, academia or … financial journalism? 'Business in Britain', 20 May 1989.

33. 'An Idea Whose Time Has Passed', 22 October 1994.

34. Blair's government returned the compliment, elevating him to the peerage as Baron Lipsey of Tooting Bec in 1999. After stepping down as Bagehot in 1997, Lipsey had stayed on part-time as social affairs editor until then: David Lipsey, *In the Corridors of Power: An Autobiography*, London 2012, pp. 173–75.

35. 'The Strangest Tory Ever Sold', 2 May 1998.

36. 'Vote Conservative', 2 June 2001. Welfare reform, public-private partnerships, university top-up fees, war in Iraq; all endeared New Labour, if not Blair or Brown, still further. See, 'There Is No Alternative (Alas)', 30 April 2005.

37. 'The Case for Gay Marriage', 26 February 2004.
38. 'Controlling Guns', 18 May 1996; 'America's Blind Spot', 24 April 1999.
39. 'The Case for Legalisation', 28 July 2001; Bill Emmott, *20:21 Vision: The Lesson of the 20th Century for the 21st*, London 2003, p. 11.
40. In 1996, it justified its choice based on the 'fiasco over health care', 'foreign policy made on the hoof', slowness to enact welfare reform and 'ethical problems'. 'What a Choice', 2 November 1996; 'If It's True, Go', 31 January 1998; 'Unwanted', 12 September 1998; 'Just Go', 19 September 1998; 'Resign, Rumsfeld', 8 May 2004.
41. Bill Emmott, *The Fate of the West: The Battle to Save the World's Most Successful Idea*, London 2017, pp. X, 61.
42. A better title, Shiina quipped privately to Emmott, would have been, 'The Japanese people's amazing ability not to be disappointed.' 'The Sun Also Rises', 8 October 2005; Emmott, *Rivals*, p. 90.
43. During a painful thirty-second handshake, attendants look on nervously. 'Do you recognize me? Bill Emmott. Lenin! Do you still think I'm a communist?' 'No, I never thought that', Berlusconi reassures him as he moves away. 'That's very generous', Emmott replies. 'We all have our part to play', replies the former prime minister. 'Exactly. Exactly.' *Girlfriend in a Coma* (2012). 'One man has been chiefly responsible for making this old Asia hand so engaged and fascinated by his country. His name is Silvio Berlusconi'. Bill Emmott, *Good Italy, Bad Italy: Why Italy Must Conquer Its Demons to Face the Future*, New Haven 2012, p. i.
44. LTCM 'did not borrow more than a typical investment bank ... nor was it especially risky'. Hedge funds were fine. 'They should be welcomed with open arms': 'A New Approach to Financial Risk', 17 October 1998.
45. For surveys by Crook see 'Trial and Error: The Third World', 23 September 1989; 'The IMF and the World Bank', 12 October 1991; 'Globalisation and Its Critics', 29 September 2001. Many other editors helped, including Frances Cairncross, who wrote favourably on globalization's environmental, technological and managerial dimensions. Her reports for the *Economist* turned into *Costing the Earth* (1993) and the *Death of Distance* (1997).
46. Weisberg, 'Tweed Jungle', *Vanity Fair*, June 1993.
47. It mocked protestors for taking their stand in such a successfully globalized city, 'home to Microsoft and Boeing, birthplace of global crazes "Frasier" and fancy coffee': 'Storm over Globalisation', 27 November 1999.
48. Environmental regulations, left unspecified, might be needed where 'greater good' was involved, but determining when would be 'tough': 'The Real Losers', 11 December 1999. Covers carrying the image of a poor child with dark skin and raised eyes became a visual trope in pro-globalisation pieces. See 'The Case for Globalisation', 23 September 2000.

49. 'Pro Logo: The Case for Brands', 8 September 2001; Naomi Klein, 15 September 2001. 'Pro Logo' argued that brands were a blessing, ensuring quality, convenience, choice and consumer protection and accountability. And people liked them. A letter from Klein appeared the next week. But this was buried in the issue of 15 September 2001. The next time she merited a verbal flogging, she had been demoted to a small column in the business section where the level of threat she now posed was indicated by the title, 'Face Value: Why Naomi Klein Needs to Grow Up', 9 November 2002.

50. 'Americans without Bank Accounts: Into the Fold', 6 May 2006. El Banco de Nuestra Comunidad 'seemed to be getting it right', Emmott wrote in 2006. As a result of the crisis, it collapsed. By 2012, only one bank had survived, Mitchell Bank in Wisconsin, and this had a strength rating of D and a troubled asset ratio of 72, when the national average was 12: Weiss Research, 'The X List: Strongest and Weakest Banks and Thrifts in the US', March 2012; Investigative Reporting Workshop: 'How Healthy Is This Bank?' banktracker.investigativereportingworkshop.org.

51. Bill Emmott, 'Crisis, What Crisis? Enough Kerfuffle, It's Just a Slowdown', *The Guardian*, 12 August 2008; Emmott's missed predictions in 2008 were also partly due, he said, to having 'spent too much time thinking about Japan'. Bill Emmott, 'I Wasn't Right. But That's OK', *The Guardian*, 3 January 2009.

52. Emmott, *Japan's Global Reach*, pp. 208–9, 199.

53. The greatest challenge for the West, Emmott argued, was 'fighting the domestic backlash against globalisation'. Not everyone on the commission agreed. Paul Wolfowitz predicted that without hard power 'the next century could eclipse the twentieth as the bloodiest in human history' and 'preponderance is a wasting asset' – 'if we don't make good use of the next ten years, events may begin to spin out of our control': Emmott et al., *Managing the International System*, pp. 13, 17–18, 44, 51. David Rockefeller and Zbigniew Brzezinski founded the Trilateral Commission.

54. 'Who Will Save Rwanda?', 25 June 1994.

55. 'First, Catch Your Gunman', 19 June 1993; 'To Bosnia's Rescue?', 24 April 1993.

56. 'Stumbling into War', 27 March 1999.

57. 'Victim of Serbia – or NATO?', 3 April 1999; 'Defining NATO's Aims', 24 April 1999. 'Making the Best of a Bungled War', 8 May 1999.

58. 'Never mind the genuine mistakes ... any dispassionate accounting of the conflict is almost certain to find the allies guilty of some terrible crimes.' 'Messy War, Messy Peace', 12 June 1999.

59. Kosovo strengthened the US-led Western alliance at a time of drift, given the collapse of the Soviet enemy, while revealing replacements for it: dictators like Slobodan Milosevic, Saddam Hussein, and those who procured them weapons. 'Other People's Wars', 31 July 1999. For Emmott's regret at being too slow to call for intervention in the

Balkan wars – 'We left it for too long. In hindsight, I think it was wrong' – see his lunch with the *Financial Times*, 10 March 2006.

60. Peter David, *Triumph in the Desert: The Challenge, the Fighting, the Legacy*, New York 1991.

61. 'The Day the World Changed', 15 September 2001; 'The Battle Ahead', 22 September 2001; 'So Far, So Good', 29 September 2001.

62. 'Propaganda War', 6 October 2001; 'A Heart-Rending but Necessary War', 3 November 2001; 'Peter David', 19 May 2012.

63. 'Bush and the Axis of Evil', 2 February 2002; 'Case for War', 3 August 2002; 'Case for War – Revisited', 19 July 2003.

64. 'Why War Would be Justified', 22 February 2003.

65. Rodenbeck, Middle East bureau chief from 2000 to 2015, is the author of a history of Cairo, where his father was a professor of comparative literature: Max Rodenbeck, *Cairo: The City Victorious*, New York 1999. Contributing regularly to the *New York Review of Books* on Lebanon, Iran, Syria, Islam, and the Arab Spring, he has used its columns to question US policy, if never the good intentions behind them. See 'The Occupation', *New York Review of Books*, 14 August 2003: 'The messiness is more a result of prewar misconceptions, wartime miscalculations and postwar misrule.' Unlike some of his colleagues, he has not just taken lessons from neoconservatives but given them some, too. For his disagreement with Bernard Lewis, see 'The Muslim Past', *New York Times*, 25 June 2010. Bill Emmott, interviewed by the author.

66. Bill Emmott, 'Present at the Creation', 29 June 2002.

67. Ibid.

68. Ibid.

69. Ibid.

70. Bill Emmott, 20:21 *Vision*, p. 16.

71. 'Such is the legacy of his misadventure in Iraq, of the continued instability of Afghanistan, of the worldwide decline in the reputation of the United States during his administration, many would rank him as having been the worst American president since Richard Nixon, or Herbert Hoover', though 'it has not been for want of ambition'. Emmott, *Rivals: How the Struggle Between China, India and Japan Will Shape Our Next Decade*, Orlando 1998, p. 1.

72. Ibid., 255.

73. This, according to a senior editor, was the reason Emmott gave Mallaby for refusing the survey, parts of which ran later in the *New Republic*. Mallaby, whose father was British ambassador to Berlin and Paris, and is married to the current editor Zanny Minton Beddoes, was hardly a heretic on economics and empire. See his subsequent post–9/11 reflection, 'The Reluctant Imperialist: Terrorism, Failed States and the Case for American Empire', *Foreign Affairs*, March 2002.

74. Maggie Brown, 'Business as Usual', *Guardian*, 27 March 2006; Ian Burrell, 'John Micklethwait: Great Minds Like a Think', *Independent*, 8 January 2007.

75. 'The naming of Mr. Micklethwait is an indication of where the *Economist* expects to find its future growth.' Katharine Q Seelye, 'The Economist Names New Editor in Chief', *New York Times*, 23 March 2006.

76. Burrell, 'John Micklethwait', *Independent*, January 8, 2007; John Micklethwait and Adrian Wooldridge, *A Future Perfect: The Challenge and Hidden Promise of Globalization*, London 2000, p. 314.

77. 'Special Report: American Politics', 3 January 2004; John Micklethwait and Adrian Wooldridge, *The Right Nation: Why America Is Different*, London 2004.

78. That enthusiasm endured: in 2018, Wooldridge published *Capitalism in America*, albeit with a new writing partner, former chairman of the Federal Reserve, Alan Greenspan.

79. Micklethwait and Wooldridge, *Future Perfect*, pp. xxii–xxiii, 232.

80. Ibid., pp. 73, 61, 32, 90, 80, 43.

81. 'Asked where he wants to be in five years, Espinosa [a young engineer at a GE plastics plant in Cartagena, Spain] points at the back of the plant manager and says "in his office". A quarter of a century ago, another young engineer, when asked a similar question in an evaluation, cockily put "chief executive officer of General Electric". His name was Jack Welch.' Ibid., pp. 139, 309.

82. Ibid., p. 97.

83. Ibid., p. 251.

84. Ibid., pp. 258–60.

85. Ibid., pp. 233, 245. It is worth noting that – to judge only from the fulsome examples given by Micklethwait and Wooldridge – this new, rising and broadening class seemed mainly to consist of the so-called older elites' children.

86. *Future Perfect*, pp. xxv, 113.

87. 'Fair trade is piffle. In fact, unfair trade is usually an oxymoron.' *The Company*, pp. 146–47, 152.

88. Companies 'gave back' by hiring people, paying wages, selling them products. 'Problems in the future may stem less from what companies do to society, than from what society does to companies.' Ibid., pp. 8, 181, 171, 170, 182.

89. Micklethwait and Wooldridge, *Right Nation*, pp. 72–73, 314, 345. For context, see 'An Exchange between Max Beloff and Irving Kristol', *Encounter*, June 1987.

90. Micklethwait and Wooldridge, *Future Perfect*, p. xiii.

91. *Right Nation*, pp. 396, 294; John Micklethwait and Adrian Wooldridge, *God Is Back: How the Global Revival of Faith Is Changing the World*, New York 2009, pp. 31–54.

92. In the *Economist*, see 'When Opium Can Be Benign', 1 February 2007.

93. *God is Back*, pp. 21, 16, 25, 1–2, 21.

94. Katharine Q. Seelye, 'The Economist Names New Editor in Chief', *New York Times*, 23 March 2006.

95. Burrell, 'John Micklethwait', *Independent*, 8 January 2007; Burrell, 'John Micklethwait: "Republicans Had the Advantage, but They Wasted It With Sleaze"', *Independent*, 3 November 2008.

96. 'Danger Time for America', 14 January 2006. Wall Street was still burdened by excessive red tape. 'What's Wrong with Wall Street', 25 November 2006. Late in 2007, it saw a possible credit crunch taking shape. But this was after Britain's Northern Rock received its first bailout. Even then, the problem was a consumer spending slowdown, not a collapse of the banking sector. 'Getting Worried Downtown', 17 November 2007.

97. Mark Blyth, *Austerity: The History of a Dangerous Idea*, New York 2013, p. 26; John Authers, *The Fearful Rise of Markets: Global Bubbles, Synchronized Meltdowns, and How to Prevent Them in the Future*, London 2010, pp. 2–3, 18, 95. For the financial, regulatory and geopolitical dynamics of the 2008 crash, see Adam Tooze, *Crashed: How a Decade of Financial Crises Changed the World*, New York 2018.

98. 'Capitalism at Bay', 16 October 2008.

99. 'I Want Your Money', 27 September 2008; 'The Credit Crunch: Saving the System', 'Rescuing the Banks: We Have a Plan', 'Global Finance: Lifelines', 9 October 2008.

100. 'Hank to the Rescue', 13 September 2008. Obama would dispel 'myths' about the US just by being president: 'it would be far harder for the spreaders of hate to denounce the Great Satan if it were led by a black man whose middle name is Hussein'; at home, 'he would salve, if not close, the ugly racial wounds left by America's history and lessen the tendency of American blacks to blame all their problems on racism': 'It's Time', 1 November 2008.

101. New Labour had many faults after thirteen years, but the financial crisis was not one of them. 'Britain was always likely to get mauled in the credit crunch': 'Bagehot', 16 October 2008.

102. See, 'The Comeback Keynes', *Time*, 23 October 2008; 'The New Big Old Thing in Economics', *Wall Street Journal*, 8 January 2009; Martin Wolf, 'Keynes Offers Us the Best Way to Think about the Financial Crisis', *Financial Times*, 23 December 2008.

103. 'Capitalism is the best economic system man has invented yet': 'Capitalism at Bay', 16 October 2008.

104. Governments must bail out, but not exert control over, Fannie Mae and Freddie Mac in the US and Northern Rock in the UK. 'Inside the Banks', 24 January 2009; 'A Short History of Modern Finance: Step by Step', 16 October 2008.

105. 'The Banks Battle Back', 29 May 2010; 'Bare-Knuckle in Basel', 29 May 2010; 'Save the City', 7 January 2012.

106. 'Bailing out Detroit would be a bad use of public money': 'Saving Detroit', 15 November 2008.

107. 13 February 2010; 8 May 2010; 'Sometimes, Austerity Makes Sense', 20 December 2010; 'Pick Your Poison', 17 June 2010.

108. 'Who Should Govern Britain?' 29 April 2010. 'Tremble, Leviathan', *World in 2011*, 22 November 2010; 'Reforming the State: The Unlikely Revolutionary', 12 August 2010.

109. 'Reforming the State: The Unlikely Revolutionary', 12 August 2010.

110. Humans possessed inherently unequal abilities: some were geniuses who 'spark a corporate renaissance', others on welfare, 'inhabiting a world of concrete events and immediate satisfactions'. Adrian Wooldridge, 'Stop the War on Wealth, We Need These Rich Few', *Sunday Times*, 12 August 2002.

111. 'Freedom Fighter', 13 April 2013.

112. 'Blood and Oil', 26 February 2011. Rejecting the 'racist assertion that Arabs cannot be democratic', it asserted 'Arabs are being asked to shed the culture of victimhood, take responsibility for themselves and uncork the creativity of their young': 'Crunch Time in Libya', 23 April 2011.

113. 'No Illusions', 19 March 2011; 'Crunch Time in Libya', 23 April 2011; 'Going, Going', 27 August 2011.

114. 'How to Set Syria Free', 11 February 2012.

115. 'Mr Obama and his allies blinked.' 'An American threat, especially over WMD, must count for something; it is hard to see how Mr Obama can eat his words without the superpower losing credibility with the likes of Iran and North Korea': 'Hit Him Hard', 31 August 2013.

116. 'Fight This War, Not the Last', 7 September 2013. 'Now every tyrant knows that a red line set by the leader of the free world is really just a threat to ask legislators how they feel about enforcing it': 'The Weakened West', 21 September 2013. A year later, Micklethwait and Wooldridge added that the West needed to reinvent itself at home to see off the threat of autocratic China and Russia – by slashing entitlements, tearing up regulations, tackling corruption and stoking innovation – in *The Fourth Revolution: The Global Race to Reinvent the State*, New York 2014.

117. 'Surprisingly sensitive about their international reputation', Russians ought to pay for their misdeeds. No energy deals, travel restrictions, exclusion from OECD, WTO and G8, with NATO extended post-haste to Georgia and Ukraine: 'Russia Resurgent', 16 August 2008.

118. 'Putin's Inferno', 20 February 2014; 'Britain, France and the United States have sometimes broken international law. But Mr Putin has emptied the law of significance': 'Kidnapped by the Kremlin', 8 March 2014; 'Mr Putin has driven a tank over the existing world order': 'The New World Order', 23 March 2014; 'Insatiable', 19 April 2014; 'The Long Game', 4 September 2014; 'A Web of Lies', 1 October 2014.

119. Edward Lucas, *The New Cold War: How the Kremlin Menaces Both Russia and the West*, London 2008, p 7; Edward Lucas, *Deception: Spies, Lies and How Russia Dupes the West*, London 2012, pp. 4–5.

120. Lucas conceded that economic shock therapy in the 1990s had entailed 'hardship and uncertainty for many'. But this was not the fault of Boris Yeltsin, a flawed yet honourable man, still less the IMF or World Bank which had devised restructuring operations for him: 'the real culprits were Lenin, Stalin and Brezhnev'. Putin won praise for, if nothing else, introducing a 13 per cent flat tax on income in 2001: Lucas, *New Cold War*, pp. 53, 42.

121. Lucas, *New Cold War*, p. 7; Lucas, *Deception*, pp. 4–5.

122. Ibid., 16, 279. Lucas, *New Cold War*, pp. 77, 284, 296, 305. 'Counter-Attacking the Kremlin', 26 April 2007. Lucas exchanges letters with 'prisoners of conscience' in Russia, and promotes embattled liberal causes in the *Economist*, *Daily Telegraph* and *Daily Mail*; see 'CEPA Stratcom Program', Center for European Policy Analysis, CEPA.org.

123. Give drone assassinations to the Army, not CIA, and have a 'secret court' sign off on them. 'Flight of the Drones', 'Drones and the Law', 8 October 2011.

124. 'The Right Reaction', 11 December 2010.

125. 'European governments should not kick up a fuss about American spying', or offer Snowden asylum: 6 July 2013.

126. Sachs justified shock therapy with the homily, 'you don't try to cross a chasm in two jumps'. 13 January 1990.

127. One reason to be optimistic about Latin America was that 'the involvement of foreign investors in domestic capital markets, which will be a permanent feature of the region, creates a new discipline on governments'. Another was private pensions, as in Chile, though it 'had the (debatable) luxury of completing the toughest part of its reforms in a non-democratic environment'. In 1995, 'Venezuela still fails to acknowledge that high-spending populism does not work': 'Latin American Finance', 5 December 1995; 'Caspian Gamble', 7 February 1998. Only tweaks to the system were possible. Citing Larry Summers, she called the prospect of designing a new financial architecture with a global capital market, a stable, regulated financial system, and national sovereignty, the 'impossible trinity'. 'Global Finance: Time for a Redesign?', 30 January 1999; 'Flying on One Engine', 20 September 2003; 'The Great Thrift Shift', 24 September 2005.

128. Ed Lucas, interviewed by the author.

129. Bank bonuses should be paid out over longer periods and tied to performance; trading divisions, which took bigger risks, ought to pay higher capital costs. Central banks, in particular the Federal Reserve, had erred: doing nothing as asset price bubbles inflated (market prices were always right, on the way up) – only to rush in with low interest rates to stop them from popping: 'Credit and Blame', 11 September 2008; 'The Bonus Racket', 29 June 2009; 'Taking von Mises to Pieces', 19 November 2010.

130. Stagnation, inflation, default, or a mix of all three, were the likeliest

outcomes: Philip Coggan, *Paper Promises: Money, Debt and the New World Order*, London 2011, p. 249.

131. Coggan, *Paper Promises*, p. 239. For the trade-off argument in the *Economist*, see 'The Question of Extractive Elites: Bankers and the Public Sector May Both Be Enemies of Growth', 13 April 2012.

132. Zanny Minton Beddoes, interviewed by the author.

133. 'True Progressivism', 13 October 2012.

134. Ibid. For a countervailing view of the neoliberal turn in Sweden, see Göran Therborn, 'Twilight of Swedish Social Democracy', *New Left Review*, no. 113, September 2018, pp. 5–26.

135. The *Economist* denied there was a crisis in living standards. Even though wages had fallen continuously since 2008, low wage, precarious work was still 'preferable, both in economic efficiency and social equity, to the French or Italian diseases of mass joblessness'. 'Britain will be a model for Europe if the Tories can boost productivity': 'Who Should Govern Britain?', 30 April 2015.

136. 'If he had his way, he would be the most economically radical premier since Margaret Thatcher': Ibid.

137. 'The Land that Labour Forgot', 5 September 2015. 'Only in the time-warp of Mr Corbyn's hard-left fraternity could a programme of renationalisation and enhanced trade-union activism be the solution to inequality.' Rent controls would 'exacerbate the shortage' in housing and a 'people's QE' – after the quantitative easing undertaken by central banks to prop up asset prices and stimulate private lending after 2008 – 'threatens to become an incontinent fiscal stimulus'. Scrapping university tuition fees 'would be regressive and counterproductive': 'Backwards Comrades', 19 September 2015.

138. 'The Way Ahead', 8 October 2016.

139. 'The West should help Saudi Arabia limit its war in Yemen': 15 October 2016.

140. In addition to a civilian death toll of at least 6,500 as a direct result of war (the actual number likely far higher, according to the UN), 85,000 children are estimated to have died of starvation since 2015. By 2018, over 1 million Yemenis were infected with cholera, and 16 million (over half the population) were 'food deficient'. Derek Watkins and Declan Walsh, 'Saudi Strikes, American Bombs, Yemeni Suffering', *New York Times*, 27 December 2018. See also the Yemen Data Project.

141. *Guardian*, 29 May 2016.

## Conclusion

1. 'UK Newspapers' Positions on Brexit', Reuters Institute for the Study of Journalism, 23 May 2016.

2. 'Some Britons despair of their country's ability to affect what happens

in Brussels. Yet Britain has played a decisive role in Europe – ask the French, who spent the 1960s keeping it out of the club. Competition policy, the single market and enlargement to the east were all championed by Britain': 'Divided We Fall', 18 June 2016.

3. 'A Tragic Split', 24 June 2016; 'Brex and the City', 24 June 2016.

4. 'Republicans should listen carefully to Mr Trump, and vote for someone else': 'Trump's America', 5 September 2015; 'Brawl Begins', 30 January 2016. 'Fortunately, Mr Trump will probably lose the general election. A candidate whom two-thirds of Americans view unfavourably will find it hard to win 65m votes … the share of women who disapprove of him is even higher.' 'Trump's Triumph'; 'Fear Trumps Hope', 7 May 2016.

5. 'The Dividing of America', 16 July 2016. 'America's Best Hope', 5 November 2016.

6. 'The Dividing of America', 16 July 2016.

7. 'America's Best Hope', 5 November 2016.

8. 'The open markets and classically liberal democracy that we defend, and which had seemed to be affirmed in 1989, have been rejected by the electorate first in Britain and now in America. France, Italy and other European countries may well follow. It is clear that popular support for the Western order depended more on rapid growth and the galvanising effect of the Soviet threat than on intellectual conviction. Recently Western democracies have done too little to spread the benefits of prosperity. Politicians and pundits took the acquiescence of the disillusioned for granted': After Trump, 'the long, hard job of winning the argument for liberal internationalism begins anew'. 'The Trump Era', 12 November 2016.

9. 'A bigger majority would leave Mrs May freer to strike sensible compromises with the EU' and 'to stand up to her ultra-Eurosceptic backbenchers, some of whom seem actively to want Britain to crash out. That explains why the pound rose this week': 'Game Change', 'Theresa May: Tory of Tories', 'Hard Work for Labour', 22 April 2017.

10. Raising the minimum wage would mean '60% of young workers' salaries are set by the state'. Free tuition was 'a vast subsidy for the middle class and a blow to the poor, more of whom have enrolled since tuition fees helped create more places': 'Britain's Missing Middle', 'Cor!', 3 June 2017.

11. 'Britain's Missing Middle', 3 June 2017; 'Europe's Saviour', 17 June 2017. Sophie Pedder, the paper's Paris chief, was a perfervid Macron-booster; for her sense of why France needed him, see her *Le déni français: les derniers enfants gatés de l'Europe*, Paris 2012, and 'France in Denial', 31 May 2012.

12. 'Mr Corbyn has revolutionised the British left': 'The Remarkable Mr Corbyn', 3 June 2017; 'The Second Eleven', 10 June 2017; 'Jeremy Corbyn, Entrepreneur', 17 June 2017.

13. 'A Regretful No', 26 November 2016; Enrico Franceschini, 'L'Economist vota No? Giornale spaccato. La sua edizione speciale è per il Sì',

*La Reppublica*, 25 November 2016; 'Renzi's Gamble', *The World in 2017*.

14. 'Paid sales fell in 2014 for the first time in 15 years': Henry Mance, 'Zanny Minton Beddoes Appointed Editor of the Economist', *Financial Times*, 22 January 2015.

15. Economist Group Annual Report 2017, pp. 3, 8.

16. Edmund Fawcett, *Liberalism: The Life of an Idea*, Princeton 2014, pp. xi, xiii–xiv, 5, 25, 293.

17. Ibid., pp. 61, 80–81, 85.

18. In Britain, the MP Robert Lowe (author of the 1856 Companies Act) warned of a threat to property and political economy in 1866, and in the next decades historians Henry Sumner Maine and W. E. H. Lecky decried democracy as 'monarchy inverted' and 'the rule of the most ignorant'. Fawcett, *Liberalism*, 152–53.

19. Ibid., pp. 144, 152–53, 156.

20. Ibid., p. 248.

21. Ibid., p. 277.

22. Ibid., p. 307.

23. Ibid., p. 380.

24. Ibid., p. 389.

25. Ibid., p. 407.

26. Letters, 14 March 2014.

27. Fawcett, *Liberalism*, p. 144.

28. Ibid., p. 22.

29. Ibid., p. 235.

30. Ibid., p. 89.

31. Ibid., pp. 113, 116.

32. Ibid., p. 215.

33. Fawcett incorrectly attributes the 'Red scares' of 1919–20 to the Harding administration; in fact, the Palmer raids took place under Wilson. Ibid., p. 231

34. Ibid., pp. 21, 227.

35. Ibid., pp. 198–200.

36. Ibid., pp. 358, 336, 353.

37. Ibid., pp. 267, 248.

38. Ibid., p. 6.

39. 'The Economist was sceptical of imperialism' and 'Liberalism was not born with the umbilical link to political democracy that it now enjoys': 'A Manifesto' and 'The Economist at 175: Reinventing Liberalism for the 21st Century', 13 September 2018. In the same issue, the Lexington columnist gave his seal of approval for Trump's cold war against China as 'popular, overdue and irrevocable'.

40. Daniel Singer, *Whose Millennium?: Theirs or Ours?*, New York 1999, p. 265.

41. Mill, *Autobiography*, London 1873, p. 239. Among Mill's Anglophone heirs, Bertrand Russell, J. A. Hobson and John Dewey all received a similar jolt that led them to embrace a version of liberal socialism.

42. 'Experience and Reform', 5 May 1860; 'Defeat of the Ministry and the Prospects of Reform', 2 April 1859; 'The Practical Difficulties of Secret Voting', 2 September 1859; 'A Simple Plan of Reform', 24 December 1864.

43. 'Conservative Criticism of Liberal Politics', 25 February 1860; 'Plurality of Votes: The True Principle of a Reform Bill', 24 March 1860; 'True Liberalism and Reform', 27 January 1866.

44. Bagehot, *CW*, Vol. V, pp. 208, 299.

45. 'Democracy and Economy', 15 August 1931.

46. 'The Way We Go to War', 26 June 1971; 'Voices', 10 July 1971.

47. 'True Purpose of the War', 2 December 1854.

48. 'As the improvement both of Turkey and Russia will be consequent on the war now happily at an end; so any war with China which should result in bringing her people more completely into trade communication with all other nations': 'Peace the Result of Free Trade', 9 May 1857.

49. Barbara Smith, 'Not So Hard Labour', 20 December 2003.

50. 'For me, Johnny never saw one he did', according to Bill Emmott.

51. 'Retiring Editor', *The Bankers' Magazine*, 1907, p. 150.

# Index

Aberdeen, Lord, George Gordon,
  George (4th Earl of Aberdeen), 50
Acheson, Dean, 273, 351, 352
Allende, Salvador, 285–9
Allison, Graham, 351, 352
Amery, Leo, 240
Amin, Hafizullah, 305
Anderson, Sir Alan, 203
Andrade, Marcos, 357
Angell, Norman, 160, 174
Arendt, Hannah, 325
Arnold, Matthew, 55
Ashley, Lord, 39, 42
al-Assad, Bashar, 364
Assange, Julian, 367
Ash, Timothy Garton, 392
Asquith, Herbert Henry, 118, 133,
  136, 139
Attlee, Clement, 207, 208, 241, 242,
  249, 272
Avebury, Lord, 150
Azaña, Manuel, 6

Bachelet, Michelle, 4
Balfour, Arthur, 132, 133, 138, 188
Bagehot, Eliza, 146, 165, 166
Bagehot, Thomas, 73
Bagehot, Walter, 12, 17, 24, 35, 70,
  71–114
Baldwin, Stanley, 188, 218
Balfour, Nancy, 262, 300

Ball, Sidney, 143
Balogh, Thomas, 205, 233
Bannon, Steve, 3
Barlow, Frank, 340
Barry, Gerald, 209
Bartlett, Vernon, 220
Bastiat, Frédéric, 10, 36
Batista, Fulgencio, 267
Beddoes, Zanny Minton, 367–72,
  373–4, 378
Beedham, Brian, 260, 267, 280–5, 287,
  289, 290, 297, 298, 299, 300, 302,
  314, 316, 318, 325–9, 330, 348,
  349, 366, 394
Bellairs, Carlyon, 192
Bell, Daniel, 290, 358
Bell, Hugh, 165
Belloc, Hilaire, 142
Beloff, Max, 358
Benenson, Peter, 383
Benn, Tony, 312
Berlin, Isaiah, 8, 239, 383
Berlusconi, Silvio, 4, 345
Berry, Gerald, 220
Berry, Vaughan, 207, 208
Bethell, Sir Richard, 77
Beveridge, Sir William, 183, 187, 203,
  225–6, 233–5, 383
Bevin, Ernest, 235, 241, 242, 248, 249,
  255, 330
Bird, Roland, 228, 254

Black, Conrad, 302
Blair, Tony, 343, 377, 378, 390
Bloomberg, Michael, 367
Bolton, John, 352
Bonham Carter, Lady Violet (Baroness
     Asquith of Yarnbury), 182, 348
Bonnemaison, Colonel Antoine, 259
Bosch, Juan, 286
Bourgeois, Léon, 382
Bowring, Sir John, 58
Boyd, Andrew, 258
Bracken, Brendan, 202, 227, 240
Brandt, Willy, 384
Bright, John, 23, 106, 113, 126
Brogan, Hugh, 266, 282
Brown, Gordon, 343, 361
Bruce, Thomas (7th Earl of Elgin), 49
Brüning, Heinrich, 6
Brunner, Sir John, 152
Bryce, James, 71
Buchanan, James, 384
Buckley, William, 358
Burgess, Anthony, 330
Burnet, Sir Alastair, 272–3, 277,
     278–80, 300, 316, 319, 342
Burns, John, 161
Bush, George H. W., 2, 324–6
Bush, George W., 18, 350, 352–3, 355,
     361, 387, 388
Butler, Rab, 261, 271
Byron, Lord George Gordon (6th
     Baron Byron), 11

Cadbury, Sir Adrian, 340
Cadbury, Laurence, 201, 202
Callaghan, James, 304, 311, 312, 317,
     343
Cameron, David, 334, 363, 372, 375
Campbell, Alex, 267
Campbell-Bannerman, Henry, 132,
     133, 138, 144, 148, 149, 152, 156,
     173
Canning, Lord John Charles (1st Earl
     Canning), 67
Cardwell, Edward, 77
Carnegie, Andrew, 146

Carlyle, Thomas, 36, 106
Carr, E. H., 232, 255
Carter, Jimmy, 305, 308, 313, 315,
     316
Castlereagh, Lord. *See* Stewart,
     Robert (Viscount Castlereagh)
Castro, Fidel, 267, 288
Catto, Lord Thomas (1st Baron
     Catto), 242
Cecil, Lord Robert (1st Earl of
     Salisbury), 179–80
Chadwick, Edwin, 41, 381
Chamberlain, Joseph, 130, 133, 137,
     138
Chapman, John, 34
Charles, Prince, 278, 342
Chávez, Hugo, 4, 377
Chesterton, G. K., 144
Chevalier, Michel, 10
Churchill, Winston, 6, 139, 149, 152,
     153, 156, 160, 173, 183, 184,
     189, 190, 202, 210, 219, 226,
     255, 387
Clinton, Bill, 331, 332, 344
Clinton, Hillary, 376
Cobden, Helena, 146
Cobden, Richard, 10, 23, 74, 381
Coggan, Philip, 369
Colchester, Nico, 319, 339
Colefax, Sibyl, 202
Comte, Auguste, 8, 92
Constant, Benjamin, 8, 9, 380
Cook, A. J., 206
Corbyn, Jeremy, 318, 372, 377, 378,
     392
Corzine, Jon, 344
Cowley, Lord. *See* Wellesley, Henry
     Richard Charles, Lord Cowley
     (1st Earl Cowley)
Craddock, John Francis (1st Baron
     Howden), 49
Croce, Benedetto, 12, 380
Cripps, Sir Stafford, 208, 238
Croly, Herbert, 382
Cronkite, Walter, 278
Crook, Clive, 319, 322, 333, 335,

339, 345, 368
Crosland, Anthony, 316, 343
Cruikshank, Margaret, 227, 257
Crowther, Geoffrey, 198, 199, 204,
206, 208, 216, 219, 227–9, 268
Crozier, Brian, 258–60, 263, 266,
267, 269, 281, 285, 287, 288,
314, 366, 394
Crump, Norman, 205

Dale, Edwin L. 257
Dalton, Hugh, 207, 228, 242
Darwin, Charles, 34–5, 72, 106, 140,
335
Davenport, Nicholas, 205–208, 232,
233, 242, 246
David, Peter, 349
Davies, Howard, 322
Dawnay, Major Guy P., 203
De Ruggiero, Guido, 380
De Staël, Madame, 9
Derby, Lord, 49, 50, 57, 59
Desjobert, Amédée, 113
Deutscher, Isaac, 232
Diaz, Porfirio, 392
Dicey, Albert, 88
Dickinson, Lowes, 183
Diem, Ngo Dinh, 282
Disraeli, Benjamin, 90–1, 108, 123,
132
Dornbusch, Rudiger, 322
Douglas-Home, Sir Alec, 271
Drucker, Peter, 290
Drummond, Eric, 183
Dufferin, Lord, 126
Dulles, Allen, 257, 261–2
Dulles, John Foster, 262
Duncan, Emma, 318, 353, 354
Durbin, Evan, 207

Eden, Anthony, 218, 261–3
Edgeworth, F. Y., 142
Einaudi, Luigi, 146, 213, 380
Elgin, Lord. *See* Bruce, Thomas (7th
Earl of Elgin)
Eliot, George, 35

Elliott, Mike, 339
Emmott, Bill, 322, 335–355, 368, 371,
378, 396–7
Eyre, Edward John, 106

Fallows, James, 2
Fawcett, Edmund, 314, 315, 379
Ferdinand, Archduke Franz, 159–60
Ferranti, Marcus de, 356
Ferry, Jules, 387
Fisher, Herbert, 204
Foot, Michael, 312, 377
Forest, William, 209
Fould, Achille, 55
Friedman, Thomas, 357
Friedman, Milton, 280, 290, 310, 358,
384, 389
Fukuyama, Francis, 327

Gaddis, John Lewis, 351
Gaitskell, Hugh, 207, 241, 261, 270,
272
Gates, Bill, 344, 356
Gaulle, General Charles de, 259, 270
George, David Lloyd 13, 144, 149,
150, 152–8, 162, 163, 165, 171–5,
178, 179, 181, 183–185, 190, 192,
199, 204, 209, 230, 382, 387
Gibson, Thomas Milner, 61
Giffen, Sir Robert, 146
Giscard d'Estaing, Valéry, 300
Gladstone, William, 12, 50, 57, 77, 79,
84, 105–6, 110, 131–2, 141–3, 147,
173, 180, 182, 381, 387
Glazer, Nathan 358
Goldring, Mary, 300
Gorbachev, Mikhail, 324–7
Gordon, David, 300
Gordon, Scott, 31
Granville, George Leveson-Gower (2nd
Earl Granville), 77
Grant, Duncan, 186, 187
Greaves, Clive, 302
Green, T. H., 134, 140, 382
Greg, Walter Wilson, 166
Greg, William Rathbone, 32, 34, 76,

79
Grimond, Jo, 348
Grimond, Johnny, 284, 300, 314, 315, 348, 349, 351, 393, 396
Guizot, François, 10, 55, 380–1, 386

Haass, Richard, 352
Halsey, Sir Lionel, 203
Hamilton, Mary Agnes, 147, 159, 166
Hammond, J. L., 142, 143
Harmsworth, Alfred Charles William (1st Viscount Northcliffe), 149, 163
Harrison, Frederic, 110
Harvey-Jones, Sir John, 340
Harris, Ralph, 309
Harrod, Roy, 244
Hastings, Max, 301, 318
Hayek, Friedrich, 232, 236, 244, 309, 314, 367–72, 382, 383, 384, 386, 389
Heath, Edward, 279, 293, 294, 309, 312, 316
Heilemann, John, 368
Helms, Richard, 308
Henderson, Hubert, 184, 226
Hersh, Seymour, 308
Higgins, Matthew, 45
Hirohito, Emperor, 291
Hirsch, Steven, 300, 356
Hirst, Francis, 17, 137, 141–3, 144–7, 147–53, 155–65, 166–9, 172–4, 177, 183, 187, 196, 225, 393–6
Hitler, Adolf, 6, 211, 214–21, 232, 284, 303
Hobhouse, Leonard, 144, 173
Hobsbawm, Eric, 390
Hobson, C. K., 147
Hobson, J. A., 141, 144, 151, 163
Hodgskin, Thomas, 32
Hodson, Henry, 205
Hogg, Sarah, 319, 320
Holmes, Stephen, 392
Holt, R. D., 165
Honecker, Erich, 327
Honey, Patrick, 269
Hooper, John, 378

Hoover, Herbert, 146, 383, 390
Howard, George William Frederick (7th Earl of Carlisle), 40
Howden, Lord. *See* Craddock, John Francis (1st Baron Howden)
Huhne, Chris, 334, 335
Hume, Cardinal Basil, 301
Hume, David, 11
Hunt, Leigh, 11
Huntington, Samuel, 326
Hussein, Saddam, 325, 350
Hutton, Graham, 70, 197, 204–206, 216, 239
Hutton, Richard, 74, 76, 133

Il, Kim Jong, 4
Inglis Palgrave, Robert Harry, 116, 117, 150

Jackson, Andrew, 102
Jackson, Frederick Huth, 150
Jacobs, Paul, 257
Jay, Douglas, 204–8, 216, 220, 226, 315
Jenkins, Roy, 272
Jenkins, Simon, 318, 319, 342
Jevons, Stanley, 117
Jintao, Hu, 4
Joffe, Adam, 352
Johnson, Lyndon B., 6, 253, 257, 284–6, 297, 384, 388, 390
Johnson, R. W., 334, 335
Johnstone, Edward, 115–37, 147, 396
Jones, Arthur Creech, 241
Joseph, Keith, 310

Kagan, Donald, 352
Kagan, Robert, 390
Kaldor, Nicholas, 205
Kant, Immanuel, 8
Babrak Karmal, 305
Kennedy, John F., 6, 257, 267, 367
Kennedy, Paul, 351
Kenyatta, Jomo, 251, 264
Keynes, John Maynard, 17, 72, 164, 171, 182–4, 185–9, 190–4, 194–9,

201, 203, 204–7, 212, 226, 227,
    231–4, 244–5, 247, 297, 309–11,
    361, 367–72, 383, 389
Khomeini, Ruholla, 305
King, Martin Luther Jr, 257
Kissinger, Henry, 6, 283, 304, 306–8,
    313, 352
Kitchener, Lord, Horatio Herbert (1st
    Earl Kitchener), 127, 172
Klein, Naomi, 346
Knight, Andrew, 289, 298, 299, 314,
    334
Koestler, Arthur, 209
Kohl, Helmut, 384–5, 390
Kristol, Irving, 358
Kyle, Keith, 256–8, 260, 261, 262,
    263, 264, 265, 277

Lamb, William (2nd Viscount
    Melbourne), 44
Lambert, Richard, 147
Lamont, Norman, 320
Lathbury, Daniel Conner, 116
Layton, Walter, 17, 147, 165, 177–221,
    226, 254, 395
Lane, David, 345
Laski, Harold, 204
Law, Andrew Bonar, 159, 170, 188
Lawrence, Sir John, 108
Lawson, Sir Wilfrid, 131
Laxton, Tim, 345
Layton, Elizabeth, 228
Layton, Gilbert, 160
Layton, Sir Walter, 209, 210
Leonard, Dick, 315, 335
Lesseps, Ferdinand de, 55
Lewis, Sir George Cornewall, 32, 43,
    50, 55, 63, 77
Lincoln, Abraham, 99–101, 103, 381
Lings, Scott, 122
Lipset, Seymour, 358
Lipsey, David, 334, 339, 343
Lipmann, Walter, 383
Locke, John, 7, 8, 15, 380
Lubbock, John, 109
Lucas, Edward, 365

Lucas, John, 365
Lula da Silva, Luiz Inácio, 4
Lumumba, Patrice, 259, 266, 322

McCulloch, J. R., 26
MacDonald, Ramsay, 142, 184, 195,
    196, 197, 205, 208, 230
Macdonell, P. J., 142
MacIntyre, Alasdair, 390
Macleod, Iain, 261
Macmillan, Harold, 72, 195, 196, 198,
    229, 244, 263, 265, 266, 270, 271
Macrae, Norman, 271, 272, 277, 280,
    289–93, 294, 295, 296, 297, 298,
    308, 309, 310, 311, 319, 325, 328,
    329, 330, 336, 337
Macron, Emmanuel, 378
Maisky, Ivan, 212
Maitland, F. W. ,146
Mallaby, Sebastian, 353
Malthus, Thomas, 27, 389
Manning, Bradley, 366
Manning, Caroline, 320
Marshall, Alfred, 170, 182–184
Martin, Kingsley, 205
Martineau, Harriet, 35
Martineau, James, 77
Marx, Karl, 6, 8, 10, 32, 40, 104,
    115–16, 147, 205, 359, 361, 391
Major, John, 320, 323–4, 333
Massingham, H. W., 144
May, Sir George, 194
May, Theresa, 377
Mayo, Katherine, 200
Mboya, Tom, 264
McCain, John, 390
McLachlan, Donald 269
Meacham, Jon, 2
Mead, Walter Russell, 352
Melbourne, Lord. *See* Lamb, William
    (2nd Viscount Melbourne)
Mendès, Pierre, 384, 388
Merkel, Angela, 2, 4, 367
Micklethwait, John, 335, 350, 353,
    354–5, 355–9, 363, 364, 367, 368,
    371, 378, 379, 397

Midgley, John, 255, 262, 267, 269, 272, 277, 300, 393
Miliband, Ed, 372
Milken, Michael, 338
Mill, James, 24, 309
Mill, John Stuart, 8, 11, 74, 82, 106, 111, 344, 381
Milne, Seumas, 318
Milner, Alfred, 129
Minh, Ho Chi, 252, 282
Mobutu Sese Seko, 259, 267
Molteno, Percy, 165
Monnet, Jean, 183
Monroe, Elizabeth, 256, 262, 269, 277
Moreton, Edwina, 350
Morley, John, 117, 131, 156
Morpeth, Lord. *See* Howard, George William Frederick (7th Earl of Carlisle)
Morris, Philip, 2
Morris, William, 78
Morrison, Herbert, 207, 241, 243, 248
Mosley, Oswald, 209
Moss, Robert, 260, 281, 286, 287, 313, 394
Mossadegh, Mohammad, 251
Mount, Ferdinand, 72
Muir, Ramsay, 188
Murdoch, Rupert, 302, 317
Murray, Gilbert, 144
Mussolini, Benito, 6, 210–14, 216, 217, 218, 221

Nagy, Imre, 262
Nasser, Abdel, 261–4, 286
Neil, Andrew, 301, 302, 316
Newmarch, William, 79
Nicolas, Tsar, 53, 124, 183
Nixon, Richard, 279, 283, 287, 298, 299, 306, 308, 377, 390
Nkrumah, Kwame, 253
Norman, Montagu, 191, 203
Northcliffe, Lord. *See* Harmsworth, Alfred Charles William (1st Viscount Northcliffe)

Northcote, Sir Stafford, 84
Nye, Joseph, 352

Oakeshott, Michael, 383
Obama, Barack, 4, 5, 361, 363, 364, 366, 372, 373, 375, 387
Orwell, George, 232, 390
Osmaston, Dorothy, 183
Owen, Robert, 39, 205

Paish, George, 150
Palin, Sarah, 3
Palmerston, Lord. *See* Temple, Henry John (3rd Viscount Palmerston)
Papadopoulos, General Georgios, 286
Parkinson, Hargreaves, 205
Parks, Rosa, 257
Parnell, Charles Stewart, 135, 136
Pasha, Colonel Arabi, 125
Pasha, Nuri, 262
Paulson, Hank, 361
Paxman, Jeremy, 278
Pearson, Clive, 209
Peel, Sir Robert, 26, 44
Pennant-Rea, Rupert, 289, 319–21, 322, 324, 332, 333, 339, 378, 398
Pethick-Lawrence, F. W., 207
Philby, Kim, 255, 268, 269, 272
Phillimore, S., 142
Pigou, Arthur, 170, 183
Pinochet, General Augusto, 260, 288
Pleydell-Bouverie, William, 29
Polanyi, Karl, 12
Popper, Karl, 383
Powell, Anthony, 2
Powell, Colin, 349
Power, Samantha, 352
Preston, Elizabeth, 25
Primrose, Archibald (5th Earl of Rosebery), 133, 143
Prochaska, Frank, 73
Putin, Vladimir, 4, 364, 365, 377, 392

Qaddafi, Muammar, 364
Quigley, Hugh, 207

Raglan, Lord. *See* Somerset, FitzRoy James Henry (1st Baron Raglan)

Rawls, John, 383

Reading, Brian, 319

Reagan, Ronald, 6, 17, 18, 306, 308, 309, 311–14, 315, 324, 336, 376, 378, 383, 390

Redlich, Josef, 146

Reid, Leonard, 147, 160

Reid, Sir Robert, 146

Renzi, Matteo, 378

Revelstoke, Lord, 155

Rhodes, Cecil, 129, 136, 145, 159

Ricardo, David, 24, 26

Ridley, Matt. *See* Wensleydale, Baron

Robbins, Lionel, 273

Robinson, Austin, 198

Robinson, Joan, 233

Rodenbeck, Max, 351

Rohwer, Jim, 353

Roosevelt, Franklin D., 6, 13, 184, 210–14, 221, 225, 239, 383, 390

Roosevelt, Theodore, 13, 387

Rosebery, Lord. *See* Primrose, Archibald (5th Earl of Rosebery)

Rothschild, Evelyn de, 300, 301, 302

Rothschild, Lord, Nathaniel Mayer (1st Baron Rothschild), 150, 152, 154, 174, 202

Rousseau, Jean-Jacques, 8

Rowntree, Seebohm, 144, 183, 201

Royer-Collard, Pierre-Paul, 10

Rumsfeld, Donald, 344

Runciman, David, 392

Runciman, Walter, 202

Rusk, Dean, 285

Ruskin, John, 72, 134, 141

Russell, Bertrand, 163, 182

Sachs, Jeffrey, 368

Sainsbury, John, 300–1

Salter, Sir Arthur, 191

Salter, Ethel, 239

Satsuma, Daimio, 107

Scardino, Marjorie, 340

Schacht, Hjalmar, 214–16

Schulze-Delitzsch, Hermann, 381

Scott, C. P., 163

Schumacher, E. F., 234

Schumpeter, Joseph, 205, 386

Schuster, Sir Felix, 150

Selassie, Emperor Haile, 217

Seldon, Arthur, 295, 309

Shawcross, William, 307

Shultz, George, 6, 308

Shiina, Motoo 344

Sihanouk, Prince, 307

Simon, Ernest, 184, 202

Simon, John A., 142, 151, 161, 202

Simon, J. E., 263

Singer, Daniel, 256

Smiles, Samuel, 381

Smiley, Xan, 345

Smith, Adam, 11, 15, 24, 27, 29, 39, 46, 51, 82, 111, 146, 309, 310, 380

Smith, Barbara, 255, 260, 264, 267, 269, 314, 315, 351, 396

Smith, Ian, 319

Smithson, Alison, 227, 228

Smuts, Jan, 180, 204

Snowden, Edward, 367

Snowden, Philip, 182, 194, 195, 208

Somerset, FitzRoy James Henry (1st Baron Raglan), 53, 54

Somoza, Anastasio, 289

Spencer, Diana 278

Sprigge, Cecil, 207

St John-Stevas, Norman, 342

Stalin, Josef, 210–14, 249, 290, 325

Stamp, Sir Josiah, 203

Standage, Tom, 367

Strakosch, Sir Henry, 191, 210

Strauss, Robert, 315

Synon, Mary Ellen, 320, 321

Stelzer, Irwin, 316

Stewart, Margaret, 228

Stewart, Robert (Viscount Castlereagh), 11

Stamp, Josiah, 183, 203

Stevenson, Adlai, 253

Stevenson, Robert Louis, 118

Stowe, Harriet Beecher, 104
Strachey, John St Loe, 118, 136
Strachey, Lytton, 118, 182
Strakosch, Henry, 191, 202, 210
Stuckey, Edith, 73
Stuckey, Herbert Spencer Vincent, 73, 75, 77, 80
Suharto, General, 285–9

Taylor, A. J. P., 176, 256
Temple, Henry John (3rd Viscount Palmerston) 32, 49, 53, 54, 59, 60, 63, 66, 147
Thatcher, Margaret, 4, 260, 281, 309, 310, 311–14, 330, 363
Thibaw, King, 126
Thiers, Adolphe, 96
Thomas, J. H., 195
Thomas, Tony, 315
Thornton, Samuel, 307
Tocqueville, Alexis de, 8, 10, 12, 29, 71, 113, 114, 380, 381, 386, 387
Tooke, Thomas, 24
Toynbee, Arnold, 141, 204, 205, 218, 248
Trevelyan, Charles, 45, 48, 70, 161
Trump, Donald, 376, 377, 378, 392
Tyerman, Donald, 235, 253, 254–6, 259, 261, 262, 264, 266, 267, 268, 269, 272, 272, 277, 393

Vallance, Aylmer, 204, 209, 210
Victoria, Queen, 66, 85, 123, 342
Villiers, Charles, 29, 30, 32
Villiers, George, 46
Voegelin, Eric, 12

Walters, Barbara, 278
Wang, Patrick, 356
Warburg, Siegmund, 254

Ward, Barbara, 228, 239, 248–53, 254, 260, 277
Ward, Dudley, 147, 152
Watson, Adam, 257
Waugh, Evelyn, 202
Webb, Beatrice, 166
Weber, Max, 359, 384
Weisberg, Jacob, 339
Welch, Jack, 356
Wellesley, Arthur (1st Duke of Wellington), 49, 337
Wellesley, Henry Richard Charles, Lord Cowley (1st Earl Cowley), 55
Wellington, Duke of. *See* Wellesley, Arthur (1st Duke of Wellington)
Wells, H. G., 183
Wensleydale, Baron, Matthew White (1st Viscount Ridley), 334–5, 339
Williams, Francis, 207, 208
Wilson, George, 30
Wilson, Harold, 72, 205, 208, 272, 279, 293
Wilson, James, 5, 17, 24–8, 28–31, 32–6, 37, 40, 65, 71, 77, 146, 194, 201, 236, 320, 341, 389, 391
Wilson, Woodrow, 13, 72, 163, 179
Will, George, 315
Withers, Hartley, 164–6, 180, 187, 225
Wood, Sir Charles, 70
Wood, Christopher, 338
Wooldridge, Adrian, 355–7, 359, 363, 371
Worth, Margaret, 227
Wright, A. W., 160

Yanukovych, Viktor, 365
Yarmolinsky, Adam, 257
Yeltsin, Boris, 325
Yew, Lee Kuan, 353
Young, G. M., 72